Sue Faulkner

Social Psychological Foundations of Health and Illness

The *Blackwell Series in Health Psychology and Behavioral Medicine* heralds the growing prominence of Health Psychology and Behavioral Medicine in preventing illness, promoting health, and enhancing quality of life.

The objectives of the series are to:

- acquaint investigators and educators with the most recent findings in diverse areas of health psychology and behavioral medicine
- offer volumes that integrate theory-guided basic and clinical research related to health promotion and maintenance and the prevention and treatment of illness
- strive for the integration of knowledge of the biomedical, psychological, and social determinants of health and illness

About the Series Editors:

Howard Tennen, PhD and **Glenn Affleck**, PhD are both Professors of Community Medicine and Psychiatry at the University of Connecticut Health Center. They have collaborated on scores of journal articles and book chapters in the area of health and human behavior.

Published:

Chronic Physical Disorders, edited by Alan J. Christensen and Michael H. Antoni
Social Psychological Foundations of Health and Illness, edited by Jerry Suls and Kenneth A. Wallston

Social Psychological Foundations of Health and Illness

Edited by

JERRY SULS

and

KENNETH A. WALLSTON

Blackwell
Publishing

350 Main Street, Malden, MA 02148-5018, USA
108 Cowley Road, Oxford OX4 1JF, UK
550 Swanston Street, Carlton, Victoria 3053, Australia

First published 2003 by Blackwell Publishing Ltd

Library of Congress Cataloging-in-Publication Data
Social psychological foundations of health and illness / edited by Jerry
 Suls and Kenneth A. Wallston.
  p. cm. – (Blackwell series in health psychology and behavioral medicine ; 2)
  Includes bibliographical references and index.
  ISBN 0-631-22515-3 (hbk : alk. paper)
  1. Social medicine. 2. Clinical health psychology. I. Suls, Jerry M.
 II. Wallston, Kenneth A. III. Series.

 RA418 .S64255 2003
 616'.001'9–dc21

                                                                    2002153501

A catalogue record for this title is available from the British Library.

Set in 10/12pt Meridien
by Graphicraft Ltd, Hong Kong
Printed and bound in the United Kingdom
by MPG Books, Bodmin, Cornwall

For further information on
Blackwell Publishing, visit our website:
http://www.blackwellpublishing.com

Contents

Part III: Personality and Health

Part IV: Adaptation to Stress and Chronic Illness

Contributors

Glenn Affleck, *Department of Community Medicine and Health Care, University of Connecticut Health Center*

Stephen Armeli, *Psychology Department, Pace University*

Andrew Baum, *Behavioral Medicine and Oncology, University of Pittsburgh*

Charles S. Carver, *Department of Psychology, University of Miami*

Robert F. DeVellis, *Department of Health Behavior and Health Education, University of North Carolina*

Kathleen A. Dwyer, *School of Nursing, Vanderbilt University*

Sara Fernandes-Taylor, *Department of Psychology, University of California, Los Angeles*

Jeffrey D. Fisher, *Department of Psychology, Center for HIV Intervention and Prevention, University of Connecticut*

William A. Fisher, *Departments of Psychology and Obstetrics and Gynaecology, University of Western Ontario*

Howard S. Friedman, *Department of Psychology, University of California, Riverside*

Linda C. Gallo, *Department of Psychology, San Diego State University*

Meg Gerrard, *Department of Psychology, Iowa State University*

Frederick X. Gibbons, *Department of Psychology, Iowa State University*

Tara L. Gruenewald, *Department of Psychology, University of California, Los Angeles*

Regan A. R. Gurung, *Department of Human Development and Psychology, University of Wisconsin*

Jennifer Harman, *Department of Psychology, Center for HIV Intervention and Prevention, University of Connecticut*

Vicki S. Helgeson, *Department of Psychology, Carnegie Mellon University*

Laura C. Klein, *Department of Biobehavioral Health, Pennsylvania State University*

David J. Lane, *Department of Psychology, Iowa State University*

Elaine Leventhal, *Division of General Internal Medicine, University of Medicine and Dentistry of New Jersey*

Howard Leventhal, *Department of Psychology and Institute for Health, Health Care Policy and Aging, Rutgers, the State University of New Jersey*

Megan A. Lewis, *Department of Health Behavior and Health Education, University of North Carolina*

Kevin D. McCaul, *Department of Psychology, North Dakota State University*

René Martin, *Department of Psychology, University of Iowa*

Amy B. Mullens, *Department of Psychology, North Dakota State University*

James W. Pennebaker, *Department of Psychology, University of Texas at Austin*

Britta Renner, *Department of Psychologie, Ernst-Moritz-Arndt-Universitaet Greifswald*

Tracey A. Revenson, *Doctoral Program in Psychology, City University of New York Graduate Center*

Nan Rothrock, *Department of Psychology, University of Iowa*

John M. Ruiz, *Department of Psychiatry, University of Pittsburgh School of Medicine*

Peter Salovey, *Department of Psychology, Yale University*

Michael F. Scheier, *Department of Psychology, Carnegie Mellon University*

Ralf Schwarzer, *Institute for Work, Organizational and Health Psychology, Free University of Berlin*

Ashley W. Smith, *Behavioral Medicine and Oncology, University of Pittsburgh*

Craig A. Smith, *Department of Psychology and Human Development, Vanderbilt University*

Timothy W. Smith, *Department of Psychology, University of Utah*

Katherine Regan Sterba, *Department of Health Behavior and Health Education, University of North Carolina*

Jerry Suls, *Department of Psychology, University of Iowa*

Shelley E. Taylor, *Department of Psychology, University of California, Los Angeles*

Howard Tennen, *Department of Community Medicine and Health Care, University of Connecticut Health Center*

Kenneth A. Wallston, *School of Nursing, Vanderbilt University*

Duane T. Wegener, *Department of Psychological Sciences, Purdue University*

Neil D. Weinstein, *Department of Human Ecology, Rutgers, The State University of New Jersey*

Preface

This volume grew out of the opinion, arrived at independently by the editors, that the social psychology of health and illness has grown from infancy to active maturity. Scores of social psychologists working at the interface of social and health psychology have provided strong theoretical and methodological orientations generating evidence relevant to the etiology, prevention, treatment and adaptation to physical illness. Furthermore, we have also seen that phenomena from the physical health arena offer challenges and inspiration to basic theories of social psychology. Of course, no claim can be made that we now have all the answers. Rather, to paraphrase some scholar, we might still be confused, but we are confused on a much higher plane and about more important questions concerning the role of the "social" in physical illness and well-being.

This volume cannot purport to be comprehensive because space limitations did not permit us to invite, and circumstances did not allow, some researchers to contribute. Nonetheless, a broad spectrum of research is presented by the series of leading scholars who contributed chapters to this volume. The pieces were written to be accessible to advanced undergraduates and graduate students but also to offer new information to new doctorates, established health psychologists, and members of the allied health professions and other social sciences. Although there is an emphasis on recent advances, we have tried to make sure that the "the classic" theories and phenomena are represented here.

We are hugely indebted to Howard Tennen and Glenn Affleck, editors of the Behavioral Medicine series, who gave us encouragement and helpful feedback. At Blackwell Publishing, Otis Dean, Steve Smith and Sarah Coleman gave us all of the support book editors should expect and more. Thanks, too, to Phyllis Wentworth for her role in the book's production.

Work on this project was aided by a grant from the National Science Foundation to J. S. But above all, the editors are grateful for the love, support and patience of their families throughout the planning and implementation of this project.

Introduction

Jerry Suls and Kenneth A. Wallston

The idea that social factors play a role in physical health and well-being is not a new one. The basis of this idea has been around for hundreds of years. Hippocrates, the father of medicine, observed that the social relationship between patient and physician was important for recovery. The ancient Greeks also believed that the balance between the four humors (i.e., air, water, fire, and phlegm) was linked to the development of particular diseases. This balance could be disturbed by many factors, including the social environment. However, an empirically based approach that focused on the role of social psychological processes for etiology, prevention, treatment and adaptation to physical illness was only pioneered in the 1950s and did not gather full-steam until the 1970s. Why did it take so long for a social psychology of health and illness to develop? At least two things needed to be in place: a conceptual framework within medicine that acknowledged the role of psychosocial influences, and a social approach within scientific psychology consisting of persuasive theories, strong methodologies and a body of empirical evidence. Both conditions did not begin to emerge until the middle of the twentieth century.

An early conceptualization that offered a role for psychosocial factors was found among the ancient Greek holistic philosophers who taught that people get sick because a combination of factors has gone askew. Physical illness was thought to be the result of interactions among the mind, physiology, and the physical and social environment. Medical treatment (rarely successful for the ancients) somehow was assumed to restore the balance of factors implying the recognition that an *entire individual* gets sick, not just a part of him and not just an organ (Nuland, 1988: 306, italics added).

Another school of thought among the ancient Greeks, however, proved to be more influential. The philosophy of dualism considered the body as part of the material world and therefore subject only to physical laws. In contrast, mind was non-material, much like the soul and not subject to physical laws. Consequently, for the dualists, the body is like a machine and physical illness or health is a function of physical causes. Interpersonal relationships, social context, and socialization were seen as distal, minor players in the competition between physical health and illness.

Dualistic philosophy dominated Western thought for centuries. When, in the 1600s, Descartes recognized that there had to be some interaction between the material body and the non-material mind, his solution was to maintain that the mind and body were separate but were connected and could communicate. (Lacking sound knowledge Descartes thought the pineal gland was a good candidate for this connection because it was located in the center of the brain.) However, the emphasis on the body as machine persisted and dominated medicine and philosophy (the precursor of psychology) until the late nineteenth century. Physicians of that era considered physical health as quite distinct from psychological health and not affected by psychological factors.

The advent of germ theory at the end of the nineteenth century reinforced this dualistic way of thinking. Germ theory, originally proposed by Galen, argued that bacteria, viruses, and other pathogens were seen as the major causes of specific diseases. Evidence for germ theory awaited the development of appropriate technologies, such as the microscope and the experimental method. Rudolf Virchow generally is credited with the first definitive evidence validating a germ theory that emphasized organs and, more specifically, processes at the cellular level. The success of germ theory reinforced the dualism where physical and psychosocial processes were seen as separate mechanisms. Medical scientists also tended to be reductionistic, ignoring the complexity of factors that influence health status, and disease-focused. In medicine at the turn of the century, health was defined as the absence of disease, and wellness received little attention. Dualistic thinking, physical mechanisms, reductionism, and disease-focus characterized the *biomedical* model of illness that became dominant through the first two-thirds of the twentieth century.

Medical scientists working from the biomedical model influenced by germ theory successfully identified pathogens for malaria, pneumonia, rabies, and tuberculosis and facilitated the development of vaccines that significantly improved the health of the human population. Other medical treatments following the biomedical perspective, such as new medications and surgical procedures, also contributed to and continue to contribute to advances in eradicating disease and prolonging life. The popularity of the biomedical approach to medicine makes sense in light of these discoveries and benefits.

Whether the biomedical approach deserves all of the credit, however, is debatable. The threat of infectious diseases began to significantly decrease several decades before the advent of effective vaccines (Grob, 1983). Declines in prevalence and mortality from infectious diseases such as tuberculosis and diphtheria appear to have occurred as a result of preventive measures such as improved personal hygiene, greater resistance to disease (owing to better nutrition) and public health measures such as sewage treatment (Runyon et al., 1982). Many of these changes were not prompted by medical science or the biomedical model but represented the results of socio-cultural changes. Nonetheless, optimism about the potential for "magic bullet" cures inspired by the biomedical model made its success more salient than more distal contributions of the physical or social environment.

Limitations of the biomedical model, however, have become apparent in part because patterns of illness changed during the twentieth century. Contagious diseases were the leading causes of death in 1900, but, by mid-century and continuing to the present, non-contagious diseases such as heart disease and cancer are the leading killers. Success of the biomedical approach and improvements in public health have played a role in this shift. People live longer which makes them more susceptible to chronic illnesses. However, the major causes of death currently involve behavior or lifestyle patterns involving health-compromising behaviors, such as smoking, overconsuming calories and alcohol, and not exercising. Once the role of behavior in health was better appreciated the biomedical model seemed incomplete. A new perspective, the biopsychosocial model (Engel, 1977), was advanced which admitted psychological and social factors as equal partners with biological factors (cf. Schwartz, 1982).

The biopsychosocial model represents a return to the "holism" that the Greeks, such as Hippocrates, advocated, but its contemporary form employs modern scientific methods. Interestingly, Rudolf Virchow, the scientist mainly responsible for the early validation of germ theory was also a holistic thinker. While tracing the role of disease to the cell, he also was a leading exponent of the thesis that man is the product of his life situation. Virchow argued as vociferously for attention to environmental influences, such as occupation and social class, as to the microbes he viewed through his microscope.

We should acknowledge that the social psychological foundations of health and illness that are described in this volume probably look very different from the social factors that Virchow thought were important. For him, social conditions pertained mainly to social class and occupation. The scientific field of social psychology, which focused on the implied, actual, or anticipated impact of people on the beliefs and behavior of others, did not emerge until some decades after Virchow's death.

Contemporary social psychologists are concerned with basic interpersonal processes such as affiliation, interpersonal attraction and attachment, comparison processes, conformity, persuasion, group decision making, and collective action. Further, social psychologists attempt to identify fundamental and general processes that apply across cultures and different eras. As such, "the social psychologist typically seeks a level of generalization that falls between broad cultural abstractions and accounts of individual learning experiences" (Jones, 1998: 8). When social psychologists turned their attention to the physical health arena, they became concerned about how basic interpersonal principles and processes influence health. Further, the areas of inquiry and application extended from the etiology of disease – Virchow's focus – to social influences on prevention, treatment of acute conditions, management of chronic illness, and delivery of medical services (Taylor, 1978).

The application of social psychology could not occur until the discipline had assembled a set of theories and experimental methodologies for the study of basic interpersonal processes. Most of the foundations of experimental social psychology emerged in the 1940s and 1950s with the efforts of Kurt Lewin, Leon Festinger, Carl Hovland, Solomon Asch and Muzifer Sherif. The beginnings of a social psychology of physical health and illness appeared in the 1950s with Irving Janis's (1958) study of patients awaiting surgery, Howard Leventhal's work on fear and health communications (e.g., Leventhal et al., 1965), and the development of the Health Belief Model (Rosenstock, 1966). Shortly afterward, Stanley Schachter (1971; 1980) and his students (e.g., Rodin, 1978) explored implications of his earlier analysis of the determinants of emotion for obesity, smoking, and other health-relevant states.

Meanwhile, David Glass and Jerome Singer (1972) were examining the role of noise and controllability in understanding effects of urban stress. The utility of the control conception to broader questions in physical health soon became apparent. Glass (1977) adapted research from learned helplessness to elucidate the nature of the Type A coronary-prone personality. These pioneers trained a cadre of researchers who combined their theoretical acumen and experimental skills to examine questions about disease etiology, prevention, treatment, and management. The application of classic theories and concepts from attitude change, person perception, social comparison, emotion, and social learning theory produced a series of new insights that brought more recruits to this new field of study.

We also should acknowledge the parallel developments in the psychology of personality (Allport, 1937; Murray, 1938). This tradition posits the existence of stable internal structures and processes in the person that explain molar behavior. Whereas social psychologists emphasize the importance of situational factors for behavior, personalogists focus on dispositional causes. Although there is a tension between these perspectives, they also have some natural intellectual affinity with the understanding that human action represents the result of dispositions playing out in the actor's social environment. In any case, many important "individuals defy an easy classification as being either a social or a personality psychologist and have theorized about one in such a way as to incorporate the other" (Jones, 1998: 6). Such persons as Adorno, Allport, Murphy and Rotter come to mind. In any case, the fuzzy boundaries between social psychology and personality psychology provided fertile ground for the study of the effects of personality on health.

Several other social sciences, of course, were concerned with physical health earlier than psychology. Medical anthropologists examined how illness is thought of differently and treated differently across cultures. Medical sociology emphasized the effects of the larger social structure and the structure of medical delivery systems. Psychiatry, early on, focused on personality- or disposition-based causes of illness. Although these fields overlap somewhat with our discipline, social psychology is unique in its examination of how basic psychological principles and processes influence the individual and the group. Furthermore, social psychology can be the vehicle by which an integration of cultural, structural, and personality factors can be achieved through its focus on the individual operating in a group and within a wider cultural context (Taylor, 1978).

As mentioned above, social psychologists began turning their attention to health-related matters in the middle of the twentieth century, but this activity received a real boost with the founding of the field of health psychology in the 1970s (see Wallston, 1993; 1997, for the history of the development of this new field). Although social psychologists make up a small minority (perhaps ~10 percent) of the membership of the Division (38) of Health Psychology of the American Psychological Association, individuals trained as social psychologists have played a disproportionate leadership role in this emerging discipline. For instance, seven of the first 20 Presidents of Division 38 were trained as social psychologists, as were three of the first five editors of the journal, *Health Psychology*. Thus, the field of health psychology today owes a great deal to social psychology which, in turn, has been enriched by a focus on physical health-related phenomena.

The Present Volume

The present volume attempts to represent the advances of the field after more than 30 years of intense activity by social/health psychologists. As such, this book represents a continuation of earlier efforts by several authors and editors. Shelley Taylor (1978) edited and contributed an influential mini-series of articles for the *Personality and Social Psychology Bulletin* that argued persuasively for the developing role of psychology in medicine. Summarizing and integrating knowledge to that point, M. Robin DiMatteo and Howard Friedman published an entire text book, entitled *Social Psychology and Medicine* in 1982. Andrew Baum, Jerome Singer and collaborators began an important edited series on health and psychology (e.g., Baum et al., 1984) that presented several notable essays reporting the developments in social aspects of health. Glenn Sanders and Jerry Suls published a collection of essays, *Social Psychology of Health and Illness* (1982) by established researchers and some of the then "young turks" of this evolving field of study. Since then, several more texts and edited volumes have appeared.

Our purpose here is to present classic and contemporary developments in the social psychology of health and illness. This includes research on symptom perception, social support, social influence, coping, individual differences, gender, stress reactivity, health behaviors, risk perception, and attitude and behavior change. The editors conceive of this volume as a compendium of the leading research in social-health psychology. To accomplish this aim, the editors have contacted several distinguished leaders in the field to provide state-of-the-art summaries of their research programs. The topics include virtually all of the major issues considered in the contemporary field of social-health psychology. Each chapter provides a brief survey of classic developments in each area of study followed by extended discussion of the authors' research programs.

Rather than impose a rigid format, the editors have allowed authors considerable flexibility in presentational style. Some contributors have chosen to present the material in the form of personal narratives. Other chapters, when the subject matter was more diverse, followed a more conventional format with more extensive reviews. Still other authors focus on a single program of research or theory. Throughout, the authors integrate past findings and offer speculations for future developments.

The editors cannot claim that the volume is comprehensive. Because of the limits of space, for example, we were unable, with one exception, to represent the many substantial efforts of European social psychologists and other colleagues around the world. Some specialized topics also do not receive attention because of the limits of space. However, we submit that social, health, social-health psychologists, physicians, nurses, allied health researchers and practitioners and laypeople can gather a broad and deep understanding of how far the social psychology of health and illness has come in a few decades by reading this volume.

Organization of the Present Volume

The chapters in this volume are organized in the four areas that we think have produced some of the most important insights and evidence for the role of psychosocial factors in physical health domain. Part I is devoted to "Models of Health/Risk Behavior and Behavior Change." The seven chapters present material on risk perception and worry, how cognitive factors influence responses to health messages, a specialized theory of adolescent health behavior and two general models of health behavior promotion.

Part II is devoted to "Social/Cognitive Processes in Health" and consists of five chapters. The material considers how people interpret and act on symptoms, how affiliation, disclosure and communication influence reactions to stress, the role of psychological factors on restoration of health, and how interpersonal comparisons influence physical well-being from disease etiology to adaptation to chronic illness.

The three chapters in Part III focus on "Personality and Health." These chapters focus on different approaches to the role of dispositions and well-being. Some perspectives are trait-based while others are rooted in general models of action and behavior such as control/systems theory and interpersonal theory.

The final part, "Adaptation to Stress and Chronic Illness" consists of four chapters. One covers restorative processes and their relationship to stress reduction. The other contributions focus on coping and social support. The need to examine the dynamics of interpersonal relationships is emphasized in this part. There also is attention paid to domain-specific measures of coping and to in situ methods to assess the coping process as it unfolds.

Although we think that our classification scheme for the chapters has heuristic value, there are many themes that extend across parts, for example between the "Social/Cognitive Processes" and the "Adaptation to Stress and

Chronic Illness" or "Personality and Illness" parts. Some chapters could just as well fit in other parts. In fact, we hope that readers will discern common threads that we overlooked and thereby inspire more research and study. Below we give a brief overview of each of the chapters organized by sections of the book.

Part I: Models of Health/Risk Behavior and Behavior Change

The seven chapters in this section fall into two subcategories, the first of which has to do with basic processes underlying health and risk behavior. Health promotion efforts are too often built around a pathology model, derived from traditional conceptions of "treating" disease. These approaches often ignore the social context of people's lives, and the psychosocial influences that push and pull them in healthy or unhealthy directions across time. In his chapter, Howard Friedman describes data from the Terman Life Cycle Study demonstrating that psychosocial and behavioral factors look different in their relation to health when they are considered across the context of the life-span than they do when considered at one point in time. Friedman contends that rather than taking a piecemeal approach and educating people about endless lists of things *not* to do, it may prove more efficient and effective to launch people onto healthy life paths. Attempts to confirm the most basic idea of prevention, that people take precautions to protect themselves from harm, have produced a morass of contradictory findings and a plethora of inappropriate research designs.

Neil Weinstein's chapter describes a careful, 20-year program of research examining the interplay between risk perceptions and behavior and the fascinating inconsistencies between what people believe about their risk and what that risk really is. Messages designed to promote healthy behaviors can be framed in different ways. Peter Salovey and Duane Wegener's chapter describes research comparing the effectiveness of messages emphasizing the benefits of adopting health behaviors (such as mammography, HIV testing, using sunblock, etc.) versus those emphasizing the risks of not adopting these behaviors. Borrowing from the social psychological literature on persuasion and attitude change, the authors then describe some of the mechanisms that might account for these framing differences.

The next chapters in Part I present four models of health behavior or health behavior change. The Information–Motivation–Behavioral Skills Model is presented in the chapter by Bill Fisher, Jeff Fisher, and Jennifer Harman as a general social psychological conceptualization for understanding and promoting health-related behavior across diverse domains of such behavior. Their chapter reviews the origins of the IMB model, the constructs and relationships it proposes, and the procedures it employs for translating this approach into conceptually based, empirically targeted, and rigorously evaluated health promotion interventions. Empirical support for the general utility of the IMB model across health behavior domains is reviewed and the chapter concludes with examples of the IMB approach to understanding and promoting diverse health behaviors. The next chapter, by Frederick Gibbons, Meg Gerrard, and David Lane, presents an outline of their prototype/willingness model of adolescent health behavior. Their model describes social and cognitive factors that influence adolescents' decisions to engage or not engage in risky behaviors, such as substance use, unprotected sex, and sun exposure. Findings from laboratory and field studies are described and implications for prevention and intervention programs are discussed.

In the following chapter, Kevin McCaul and Amy Boedicker Mullens suggest that most theoretical models used to explain self-protective health behaviors overemphasize cognitive variables (e.g., beliefs) at the expense of affective variables (e.g., worry). They make the point concretely by showing that worry is an important predictor of screening for cancer. The culminating chapter in this section, by Britta Renner and Ralf Schwarzer, describes some psychosocial factors that influence health behavior change. The role of risk perceptions, outcome expectancies, perceived self-efficacy and behavioral intentions is explored in conjunction with a stage model that lends a special focus on post-intentional processes. Research examples from the domain of preventive nutrition are used to illustrate such a health behavior change process.

Part II: Social/Cognitive Processes in Health

The opening chapter in this section, by René Martin, Nan Rothrock, Howard Leventhal and Elaine Leventhal, reviews how common sense models of illness influence symptom perception and people's decisions about illness self-management and treatment seeking. The authors explore how characteristics of the social environment shape symptom interpretation. Most interesting, they describe how stereotypes about gender and heart disease vulnerability encourage symptom misattribution and treatment delay for female heart attack sufferers. Next, Jerry Suls' chapter reviews health-related research emanating from Festinger's theory of social comparison of opinions and abilities and Schachter's extensions to affiliation and emotion. The chapter reviews evidence showing how comparisons are involved in a broad range of illness-related phenomena. Interpersonal comparison can make people ill, affect prevention efforts, and facilitate coping with acute and chronic health threats.

The following chapter by Bob DeVellis, Megan Lewis, and Katherine Regan Sterba examines specific theories related to dyadic processes and mood management that are well established in social psychology but have been largely overlooked by health researchers. The authors summarize how interpersonal and emotional factors have been viewed historically, give overviews of selected theoretical approaches, and provide examples of how these theories can be applied in the context of health research. Ever since the mid-1980s, James Pennebaker and other researchers have been investigating the mental and physical health benefits of writing or talking about upsetting emotional experiences. In his chapter for this volume, Pennebaker explores the social, linguistic, physiological, and personality correlates of writing about traumatic or emotional experiences as opposed to writing about non-emotional control topics. Finally, the chapter by Shelley Taylor, Laura Klein, Tara Gruenewald, Regan Gurung, and Sara Fernandes-Taylor addresses social support and the fact that people often cope with stress by turning to others for advice and comfort. The authors review evidence of potential biological underpinnings, suggesting that oxytocin, endogenous opioid peptides, and other hormones may promote these social responses to stress, especially in women.

Part III: Personality and Health

Although many of the chapters in this volume are concerned with individual difference factors, three in particular deal explicitly with what might be termed personality traits. Personality traits (e.g., anger and hostility) and features of the social environment (i.e., isolation versus support) confer risk of coronary heart disease, presumably through mechanisms involving heightened cardiovascular reactivity to interpersonal stressors. The chapter by Tim Smith, Linda Gallo, and John Ruiz illustrates the conceptual and methodological value of the interpersonal tradition in social and personality psychology for refining what is known about the social psychophysiology of cardiovascular risk. Next, Vicki Helgeson's chapter examines the implications of two gender-related traits, unmitigated agency (focus on self to the exclusion of others) and unmitigated communion (focus on others to the exclusion of self), for psychological and physical well-being. Evidence on the relationship of these traits to health is presented along with an examination of behavioral and interpersonal mechanisms that explain these relationships. Finally, the chapter by Michael Scheier and Charles Carver presents basic elements of current models of behavioral self-regulation. A central point is that coping, at its core, reflects self-regulatory processes during times of stress. Empirical findings are reviewed that link dispositional optimism, a personality-like trait, to physical and psychological well-being, and show how those linkages seem to be mediated by variations in the coping tactics that people use to respond to threat (both illness-related and non-illness-related in nature).

Part IV: Adaptation to Stress and Chronic Illness

The first chapter in this section is by Ashley Smith and Andy Baum. Smith and Baum discuss the importance of engaging in restorative activities as a means of reducing stress and promoting physical and emotional functioning. Restorative activities appear to be effective ways of reducing stress and promoting improved mental and physical health. Their chapter reviews research on sleep, exercise, relaxation, vacation, social interaction, and spending time in natural environments that support restoration, and discusses potential psychological mechanisms that may be involved in the relationship between restoration and health. Emotional response and social processes, particularly those related to interpersonal relationships, offer explanations for the restorative effects of many of these activities. Next, Craig Smith, Ken Wallston, and Kathy Dwyer examine the advantages and disadvantages of using coping checklists in the study of adaptation to chronic illnesses. A number of theoretical and methodological issues related to this use are considered, and several research recommendations are made. The potential value of using increasingly sophisticated statistical techniques to analyze checklist data, and of using checklists in concert with alternative methodologies (e.g., qualitative analysis, experimental interventions), are illustrated with examples drawn from the authors' work on coping and adjustment to rheumatoid arthritis.

The next chapter in this section is by Howard Tennen and Glenn Affleck, the series editors for this volume, along with Stephen Armeli. Their chapter describes a daily process approach to studying health-related phenomena. They review studies of daily stress and risk for cardiovascular disease, the dynamics of coping, adjustment to chronic pain, and substance use. The contribution by Tennen, Affleck, and Armeli highlights the ability of daily process designs to address clinically relevant questions, and evaluates a variety of methods and statistical approaches unique to daily process studies.

As many chronic stressors and life strains involve the whole family – if not the neighborhood, community and school – it is often advantageous to extend the study of stress, coping, and adaptation beyond the individual level of analysis. Tracey Revenson's chapter presents a framework for studying dyadic coping processes among married couples coping with chronic illness. Two themes central to understanding marital coping processes are woven throughout the chapter. First, how do contexts – specifically, the interpersonal, medical, and temporal contexts – affect couples' patterns of coping with chronic illness? Second, how does gender fit into the equation? Is the experience of living with a chronically ill spouse the same for men and women?

Conclusion

In 1982, Sanders and Suls' aim was to convince the reader "that a social psychological orientation is a useful conceptual tool for the analysis of health and illness" (p. ix). The present editors no longer think readers will need to be persuaded. The authors of the chapters in this volume document the many important contributions to the understanding of the causes, adaptation, prevention, and treatment of physical illness made by social psychologists. It is our hope that this volume will spur even more work in the field of social/health psychology.

Acknowledgments

Both authors contributed equally to the content and writing of this chapter and are listed alphabetically. We thank Craig Smith and Howard Tennen and for their comments on an earlier draft.

References

Allport, G. W. (1937). *Personality: A Psychological Interpretation*. New York: Henry Holt.

Baum, A., Taylor, S., and Singer, J. (Eds.) (1984). *Handbook of Psychology and Health: Social Psychological Aspects of Health* (Vol. 4). Hillsdale, NJ: Lawrence Erlbaum.

DiMatteo, R., and Friedman, H. (1982). *Social Psychology and Medicine*. Cambridge, MA: Oelgeschlager, Gunn, & Hain.

Engel, G. L. (1977). The need for a new medical model: A challenge for biomedicine. *Science*, 196, 129–36.

Glass, D. (1977). *Behavior Patterns, Stress and Coronary Disease*. Hillsdale, NJ: Lawrence Erlbaum.

Glass, D. C., and Singer, J. E. (1972). *Urban Stress*. New York: Academic Press.

Grob, G. N. (1983). Disease and environment in American history. In D. Mechanic (Ed.), *Handbook of Health, Health Care and the Health Professions*. New York: Free Press.

Janis, I. L. (1958). *Psychological Stress*. New York: Wiley.

Jones, E. E. (1998). Major developments in five decades of social psychology. In D. Gilbert, S. Fiske, and G. Lindzey (Eds.), *Handbook of Social Psychology* (4th edn, pp. 3–57). Boston: McGraw-Hill.

Leventhal, H., Singer, R., and Jones, S. (1965). Effects of fear and specificity of recommendations upon attitudes and behavior. *Journal of Personality and Social Psychology*, 2, 20–9.

Murray, H. (1938). *Explorations in Personality*. New York: Oxford University Press.

Nuland, S. B. (1988). *Doctors: The Biography of Medicine*. New York: Vintage Books.

Rodin, J. (1978). Somatopsychics and attribution. *Personality and Social Psychology Bulletin*, 4, 531–40.

Rosenstock, I. M. (1966). Why people use health services. *Milbank Memorial Fund Quarterly*, 44, 94–127.

Runyon, C. W., DeVellis, R. F., DeVellis, B. M., and Hochbaum, G. M. (1982). Health psychology and the public health perspective: In search of the pump handle. *Health Psychology*, 1, 169–80.

Sanders, G., and Suls, J. (Eds.) (1982). *Social Psychology of Health and Illness*. Hillsdale, NJ: Lawrence Erlbaum.

Schachter, S. (1971). Some extraordinary facts about obese humans and rats. *American Psychologist*, 26, 129–44.

Schachter, S. (1980). Urinary pH and the psychology of addiction. In P. O. Davidson and S. M. Davidson (Eds.), *Behavioral Medicine: Changing Health Lifestyles*. New York: Brunner/Mazel.

Schwartz, G. (1982). Testing the biopsychosocial model: The ultimate challenge facing behavioral medicine. *Journal of Consulting and Clinical Psychology*, 50, 1040–53.

Taylor, S. (1978). A developing role for social psychology in medicine and medical practice. *Personality and Social Psychology Bulletin*, 4, 515–24.

Wallston, K. A. (1993). Health psychology in the USA. In S. Maes, H. Leventhal, and M. Johnston (Eds.), *International Review of Health Psychology* (Vol. 2, pp. 215–28), Chicester, England: John Wiley & Sons.

Wallston, K. A. (1997). A history of Division 38 (Health Psychology): Healthy, wealthy, and Weiss. In D. A. Dewsbury (Ed.), *Unification through Division: Histories of the Divisions of the American Psychological Association* (Vol. 2, pp. 239–67). Washington, DC: American Psychological Association.

PART I

Models of Health/Risk Behavior and Behavior Change

CHAPTER 1

Healthy Life-style Across the Life-span: The Heck with the Surgeon General!

Howard S. Friedman

University of California, Riverside

Introduction

Health times are changing. Eggs are again a healthy food. Avoiding cholesterol-laden eggs won't solve elevated-cholesterol problems for most people. Salt intake, however, can lead to high blood pressure, and thereby perhaps threaten cardiovascular health. Except, maybe eggs are not so healthy, possibly because of their high levels of saturated fat. And the threat from salt intake seems only true for certain people who are sodium sensitive. Butter is full of saturated fat, so you should switch to margarine. Wait. Margarine, containing hydrogenated oils, is loaded with trans fatty acids, which makes it a poor alternative to butter. Try the new and expensive kind of cholesterol-lowering margarine.

Where does all of this conflicting health advice come from? Some of this changing advice results from new scientific discoveries. New studies constantly address a piece of the puzzle of the development of chronic illness. Since cardiovascular disease is by far the greatest killer in the Western world, it and its risk factors (serum cholesterol, blood pressure, diet, stress) receive lots of research attention, usually fragmentary. Another part of this contradictory advice results from clinicians and reporters who overstate their findings. Individual studies are rarely multi-faceted, long-term, and definitive. So as each finding emerges, it receives more attention than justified; then later, another, different piece of the picture is revealed.

But part of the confusion results from scientists who misunderstand their findings. It is this scientific mis-step that is the subject of this chapter.

In 1989 I wrote a book entitled *The Self-Healing Personality*. I wrote:

"Since eggs are high in cholesterol, some scientists have urged people to make drastic changes in their diets – avoid all eggs. However, cholesterol does not go

directly from our stomachs into our blood. The human body processes the cholesterol in food and makes its own cholesterol. The level of cholesterol in our
blood is affected by hereditary factors, by the amount of fat (especially saturated
fat) in the diet, by exercise, and by stress. It is also affected by other, as yet
unknown, factors. Avoiding eggs will by itself have little or no effect on blood
cholesterol in most people.

Many products on the supermarket shelves are now advertised with the
ridiculous slogan, 'No cholesterol!' Believe it or not, I recently purchased a bunch
of bananas that had a 'No cholesterol' sticker attached to them. This labelling
indicates a grave public misconception of the best ways to promote health.

For a whole host of reasons, it is healthy to eat lots of fruit and vegetables.
Bananas do fall into this category, but no scientist really knows all the exact
details of why fruits and vegetables are good to eat. Certainly a lot more than
cholesterol content is involved . . .

How many people are now feeling guilty when they eat a steak? The guilt is
likely a greater problem than the steak. It is true that there is substantial evidence that high animal fat intake is unhealthy. At a restaurant near my home,
I observed a fat man devour a huge fatty chunk of prime rib. He concluded the
meal with a large piece of chocolate cake a la mode. If he does this often (as he
evidently did), his arteries may pay the consequences. But people who occasionally enjoy eating a trimmed piece of broiled steak as part of a varied diet are
giving themselves an excellent source of protein and minerals" (Friedman, 1991/
2000: 130).

Now, more than a decade later, both the popular and scientific literatures are
filled with articles questioning the "ban" on eggs and steak. They claim there
is "new research" (e.g., "Eat your heart out: Forget what you know about
eggs, margarine and salt", *Time* magazine, 1999). So how could I presciently
write those words so long ago? All I had to do was read the scientific literature
and think about its full context. There was never any convincing study even
remotely indicating that eliminating high-cholesterol eggs from breakfast would
improve the health of the population. Similarly, eating an occasional steak
(full of essential proteins and minerals) was never shown to be worse for
one's arteries than many other common foods, including drinking milk. But
scientists misunderstood their own findings.

As we shall see, our health promotion efforts and our public health systems
are too often built around a pathology model, derived from traditional conceptions of "treating" disease. These approaches often ignore the social context
of people's lives, and the psychosocial influences that push and pull them in
healthy or unhealthy directions across time. In the scientific arena, this orientation often means that each result from a particular scientific study is seen
as an important and direct causal step on the road to disease. Anything that
seems to be associated with an increase in a risk factor is a threat! Thus
we encounter a litany of health advice – do's and don't's sometimes relevant
to the proximal causes of ill health but ignorant of the long-term causal
patterns.

Furthermore, such advice appears in isolation, disease by disease. All together, in the popular arena, this faddish approach produces people who have
had it up to their noses with conflicting medical advice. They have had their

fill of half-baked baloney casseroles. So they junk all the advice and return to eating junk food. They say, "The heck with the Surgeon General!"

The truth be told, this exclamatory subtitle is not original. Rather, it was stolen from a huge billboard on the highway between San Diego and Riverside. The huge letters proclaim, "The heck with the Surgeon General." This is followed by the phrase "Inhale a big juicy star." It is an advertisement for Carl's Junior star hamburgers. Forget about warnings, and inhale loads of fatty hamburgers! Millions do. The burgers are accompanied by fries and shakes.

Backlash

A study in the *Journal of the American Dietetic Association* documented this backlash against promulgated nutritional advice (Patterson et al., 2001). This research used a random digit telephone survey of residents of Washington state, weighted to be representative of the population. More than two-thirds of the respondents asserted that the government should not tell people what to eat, and many complained about low-fat diets. More importantly, people evidencing high "nutrition backlash" ate more fat and fewer servings of fruits and vegetables.

The causal direction of these associations with nutrition backlash is not established. Patterson et al. (2001) concluded that it is likely that people who are annoyed with constant government and media harping on low-fat diets are more likely to disregard the advice altogether, and eat a fat-laden and low-fruit diet. The government advice backfires. This is also the prediction of psychological reactance models, which forecast that threats to one's personal freedom produce negative reactions that increase one's resistance to persuasion. This reactance against health advice may be especially true among people concerned with control issues (Rhodewalt and Davison, 1983). It is also the case that people may generally see themselves as less susceptible to such influence when the persuading entity is an irrelevant "outgroup" such as the government (Terry et al., 1999).

On the other hand, social psychological theory and research on cognitive consistency predicts that people who know they are eating high-fat, low-fruit diets will be more likely to evidence this "nutrition backlash" when asked about their diet. That is, if one is eating French fries, pork chops, and ice cream on a regular basis, then one is unlikely to assert that the government is doing a fine job in warning people about the health risks of such diets. Such thoughts and behaviors would be inconsistent, dissonant, and unperceptive. In this case, it is not annoyed people who ignore health advice, but rather misbehaving people who become annoyed with the advice (Abelson et al., 1968).

It is likely, however, that both sorts of causal directions account for the association between poor dietary habits and dissatisfaction with government preaching and scientific reversals. Some people will not attend to health messages, will not believe them if they hear them, and will not change their behaviors even if they hear and believe the message. Various cognitive, emotional, and informational processes are at work. On the other hand, other people will form unhealthy habits and behave in unhealthy ways for a variety of inter-personal and situational reasons, and they then will form negative attitudes about health promotion as a function of these behaviors (Rodin et al., 1990).

The Skinny on Fat

Human beings have evolved to enjoy eating fat. In fact, people cannot live without fat in their diets. There are many different types of fats. There are fats from dairy products and fats from meats, there are artificial fats from food processors, and there are fats from produce ranging from soy and nuts to olives and avocados.

There are fat people who do not eat much fat, and there are skinny people who eat a lot of fat. Many people gain weight as they age, but many do not. Although it is known that some people who eat a lot of saturated fat will raise their cholesterol levels, a subsequent long-term causal link to all-cause pre-mature mortality from this single behavior has not been directly documented as a major risk to the population.

Medical advisors who recommend addressing high serum (blood) cholesterol in people at high risk for cardiovascular disease through dietary changes in fat intake are piecing together different sorts of findings. But it has always been controversial whether simple diet-based attempts (such as avoiding eggs) at serum cholesterol reductions are needed for healthy young or middle-aged adults, especially given the often minimal or unexpected effects on serum cholesterol and health of moderate dietary changes (Kaplan et al., 1992; Taubes, 2001; Taylor et al., 1987). Further, any beneficial effects preventing deaths from cardiovascular disease might be offset by increased risk from other diseases.

Fat and carbohydrate metabolism in the body is complicated, and it is not clear that a high carbohydrate diet is especially healthy as a replacement. Add in considerations of physical activity, stress, alcohol, and culture, and the complexity multiplies dramatically (Epel et al., 2001). Note that during the years since the government and some health advisors have begun preaching fat intake reduction, the incidence of obesity among Americans has increased dramatically.

Of course such issues do not negate the documented associations between certain habits and disease. For example, there is a vast amount of evidence associating fruit intake with good health, and increasing one's fruit consumption of delicious fresh fruit might yield better health as a lagniappe (extra gift) for the lucky.

Other Health Promotions

Strangely reminiscent of the fat controversies, there is currently a govern-mental effort to increase the amount of exercise individuals do, as part of "Healthy People 2010" (http://www.aoa.gov/factsheets/LONGEVITY.html).

There is good correlational evidence that people with good cardiovascular fitness are at lower short-term risk of morbidity and premature mortality (US Department of Health and Human Services, 1996). But what will happen if we attempt massive public persuasion campaigns? Will we increase the numbers of anorexics? Will we increase the use of diet pills or weird diets? More bulimia? Will we have people injuring themselves running, or dropping dead from heart attacks? There are sure to be unintended consequences. A similar campaign was launched when John Kennedy was president, and now, 40 years later, many segments of the population are more obese and less fit than ever.

Many other health campaigns, similarly based on short-term and fragmentary evidence, are now underway. People are advised to use liberal doses of sunscreen when out in the sun. They may hear that an alcoholic drink a day is a good idea. They are advised to seek friends, go to church, stay married, meditate, lift weights, take vacations, get more sleep, eat breakfast, express their feelings, be cheerful, get more hugs, massage their children, floss their teeth, use disinfectant soaps, take supplements and herbs, and make other substantial (and often expensive) changes in their lives so that they will live longer. In all of these cases, there is mixed evidence, sometimes suggesting that the recommended interventional practices can be harmful, economically wasteful, or have unanticipated consequences over the long term. The clearest exception here is cigarette smoking, for which there is excellent evidence that avoiding or stopping smoking will improve health and longevity.

Scientific Inferences about Health

Much of the difficulty with health promotions derives from that abiding bugaboo of epidemiology, namely the conundrum that correlation does not mean causation. We observe associations among peoples, behaviors, customs, places, and health, but we do not usually know whether a corresponding intervention will have long-term salutary effects. For example, although it has been recognized for more than half a century that people better integrated into the community have better health, the implications for intervention are still unclear (Burg and Seeman, 1994; House et al., 1988; Stout et al., 1964).

Even with cigarette smoking, causal relations to health were controversial for decades, as we could not randomly assign half of the teenage population to be smokers, and then follow them for 50 years. What sort of evidence was finally mustered? First, there is a much higher incidence of disease and premature death among those engaging in the behavior. Second, there is clear temporal priority (e.g., smoking precedes lung cancer). Third, there is a dose to response relationship (heavier smokers have greater risks). Fourth, the relationship is consistent with other existing physiological knowledge (cigarette smoke has substances that damage living cells). Fifth, the association is consistent in different populations (men, women, in different ethnic groups, and in countries around the world). Sixth, there are animal analogs. Seventh, intervention seems to have an effect (people who stop smoking often have better subsequent health than those who continue smoking). Together, these sorts of evidence almost completely rule out competing explanations for the observed relationship between smoking and cancer and premature mortality, and so make us very confident in our casual inference. Even here, however, it may be that there are complex relations among genetics, personality, smoking, and disease (Eysenck, 1985).

In an attempt to address the complexity, indeed messiness, of the naturally occurring interactions of individuals and varying environments, the medical community has increasingly turned to the randomized clinical trial. This has led to some odd, artificial, and perhaps dangerous studies. For example, the drugs tamoxifen and raloxifene are being studied (and used) for the prevention of breast cancer in healthy women who are at risk of breast cancer, despite sometimes significant side effects and risks (National Cancer Institute, 2001). Will we go down similar paths for personality and social psychology and health? That is, will we pursue similar litanies of healthy psychosocial characteristics? Will we then pursue drug or genetic interventions on personality and social relations?

How could we possibly pursue randomized clinical trials of personality, stress, social relations, and community? Should we make certain children more cheerful and optimistic, make certain adults more sociable and extroverted (preventive Prozac?), and test effects of divorce, recession, and community disharmony through randomized clinical trials? I hope not.

In many ways and for many reasons, the best means of ascertaining healthy lifestyles and understanding health-promoting life pathways is through long-term longitudinal study. By amalgamating the lessons of careful and comprehensive longitudinal research, a sensible and scientific approach to psychosocial health promotion can be constructed. Such longitudinal research often yields unexpected implications. The remainder of this paper reports illustrative findings from one such comprehensive effort, the eight-decade Terman Life Cycle Study.

The Terman Cohort

The Terman Gifted Children Study (later renamed the Terman Life Cycle Study) began in 1921–22 when most of the 1,528 participants were in elementary school. Continued until the present, it is the longest study of a single cohort ever conducted, and the only such major study with rich data collected regularly throughout the life-span (from childhood to late adulthood and death). My colleagues and I (especially Kathleen Clark, Michael Criqui, Leslie Martin, Joseph Schwartz, Carol Tomlinson-Keasey, and Joan Tucker) have made major efforts to follow up on and improve the data set. Data have been collected and refined on the subjects' social relations, education, personality, habits, careers, families, mental health, life stress, physical activities, and physical health; most importantly, we have collected death certificates and coded date and cause of death (Friedman et al., 1995c). Until our project began, the study aimed primarily to describe the life course of gifted individuals (Terman and Oden, 1947). That is, the study was originally focused on addressing such issues as whether bright children were introverted eggheads (it turned out that they were not). Few predictive studies using the data had been undertaken, with little or no study of health as a function of individual differences. Because of the richness of the psychosocial data across many decades, and because of hard health outcomes (especially longevity and cause of death), these data provide an excellent opportunity to tease apart interacting factors relevant to health.

The Sample

Terman's aim was to secure a reasonably random sample of bright California children, and so most public schools in the San Francisco and Los Angeles areas in the 1920s were searched for bright children, nominated by their teachers and tested by Terman. The sample was later characterized as a productive, intelligent segment of twentieth-century middle-class American men and women. The average birth date was 1910. Most were pre-adolescent when first studied; those still living are now in their 90s. Most important is the fact that the data are collected prospectively, without any knowledge of the eventual health outcome, thus avoiding several common sources of bias in the data collection phase of such studies.

The sample is relatively homogeneous on dimensions of intelligence and social class. A resulting advantage is that these people had the ability to understand medical advice, had a place to exercise, had routine health care, and so on; the sample thus allows a clearer focus on the effects of psychosocial variables. The results are not directly generalizable to other groups, in other times, in other circumstances, but there is little reason to suspect that most relationships analyzed will be strongly influenced by the characteristics of this sample. For example, there is no reason to suspect that the relationship between personality traits and longevity is different for bright people than it is for people of average intelligence. (The sample is actually much more representative of the population than the various prospective studies that have followed samples of physicians or nurses.) The homogeneous nature of the sample might restrict the range on the predictor variables; however, our work shows that this is not the case for most variables of interest; there is generally a more than adequate range of individual differences and environmental stressors. Nevertheless, caution is obviously needed in generalizing from any single sample, especially when social or cultural variables are likely to affect a particular relation or finding. For example, socioeconomic status is very relevant to health in the US population as a whole, but is not so important in this restricted sample.

Overall, the data are remarkably complete. A low attrition rate of only 6 percent applies to most longevity analyses. Those lost from the sample did not differ in any known ways on relevant variables.

Neglect of Precursors and Complex Causal Pathways, Including Self-selection into Environments

I have noted that our health promotion efforts and public health systems are too often built around a pathology model, derived from traditional conceptions of "treating" disease. These approaches, which ignore the social context of people's lives, often arise from the unrealistic causal models implicitly assumed. For example, they may say, "Here we have a person with high serum cholesterol and so we need to reduce cholesterol intake"; "Here we have a person who is overweight and so we need to teach weight loss skills"; "Here we have a person with high stress and we need to teach relaxation skills." These approaches assume that the program begins at time zero – that you exist with certain risks at a certain point in time. But, in fact each person is on a certain trajectory that comes from previous characteristics and experiences, which are often quite different and unique. All overweight adults have not come from the same place, nor for the same reasons. So the causal *intervention* models are often wrong, or at least very imprecise or limited (Friedman, 1990; Suls and Rittenhouse, 1990).

Importantly, there is *self-selection* or pull into risk conditions. That is, people seek out healthier or unhealthier situations as a function of personality and pre-existing stress. I call the forces that pull some individuals towards healthy or unhealthy situations *tropisms* (Friedman, 2000). Just as phototropic plants move towards a source of light, some individuals grow towards more fulfilling and health-promoting spaces while other individuals remain subject to darker, health-threatening environments. A person's personality and temperament (psychophysiological reactivity resulting from genes, early hormonal exposures, and early experiences) is not independent of the environment (Snyder and Cantor, 1998). For example, neuroticism (a tendency towards anxiety and depression) and aspects of temperament tend to predict to negative life events, thus making it misleading to think of personality, located within the individual, as randomly encountering various stressful or unstressful events (Bolger and Zuckerman, 1995; Magnus et al., 1993; McCartney et al., 1990; Scarr and McCartney, 1984; Van Heck, 1997; Wills et al., 2000).

Such more complex paths to health risks clearly emerge from analyses of the participants in the Terman Life-Cycle study. Let us first consider a significant factor of adulthood stability and stress, and then consider certain relevant aspects of personality.

Marriage and Divorce

Numerous epidemiological studies have found that married individuals, especially married men, have a significantly lower mortality risk than single and divorced individuals. It is usually assumed that this association reveals a protective effect of marriage. Perhaps a spouse serves as a buffer against stress.

Perhaps a spouse helps insure co-operation with medical regimens like taking pills on time. Perhaps a spouse is quick to call for emergency help when needed. (In fact, there is also evidence to support each of these associations – Friedman, 2002.) But studies of causal mechanisms have been difficult without access to a lifelong study. The resulting advice is "get married" or "stay married" to be healthy, an inference not justified by such data.

Using the Terman archives, supplemented by death certificates we collected and coded, the association between marital history at mid-life and mortality (as of 1991) was studied in the sample of participants (Tucker et al., 1996) ($N = 1,077$). As of 1950 (when they were about 40 years old), the vast majority of the participants were alive, mature, and had married if they were ever going to marry. We classified them as to whether they were currently and steadily married ($N = 829$), married but not in the first marriage (inconsistently married) ($N = 142$), never married ($N = 102$), or currently separated, widowed or divorced ($N = 70$). Very few had been widowed by this point.

Results confirmed that consistently married people (especially men) live longer than those who are single due to marital breakup. But intriguingly, the results suggested that this is not necessarily due to the protective effects of marriage itself. Controlling for gender and self-reported health, we found (in survival analyses) that the inconsistently married people were at higher risk for premature mortality than the steadily married, and that the currently split people were at even higher risk. Inconsistently married men had a relative hazard of mortality of almost 1.4 (40 percent greater risk), and separated or divorced men had a relative hazard of 2.2. That is, men who were currently married, but had previously experienced a divorce, were at significantly higher mortality risk compared with consistently married individuals. Since both groups were currently married (in 1950), the marriage itself could not be the relevant protective factor. Furthermore, controlling for number of years married had minimal effect on the association between marital history and mortality risk.

Since divorce is recognized as one of the greatest social stressors, perhaps the stress of the divorce harms health or sets in motion other harmful behaviors. If this is true, this divorce effect may dissipate over time, as those who erred (or had bad luck) the first time around, settle into stable remarriages. In fact, this is the case, as men who experienced marital dissolution and remarried were at higher risk prior to age 70, and then their relative mortality risk declines (Tucker et al., 1999). To the extent that the stress of divorce increases mortality risk, strong advice to "get married" (for social support) ironically may increase rather than decrease one's risk, since one cannot face the stress of divorce if one has not married.

What about tropisms, the pull into certain social environments? Interestingly, part of the relationship between marital history and mortality risk in the Terman participants may be explained by childhood psychosocial variables, which were associated with both future marital history and mortality risk (Tucker et al., 1996). Some people evidently are poor bets both for stable marriage and a long life.

In sum, it is possible that the stress of divorce and its concomitants, coupled with selection into stable or unstable married roles, are more important health mechanisms than the sustenance provided by marriage itself. An incorrect causal inference might be drawn from simple observation of the association between marriage and health. And an invalid, simple preventive intervention ("Get married to promote health") may be designed.

Precursors

What are these lifelong pathways that the adults with a consistent and stable marriage are traveling? In other words, where have they come from, both psychologically and socially? Individuals who were divorced or remarried reported (retrospectively) that their childhoods were significantly more stressful than those who got and stayed married. (They scored highly on such items as "marked friction among family members during childhood.") Is there any more objective, prospective evidence for this?

Because there has never before been a lifelong prospective study of family stress predictors of mortality risk, the Terman cohort provides a unique opportunity to examine longer-term pathways. Family stress (particularly parental divorce) is known to predict unhealthy behaviors such as smoking and drug use in adolescence as well as poor psychological adjustment (Amato and Keith, 1991; Block et al., 1988a; 1988b; Chassin et al., 1984; Hawkins et al., 1992). Could such detrimental effects of parental divorce reach across the lifespan and affect (or at least predict) one's own marital relations and eventual mortality risk?

Divorce of one's parents during childhood can certainly affect one's future mental health. There is good longitudinal evidence that children of divorce, especially boys, are at greater risk for observable behavior and adjustment problems (Amato and Keith, 1991; Block et al., 1988a; Hetherington, 1991; Jellinek and Slovik, 1981; Shaw et al., 1993; Zill et al., 1993). Most of the conceptual analyses concern a lack of social dependability or ego control – impulsivity and nonconformity, although neuroticism and low emotional stability are also often implicated.

We examined the Terman children ($N = 1285$) whose parents either did or did not divorce before the child reached age 21, who were of school age in 1922, and who lived at least until 1930 (Schwartz et al., 1995), using hazard regression analyses (survival analyses) to predict longevity, controlling for gender. Children of divorced parents faced one-third greater mortality risk than people whose parents remained married at least until they reached age 21. In light of the overwhelming evidence from other studies indicating damaging *psychological* impacts of parental divorce, this finding does provoke serious consideration. Death of a parent had very little effect, consistent with other research indicating that parental strife and divorce is a greater influence on subsequent psychopathology than is parental death (Tennant, 1988).

Importantly, the Terman study participants who experienced a marital breakup were more likely to have seen the divorce of their own parents.

Given that parental divorce is associated with one's own future divorce risk, and given that one's divorce is predictive of increased mortality risk, it is the case that one's unstable adult relations "explains" some of the detrimental effect of parental divorce. However, even after controlling for one's (adult) divorce, parental divorce during childhood remains a significant predictor of premature mortality, suggesting that it may have additional adverse consequences in adulthood.

Is childhood personality also relevant to these pathways? Indeed, part of the association between marital status and mortality risk seems to be due to a selection into steady marriages. Terman participants who were impulsive children, grew up to be both less likely to be consistently married and more likely to die younger (Tucker et al., 1996; 1999).

Thus, there do seem to be precursor selection effects at work. Childhood impulsivity and parental divorce predicted marital instability, and these are also predictive of earlier mortality. These variables explain some of the mortality differential between consistently and inconsistently married participants.

Personality

Perhaps we should therefore turn to personality as a key determinant of health. Here too we find that long-term patterns are most important.

Sociability

As a more general aspect of the well-documented associations between marriage and health, a large amount of evidence establishes that people with various personal and community ties, usually termed *social support*, are generally healthier (Cohen, 1991). It thus seems sensible that more sociable people would be healthier, and that development of sociability in children and adolescents should be encouraged. This conclusion again neglects precursors and complex causal pathways, including self-selection into environments. It turns out that there is little evidence that sociability itself predicts health and longevity. This is confirmed by the Terman data.

In 1922, the participant's teacher and parents (usually the mother, or both parents together) rated the subject (on 13-point scales) on trait dimensions chosen to measure intellectual, volitional, moral, emotional, aesthetic, physical, and social functioning. The scales used are remarkably modern in their appearance. Several other rated variables from the 1922 Terman assessment were also chosen for their similarity to some of the 25 trait ratings. Based on correlational and factor analyses, we defined Sociability as: fondness for large groups, popularity, leadership, preference for playing with several other people, and preference for social activities such as parties. We later showed that Sociability was strongly related to Extraversion but also significantly correlated with Agreeableness, as measured by the NEO Personality Inventory (Martin and Friedman, 2000).

In terms of life-span mortality risk, the Terman children who were rated by their parents and teachers as popular, fond of large groups and social activities, and so on did not live longer than their unsociable peers (Friedman et al., 1993). There was simply no evidence that sociable children were healthier or lived longer across many decades. In fact, sociable children were somewhat more likely to grow up to smoke and drink (Tucker et al., 1995).

To confirm this finding, we also examined Terman's own grouping of the men in the sample into "scientists and engineers" versus "businessmen and lawyers." Terman found marked personality differences, with the former group much more unsociable and less interested in social relations at school and in young adulthood. When we analyzed mortality risk, however, we found the scientist and engineer group at slightly *less* risk of premature mortality (Friedman et al., 1994). Examination of the pathways and tropisms suggests that these studious men often wound up well adjusted, working in positions well integrated into society.

Conscientiousness and Neuroticism

Conscientiousness – a tendency to be prudent, planful, persistent, dependable – is not highly related to the personality measures typically used in health research (Friedman et al., 1995a; Marshall et al., 1994). It turns out, however, to be relevant to understanding pathways to health.

Teachers and parents rated the Terman children on items that formed a scale of "Conscientiousness-Social Dependability" (comprised of prudence-forethought, freedom from vanity-egotism, conscientiousness, and truthfulness). This childhood measure was a good predictor of mortality risk across the life-span (Friedman et al., 1993; Tucker et al., 1995). Survival analyses suggest that the protective effect of conscientiousness is not primarily due to accident avoidance, although injury deaths do tend to be higher among the unconscientious. Conscientiousness seems to have more far-reaching and general effects. Childhood unconscientiousness predicts a host of unhealthy mechanisms and tropisms, including adult smoking, adult alcohol consumption, and less social and work stability and accomplishment. Subsequent studies by others confirm the health importance of conscientiousness. For example, a study of conscientiousness and renal deterioration in patients with diabetes found that time to renal failure was much longer in those with high conscientiousness (Brickman et al., 1996).

Interestingly, Conscientiousness, which exhibited the strongest predictive power in childhood was also the best predictor of mortality risk when personality was assessed in adulthood (Friedman et al., 1995c; Martin and Friedman, 2000). Yet childhood conscientiousness was reliably, but not strongly, related to adult conscientiousness ($r = 0.13$). This set of findings points again to the need to look at the larger context. In childhood, conscientiousness as measured by parental ratings is a key personality predictor of longevity, and in adulthood, conscientiousness as measured by self-report items is a key predictor of longevity. Yet this is more of an orientation to life than a "risk factor" like serum cholesterol. (Note that both of these conscientiousness measures are highly associated with both rational judgments about what it means to measure conscientiousness and with NEO PI-R measurement of Conscientiousness – Martin and Friedman, 2000).

What about neuroticism, since there is all sorts of evidence that many diseases are associated with higher levels of hostility, anxiety, and depression (Friedman, 1991/2000; Friedman, 2002; Friedman and Booth-Kewley, 1987)? Having more emotional stability as a child was somewhat protective in the Terman sample, but adult neuroticism did not turn out to be a simple risk factor for earlier mortality. (And permanency of moods in childhood was not strongly related to adulthood neuroticism.) It may be the case that there are two or more types of health-relevant neuroticism. For example, an unhealthy neurotic may smoke, drink, take pills, oversleep, overeat, and seek self-destructive pleasure, all in an attempt to reduce anxiety, improve depressed mood, or cope with feelings of anger. A healthy neurotic, on the other hand, might direct worry and anxiety toward avoiding germs, seeking lots of medical care, wearing seat belts, saving money, buying insurance, and so on. Furthermore, some people thrive on challenge and competition, and so there are "healthy Type A's" (Friedman et al., 1985). The construct of neuroticism may be too broad to distinguish such subtypes, without knowing more about the situation and life pathway. For example, among the Terman children, those neurotics who grew up in stable families were not more or less prone to premature mortality; but those neurotics who faced parental divorce were at increased risk (Martin et al., submitted).

A further example comes from religiosity, sometimes offered as the royal road to health. The Terman women who viewed themselves as more religious in adulthood (approximately age 40) had a somewhat lower risk for premature mortality over the next several decades than those who were less religiously inclined. These women had healthier behaviors, more definite purposes and goals, more positive feelings about their futures, and reported being somewhat happier than their less religiously inclined peers. But such women were so inclined in childhood, often grew up in more positive families, joined more organizations, smoked less, drank less, and so on. In this particular circumstance of twentieth-century middle-class women, religiosity appeared to be part of a generally healthy lifestyle, but not a direct cause of it (Clark et al., 1999).

Even gender effects can be complex. As is typical, females do significantly outlive males in the Terman sample. However, in both men and women, individuals who were more male-typical in their occupational preferences tended to show higher mortality rates than individuals who were more female-typical. These associations were not due to a specific cause of death (Lippa et al., 2000).

Generality

As noted, the Terman Life-cycle sample is not directly representative of the current US population. First, as in any longitudinal cohort study, the Terman study participants were born in a certain era and grew up in specific social times. Second, Terman sampled only bright Californians, and few ethnic minorities were present in the classrooms Terman sampled, often because they were not allowed to be present. It is therefore important to ask what limits on generality may result. Any variable that impacts both our predictors and our outcomes could alter the relations. For example, the sample members have good education, access to medical care, and ability to understand the American medical system and medical prescription; therefore in no case should the findings be directly generalized to people who face significant deficiencies in any of these areas. In addition, *effect size* estimates from this research should not be directly generalized to the US population as a whole. Nevertheless, there is a wide range of usual personality, life challenges, and social relations within the sample, and so it is well suited to explore such issues. It is especially valuable for pointing out some of the complexities that occur as certain life-paths unfold across time. Although bright children growing up in California in the 1920s faced some unique challenges and so the results should not be carelessly generalized to other groups of people in other historical contexts, it is also the case that the findings fit in an understandable way with what is already known about the correlates of better or worse mental and physical health.

Co-morbidity

One would undoubtedly find it odd to be administered a treadmill test for cardiovascular fitness as a screening test for cancer. Activity and fitness are believed to be ways to prevent cardiovascular disease, by lowering blood pressure, raising levels of high density lipoprotein, decreasing reactivity, reducing stress, improving fat metabolism, and a host of other postulated (and often documented) mechanisms to keep arteries clean and supple. Yet a large prospective study of middle-aged men, not atypically, found that physically fit men (as assessed by maximal oxygen uptake at baseline, and also by exercise test duration) were much less likely to die prematurely not only from cardiovascular disease, but also from all-causes and non-cardiovascular causes (Laukkanen et al., 2001).

This study was not published in an oncology journal. Analogously, a study of activity effects (or stress effects) on immune system response to tumor growth would not be published in a cardiology journal. Yet, recently, many in the biomedical research community have come to be surprised by what are termed "co-morbidity effects." This usually means that people at high risk of or having a high incidence of one disease are also at high risk of or have a high incidence of other, seemingly unrelated, diseases. People with so-called mental diseases are more likely to have so-called physical diseases (and vice versa). People with diabetes are more likely to have cardiovascular disease, and so on. In the psychological sphere, it is not only the case that hostile people are at higher risk of cardiovascular diseases and depressed people are at higher risk for cancer, but that hostile people are at higher risk of cancer and depressed people are at higher risk for cardiovascular diseases (Friedman, 1998; 2002).

Such findings are only surprising if you are a cardiologist who never studies cancer, an oncologist who never studies heart disease, a cancer-prevention psychologist who never studies diabetes, or a diabetes prevention-and-control psychologist who never studies cancer. They are not surprising to health psychologists studying resilience and self-healing, nor are they surprising to many developmental health psychologists. For example, Jessor's work on adolescents clearly demonstrates that those who like and value school, participate in family and church activities, have good kids as friends, and value health are more likely to engage in a host of healthy behaviors like healthy diet, exercise, and seat-belt use (Jessor et al., 1998). Although these conclusions, which I term *co-salubrious* effects, seem eminently sensible when pointed out in this manner, many health promotion conceptions are not socially or developmentally or contextually sensitive.

Conclusion

What conclusions can be drawn? First, we need to examine individual life patterns. Rather than taking a piecemeal approach, rather than educating people about endless lists of things not to do, it may prove more efficient and effective to launch people onto healthy life paths, and intervene intensively only for those few people at special high risk. Although the proof is not yet in, it may be that the more likely people are to be doing a few important things earlier in life, the more likely it is that other healthy styles and behaviors will follow later in life.

Second, we need greater focus on the social context – the person in the situation, and situation selection. This means studying the match between people and their environments, and why people wind up in certain unhealthy environments. In many ways, a self-healing personality is one in which there is a healing emotional style involving a match between the individual and the environment, which maintains a physiological and psychosocial homeostasis, and through which good mental health promotes good physical health (Friedman, 1991/2000).

Third, we need to consider cultural changes, both in the medical culture and in the broader societal culture. In terms of medical culture, we also need to break down the walls between different health institutes and narrow approaches to disease. We need to include *overall* health (not going system by system or disease by disease), as well as overall quality of life, as outcomes in our research.

In the broader societal culture, we need to recognize the complexities of socialization. As one example, there is a lot of smoking and a lot of lung cancer in Kentucky, but little smoking and little lung cancer in Utah. Should we spend a lot of time and money on designing anti-smoking newspaper ads in Kentucky, or might we focus more on comparing the tobacco farm southern culture to the LDS (Mormon) culture of Utah?

How is culture changed? It is not just more education. Rather, structural changes are often more efficient and effective. Yet no one objects to spending billions and billions on treating cancer, and millions and millions on research on cancer, but how about subsidizing the many public health structures that affect behavior? But it is not only a role for government. The cruise industry is booming as people spend thousands of dollars to sit and eat 24 hours a day, but they do not have time or money to stay in shape, swim with their children, cook dinners, or go to church or their yogi. These are lifelong community values.

In sum, when psychosocial aspects of health are considered at a deep and time-sensitive perspective, we already know a lot about how to promote health, and it does not mainly involve campaigns against eggs, more warning labels on margarine, or even more exercise campaigns. Although we do need to keep researching healthy behavior and nutrition, physiology, immunology, infections, safety engineering, and so on, that is not where many of the greatest payoffs likely will come. Rather, the Terman data and many other sources of information suggest that stable people, well-integrated socially and with their community, living in a healthy culture – a healthy lifestyle across the life-span – will mostly have long, productive lives. But the context for each individual cannot be ignored. The bottom line is that psychosocial and behavioral factors look different in their relation to health when they are considered across the context of the life-span, than they do when considered at one point in time.

Acknowledgments

I would like to thank Leslie Martin for collaborative work on some points made herein. This project was supported by research grant #AG08825 from the National Institute on Aging.

Correspondence should be addressed to: Howard S. Friedman, Distinguished Professor of Psychology, University of California, Riverside, CA 92521, USA.

References

Abelson, R. P. (Ed.). (1968). *Theories of Cognitive Consistency: A Sourcebook*. Chicago: Rand McNally.

Amato, P. R., and Keith, B. (1991). Parental divorce and the well-being of children: A meta-analysis. *Psychological Bulletin*, 110, 26–46.

Block, J., Block, J. H., Gjerde, P. F. (1988). Parental functioning and the home environment in families of divorce: Prospective and concurrent analyses. *Journal of the American Academy of Child and Adolescent Psychiatry*, 27, 207–13.

Block, J., Block, J. H., and Keyes, S. (1988). Longitudinally foretelling drug usage in adolescence: Early childhood personality and environmental precursors. *Child Development*, 59, 336–55.

Bolger, N., and Zuckerman, A. (1995). A framework for studying personality in the stress process. *Journal of Personality and Social Psychology*, 69, 890–902.

Brickman, A. L., Yount, S. E., Blaney, N. T., and Rothberg, S. T. (1996). Personality traits and long-term health status: The influence of neuroticism and conscientiousness on renal deterioration in Type-1 diabetes. *Psychosomatics*, 37, 459–68.

Burg, M. M., and Seeman, T. E. (1994). Families and health: The negative side of social ties. *Annals of Behavioral Medicine*, 16, 109–15.

Chassin, L., Olshavsky, R. W., Presson, C., Sherman, S., and Corty, E. (1984). Predicting the onset of cigarette smoking in adolescents: A longitudinal study. *Journal of Applied Social Psychology*, 14, 224–43.

Clark, K. M., Friedman, H. S., and Martin, L. M. (1999). The impact of religiosity on mortality risk. *Journal of Health Psychology*, 4, 381–91.

Cohen, S. (1991). Social supports and physical health: Symptoms, health behaviors, and infectious disease. In E. M. Cummings and A. L. Greene (Eds.), *Life-span Developmental Psychology: Perspectives on Stress and Coping* (pp. 213–34). Hillsdale, NJ: Lawrence Erlbaum.

Epel, E., Lapidus, R., McEwen, B., and Brownell, K. (2001). Stress may add bite to appetite in women: A laboratory study of stress-induced cortisol and eating behavior. *Psychoneuroendocrinology*, 26, 37–49.

Eysenck, H. J. (1985). Personality, cancer and cardiovascular disease: A causal analysis. *Personality and Individual Differences*, 6, 535–56.

Friedman, H. S. (Ed.) (1990). *Personality and Disease*. New York: Wiley & Sons.

Friedman, H. S. (1991/2000). *Self-Healing Personality: Why Some People Achieve Health and Others Succumb to Illness*. New York (www.iuniverse.com).

Friedman, H. S. (Editor-in-chief) (1998). *Encyclopedia of Mental Health* (3 vols.). San Diego: Academic Press.

Friedman, H. S. (2000). Long-term relations of personality and health: Dynamisms, mechanisms, tropisms. *Journal of Personality*, 68, 1089–108.

Friedman, H. S. (2002). *Health Psychology* (2nd edn). Upper Saddle River, NJ: Prentice Hall.

Friedman, H. S., and Booth-Kewley, S. (1987). The "disease-prone personality": A meta-analytic view of the construct. *American Psychologist*, 42, 539–55.

Friedman, H. S., Hall, J. A., and Harris, M. J. (1985). Type A behavior, nonverbal expressive style, and health. *Journal of Personality and Social Psychology*, 48, 1299–315.

Friedman, H. S., Tucker, J. S., Martin, L. R. et al. (1994). Do non-scientists really live longer? *The Lancet*, 343, 296.

Friedman, H. S., Tucker, J. S., and Reise, S. (1995a). Personality dimensions and measures potentially relevant to health: A focus on hostility. *Annals of Behavioral Medicine*, 17, 245–53.

Friedman, H. S., Tucker, J. S., Schwartz, J. E., Martin, L. R., and Criqui, M. (1995b). Childhood conscientiousness and longevity: Health behaviors and cause of death. *Journal of Personality and Social Psychology*, 68, 696–703.

Friedman, H. S., Tucker, J. S., Schwartz, J. E. et al. (1995c). Psychosocial and behavioral predictors of longevity: The aging and death of the "Termites." *American Psychologist*, 50, 69–78.

Friedman, H. S., Tucker, J., Tomlinson-Keasey, C., Schwartz, J., Wingard, D., and Criqui, M. H. (1993). Does childhood personality predict longevity? *Journal of Personality and Social Psychology*, 65, 176–85.

Hawkins, J. D., Catalano, R. F., and Miller, J. Y. (1992). Risk and protective factors for alcohol and other drug problems in adolescence and early adulthood: Implications for substance abuse prevention. *Psychological Bulletin*, 112, 64–105.

Hetherington, E. M. (1991). Presidential address: Families, lies, and videotapes. Presidential Address of the Society for Research in Adolescence. *Journal of Research on Adolescence*, 1, 323–48.

House, J. S., Landis, K. R., and Umberson, D. (1988). Social relationships and health. *Science*, 241, 540–45.

Jellinek, M. S., and Slovik, L. S. (1981). Current concepts in psychiatry. Divorce: impact on children. *New England Journal of Medicine*, 305(10), 557–60.

Jessor, R., Turbin, M. S., and Costa, F. M. (1998). Protective factors in adolescent health behavior. *Journal of Personality and Social Psychology*, 75, 788–800.

Kaplan, R. M., Manuck, S. B., and Shumaker, S. (1992). Does lowering cholesterol cause increases in depression, suicide, and accidents? In H. S. Friedman (Ed.), *Hostility, Coping, and Health* (pp. 117–23). Washington, DC: American Psychological Association.

Laukkanen, J. A., Lakka, T. A., Rauramaa, R. et al. (2001). Cardiovascular fitness as a predictor of mortality in men. *Archives of Internal Medicine*, 161(6), 825–31.

Lippa, R. A., Martin, L. R., and Friedman, H. S. (2000). Gender-related individual differences and mortality in the Terman longitudinal study: Is masculinity hazardous to your health? *Personality and Social Psychology Bulletin*, 26, 1560–70.

Magnus, K., Diener, E., Fujita, F., and Payot, W. (1993). Extraversion and neuroticism as predictors of objective life events: A longitudinal analysis. *Journal of Personality and Social Psychology*, 65, 1046–53.

Marshall, G. N., Wortman, C. B., Vickers, R. R., Kusulas, J. W., and Hervig, L. K. (1994). The five-factor model of personality as a framework for personality-health research. *Journal of Personality and Social Psychology*, 67, 278–86.

Martin, L. R. and Friedman, H. S. (2000). Comparing personality scales across time: An illustrative study of validity and consistency in life-span archival data. *Journal of Personality*, 68, 85–110.

Martin, L. R., Friedman, H. S., Clark, K. M., and Tucker, J. S. (submitted). Personal resilience: Health and longevity in the face of parental divorce.

McCartney, K., Harris, M. J., and Bernieri, F. (1990). Growing up and growing apart: A developmental meta-analysis of twin studies. *Psychological Bulletin*, 107, 226–37.

National Cancer Institute (2001). http://cis.nci.nih.gov/fact/7_16.htm

Patterson, R. E., Satia, J. A., Kristal, A. R., Neuhouser, M. L., and Drewnowski, A. (2001). Is there a consumer backlash against the diet and health message? *Journal of the American Dietetic Association*, 101(1), 37–41.

Rhodewalt, F., and Davison, J. (1983). Reactance and the coronary-prone behavior pattern: The role of self-attribution in responses to reduced behavioral freedom. *Journal of Personality and Social Psychology*, 44(1), 220–8.

Rodin, J., Schooler, C., and Schaie, K. W. (Eds.) (1990). *Self-directedness: Cause and Effects Throughout the Life Course*. Hillsdale, NJ: Erlbaum Associates.

Scarr, S., and McCartney, K. (1984). How people make their own environments: A theory of genotype–environment effects. *Annual Progress in Child Psychiatry and Child Development*, 98–118.

Schwartz, J. E., Friedman, H. S., Tucker, J. S., Tomlinson-Keasey, C., Wingard, D. L., and Criqui, M. H. (1995). Childhood sociodemographic and psychosocial factors as predictors of longevity across the life-span. *American Journal of Public Health*, 85, 1237–45.

Shaw, D. S., Emery, R. E., and Tuer, M. D. (1993). Parental functioning and children's adjustment in families of divorce: A prospective study. *Journal of Abnormal Child Psychology*, 21, 119–34.

Snyder, M., and Cantor, N. (1998). Understanding personality and social behavior: A functionalist strategy. In D. T. Gilbert, S. T. Fiske, and G. Lindzey (Eds.), *The Handbook of Social Psychology* (Vol. 1, 4th edn, pp. 635–79). New York: McGraw-Hill.

Stout, C., Morrow, J., Brandt, E., and Wolf, S. (1964). Unusually low incidence of death from myocardial infarction in an Italian-American community in Pennsylvania. *Journal of the American Medical Association*, 188, 845–9.

Suls, J., and Rittenhouse, J. D. (1990). Models of linkages between personality and disease. In: H. S. Friedman (Ed.), *Personality and Disease* (pp. 38–64). New York: John Wiley & Sons.

Taubes, G. (2001). The soft science of dietary fat. *Science*, 291, 2536–45.

Taylor, W. C., Pass, T. M., Shepard, D. S., and Komaroff, A. L. (1987). Cholesterol reduction and life expectancy. A model incorporating multiple risk. *Annals of Internal Medicine*, 106(4), 605–14.

Tennant, C. (1988). Parental loss in childhood: Its effect in adult life. *Archives of General Psychiatry*, 45, 1045–50.

Terman, L. M., and Oden, M. H. (1947). *Genetic Studies of Genius: The Gifted Child Grows Up*. (Vol. 4). Stanford, CA: Stanford University Press.

Terry, D. J., Hogg, M. A., and Duck, J. M. (1999). Group membership, social identity, and attitudes. In D. Adams and M. A. Hogg (Eds.), *Social Identity and Social Cognition* (pp. 280–314). Malden, MA: Blackwell.

Time magazine (1999). Eat your heart out: Forget what you know about eggs, margarine and salt. July 19.

Tucker, J. S., Friedman, H. S., Tomlinson-Keasey, C., Schwartz, J. E., Wingard, D. L., and Criqui, M. H. (1995). Childhood psychosocial predictors of adulthood smoking, alcohol consumption, and physical activity. *Journal of Applied Social Psychology*, 25, 1884–99.

Tucker, J. S., Friedman, H. S., Wingard, D. L., and Schwartz, J. E. (1996). Marital history at mid-life as a predictor of longevity: Alternative explanations to the protective effect of marriage. *Health Psychology*, 15, 94–101.

Tucker, J. S., Schwartz, J. E., Clark, K. M., and Friedman, H. S. (1999). Age-related changes in the association of social network ties with mortality risk. *Psychology and Aging*, 14, 564–71.

US Department of Health and Human Services (1996). *Physical Activity and Health: A Report of the Surgeon General*. Atlanta, GA: US Department of Health and Human Services, Centers for Disease Control and Prevention.

Van Heck, G. L. (1997). Personality and physical health: Toward an ecological approach to health-related personality research. *European Journal of Personality*, 11, 415–43.

Wills, T. A., Sandy, J. M., and Yaeger, A. (2000). Temperament and adolescent substance use: An epigenetic approach to risk and protection. *Journal of Personality*, 68, 1127–51.

Zill, N., Morrison, D. R., and Coiro, M. J. (1993). Long-term effects of parental divorce on parent-child relationships, adjustment, and achievement in young adulthood. *Journal of Family Psychology*, Special Section: *Families in Transition*, 7, 91–103.

CHAPTER 2

Exploring the Links Between Risk Perceptions and Preventive Health Behavior

Neil D. Weinstein

The State University of New Jersey

Introduction

"People take precautions in order to reduce their risks." This statement may seem obvious, but it is not necessarily true. Just because people act in ways that protect their health does not mean that risk reduction is the reason for these actions. Most health promotion and health education programs assume that people take precautions to avoid harm, but the actual links between risk perceptions and health behaviors are far from obvious.

This chapter describes my attempts over several decades to investigate these links. Neither an empirical review nor a description of a single theory, the chapter is more personal and historical. This approach allows me to present some of the thinking that has guided this research, including such subjects as why particular topics were chosen, how ideas and results led from one project to the next (or sometimes led nowhere!), and how resources and opportunities shaped the research progression.

Initial Steps

Always interested in how people react to stressful conditions, I was especially intrigued when the United States Government published the *Atlas of Cancer Mortality* in 1975 (Mason et al., 1975). For the first time separate cancer rates were available for each state and county in the country. New Jersey, where I was teaching, had the highest overall cancer rate (that questionable honor has since fallen upon other states), and the *Cancer Atlas* was front-page news throughout New Jersey. Surprisingly, my students did not seem particularly concerned, and I decided to study their reactions to what I thought was quite alarming news.

In a quick-response, low-budget investigation (Weinstein, 1978), under-graduate assistants interviewed more than 500 of their peers. The interviewers asked whether respondents had heard that New Jersey's cancer rate was among the highest in the country and then asked, "What's your reaction to that? Do you think that by living in New Jersey you would be increasing your chances of getting cancer?" Answers to this open-ended question were coded along an "acknowledgment of risk" scale, from "definitely yes" at one end to "definitely no" at the other. When an interview was finished, the respondent was given a postcard that could be mailed back to receive information about the cancer rates in different counties in New Jersey and surrounding states.

The interviews revealed that many students did not believe the news re-ports. They challenged the accuracy of the information, saw cancer as caused by non-environmental factors, or thought that they were personally excluded from risk because of the region of New Jersey where they expected to live or work. Interestingly, students who planned to leave the state after graduation were more likely to believe in the risk than those who planned to remain. Postcard requests for information came mainly from those who either ac-cepted or denied that they would be at risk (return rates of 49 percent and 41 percent, respectively). Only about 26 percent of the people in the middle of the risk acknowledgment scale (people who gave such responses as, "I don't think so," "can't say," "maybe," "it's a possibility") returned the postcard. At the time I speculated that people in the middle of the scale might hold conflicting feelings – finding the threat real and disturbing, but trying to deny it by avoiding further information – or they might simply be people who had never been engaged by the issue and simply had little interest in learning more.

This investigation and a follow-up study (Weinstein, 1979) that was also prompted by the *Cancer Atlas* convinced me that people have many ways of discounting unwelcome messages. These projects heightened my interest in understanding how people use and misuse information about their own vulnerability to harm.

Unrealistic Optimism about Personal Risk

A substantial and persistent bias in how people perceived their own risks appeared unexpectedly while studying an unrelated issue, mood. One factor that might influence feelings of vulnerability is a person's mood (e.g., Johnson and Tversky, 1983). People might feel more risk if other events had already made them worried or depressed. Attempting to induce moods in a laboratory experiment could be difficult and slow, so I tried to study this issue by taking advantage of a naturally occurring, mood-altering event, a college examina-tion. A few minutes after students in a large lecture class received their mid-semester test grades, I distributed a risk questionnaire. I expected that some of the students would be pleased by their grades whereas others would be disappointed, and these moods might affect their perceived vulnerability to a variety of negative events.

The data were collected in the era of punch cards and mainframe computers, and I remember sitting at the keypunch machine entering the data from the questionnaires: an expected grade, received grade, feelings of happiness or disappointment, and ratings of personal vulnerability. As I worked, I did not notice any difference between those students who were pleased with their grades and those who were not (and never did find any), but I did notice something strange about the risk judgments. For no particular reason, I had asked the students about their *relative* risk. In other words, were their chances of experiencing each of these illnesses, accidents, and other problems lower than the risk of a typical student, greater than the risk of a typical student, or about average? Overwhelmingly, students had reported their risk to be average or below average. Hardly any admitted that they might be above average in risk.

Although some students' risks truly could be below average, others' risks had to be above average. The mean of these relative risk judgments, if they had been unbiased, should have fallen at the midpoint of the scale (i.e., at "average"). Instead, for every hazard on the questionnaire, the mean rating fell between "average" and "less than average." In fact, in some cases nearly all the students thought they were below average in risk. Thus, these ratings were clearly and strongly biased in an optimistic direction. The group as a whole was unrealistically optimistic about avoiding harm.

The reluctance of individuals to acknowledge risk, often called "denial," is a familiar Freudian concept. However, denial is difficult to measure; complete denial is seldom observed, and the denial concept has not provided much insight into why and when people resist information about their risk. By a fortuitous choice of a rating scale involving relative risk judgments, I had stumbled upon a simple, quantitative measure of risk perception bias.

It is important to recognize that using a relative risk scale does not reveal which individuals are biased. A man who says that his risk of heart disease is "a little above average" is giving a somewhat pessimistic risk rating, but if he smokes heavily, even this rating may be unrealistically optimistic. In contrast, a non-smoker with low cholesterol levels, normal blood pressure, and no family history of heart disease may be accurate in claiming that his risk is "much below average." Thus, we need to distinguish between optimism (or pessimism), which can be determined from a single individual's relative risk judgment, and unrealistic optimism (or unrealistic pessimism), which can be determined only by reference to an objective standard of accuracy.

Two different standards can be used. A person's actual risk can sometimes be obtained from detailed knowledge about his or her risk factors and the epidemiological risk of similar people (e.g., Strecher et al., 1995). More often, however, the standard of accuracy is derived from the fact that a group of individuals who compare their risk to that of their peers should give relative risk ratings whose mean is "average." This standard refers to group, not individual, data.

A series of subsequent studies (Weinstein, 1982; 1984; 1989) used this relative risk approach to measure the magnitude of optimistic biases. These studies demonstrated that unrealistic optimism appears for a wide range of hazards and populations, and it is insensitive to the exact wording of the risk questions or measurement procedures. For most hazards, people claim that they are less at risk than others like them. The amount of bias in these studies varied from hazard to hazard. It was strongest with hazards that people think are controllable, that they believe appear early in life, that occur infrequently, and with which people have little experience. Contrary to the idea that such biases are a defense against anxiety, they were no greater for serious, life-threatening hazards than for more mundane problems.

These initial studies were all conducted with college students, and I began to feel very uncomfortable about this limitation. College students are probably healthier than the average person their age, and since they are getting college degrees, they probably have brighter futures than the average person as well. If, in filling out my questionnaires, they had compared themselves to the average person their age, rather than to the average student at their college, as the instructions had requested, they could be correct in claiming that their futures looked better than average. Thus, rather than representing a bias in risk perceptions, the pattern I observed might just represent students' difficulty in focusing on the correct comparison group. Another possibility was that the students really were unrealistically optimistic, but that unrealistic optimism is limited to teens and young adults. After all, it is widely believed that teenagers think they are invulnerable (see Quadrel and Fischhoff, 1993). I thought it was time to move this research outside the university.

Such a study would require funding, but the two applications I submitted to Federal agencies were both unsuccessful. One set of reviewers thought that the phenomenon was already so well established that it was unnecessary to see if unrealistic optimism would appear in a non-student population. Another critical reviewer faulted my coverage of the relevant literature. I asked the program officer to contact the reviewer to find out what I had overlooked. He later told me that I had neglected the research on the topic by a psychologist named Neil Weinstein! I finally managed to carry out the project on a minimal budget, without outside funding (Weinstein, 1987). I restricted the sample to communities within the free telephone dialing area around Rutgers (which happened to be an area with a quite diverse population), had all questionnaires printed by the university's mainframe computer (at a time when an unlimited number of pages could be printed for free), and found student assistants to pick people from the local phone book, call them, and ask if they would complete a questionnaire that we would mail to them. With this approach, and follow-up calls and mailings, we achieved a 68 percent completion rate.

The results of this study (shown in Table 2.1) confirmed all the previous research. Optimistic biases in relative risk ratings for health and safety risks were independent of age, education, and occupational prestige. The same hazard attributes that had affected the size of the bias in student populations affected the size of the bias in this broader population as well.

These studies and those of many other investigators (Weinstein, 1998b) have provided a great deal of information about biases in personal risk ratings. Still, although errors in people's beliefs are interesting, more important

Table 2.1   Comparative risk judgments for health problems and other hazards

Hazard	Mean comparative risk judgment
Drug addiction	−2.17***
Drinking (alcohol) problem	−2.02***
Attempting suicide	−1.94***
Asthma	−1.36***
Food poisoning	−1.25***
Poison ivy rash	−1.19***
Sunstroke	−1.17***
Nervous breakdown	−1.15***
Homicide victim	−1.14***
Gallstone	−0.84***
Deaf	−0.82***
Pneumonia	−0.80***
Lung cancer	−0.77***
Skin cancer	−0.77***
Cold sores	−0.77***
Senile	−0.76***
Laryngitis	−0.71***
Gum disease	−0.69***
Tooth decay	−0.58***
Insomnia	−0.57***
Ulcer	−0.55***
Mugging victim	−0.54***
Diabetes	−0.53**
Overweight 30 or more pounds	−0.40
Influenza	−0.31**
Stroke	−0.29
Serious auto injury	−0.27*
Heart attack	−0.24
Arthritis	−0.24
Falling and breaking a bone	−0.10
High blood pressure	−0.02
Cancer	0.08

Notes: Comparative risk judgments could range from −3 ("much below average") to +3 ("much above average"). A mean less than zero indicates an optimistic tendency to claim that one's own risk is less than average. Significance levels refer to t tests of the hypothesis that the mean is different from zero.
$N = 87$–104.
* $p < 0.05$.
** $p < 0.01$.
*** $p < 0.001$.

is whether these errors have consequences for real world decisions and behaviors. Does unrealistic optimism increase the likelihood of subsequent illness or injury? If it does, then understanding this bias may show investigators how to help people avoid significant personal harm. So the question remained, are optimistic biases about risk merely curiosities, or do they make a difference in people's lives?

Finding the Right Context for Health Behavior Research

Studying consequential *behaviors* is much more difficult than simply asking people about their beliefs, attitudes, or decisions. Self-reports of behavioral intentions always have an uncertain relation to the behaviors people eventually perform. Laboratory studies of behavior, however, usually have an air of unreality. When a laboratory intervention fails to produce the effects hypothesized, I always wonder whether the hypothesis was incorrect or whether the hypothesis would have been supported if the research had been carried out in a more natural setting. After all, the length of time in the laboratory is brief; the responses available to participants are greatly restricted; and these responses seldom have consequences once participants leave the laboratory.

Some researchers appear able to design laboratory experiments that participants find engaging and realistic. However, I have never felt confident that my experiments would elicit the same behaviors people would show in their own worlds, and I certainly do not want to end every unsuccessful experiment second-guessing my own results. As a consequence, I seldom use the laboratory to investigate health behavior.

In order to conduct experimental studies of health behavior outside the laboratory, researchers have two main options. The first is to obtain substantial outside funding so that you can create the events you want to study. For example, you might recruit pediatricians to take part in a smoking prevention study, teach them how to counsel their patients against smoking, and monitor how they use this training and what impact their counseling has on smoking initiation.

The second option is to take advantage of naturally occurring opportunities for research, waiting for some event (such as an institutional decision or a news announcement) that provides an intervention similar to the one that had interested you. For example, a celebrity might become ill, a new cure might be announced, or risk estimates might be revised. The "interventions" in this second approach are free, requiring less time writing grant proposals. However, you must wait for an event to occur that allows you to test your hypothesis, and a suitable event may never be found. As a variation, you might watch for some widely publicized, health-relevant event (such as the discovery of a new genetic marker for disease susceptibility) and then, when the event occurs, develop a hypothesis that might be investigated in the context of that event.

If you do not create the impactful event, you have little control over the situation, so confounding variables may be difficult to rule out. Nevertheless, when possible, I have tried to use the latter strategy. For example, to study the impact of hazard experience on perceptions of risk, I interviewed people after their hometown had been struck by a tornado (Weinstein et al., 2000b). Obviously, I did not create the tornado.

Another question facing health researchers is which behaviors to study. This question is particularly salient for researchers who hope to identify principles that will explain health behavior in general. The question is less relevant for researchers interested in either a specific disease (such as cancer, heart disease, asthma, or AIDS) or a specific type of behavior (such as smoking, diet, or exercise). Societal institutions (e.g., schools, charitable organizations, funding agencies, politicians, mass media) usually pay the greatest attention to those behaviors that cause the greatest harm, ones like smoking, unprotected sex, and alcohol abuse. Consequently, members of the public are exposed to hundreds or thousands of messages about these behaviors. Some members of the public have listened to these admonitions and have modified their behavior, but the people who continue these risky actions despite the warnings either don't want to change or are unable to change. Behaviors resistant to change may be supported by peer reinforcement, may be actively encouraged by manufacturers of hazardous products, or may involve deeply ingrained habits or addictive substances. Cigarette smoking provides an example of all three.

Thus, the behaviors to which society pays the most attention are not problems merely because of their negative health consequences but because they have resisted previous interventions. Nearly all researchers have a limited time in which to carry out their investigations and limited budgets. Consequently, the probability that their interventions will make an impact is relatively small. Choosing to investigate difficult-to-change behaviors can be a risky research strategy. One could choose to study risky behaviors that have not yet received much attention, but if the reason for this inattention is that the actual health risk is small, it will be difficult to design a motivating intervention.

Some consequential risks have received relatively little attention, despite their significant magnitude, because they affect only a small number of people (for example, a genetic variation confined to a single ethnic group). Choosing to study such risks exposes the researcher to the cost of locating the people for whom it is relevant. Thus, deciding which health-related behaviors to investigate requires attention to the magnitude of the risk, the cost of the desired intervention (or the possibility of a naturally occurring intervention), and the likelihood that this intervention will make a difference.

Risk Perceptions and Precautions for Radon

One day in 1985 an article appeared on the front page of the *Home News*, my local newspaper. It described a serious, *new* health hazard, the risk of lung cancer from radon gas. Actually, radon had been recognized as an occupational health problem for miners, but it had just been discovered that levels in homes could be as high as those in mines. Radon is produced by the decay of naturally occurring uranium in the soil. Researchers found that it could concentrate in houses and reach unsafe levels. In fact, in millions of homes in the United States and other countries the lifetime probability of lung cancer from radon is comparable to that of dying in an automobile accident.

This certainly seemed like a major health issue. A map accompanying the article showed that a substantial portion of New Jersey had high levels of uranium in the soil and hence unusually high radon risks. Because the level of radon in a building is influenced by a variety of factors, homes next to one another can have quite different levels. Therefore, the recommendation offered by health experts was straightforward: all homeowners in New Jersey should test for radon.

This hazard seemed to offer the perfect opportunity to study the relationship between risk perceptions and a concrete, easily measurable, health behavior – home radon testing. Furthermore, because the hazard was new, radon provided an opportunity to study the adoption of a precaution from the very beginning, before hardly anyone had tested his or her home. I could examine the behavior of the public in general, not just the behavior of those who had resisted previous warnings.

Radon testing is not really a preventive behavior. Like checking the level of cholesterol in your blood or the amount of lead in your tap water, radon testing is intended to detect a risk factor for an illness before that illness occurs. This type of action can be distinguished from two other types of health protective behaviors: true preventive behaviors that reduce the likelihood or severity of victimization (e.g., taking cholesterol-lowering drugs), and screening behaviors that detect the presence of an existing illness (e.g., getting a mammogram). Screening behaviors, because they might find a serious illness, can be very frightening, whereas detecting a risk factor for an illness is likely to be much less frightening (since a positive test indicates only an increased chance of future harm). Finally, preventing an illness before it or any risk factor is present seems to be the least frightening of all.

For these reasons, researchers believe that prevention and screening behaviors may have different determinants – with risk factor detection behaviors as a potentially intermediate case. Still, there does not seem to be any agreement on what the differences are. In fact, I am not aware of any empirical reviews, or even thorough discussions, of the ways that the *determinants of preventive behaviors* differ from *the determinants of screening behaviors*. Thus, one should keep in mind that conclusions about health behavior gained from studying radon testing might not apply to prevention and screening behaviors, although these conclusions probably would apply to other risk factor detection behaviors.

Radon testing was "recommended" by public authorities, not required, so it was obvious to the New Jersey Department of Environmental Protection (NJDEP) that research on ways to encourage this behavior could be useful. With funding from NJDEP, and in collaboration with colleague Peter Sandman, I carried out several surveys of homeowners in high-risk areas of New Jersey (Sandman et al., 1987; Weinstein et al., 1987; 1989). People in these regions of the state had at least a 25 percent chance of finding radon concentrations above the suggested action level in their houses. The surveys assessed residents' knowledge about radon, beliefs about the risk from radon (including questions about the probability that they might have a high level in their own home and questions about the relative probability of a problem in their home compared to other homes in the same community), thoughts about the difficulty of reducing radon levels if high concentrations were found, and interest in radon testing. Given the nature of the questions, it was sent only to people who, during an initial phone call, said that they had heard of radon.

This early in the home radon story few people had tested their homes, and large numbers had never even thought about testing, despite knowing that it was possible. On many questions, people were allowed to choose "no idea" as their answer, and this response was common. When asked why they had not tested, people frequently said that they did not think there were radon problems in their area or that they did not think they had problems in their own homes.

These particular choices were consistent with the positive correlation we found between interest in testing and perceptions of the likelihood of having a problem (Sandman and Weinstein, 1993). Such correlations could not, however, prove that perceptions of personal risk had a causal role and created this interest in testing. Thinking their risk was high might lead homeowners to be interested in testing, but it was possible that some third factor, for example, concern expressed by neighbors, was responsible for both variables.

The survey respondents were also asked if they thought their own homes were more likely or less likely to have radon problems than other homes in the community. At this early stage in the radon issue, many people said they had no idea about their risk, but of those who answered, the number claiming below-average risk greatly outnumbered those believing that their risk was above average. Thus, the familiar optimistic bias appeared again (Weinstein et al., 1988). The reasons people gave for believing their risk was low were interesting. Some thought their risk was lower because their house was new; others thought their risk was lower because their house was old. Some mentioned that they had good insulation, others that they had good ventilation. Homeowners had an impressive ability to focus on (and frequently distort) factors that suggested their risk was low and to ignore or minimize the importance of any unfavorable risk factors. They seemed to go out of their way to convince themselves that they were less at risk than their peers.

Radon Experiments

If underestimating risk does indeed decrease homeowners' interest in testing, convincing homeowners that their risk is substantial should increase their motivation to test. Could a message that described the actual risk succeed in increasing perceived vulnerability, decreasing optimistic biases, and increasing health protective behavior? To answer this question we planned a field experiment (Weinstein et al., 1990). Homeowners in high-risk areas of New Jersey ($N = 271$) were mailed a radon brochure, a questionnaire, and a form for ordering a $20 radon test kit from the American Lung Association. Various versions of the brochures were created that differed in their portrayal of the magnitude of the radon threat (brief mentions of the probability and serious-ness of having radon problems versus detailed and emphatic discussions) and what they said about the ease of reducing radon levels (brief versus detailed and emphatic). Combinations of these two variables (threat and radon reduc-tion) created a 2 × 2 experimental design.

As intended, the effects of the brochure manipulations on questionnaire ratings of threat and mitigation difficulty were highly significant. Neverthe-less, the radon test order rate stayed constant across brochures; approximately 19 percent of people in each condition ordered a test kit. The independent variables had no measurable impact on either test kit orders or on the inten-tions to test of those who did not order a kit.

Despite the absence of intervention effects, perceptions of risk likelihood and risk seriousness were highly correlated with testing intentions and test orders within each experimental group. Further calculations helped to explain how the manipulation of perceived risk could have produced negligible effects even if the initial hypothesis – that risk perceptions lead to action – was correct.

Let us assume that an intervention (I'll call it "variable 1") successfully increases risk perceptions (variable 2) and that this increase in risk percep-tions causes an increase in action (variable 3). Path analysis shows that the overall effect (i.e., the expected correlation between variable 1 [intervention] and variable 3 [test orders or test plans]) is simply the product of the correla-tions for the two separate steps, that is, $r_{12} \times r_{23}$.

Even though the effect of the intervention on risk perceptions was signific-ant beyond the 0.0001 level in our experiment, the magnitude of the effect was only moderate in size (the correlation between intervention condition and risk perceptions was 0.25). The correlation of risk perceptions with test orders was 0.31 and the correlation with testing intentions was 0.55. Because two correlations are multiplied together to get the overall correlation, even if each step is moderately strong, the overall effect will be relatively weak. We calculated an expected effect of our intervention on test orders of 0.25 × 0.31 = 0.08 and an expected effect on testing intentions of 0.25 × 0.55 = 0.14), both of which would be too small to be statistically significant with the sample sizes used. The observed correlations between condition and orders or intentions were 0.03 and 0.14, respectively, essentially the same as the two-step model predicted. These calculations taught us an important lesson: experimental tests of suspected causal variables may be inadequate despite apparently successful manipulation checks. Our theories may sometimes be better than our tests make them appear.

A second field experiment (Weinstein et al., 1991) tried even harder to increase radon testing by increasing risk perceptions. It used a much larger sample of 641 homeowners, a simpler design with only high-risk and control conditions. It also used a more intensive intervention to raise perceived risk. Each high-risk condition participant received a personalized letter which stated that "radon is a real problem in your area of [county name] . . . As you can see [from the map enclosed and the accompanying list of towns with high risk], there is a substantial risk that you have high radon levels in your home." A personal telephone call then reinforced the risk message. The caller said, for example, that "We felt that we should call you . . . because you might not realize that a lot of houses in [respondent's hometown] have radon problems."

Despite these attempts to increase the strength of the intervention and the statistical power of the design, the results were essentially the same as in the previous experiment. Once again the intervention succeeded in increasing risk perceptions, and risk perceptions within each condition were correlated with both interest in testing and actual test purchases. Still, as before, people in the high-risk condition showed no more interest in testing or test orders than people in the control condition. Fifteen percent of the participants ordered test kits, independent of the condition they were in. When the calculations described earlier were repeated, that is, the effect of the intervention on perceived risk (as a correlation) was multiplied by the within-condition correlation between risk perceptions and action (or interest in action), we again found that the predicted effect of the risk intervention on testing was too small to be detected with our research design. In other words, though the experimental results were negative, they were still consistent with the idea that risk perceptions were a causal factor in the behavioral response.

By now, two well-controlled field experiments in high risk areas had failed to demonstrate that perceptions of either absolute risk or relative risk were important causes of precautionary behavior. At this point my colleagues, students, and I decided to proceed in three directions. First, we would re-examine the literature relating risk perceptions to risk behavior. Second, we would try to develop interventions that would be more successful in increasing risk perceptions and reducing unrealistic optimism, allowing us to generate better experimental tests of the risk perception-risk behavior relationship. Third, we would review the large body of data already collected in our radon surveys and experiments to see if we had overlooked something important.

The Risk Perception–Risk Behavior Literature

An enormous number of empirical investigations, certainly several thousand, have examined precautionary behavior. A large proportion have included perceived risk among the variables they examine, so one might think that the links between risk perceptions and action would be thoroughly understood by now. However, very few of these studies, less than 10 percent, have used experimental research designs, and only a small fraction of these have employed interventions in which perceived risk was manipulated independently of other factors. Even in this tiny group, as we saw in our own experiments, interventions intended to alter risk perceptions may have failed to affect behavior simply because they did not change these perceptions enough.

With cross-sectional or prospective surveys, by far the most commonly used research designs, there is often a considerable range in the risk perceptions of the study participants, which should help in determining whether risk perceptions have consequences for action. Yet, determining causality with survey data is notoriously difficult. There is the well-known possibility that a third, unrecognized variable might be the real cause of an apparent link between the two variables studied. Yet, correctly interpreting risk perception–health behavior correlations poses other serious problems that are recognized by few researchers. An example from our radon research can illustrate their nature.

In our radon surveys, we always included questions that asked people about their risk – in particular, their thoughts about the likelihood that they had unsafe radon levels in their homes. It would have been silly, though, to compare the risk perceptions of people who had already tested for radon with those who had not tested in order to learn if perceptions of high risk are associated with (and would therefore be a possible cause of) testing. The people who had already tested *knew* their radon levels from the tests they had conducted. Their test results had undoubtedly affected their perceptions, convincing people with high test results that they definitely or probably had a radon problem and convincing people with low test results that they definitely or probably did not have a problem. In other words, among people who had carried out this precautionary behavior testing, the perceptions of risk measured in our cross-sectional surveys were not the perceptions that might have led to the behavior but the consequences of that behavior. The original perceptions were gone. (It did make sense, however, to look at the difference in risk perceptions between those who had not tested and those who had a test in progress.)

This same issue is relevant to many health behavior studies. If it is true that people take precautions to reduce their risk, then, after they have taken these precautions, they should feel that their risk is lower than it had been before these precautions. With cross-sectional data, it would be patently incorrect to look at the correlation between current perceptions and current behavior to test the idea that prior perceived risk may have produced this behavior. Nevertheless, many studies have proceeded in exactly this fashion.

The problem is not that the correlations from such cross-sectional studies are slightly inaccurate. Instead, the effect of this mistake is so serious that the sign of the calculated correlation can actually be the reverse of what it should be. As might be expected from the use of such incorrect analyses, the associations between risk perceptions and behavior reported in the literature are very inconsistent. Usually, when studies of the same issue are inconsistent, it is because some studies find the relationship hypothesized and others find a weaker or no relationship. In studies of health behavior, however, some studies report significant positive associations between perceived risk and health behavior, whereas others report significant negative associations (see Kirscht, 1988). Researchers have even claimed to have found that low perceived risk leads people to act (e.g., Simon et al., 1993), when it was probably the high perceived risk of these people before they acted that had motivated their behavior.

Table 2.2   Correlations recommended for studying effects of risk perceptions on behavior

---

Cross-sectional data

I.	Temporal context	Soon after an event or intervention, so that few people have had time to change their behavior
	Hypothesis tested	"People with higher perceived risk are more likely to adopt precautions than people lower in risk"
	Type of behavior	Case A. Precaution or test result affects risk: No correlation is appropriate for testing the hypothesis Case B. Precaution or test result does not affect risk: No correlation is appropriate for testing the hypothesis
II.	Temporal context	After people have had time to act and current behavior change rates are low
	Hypothesis tested	"People who think it is risky to not take precautions will behave more cautiously than those who do not think it is risky"
	Type of behavior	Case A. Precaution or test result affects risk: $R_H B$ Case B. Precaution or test result does not affect risk: $R_C B$ or $R_H B$

Prospective data

III.	Temporal context	Soon after an event or intervention, so that few people have had time to change their behavior
	Hypothesis tested	"People with higher perceived risk are more likely to adopt precautions than people with lower perceived risk"
	Type of behavior	Regardless of whether precaution or test result affects or does not affect risk: $R_{Ct} B_{t+1}$ controlling for B_t or $R_{Ht} B_{t+1}$ controlling for B_t
IV.	Temporal context	After people have had time to act and current behavior change rates are low
	Hypothesis tested	"People who think it is risky to not take precautions behave more cautiously than those who do not think it is risky" Because cross-sectional correlations are recommended under these conditions there is no advantage to prospective data (see section II for specific recommendations). If prospective data are available, $R_{Ht} B_{t+1}$ can be used (or $R_{Ct} B_{t+1}$ if the precaution or test result does not affect risk).

Notes: The appropriateness of the correlations listed for cross-sectional data is based on the assumption that the risk perception observed is essentially the same as it was before people took action. When correlated variables do not have subscripts to indicate time, they refer to measurements made at the same time. Wherever R_H appears, R_L or R_H–R_L can also be used. Wherever R_C appears, R might be used, but the former is preferable. These various risk perceptions are not interchangeable; the information obtained will be different.
B = Pattern of precautionary behavior at a specific time point. Includes both performance of risk-decreasing behaviors (e.g., using condoms) and non-performance of risk-increasing behaviors (e.g., avoiding unprotected sex).
ΔB = Change in precautionary behavior between two time points.
R = Perceived personal risk (e.g., "What is your risk of getting AIDS?").
R_C = Perceived personal risk if current behavior continued (e.g., "If you continue your current pattern of behavior, what is your risk of getting AIDS?").
R_H = Perceived personal risk from engaging in a *high*-risk behavior (e.g., "What would be your risk of getting AIDS if you never used condoms?").
R_L = Perceived personal risk if engaging in *low*-risk behavior (e.g., "What would be your risk of getting AIDS if you always used condoms?").

At first, I thought that I could explain this data analysis problem in a brief note, and I agreed to write a short article for a special issue of the journal *Psychology and Health* that would focus on theory. The more I thought about the problem, however, the more complicated it became. What if the risk perception dealt not with hazard likelihood but with hazard severity or illness treatability? A woman might get a mammogram to increase the likelihood that she could be cured (i.e., decrease the likelihood that she would die) if breast cancer were found, but a negative mammogram does not decrease the likelihood of eventually developing breast cancer. In this case, a woman's risk judgment after the screening would have no reason to be different from what it was beforehand. What about studies using prospective data or those using intentions to act as the outcome variable, rather than action itself? And what about different kinds of risk questions, such as those that involve conditional statements: "What would be your risk of lung cancer *if you had not quit smoking*?"

With the aid of colleagues Mark Nicolich and Alex Rothman I gradually worked through these issues. Eventually, several years after the special issue of *Psychology and Health* had gone to press without us, we finished our articles and guided them into print (Weinstein and Nicolich, 1993; Weinstein et al., 1998b). Table 2.2 summarizes our conclusions about the best ways to analyze correlational data. (The table only shows recommendations for correlations in which behavior is the outcome variable. The original articles also include recommendations for what to do when only self-reports of intentions to act are available.) The analyses that we recommend still do not prove causality, but at least they are not testing the idea that high perceived risk motivates people to take precautions with an analysis that blatantly violates the hypothesis it is intended to test. The best that the recommended analyses *can* determine is whether the data are *consistent with* the hypothesis.

In the course of this work we decided to find out how prevalent were these data analysis problems. We reviewed five years of four respected journals in the health behavior field, *Health Psychology, Psychology and Health, Journal of Behavioral Medicine,* and *Health Education Quarterly* (Weinstein et al., 1998b). In this select group, more than 30 percent of the articles that examined the risk perception–health behavior relationship had used analyses that were clearly invalid. Subsequently, colleagues have told me that the situation is even worse in journals that are not so selective. Thus, this is a very widespread problem in correlational studies of health behavior.[1]

Reducing Unrealistic Optimism about Personal Risk

Early investigations had identified several ways that unrealistic optimism could be reduced. Two similar experiments (Lachendro and Weinstein, 1982; Weinstein, 1980, study 2) accomplished this by creating a more realistic (i.e., less pejorative) view of the average person. As a preliminary step, a large group of individuals prepared handwritten lists of all the factors that increased and decreased their chances of experiencing specific problems in the future. Half of the study participants (none of whom had prepared a list) read five of the handwritten lists and then all estimated their own relative risk. The data showed that learning what others had listed significantly reduced participants' optimistic biases.

In one of the studies (Lachendro and Weinstein, 1982), just asking people to imagine what a typical peer might list as reducing and increasing his or her risk was enough to reduce biases, suggesting further that part of people's unrealistic optimism comes from a failure to think carefully about the person to whom they are comparing themselves. Yet, though reduced in size, the optimistic biases remained substantial. The interventions changed judgments that were highly optimistic to ones that were only moderately optimistic or neutral, but there was no increase in the number of people who acknowledged above-average risk. We also found that simply asking study participants to list all the factors that increased or decreased their own risk had no effect on their risk judgments.

A third study (Weinstein, 1983) was designed to provide more structured feedback about the risk status of peers. College students recorded their standing on a variety of risk factors for a number of hazards. One point along each scale was marked in red to show participants the average standing of fellow students on the risk factor. When those in the study proceeded to estimate their own relative risk for these health problems, biases were eliminated. Interestingly, students who filled out a version of the same risk factor questionnaire that was not marked to show the standing of peers became more optimistic, not less, as if learning of additional risk factors simply gave people more opportunities to think of reasons why their own risk was low.

Bill Klein and I decided to look further into ways of reducing optimistic biases (Weinstein and Klein, 1995). In one investigation we tried to present risk factors in a way that would highlight the fact that our study participants' risk factor profiles were less than ideal. The effects of focusing attention on the positive end of a risk factor dimension (e.g., "I have never gotten drunk") were contrasted with those of an approach that focused attention on the negative end of the dimension (e.g., "I get drunk three or more times each week"). Our hypothesis was that the "positive end" approach would decrease optimistic biases by helping people see that there were many risk-decreasing attributes that they did not have.

Seven attributes related to heart disease and eight related to drinking problems were presented in a checklist format, with only the high-risk or low-risk attributes listed. After checking the attributes that described them, our college student participants rated their own risk and the average student's risk on scales that ranged from "no chance" to "certain to happen." Examination of the results showed that neither experimental group's optimistic bias had decreased relative to that of a no-list control group. Instead, both interventions had a tendency to increase the optimistic biases.

Our next study again tried to reduce biases by altering the standard of comparison people use when making risk judgments. We hypothesized that people tend to compare themselves to someone who is especially vulnerable to a hazard, someone who embodies all the high-risk factors for that hazard (see Perloff and Fetzer, 1986). If, instead, we could make a low-risk person the target of comparison, people might realize that their risk was not necessarily less than that of the average person.

We recruited college students for an experiment that was described as a study of visualization. Our goal was to get our participants to form a vivid mental image of one of two people: either someone who had many attributes that increased the risk of becoming seriously overweight (such as being from an overweight family, loving snack foods, and hating to exercise) or someone who had many attributes that decreased the risk of becoming seriously over-weight (such as being from a thin family, following a vegetarian diet, and enjoying exercise). We supplied these attributes to participants so that we could be certain that the high-risk and low-risk images were based on the same factors. There was also a no-visualization control group. After the visualization experience, our participants rated their own chances of becoming overweight. Contrary to predictions, but consistent with Study 1, participants encouraged to think about someone at low risk did not decrease their tendency to claim that they were less likely to have weight problems than their peers. However, participants who had formed a mental image of a high-risk person showed a significant *increase* in optimistic bias.

A final study tried still another approach. Several investigators (Levi and Pryor, 1987; Sherman et al., 1981) have shown that if people generate reasons to explain why a particular outcome might happen to them or think through a series of events that could lead to this outcome, their perceptions of the likelihood that the outcome will occur increases. We applied this same technique to perceptions of personal risk. Our participants were asked to list all the factors they could think of that tend to increase (or, in another condition, to decrease) the likelihood that they would eventually become 30 or more pounds overweight or would develop a drinking problem. Then they were asked about the likelihood that they would experience these problems in the future.

Once again, we found that asking people to focus on factors that made a problem more likely did not reduce their optimistic biases. The only significant effect in this experiment was a decrease in the perceived risk of weight problems for people in the risk-decreasing condition. Thus, an approach that had proved effective in changing attitudes or predictions about future events in other research was not able to reduce unrealistic optimism in people's predictions about their own futures.

Overall, our results were depressingly consistent. None of the experiments Klein and I conducted had succeeded in raising perceptions of relative risk or decreasing optimistic bias. Nevertheless, in several cases, the same kind of intervention applied in an opposite manner was able to *increase* optimistic biases. This imbalance in the consequences of two conceptually identical interventions strongly suggests that these are, at least in part, motivated biases. In other words, people welcome the idea that their relative risk is low but resist the idea that their relative risk is high. We thought about calling the article that described this series of experiments, "Four failures to reduce unrealistic optimism," but settled on the more serious-sounding title, "Resistance of personal risk perceptions to debiasing interventions."

Klein and I had tried to find approaches that, by shaping the way in which people thought about their risk, would help them realize *on their own* that they were not necessarily better off than their peers. Such approaches could be incorporated directly into public education campaigns. The successful, earlier experiments that had provided people with actual information about their peers would be more difficult to implement in mass campaigns, although they might be used in small-scale interventions.

A more direct and potentially more powerful approach for reducing unrealistic optimism would be to provide explicit, personalized feedback about a person's relative risk. To determine relative risk, one needs information about the individual's risk factors, a way to combine these factors to arrive at a summary risk estimate, and information about the risk of a relevant peer group. These requirements make it difficult to use this strategy in mass campaigns, but it does not seem impossible to have messages telling smokers, and even smokers with different levels of tobacco use, how much their risk of heart disease and cancer is increased above that of their non-smoking peers.

Personalized feedback to increase recognition of personal risk is well suited to settings that provide direct contact with your intended audience, for example, during a doctor's visit or through an interactive computer program, and it is beginning to be evaluated in such settings. However, the issues and effects are complex. For example, Lipkus et al. (2000) found that giving women personalized estimates of absolute breast cancer risk, estimates that were much smaller than study participants' initial expectations – increased optimistic biases in comparative risk. Recently, my colleagues and I (Weinstein et al., 2001) found that participants in our study of colon cancer perception overestimated their comparative risk and were reluctant to believe the lower values they received despite the detailed risk factor information that accompanied these communications.

Stages of Precaution Adoption

Evidence from Radon Research

Our surveys and experiments had generated a mass of data dealing with radon beliefs and testing, but no clear causal link between perceptions of risk and action had emerged. Looking through these data once again, three points caught our attention. First, large numbers of people had either never heard of radon or said that they had never even thought about testing. This observation raised doubts about the relevance of the most widely used theories of preventive health behavior to this situation.

Because any significant change in behavior seems to require conscious decision-making, it appears appropriate to view action as the outcome of a cognitive process that considers the expected advantages and disadvantages of this action. The most obvious advantage of precaution taking is the risk that can be avoided (i.e., the decrease in the likelihood or severity of harm). Other advantages could include peer and family approval, decreases in anxiety, or increased feelings of self-efficacy. The disadvantages and problems of precaution taking include the difficulties of successfully changing behavior and the possible need to give up a pleasurable habit (such as smoking or snacking). The most popular current theories of health behavior (e.g., Theory of Reasoned Action – Ajzen and Fishbein, 1980; Fishbein and Ajzen, 1975; Fishbein and Middlestadt, 1989; Theory of Planned Behavior – Ajzen, 1985; Ajzen and Madden, 1986; Health Belief Model – Janz and Becker, 1984; Kirscht, 1988; Rosenstock, 1974; Protection Motivation Theory – Rogers, 1983; Prentice-Dunn and Rogers, 1986; Subjective Expected Utility Theory – Edwards, 1954; Ronis, 1992; Sutton, 1982) adopt this decision-making perspective, predicting action from the individual's views about costs and benefits and incorporating most of the variables just mentioned.

Obviously, it is possible to explain someone's action in terms of his or her expectations about positive and negative outcomes only if the person *has* thoughts and expectations about these outcomes. Yet, it was clear that the many people in our research who knew nothing about radon or who said they had never thought about testing did not have any position on these issues. Rather than having considered the pros and cons of testing and having decided not to act, they had not made any decision about testing.

The studies of reactions to the *Cancer Atlas* that I described earlier in this chapter had also found many people who were uncertain and answered questions about risk with phrases like "can't say" or "maybe." These people, too, seemed predecisional, and they showed less interest in learning about the environmental cancer threat than those who held more definite beliefs.

The dominant theories of preventive health behavior might be appropriate for people who are trying to decide whether to act, but these theories appeared irrelevant to people who never heard of the hazard, had never considered whether they might be at risk, or had never thought about taking any precautions. Any complete theory of health behavior would somehow have to include all these groups (Weinstein, 1988).

The second thing we noticed (Weinstein and Sandman, 1992) was that many variables in our radon studies were able to predict *interest* in testing. A person's perceived risk, that is, the belief that his or her home was likely to have hazardous radon levels – was the single best predictor. Yet, none of the variables we measured, including perceived risk, differentiated between the people who said they had decided to test and those who had actually gone ahead to purchase a test kit.

Our guess was that the transition from intention to action in our studies was not determined by a person's beliefs and expectations, factors internal to the person, but by situational factors that helped them carry out their intentions. Although health experts know that it is easy and inexpensive to test one's home for radon, did homeowners know this? Were they deterred by doubts about the kind of test kit to buy, how much they cost, where to get them, how many to get, where to put them, how to use them, and so forth? Contact with people who could answer their questions about testing, such as friends who had already tested, could be crucial in helping people resolve these uncertainties. In other words, it seemed to us that the factors that facilitated the purchase of test kits were different from those that had led to decisions to test.

A final observation from the two experiments and the one prospective survey that we had conducted concerned the state of mind that leads to action. After screening out people who had never heard of radon, we had asked respondents for their thoughts about testing, giving them five options. These included four pre-action choices ("I never thought about testing my home"; "I'm undecided about testing"; "I've decided I *don't* want to test"; and "I've decided I *do* want to test") plus one post-action choice ("I have already completed a test, have a test in progress, or have purchased a test").

After the experiments had been completed and the follow-up survey in the prospective study was finished, we looked to see which people in the pre-action groups had bought radon tests. We thought that the order of three of the categories was quite clear: never thinking about acting was the furthest from action, being undecided was somewhat closer, and having decided to act was closest of all. (The people who had decided not to act did not have any obvious location among these categories, and, because we expected it to be very difficult to get them to test, we had screened them out of the experiments.)

What we found was that nearly all the testers came out of the "decided to test" group. The likelihood of action did not increase gradually from group to group, as one would expect if the groups represented different locations along a continuum of action likelihood. For example, in a prospective study of 453 people who had not yet tested (Weinstein and Sandman, 1992), the rates of testing for those who said they had "never thought about it," "thought it was not needed," or were "undecided" were 5.3 percent, 4.8 percent, and 3.5 percent, respectively. However, 28.2 percent of those who had said that they planned to test did purchase a test kit. Thus, deciding to test appeared to be qualitatively different, and reaching this stage appeared to be a precondition for radon testing.

Formulation of the Precaution Adoption Process Model (PAPM)

The decision-oriented theories mentioned earlier combine the variables they consider important in an algebraic equation that is either prescribed by the theory or derived empirically from collected data (for examples, see Weinstein, 1993). Each theory has a single prediction equation. Substituting a person's standing on the relevant variables into this equation leads to a single numerical value for this individual, and this value is interpreted as the relative probability that this person will act. Thus, the prediction rule places each person along a *continuum* of action likelihood, and such theories might be called "continuum theories." The goal of interventions, according to this perspective, is to move people along the continuum, increasing the probability of action, though action can occur from any point along the continuum. If different interventions increase the value of the prediction equation by the same amount, they are all expected to produce the same change in behavior.

Such theories seemed inadequate to explain our observations. First, many of the people we studied did not have opinions about the variables that would have to go into the prediction equations of current models and could not be placed anywhere along the action continuum. Second, in the process of coming to adopt a precaution, it appeared to us that the barriers changed as a person moved closer to action. With a single prediction rule, however, whichever variable is the most important determinant of the value of the equation (it might, for example, be the one that had the largest regression coefficient) would be most important for everyone, regardless of where along the action continuum the equation had placed them. Finally, the pre-action categories we identified, "never thought about it," "undecided," "decided to act," certainly seemed to represent progress toward testing, but they could not be said to occupy different places along a continuum of action likelihood since the data suggested that action could only come from the people who had moved through all the preceding categories and had decided to act.

To explain our data one needs a different kind of theory, a stage theory of precaution adoption (Weinstein et al., 1998c). Stage theories are based on an ordered sequence of qualitatively different categories ("stages"), and they assume that people have to move through all the stages to get to the end point. The barriers impeding progress toward the next stage change as people move from one stage to the next. For example, general education may be needed by people who are unaware of a risk, but those who have already decided to act may need guidance in how to carry out their decision. Thus, the goals of a stage theory are: first, to correctly identify the characteristics of the stages (so that people can be classified) and, second, to identify the barriers between stages (so that they can be helped to act). In effect, the second goal requires us to develop a *series* of prediction equations, one for each stage transition.

Proposing a sequence of stages does not imply that progression is necessarily inevitable or irreversible, as Bandura (1995) has asserted. In this respect, behavior change is different from biological development. Furthermore, because of the flexibility of human behavior, people do not need to spend a fixed or minimum length of time in any stage. If all the factors needed to convince people to act and to carry out an action are present simultaneously, people may pass through all of the stages in a few moments. Yet, if an essential component is missing, people may never get beyond their current stage.

Rather than resembling stages of biological development, stages of health behavior are more like the stages of buying a house. First people decide that they need a new home. Then they search for a house that matches their needs. Once such a house is found, they enter into negotiations with the owner over the final price and the terms of sale. Next, they need to obtain a mortgage. Finally, the sale is completed and they own a new home. Acquiring a new house is not a steady, incremental process. Quite different issues are important at different times, and at any point the process can be halted,

Table 2.3   Precaution adoption process model and its application to home radon testing

Precaution adoption process model stages			Precaution adoption process model for radon testing	
Stage 1	Unaware of issue ∴		Never heard of radon ∴	
Stage 2	Unengaged by issue ∴		Never thought about testing ∴	Ψ Decided not to test
Stage 3	Deciding about acting ∴	Stage 4 Ψ Decided not to act	Undecided about testing ∴	
Stage 5	Decided to act ∴		Decided to test ∴	
Stage 6	Acting ∴		Testing ∴	
Stage 7	Maintenance		Not applicable	

reversed, or even abandoned. Like buying a house, people may pass through some stages of health behavior several times before they succeed in reaching the final endpoint. Attempting to use a single equation to model the process of purchasing a house would distort the complex and changing issues involved.

If health behavior change proceeds through a series of stages, a theory that correctly describes these stages makes possible the matching of treatments to individuals – because people in different stages have different needs – and the sequencing of treatments – because the stages have a temporal order. Furthermore, a variable could be extremely important in determining whether people are able to make a particular transition between stages, but this variable may be much less important at other points in the process. If so, the ability of this variable to predict action would appear to be modest in a study that disregarded stages because the study would be mixing together people from all the pre-action stages. Thus, to the extent that stage theories are true, standard correlational and experimental research designs blur the role of particular variables by merging together many different stage transitions.

Sandman and I suggested that the categories in Table 2.3 represent the stages that people pass through as they progress from ignorance to action. We called this theory the Precaution Adoption Process Model, using the word "process" to emphasize that multiple steps are involved and to differentiate this approach from models that reduce action to the single step of making a decision. Furthermore, this is a model of how people come to adopt health precautions and does not try to explain how other health-related behaviors, such as patterns of exercise or diet, are initially acquired.

Other stage or process models of health behavior, such as the Transtheoretical Model (Prochaska and DiClemente, 1983) or the Health Action Process Approach (Schwarzer, 1992), propose different numbers of stages and use different criteria to define these stages. For example, the Transtheoretical Model defines stages in terms of when a person plans to change a behavior (not within the next six months; within the next six months but not within the next month; within the next month; currently acting; maintaining action). Although these stages have names that make them appear quite similar to the stages of the PAPM (pre-contemplation, contemplation, preparation, action, and maintenance), it is clear from the definitions of the stages that the two theories are quite different. There is growing evidence (Farkas et al., 1996; Herzog et al., 1999; Quinlan and McCaul, 2000; Sutton, 2000) that the arbitrary time points used in the first three categories of the Transtheoretical Model do not refer to qualitatively different stages and, if anything, represent variations in the strength of a person's intention to act.

Testing the Precaution Adoption Process Model

Testing stage models, with their multiple transitions, is more difficult than testing continuum theories (Weinstein et al., 1998c). A key feature of stage theories is the idea that different variables influence movement at different stages. If this idea is correct, a treatment designed to change one of these variables should be most effective when applied to people in the correct stage. Thus, individuals in a given stage should respond better to an intervention that is *matched* to their stage than to one that is *mismatched* (i.e., matched to a different stage). To test the Precaution Adoption Process Model we decided to carry out just such an experiment. Only the main features of the experiment are described here; additional details are available in the full report of the study (Weinstein et al., 1998a).

The experiment focused on two stage transitions: from being undecided about testing one's home for radon (Stage 3) to deciding to test (Stage 5), and from deciding to test (Stage 5) to actually ordering a test (Stage 6).

Increasing homeowners' perceptions of the likelihood of having unhealthy radon levels in their homes appeared to be important in getting undecided people to decide to test. Consequently, this was chosen as the goal of one intervention ("High-likelihood"). Interventions focusing on risk had not been effective, however, in getting people to actually order tests (Weinstein et al., 1990, 1991). Instead, several studies had found that test orders could be increased by increasing the ease of testing (Doyle et al., 1991; Weinstein et al., 1990, 1991). Thus, for people who had already decided to test, the second intervention was intended to lower barriers to action by providing information about do-it-yourself test kits and a form that could be used to purchase a test kit from the American Lung Association ("Low-effort"). These two treatments were combined factorially to create four conditions: Control (no

Table 2.4 Radon testing as a function of experimental condition and pre-intervention stage

Pre-intervention stage	Condition			
	Control	High-likelihood	Low-effort	Combination
Progressed one or more stage toward acting (%)[a]				
Undecided	18.8	41.7	36.4	54.5
	(138)	(144)	(130)	(139)
Decided-to-test	8.0	10.4	32.5	35.8
	(339)	(338)	(329)	(345)
Purchased radon test kit (%)				
Undecided	(a) 5.1	(b) 3.5	(c) 10.1	(d) 18.7
Decided-to-test	(e) 8.0	(f) 10.4	(g) 32.5	(h) 35.8

[a] The group size in each cell is shown in parentheses.

intervention), High-likelihood, Low-effort, and Combination (High-likelihood + Low-effort).

The investigation took place in Columbus, Ohio, a city with high radon levels, and study participants were initially contacted by telephone. Those individuals who were either in the "undecided" stage or "decided to test" stage were assigned at random to one of the four experimental conditions. The experimental interventions were delivered by videotapes sent to each participant. Follow-up telephone interviews were carried out 9–10 weeks after respondents returned a post-video questionnaire. The interviewers determined whether participants had purchased a radon test kit and, if not, determined their final stage.

Predicting Progress Toward Action

The upper half of Table 2.4 shows the percentage of people from each preintervention stage who progressed *one or more* stages toward testing. This criterion (rather than progress of only one stage toward testing) was chosen because although people stopped at one stage were hypothesized to lack the requirements to get to the next stage, there was no a priori reason to assume that they did not already possess the information or skills needed to overcome later barriers. The first row of the table indicates the percentage of people at follow-up who had moved from the undecided stage to either the decided-to-test or the testing stage. The second row of the table shows the percentage of decided-to-test people who had moved on to the testing stage.

As expected, the High-likelihood treatment was much more effective for undecided participants than for decided-to-act participants. Also as predicted, the Low-effort treatment had a relatively bigger effect on people already planning to test than on people who were undecided.

Predicting Test Orders

The follow-up interviews revealed that radon tests were ordered by 342 study participants or 18 percent of the sample. The data concerning test orders are presented in the bottom half of Table 2.4. One of the powers of a stage model is its potential for predicting how people in different stages will react to interventions. In subsequent paragraphs the predictions are presented in brackets and experimental groups are labeled with letters that refer to the cells in the table. Test order rates of both undecided and decided-to-test participants in the Control condition were expected to be quite low since both groups were viewed as lacking information needed to progress to action [(a) ≈ (e), both small]. The main problems facing people who had decided to test were hypothesized to be the difficulties in choosing, purchasing, and using radon test kits. Thus, the Low-effort treatment was expected to be much more helpful than the High-likelihood treatment in getting people in this stage to actually order tests [(g) > (f)]. In fact, past research (Weinstein et al., 1990, 1991) suggested that the High-likelihood treatment would be ineffective in eliciting testing from people planning to test [(f) ≈ (e)], and, more obviously, unable to elicit test orders from undecided people [(b) ≈ (a)]. Furthermore, since it was anticipated that people in the decided-to-test stage did not need further information about risk, we predicted that testing in the Combination condition would not be significantly greater than testing in the Low-effort condition [(h) ≈ (g)].

According to the PAPM, people who are undecided have to decide to test before acting, so a Low-effort intervention alone was not expected to produce test orders from this group [(c) ≈ (a)]. However, undecided people in the Combination condition received both high-likelihood information (seen as important in deciding to test) and low-effort assistance (seen as important for carrying out action intentions). Some of these people might be able to make two stage transitions [(d) > (c)], but not as many as decided-to-test people in the Combination condition who needed to advance only one stage [(d) < (h)]. When these predictions were compared to the data, it was found that none of the pairs expected to be approximately the same were significantly different (p's > 0.3), but all the pairs predicted to be different were significantly different (all p's < 0.0001 except for the hypothesis that (d) > (c), p = 0.03). Although it is theoretically possible for the same predictions to be generated from a theory based on a single, algebraic equation, the equation would need to have a large number of interaction terms, terms that would produce large impacts for some individuals and small impacts for others. No other current theory is able to predict the pattern shown in Table 2.4.

Although hypotheses derived from the Precaution Adoption Process Model were strongly supported, the experiment looked only at a small part of the model – two stage transitions. Other transitions and other hazards obviously need to be examined. In such work it is important to keep in mind that even though I believe that the stages of the PAPM are relevant to all precaution adoption, there is no reason to believe that the barriers between stages will be the same across hazards. Thus, each study of a new hazard must discover anew the issues limiting progress between stages.

Another limitation of this experiment is that all participants knew they were part of a research study, so they undoubtedly paid more attention to the interventions than they would have otherwise. In fact, we might expect that in real life messages that are irrelevant to someone's stage would be largely ignored, so stage effects might be even greater if observed under more natural conditions.

What We Don't Know

Although much has been learned about risk perceptions and health behavior, progress in understanding the links between them has been slow. Earlier I discussed several reasons for this state of affairs. These include the excessive use of correlational research designs, with their attendant ambiguity about causation; the frequent failure to analyze cross-sectional data correctly; the difficulties experimenters encounter in manipulating risk perceptions; and the absence of valid reviews of the risk perception–risk behavior literature. I would add to these problems the over reliance on behavioral intentions, rather than actual behavior, as the outcome criterion, and the failure of researchers who believe in one theory to ask whether their data could be explained just as well by other theories. This last has several causes, including ignorance of theories other than the one selected for study, reluctance to gather additional data (though several theories are so similar that hardly any additional data would be needed), and unrealistic page limitations imposed by journal editors. The foregoing problems concern the choice of research designs, the manipulation of variables, and the analysis and interpretation of data.

Correcting these problems should not be too difficult, requiring researchers who are informed about and willing to address these methodological deficiencies and to focus more on theory-oriented, experimental research. But even if these problems are addressed, there remain other issues that cannot be resolved by improved methodology. In this concluding section I describe briefly some of the substantive and conceptual issues that will need attention and resolution before anyone will really understand the risk perception–preventive behavior relationship.

The Multi-dimensionality of Risks

For the most part, the word "risk" in this chapter referred to a specific issue, the probability that a harmful event will occur. *Severity* is another attribute of harmful events that is included in most theories of preventive health behavior. Severity is usually assessed by one or two questions that ask for an overall judgment about how bad it would be to experience the problem. This approach glosses over the separate and perhaps different roles that expectations of disability, pain, duration, death, curability, dependency and disfigurement might play. Some of these issues may be more influential than others, and a summary judgment of severity may miss what is really important to people. (For an empirical study of hazard attributes other than severity see Klohn and Rogers, 1991.)

Nearly all of the studies that have examined the links between risk perceptions and precautionary behavior have considered just these two aspects of risk perceptions – likelihood and severity – and they have assessed such perceptions through only one method – direct questioning (e.g., "How serious would it be to have it happen to you?"). However, no real hazards can be adequately described by just these two dimensions (Weinstein, 1999).

As an example, consider cigarette smoking. Smoking can lead to many different negative outcomes – including wrinkles, sick family members, shortness of breath, heart disease, and cancer – and these vary greatly in the likelihood that they will lead to disability or death. These outcomes vary in the delay between beginning smoking and experiencing harm, in the degree to which they are reversible by quitting, and in the extent to which there are warning signals of approaching harm. It is highly questionable whether these issues are adequately described by summary judgments of the likelihood and severity of health problems from smoking.

Other hazard attributes that may influence behavior (and that certainly influence risk perceptions; Slovic, 1987) include whether the hazard is perceived to be familiar or unfamiliar; natural or manmade; appearing slowly or gradually; understood by science or poorly understood; infectious or not infectious; and so on. All of these are aspects of "risk perception" and need consideration.

Understanding Perceived Likelihood

Even though perceptions of hazard likelihood have been recognized as important since the earliest theories of health behavior were formulated (e.g., Hochbaum, 1958), we still know almost nothing about how people process, store, and retrieve information about the probability of harm. One thing is clear; people have great difficulty using the odds and percentages that form the scientist's language of probability (Weinstein, 1998a). Even if people are able to cite a probability statistic accurately, it does not mean they understand what this number really means or that they actually use this number in making decisions. This fact should not be surprising. Aside from weather forecasts, hardly ever does the public receive, generate, or make choices on the basis of numerical probability data.

How do people normally think about probability? Is it more natural to think about the absolute magnitude of a risk, or do people tend to think in terms of risk comparisons (i.e., which risks are bigger or smaller than others)? Do people focus on whether their own risks are higher or lower than those of their peers? Since people have such difficulty with numerical probabilities, do they have some kind of verbal or non-verbal category system for risk? Do different people use different kinds of cognitive structures to understand their vulnerability, so that some rely on between-hazard comparisons and others

on a small number of probability categories? We can neither assess perceptions of likelihood well nor communicate perceptions of likelihood effectively
without a better understanding of how people process and use probability
information.

Factors Other than Beliefs that Affect Behavior

An implicit assumption of current decision-oriented theories of preventive
health behavior is that cognitive appraisals (i.e., judgments about hazard
attributes and other situational features) are the sole determinants of precautionary behavior. I seriously doubt, however, that responses to hazards can
ever be predicted adequately from our judgments alone. Hazards also produce
emotional reactions, such as fear, and can have persistent effects on mood.
They can produce unbidden thoughts that vary in their vividness, frequency,
and intrusiveness. In current theories, these factors would be relevant to
action only if they influenced hazard perceptions.

Considerable evidence exists demonstrating that worry (a poorly defined
concept containing elements of both emotion and attention) is often a good
predictor of action (e.g., McCaul et al., 1996) and that worry provides predictive power beyond that provided by judgments of likelihood and severity.
Similarly, in a study of the steps people take to protect themselves against
tornadoes (Weinstein et al., 2000a), my colleagues and I found that a dimension we called "preoccupation," a combination of intrusive thoughts, vigilance, and frequency of thoughts, predicted action better than did ratings of
tornado likelihood, control, self-reported anxiety, or self-reported depression.
Thus, reactions to risk involve more than beliefs and expectations, so even if
one were to collect ratings of all the hazard attributes mentioned earlier, we
would still have an incomplete picture of its impact on an individual.

Toward the Future

Do people take precautions to reduce their risks? It seems obvious that risk
influences preventive actions some of the time, but attempts to investigate
this relationship, how its strength various from person to person and from
hazard to hazard – have not been very successful. My research has helped to
clarify how we should (and should not) study these issues and to reinforce
the belief that under-estimations of risk encourage risky behavior. What is
not yet clear is how much our tendency to construct comforting assessments
of our own vulnerability limits preventive health behavior. It appears that
absolute risk judgments (e.g., it is "very unlikely") sometimes predict action
better than relative risk judgments (e.g., it is "less likely for me than for other
people"), but these absolute judgments are often constructed by starting
with the perceived absolute risk for others and adjusting downward (thereby

demonstrating biased perceptions of relative risk) to arrive at an absolute risk for oneself (Chandler and Greening, 1995; Greening and Chandler, 1997; Rothman et al., 1996; Weinstein and Lyon, 1999).

Risk reduction appears to be one of the most important reasons why people adopt behaviors that protect them from harm, but it is not the only reason. Better research, especially experiments examining the change in behavior that can be achieved by altering perceptions of risk, could go a long way toward helping us understand the risk perception–preventive behavior link. If, as I believe, precaution adoption occurs through a series of stages, there may be multiple points at which risk perceptions are important, and successful attempts to explain the perception–behavior link (and to encourage self-protective behavior) will have to incorporate these stages into research designs and analyses.

Acknowledgments

This chapter benefited greatly from the suggestions of Cara Cuite, Jerry Suls, and Kenneth Wallston. I also wish to acknowledge the contributions made by my collaborators in this research, especially Cara Cuite, Bill Klein, Judith Lyon, Alexander Rothman, and Peter Sandman. Support for this work from the New Jersey Department of Environmental Protection, the New Jersey Agriculture Experiment Station, the US Environmental Protection Agency, and the National Cancer Institute is gratefully acknowledged.

Correspondence concerning this chapter should be sent to: Neil Weinstein, Department of Human Ecology, Cook College, Building 202, Rutgers, The State University of New Jersey, New Brunswick, MJ 08903-0231, USA; e-mail: neilw@aesop.rutgers.edu

Note

1. To my knowledge, in the past couple of decades there have been only a few reviews of studies examining the link between risk perceptions and action (e.g., Harrison et al., 1992; Janz and Becker, 1984; Floyd et al., 2000). Unfortunately, none of these reviews excluded studies that used incorrect analyses. Thus, despite the existence of a huge non-experimental literature, there are no trustworthy summaries of this research. To find out whether high levels of perceived risk are associated with a greater likelihood of subsequent action in correlational research, one would need to carefully review hundreds of studies, screening out those that used incorrect analyses and ones that are weak in other ways (for example, inadequate sample sizes, questionable measurements, use of behavioral intentions rather than actual behavior as the outcome variable, or low within-sample variance in the independent variables). Such a review would be an extremely valuable contribution to the field, but it has yet to be carried out. Equally valuable would be a review of the experimental literature on this topic, and because of the much smaller number of studies, it would be a less daunting task.

References

Ajzen, I. (1985). From intentions to actions: A theory of planned behavior. In J. Kuhl and J. Beckmann (Eds.), *Action Control: From Cognition to Behavior* (pp. 11–40). Berlin: Springer-Verlag.

Ajzen, I., and Fishbein, M. (1980). *Understanding Attitudes and Predicting Behavior*. Englewood Cliffs, NJ: Prentice-Hall.

Ajzen, I., and Madden, T. J. (1986). Prediction of goal-directed behavior: Attitudes, intentions, and perceived behavioral control. *Journal of Experimental Social Psychology*, 22, 453–74.

Bandura, A. (1995). Moving into forward gear in health promotion and disease prevention. Address presented at the annual meeting of the Society of Behavioral Medicine, San Diego, CA, March.

Chandler, C. C., and Greening, L. A. (1995). It can't happen to me . . . Or can it? Poster presented at the annual meeting of the Society for Judgment and Decision Making, Los Angeles, CA.

Doyle, J. K., McClelland, G. H., and Schulze, W. D. (1991). Protective responses to household risk: A case study of radon mitigation. *Risk Analysis*, 11, 121–34.

Edwards, W. (1954). The theory of decision making. *Psychological Bulletin*, 51, 380–417.

Farkas, A. J., Pierce, J. P., Gilpin, E. A., Zhu, Shu-Hong, Rosbrook, B., Berry, C., and Kaplan, R. M. (1996). Is stage-of-change a useful measure of the likelihood of smoking cessation? *Annals of Behavioral Medicine*, 18, 79–86.

Fishbein, M., and Ajzen, I. (1975). *Belief, Attitude, Intention and Behavior: An Introduction to Theory and Research*. Reading, MA: Addison-Wesley.

Fishbein, M., and Middlestadt, S. E. (1989). Using the theory of reasoned action as a framework for understanding and changing AIDS-related behaviors. In V. M. Mays, G. W. Albee and S. F. Schneider (Eds.), *Primary Prevention of AIDS: Psychological Approaches* (pp. 93–110). Newbury Park, CA: Sage.

Floyd, D. L., Prentice-Dunn, S., Rogers, R. W. (2000). A meta-analysis of research on protection motivation theory. *Journal of Applied Social Psychology*, 30, 407–29.

Greening, L., and Chandler, C. C. (1997). Why it can't happen to me: The base rate matters, but overestimating skill leads to underestimating risk. *Journal of Applied Social Psychology*, 27, 760–80.

Harrison, J. A., Mullen, P. D., and Green, L. W. (1992). A meta-analysis of studies of the health belief model with adults. *Health Education Research: Theory and Practice*, 7, 107–16.

Herzog, T. A., Abrams, D. B., Emmons, K. M., Linnan, L. A., and Shadel, W. G. (1999). Do processes of change predict smoking stage movements? A prospective analysis of the transtheoretical model. *Health Psychology*, 18, 369–75.

Hochbaum, G. M. (1958). Public participation in medical screening programs: A sociopsychological study. US Public Health Service Publication No. 572. Washington, DC: US Government Printing Office.

Janz, N. K., and Becker, M. H. (1984). The Health Belief Model: A decade later. *Health Education Quarterly*, 11, 1–47.

Johnson, E. J., and Tversky, A. (1983). Affect, generalization, and the perception of risk. *Journal of Personality and Social Psychology*, 454, 20–31.

Kirscht, J. P. (1988). The health belief model and predictions of health actions. In D. S. Gochman (Ed.), *Health Behavior: Emerging Research Perspectives* (pp. 27–41). New York: Plenum Press.

Klohn, L. S., and Rogers, R. W. (1991). Dimensions of the severity of a health threat: the persuasive effects of visibility, time of onset, and rate of onset on young women's intentions to prevent osteoporosis. *Health Psychology*, 10, 323–9.

Lachendro, E., and Weinstein, N. D. (1982). Egocentrism as a source of unrealistic optimism. *Personality and Social Psychology Bulletin*, 8, 195–200.

Levi, A. S., and Pryor, J. B. (1987). Use of the availability heuristic in probability estimates of future events: The effects of imagining outcomes versus imagining reasons. *Organizational Behavior and Human Decision Processes*, 40, 219–34.

Lipkus, I. M., Biradavolu, M., Fenn, K., Keller, P., and Rimer, B. K. (2001). Informing women about their breast cancer risks: Truth and consequences. *Health Communication*, 13, 205–26.

Mason, T. J., McKay, F. W., Hoover, R., Blot, W. J., and Fraumeni, Jr., J. F. (1975). *Atlas of Cancer Mortality in US Counties: 1950–1969*. US Department of Health, Education, and Welfare, HEW Publication No. NIH 75–780. Washington, DC: US Government Printing Office.

McCaul, K. D., Schroeder, D. M., and Reid, P. A. (1996). Breast cancer worry and screening: Some prospective data. *Health Psychology*, 15, 430–3.

Perloff, L. S., and Fetzer, B. K. (1986). Self-other judgments and perceived vulnerability to victimization. *Journal of Personality and Social Psychology*, 50, 502–11.

Prentice-Dunn, S., and Rogers, R. W. (1986). Protection motivation theory and preventive health: Beyond the Health Belief Model. *Health Education Research*, 1, 153–61.

Prochaska, J. O., and DiClemente, C. C. (1983). Sages and processes of self-change in smoking: Toward an integrative model of change. *Journal of Consulting and Clinical Psychology*, 51, 390–5.

Quadrel, M. J., and Fischhoff, B. (1993). Adolescent (in)vulnerability. *American Psychologist*, 48, 102–17.

Quinlan, K. B., and McCaul, K. D. (2000). Matched and mismatched interventions with young adult smokers: Testing a stage theory. *Health Psychology*, 19, 165–71.

Rogers, R. W. (1983). Cognitive and physiological processes in fear appeals and attitude change. In J. T. Cacioppo and R. E. Petty (Eds.), *Social Psychophysiology* (pp. 153–76). New York: Guilford Press.

Ronis, D. L. (1992). Conditional health threats: Health beliefs, decisions, and behaviors among adults. *Health Psychology*, 11, 127–34.

Rosenstock, I. M. (1974). The health belief model: Origins and correlates. *Health Education Monographs*, 2, 336–53.

Rothman, A. J., Klein, W. M., and Weinstein, N. D. (1996). Absolute and relative biases in estimations of personal risk. *Journal of Applied Social Psychology*, 26, 1213–36.

Sandman, P. M., Klotz, M. L., and Weinstein, N. D. (1987). Public response to the risk from geological radon. *Journal of Communication*, 37(3), 93–108.

Sandman, P. M., and Weinstein, N. D. (1993). Predictors of home radon testing and implications for testing promotion programs. *Health Education Quarterly*, 20, 1–17.

Schwarzer, R. (1992). Self-efficacy in the adoption and maintenance of health behaviors: Theoretical approaches and a new model. In R. Schwarzer (Ed.), *Self-efficacy: Thought Control of Action* (pp. 217–42). Washington, DC: Hemisphere.

Sherman, S. J., Skov, R. B., Hervitz, E. F., and Stock, C. B. (1981). The effects of explaining hypothetical future events: From possibility to probability to actuality and beyond. *Journal of Experimental Social Psychology*, 17, 142–58.

Simon, P. M., Morse, E. V., Balson, P. M., Osofsky, H. J., and Gaumer, H. R. (1993). Barriers to human immunodeficiency virus related risk among male street prostitutes. *Health Education Quarterly*, 20, 261–73.

Slovic, P. (1987). Perception of risk. *Science*, 236, 280–5.

Strecher, V. J., Kreuter, M. W., and Kobrin, S. C. (1995). Do cigarette smokers have unrealistic perceptions of their heart attack, cancer, and stroke risks? *Journal of Behavioral Medicine*, 18, 45–54.

Sutton, S. R. (1982). Fear arousing communications: A critical examination of theory and research. In J. R. Eiser (Ed.), *Social Psychology and Behavioral Medicine* (pp. 303–38). New York: Wiley.

Sutton, S. R. (2000). A critical review of the transtheoretical model applied to smoking cessation. In P. Norman, C. Abraham, and M. Conner (Eds.), *Understanding and Changing Health Behaviour: From Health Beliefs to Self-regulation* (pp. 207–25). Reading, UK: Harwood Academic Press.

Weinstein, N. D. (1978). Cognitive processes and information seeking concerning an environmental health threat. *Journal of Human Stress*, 4, 32–41.

Weinstein, N. D. (1979). Seeking reassuring or threatening information about environmental cancer. *Journal of Behavioral Medicine*, 2, 125–39.

Weinstein, N. D. (1980). Unrealistic optimism about future life events. *Journal of Personality and Social Psychology*, 39, 806–20.

Weinstein, N. D. (1982). Unrealistic optimism about susceptibility to health problems. *Journal of Behavioral Medicine*, 5, 441–60.

Weinstein, N. D. (1983). Reducing unrealistic optimism about illness susceptibility. *Health Psychology*, 2, 11–20.

Weinstein, N. D. (1984). Why it won't happen to me: Perceptions of risk factors and illness susceptibility. *Health Psychology*, 3, 431–57.

Weinstein, N. D. (1987). Unrealistic optimism about susceptibility to health problems: Conclusions from a community-wide sample. *Journal of Behavioral Medicine*, 10(5), 481–500.

Weinstein, N. D. (1988). The precaution adoption process. *Health Psychology*, 7(4), 355–86.

Weinstein, N. D. (1989). Optimistic biases about personal risks. *Science*, 246, 1232–3.

Weinstein, N. D. (1993). Testing four competing theories of health-protective behavior. *Health Psychology*, 12, 324–33.

Weinstein, N. D. (1998a). Accuracy of smokers' risk perceptions. *Annals of Behavioral Medicine*, 20, 135–40.

Weinstein, N. D. (1998b). References on perceived vulnerability and optimistic biases about risk or future life events. Unpublished bibliography, Department of Human Ecology, Rutgers University, New Brunswick, NJ.

Weinstein, N. D. (1999). What does it mean to understand a risk? Evaluating risk comprehension. *Journal of the National Cancer Institute*, Monograph 25, 15–20.

Weinstein, N. D., Atwood, K., Puleo, E., Fletcher, R., Colditz, G., and Emmons, K. M. (2001). Colon cancer: Risk perceptions and risk communication. Unpublished paper. Department of Human Ecology, Rutgers University, New Brunswick, NJ.

Weinstein, N. D., and Klein, W. M. (1995). Resistance of personal risk perceptions to debiasing interventions. *Health Psychology*, 14, 132–40.

Weinstein, N. D., and Klein, W. M. (1996). Unrealistic optimism: Present and future. *Journal of Social and Clinical Psychology*, 15, 1–8.

Weinstein, N. D., Klotz, M. L., and Sandman, P. M. (1988). Optimistic biases in public perceptions of the risk from radon. *American Journal of Public Health*, 78, 796–800.

Weinstein, N. D., and Lyon, J. E. (1999). Mindset, optimistic bias, and preventive behavior. *British Journal of Health Psychology*, 4, 289–300.

Weinstein, N. D., Lyon, J. E., Rothman, A. J., and Cuite, C. L. (2000a). Preoccupation and affect as predictors of self-protective behavior following natural disaster. *British Journal of Health Psychology*, 5, 351–63.

Weinstein, N. D., Lyon, J. E., Rothman, A. J., and Cuite, C. L. (2000b). Changes in perceived vulnerability following natural disaster. *Journal of Social and Clinical Psychology*, 19, 372–95.

Weinstein, N. D., Lyon, J. E., Sandman, P. M., and Cuite, C. L. (1998a). Experimental evidence for stages of precaution adoption. *Health Psychology*, 17, 445–53.

Weinstein, N. D., and Nicolich, M. (1993). Correct and incorrect interpretations of correlations between risk perceptions and risk behaviors. *Health Psychology*, 12, 235–45.

Weinstein, N. D., Rothman, A. J., and Nicolich, M. (1998b). Using correlations to study relationships between risk perceptions and preventive behavior. *Psychology and Health*, 13, 479–501.

Weinstein, N. D., Rothman, A., and Sutton, S. (1998c). Stage theories of health behavior. *Health Psychology*, 17, 290–9.

Weinstein, N. D., and Sandman, P. M. (1992). A model of the precaution adoption process: Evidence from home radon testing. *Health Psychology*, 11, 170–80.

Weinstein, N. D., Sandman, P. M., and Klotz, M. L. (1987). *Public response to the risk from radon, 1986*. Report to the Division of Environmental Quality, New Jersey Department of Environmental Protection, Trenton, NJ.

Weinstein, N. D., Sandman, P. M., and Roberts, N. E. (1989). *Public response to the risk from radon, 1988–89*. Report to the Division of Environmental Quality, New Jersey Department of Environmental Protection, Trenton, NJ.

Weinstein, N. D., Sandman, P. M., and Roberts, N. E. (1990). Determinants of self-protective behavior: Home radon testing. *Journal of Applied Social Psychology*, 20, 783–801.

Weinstein, N. D., Sandman, P. M., and Roberts, N. E. (1991). Perceived susceptibility and self-protective behavior: A field experiment to encourage home radon testing. *Health Psychology*, 10, 25–33.

CHAPTER 3

Communicating about Health: Message Framing, Persuasion, and Health Behavior

Peter Salovey

Yale University

and

Duane T. Wegener

Purdue University

Introduction

For several decades, public health experts and communication researchers have been concerned about whether health campaigns – sometimes very costly efforts – were actually having their intended impact. There have been some notable failures: the campaign to "Just Say No" to drugs probably did little to turn adolescents away from marijuana, cocaine, or heroin. Over the years, marketing principles generally thought to be effective have been articulated, but often they have been deduced from the ground up, that is, without guidance from overarching theories of persuasion or decision making. Many such theories have been developed and tested within social psychology, and such theories might do a great deal to inform applied work in health communication (and to motivate future research on health communication). In this chapter, we discuss social psychological research and theory that can be used to optimize the influence of health messages. In particular, we discuss research on message framing that was initially inspired by Prospect Theory (Kahneman and Tversky, 1979). Much of this research, and the persuasion literature in general, might be organized by overarching models such as the Elaboration Likelihood Model (Petty and Cacioppo, 1986b), and we describe in some detail how such models might guide future attempts to understand effects of health-relevant communications.

Social psychological research on attitude change has studied many aspects of persuasive communication (see Eagly and Chaiken, 1998; Petty and Wegener, 1998a, for recent reviews). The variables studied can be classified into four broad categories of (a) the source of the persuasive message (e.g., expertise, credibility, trustworthiness, attractiveness, and similarity to the recipient), (b) the recipient of the message (e.g., knowledge about the attitude domain, experience with the attitude object, and demographic and dispositional characteristics expected to be associated with influenceability), (c) aspects of the message itself (e.g., personal relevance of the message topic, discrepancy of the message position from recipient opinions, use of rhetorical questions), and (d) the context in which the message is encountered (e.g., distraction, audience reactions to a message). (For more thorough reviews, see McGuire, 1969; 1985; Petty and Wegener, 1998a.) In the present chapter we focus on message factors in health communications.

Background: Fear Appeals

Though many message factors have been studied within the realm of health communications, one of the oldest and most studied topics is the inclusion of threatening (fear-producing) material in persuasive messages. Over the years, there have been a number of approaches to fear-inducing messages. Hovland et al. (1953) treated fear as a drive state that would motivate attempts to reduce the state, including acceptance of a "reassuring recommendation" from the persuasive appeal. However, high levels of fear were also thought to motivate defensive behaviors such as inattention to the message, aggression toward the source, and future defensive avoidance of the topic altogether. Therefore, this drive-reduction approach predicted curvilinear effects of fear (with moderate levels of fear producing the greatest message effectiveness), and later work by Janis (1967) and McGuire (1968; 1969) conceptualized such curvilinear effects as related to reception (understanding) of message arguments juxtaposed with yielding to (acceptance of) the message.

Despite the centrality of emotional experiences in these early treatments of threatening appeals, the cognitive revolution in psychology was accompanied by views of fear appeals that were much more "cold" and cognitive. This began with Leventhal's (1970) parallel response model, in which cognitive attempts at "danger control" operated as conceptually separate processes from the "fear control" aimed at reducing emotional tension. Even more "cognitive" treatments of threat/fear appeals were developed by Rogers (1975; 1983), Beck and Frankel (1981), and Sutton (1982). These theories are generally consistent with the expectancy-value notions that persuasive appeals will be most successful when they describe likely positive consequences of action or likely negative consequences of failing to take the recommended action (see Eagly and Chaiken, 1998; McCaul this volume; Petty and Wegener, 1998a, for discussions). In such approaches, the cognitive assessments of such variables as the severity of the threat or one's vulnerability to that threat take center stage. The direct role of fear per se is minimized, though emotional reactions could influence one's perceptions of the threat or the consequences of action (Keller, 1999; Petty and Wegener, 1991; Rogers, 1983; Witte, 1998).

There are certainly parallels between the work on fear appeals and the work on message framing – the focus of the current chapter. For example, framing of messages in terms of negative consequences of inaction can be more threatening than framing in terms of positive consequences of action. In addition, the former framing can often lead to increases in experienced negative emotion on the part of message recipients. However, much of the existing research on message framing has failed to document direct effects of experienced emotion on message effectiveness.

Message Framing: Theoretical Background

Message framing refers to the emphasis in the message on the positive or negative consequences of adopting or failing to adopt a particular behavior (Rothman and Salovey, 1997). Therefore, appeals aimed at persuading individuals to perform a particular health behavior can be *framed* in different ways. *Gain-framed* messages usually present the benefits that are accrued through adopting the behavior (e.g., "a diet high in fruits and vegetables but low in fat can keep you healthy"). *Loss-framed* messages generally convey the costs of not adopting the requested behavior (e.g., "a diet low in fruits and vegetables but high in fat can lead to cancer").[1] Although these two messages convey essentially the same information about diet and health, one of these messages might be more persuasive than the other in certain settings.

The initial point of departure for investigating the effects of framed persuasive messages on health behaviors was provided by Prospect Theory (Kahneman and Tversky, 1979; 1982; Tversky and Kahneman, 1981). Prospect Theory was developed to predict decision-making under conditions of risk. The framing postulate suggests that decision makers organize information in memory relevant to such decisions in terms of potential gains (i.e., benefits) or potential losses (i.e., costs) as compared to a reference point (e.g., one's present level of health). Factually equivalent material can be presented differentially to individuals such that they encode it as either a gain or a loss.

In a famous example of how framing can cause preference reversals, Tversky and Kahneman (1981) presented individuals with a situation in which the outbreak of a disease is expected to kill 600 people. In one condition, participants were presented with gain-framed information. They decided whether to endorse a program guaranteeing that 200 people will be *saved* out of the original 600 people or one that claims there is a 0.33 probability that all 600 will be saved but also a 0.67 probability that no one will be saved. Note that although the "expected value" of the two programs is identical, the first option emphasizes a *certain* outcome, but the second emphasizes a *probabilistic* or risky outcome. Participants presented with these choices overwhelmingly selected the first option, the certain outcome, in which 200 people are guaranteed to be saved.

A second group of participants was presented with the same two options. However, in this version, the potential losses were emphasized. Participants had to choose between a first program in which 400 people out of the original 600 will certainly *die* or one in which there is the same 0.33 probability that no one will die and a 0.67 probability that all will die. Once again, the "expected value" of these two options is identical. Furthermore, these two options differ from the two previous options only in that they make salient potential costs or losses – deaths – as compared with the options that made salient potential benefits or gains – lives saved. In the loss-salient situation, participants overwhelmingly choose the second option, in which there is a 0.67 probability that everyone will die. When losses are anticipated, people no longer prefer the option that is a sure bet (400 will die, but 200 will live). Rather, they choose the option that involves risk or uncertainty (all might die, but all might live).

Prospect Theory summarizes these decision strategies by noting that individuals are, in general, *risk-seeking* in the domain of losses but *risk-averse* in the domain of gains. Prospect Theory assumes that an S-shaped function relates objective outcomes to their subjective values, and that the function is concave for gains and convex for losses and steeper in the loss domain. This function suggests that when behavioral choices involve some risk or uncertainty, individuals will be more likely to take these risks when information is framed in terms of the relative disadvantages (i.e., losses or costs) of the behavioral options.

Framing and the Prevention/Detection Distinction
The literature on framing and health promotion has yielded an interesting pattern of findings (reviewed in Rothman and Salovey, 1997; Wilson et al., 1988). Although loss-framing has been especially effective when promoting breast self-examination (Meyerowitz and Chaiken, 1987), HIV screening (Kalichman and Coley, 1995), and mammography utilization (Banks et al., 1995; Schneider et al., 2001a), gain-framed messages have encouraged preferences for certain surgical procedures (Levin et al., 1988, Experiment 2; Marteau, 1989; McNeil et al., 1982; Wilson et al., 1987), the use of infant car restraints (Christophersen and Gyulay, 1981; Treiber, 1986), regular physical exercise (Robberson and Rogers, 1988) and sunscreen utilization (Detweiler et al., 1999; Rothman et al., 1993).

Despite the disparate behavioral domains, considering the *type* of behavior being promoted can simplify the pattern of message framing effects on health behaviors. Loss-framed messages have been effective in promoting mammography, BSE, and HIV testing, all early-detection behaviors. Conversely, gain-framed messages have been effective in promoting the use of infant car restraints and sunscreen, both prevention behaviors. From a Prospect Theory point of view, the perceived risk (of finding an abnormality) could make loss-framed messages more persuasive in promoting the detection behaviors. However, prevention behaviors may not be perceived as risky at all; they are performed to deter the onset or occurrence of a health problem. Choosing to perform prevention behaviors is a conservative option – it maintains good health. From the view of Prospect Theory, because risk-averse options are preferred when people are considering benefits or gains, gain-framed messages might be more likely to facilitate performing prevention behaviors. Therefore, our initial empirical work tested whether the *match* between a message frame (gain or loss) and the required health behavior (prevention or detection) effectively creates behavior change. That is, are gain-framed messages more persuasive when promoting prevention behaviors, but loss-framed messages more persuasive when promoting early detection (screening) behaviors?

Highlights from a Ten-year Program of Research on Health Message Framing

Since 1990, we (the Health, Emotion, and Behavior [HEB] Laboratory in the Department of Psychology at Yale University)[2] have conducted a program of research investigating the influence of variously framed messages on behaviors relevant to cancer or HIV/AIDS. Many of these experiments have been conducted in field settings – such as community medical clinics, housing developments, and public beaches – often under the auspices of some kind of health promotion program. Other experiments have been conducted in the laboratory, in which we have sacrificed some ecological validity, but have gained greater control over the experimental setting and greater opportunity to explore potential mediators and moderators of framing effects. In the pages to follow, we organize the presentation of these experiments in the following way. First, we describe two field experiments demonstrating that loss-framed messages are especially effective in promoting early detection behaviors such as screen mammography. Then we describe two experiments showing that gain-framed messages are persuasive when the target behavior is a prevention-oriented activity such as the use of sunscreen. Third, we discuss health behaviors that can be described as having either prevention or detection functions, and we show that gain-framed messages are more persuasive in the former case but loss-framed messages are more persuasive in the latter. Finally, we present some findings from our program of research focused on HIV/AIDS, and argue that some behaviors, like HIV-testing, might be construed as having different functions by different message recipients and that the effectiveness of one frame or the other depends on these a priori construals (for a more complete review, see Salovey et al., 2002).

Loss-framed Messages Promote Detection Behaviors: Mammography

In many ways, screening mammography is the quintessential early-detection behavior. Women are encouraged to obtain mammograms annually (especially after age 50), and most seek screening believing that they are healthy. Obtaining a mammogram, then, is a psychologically risky behavior – a woman runs the risk of finding out she has an abnormality that could be cancerous when previously she thought she was healthy. Because mammography involves a probabilistic, uncertain outcome, it should be better motivated by loss-framed messages than gain-framed messages.

Our first experiment focused on mammography screening was conducted as part of a workplace health-promotion program at a large telephone company (Banks et al., 1995). Women were recruited through announcements in their paycheck envelopes. Anyone who had obtained fewer than 50 percent of the mammograms that they should have for someone of their age (assuming one every other year between age 40 and 50, and then one annually after age 50) was invited to view a 15-minute videotape on breast cancer and mammography. A sample of 133 women were assigned randomly to view a video during their lunch hour in which most of the information was presented either in gain-framed terms (e.g., the title was "The Benefits of Mammography") or in loss-framed terms (e.g., titled, "The Risks of Neglecting Mammography"). The sample was about 80 percent white and mostly Catholic. These women were generally from middle-class families and had moderate levels of education. We assessed attitudes relevant to breast cancer and mammography before and after the video presentation and, more importantly, assessed utilization of screening mammography 6 and 12 months later. Sample sentences from the two videos are provided in Banks et al. (1995, Table 1).

Interestingly, women who viewed the gain- or loss-framed video did not differ in their liking for the video or knowledge gleaned from it. However, after 12 months, it was clear that the loss-framed video had been more persuasive: 66.2 percent of the women had obtained a mammogram compared to 51.5 percent of the women who had viewed the gain-framed video. Similar differences, though not as large, were also obtained after just 6 months.

Some years later, we replicated this experiment but with a very different population of women (Schneider et al., 2001a). We recruited 752 women from two inner-city health clinics and several public housing developments in the same neighborhoods. About 43 percent were African American, 27 percent Anglo, and 25 percent Latina. Most of the participants were from low-income families (less than $13,500 per year) with a mean age of 56. Once again, women viewed a 15-minute video about breast cancer and mammography that was gain- or loss-framed. We made different pairs of framed videos, one pair emphasized the problem of breast cancer for all women, black, white or Latina. The other videos were targeted especially for either black, white, or Latina women and provided statistics and pictured models drawn only from those groups. We called these pairs of videos "multicultural" versus "targeted."

As measured 6 months later, the advantage for loss- over gain-framed messages seen in the telephone company study (Banks et al., 1995) was replicated here. With the multicultural messages, which were most like the ones used at the telephone company, 50 percent of the women who viewed the loss-framed message had received a mammogram compared to only 36 percent in the gain-framed version. However, there were no differences due to framing when the messages were targeted to the specific ethnicity of the participants, and neither version of the targeted video was as effective as the loss-framed, multicultural one. After 12 months, the pattern of findings was still the same, but the size of the effect had attenuated to some extent. Perhaps loss-framed messages that are so explicitly targeted to a particular ethnic group elicit some defensiveness that counteracted their expected effectiveness.

Taken together, loss-framed videos designed to promote screening mammography are more effective than gain-framed videos provided they are designed for a multicultural audience rather than specifically targeted for a particular ethnic group. This effect has been obtained in two quite different samples. Given that mammography is a health behavior that involves a psychological risk – the uncertainty associated with the potential to find cancer – these findings are consistent with the Prospect Theory prediction that risk (uncertainty) should be preferred over certainty when losses are made salient.

Gain-framed Messages Promote Prevention Behavior: Sunscreen

In comparison to screening mammography, the use of sunscreen at the beach, like most prevention-oriented health behaviors, involves few uncertainties and little psychological risk. One can be fairly sure that using sunscreen is a low-cost way of reducing skin cancer risk. Prospect Theory suggests that individuals should prefer options with certain outcomes (to options with probabilistic or uncertain outcomes) after considering potential gains, that is, when the advantages of the option are made salient. So in contrast with the findings obtained for screening mammography, we expected that the best way to promote the use of sunscreen is with gain-framed messages.

Over the years, we have conducted several studies of framed messages and interest in sunscreen, some among college students and others with more diverse samples of sunbathers on public beaches. In one study, 146 undergraduates read gain- or loss-framed pamphlets about skin cancer and sunscreen use (Rothman et al., 1993, Experiment 2). After reading the pamphlets, participants were given postage-paid postcards that they could mail to our laboratory requesting sunscreen samples and more information about skin cancer prevention. Interest in the pamphlet was high and did not differ across the two framing conditions. The gain-framed pamphlet did arouse more positive emotions, whereas the loss-framed pamphlet led to more negative feelings as well as higher estimates of one's risk for skin cancer. However, as Prospect Theory led us to predict, it was the gain-framed pamphlet that motivated more requests for sunscreen. The advantage of gain-framed messages over loss-framed ones was small for the men in the study, but quite sizable for the women. For instance, 79 percent of the women who read a gain-framed pamphlet subsequently requested sunscreen as compared to 45 percent who read the loss-framed pamphlet. For men, request rates were 50 percent and 47 percent, respectively. This might have occurred because the skin cancer topic was viewed as more personally relevant by the women in the study.

For people sunbathing on the beach, however, skin cancer might be a relatively involving topic for both genders. The beach certainly represents an ecologically valid (and enjoyable) setting in which to collect data about interest in sunscreen. In one experiment, we recruited 217 sunbathers on a public beach to read either gain- or loss-framed brochures about sunscreen and the prevention of skin cancer. After reading the brochure, they were given a coupon that could be exchanged later for a free bottle of sunscreen. When the sunscreen "vender" (actually, graduate students from the Health, Emotion, and Behavior Laboratory) appeared on the beach about half-hour later, we could observe, simply, which beach goers actually turned in their coupons. Seventy-one percent of the participants who read a gain-framed pamphlet subsequently requested sunscreen, but only 53 percent of those who read a loss-framed pamphlet did likewise. This difference remained reliable even when prior intentions to use sunscreen that day were statistically controlled. The advantage of gain-framed messages over loss-framed messages was especially apparent among beach goers who indicated that they had no prior intention to use sunscreen that day. In the more psychologically involving setting of the beach, these framing effects were seen in both men and women (Detweiler et al., 1999).

Unlike our experiments targeting mammography in which an early detection behavior was best promoted using loss-framed messages, the sunscreen experiments suggest that prevention behaviors might be best promoted with gain-framed messages. This was exactly the pattern of effects predicted based on the notions gleaned from Prospect Theory, but this pattern was only obtained across very different experiments targeting very different behaviors. More convincing data would require observing both the loss-frame and gain-frame advantages within the same study when participants are randomly assigned to conditions.

Some Behaviors Can Be Described as Detection *or* Prevention: Mouthwash, Pap Testing, and Hypothetical Actions

Ideally, we would like to show that when a health behavior is described as serving a prevention function, gain-framed messages are more effective than loss-framed messages. But when the same action is described as an early detection or screening behavior, loss-framed messages should be more effective. We have conducted this type of laboratory experiment in three different domains – promoting the use of dental mouthwash, pap testing, and behaviors relevant to a fictitious health problem.

Mouthwash
In our study promoting mouthwash, we described a mouth rinse product to 120 University of Minnesota undergraduates (Rothman et al., 1999,

Experiment 2). Half of these students heard about a typical mouthwash, one that removes plaque from teeth and thus prevents tooth decay and gum disease. The other half heard about a slightly more unusual mouthwash, one that detects the buildup of plaque by leaving red discolorations on the teeth where better brushing is needed (much like those red disclosing tablets that many baby boomers were given in elementary school). As usual, arguments in favor of either the prevention mouthwash or the disclosing mouthwash were framed in gain or loss terms, and participants were assigned randomly to receive one set or the other. Once again, ratings of the quality of the pamphlet were unaffected by either the behavior-type or framing manipulations, although participants reported having more positive affective reactions to the gain-framed pamphlet.

Participants were asked about their intentions to buy the mouthwash in the next week. As predicted, intentions to purchase the product were strongest when the preventive mouthwash was described in terms of benefits of using the mouthwash (gain-frame) and when the disclosing (detection) mouthwash was described in terms of costs of not using the mouthwash (loss-frame). For the prevention mouthwash, 67 percent of the participants planned to purchase it after reading the gain-framed pamphlet, but only 47 percent planned to purchase it after reading the loss-framed pamphlet. In the detection condition, 73 percent of the participants said they would buy the disclosing mouthwash after reading the loss-framed pamphlet, but only 37 percent of them said they would purchase it after reading the gain-framed pamphlet. These are some of the largest framing effects we have observed.

Pap testing
Pap testing is generally thought of as a behavior designed to detect cervical cancer. But actually, pap tests can be described in two different ways, emphasizing their early detection function, which is typical of most pap messages, or their preventive function. For example, health communicators can emphasize the *prevention* of cervical cancer through the detection of pre-cancerous abnormalities with regular pap testing (this is similar to the prevention of skin cancer through regular skin exams, detection and removal of pre-cancerous moles). In a study that we just completed, we developed four different videotape programs about the benefits of pap testing, gain- and loss-framed versions of a program emphasizing the early detection of cervical cancer, and gain- and loss-framed versions of a program emphasizing the prevention of cervical cancer through the detection of pre-cancerous lesions that could then be treated. Although this latter message is not exclusively focused on prevention, it does include more information about cancer prevention than the more typical pap test-promoting communications.

We showed one of these four videos to 497 women over age 18 attending a community health clinic. Most of these women were from relatively poor families; 59 percent were African American, 26 percent were Latina, and 12 percent were white. Six months later, rates of pap testing were highest in the prevention-gain and detection-loss conditions as expected, though the effect is not large.

A Hypothetical Health Problem

No chapter about health communication and social psychology would be complete without highlighting a study using a fictitious ailment. In this experiment, we described to 176 undergraduates a new disease called the letrolisus virus, that was much like the common flu but with much more health damaging consequences. Half of these participants heard about a program for preventing the letrolisus virus, while the other half heard about a letrolisus virus early-detection program. The actual behaviors required for either program were kept constant. Written arguments for the two health programs were either gain- or loss-framed (Rothman et al., 1999, Experiment 1).

Overall, there was a preference for engaging in prevention behaviors over detection behaviors, even though the same effort was required for each. This study also measured participants' need for cognition (Cacioppo et al., 1984), the willingness to engage in effortful cognitive activities. For participants high in need for cognition, the predicted pattern of behavioral intentions was observed. Individuals expressed stronger intentions to perform the detection behavior after reading the loss- rather than gain-framed information, and this pattern of means was reversed in the prevention condition. The behavioral intentions of people who tended not to think carefully about persuasive messages – people low in need for cognition – were unaffected by either the message-framing or behavior-type manipulations. As discussed later, this result is consistent with the idea that many of the observed framing effects require relatively high levels of information processing.

HIV Testing Can Be Construed as Having Certain or Uncertain Outcomes

As we have been discussing, the perceived function – as prevention or detection – of performing a health behavior appears to determine whether a gain- or loss-framed message is more persuasive in promoting it. Prevention and early detection behaviors differ in terms of the risk or uncertainty typically associated with them. Prevention behaviors are usually construed as safe, risk-averse choices. The decision to initiate a detection behavior often involves uncertainty and risk, as one generally does not know the outcome (health/illness) in advance.

Being tested for HIV would seem to be a typical detection behavior with attendant psychological risks and uncertainty, and thus should be better motivated by loss-framed messages. However, because HIV is tied, in large part, to behavior, some individuals might reasonably believe, based on their past behavior, that they are not at risk for HIV. For these individuals, HIV testing is a psychologically safe behavior (there is little chance of testing positive); the behavior has a relatively certain outcome. Therefore, these individuals might be more persuaded by gain-framed messages.

We recently completed a field experiment in which we tested whether individuals who differed in their views of HIV testing in this way would likewise differ in the framed message that would be most effective in motivating them to obtain an HIV test (Apanovitch et al., 2003). Prior to our work in this area, there has been little framing research in the domain of HIV/AIDS. One study, cited earlier, reported that 63 percent of African American participants volunteered for HIV testing after watching a loss-framed videotape targeted to participant's sex and ethnicity as compared to 23 percent who watched an "unframed" video featuring sex- and ethnic-matched models and 0 percent who viewed an "unframed" video in which ethnicity but not sex was matched (Kalichman and Coley, 1995). Kalichman and Coley did not provide a systematic test of message framing, however, as the groups varied on both message framing and targeting, and a gain-framed message was not included in the study. In other research, when condoms were described as 95 percent effective in preventing the spread of HIV (gain-frame), college students said they were more likely to use them than when they were described as having a 5 percent failure rate (loss-frame), even though the two statements are factually equivalent (Linville et al., 1993). However, Linville et al. did not recruit participants from a particularly vulnerable population, nor did they include a report of actual safer sex practices.

In our recently completed experiment, we examined whether gain- or loss-framed messages were more effective in encouraging women living in public housing or attending a community health center to obtain an HIV test (Apanovitch et al., 2003). We expected women who viewed HIV testing as a risky behavior with uncertain outcomes to be more persuaded by a loss-framed message, whereas women who viewed HIV testing as a safe behavior with certain outcomes would be more persuaded by gain-framed messages.

All participants were women from a low-income neighborhood of New Haven, Connecticut, either living in one of four public housing developments or attending a community health center. Of the 480 participants included in our analysis, most were ethnic minority group members: 66 percent African American, 21 percent Latino, 9 percent White, 1 percent Asian, 1 percent American Indian/Alaskan Native, and 2 percent other. The average age of the women in this sample was 32. Most (65 percent) of the women were single (never married), 82 percent had a high school diploma or less education, and the average annual income was $8,076.

We developed four videotaped educational programs, identical in informational content, but framed differently. Two types of gain-framed and two types of loss-framed videotapes promoting HIV testing were created. That is, gain-framed messages either noted that HIV testing would bring positive consequences or would make negative outcomes unlikely. Loss-framed messages either noted that not testing for HIV would make negative consequences likely or would make positive outcomes unlikely (see also Detweiler et al., 1999; Rothman and Salovey, 1997). There were no differences across the two types of gain-framed or loss-framed videos, so they were combined in all subsequent analyses.

At 6 months, results generally conformed to the pattern previously discussed. There was a significant gain-frame advantage among women who viewed

HIV testing as a behavior with a certain outcome such that 38 percent of those who saw a gain-framed video were tested, compared to 26 percent who saw a loss-framed video. Participants who viewed HIV testing as a risky behavior with uncertain outcomes showed a trend in the other direction, toward loss-framed messages being more persuasive. Forty percent of participants who saw a gain-framed video were tested compared with 47 percent who saw a loss-framed video.

HIV, compared to breast cancer, for example, seems to be a unique disease in that individuals have a greater chance of surmising their HIV status, based on their behavioral history, without testing. In other words, to some extent, individuals can assess their risk independently without reference to a medical test. Differences in the perceptions of the riskiness of being tested for HIV naturally follow, with those engaging in high-risk behavior having more uncertainty as to their HIV status and test outcome, and those not engaging in high-risk behavior perceiving the test as an opportunity to confirm their present health status. Loss-framed messages appear more persuasive to the former group of individuals, while gain-framed messages are more effective for the latter group.

Mechanism

We hope, so far, that we have been fairly convincing with respect to the relatively robust effects of framing on the persuasiveness of health messages. Because many of these experiments have taken place in field settings with vulnerable and often hard-to-reach populations, we have not always had the luxury of pursing potential mediators of framing effects. Even in our laboratory studies, it has been difficult to find consistent evidence for any one mediator being critical to understanding the impact of framing on health behavior. Although Prospect Theory provided a point of departure for studying effects of message framing, the theory provides more of a description of outcomes than it does a discussion of mediating (or moderating) process. A number of more process-oriented theories of attitude change have held center stage in the attitudes domain since the development of Prospect Theory, however. In fact, around the time Prospect Theory was introduced, overarching theories of attitude change were also developed that include ways to organize the effects of many persuasion variables and processes. In the following sections, we present a general overview of basic attitudes work in social psychology, and we attempt to provide a "road map" for how the existing organizing themes could be brought to bear on the topic of framing of health communications. Integrating research on message framing with the extant persuasion theories serves to suggest a number of potential mediators and moderators of framing effects. It is our hope that consideration of these variables and processes will provide greater understanding of potential mechanisms that account for the differential effectiveness of gain- and loss-framed messages in different behavioral domains.

Basic Research on Attitude Change

Over the past 20 years, the social psychological literature has come to organize attitude change phenomena within so-called "dual-process" models such as the Elaboration Likelihood Model (ELM; Petty and Cacioppo, 1986a; 1986b) and the Heuristic-Systematic Model (HSM; Chaiken et al., 1989; see Chaiken and Trope, 1999 for presentation and discussion of a variety of dual-process models in social psychology). These models emphasize that different persuasion processes require differing levels of cognitive effort, and that, in part due to these different levels of effort, such processes differ in their long-term consequences for attitude change. Another important aspect of these models is that a given persuasion outcome (e.g., greater persuasion to obtain a mammogram by a loss-framed message) can come about for many different reasons. Because some of the processes that lead to this result might be relatively thoughtful, whereas others might be relatively non-thoughtful, the different processes leading to this persuasion outcome could hold the key to predicting whether that outcome would or would not persist over time (and, therefore, be capable of influencing later behavior; see Petty et al., 1995). In part because such predictions for lasting persuasive influence have been addressed very specifically within the ELM (Petty and Cacioppo, 1986a; 1986b), we use the ELM as an organizing framework for the following section (although an alternative approach, such as the HSM, could also be used to organize effects of persuasion variables, e.g., Chaiken et al., 1996).

The Elaboration Likelihood Model

Perhaps the most critical construct in the ELM is the elaboration continuum. This elaboration continuum is defined by how motivated and able people are to assess the central merits of a person, issue, or a position (i.e., the attitude object). The more motivated and able people are to assess the central merits of the attitude object (i.e., to determine how good the object really is), the more likely they are to scrutinize all available object-relevant information effortfully. Thus, at the high end of the elaboration continuum, people assess object-relevant information in relation to knowledge that they already possess, and arrive at a reasoned (though not necessarily unbiased) attitude that is well articulated and bolstered by supporting information. Especially in early depictions of the ELM, the high end of the elaboration continuum has been referred to as the "central route" to attitude change (see Petty and Wegener, 1999).

At the low end of the elaboration continuum (the so-called "peripheral route"), information scrutiny is reduced (see Petty and Wegener, 1999). Nevertheless, attitude change can still result from a low-effort scrutiny of the information available (e.g., examining less information than when elaboration is high or examining the same information less carefully), or attitude change can result from a number of less resource demanding processes such as classical conditioning (Staats and Staats, 1958), self-perception (Bem, 1972), or the use of heuristics (Chaiken, 1987). Attitudes that are changed with minimal object-relevant thought are postulated to be weaker than attitudes that are changed to the same extent as a result of maximal object-relevant thought.

Multiple Roles for Persuasion Variables
According to the ELM, at different points along the elaboration continuum, the same variables can have an impact on attitudes through different processes. When elaboration is high (when people think extensively about the attitude object), variables can influence attitudes by serving as "central merits" of an attitude object – serving as an "argument" that the object is good or bad – or by biasing information processing – making certain positive or negative interpretations of information more likely than other interpretations. When elaboration is low, however, the same variables might serve as relatively direct peripheral cues. That is, even if a variable is "peripheral" to the perceived central merits of the object, that variable might provide some simple indication that the attitude object is good or bad. Especially when elaboration is not constrained to be high or low, variables can influence where a person falls on the elaboration continuum (i.e., variables can influence motivation and/or ability to process information). In order to illustrate these multiple roles (central merit, biased processing, peripheral cue, amount of processing), we note examples of each role in the study of affect (mood) in persuasion. We do this in part because mood has been studied across each of the roles postulated by the ELM (see Wegener and Petty, 1996, 2001). In addition, affect might potentially play a role in message framing effects (e.g., see Petty and Wegener, 1991; Wegener et al., 1994, and later discussions in this chapter).

Mood as Central Merit
When motivation and ability to process information are maximally high, all information about the attitude object is effortfully scrutinized for its "central merits" relevant to the object. Therefore, one way for a variable to influence judgments is for the variable to represent a "central merit" of the object. For example, consider a situation in which one wants to assess whether or not a particular treatment for anxiety or depression is effective. How the person feels when using that treatment is clearly a central dimension of the merits of that treatment (see also Petty and Cacioppo, 1986a; Wegener and Petty, 1996).

Mood Biasing Information Processing
Another way for a variable to influence judgments when motivation and ability to think are high is to bias the processing of judgment-relevant information. That is, if multiple interpretations of judgment-relevant information are possible, a variable might make one interpretation more likely than other equally plausible interpretations, especially if available judgment-relevant information is somewhat ambiguous (e.g., see Chaiken and Maheswaran, 1994; Petty et al., 1991). For example, happy moods have often been found to make events or objects seem more desirable and/or more likely than the same events or objects appear when in sad or neutral moods (e.g., Forgas and

Moylan, 1987; Mayer et al., 1992; Wegener and Petty, 1996). These perceptions could make happy people likely to generate positive thoughts when
thinking carefully about a persuasive message (e.g., Petty et al., 1993).

When moods influence thoughts, however, the result is not always positive
moods leading to more persuasion. In some circumstances, negative moods
can actually lead to more favorable attitudes (Petty and Wegener, 1991;
Wegener et al., 1994). As noted earlier, mood can bias judgments by influencing estimates of the likelihood that the target possesses desirable or undesirable characteristics. In fact, this type of outcome has been shown when studying
effects of mood on the persuasiveness of gain- and loss-framed information.

Wegener et al. (1994) provided some research participants with a message
stating that adoption of the recommended position was likely to make good
things happen (a gain frame) and provided others with a message that failing
to adopt the position would make bad things happen (a loss frame). Wegener
et al. (1994) also included a measure of need for cognition (Cacioppo et al.,
1984). For participants who naturally enjoyed thinking (people high in need
for cognition), mood had opposite effects on the effectiveness of gain- versus
loss-framed messages. For gain-framed messages ("If you do this, good things
will happen"), happy mood led to more favorable views of the advocacy than
a sad mood. However, for loss-framed messages ("If you don't do this, bad
things will happen"), sad mood led to more favorable views of the advocacy
than a happy mood. Happy mood made the positive consequences of adopting the advocacy seem more likely, and the sad mood made the negative
consequences of *not* adopting the advocacy seem more likely.

Mood as a Peripheral Cue
For some situations, people, or objects, motivation and/or ability to process
information is lacking. When this is the case, people devote less effort to
assessing the central merits of an object. For example, they might consider
fewer pieces of evidence than individuals who are highly motivated and able
to think, or they might consider the same pieces of evidence, but do so in a
less thorough, more cursory way. In addition, when motivation or ability is
low, people are more likely to use some kind of short-cut based on aspects of
the message or setting that are "peripheral" to the central merits of the target.
In such settings, mood can have an impact on attitudes through relatively
simple associations or heuristics (Wegener and Petty, 1996; 2001).

Associating feelings with an object by classical conditioning would be one
example of low-effort processes providing a link between mood and judgment
(Griffitt, 1970; Zanna et al., 1970) because classical conditioning does not rely
on effortful scrutiny of information about the target (Cacioppo et al., 1992).
Mood might also affect attitudes relatively directly if mood is consulted in a
"How do I feel about it?" heuristic (Schwarz, 1990).[3]

Mood Influencing Amount of Processing
Finally, variables can affect motivation and/or ability to think carefully about
attitude-relevant information. A variety of processes might enable mood to
influence amount of processing. For example, some have postulated that certain

moods are associated with decreased cognitive capacity (Ellis and Ashbrook, 1988; Mackie and Worth, 1989; an "ability" hypothesis). One motivational hypothesis is that moods "inform" people whether or not processing is necessary. Positive moods are said to inform the person that the environment is safe and scrutiny of that environment is not necessary, whereas negative moods inform the person that there is a problem that deserves attention and thought (Clore et al., 1994; Schwarz, 1990).[4] Other hypothesized motives include mood-management (staying happy or feeling better, e.g., Isen and Shalker, 1982; Wegener et al., 1995).

Of course, the likelihood of mood or any variable influencing amount of thought is constrained by other variables in the setting – factors both internal and external to the social perceiver. If the baseline likelihood of elaboration is already quite low (e.g., because the person is distracted, Kiesler and Mathog, 1968; Petty et al., 1976) or quite high (e.g., because the judgment target is quite important or personally relevant, Leippe and Elkin, 1987; Petty et al., 1981), then impact of a variable on attitudes is most likely to occur through the low- or high-elaboration roles outlined earlier. If background variables do not constrain elaboration to be particularly high or low, and especially if a person is not sure whether or not effortful scrutiny is merited, however, then the variable might affect attitudes by increasing or decreasing the level of thought given to the available information.

In sum, the ELM posits that the same overall judgment outcome can take place for very different reasons. Thus, for example, positive mood could lead to increases in favorability of judgment because (a) elaboration was low but the positive mood was used as a favorable peripheral cue or easy-to-process piece of information (Petty et al., 1993), (b) elaboration was high and the positive mood served as a favorable piece of judgment-relevant information (Martin et al., 1997; see Wegener and Petty, 2001), (c) elaboration was high and the positive mood biased scrutiny of judgment-relevant information in a favorable direction (Wegener et al., 1994), (d) the positive mood increased the amount of scrutiny of cogent (strong) information (Wegener et al., 1995), or (e) the positive mood decreased the amount of scrutiny of specious (weak) information (Wegener et al., 1995a). As one can easily derive from the previous statements, a given variable (e.g., positive mood) can also assume different roles in different situations and therefore lead to different outcomes (see also Petty and Cacioppo, 1986b; Petty and Wegener, 1998a; 1999). Therefore, an overall attitudinal outcome alone (e.g., greater persuasion by a loss-framed message) often provides rather ambiguous evidence regarding processes that might underlie the outcome. Yet according to the ELM, the process by which any outcome is achieved is important because of the consequences for the judgment.

The ELM provides a useful organizing framework for attitude change. However, for many process-level predictions regarding effects of specific variables, the ELM depends on additional theoretical and empirical developments. For instance, the ELM itself does not predict whether gain-framed or loss-framed messages would be the most effective or whether gain- or loss-framed messages would increase or decrease processing. However, such questions follow logically

from considerations of the ELM multiple roles. Moreover, the ELM hypotheses about the strength of attitudes formed via high- versus low-elaboration
processes would suggest important consequences of the answers to such
research questions (see Petty et al., 1995). In the following section, we discuss
the possible relations between message framing effects and ELM predictions.
We also note some of the ELM-inspired techniques that would allow future
research to situate message framing within the multi-process landscape of
contemporary attitudes research. Finally, we also speculate about the most
likely mechanisms responsible for observed effects of message framing in
health communication contexts.

Understanding Message Framing Effects

As reviewed earlier, there are a number of effects of message framing
that have been consistently obtained. Detection behaviors generally are better
promoted by loss-framed messages, but prevention behaviors seem better
promoted by gain-framed messages. The next important step in this work is to
gain a firm grasp on the mechanism(s) responsible for such effects. Consistent
with the purpose of this chapter, one reasonable place to start in such an
endeavor would be to ask how basic theory in attitude change would inform
the understanding of the mechanisms underlying these framing effects.

Recall that the ELM poses a number of possible reasons for a given persuasion outcome, depending on the level of elaboration in that persuasion
setting. Let us consider the consistent advantage of gain-frame messages in
the arena of prevention behaviors (e.g., Christophersen and Gyulay, 1981;
Detweiler et al., 1999; Rothman et al., 1993; Schneider et al., 2001b). Without considering the specific factors that might make one explanation better
than others, the general ELM framework might suggest that gain-frame
messages increase persuasion for one or more of the following reasons:
(a) elaboration was low but the positive tone of gain-frame communications
served as a favorable peripheral cue or easy-to-process piece of information
(cf. Maheswaran and Meyers-Levy, 1990); (b) elaboration was high and gain-
frame messages generally constituted "stronger" (more compelling) arguments
than loss-frame messages when arguing for prevention behaviors; (c) elaboration was high and some aspect of the prevention setting biased scrutiny of the
information to make gain-frame communications more effective or loss-frame
information less effective (cf. Wegener et al., 1994); (d) the gain-frame messages received greater scrutiny than the loss-frame messages and there were
cogent (strong) arguments in the message, or (e) the gain-frame messages
received less scrutiny than the loss-frame messages and there were specious
(weak) arguments in the message.

Cue Effects?
These possible explanations are certainly not all equally plausible. Based on
the existing research, it seems unlikely that the enhanced effectiveness of
gain-frame messages in prevention settings (or loss-frame effectiveness in

detection settings) would be driven by low-effort "cue" effects of the message frame. The strongest argument against framing being a function of peripheral cues, however, is that the observed effects have been long lasting. Not only have the framing effects influenced relatively immediate behavior or judgment (as in Detweiler et al., 1999; Rothman et al., 1999), but many of the observed effects have influenced behaviors performed weeks, months, or up to a year after the framed communication (e.g., Banks et al., 1995; Schneider et al., 2001a; Schneider et al., 2001b). It should be noted that the loss-frame advantages for detection behaviors have been more extensively studied following long delays (e.g., Banks et al., 1995; Schneider et al., 2001a), but even the gain-frame advantages on sunscreen requests have measured behavior outside the immediate questionnaire context (Detweiler et al., 1999) or using return of postcards some time after the experimental session (Rothman et al., 1993). Strong impact on behavior is a likely consequence of attitudes based on high levels of information scrutiny (e.g., Petty et al., 1995), so the existing behavioral results suggest that the observed framing effects are probably the result of one or more processes operating at relatively high levels of message scrutiny.

Differential Argument Strength?

One might consider whether gain-framed messages are stronger arguments for prevention behaviors and whether loss-framed messages are stronger arguments for detection behaviors. For example, consider a choice about where to have heart surgery. Even if levels of scrutiny are equally high for each type of argument, it could be that arguments to have the surgery at one hospital would be "stronger" if focused on positive health outcomes (e.g., successful surgeries or recovery rates) at that hospital rather than negative health outcomes (e.g., deaths) avoided by the hospital. Even if the information provided is held constant across arguments, it could be that successful surgeries and recovery would conjure images of health and living, whereas avoiding deaths might conjure images of patients struggling to stay alive. Because elaboration of information in persuasive appeals often entails going beyond the information in the appeal (see Petty and Cacioppo, 1986a: 7–8; Wegener and Claypool, 1999), such "argument strength" effects of gain- versus loss-frame messages might be possible for some topics.

Considering a prevention behavior often occurs when people think themselves to be healthy. Information about continued health might seem appropriate and applicable to a person in that setting. Perhaps information about lack of health or about becoming sick appears less appropriate or applicable. When considering a detection behavior, however, this is often done when there is some possibility of disease (or at least the message is arguing for such a possibility). Therefore, messages about attaining undesirable outcomes might appear more applicable or appropriate.

One might also think of this in terms of chronological frames of reference. That is, gain-framed messages tend to imply current health and continued health, whereas loss-framed messages tend to imply current or impending lack of health. When healthy individuals consider preventive behaviors, they might naturally take on a long-term perspective, and gain-framed information might fit that view of illness as a future rather than current consideration. Similarly, when people consider actions that might detect a current illness, they might naturally take on a more short-term perspective, and loss-framed information that implies current or impending illness might resonate with that perspective.

Some existing framing data might be considered consistent with this possibility. That is, for healthy women who viewed HIV testing as unlikely to reveal disease, gain-framed messages were actually more effective than loss-framed messages. It could be that the gain-framed arguments appeared more appropriate or applicable when the women thought they were already healthy (and when they could actually use the detection behavior as a way to keep their partners healthy; Apanovitch et al., 2003).

There might also be differential affective consequences of performing (or not performing) particular behaviors within prevention or detection settings. As noted earlier, prevention settings and gain-framed information each seem to focus on a current status of health. Given that prevention behaviors are quite likely to be beneficial according to the gain-framed arguments, one might feel particularly bad if one failed to engage in those prevention behaviors and later found oneself to be ill. In comparison, loss-framed arguments stress that the status quo or current situation is dangerous (i.e., doing nothing, bad things will happen or good things will fail to happen). Given this danger, one might feel particularly compelled to discover one's current health status, and would feel bad if discovery of illness is not attempted given the obvious possible danger (see also Salovey et al., 2002).

Biased Processing of Gain- versus Loss-framed Arguments?
Perhaps something associated with considering prevention or detection behaviors creates bias in processing of gain- versus loss-framed messages. That is, instead of the gain- or loss-framed arguments seeming more appropriate or applicable for a given type of behavior, it could be that something in the persuasion setting changes perceptions of the desirability of action and/or the likelihood of consequences of acting or failing to act.

Such an effect might be similar to the observed influence of mood on the effectiveness of gain- versus loss-framed messages (see earlier discussion of Wegener et al., 1994). Perhaps something similar could occur when comparing messages about prevention versus detection behaviors. Consider, for example, the gain-frame advantage for skin-protective behaviors at a public beach (Detweiler et al., 1999) compared with the loss-frame advantage for mammography (Banks et al., 1995). It could well be that message recipients are in a better mood when at the public beach rather than at work preparing to attend a lunchtime discussion of mammography. If so, then some part of the prevention-detection differences observed in past studies might be due to differences in feelings that co-vary with the settings in which message framing has been investigated. Even if feeling states per se do not markedly differ across the settings, it is almost assuredly true that people are more likely to be thinking about positive events when at the beach than when at work, especially if one is giving up one's lunch hour to hear about mammography. In fact, part of the prevention-detection difference itself might be that prevention is inherently more positive (less negative) than detection. When studies describe even the same behavior as being prevention, rather than detection, before presenting a message, it could be that the difference in positivity of prevention (versus negativity of detection) determines whether the gain- versus loss-framed information will be more effective (cf. Rothman et al., 1999). If this is so, then it may well be possible to influence whether gain- or loss-framing will be most effective even for the same prevention or detection behavior and without necessarily reinterpreting the prevention behavior as detection or vice versa.

Affecting Amount of Processing?
The messages used in past studies of message framing and health settings were undoubtedly designed to include strong arguments to support the advocacy. Given this fact, as well as the lasting impact of the framing effects investigated, it seems unlikely that the observed framing effects on behavior would be due to decreases in processing of weak (specious) information. They could be due to differences in amount of processing given to the critical aspects of the various messages. There might be a variety of factors that influence whether gain- or loss-framed information receives high levels of scrutiny. For example, Smith and Petty (1996) showed that creating expectations of gain or loss framing (through framing of article titles) increased processing of messages framed in the unexpected manner (i.e., gain-framed messages encountered after a loss-framed title or loss-framed messages encountered after a gain-framed title).

It seems unlikely that people would strongly expect loss-framed information for prevention behaviors and gain-framed information for detection behaviors, so processing of unexpected frames would seem unlikely to be a general explanation for framing effects. However, there are some processing effects that might apply. Messages "matching" the functional basis of the attitude result in greater scrutiny of that information (Snyder and DeBono, 1989). There may be a number of ways in which gain-framed information better "matches" the way people tend to think about the prevention behaviors (e.g., implying current health, long-term time perspective, affectively pleasant). It could also be that loss-framed information better "matches" the way people tend to think about detection behaviors (e.g., implying possible illness, short-term time perspective, affectively unpleasant).

Perhaps the affective differences between prevention and detection would also create differences in amount of processing of gain- versus loss-framed information. Information expected to be uplifting – such as about prevention – can receive greater processing by people in a positive rather than negative mood, whereas information expected to be depressing – such as having to contemplate disease detection – can receive greater processing by people in a negative rather than positive mood (Wegener et al., 1995; see Wegener and Petty, 1996, for a review). Gain- versus loss-framed information might be better processed, then, in the more positive versus negative moods generated, respectively, by having to think about prevention and detection.

Distinguishing among the Possibilities

Current attitude theory suggests two broad classes of effects that might account for the observed message framing effects. First, it could be that framing effects occur when people are thinking carefully about all the messages but something about the messages or setting makes one message more effective than the other. We refer to these explanations as the "high-elaboration" explanations. That is, either the gain- or the loss-framed message might appear more applicable or generally "stronger" (more compelling) than the other in a given setting (i.e., prevention or detection). Within the same class of effects, it could also be that the consequences of action specified in the message are viewed as more likely and/or more desirable when the message addresses certain types of behaviors. As a second type of explanation, it could be that something in the persuasion setting creates differences in how much people think about gain- or loss-framed information about the different behaviors. We refer to this explanation as the "amount of processing" explanation.

How might we distinguish between these possibilities, based on the existing research or on future data? One might begin by thinking about attitudinal responses immediately after the persuasive appeal that might distinguish "high-elaboration" from "amount of processing" accounts. If high levels of elaboration are present for both gain- and loss-framed messages, then differences in attitudes toward the prevention or detection behavior should be present soon after the message is encountered. However, if studies consistently show the same immediate post-message attitudes across conditions (despite finding different effects of message frames over time), this would make the "high-elaboration" explanations less plausible. This result could be consistent with an "amount of processing" explanation, however. As noted earlier, the same attitudes can come about for thoughtful versus non-thoughtful reasons. If the framing conditions differ in the amount of processing they receive, one could often find the same attitudes immediately after the message, but find differences in behavior over time because of the differential persistence of attitudes over time and differential use of attitudes to guide behavior across levels of processing. The existing framing studies do not allow one strongly to prefer one type of explanation over the other. One way to address such questions would be to incorporate traditional means of assessing the amount of processing of persuasive communications. These could include indices of cognitive responses and recall of message arguments, manipulations of argument quality, and assessments of cognitive effort given to scrutiny of the persuasive message (see Wegener et al., 1995a).

In the types of health settings described in this chapter, one would generally not introduce weak arguments supporting a health behavior. However, this is easily and commonly done when studying fictitious topics in the general persuasion literature (e.g., see Smith and Petty, 1996, using a fictitious vitamin supplement). Such techniques might be put to good use in studying message framing in the context of fictitious prevention or detection behaviors.

If message processing is greater for gain-framed messages in prevention settings (and/or for loss-framed messages in detection settings), then one should show greater impact of argument quality in these conditions.

It could well be, however, that the observed framing effects are due to the "high-elaboration processes" that would not be documented by assessments of "amount of processing." One could attempt to document this in a number of ways. Some experimental research already suggests that loss-frame advantages for a detection behavior are more likely under high levels of involvement or personal relevance (Maheswaran and Myers-Levy, 1990). Also, as noted earlier, some research using gender as a proxy for involvement has shown loss-frame advantages for detection and gain-frame advantages for prevention under high levels of involvement (Rothman et al., 1993). Additional research manipulating involvement (motivation to process) or manipulating ability to scrutinize information (e.g., through introduction of cognitive load, Petty et al., 1976) would certainly bolster support for such a conclusion. Additional support for "high-elaboration processes" could also be found through indices aimed at documenting the underlying judgmental processes (e.g., Wegener et al., 1994).

Summary

We adhere wholeheartedly to Kurt Lewin's edict that there is nothing so practical as a good theory. Understanding the mechanisms responsible for framing effects in health communications will be crucial to maximizing the effectiveness of applications of message framing to address important health crises (e.g., HIV/AIDS, cancer, teen pregnancy). It is our hope that current theorizing and methods from the area of attitudes and persuasion can enhance our understanding of message framing effects to encourage valuable and effective interventions through health communication.

We believe that many of the reported findings fit well within existing persuasion theories and that these theories suggest fruitful directions for future research. It should be noted, however, that this approach also raises many possibilities for changing one's general strategy with respect to the problem of prevention versus detection differences and message framing. That is, consistent with Salovey et al. (2002), we would note that the prevention-detection distinction is quite likely to be a specific (and imperfect) instance of some more general and abstract principle(s). Although the prevention-detection distinction has provided a ready shorthand or heuristic for organizing existing work, it is likely that more general dimensions will be found. Some current possibilities include the mood of the message recipient, the overall pleasantness of the setting preceding and surrounding the persuasive appeal, and/or the anticipated affective consequences of supporting or opposing the message advocacy (i.e., enacting or failing to enact the advocated action). We look with excitement toward the future work that will address these general principles as we continue to pursue understandings of health communication that facilitate effective intervention.

Acknowledgments

We thank the graduate students, undergraduates, and, especially, the research staff associated with the Health, Emotion, and Behavior (HEB) Laboratory in the Department of Psychology at Yale University who were instrumental in conducting much of the research reported here. Experiments on the framing of messages about behaviors relevant to the prevention or early detection of HIV and AIDS were conducted under the auspices of the Center for Interdisciplinary Research on AIDS (CIRA) at Yale University.

The research on the framing of health messages reported in this chapter was supported by grants to Peter Salovey from the American Cancer Society (RPG-93-028-05-PBP), the National Cancer Institute (R01-CA68427), and the Donaghue Women's Health Investigator Program at Yale University, and by a grant to both authors from the National Institute of Mental Health (P01-MH/DA56826).

Correspondence concerning this article should be addressed to Peter Salovey, Department of Psychology, Yale University, P.O. Box 208205, New Haven, Connecticut 06520-8205, USA; e-mail: peter.salovey@yale.edu.

Notes

1. These types of messages are also sometimes called positively framed and negatively framed messages, respectively (e.g., Petty and Wegener, 1991), but we will use the gain- and loss-frame terminology throughout this chapter.
2. From 1994 to 1997, this group included Duane Wegener and his students, whose work focused on attitudes and attitude change.
3. A key difference between use of mood under low and high elaboration conditions is that under low elaboration conditions, people would likely stop after inferring that "if I feel good, I must like it." Under high elaboration conditions, people would also consider any other judgment-relevant information that was available, and would be more likely to assess whether current feelings were really informative about the attitude object (i.e., they would assess the central merit of feelings for the judgment at hand).
4. Recently, a number of variants on such "informational" effects have been proposed (e.g., Bless et al., 1996; Martin et al., 1993; Wyer et al., 1999). Some of these variations propose that mood can answer questions other than whether processing is necessary, such as "do I still enjoy this activity," "do I need to work more," or "is this strategy sufficient."

References

Apanovitch, A. P., McCarthy, D., and Salovey, P. (2003). Using message framing to motivate HIV testing among low-income, ethnic minority women. *Health Psychology*, in press.

Banks, S. M., Salovey, P., Greener, S. et al. (1995). The effects of message framing on mammography utilization. *Health Psychology*, 14, 178–84.

Beck, K. H., and Frankel, A. (1981). A conceptualization of threat communications and protective health behavior. *Social Psychology Quarterly*, 44, 204–17.

Bem, D. J. (1972). Self-perception theory. In L. Berkowitz (Ed.), *Advances in Experimental Social Psychology* (Vol. 6, pp. 1–62). New York: Academic Press.

Bless, H., Clore, G. L., Schwarz, N., Golisano, V., Rabe, C., and Woelke, M. (1996). Mood and the use of scripts: Does being in a happy mood really lead to mindlessness? *Journal of Personality and Social Psychology*, 71, 665–79.

Cacioppo, J. T., Marshall-Goodell, B. S., Tassinary, L. G., and Petty, R. E. (1992). Rudimentary determinants of attitudes: Classical conditioning is more effective when prior knowledge about the attitude stimulus is low than high. *Journal of Experimental Social Psychology*, 28, 207–33.

Cacioppo, J. T., Petty, R. E., and Kao, C. (1984). The efficient assessment of need for cognition. *Journal of Personality Assessment*, 48, 306–7.

Chaiken, S. (1987). The heuristic model of persuasion. In M. P. Zanna, J. M. Olson, and C. P. Herman (Eds.), *Social Influence: The Ontario Symposium* (Vol. 5, pp. 3–39). Hillsdale, NJ: Erlbaum.

Chaiken, S., Liberman, A., and Eagly, A. H. (1989). Heuristic and systematic processing within and beyond the persuasion context. In J. S. Uleman, and J. A. Bargh (Eds.), *Unintended Thought* (pp. 212–52). New York: Guilford Press.

Chaiken, S., and Maheswaran, D. (1994). Heuristic processing can bias systematic processing: Effects of source credibility, argument ambiguity, and task importance on attitude judgment. *Journal of Personality and Social Psychology*, 66, 460–73.

Chaiken, S. and Trope, Y. (Eds.) (1999). *Dual Process Theories in Social Psychology*. New York: Guilford Press.

Chaiken, S., Wood, W., and Eagly, A. H. (1996). Principles of persuasion. In E. T. Higgins, and A. W. Kruglanski (Eds.), *Social Psychology: Handbook of Basic Principles* (pp. 702–42). New York: Guilford Press.

Christophersen, E. R., and Gyulay, J. E. (1981). Parental compliance with car seat usage: A positive approach with long term follow-up. *Journal of Pediatric Psychology*, 6, 301–12.

Clore, G. L., Schwarz, N., and Conway, M. (1994). Affective causes and consequences of social information processing. In R. S. Wyer, and T. K. Srull (Eds.), *Handbook of Social Cognition*, Vol. 1: *Basic Processes* (pp. 323–417). Hillsdale, NJ: Erlbaum.

Detweiler, J. B., Bedell, B. T., Salovey, P., Pronin, E., and Rothman, A. J. (1999). Message framing and sunscreen use: Gain-framed messages motivate beach-goers. *Health Psychology*, 18, 189–96.

Eagly, A. E., and Chaiken, S. (1998). Attitude structure and function. In D. T. Gilbert, S. T. Fiske, and G. Lindzey (Eds.), *The Handbook of Social Psychology* (4th edn, pp. 269–322). Boston: McGraw-Hill.

Ellis, H. C., and Ashbrook, P. W. (1988). Resource allocation model of the effects of depressed mood states on memory. In K. Fiedler and J. Forgas (Eds.), *Affect, Cognition, and Social Behavior* (pp. 25–43). Toronto: C. J. Hogrefe.

Forgas, J. P., and Moylan, S. (1987). After the movies: The effects of mood on social judgments. *Personality and Social Psychology Bulletin*, 13, 467–77.

Griffitt, W. B. (1970). Environmental effects on interpersonal affective behavior: Ambient effective temperature and attraction. *Journal of Personality and Social Psychology*, 15, 240–4.

Hovland, C. I., Janis, I. L., and Kelley, H. H. (1953). *Communication and Persuasion: Psychological Studies of Opinion Change*. New Haven, CT: Yale University Press.

Isen, A. M., and Shalker, T. E. (1982). The effect of feeling state on evaluation of positive, neutral, and negative stimuli: When you "accentuate the positive," do you "eliminate the negative"? *Social Psychology Quarterly*, 45, 58–63.

Janis, I. L. (1967). Effects of fear arousal on attitude change: Recent developments in theory and experimental research. In L. Berkowitz (Ed.), *Advances in Experimental Social Psychology* (Vol. 3, pp. 166–224). San Diego, CA: Academic Press.

Kahneman, D., and Tversky, A. (1979). Prospect theory: An analysis of decision under risk. *Econometrica*, 47, 263–91.

Kahneman, D., and Tversky, A. (1982). The psychology of preferences. *Scientific American*, 247, 160–73.

Kalichman, S. C., and Coley, B. (1995). Context framing to enhance HIV-antibody-testing messages targeted to African American women. *Health Psychology*, 14, 247–54.

Keller, P. A. (1999). Converting the unconverted: The effect of inclination and opportunity to discount health-related fear appeals. *Journal of Applied Psychology*, 84, 403–15.

Kiesler, S. B., and Mathog, R. (1968). The distraction hypothesis in attitude change. *Psychological Reports*, 23, 1123–33.

Leippe, M. R., and Elkin, R. A. (1987). When motives clash: Issue involvement and response involvement as determinants of persuasion. *Journal of Personality and Social Psychology*, 52, 269–78.

Leventhal, H. (1970). Findings and theory in the study of fear communications. In L. Berkowitz (Ed.), *Advances in Experimental Social Psychology* (Vol. 5, pp. 119–86). New York: Academic Press.

Levin, I. P., Schnittjer, S. K., and Thee, S. L. (1988). Information framing effects in social and personal decisions. *Journal of Experimental Social Psychology*, 24, 520–9.

Linville, P. W., Fischer, G. W., and Fischhoff, B. (1993). AIDS risk perceptions and decision biases. In J. B. Pryor and G. D. Reeder (Eds.), *The Social Psychology of HIV Infection* (pp. 421–32). Hillsdale, NJ: Erlbaum.

Mackie, D. M., and Worth, L. T. (1989). Processing deficits and the mediation of positive affect in persuasion. *Journal of Personality and Social Psychology*, 57, 27–40.

Maheswaran, D., and Myers-Levy, J. (1990). The influence of message framing and issue involvement. *Journal of Marketing Research*, 27, 361–7.

Marteau, T. M. (1989). Framing of information: Its influence upon decisions of doctors and patients. *British Journal of Social Psychology*, 28, 89–94.

Martin, L. L., Abend, T. A., Sedikides, C., and Green, J. (1997). How would I feel if . . . ? Mood as input to a role fulfillment evaluation process. *Journal of Personality and Social Psychology*, 73, 242–53.

Martin, L. L., Ward, D. W., Achee, J. W., and Wyer, R. S. Jr. (1993). Mood as input: People have to interpret the motivational implications of their moods. *Journal of Personality and Social Psychology*, 64, 317–26.

Mayer, J. D., Gaschke, Y. N., Bravermen, D. L., and Evans, T. W. (1992). Mood-congruent judgment is a general effect. *Journal of Personality and Social Psychology*, 63, 119–32.

McGuire, W. J. (1968). Personality and attitude change: An information-processing theory. In A. G. Greenwald, T. C. Brock, and T. M. Ostrom (Ed.), *Psychological Foundations of Attitudes* (pp. 171–96). New York: Academic.

McGuire, W. J. (1969). The nature of attitudes and attitude change. In G. Lindzey, and E. Aronson (Eds.), *Handbook of Social Psychology* (2nd edn, Vol. 3, pp. 136–314). Reading, MA: Addison-Wesley.

McGuire, W. J. (1985). Attitudes and attitude change. In G. Lindzey, and E. Aronson (Eds.), *Handbook of Social Psychology* (3rd edn, Vol. 2, pp. 233–346). New York: Random House.

McNeil, B. J., Pauker, S. G., Sox, H. C., and Tversky, A. (1982). On the elicitation of preferences for alternative therapies. *New England Journal of Medicine*, 306, 1259–62.

Meyerowitz, B. E., and Chaiken, S. (1987). The effect of message framing on breast self-examination attitudes, intentions, and behavior. *Journal of Personality and Social Psychology*, 52, 500–10.

Petty, R. E., and Cacioppo, J. T. (1986a). *Communication and Persuasion: Central and Peripheral Routes to Attitude Change*. New York: Springer-Verlag.

Petty, R. E., and Cacioppo, J. T. (1986b). The elaboration likelihood model of persuasion. In L. Berkowitz (Ed.), *Advances in Experimental Social Psychology* (Vol. 19, pp. 123–205). New York: Academic Press.

Petty, R. E., Cacioppo, J. T., and Goldman, R. (1981). Personal involvement as a determinant of argument-based persuasion. *Journal of Personality and Social Psychology*, 41, 847–55.

Petty, R. E., Gleicher, F., and Baker, S. (1991). Multiple roles for affect in persuasion. In J. Forgas (Ed.), *Emotion and Social Judgments* (pp. 181–200). Oxford: Pergamon.

Petty, R. E., Haugtvedt, C., and Smith, S. M. (1995). Elaboration as a determinant of attitude strength: Creating attitudes that are persistent, resistant, and predictive of behavior. In R. E. Petty and J. A. Krosnick (Eds.), *Attitude Strength: Antecedents and Consequences* (pp. 93–130). Mahwah, NJ: Erlbaum.

Petty, R. E., Schumann, D., Richman, S., and Strathman, A. (1993). Positive mood and persuasion: Different roles for affect under high and low elaboration conditions. *Journal of Personality and Social Psychology*, 64, 5–20.

Petty, R. E., and Wegener, D. T. (1991). Thought systems, argument quality, and persuasion. In R. S. Wyer and T. K. Srull (Eds.), *Advances in Social Cognition* (Vol. 4, pp. 143–61). Hillsdale, NJ: Erlbaum.

Petty, R. E., and Wegener, D. T. (1998a). Attitude change. In D. Gilbert, S. Fiske, and G. Lindzey (Eds.), *The Handbook of Social Psychology* (4th edn, Vol. 1, pp. 323–90). New York: McGraw-Hill.

Petty, R. E., and Wegener, D. T. (1998b). Match versus mismatch of persuasive appeals to functional bases of attitudes: Effects on processing of message content. *Personality and Social Psychology Bulletin*, 24, 227–40.

Petty, R. E., and Wegener, D. T. (1999). The elaboration likelihood model: Current status and controversies. In S. Chaiken and Y. Trope (Eds.), *Dual process theories in social psychology* (pp. 41–72). New York: Guilford Press.

Petty, R. E., Wells, G. L., and Brock, T. C. (1976). Distraction can enhance or reduce yielding to propaganda: Thought disruption versus effort justification. *Journal of Personality and Social Psychology*, 34, 874–84.

Robberson, M. R., and Rogers, R. W. (1988). Beyond fear appeals: Negative and positive persuasive appeals to health and self-esteem. *Journal of Applied Social Psychology*, 13, 277–87.

Rogers, R. W. (1975). A protection motivation theory of fear appeals and attitude change. *Journal of Psychology*, 91, 93–114.

Rogers, R. W. (1983). Cognitive and physiological processes in fear appeals and attitude change: A revised theory of protection motivation. In J. T. Cacioppo, and R. E. Petty (Eds.), *Social Psychophysiology: A Sourcebook* (pp. 153–76). New York: Guilford Press.

Rothman, A. J., Martino, S. C., Bedell, B., Detweiler, J., and Salovey, P. (1999). The systematic influence of gain- and loss-framed messages on interest in different types of health behavior. *Personality and Social Psychology Bulletin*, 25, 1357–71.

Rothman, A. J., and Salovey, P. (1997). Shaping perceptions to motivate healthy behavior: The role of message framing. *Psychological Bulletin*, 121, 3–19.

Rothman, A. J., Salovey, P., Antone, C., Keough, K., and Martin, C. (1993). The influence of message framing on health behavior. *Journal of Experimental Social Psychology*, 29, 408–33.

Salovey, P., Schneider, T. R., and Apanovitch, A. M. (2002). Message framing in the prevention and early detection of illness. In J. P. Dillard and M. Pfau (Eds.), *The Persuasion Handbook: Theory and Practice* (pp. 391–406). Thousand Oaks, CA: Sage Publications.

Schneider, T. R., Salovey, P., Apanovitch, A. M., Pizarro, J., McCarthy, D., Zullo, J., and Rothman, A. J. (2001a). The effects of message framing and ethnic targeting on mammography use among low-income women. *Health Psychology*, 20, 256–66.

Schneider, T. R., Salovey, P., Pallonen, U., Mundorf, N., Smith, N. F., and Steward, W. (2001b). Visual and auditory message framing effects on tobacco smoking. *Journal of Applied Social Psychology*, 31, 667–82.

Schwarz, N. (1990). Feelings as information: Informational and motivational functions of affective states. In R. M. Sorrentino and E. T. Higgins (Eds.), *Handbook of Motivation and Cognition: Foundations of Social Behavior* (Vol. 2, pp. 527–61). New York: Guilford Press.

Smith, S. M., and Petty, R. E. (1996). Message framing and persuasion: A message processing analysis. *Personality and Social Psychology Bulletin*, 22, 257–68.

Snyder, M., and DeBono, K. G. (1989). Understanding the functions of attitudes: Lessons from personality and social behavior. In S. J. Pratkanis, S. J. Breckler, and A. G. Greenwald (Eds.), *Attitude Structure and Function* (pp. 339–59). Hillsdale, NJ: Erlbaum.

Staats, A. W., and Staats, C. K. (1958). Attitudes established by classical conditioning. *Journal of Abnormal and Social Psychology*, 57, 37–40.

Sutton, S. R. (1982). Fear-arousing communications: A critical examination of theory and research. In J. R. Eiser (Ed.), *Social Psychology and Behavioral Medicine* (pp. 303–37). Chichester, England: Wiley.

Treiber, F. A. (1986). A comparison of positive and negative consequences approaches upon car restraint usage. *Journal of Pediatric Psychology*, 11, 15–24.

Tversky, A., and Kahneman, D. (1981). The framing of decisions and the psychology of choice. *Science*, 211, 453–8.

Wegener, D. T., and Claypool, H. M. (1999). The elaboration continuum by any other name does not smell as sweet. *Psychological Inquiry*, 10, 176–81.

Wegener, D. T., and Petty, R. E. (1996). Effects of mood on persuasion processes: Enhancing, reducing, and biasing scrutiny of attitude-relevant information. In L. L. Martin and A. Tesser (Eds.), *Striving and Feeling: Interactions among Goals, Affect, and Self-regulation* (pp. 329–62). Mahwah, NJ: Erlbaum.

Wegener, D. T., and Petty, R. E. (2001). Understanding effects of mood through the Elaboration Likelihood and Flexible Correction Models. In L. L. Martin and G. L. Clore (Eds.) *Theories of Mood and Cognition: A User's Guidebook* (pp. 177–210). Mahwah, NJ: Erlbaum.

Wegener, D. T., Petty, R. E., and Klein, D. J. (1994). Effects of mood on high elaboration attitude change: The mediating role of likelihood judgments. *European Journal of Social Psychology*, 24, 25–44.

Wegener, D. T., Petty, R. E., and Smith, S. M. (1995). Positive mood can increase or decrease message scrutiny: The hedonic contingency view of mood and message processing. *Journal of Personality and Social Psychology*, 69, 5–15.

Wilson, D. K., Kaplan, R. M., and Schneiderman, L. (1987). Framing of decisions and selections of alternatives in health care. *Social Behavior*, 2, 51–9.

Wilson, D. K., Purdon, S. E., and Wallston, K. A. (1988). Compliance to health recommendations: A theoretical overview of message framing. *Health Education Research: Theory and Practice*, 3, 161–71.

Witte, K. (1998). Fear as motivator, fear as inhibitor: Using the extended parallel process model to explain fear appeal successes and failures. In P. E. Anderson and L. K. Guerrero (Eds.), *Handbook of Communication and Emotion: Research, Theory, Applications, and Contexts* (pp. 423–50). San Diego, CA: Academic Press.

Wyer, R. S., Clore, G. L., and Isbell, L. M. (1999). Affect and information processing. In M. P. Zanna (Ed.), *Advances in Experimental Social Psychology* (Vol. 31, pp. 1–77). San Diego, CA: Academic Press.

Zanna, M. P., Kiesler, C. A., and Pilkonis, P. A. (1970). Positive and negative attitudinal affect established by classical conditioning. *Journal of Personality and Social Psychology*, 14, 321–8.

CHAPTER 4

The Information–Motivation–Behavioral Skills Model: A General Social Psychological Approach to Understanding and Promoting Health Behavior

William A. Fisher,

University of Western Ontario

Jeffrey D. Fisher and Jennifer Harman

University of Connecticut

Introduction

Over the past half-century, a number of conceptualizations (e.g., the Health Belief Model, Hochbaum, 1958, Rosenstock, 1990; the Transtheoretical Model, Prochaska and Velicer, 1997) have been developed as general theories of the determinants of the range of health-related behaviors. Other conceptualizations, such as the AIDS Risk Reduction Model (Catania et al., 1990), have been created for the specific purpose of understanding and changing a particular health behavior. In addition, social psychological conceptualizations such as the Theory of Reasoned Action (e.g., Fishbein and Ajzen, 1975; W. Fisher et al., 1995), the Theory of Planned Behavior (e.g., Ajzen, 1991; Godin and Kok, 1996), and Social-Cognitive Theory (e.g., Bandura, 1989; 1992) that have been formulated in contexts other than health behavior have been applied in efforts to understand and modify a range of health-related actions.

Building on existing work concerning the social and individual determinants of health behavior, and seeking to extend these efforts, the current chapter presents the Information–Motivation–Behavioral Skills (IMB) Model (J. Fisher and Fisher, 1992; 2000; W. Fisher and Fisher, 1993; 1999) as a general social psychological conceptualization for understanding and promoting health-related behavior. We first describe the origins of the IMB model and the constructs and relationships it proposes. Next, we discuss procedures for translating the IMB approach into conceptually based, empirically targeted, and rigorously evaluated health promotion intervention efforts. We then review empirical support for the IMB model in the context of correlational and experimental intervention research in the area of HIV prevention. Based upon this conceptual and empirical foundation, we suggest the general utility of the IMB model as an approach to understanding social and psychological factors that influence the range of health-related behaviors. We support the general utility of the IMB approach with a literature review emphasizing the significance of the factors central to this model as critical elements in the prediction and promotion of health behavior broadly conceived. As examples of the general conceptual and empirical utility of the IMB approach to understanding and promoting health behaviors, we conclude with examples of its application in diverse health domains. Specifically, we review applications of the IMB model in the prediction and understanding of breast self-examination and motorcycle safety gear utilization, and end with an IMB model-based conceptualization of adherence to complex medication regimens.

The Information–Motivation–Behavioral Skills Model

The IMB model (J. Fisher and Fisher, 1992; 2000; W. Fisher and Fisher, 1993; 1999) conceptualizes psychological determinants of the performance of behaviors that have the capacity to impair or to improve health status. The model was originally developed to provide an account of the psychological determinants of HIV risk and preventive behavior (J. Fisher and Fisher, 1992; W. Fisher and Fisher, 1993), and is based on a critical review and integration of the constructs of relevant theories in social and health psychology (e.g., Bandura, 1989, Fishbein and Ajzen, 1975; Hochbaum, 1958) and on an analysis of successes and failures reported in the HIV prevention intervention literature (J. Fisher and Fisher, 1992). The IMB conceptualization seeks to address limitations of existing theory in social and health psychology (J. Fisher and Fisher, 1992). These include the absence of specification of the relationships among critical constructs (e.g., Bandura, 1989; Rosenstock, 1974; 1996); lack of predictive validity of key constructs (e.g., Rosenstock, 1974; 1996; Gerrard et al., 1996); lack of conceptual parsimony (e.g., Prochaska et al., 1994); and absence of constructs that may be central to understanding and changing health-related behavior (e.g., Fishbein and Ajzen, 1975; Ajzen, 1991). The IMB model was also designed to be easy to translate into theoretically based and empirically targeted intervention operations. (For current purposes, an empirically targeted intervention refers to an intervention that is directed specifically at objectively identified information, motivation, and behavioral skills needs of a particular population requiring health promotion efforts. See J. Fisher and Fisher, 1992; 2000, for a critical discussion of conceptual and methodological issues in health behavior change research).

The IMB model focuses comprehensively on the set of information (e.g., US Department of Health and Human Services, 1988), motivation (e.g., Fishbein and Ajzen, 1975), and behavioral skills (e.g., Kelly and St. Lawrence, 1988) factors that are conceptually and empirically associated with performance of health-related behavior, but which are often dealt with in isolation from one another in both conceptual and health promotion intervention efforts (J. Fisher and Fisher, 1992). The model specifies a set of causal relationships among these constructs (J. Fisher and Fisher, 1992) as well as a set of operations (W. Fisher and Fisher, 1993) that may be used for translating the IMB approach into health promotion interventions.

Assumptions of the IMB Model

The IMB model asserts that health-related information, motivation, and behavioral skills are fundamental determinants of performance of health behaviors. To the extent that individuals are well informed, motivated to act, and possess the requisite behavioral skills for effective action, they will be likely to initiate and maintain health-promoting behaviors and to experience positive health outcomes. In contrast, to the extent that individuals are poorly informed, unmotivated to act, and lack behavioral skills required for effective action, they will tend to engage in health risk behaviors and to experience negative health outcomes.

According to the IMB model, *information* that is directly relevant to the performance of health behavior and that can be easily enacted by an individual in his or her social ecology is a critical determinant of health behavior performance (J. Fisher and Fisher, 1992; 2000; W. Fisher and Fisher, 1993; 1999). Information can include specific facts about health promotion as well as relevant heuristics (simple rules which permit automatic and cognitively effortless – but often incorrect – decisions about whether or not to engage in a health promotion behavior). Health promotion information can also involve relatively elaborate implicit theories (complicated sets of beliefs that require cognitive effort to process and which are also often incorrect) in making decisions about health-related action. In the area of HIV preventive behavior, for example, specific facts (e.g., "Condom use prevents HIV transmission"), heuristics ("Monogamous sex is safe sex"), and implicit theories ("Known and trusted people who dress and act reasonably and who possess a variety of normative characteristics are safe partners") appear to exert powerful influences on HIV preventive behavior performance (Hammer et al., 1996; Misovich et al., 1996; Williams et al., 1992). In other areas of health behavior, such as disease prevention and screening, the IMB model asserts that information can be important as well. For example, the model would direct our attention to exploring the impact of possessing specific facts (e.g., "Genetic testing for BRCA1 and BRCA2 can clarify the risk of breast and ovarian cancer"); heuristics ("Ashkenezic Jewish woman should all seek BRCA1 and BRCA2 testing"); and implicit theories ("I have small breasts and women with small breasts don't get breast cancer") on individuals' levels of disease prevention and screening.

The IMB model specifies that *motivation* is an additional determinant of the performance of health-related behaviors, and influences whether even well-informed individuals will be inclined to undertake health promotion actions. According to the model, personal motivation (attitudes toward personal performance of health promotion behaviors) and social motivation (social support for enactment of health promotion behaviors) are critical influences on performance of health-related behavior. In the HIV prevention domain, for example, personal attitudes towards condom use and perceptions of social support for it are strongly predictive of condom use behavior (e.g., Albarracin et al., 2001). In parallel fashion, and consistent with the IMB model, in the area of disease screening and prevention, attitudes and social support regarding breast self-examination predict its performance (e.g., Champion, 1990; Lierman et al., 1991; Misovich et al., 2001). In the area of adherence to medical regimen, attitudes and social norms towards hormone replacement therapy are strong correlates of postmenopausal women's continued use of this therapy (e.g., W. Fisher et al., 2000b).

Behavioral skills for performance of health promotion actions are an additional critical determinant of whether well-informed and well-motivated individuals will be capable of effectively enacting health promotion behaviors. The IMB model's behavioral skills component focuses on an individual's objective abilities and his or her sense of self-efficacy (Rye, 1990; 1998) concerning performance of a given health-related behavior. Behavioral skills for the performance of HIV preventive behavior, for example, may include an individual's actual and perceived ability to bring up and negotiate HIV prevention with a partner; to acquire and use condoms comfortably; to maintain condom use over extended periods of time; and to shift prevention patterns appropriately. Behavioral skills are implicated in a wide range of health practices, from breast and testicular self-examination (actual and perceived tactile skills are required for effective self-examination), to medication adherence (actual and perceived ability to utilize naturally occurring daily life events to cue medication taking may be critical to adherence), to cardiovascular health (actual and perceived skills for smoking cessation and relapse prevention can be critical to maintaining lowered levels of cardiovascular risk).

The IMB model specifies that health promotion information and motivation work primarily through health promotion behavioral skills to influence health promotion behavior. In essence, the effects of health promotion information and motivation are seen primarily as a result of the application of health promotion behavioral skills to the initiation and maintenance of health promotion behavior. The model also asserts that health promotion information and motivation may have direct effects on health promotion behavior performance, when complicated or novel behavioral skills are not required to enact the health promotion behavior in question. For example, acquiring information about the fact that anti-retroviral medication can prevent mother to child transmission of HIV might have a direct effect on HIV+ pregnant women seeking such treatment. Or, high levels of motivation could incline an individual to maintain an existing sexually abstinent pattern of behavior. In addition, we note that the IMB model regards health promotion information

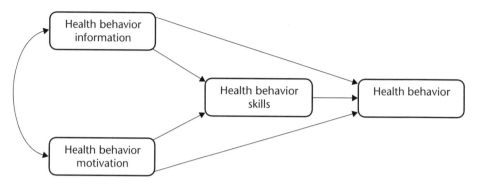

Figure 4.1   The Information–Motivation–Behavioral Skills Model of health behavior.
From J. D. Fisher and W. A. Fisher (1992). Changing AIDS risk behavior.
Psychological Bulletin, 111, 455–74. Copyright by APA. Reprinted with permission.

and motivation as potentially independent constructs, insofar as well-informed individuals are not necessarily motivated to engage in health promotion behaviors, and highly motivated individuals are not necessarily well informed about health promotion practices (J. Fisher and Fisher, 1992; J. Fisher et al., 1994). The constructs and relationships of the IMB model are presented in Figure 4.1.

In the case of HIV preventive behavior, we would anticipate that in general, individuals who possess accurate and relevant information, and personal and social motivation to act on it, would assemble and apply requisite behavioral skills to initiate and maintain patterns of safer sexual behavior. We would also anticipate that in some cases, when complex behavioral skills may be less critical, HIV prevention information and HIV prevention motivation may have a direct effect on behavior, as noted above.

In another health domain – disease screening and prevention – the IMB analysis would suggest that in general, individuals who possess relevant information about breast or testicular self-examination and personal and social motivation to carry out these behaviors will assemble and utilize behavioral skills for doing so effectively, and will likely engage in these health promotion actions regularly. Nevertheless, there will be cases in which health promotion information concerning breast or testicular examination, or health promotion motivation concerning such examination, is directly linked with health behavior in a fashion not mediated by health promotion behavioral skills. Such a situation would occur when a well-informed or -motivated individual accepts a professional's offer to provide breast or testicular examination to screen for malignancy in the context of an annual physical examination.

The IMB model's information, motivation, and behavioral skills constructs and the relationships among them are regarded as highly generalizable determinants of health promotion behavior, across populations and health promotion behaviors of interest (J. Fisher and Fisher, 1992; W. Fisher and Fisher, 1999). Within this approach, however, it is asserted that the model's information, motivation, and behavioral skills constructs will have specific content that is most relevant to specific populations' practice of specific health promotion behaviors. Thus, for example, specific sets of information, personal and social motives, and behavioral skills will be most relevant to understanding HIV preventive behavior for men (versus women), for heterosexual (versus homosexual) individuals, for African-American (versus Hispanic-American) individuals, etc. By the same token, particular sets of information, personal and social motives, and behavioral skills will be most relevant to understanding specific health promotion behaviors (e.g., safer sexual practices versus safer needle-use practices).

The IMB approach asserts that particular constructs of the model, and particular causal pathways among them, will emerge as more or less influential determinants of health promotion behavior for given populations and health promotion behaviors (J. Fisher and Fisher, 1992; 2000; W. Fisher and Fisher, 1993). The model specifies procedures that may be used to identify constructs and causal links among them that are especially influential in determining a given population's practice of a health promotion behavior of interest (J. Fisher and Fisher, 1992; 2000; J. Fisher et al., 1994; W. Fisher and Fisher, 1993). From the IMB perspective, specification of the information, motivation, and behavioral skills elements most relevant to a population's practice of a particular health-related behavior, and identification of model constructs which most strongly influence that population's practice of the behavior, is crucial to designing targeted interventions effective for the population and health promotion behavior of interest (J. Fisher and Fisher, 1992; 2000).

The IMB approach to understanding and promoting health behavior specifies a set of generalizable operations for constructing, implementing, and evaluating health promotion interventions for specific populations and health promotion behaviors of interest (J. Fisher and Fisher, 1992; 2000; W. Fisher and Fisher, 1993; 1999). The first step in the process of promoting health behavior – which can involve either initiation or maintenance of health promotion practices *or* the reduction of health risk behaviors – involves the conduct of *elicitation research* with a representative subsample of a target population. Elicitation research seeks to empirically identify the target population's information, motivation, and behavioral skills deficits and assets, and level of health promotion or health risk behavior per se, in a specific health domain. The use of open-ended data collection techniques such as focus groups is advocated, in addition to the use of close-ended techniques, in order to avoid prompting responses that may not be salient or ecologically valid representations of the information, motivation, and behavioral skills factors operating within a target population.

The second step in the IMB approach to health promotion involves the design and implementation of *conceptually based, empirically targeted, population-specific interventions* constructed on the basis of elicitation research findings. Such targeted interventions are designed to address empirically identified deficits in health behavior information, motivation, and behavioral skills, relative to the health behavior at issue, and to capitalize on information, motivation, and behavioral skills assets that exist within a target population and that can be mobilized to encourage health behavior performance.

The third step in the IMB approach to health promotion involves the conduct of methodologically rigorous *evaluation research* to determine whether an intervention has had significant effects on the information, motivation, and behavioral skills determinants of a targeted health behavior, and whether it has had significant and sustained effects on the performance of this health behavior per se. The IMB approach advocates evaluation research which utilizes multiple convergent sources of evaluation outcome data, at least someof which are relatively non-reactive, and at least some of which are collected in a context that appears to intervention participants to be unrelated to the health promotion intervention itself. The IMB model's elicitation–intervention–evaluation approach to the promotion of health behavior is illustrated in Figure 4.2 and is discussed in detail in J. Fisher and Fisher (1992; 2000) and W. Fisher and Fisher (1993; 1999).

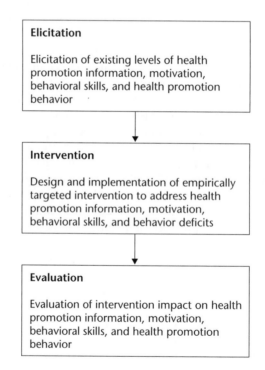

Figure 4.2   The Information–Motivation–Behavioral Skills Model approach to the promotion of health behavior.
From W. A. Fisher and J. D. Fisher (1993). A general social psychological model for changing AIDS risk behavior. In J. Pryor and G. Reeder (Eds.), *The Social Psychology of HIV Infection* (pp. 27–53). Copyright by Lawrence Erlbaum Associates. Reprinted with permission.

Empirical Support for the IMB Model

Considerable empirical support for the assumptions of the IMB model has been accumulated in multivariate correlational research concerning information, motivation, and behavioral skills determinants of HIV preventive behavior, across populations and behaviors of interest (e.g., Bryan et al., 2001; J. Fisher et al., 1994; W. Fisher et al., 1999; see J. Fisher and Fisher, 2000, for a review of this literature). For example, J. Fisher et al. (1994) examined the determinants of HIV preventive behavior, from the perspective of the IMB model, in a sample of heterosexual university students. Structural equation modeling revealed that HIV prevention information and HIV prevention motivation were statistically independent constructs; each was significantly related to HIV prevention behavioral skills; and HIV prevention behavioral skills were significantly related to HIV preventive behavior performance per se, precisely as predicted by the IMB conceptualization. In an additional IMB model-based study, J. Fisher et al. (1994) examined HIV preventive behavior in a sample of homosexual men. Once again, structural equation modeling indicated that HIV prevention information and HIV prevention motivation were statistically independent constructs; each was related to HIV prevention behavioral skills; and HIV prevention behavioral skills were again related to performance of HIV preventive behavior. In addition, and also as predicted by the model, in this sample, a direct link was observed between HIV prevention motivation and HIV preventive behavior. Additional research has confirmed the assumptions of the IMB model in research concerning the information, motivation, and behavioral skills determinants of HIV preventive behavior in samples of sexually active minority high school students (Bryan et al., 2001; W. Fisher et al., 1999), African-American and white very low income women (Anderson et al., 1997), Dutch homosexual men (DeVroome et al., 1996), and truck drivers from the Indian subcontinent (Bryan et al., 2000; 2001).

Empirical tests of the IMB model's assumptions, in the context of correlational research concerning HIV preventive behavior, are summarized in Table 4.1. It can be seen that, as predicted by the IMB model, HIV prevention information and HIV prevention motivation are associated with the application of HIV prevention behavioral skills to promote HIV preventive behavior. It is also apparent that there is often a direct link between HIV prevention motivation and HIV preventive behavior, consistent with the model's assertion that motivation may directly affect behavior when complicated or novel behavioral performances are not necessary for prevention. As can also be seen in Table 4.1, across diverse populations under study, the IMB model's information, motivation, and behavioral skills components generally account for a substantial proportion of the variance in health behavior performance.

Confirmation of the IMB model's health promotion implications has been provided in model-based experimental intervention research. This work, which has targeted population-specific deficits in HIV prevention information, motivation, and behavioral skills, has resulted in significant and sustained increases

Table 4.1 Tests of the Information–Motivation–Behavioral Skills Model: summary of reported associations

Sample	Information–motivation	Information–behavioral skills	Motivation–behavioral skills	Behavioral skills–behavior	Information–behavior	Motivation–behavior	Percentage variance
Heterosexual university males and females (Fisher et al., 1994)		✓	✓	✓		✓	10
Homosexual adult males (Fisher et al., 1994)		✓	✓	✓		✓	35
Urban minority high school males (Fisher et al., 1999)			✓	✓		✓	75
Urban minority high school females (Fisher et al., 1999)		✓	✓	✓		✓	46
Netherland adult homosexual males (deVroom et al., 1996)	✓	✓	✓	✓	✓	✓	26
Low-income African-American females (Anderson et al., 1997)	✓	✓	✓	✓		✓	36
Low-income white female (Anderson et al., 1997)	✓		✓	✓		✓	57
Indian truck drivers[a] (Bryan et al., in press)				✓	✓	✓	40–51

[a] Findings from Bryan et al. (in press) represent tests of relationships of information, motivation, behavioral skills with behavior, and percent of variance accounted for in condom use with wives and with commercial sex workers.

Source: J. D. Fisher and W. A. Fisher (2000). Theoretical approaches to individual level change in HIV risk behavior. In J. L. Peterson and R. J. DiClemete (Eds.), *Handbook of HIV Prevention* (pp. 3–55). New York: Kluwer Academic/Plenum. Reprinted with permission.

in HIV preventive behavior across a number of intervention target populations (e.g., Carey et al., 1997; J. Fisher et al., 1996; J. Fisher et al., 2002;
Kalichman et al., 1999a; 1999b, 2001; see also J. Fisher and Fisher, 2000, for
a review of this literature). For example, J. Fisher et al. (1996) conducted
IMB model-based experimental intervention research with samples of primarily heterosexual university students. In this work, elicitation research was
used to identify HIV prevention information deficits, motivational obstacles,
and behavioral skills limitations that were related to patterns of HIV risk
behavior observed in this population. Based on elicitation findings, an IMB
model-based population-specific intervention was created and delivered to
remediate identified gaps in HIV prevention information, motivation, and
behavioral skills. The intervention was delivered in the context of a field
experiment in male and female dormitories and included slide shows, videos,
group discussions, and role-plays conveyed by a health educator and peer
educators. Rigorous evaluation outcome research showed that the intervention had a significant impact on multiple indicators of HIV prevention information, motivation, and behavioral skills at four weeks post-intervention. At a
2–4 month follow-up, the intervention had significant effects on HIV prevention behavioral performance, including condom accessibility (keeping condoms available for use), condom use during intercourse, and the seeking of
HIV antibody testing.

Recent research (J. Fisher et al., 2002) has indicated that an IMB model-
based intervention, guided by elicitation research and delivered in entire, intact
inner-city high school classes, had significant effects on HIV prevention information, motivation, and behavioral skills at one month post-intervention.
More importantly, the intervention had significant, sustained effects on HIV
preventive behaviors such as condom use fully one-year post-intervention.
Additional IMB model-based intervention research has demonstrated outcome efficacy in a sample of African-American economically disadvantaged
urban women (Carey et al., 1997), with experimental (versus control) participants showing reductions in unprotected vaginal intercourse three months
post-intervention. In further work, St. Lawrence et al. (1995) found strong
support for the efficacy of an IMB model-based HIV prevention intervention
with minority adolescents, and Weinhardt et al. (1997) report encouraging
results of an IMB model-based pilot intervention for the reduction of HIV
risk behavior in a sample of chronically mentally ill individuals. Kalichman
et al. (1999a) also report that an IMB model-based intervention led to lower
rates of unprotected vaginal intercourse and higher condom use among
minority men recruited from a public clinic, and Kalichman et al. (1999b)
observed that an intervention with information, motivation, and skills elements led to greater use of female condoms among women. Recent research
by Kalichman and associates (Kalichman et al., 2001) also found that an
intervention containing IMB elements was effective at reducing HIV transmission risk behaviors among HIV+ individuals. Finally, meta-analytic work
has strongly supported the efficacy of including information, motivation, and
behavioral skills-based elements in HIV risk behavior change interventions
(Johnson et al., 2001).

Establishing the Generality of the IMB Model as an Approach to Understanding and Promoting Health Behavior

Beyond its empirical strength in the prediction and promotion of HIV preventive behavior, the IMB model is viewed as a highly generalizable approach to understanding and promoting health behavior across health behavior domains. As an initial step in establishing the generality of the model, we have conducted a systematic review of the literature concerning psychological factors linked to health behavior performance and change in a number of areas. The findings of this review are reported in the following section, and their implications for the generalizability of the IMB model across health behaviors are considered.

Review of Correlational and Intervention Research Concerning Information, Motivation, Behavioral Skills, and Health-related Behavior

We have surveyed correlational and experimental intervention research across several areas of health behavior, published since 1990, from the perspective of the IMB model. (For a detailed description of the method, scope and findings of this literature review, see the publications section of http://psych.uconn.edu/chip.html. Space considerations preclude our presenting this information fully in the text of this chapter). Our review of the correlational literature clearly indicates that information, motivation, and behavioral skills are consistently correlated with health behavior performance across diverse domains such as exercise behavior, smoking cessation, nutrition, breast health, cardiovascular health, and other areas. Findings revealed that information was correlated with health behavior performance in 19 of 25 (76 percent) associations of these factors that were examined; motivation was associated with health behavior performance in 41 of 46 (89 percent) of associations examined; and behavioral skills were associated with health behavior performance in 37 of 41 (90 percent) of associations examined. Our review of the correlational literature was highly consistent with the IMB model's assertion that information, motivation, and behavioral skills are fundamental determinants of health behavior across broad domains of such behavior that extend well *outside* the HIV prevention literature in which the IMB model was initially developed and tested. The relatively more modest consistency with which information is correlated with health behavior performance (compared to motivation and behavioral skills) is in accord with the IMB model's assertion (J. Fisher and Fisher, 1992; W. Fisher and Fisher, 1993) that only information which is easily translated into health behavior in an individual's social ecology is expected to be related to health behavior performance. Unfortunately, much of the information disseminated by public health officials and assessed in health promotion research is actually irrelevant to the practice of health behavior and would not be expected to predict such behavior (J. Fisher and Fisher, 1992).

We next reviewed experimental health promotion intervention research across several health behavior domains (again, for a summary table and a detailed description of the method, scope, and results of this literature search, see the publications section of http://psych.uconn.edu/chip.html). Our review provided a basis for several important conclusions relevant to the IMB conceptualization and to health behavior change research in general. First, although the IMB approach emphasizes the critical importance of health promotion interventions which are conceptually based and targeted at identified needs of an intervention population, little more than half (35 out of 59, or 59 percent) of the interventions reviewed were based on a formally stated theory or conceptualization. Further, very few (7 out of 59, or 12 percent) were based on formal elicitation research conducted to identify target population characteristics or needs which can be critical to creating an effective health promotion intervention for a specific population and preventive behavior of interest.

Second, although the IMB model asserts that successful interventions to promote health behavior change will generally require information, motivation, *and* behavioral skills components, many of the intervention efforts reviewed contained only informational content, with motivation- and behavioral skills-related intervention content far less often present. There is consistent evidence in the literature that "information only" interventions are unlikely to change health behavior (J. Fisher and Fisher, 2000). Further, we found that interventions with information *and* motivation *and* behavioral skills content were more effective in promoting health behavior change than interventions that did not have all three elements. To quantify, at least crudely, our impression that interventions that contained all three components had a greater impact than those that did not, intervention effects were rated on a 3-point scale of intensity (0 = no effects observed, 3 = strongest effects observed). We then compared the average intensity of intervention effects in health promotion interventions that contained information, motivation, and behavioral skills elements versus those that did not contain all three elements. When all three intervention elements specified by the IMB model were present, the average intensity of intervention effect observed (1.80) was significantly greater than when these three elements were not all present (1.13), $t = -2.39$, $df = 27.50$, $p = 0.027$.

In another approach to quantify the relationships between health promotion intervention information, motivation, and behavioral skills content and health promotion intervention impact, the strength of the information, motivation, and behavioral skills content reflected within an intervention was rated (0 = no content present to 3 = content strongly represented). We then compared the strength of the information, motivation, and behavioral skills content represented in those health promotion interventions that had strong or relatively strong effects (3 or 2 on our scale of intervention effect intensity) versus those with weak or null effects (1 or 0 on our scale of intervention effect intensity). Statistical tests indicated that interventions that had stronger compared to weaker effects also possessed stronger information (2.29 versus 1.65, $t = -2.51$, $df = 32.27$, $p = 0.017$), motivation (2.00 versus 1.30, $t = -3.19$,

$df = 50.56$, $p = 0.002$), and behavioral skills (2.35 versus 1.30, $t = -3.54$, $df = 33.70$, $p = 0.001$) content.

The experimental intervention literature reviewed is highly consistent with the IMB model's assertions concerning information, motivation, and behavioral skills as fundamental determinants of health promotion behavior change across widely varying domains of behavior. Our review of the literature detected these findings outside of the HIV prevention context in which the IMB model has been developed and extensively tested. In a broad sense, then, the presence of health promotion information, motivation, and behavioral skills elements appears to be associated with health promotion intervention impact, and the more strongly these elements are represented, the greater the intervention's impact on health promotion behavior change.

Application of the IMB Model to Breast Self-examination Behavior

As an additional step in establishing the generality of the IMB model across health behavior domains, we report the findings of model-based research concerning information, motivation, and behavioral skills determinants of breast self-examination (BSE) practices (Misovich et al., 2001). BSE is a critical health behavior for our purposes, both because it is regarded as potentially effective in the early detection and cure of breast cancer (American Cancer Society, 1998) and because it is presently practiced by relatively few women (W. Fisher et al., 2000a; Misovich et al, 2001). Moreover, for the purpose of establishing the generality of the IMB model, we note that BSE takes place in the domain of disease detection and screening, while most work on the IMB model, in the area of HIV prevention, has focused on disease prevention.

In research reported by Misovich et al. (2001), women ($N = 166$) aged 22 to 64 ($M = 42.6$) were recruited in workplace settings and completed questionnaire measures of BSE related information, motivation, behavioral skills, and behavior (practice of BSE, discussion of BSE, and having a friend remind the individual to engage in BSE). Findings from this cross-sectional study revealed that women had significant information deficits relative to BSE (women's average score on a 40-item information measure concerning BSE was 67 percent and important gaps existed with respect to items such as the correct time during the menstrual cycle to examine one's breasts). Motivation concerning BSE practice ranged from neutral to positive, with more positive attitudes and social norms toward learning and practicing BSE and less positive attitudes and social norms toward discussing BSE and being prompted by friends to practice BSE. A parallel pattern emerged for assessments of women's BSE-related behavioral skills. Women perceived high levels of skills for learning and practicing BSE and lower levels of skills for discussing or asking others to remind them to practice BSE. Women's practice of BSE was modest, with only 54 percent indicating BSE at a level even approaching monthly frequency.

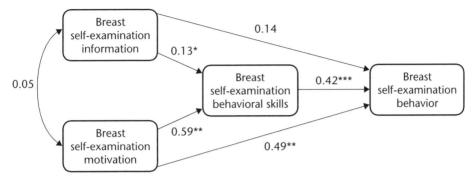

Figure 4.3 Empirical test of the Information–Motivation–Behavioral Skills Model of the determinants of breast self-examination behavior (after Misovich et al., 2001).

Determinants of BSE, from the perspective of the IMB model, were examined using structural equation modeling. Results showed that each of the relationships specified by the model was confirmed, and that it provided an acceptable fit to the data (CFI = 0.96, RMSEA = 0.07). As can be seen in Figure 4.3, BSE information and motivation are statistically independent constructs; each is significantly linked with BSE behavioral skills; and BSE behavioral skills are significantly associated with performance of BSE-related behavior, all as specified by the IMB model. In addition, and also predicted by the model, there is an independent link between BSE motivation and BSE-related behavioral performance. The three components of the IMB model account for 70 percent of the variance in BSE-related behaviors, which is regarded as a large effect size for a prediction model in the behavioral sciences (Cohen, 1988).

These findings illustrate the generalizability and strength of the IMB model across domains of health behavior including preventive behavior (e.g., HIV prevention) and screening and detection behaviors (e.g., BSE-related behaviors). Moreover, these findings can serve as elicitation research to guide future intervention efforts to increase BSE. On the basis of our observations, such interventions should focus comprehensively on the set of information, motivation, and behavioral skills factors and their interrelations that have been empirically demonstrated to account for substantial variance in BSE-related behaviors. The present work can also serve to assist with the identification of specific information, motivation, and behavioral skills intervention deficits that are relevant to BSE and that could be targeted in health promotion interventions to encourage initiation and maintenance of this practice.

Application of the IMB Model to Motorcycle Safety Gear Utilization

As a further step in establishing the IMB model as a generalizable account of the psychological determinants of health behavior performance, we report the findings of IMB model-based research concerning the determinants of motor-cycle safety gear utilization (Murray, 2000). Motorcycle accidents and associated injury and death are very common occurrences (US Department of Transportation, 1997). Although motorcycle safety gear has the potential to save hundreds of lives annually (US Department of Transportation, 1997), it is inconsistently used by those at risk. For the purpose of broadening the generality of the IMB model, we note that motorcycle safety gear use represents a very different type of health behavior than those in our previous studies (i.e., it is an *injury prevention* behavior, as opposed to a disease prevention or disease detection practice). Findings that the IMB approach can provide an empirically strong account of motorcycle safety gear use would provide additional evidence of the general utility of this model for understanding health behavior performance.

In a correlational study reported by Murray (2000), elicitation research-based sets of information, motivation, behavioral skills and behavior items relating to motorcycle safety gear use were generated and pilot tested. Data collection from an Internet-based sample of motorcycle riders took place through motorcycle-related websites and web-based mailing lists, and questionnaires which were completed through the Internet were returned by email.

Findings from this cross-sectional study revealed that motorcycle riders had significant information deficits relative to motorcycle safety gear utilization (the average score on a 33-item information measure was 73 percent). Mean motivation (attitudes, social norms, and intentions) and behavioral skills (4.37, 3.90, 3.93, and 4.11, respectively, on 1–5 scales) concerning motorcycle safety gear use were generally high. However, motorcycle safety helmet utilization, which is critical for saving lives, was variable, with mean use of helmets 81 percent of the time when riding, and a range of 0–100 percent.

Structural equation modeling was employed to examine determinants of motorcycle safety helmet use among respondents who resided in states that did not have laws *requiring* them to wear helmets ($N = 197$). Comfortable and non-intrusive motorcycle safety helmet use can require application of complex and novel behavioral skills, since it can be difficult to find the "right fit" for helmets, they can be challenging to put on comfortably, and they can impair one's sense of control and mobility when riding. For health-related behaviors that involve the application of significant behavioral skills, the IMB model specifies a mediational relationship between information and motivation and behavioral skills and behavior.

Results of structural equation modeling showed that the relationships specified by the IMB model were confirmed, and suggested that the model may provide an acceptable fit to the data (CFI = 0.93; RMSA = 0.13). As can be seen in Figure 4.4, information and motivation concerning motorcycle safety gear use were statistically related constructs. (While the IMB model suggests that information and motivation may be independent constructs, because well-informed persons are not necessarily well motivated to practice health behaviors, the model does not require the statistical independence of the information and motivation constructs). Further, and as predicted by

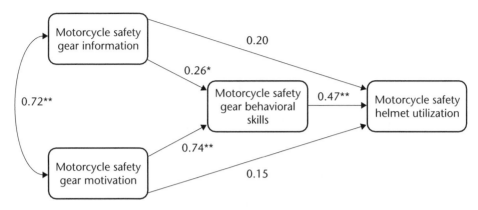

Figure 4.4   Empirical test of the Information–Motivation–Behavioral Skills Model of the determinants of motorcycle safety helmet utilization (based upon data collected by Murray, 2000).

the IMB model, information and motivation were associated with behavioral skills for motorcycle safety gear use, and behavioral skills were significantly associated with the criterion of motorcycle safety helmet use per se. The information, motivation, and behavioral skills components of the IMB model accounted for 61 percent of the variance in motorcycle safety helmet utilization, indicating substantial predictive power of the IMB model in this health behavior domain. Once again, this IMB model-based exploration of the determinants of motorcycle safety gear use can serve as elicitation research to guide targeted interventions to encourage motorcycle safety gear utilization. Moreover, these findings further establish the generalizability and strength of the IMB model across domains of health behavior, including disease preventive behavior (e.g., HIV prevention), disease detection behavior (e.g., BSE), and injury prevention behavior (e.g., motorcycle safety helmet use).

An IMB Model Analysis of Adherence to Medication Regimen

In addition to establishing the empirical generalizability of the IMB model, we wish to demonstrate conceptual utility as a basis for analysis of the determinants of still other health-related behaviors. To illustrate, we present an IMB model conceptualization of factors implicated in adherence to anti-retroviral therapy among people living with HIV infection. Understanding and promoting adherence to anti-retroviral therapy among HIV+ individuals is of enormous individual health and public health significance. On the one hand, anti-retroviral therapy has proven dramatically effective in reducing the viral load and associated morbidity among persons living with HIV, and has contributed directly to dramatic declines in HIV-related mortality (Greenberg et al., 1999;

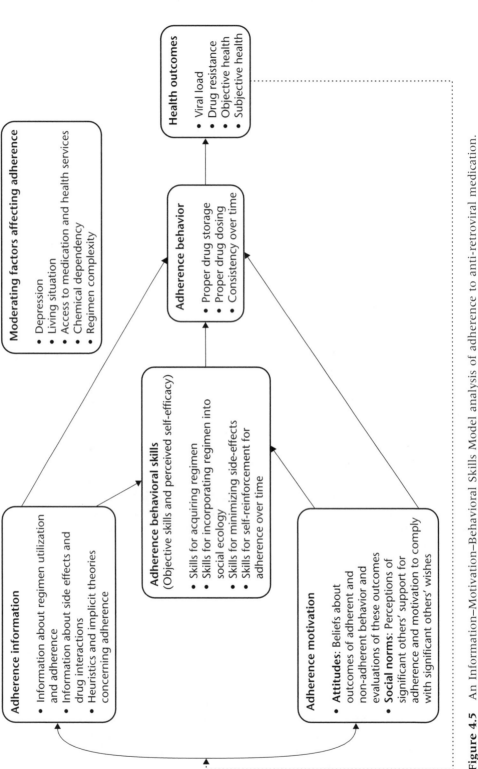

Figure 4.5 An Information–Motivation–Behavioral Skills Model analysis of adherence to anti-retroviral medication. From J. D. Fisher, W. A. Fisher, K. Amico and J. Harman (2001). An information–motivation–behavioral skills model of adherence to highly active antiretroviral therapy. Manuscript submitted for publication. Reprinted with permission.

Montaner et al., 1998). On the other hand, anti-retroviral therapy adherence – which can involve taking numerous pills per day, some fasting and some with food, many of which produce significant side effects, and all of which are expensive and can indirectly disclose one's illness to others – must occur with a great deal of consistency and for an HIV+ individual's entire foreseeable future.

Although adherence to anti-retroviral therapy must be in the 95 percent range, in actuality adherence to therapy is often much lower (W. Fisher et al., 2002; Montessori et al., 2000). When anti-retroviral adherence is suboptimal, treatment failure, viral mutation, and development of multidrug resistant HIV may take place (Boden et al., 1999; Eron, 2000; Hogg et al., 2000). HIV+ individuals who are intermittently adherent therefore are at significant personal health risk and may pose a substantial public health risk involving the potential development and transmission of multidrug resistant HIV to others.

From the perspective of the IMB model, adherence to medication regimen shares much in common with maintenance of other critical health behaviors. Therefore, anti-retroviral adherence is conceptualized to occur as a function of the presence of a specific set of relevant information, motivation, and behavioral skills elements. All else being equal, to the extent that an HIV+ individual is well informed about anti-retroviral therapy, motivated to act, and possesses the requisite behavioral skills to act effectively, he or she will be likely to adhere to anti-retroviral regimens, and to reap the substantial health benefits of adherence. To the extent that HIV+ individuals are poorly informed, unmotivated to act, and lack the requisite behavioral skills for effective adherence, they are expected to be non-adherent to anti-retroviral therapy and will fail to realize the substantial health benefits of this therapy. An IMB model analysis of anti-retroviral adherence is presented in Figure 4.5, which describes specific information, motivation, behavioral skills, and adherence behavior parameters and the relationships among them, as well as a set of moderating factors that are relevant in the context of anti-retroviral adherence.

According to the IMB model, *information* which is directly relevant to anti-retroviral medication utilization is a prerequisite for adherence. At a minimum, information about one's anti-retroviral regimen, including when (e.g., dosing intervals) and how (e.g., food and fasting requirements) to take the regimen, is required for adherent behavior. In addition, information about adequate adherence levels (e.g., about the relative effectiveness of anti-retroviral medication at 95 percent versus 50 percent adherence), information about side effects, and information about interactions with other prescription or recreational drugs are also thought to be critical to anti-retroviral adherence (J. Fisher et al., 2001). In addition to specific information that is fundamental to anti-retroviral adherence, the IMB model also directs our attention to adherence-related heuristics that permit automatic and cognitively effortless (but often incorrect) adherence-related decision making (e.g., "If I feel good I must be adhering at a sufficient level"). Adherence-related implicit theories – more complicated sets of beliefs that require cognitive effort to apply to anti-retroviral therapy decision-making – may also affect behavior. For example, the adherence-related implicit theory reflected in the view that "Periodic drug holidays (e.g., not taking drugs on weekends or vacations) approximate the structured interruptions of therapy that cutting edge science is experimenting with, so they are not only acceptable but desirable adherence interruptions" might exert a substantial effect on adherence behavior.

Motivation to adhere to anti-retroviral therapy is an additional factor which is expected to strongly influence whether even well-informed individuals will be inclined to adhere to therapy (e.g., J. Fisher et al., 2001; Richter et al., 1998). From an IMB model perspective, personal attitudes towards adherence – based upon perceptions of the outcomes of adherent behavior and evaluations of these outcomes (Fishbein and Ajzen, 1975) – represent an individual's personal motivation to adhere to anti-retroviral therapy. Social motivation – based upon perceived support for adherence to anti-retroviral therapy from salient referent others and motivation to comply with these referents' wishes – represents an individual's source of social motivation to adhere to therapy. Examination of circumstances under which personal motivation, social motivation, or both serve as especially strong influences on adherence will be an important focus for understanding and, critically, for promoting adherence to anti-retroviral therapy.

Behavioral skills for adhering to complicated, costly, side effect laden, and potentially illness-disclosing anti-retroviral regimens are an additional critical influence on adherence and determine whether well-informed and motivated individuals will be capable of adhering effectively to therapy over time (Albert et al., 1999; J. Fisher et al., 2001; Gallant and Block, 1998). Behavioral skills include objective abilities and perceptions of self-efficacy (J. Fisher and Fisher, 1992; J. Fisher et al., 2001) for performing a sequence of critical adherence behaviors. These may include acquiring anti-retroviral medication in an affordable and timely fashion and storing it appropriately; incorporating adherence into the social ecology of daily life (e.g., utilizing routine events to self-cue medication dosing; taking medication while at work without disclosing that one is HIV+); avoiding or minimizing side-effects and drug interactions; continuously updating adherence-related knowledge; and reinforcing one's self for adhering to anti-retroviral therapy over time and in the face of the multiple challenges that adherence to therapy represents.

As is the case for other health behaviors, the IMB model specifies that adherence information and motivation are often statistically independent factors that work primarily through behavioral skills to affect adherence behavior per se (see Figure 4.5). In essence, effects of adherence information and motivation will be expressed primarily through the application of adherence behavioral skills to the task of maintaining adherence to anti-retroviral therapy over time. As with other health behaviors, the model also specifies that adherence information and motivation may potentially have direct effects on adherence behavior, in situations in which novel or complicated behavioral skills are not required for adherence. At present, anti-retroviral therapy adherence clearly *does* require complex behavioral skills. If in the future, however, anti-retroviral regimens are developed which are delivered via once a day or weekly dosages or transdermal patches, and which have very low cost and few side effects, the IMB model would anticipate that adherence information and/or motivation could have direct effects on adherence behavior.

The IMB approach described in Figure 4.5 includes some critical additional elements. Clearly, adherence behaviors ultimately have direct effects on individual health outcomes (e.g., viral load, objective health, subjective health; Arnsten et al., 2000; Bangsberg et al., 2000). These outcomes, in turn, can feed back into the system and influence the information, motivation, and behavioral skills determinants of adherence behavior (see Figure 4.5). Thus, a positive objective and/or subjective health outcome may strengthen individuals' reliance on their adherence information, strengthen their personal and social motivation to adhere to therapy, and strengthen their objective and perceived efficacy for applying their behavioral skills to maintain adherent behavior. Such positive feedback should result in the maintenance and strengthening of anti-retroviral adherence among HIV+ patients in the context of good health outcomes. In contrast, a poor objective and/or subjective health outcome could cause weakened reliance on adherence information, lessened motivation to adhere, and lower objective and perceived self-efficacy with respect to applying behavioral skills to the challenge of anti-retroviral adherence. Such a negative feedback process could ultimately result in weakened adherence to therapy. Potential time lags between an individual's adherent or non-adherent behavior and his or her health outcomes are also accommodated within this IMB model analysis. For example, a fully adherent individual who does not achieve a discernable positive health outcome due to a medication response time lag may lose confidence in his or her adherence information base, lose motivation to adhere, and suffer a decline in perceived adherence behavioral skills, all of which will effect a decrease in adherence. By the same token, an intermittently adherent individual who does not observe a linked health decline may conclude that intermittent adherence is acceptable and may alter his or her adherence-related information, motivation, and behavioral skills in a way that results in continued deterioration of adherence to therapy.

Beyond these relationships, the IMB model of adherence also recognizes that relevant situational and individual factors will moderate the relationships in the model. Situational and personal affordances such as supportive and stable versus unstable living situations, easy versus limited access to medication and medical care, positive versus distressed psychological health status, and simplicity versus complexity of medication regimen will act to moderate effects of adherence information, motivation and behavioral skills on adherence behavior and health outcomes. For example, in the context of stable and supportive living circumstances (versus homelessness), adherence information, motivation, and behavioral skills are expected to be relatively strongly related to adherence behavior and health outcomes and should account for a substantial proportion of the variance in these parameters. In contrast, in the context of a non-supportive living situation such as homelessness, adherence information, motivation and behavioral skills are not expected to be capable of having strong effects on adherence behavior and health outcomes unless and until homelessness is remedied. Similarly, good access to medication, psychological health, and a lack of alcohol or drug dependence are expected to moderate strong relationships of adherence information and motivation through behavioral skills to adherence behavior and health outcomes. Conversely, poor access to medication, psychological ill health, and presence of alcohol or drug addiction are expected to moderate weak relationships of adherence information, motivation, behavioral skills, behavior, and health outcomes.

Finally, following the IMB analysis of the determinants of health behavior, we note that the model's information, motivation, and behavioral skills constructs are expected to have specific content that is especially relevant to the understanding and promotion of anti-retroviral adherence for particular populations and adherence behaviors of interest. For example, within the IMB approach, it is expected that specific adherence-related information, motivation, and behavioral skills factors will have special relevance to understanding and promoting adherence among individuals who have or who have not disclosed their HIV status, and among individuals who differ in gender, ethnicity, sexual orientation, chemical dependency, and like characteristics. For example, specific information about anti-retroviral medication and methadone interactions might be crucial to a heroin-addicted individual's adherence to anti-retroviral therapy; specific motivational factors might be associated with anti-retroviral adherence among HIV+ men and women with young children; and specific behavioral skills might be implicated in adherence behavior for individuals who have not disclosed their HIV status. Similarly, specific information, motivation, and behavioral skills may prove to be relevant to specific adherence behaviors, such as obtaining anti-retroviral medications, self-dosing at correct intervals, and avoiding or addressing drug side-effects.

Concluding Comments

The current chapter has outlined constructs and relationships of the IMB approach to understanding and promoting health behavior performance. We have reviewed considerable empirical evidence establishing the conceptual and predictive utility of the IMB approach in the context of understanding and promoting HIV preventive behavior. In addition, we have asserted that the IMB approach is a conceptually and empirically generalizable approach across health behavior domains. This assertion of generalizability has consistently been supported with evidence from reviews of the correlational and intervention literature across domains of health behavior, in focused empirical studies of health behaviors as diverse as breast self-examination and motorcycle safety gear use, and in focused conceptual efforts such as an IMB analysis of adherence to complex medication regimens. It is hoped that this evidence for the generalizability of the IMB approach will stimulate applications of the model to understanding and promoting health behavior across diverse domains of health related action.

Acknowledgments

The authors would like to acknowledge a National Institute of Mental Health grant RO1 MH59473 that supported work on this manuscript.

Correspondence should be directed to William A. Fisher, PhD, Department of Psychology and Department of Obstetrics and Gynaecology, Social Sciences Centre 6430, University of Western Ontario, London, Ontario, Canada, N6A 5C2; e-mail: fisher@uwo.ca.

References

Ajzen, I. (1991). The theory of planned behavior. *Organizational Behavior and Human Decision Processes*, 50, 179–211.

Albarracin, D., Johnson, B. T., Fishbein, M., and Muellerleile, P. A. (2001). Theories of reasoned action and planned behavior as models of condom use: A meta-analysis. *Psychological Bulletin*, 127(1), 142–61.

Albert, S. M., Weber, C. M., Todak, G. et al. (1999). An observed performance test of medication management ability in HIV: Relation to neuropsychological status and medication adherence outcomes. *AIDS and Behavior*, 3, 121–8.

American Cancer Society (1998). *What are the key statistics about breast cancer?* http://www.cancer.org/ben/info/brstats.html.

Anderson, E. S., Wagstaff, D. A., Sikkima, K. J., et al. (1997). AIDS prevention among low-income, urban African-American and white women: Testing the Information–Motivation–Behavioral Skills model. Poster presented at the 18th Annual Scientific Sessions of the Society of Behavioral Medicine, San Francisco, CA, April, 1997.

Arnsten, J., Demas, P., Gourevitch, M., Buono, D., Farzadegan, H. and Schoenbaum, E. (2000). Adherence and viral load in HIV-infected drug users. Comparison of self-report and medication event monitors (MEMS). 7th Conferences on Retroviruses and Opportunistic Infections. San Francisco, CA.

Bandura, A. (1989). Perceived self-efficacy in the exercise of control over AIDS infection. In V. M. Mays, G. W. Albee, and S. M. Schneider (Eds.), *Primary Prevention of AIDS* (pp. 128–41). Newbury Park, CA: Sage.

Bandura, A. (1992). A social cognitive approach to the exercise of control of AIDS infection. In R. J. DiClemente (Ed.), *Adolescents and AIDS: A Generation in Jeopardy* (pp. 89–116). Newbury Park, CA: Sage.

Bangsberg, D. R., Hecht, F. M., Charlebois, E. D. et al. (2000). Adherance to protease inhibitors, HIV-1 viral load, and development of drug resistance in an indigent population. *AIDS*, 14 (4), 357–66.

Boden, D., Hurley, A., Zhang, L. et al. (1999). HIV-1 drug resistance in newly infected individuals. *Journal of the American Medical Association*, 282(12), 1135–41.

Bryan, A. D., Fisher, J. D., and Benziger, T. J. (2000). HIV prevention information, motivation, behavioral skills and behaviour among truck drivers in Chennai, India. *AIDS*, 14(6), 756–8.

Bryan, A. D., Fisher, J. D., and Benziger, T. J. (2001). Determinants of HIV risk among Indian Truck drivers: An Information-Motivation-Behavioral Skills approach. *Social Science and Medicine*, 53, 1413–26.

Carey, M. P., Maisto, S. A., Kalichman, S. C., Forsyth, A. D., Wright, E. M., and Johnson, B. T. (1997). Enhancing motivation to reduce the risk of HIV infection for economically disadvantaged urban women. *Journal of Consulting and Clinical Psychology*, 65(4), 531–41.

Catania, J. A., Kegeles, S. M., and Coates, T. J. (1990). Towards an understanding of risk behavior: An AIDS risk reduction model (ARRM). *Health Education Quarterly*, 17, 53–72.

Catz, S. L., Kelly, J. A., Bogart, L. M., Benotsch, E. G., and McAuliffe, T. L. (2000). Patterns, correlates, and barriers to medication adherence among persons prescribed new treatments for HIV disease. *Health Psychology*, 19(2), 124–33.

Champion, V. L. (1990). Breast self-examination in women 35 and older: A prospective study. *Journal of Behavioral Medicine*, 13(6), 523–38.

Centers for Disease Control (2000). http://www.cdc.gov/health/injuries.htm.

Cohen, J. (1988). *Statistical power analysis for the behavioral sciences* (2nd edn.). Hillsdale, NJ: Erlbaum.

DeVroome, E. M., deWit, J. B., Sandfort, T. G., et al. (1996). Comparing the Information–Motivation–Behavioral Skills Model and the Theory of Planned Behavior in Explaining Unsafe Sex Among Gay Men. Unpublished manuscript, Utrecht University, Department of Gay and Lesbian Studies and Department of Social and Organizational Psychology, Utrecht, Netherlands.

Eron, J. (2000). *The Prospect for New Agents in the Management of Treatment Failure.* Program and abstracts of the 7th Conference on Retroviruses and Opportunistic Infections, San Francisco, CA, January 30–February 2, 2000, Abstract S34.

Fishbein, M., and Ajzen, I. (1975). *Belief, Attitude, Intention and Behavior: An Introduction to Theory and Research.* Reading, MA: Addison-Wesley.

Fisher, J. D., and Fisher, W. A. (1992). Changing AIDS risk behavior. *Psychological Bulletin*, 111, 455–74.

Fisher, J. D., and Fisher, W. A. (2000). Theoretical approaches to individual level change in HIV risk behavior. In J. L. Peterson and R. J. DiClemente (Eds.), *Handbook of HIV Prevention*. Kluwer Academic/Plenum: New York.

Fisher, J. D., Fisher, W. A., Amico, K., and Harman, J. (2001). An information–motivation–behavioral skills model of adherence to highly active antiretroviral therapy. Manuscript submitted for publication.

Fisher, J. D., Fisher, W. A., Misovich, S. J., and Bryan, A. D. (2002). Information–motivation–behavioral skills model-based HIV risk behavior change intervention for inner-city high school youth. *Health Psychology*, 21(2), 177–86.

Fisher, J. D., Fisher, W. A., Misovich, S. J., Kimble, D. L., and Malloy, T. E. (1996). Changing AIDS risk behavior: Effects of an intervention emphasizing AIDS risk reduction information, motivation, and behavioral skills in a college student population. *Health Psychology*, 15, 114–23.

Fisher, J. D., Fisher, W. A., Williams, S. S., and Malloy, T. E. (1994). Empirical tests of an information–motivation–behavioral skills model of AIDS preventive behavior with gay men and heterosexual university students. *Health Psychology*, 13(3), 238–50.

Fisher, W. A., Dervatis, K. A., Bryan, A. D., Silcox, J. and Kohn, H. (2000a). Sexual health, reproductive health, sexual coercion, and partner abuse indicators in a Canadian obstetrics and gynaecology outpatient population. *Journal of the Society of Obstetricians and Gynaecologists of Canada*, 22, 714–24.

Fisher, W. A., and Fisher, J. D. (1993). A general social psychological model for changing AIDS risk behavior. In J. Pryor and G. Reeder (Eds.), *The Social Psychology of HIV Infection* (pp. 27–53). Hillsdale, NJ: Erlbaum.

Fisher, W. A., and Fisher, J. D. (1999). Understanding and promoting sexual and reproductive health behavior: Theory and method. In R. Rosen, C. Davis, and

H. Ruppel (Eds.) *Annual Review of Sex Research* (Vol. IX, pp. 39–76). Mount Vernon, IO: Society for the Scientific Study of Sexuality.

Fisher, W. A., Fisher, J. D., and Rye, B. J. (1995). Understanding and promoting AIDS preventive behavior: Insights from the Theory of Reasoned Action. *Health Psychology*, 14, 255–64.

Fisher, W. A., Gilmore, J., Clark, F. et al. (2002). Patterns and correlates of HIV transmission risk behavior among HIV+ patients in clinical care. Manuscript in preparation.

Fisher, W. A., Sand, M., Lewis, W., and Boroditsky, R. (2000b). Canadian Menopause Study – I. Understanding women's intentions to utilize hormone replacement therapy. *Maturitas*, 37, 1–14.

Fisher, W. A., Williams, S. S., Fisher, J. D., and Malloy, T. E. (1999). Understanding AIDS risk behavior among sexually active urban adolescents. An empirical test of the Information–Motivation–Behavioral Skills model. *AIDS and Behavior*, 3, 13–23.

Gallant, J. E., and Block, D. S. (1998). Adherence to antiretroviral regimens in HIV-infected patients: Results of a survey among physicians and patients. *Journal of the International Association of Physicians in AIDS Care*, 4, 32–5.

Gerrard, M., Gibbons, F. X., and Bushman, B. J. (1996). Relation between perceived vulnerability to HIV and precautionary sexual behavior. *Psychological Bulletin*, 119, 390–409.

Godin, G., and Kok, G. (1996). The theory of planned behavior: A review of its applications to health-related behaviors. *American Journal of Health Promotion*, 11, 87–98.

Greenberg, B., Berkman, A., Thomas, R. et al. (1999). Evaluating supervised HAART in late-stage HIV among drug users: a preliminary report. *Journal of Urban. Health*, 76(4), 468–80.

Hammer, J. C., Fisher, J. D., Fitzgerald, P. C. (1996). When two heads aren't better than one: AIDS risk behavior in college-age couples. *Journal of Applied Social Psychology*, 26, 375–97.

Hochbaum, G. M. (1958). *Public Participation in Medical Screening Programs: A Sociopsychological Study*. (PHS Publication No. 572). Washington, DC: US Government Printing Office.

Hogg, R. S., Yip, B. K. C., O'Shaughnessy, M. V., and Montaner, S. G. (2000). *Nonadherence to Triple Combination Therapy is Predictive of AIDS Progression and Death in HIV-positive Men and Women*. Program and abstracts of 7th Conference on Retroviruses and Opportunistic Infections. San Francisco, CA. January 30–February 2, 2000.

Johnson, B. T., Marsh, K. L., and Carey, M. P. (2001). Factors underlying the success of behavioral interventions to reduce sexual HIV transmission. Paper presented at the 5th International Conference of AIDS Impact, Brighton, UK.

Kalichman, S. C., Cherry, C., and Browne-Sperling, F. (1999a). Effectiveness of a video-based motivational skills-building HIV risk-reduction intervention for inner-city African American men. *Journal of Consulting and Clinical Psychology*, 67(6), 959–66.

Kalichman, S. C., Rompa, D., Cage, M. et al. (2001). Effectiveness of an intervention to reduce HIV transmission risks in HIV-positive people. *American Journal of Preventive Medicine*, 21(2), 84–92.

Kalichman, S. C., Williams, E., and Nachimson, D. (1999b). Brief behavioral skills building intervention for female controlled methods of STD-HIV prevention: outcomes of a randomized clinical field trial. *International Journal of STD and AIDS*, 19, 174–81.

Kelly, J. A., and St. Lawrence, J. S. (1988). *The AIDS Health Crisis: Psychological and Social Interventions*. New York: Plenum Press.

Lierman, L. M., Kasprzyk, D., and Benoliel, J. Q. (1991). Understanding adherence to breast self-examination in older women. *Western Journal of Nursing Research*, 13(1), 46–61.

Misovich, S. J., Fisher, J. D., and Fisher, W. A. (1996). The perceived AIDS-preventive utility of knowing one's partner well: A public health dictum and individual's risky sexual behaviour. *Canadian Journal of Human Sexuality*, 5, 83–90.

Misovich, S. J., Martinez, T., Fisher, J. D., Bryan, A. D., and Catapano, N. (2001). Breast self-examination: A test of the Information, Motivation, and Behavioral Skills Model. Manuscript submitted for publication.

Montessori, V., Heath, K. V., Yip, B., Hogg, R. S., O'Shaughnessy, M. V., and Montaner, S. G. (2000). *Predictors of Adherence with Triple-combination Antiretroviral Therapy*. Program and abstracts of the 7th Conference on Retroviruses and Opportunistic Infections, Abstract 72.

Montaner, J. D., Reiss, P., Cooper, D. et al. (1998). A randomized, double-blind trial comparing combinations of nevirapine, didanosine, and zidovudine for HIV-infected patients. *Journal of the American Medical Association*, 279, 930–7.

Murray, D. M. (2000). Exploring motorcycle safety gear use: A theoretical approach. Unpublished master's thesis, Department of Psychology, University of Connecticut, Storrs, CT.

Prochaska, J. O., and Velicer, W. F. (1997). The transtheoretical model of health behavior change. *American Journal of Health Promotion*, 12, 38–48.

Prochaska, J. O., Velicer, W. F., Rossi, J. S. et al. (1994). Stages of change and decisional balance for 12 problem behaviors. *Health Psychology*, 13, 39–46.

Richter, R., Michaels, M., Carlson, B., and Coates, T. J. (1998). Motivators and barriers to use of combination therapies in patients with HIV disease. HIV InSite Knowledge Base. [On-Line]. http://hivinsite.ucsf.edu/InSite?page=KB.

Rosenstock, I. M. (1974). Historical origins of the health belief model. *Health Education Monographs*, 2, 328–35.

Rosenstock, I. M. (1990). The health belief model: Explaining health behavior through expectancies. In K. Glanz, F. M. Lewis, and B. K. Rimer (Eds.), *Health Behavior and Health Education* (pp. 39–62). San Francisco: Jossey-Bass.

Rosenstock, I. M. (1996). Why people use health services. *Milbank Mem Fund Quarterly*, 44, 94–124.

Rye, B. J. (1990). Affective and cognitive predictors of AIDS preventive behaviors among female university students. Unpublished master's thesis, University of Western Ontario, London, Ontario, Canada.

Rye, B. J. (1998). Impact of an AIDS prevention video on AIDS-related perceptions. *Canadian Journal of Human Sexuality*, 7(1), 19–30.

St. Lawrence, J. S., Brasfield, T. L., Jefferson, K. W., et al. (1995). Cognitive-behavioral intervention to reduce African American adolescents' risk for HIV infection. *Journal of Consulting and Clinical Psychology*, 63, 221–37.

US Department of Transportation: National Highway Traffic Safety Administration (1997). Traffic safety facts: Motorcycles.

US Department of Health and Human Services (1988). *Understanding AIDS*. HHS-88-8404. Rockville, MD: Centers for Disease Control.

Weinhardt, L. S., Carey, M. P., and Carey, K. B. (1997). HIV risk reduction for the seriously mentally ill: Pilot investigation and call for research. *Journal of Behavior Therapy and Experimental Psychiatry*, 28 (2), 87–95.

Williams, S. S., Kimble, D., Covell, N. et al. (1992). College students use implicit personality theory instead of safer sex. *Journal of Applied Social Psychology*, 22, 921–33.

CHAPTER 5

A Social Reaction Model of Adolescent Health Risk

Frederick X. Gibbons, Meg Gerrard, and
David J. Lane

Iowa State University

Introduction

As parents of a current and a former teenage daughter, it often seems to us
(FG and MG) that the lives of adolescents revolve around risk. We realize that
may be somewhat of an exaggeration, but the fact is that the social activities
that young people engage in frequently include risk *opportunities* – in the form
of available substances, such as drugs, or alcohol; or a car; or a potential
sexual partner; or some combination of all of these. More so than with adults,
health risk behaviors for young people involve others; they are done in the
presence of – and often for the benefit of – friends and peers. It is surprising
then, given the significance of the behavior, that relatively few social psychologists have concerned themselves with the questions of why young people
engage in risky behavior and how these behaviors might be reduced or inhibited. In this chapter we will present a social psychological model of adolescent
health risk that is based on two fundamental beliefs. One is that risk behavior
among young people is largely a social activity, and therefore is best approached
from a social psychological perspective. The second is that this particular
behavior, in many respects, is unique. It is different than other adolescent
behaviors, and it is different from the same behavior in adults, which means
that the models and theories that have been developed for older individuals
do not apply as well to younger people.

Our model is oriented toward social cognition, but its theoretical foundation is in basic social psychology. Its genesis had an ad hoc nature: it was
specific to the health risk behavior of adolescents, and the research it has
generated reflects this focus. We believe, however, that the model has something to say about other types of behavior besides substance use and sex,
and that it is applicable to individuals other than those in their teens. We
will begin by describing the model, focusing on its refinements since we last

described it (Gibbons and Gerrard, 1997), along with the more recent research it has generated. Because of the nature of the behavior involved, we will spend some time discussing the intervention implications of this work, and then conclude with some thoughts on future research directions.

Reasoned Approaches

Although there have not been a lot of social psychologists who have been interested in health behavior, an argument could be made that the work they have produced has had as much impact as that from any area of psychology. This is largely attributable to the efforts of a few researchers, such as Fishbein and Ajzen, whose theory of reasoned action (Fishbein and Ajzen, 1975) and its update, the theory of planned behavior (Ajzen, 1985; 1991), are arguably the most popular theories in the health behavior arena (and perhaps in the domain of all human social behavior).[1] Most readers of this volume are likely to be familiar with both theories, and so a brief review should suffice. The theory of reasoned action is an extension of earlier expectancy value theories, which view human social behavior from a decision-making perspective. The process outlined by the theory involves consideration and evaluation of two factors: *attitudes* toward the behavior, which includes perceptions of the behavior and the anticipated outcomes associated with it; and *subjective norms*, which is perceptions of what others would want one to do. This assessment leads to a decision to act or not act, referred to as *behavioral intention* (BI). As the theory's name implies, this process is thought to be a reasoned (though not necessarily rational) one that involves some premeditation and planning. In Ajzen's words, intentions are "behavioral plans that, in combination with appropriate opportunities and resources, enable attainment of a behavioral goal" (1999: 312). Taking breast self-examination as an example, the decision to examine or not would depend on the woman's beliefs about the efficacy of the act, her reaction to it (e.g., is it unpleasant or embarrassing?), and her perceptions of whether or not significant others would want her to do it. The theory of planned behavior would add to these two factors perceived behavioral control, or the woman's perceptions of her ability to effectively carry out the examination (McCaul et al., 1993).

There are hundreds of published studies in which one or both theories has been used effectively to predict health-relevant behaviors, ranging from flossing and vegetable consumption to seat belt use. The last meta-analysis of reasoned action theory, a doctoral dissertation by van den Putte (1993), indicated that, on average, BI explains about 38 percent of the variance in health behavior. A more recent meta-analysis of planned behavior theory (Armitage and Conner, 2001) suggested the figure may be closer to 31 percent – still a very impressive amount.

Moderators of the BI–behavior Relation

In these and other reviews of the two theories, a number of important moderators of the BI–behavior relation have been identified. One has to do with the way the behavior is assessed. Armitage and Conner reported that these theories do better at predicting behavioral self-reports than actual observations of behavior. Similarly, they are more effective at predicting intentions than behavior, especially when the behavior involves substance use (Morojele and Stephenson, 1994), such as smoking (Stacy et al., 1994) or excessive drinking (Schlegel et al., 1992).

The fact that these theories predict intentions better than behavior is certainly not a fatal flaw, and the same criticism could be leveled at any model of attitude/behavior consistency. The point here is only that reasoned or deliberative models work better at explaining and predicting behavior that is reasoned or deliberated. They are less effective at explaining behaviors that are irrational or impulsive (Ingham et al., 1992), or socially undesirable (Beck and Ajzen, 1991), or have a significant affective component (Eiser et al., 1993), all of which are characteristics of adolescent health-risk behaviors.

Another moderator of the BI–behavior relation is *experience*. Generally speaking, the relation between intention and behavior is lower among young people, and it increases over time, up to about age 19 or 20 (Albarracin et al., 2001; Chassin et al., 1992; Sheeran and Orbell, 1998). A study from our lab, which included seven annual waves of data from a panel of adolescents, from age 13 to age 19 (Reis-Bergan et al., 2003), found that the relation between smoking and drinking and behavioral expectation (BE; see discussion below) increased almost linearly with age and experience. At earlier ages, however, a construct from our model, behavioral willingness (BW) was a stronger predictor than either BE or previous behavior; we will return to this point later.

Because of the visibility of reasoned action and planned behavior theories, they have been frequent targets of conceptual and theoretical "potshots," yet their continued popularity clearly suggests they have withstood the tests of empirical scrutiny quite well (Norman et al., 2000). Nonetheless, we would argue that some assumptions of the expectancy value approach limit its applicability for certain kinds of behavior and certain populations (Cho et al., 1999; Eagly and Chaiken, 1993; Sutton, 1987). In particular, adolescents' (i.e., through age 20 or 21) decision-making "strategies" often do not follow the planful and deliberative sequence outlined by reasoned action or planned behavior, or other expectancy-value theories. To a lesser extent, that is also true for some behaviors throughout adulthood.

The Prototype/Willingness Model

When asked if they intend to use drugs, or drink to excess, or have sex without protection, the vast majority of adolescents will say no. Statistics indicate, however, that many of them will engage in these behaviors, and a fair number will do so repeatedly (Johnston et al., 2000). It is certainly possible that some of them are lying or impression managing, and that for others, plans changed. In most cases, however, we would argue that up until the time they indulged, they actually had no intention of doing so. Instead, they found themselves in situations – that they may not have sought – in which the opportunity to smoke or drink presented itself, and they responded. To the extent that these behaviors occur without forethought or premeditation, they do not fit well into the decision-making sequence outlined by expectancy value theories (Ingham et al., 1992; Kippax and Crawford, 1993), most of which maintain that intentions are the *only* proximal antecedent to behavior.

The basis of the prototype/willingness (P/W) model is the belief that there are actually two pathways to risk behavior, one of which is reasoned, the other is not. The former path involves many of the elements of expectancy value theories; it reflects the fact that sometimes adolescents engage in risky behaviors because they have made a conscious decision ahead of time to do so. The latter pathway is much less deliberative and much more reactive; this is the social reaction pathway and it is the focus of the model. This second pathway reflects the first and most fundamental of three assumptions of the model, which is that much adolescent risk behavior is a reaction to risk-conducive circumstances rather than a preplanned event. The second assumption of the model is that because these situations are both public and social – unlike adults, young people almost always smoke, drink, or drive recklessly with friends rather than by themselves – they have clear social images associated with them that are widely recognized by adolescents and even pre-teens. The third assumption is that because young people are very image-conscious (Carroll et al., 1997; Elkind, 1978; Lloyd and Lucas, 1998), these risk images or prototypes (the terms are used interchangeably in this chapter) have a significant influence on their risk behavior. That influence works via a social comparison process in which the adolescent compares him/herself with the image. The more comparison the adolescent engages in, the more influential his/her image will be. An outline of the model is presented in Figure 5.1.

The model includes previous behavior, which reflects its primary goal: to examine the cognitive factors that *mediate change* in behavior, including onset and escalation, as well as decline. With the exception of inclusion of previous behavior, the rest of the top half of the model has been borrowed directly from reasoned action theory, and is generally consistent with the expectancy-value perspective. The operationalization of these constructs is somewhat different than in reasoned action theory, however, given the nature of the behavior. First, regarding *subjective norms*, adolescents typically identify two significant sources of social influence: parents and peers. Realistically, the former group yields very little variance on this dimension, because few parents are accepting of these behaviors and their children know that. The peer group may accept and even facilitate the behavior, but seldom do young people report that their friends or peers *want* them to engage (boyfriends perhaps being an exception). Consequently, the model includes descriptive rather than injunctive norms (Deutsch and Gerard, 1955) – i.e., what the adolescent thinks his/her friends are doing rather than what they want him/her to do.[2]

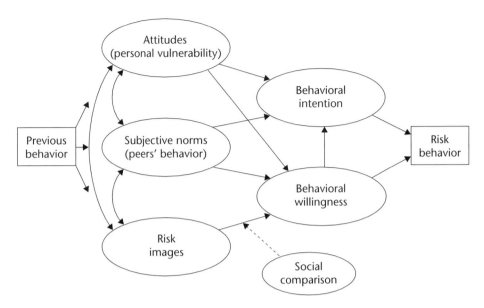

Figure 5.1   The prototype/willingness model.

The *attitude* construct has been operationalized in a manner that is generally consistent with the expectancy value approach, but slightly different from that in the planned behavior or reasoned action theories. We have assumed that most young people are ambivalent toward these actions. They find the behaviors enticing and exciting, on the one hand, but they recognize at least some of the inherent risks, and so they also view the behaviors as somewhat frightening. This ambivalence is quite common and so there is typically not a lot of variance on the affective dimension. There are more pronounced differences, however, in the extent to which young people view themselves as personally vulnerable to the negative outcomes that could accompany these actions, largely because there are considerable differences in the extent to which they have actually thought about these consequences. Some consider themselves "uniquely invulnerable" – a form of optimistic bias (Weinstein, 1984); others do not. For this reason, attitude operationalization in the model focuses on perceived *personal vulnerability* to negative consequences. These items are worded in the subjunctive (e.g., "If you *were* to . . . [drink and drive], what do you think the chances are that you would . . . [have an accident]?"). Otherwise, responses are confounded with intention: those who are not intending to do the behavior will deny risk in response to a direct question, such as "What is the likelihood that you will have an accident?"

We typically use expectation (BE) measures rather than intention (BI) measures when assessing these behaviors. BE is a modified version of BI, which gets at the individual's perceived *likelihood* that he/she will actually engage in a behavior rather than his/her plan to engage. Because it is less restrictive than BI, it often has more variance and does a better job of predicting less appropriate behaviors, such as heavy drinking and speeding (Parker et al., 1992; Schlegel et al., 1992). In fact, this practice (using BE measures) is typical of research in this area. Of the 154 studies included in the meta-analysis of planned behavior theory by Armitage and Conner (2001), only 20 used "pure" BI measures, whereas 40 used BE measures, and 88 used a combination of the two. Combining the two types of measures is not always a good idea, however, because it can conceal some important information. Acknowledging that one is likely to drink and drive or have unprotected sex is not the same as planning to do so, and it is quite different from having these actions as goals or "desires" (Bagozzi, 1992). For this reason, we suggest that future studies in this area, especially with adolescents, use both measures, along with a third proximal antecedent from our model, behavioral willingness (BW). This construct, and prototypes, are the two remaining and unique elements of the P/W model.

Risk Images

Actions speak louder than words – and they say a lot more as well. One reason for this has to do with the images that people associate with different behaviors – the prototype or cognitive representation of the type of person who engages in the behavior (Cantor and Mischel, 1979; Setterlund and Niedenthal, 1993). Generally speaking, the more extreme the behavior, the more vivid the associated image or prototype, and the more impact it is likely to have on impressions that are formed by others (Skowronski and Carlston, 1989). Riding a Harley-Davidson at age 60 says something different about a person – i.e., presents a different image – than does riding a bike at the same age or riding a Harley at age 20. Awareness of the image and the impact that it has can influence the decision to ride. Of course, by age 60, concern about others' opinions of the self usually has waned, which means the Harley image may have lost some of the influence (on behavioral decisions) that it had earlier in life. In fact, concern about social images and presumably their impact on behavior appear to peak during the teen years (Kelly and Edwards, 1998; Krosnick and Judd, 1982). Moreover, because adolescent risk behavior is unusual, in most instances public, and typically very salient, risk images tend to have more of an impact on teens than any other kind of image (Gibbons and Gerrard, 1997), and they have more of an impact on teens than they do on adults (Beyth-Marom et al., 1993). There is consensus among young people, for example, as to the type of person their age who drinks heavily, takes drugs, or has multiple sexual partners. It is not surprising, then, that numerous studies have shown that these images are associated with the decision to engage or not engage in risky behaviors (Chassin et al., 1981; 1985; Burton et al., 1989).

Early work in this area, much of it prompted by Leventhal and Cleary's (1980) seminal article that discussed the impact of smoker images on adolescents' smoking behavior, was based on an assumption that these images act as goal states and therefore have a motivating effect. This makes sense. Some boys play basketball because they want to "be like Mike" (Jordan), whereas some girls decide to become lawyers because they see themselves as Ally McBeal or (Judge) Amy Grey types. With regard to smoking, the argument was that young people take up the habit in order to be seen by others as tough or independent. Support for this perspective came from a series of "prototype-matching" studies indicating that the more similar adolescents' smoking or drinking images and self-images were, the greater their intention to smoke or drink (Chassin et al., 1981; 1985). Becoming like the image was, and undoubtedly for some, still is a motive for this behavior. One encouraging result of public health campaigns of the last 25 years, however, is that the images associated with health-impairing behaviors, such as smoking and drinking, have become more negative (Harms and Wolk, 1990; Lloyd and Lucas, 1998). Moreover, there is evidence that individuals who engage in risky behaviors are now more likely to be blamed for the negative outcomes associated with those behaviors (Brandt, 1997). As a result of this change in attitudes, it appears that risk images do continue to be influential, but the process whereby that influence takes place is more complex than was first thought.

Our data indicate that adolescents' risk images tend to be fairly negative. Even among those who are currently engaging, risk images are decidedly more negative than self-images on virtually every evaluative dimension that we have assessed. This suggests that most young people do not engage in order to acquire an image or certain characteristics of an image – why seek an image that is more negative than the one you currently have? On the contrary, many of them do *not* smoke or drink largely because of the image associated with these behaviors. They may view smoking and drinking as novel and appealing for a variety of reasons (Shapiro et al., 1998), but experimentation is inhibited because of the social costs involved.

These early image studies focused on drinking and especially smoking, presumably because these images are most vivid – their iconic representations are most clearly defined. It is easy to picture a young boy with a cigarette in his mouth or a teenage girl with a can of beer. It is much more difficult to describe the visual image one has of the typical drunk driver or the typical young woman who engages in casual sex (Ouellette et al., 2002). Nonetheless, although students have trouble describing what a "typical promiscuous female student" looks like, they have very little difficulty describing the *type* of young woman their age who does this behavior, and so this prototype does have an impact (Gibbons et al., 1995a; 1998a). In this sense, the P/W model is a typology, rather than a theory of visual images. Finally, because they tend to work more in an inhibitory than a facilitating fashion, and are seldom goal states, we would expect that risk images would not have a strong relation with intentions, and that is the case (Gibbons et al., 1998a). Instead, they are more strongly associated with a different proximal antecedent to behavior, behavioral willingness (BW).

Behavioral Willingness

The idea that risk-taking behavior by young people is often not intentional is not a new one. The same observation has been made by a number of researchers examining the sexual behavior of young men and women (Brooks-Gunn and Furstenberg, 1989; Chilman, 1983; Zelnick and Shah, 1983). Cobliner (1974), for example, found that less than half of the pregnant adolescents in their study said that their sexual behavior was deliberate (cf. Murry, 1994). Similarly, when we asked members of one of our adolescent panels (at age 18) if they had any plans to engage in casual or unprotected sex in the next year, 43 percent indicated they had no such intentions at all (i.e., marked a 1 on a 7-point BI scale), and yet when we asked them a year later if they had done this, 31 percent of these non-intenders said yes. Similar results occurred on the BE scale. We also asked them (at age 17) if there was any *likelihood* that they would have casual or unprotected sex, and more than half indicated no likelihood, by circling a 1 on the 7-point BE scale. Nonetheless, 26 percent of the group that had said no indicated a year later that they had engaged in the behavior. This inconsistency is not unique to sex. These same adolescents were also asked if they had any intentions to drive after drinking, and 58 percent said definitely not; yet a year later, 57 percent of this same group said they had done it. When asked why, a common response – probably all too familiar to parents of teens – was simply ". . . it just happened, that's all" (Mitchell and Wellings, 1998), which, of course, is another way of saying it was not intentional. In each instance, however, a significant percentage of these unintending adolescents had indicated some willingness to engage in the behavior.

BW versus BI/BE
BW is an openness to risk opportunity. It is an acknowledgment by the individual that he/she might do the behavior under some circumstances. As might be expected, BW is usually highly correlated with BI and BE, but it is not the same thing. Thus, it predicts risk behavior and does so independently of both BI and BE. In general, adolescents, and to a lesser extent adults, are willing to do riskier things than they intend or expect to do. In this sense, BW represents a "latitude of acceptance" (Sherif and Hovland, 1961). Moreover, the BW/BI relation is recursive: intention implies willingness, but the opposite is not the case. Indeed, this is a central focus of the model – the idea that there are a number of individuals, usually young, who are willing to do behaviors that they are not intending to do. In many respects, these adolescents are an at-risk group. Because they are not intending to take risks, they do not prepare for them – they do not carry condoms, or arrange for a designated driver, for example. But they are willing to take risks, and they sometimes do (depending on the circumstances they encounter), and that can be problematic. This at-risk group has been the focus of some of our recent research, and, we believe, should also be a focus of intervention efforts. Other ways in which BW and BI differ, besides focus of attention and locus of attribution

(discussed below), include the fact that BW is more affect-laden (the excitement and fear associated with risk), and that BW applies only to risky behavior, although the risk can be positive (e.g., willingness to intervene in an emergency). The primary way in which the two differ, however, is the fact that BI involves more forethought and planning than BW does. In fact, BW is often characterized by an *avoidance* of such considerations, as adolescents who are willing often avoid thinking about the potential consequences of their actions (Gerrard et al., 1996; Gibbons et al., 1998b).

Measurement

BW

Tapping into adolescents' BW involves several steps. First, we ask them to think about a risk-conducive situation (e.g., an older sibling left some marijuana in the house), making clear that there is no presumption about whether they would ever be in such a situation. This instruction is intended to shift attention away from the self and toward the context. In so doing, it helps get over the initial hurdle of implied responsibility inherent in most intention measures ("I didn't intend to do this, so I really can't be blamed for what happened . . ."), which is a major issue for young people when it comes to risky behaviors (Covington and Omelich, 1988). It also helps them appreciate some of the persuasive power of the situation. They are then asked to indicate what they would be willing to do by responding to a series of options, each increasing in risk level (e.g., take a puff . . . get stoned), which are aggregated into an index.

Images

To assess images, we ask respondents to first spend some time thinking about the typical person their age who engages in the behavior (e.g., drinks heavily). It is acknowledged that not all people who do this are alike, but it is suggested that they may share some characteristics. Respondents are then asked to evaluate this prototype using a list of from 6 to 20 adjectives (e.g., attractive, popular, inconsiderate), each with a scale from "not at all" to "very," sometimes followed by an open-ended evaluation. Responses on the adjectives and content analysis of the open-ended responses, if they are used, are aggregated to form an image index.[3]

Prototype/Willingness versus Other Models

Dual Processing

As indicated earlier, the two pathways to risk behavior, reasoned and reactive, involve different processing styles, which suggests that the P/W model might share some features with "dual-processing" models that have proliferated in social psychology in the last 10–15 years. Prominent among these would be Petty and Cacioppo's elaboration likelihood model (Petty and

Cacioppo, 1986), Fazio's MODE model (Fazio, 1990), Chaiken's heuristic-systematic model (Chen and Chaiken, 1999), and Gollwitzer's mind-set model (Gollwitzer and Bayer, 1999). There are two elements that are common to each of these models: (a) the contention that processing is more mindful (or systematic) in one mode and more heuristic-based in the other, and (b) beliefs about what factors determine which route is likely to be activated. The two route-determining factors are illustrated clearly in the MODE model; they are: motivation and opportunity (the full name of the model is *Motivation and Opportunity as Determinants*). The basic idea is that incentive and cognitive resources are both necessary to induce individuals to engage in the "effortful reflection" that is required by the deliberative-processing alternative. If one doesn't have the time or the inclination, then the heuristic processing mode is preferred (or is the default; Bagozzi and Yi, 1989).

This distinction does sound similar to the description of the reasoned versus reactive pathways. The factors that determine response mode are different in these models than in the P/W model, however. Although time and motivation are prerequisites for forming *intentions* to engage or not engage in risk, the absence of these factors does not lead to reactive processing. For one thing, as suggested earlier, risk opportunity and risk behaviors are an important part of the lives of many adolescents, and the consequences of these behaviors are potentially very significant. For most adolescents, then, the motivation level surrounding risky behavior and decision-making is often very high. Second, it is true that risk decisions are sometimes made "on-line," without much opportunity to deliberate; under these circumstances, processing will necessarily be abbreviated, and images – whether favorable or not – are likely to be more influential (Epstein, 1994). Nonetheless, it is also the case that adolescents have ample opportunity to form intentions not to engage in risky actions, and yet they frequently do not. In fact, it is the appeal of these behaviors that leads young people to *avoid* thinking seriously about them and especially about their consequences (Gibbons et al., 1998b). Theoretically, inducing careful contemplation of the behavior or its associated images should lead to consideration of consequences and a reduction in BW, along with an increase in intention not to engage (Gibbons et al., 2002c; see below).

CEST

The dual-processing model that is most similar to the P/W model is Epstein's cognitive experiential self theory (CEST; Epstein, 1990; Epstein and Pacini, 1999). Briefly, the two processing systems in Epstein's theory – rational and experiential – exist simultaneously. The rational system is deliberative and analytical and involves logical rules of inference. The experiential system is affect-based; it operates according to heuristic principles and involves images and intuition. The two systems share a number of characteristics with the reasoned and reactive pathways in the P/W model. Because they are both rooted in expectancy value approaches, the similarities between the rational system and the reasoned pathway are more obvious and more intuitive: both involve deliberation and intentions, and both are reason-oriented. The relations between the experiential system and the reactive path are more complex, but also more interesting. Both involve influential images (objects or exemplars in one case, prototypes in the other) and deliberation that is usually more restricted than that of the alternative path or processing mode. Both involve processing that is affect-based and less consistent over time than the alternative. With age and experience, both give way somewhat, though not completely, to the other, more reasoned and/or deliberative system (i.e., adults' behavior is more rational and more reasoned than adolescents' behavior).

Another important similarity has to do with cognizance of the two paths and systems. Not only are individuals aware of the (simultaneous) existence of the experiential and rational systems, as well as the difference between intentions and willingness, they also acknowledge that the reasoned path and rational system involve more "appropriate" responding – what should be done or the most reasonable response – whereas the experiential system and reactive pathway often reflect reality – what would or could be done under certain circumstances. As suggested earlier, young people (especially) will report levels of risk willingness that are a fair amount higher than their levels of risk intention and yet pointing out the discrepancy between the two seems to create little dissonance. Apparently, the fact that one is willing to accept a higher level of risk than one intentionally seeks is not perceived as a contradiction. Also, the reliability of BW over time and its predictive validity both suggest that it is a fairly stable construct, one that individuals are aware of and can report on fairly accurately.

There are differences between the CEST and P/W model, most of which reflect the more specific focus of the latter (on adolescent health risk). For example, although experiential processing is usually faster than rational processing, reactive processing is not necessarily faster than reasoned processing. Contemplation of one's willingness (during assessment) is truncated, because it includes minimal consideration of risk consequences. It does include consideration of social consequences (the typology element of the P/W model), however, and it involves social comparison (with the image), and that takes time. In fact, *initial* responses, which are typical of the experiential system, often reveal intended or reasoned behavior – what one should do or hopes to do. It is only when encouraged to take the next step and consider risk opportunities afforded by the context that BW is likely to emerge (cf. Gilbert, 1991). Thus, unlike the experiential system, the reactive path includes some recognition of (risk-conducive) circumstances, or the power of the situation. Similarly, images that guide behavior in the experiential system develop out of previous personal experience, whereas in the P/W model, those images are socially based (largely because most adolescents have had minimal personal experience with risk). Although similar to the CEST, we would argue that the unique elements of the P/W model make it more useful within its intended domain.

Stage Theories
Intention to engage in risk is usually preceded by willingness to do so; and it is often the case that with age and experience, an adolescent's willingness to

engage in risk will translate into an intention to do so. That is not necessarily the case, however, as curiosity about some behaviors, and willingness to engage in those behaviors wanes with maturity. Moreover, the reasoned and reactive paths often exist simultaneously, and neither one is a prerequisite for the other. Thus, the P/W model is not a stage theory of risk, and it does differ from existing stage theories, most of which are concerned with health promotion rather than health risk (e.g., the transtheoretical model; Prochaska et al., 1992). There are some similarities with Weinstein's (1988) precaution adoption model with regard to *risk perception*, however. Specifically, Weinstein argues that individuals must perceive that they are *personally* vulnerable to a health risk before they will act to protect themselves. Young people who are willing but not intending to engage in risk most likely are at this pre-acknowledgment stage, largely because they have avoided thinking about the potential risk. Presumably, encouraging consideration of the risk and its consequences would facilitate recognition of personal vulnerability and therefore reduce willingness.

Empirical Support

BW and Images
Research conducted in the first five or six years of the P/W model's development focused on its individual elements. Because that research is described in some detail elsewhere (Gibbons and Gerrard, 1997), we will summarize it briefly and then move to a discussion of the more recent work. These earlier studies, which involved several different panels of Iowa (i.e., white) adolescents, established links between risk images and risk willingness, including smoking and sex (Gibbons and Gerrard, 1995; Gibbons et al., 1995a; 1995b); and between risk images and risk behaviors, including drinking (Blanton et al., 1997; Gibbons and Gerrard, 1995), smoking (Gibbons et al., 1995b; Gibbons and Eggleston, 1996), and contraceptive use (Gibbons and Gerrard, 1995). Several studies also included assessments of BW and BI/BE as proximal antecedents (i.e., mediators of distal predictors) of risk behavior, and all of them demonstrated the ability of BW to predict behavior and do so independently of BI/BE (Blanton et al., 1997; Gibbons et al., 1998a; Gerrard et al., 1999).

Social Comparison
In addition, in one of those earlier studies (Gibbons and Gerrard, 1995), an ad hoc measure of social comparison tendencies was included in order to determine if this measure moderated the relation between risk images and behavior, as the P/W model would predict. Actually, the model suggests that images influence behavior *through* a social comparison process, but this type of mediation cannot be assessed effectively with correlational field data. Moderation by individual difference measures does allow for inferences about process, however, and in fact, the impact of images on subsequent behavior was significantly stronger for those students who had indicated that they frequently engaged in social comparison. The same results were found in two

recent studies, one of which (Gerrard et al., 2002) used a full version of the INCOM social comparison scale (Gibbons and Buunk, 1999), the other (Gibbons et al., 2002b) an abbreviated version. Finally, the pattern of the data appeared to be in line with the belief that risk images work primarily in an inhibitory fashion. In particular, the least amount of willingness to use substances and to have casual sex – essentially no willingness at all – was reported by adolescents and college students who were high in comparison tendencies and had negative risk images.

From an intervention perspective, there is good news in these negative images. Given their influence and the fact that they tend to be unfavorable, even among risk-takers, there is reason to believe that these images may be incorporated effectively into prevention and intervention programs aimed at delaying onset and escalation among pre-teens and adolescents. With this idea in mind, we have expanded the focus of our research over the last three or four years, to include factors that retard risk and/or promote health. In fact, a number of new empirical questions were raised by this earlier work, including: Can risk images be altered and, if so, does this reduce BW and, in turn, risk behavior? Do positive or healthy images exist; are they influential? Finally, where do these images come from?

Sources of Risk Images

High Risk

The question about the origins of risk images seems especially important because of the potential that this kind of information has to guide prevention efforts. As Figure 5.1 indicates, images are influenced by previous actions, but this is certainly not where they originate. Instead, they emanate from a number of sources, such as friends, school, parents, and TV/media. In fact, our data indicate that all of these sources contribute, though in different ways, and to varying degrees at different ages. We began asking relevant questions of one of the adolescent panels ($N = 500$) when they were 15. By that age, the most influential source of substance use images was clearly the peer group. Others have suggested, however, that adolescents may have fairly well-developed smoking and drinking images well before their friends are using, perhaps as early as age 10 or 11 (Aloise-Young and Hennigan, 1996). To explore this question more thoroughly, we are examining the development of risk images and their impact on behavior in two panels of African American children, both of which are part of the Family and Community Health Study (FACHS). One panel comprises 897 target children, age 10 or 11 at Wave 1; and the other, 297 of their siblings, who were age 13 or 14 at that time (Gibbons et al., 2002b; Wills et al., 2000; in press). The advantage of having a sample as young as these targets is that very few of them or their friends have started to engage in risk behaviors (Wills et al., 1999), so it is possible to determine the impact (on use) of factors other than peers, some of which are at least potentially more controllable, such as parenting or education. As expected, only 3 or 4 percent of the younger children reported having used substances at Wave 1 (although about 15 percent reported some willingness to use), and 95 percent reported either no use or only minimal use by their friends. Not surprisingly, then, norm perceptions were not related to risk images. Nonetheless, the evidence suggested that even at this young age, the images were fairly well developed and distinct.

Several influential sources of these images were identified. First, when asked directly where their substance images had come from, the top choice for both groups was TV/movies followed by peers and friends. The former is somewhat surprising given that we were asking about images of users *their own age*, and such precocious use is rare on TV (Grube, 1995). Most of the other sources involved individual differences. As expected, those who were high in a tendency toward *risk-taking* (Eysenck and Eysenck, 1977) had more favorable images, whereas those who were more *academically oriented* had less favorable images. Less intuitive was the third individual difference factor: the children's perceptions of their previous experience with *racial discrimination* (Landrine and Klonoff, 1996) was a significant predictor of both their BW to use and their risk images. Moreover, in the first two waves, perceived discrimination was far and away the strongest predictor of perceived peer usage ($p < 0.001$), which is a reflection of affiliation preferences.

The fourth influential factor was one that we had detected as an indirect effect in previous studies with older, white samples (Blanton et al., 1997), and that was the *parenting style* of the primary caregiver. If the parents had an involved parenting style, meaning they monitored the child's activities, provided warmth and support, and communicated with the child about sex and substance use, then their children were much less willing to use substances ($p < 0.001$). In addition, there was a strong indirect effect of parenting on risk images, in the expected (positive) direction, through academic orientation. Finally, the impact of both risk images and parenting style on BW was moderated by *context*. Among families living in neighborhoods in which there was more crime and public use of substances, the children had more favorable risk images and more willingness to use, in general, *and* the impact of parenting style – both good and bad – and risk images on BW were also significantly stronger than in the less risky neighborhoods. Thus, parents were able to have more of an impact when it counted most (Baldwin et al., 1990).

Positive (Healthy) Images

Almost all of the work done in this area has focused on images associated with risky behaviors; very few studies have looked at the impact of low risk or healthy images. In fact, there is reason to question whether such images even exist among young people. The image of a teen smoker is fairly vivid, but it is much harder to envision a teen non-smoker or non-drinker (Fazio et al., 1982; Nisbett and Ross, 1980). Still, it is likely that by a certain age, adolescents have formed an impression of the *type* of young person who has made a conscious decision to not use substances or not have sex. The question is when – at what age is the behavior common enough that choosing not to engage in it makes some kind of statement to others? We have addressed this question in several studies. Before beginning the FACHS project, we ran a series of focus groups with 10-year old African American children in which they were asked to describe the type of child their age who smokes or drinks and the type who chooses not to do either one. As was the case with the panel, these adolescents had formed user images and, in general, had relatively few problems with the questions about users. But they had difficulty describing their image of a 10/11 year-old non-user – the category was much too large for it to have a distinct image or prototype (Linville and Fischer, 1993; Smith and Zarate, 1992).

Social versus Conventional Sources
The situation was different with the older siblings. By their age (13 or 14), enough of them and their friends had at least minimal experience with some substance (54 percent and 69 percent, respectively), that a clear image of a non-user had been formed, and their descriptions of both users and non-users were internally reliable. The two types of images had different antecedents, however. High-risk images were most strongly linked to friends' use and risk-taking disposition. The low-risk images were linked to more conventional sources, the two primary ones being academic orientation and communication (about risk) from their primary caregiver. Our interpretation of this difference was that these non-user images were a reflection of a more careful deliberative process, characteristic of the reasoned pathway, which was induced or encouraged by teachers and parents. The user image, on the other hand, came mostly from TV and older peers, and did *not* include consideration of the behavior and its consequences.

   This hypothesis was tested more directly with analyses of longitudinal data from one of the white panels (ages 16–18), which included several additional measures that allowed us to get a better idea of image influence (Gerrard et al., 2002). Participants' self- and ideal self-images were assessed with the same set of adjectives that had been used with the prototypes, and they were also asked directly how much they had thought about the risk and the non-risk (drinker and non-drinker) images.[4] The panel was divided into two roughly equal-sized groups comprising those who had and those who had not had experience with drinking, and then comparisons were made between them. The self-images of the two groups were virtually identical, and in both groups, risk images were less favorable than either the self- or the non-risk images. In contrast, the non-risk image was less favorable than the self-image for drinkers, but it was significantly *more favorable* than the self for abstainers – the first time we have seen evidence of a prototype being more favorable than the self-image in any of our studies. Also, the ideal self correlated with the non-risk image for both groups; however, the risk image was negatively correlated with the self for the abstainers and not related to the self for the drinkers. Thus, the study provided no evidence that risk images represented goal states for any of the adolescents, regardless of their behavior; instead, these images had an inhibitory effect – albeit for some more than others. In contrast, the non-risk images did appear to be acting as goal states, but, again, more so for some than for others.

Cognitive mediation was also assessed in this study by means of a structural equation analysis that examined the relations among image favorability, image contemplation, and both BW and alcohol consumption. First, all students reported that they had thought more about the non-risk than about the risk image. In addition, and consistent with expectations, the non-risk image was related to BW and to use, but that impact was totally mediated by the extent to which the adolescents reported they had thought about (contemplated) the image. In contrast, although the risk image did have a strong impact on BW and behavior, this effect was *not* mediated by the relevant image-contemplation measure. In short, non-risk image influence involves image contemplation (a more reasoned process) much more than does risk image influence (a more reactive process).

Sexual Images
Finally, another study examined antecedents of the older siblings' sexual images, i.e., sexually active versus abstinent (Wills et al., in press). Once again, parents had significant input. Teens who reported having a good relationship with their parents and whose parents communicated with them about sexual topics, such as birth control and AIDS, had less favorable sexual prototypes. In addition, the teens' self-control (Rothbart and Bates, 1998) was related to their abstinence images in the anticipated fashion: good self-control (also called "planfulness") was positively related and poor self-control was negatively related. Although self-control had more of an impact on the siblings' sexual images than on their substance use images, the antecedents of both types of images were, for the most part, similar. More generally, it would appear that to varying extents, parents, peers, and personality all play a role in the development of both risky and healthy images.

Interpretation and Summary

Risk images, for the most part, are negative. They are more negative than the self- or the ideal self-image, and that is true for most adolescents whether they are engaging in the behavior or not. Thus, the images work primarily in an inhibitory fashion. Although many adolescents find the prospects of substance use or early/risky sexual behavior to be enticing or exciting, they choose not to participate because they don't want to pay the price – the social or personal consequences that come with being identified as the type of kid who uses drugs or sleeps around (Beyth-Marom et al., 1993). This inhibitory effect requires relatively little processing effort. Most of those who do choose to engage in these behaviors do so in spite of the image. If anything, they tend to avoid thinking about the image as well as the behavior and its consequences (Gerrard et al., 2002; Gibbons et al., 1997). Were they to seriously consider the images, they would probably be less inclined to engage (Gibbons et al., 2002c).

In contrast, non-risk images have all the earmarks of goals or goal states. They are correlated with adolescents' ideal selves, even for those who are doing the behaviors. These positive or healthy images are also more favorable than the self-images of those who have chosen not to use; and their impact is mediated by contemplation, which would be expected of a goal state (Ajzen, 1991). In short, it would appear that there are two pathways to risk avoidance, just as there are two pathways to risk behavior. Some adolescents intend to avoid risk (and follow the reasoned path); some are simply unwilling to accept the social consequences that come with risk behavior (and thus follow the social reaction path). Before discussing the intervention and prevention implications of these findings, we will discuss some recent studies that have examined the effects of altering risk images on behavior.

Changing Risk Cognitions and Risk Behavior

Images and Willingness

The image and behavior change studies have been conducted with college students. By this age, certain risk behaviors, such as social drinking and smoking, are becoming habitual, more or less, and so BW is likely to be less of an issue. Other behaviors, however, such as casual sex, drunk driving, or binge drinking, are not well engrained (and may never become so; see discussion below) and so are good candidates for alteration. The first study in this area was a dissertation (Eggleston, 1997) in which an attempt was made to alter college women's perceptions of the casual sex prototype to see what effect it would have on their BW and BI to have unprotected sex. This was done by presenting accurate information about the percentage of their peers who were having unprotected sex – a percentage that is consistently overestimated by college students (Gibbons et al., 2002c; cf. Baer et al., 1991). As expected, BW to have casual sex declined in the lab session (relative to pre-testing) and the associated prototype became more negative. Changes in these two constructs were correlated, and change in the image did mediate change in BW, as predicted. BI to have casual sex also declined over time, but this change was not related to the decline in image favorability. In a similar study, Blanton et al. (2001, Study 4) presented college students with a bogus newspaper article reporting the results of a personality survey indicating either that people who use condoms are less selfish and more responsible than those who do not (positive non-risk image), or that those who do not use condoms are more selfish and less responsible than those who do (negative risk image). A control condition was also included in which no information about condom users was provided. Participants were then presented with a casual sex scenario and asked what they thought they might do under those circumstances (a BW/ BE combination). As expected BW was significantly lower in the negative image condition than in either the control or favorable image conditions.[5]

In another variation of this same theme, Gibbons et al. (2002c, Study 2) presented college students with a bogus audiotape in which a student was described by two others who supposedly knew him/her fairly well. The description varied according to a 2 × 2 design. It was either very favorable (e.g., successful student, athlete, volunteer) or unfavorable, and it indicated that the student either was a virgin or had had a number of casual sexual partners. The relevant prototype and BW were assessed and compared with the same measures taken in pretesting, 2–4 weeks earlier. This procedure also allowed exploration of a basic question from the social comparison literature that is relevant to the P/W model: can exposure to an exemplar affect perceptions of a prototype? In other words, can comparison with a specific individual who represents a category change one's perception of that category? Results suggested the answer is yes, as the most negative prototype evaluations were provided for the high risk exemplar described in unfavorable terms. In addition, the lowest BW for casual sex (controlling for pretest BW) also occurred in this condition, and change in the image mediated change in BW, as expected. There were no significant changes in BI, which remained at a lower level than BW at both assessments. Finally, although the differences were not significant, the effects were stronger for participants who had high pretest scores on a measure of social comparison tendencies (the INCOM).

In another study, target similarity (to the subject) was manipulated rather than favorability (Thornton et al., 2002; Study 2). Female subjects read a description of a student their age who was sexually active but erratic in her use of contraception, and described as either very similar to them or very dissimilar, based on an attitude questionnaire completed in pretesting. The assumption was that the similarity manipulation would influence the extent to which participants socially compared with the target, with more comparison occurring in the similar than the dissimilar condition (Goethals and Darley, 1977). Subjects also indicated how similar they thought they were to the target, provided a general evaluation of her, and then indicated their own BW for unprotected sex. As expected, target (image) evaluations interacted with perceived similarity in determining BW: the more favorable subjects' evaluations of the target, the higher their BW, but only when perceived similarity with the target was high and, therefore, social comparison was encouraged.

Changing Behavior

Although these studies demonstrated that alteration of risk images and, in turn, BW is possible, the question remains as to whether image manipulation or modification can be used to induce behavior change. Theoretically, this should work, and previous studies documenting a link between images and behavior offer support for this presumption. Inducing and studying behavior change in the lab is difficult, however, and that is especially true for behaviors of this nature. There have been two attempts to do this, both of which provided affirming but indirect evidence that images can be used to produce change in health-relevant behavior.

In the first of the studies, Ouellette et al. (2002) used different kinds of images in an effort to increase a positive health behavior, namely exercise.

College students spent about 25 minutes visualizing and answering questions about one of four images in a 2 × 2 design: either the prototypical exerciser or non-exerciser; or themselves in the future (a "possible self," Markus and Nurius, 1986), also as either a regular exerciser or as a non-exerciser. Their exercise behavior had been assessed in pretesting, along with two individual difference measures that were expected to moderate the impact of each type of image on behavior: the INCOM and the Consideration of Future Consequences scale (CFC, Strathman et al., 1994). Because the INCOM measures social comparison tendencies, it was expected to moderate the impact of the prototype. The CFC assesses current versus future time orientation and therefore was expected to moderate the impact of consideration of future self. The students had little difficulty envisioning either the prototype or themselves in the future, as they wrote fairly detailed descriptions in both conditions. A month after the lab session, they were called, supposedly as part of a recreation survey, and asked questions about their exercise behavior during the previous month. These self-reports of exercise behavior supported both assumptions. In the prototype consideration condition, significant increases in exercise were reported only by participants who were high in social comparison, whereas in the future-self condition, significant increases in exercise were reported only by those who were high in CFC.[6]

The most recent behavior change study took a different approach. The health risk in this instance was ultraviolet (UV) ray exposure from sunbathing and tanning booth use – behaviors that are contributing to what is now the fastest growing form of cancer in the US (Jemal et al., 2000). This study (Gibbons et al., 2002a) was one of a series of studies run in Iowa and southern California, in which half the student participants received a lab-based intervention in the form of a photograph of their faces taken by a camera with a UV filter. These photographs graphically depict existing skin damage, due to previous UV exposure, that is not yet visible to the naked eye (Fulton, 1997). It was assumed that these photographs would affect two components of the P/W model: attitudes toward tanning (including perceived risk) and risk image (i.e., the "typical tanner" prototype). In fact, in each of the studies, the photographs significantly increased perceptions of personal vulnerability, decreased favorability of the tanner image, and lowered willingness for UV exposure.

Most relevant to the current discussion, however, were the results on the one-month follow-up visits back in the lab. First, most of the initial changes in cognitions (tanner prototype, perceived vulnerability, BW) persisted over the interim. Changing behavior presented more of a challenge: *reducing* sunbathing in Iowa in March is not feasible. A large percentage of Iowa college students (as high as 40 percent) visit tanning booths around spring break, however, and so there was some variance to work with on that behavior. In fact, those who had received the UV photo, reported a significantly greater drop in tanning booth use in both studies (p's < 0.01), and that change in behavior was mediated by the change in their tan attitudes and prototypes. In other words, seeing a photo of themselves in which their UV-induced skin damage was made salient, resulted in a more negative opinion of the prototypical tanner, and this, in turn, was associated with a decline in their use of tanning booths.

Intervention Implications

Researchers in the area of adolescent health know a great deal about why young people smoke and drink and have unprotected sex, but efforts to turn that knowledge into effective programs that can prevent or change those behaviors have met with mixed success, at best. A prime example is the DARE program, which is based on a refusal efficacy model (i.e., empower young people to "just say no" in response to social pressure). This approach has enjoyed considerable popularity and financial support in spite of the fact that evaluations of its efficacy have consistently produced disappointing results (Lynam et al., 1999). More encouraging results have come from evaluations of programs that are based on normative theories (Hansen, 1992; Tobler and Stratton, 1998), which target adolescents' *perceptions* of the extent to which their peers condone and participate in substance use of one kind or another (i.e., subjective norms). As suggested earlier, these perceptions are often inflated (Suls et al., 1988; Prentice and Miller, 1993), and this inflated perception, in turn, appears to be related to subsequent increases in use (Gerrard et al., 1996). Theoretically, then, disabusing adolescents of these faulty cognitions should result in a decrease in use, and that does appear to be the case (Schroeder and Prentice, 1998).

In an evaluation of the Adolescent Alcohol Prevention Trial, which included both normative education and refusal training administered separately or together in a 2 × 2 design, Donaldson et al. (1995) reported that refusal training worked well, but only among those adolescents who had already decided that alcohol consumption is inappropriate. It was less effective, and may have even backfired, among those who had not made that decision. Donaldson et al. suggested that the reversal is due to the fact that presenting refusal training without normative enlightenment results in a significant increase in prevalence estimates (i.e., "there must be *some* reason why they are putting so much effort into this training . . ."), and that, in turn, leads to more acceptance of the behavior and eventually to more behavior.

This "preaching to the choir" criticism of the DARE program is consistent with the P/W model. Adolescents who have already decided that drinking is bad are, most likely, using the reasoned path. They are not only not intending to consume, many of them have probably developed intentions *not* to do so. On the other hand, most of those who are not opposed to drinking are using the social reaction pathway – they do not have any intentions to drink (at age 14 or 15), but they are willing to do so. As suggested earlier, these are the adolescents who should be targeted in future interventions. Some suggestions on how that might be done come from the P/W model, and involve its two core elements: prototypes and BW.

First, adolescents' tendency to overestimate the extent to which their peers condone substance use also applies to their beliefs about peers' risk images – kids think other kids have more favorable risk images *and* less favorable non-risk images than is actually the case. Given that these images are malleable, that we have some idea of where they originate or what influences them, and that promoting change in the direction of reality involves telling the truth, there is reason for optimism about the prospects for effective intervention. Second, as suggested earlier, adolescents apparently can understand the difference between BW and BI. What they are not aware of is the *extent* to which their own behavior, as well as that of their friends and peers, is willingness based. They may decide that because they are not intending to engage in a particular behavior, they don't have to worry about it. In addition, those with some inclination to engage may actively avoid thinking about the behavior and especially its consequences. In either case, focusing adolescents' attention on the issue of willingness is likely to be enlightening for them.

We are now beginning an intervention with a new panel of 400 African American youths and their families that is based, in part, on the P/W model. In addition to altering risk images, the program will focus on BW; the following strategies will be employed:

- Educate young people about the differences between BI and BW, and the fact that much of their risk behavior is not intended. Encourage consideration of their willingness to put themselves in risk-conducive situations; plan ahead to avoid these situations.
- When considering the difference between BW and BI, focus on internal attributions of responsibility for behavior, especially for behavior that is willingness based.
- Help them devise a plan for resisting risk opportunity that is internally based; i.e., recognizes interest in the behavior and goes beyond "just" resisting social pressure.

Future Directions

Image Composition
There are a number of general topics and specific research questions that are likely to produce useful information that can improve the model. These topics can be divided into two general categories reflecting the two primary components of the model. First, regarding *risk images*, one specific question has to do with their nature – are there individual attributes associated with certain risk images that are more impactful? To date, our analyses have consistently shown that the overall favorability index predicts behavior better than any subset of adjectives (see note 4), which is consistent with the assumption that it is not specific characteristics of the images that motivate behavior (as goals), but rather the general impression of the type of person who engages that is influential (a typology). More detailed exploration of image composition should shed additional light on the process of image influence and also inform efforts at prevention.

Social Comparison

A second issue in need of attention has to do with the role that social comparison plays in this process. As suggested earlier, we know that images are more of a factor for persons who are prone to socially compare (Gerrard et al., 2002; Ouellette et al., 2002), but we have yet to isolate the process of comparison in a controlled experiment (the fact that the similar image had more impact on BW in Thornton et al. 2002 is consistent with the assumption of social comparison mediation but again it is only indirect evidence). By experimentally manipulating comparison, we should be able to learn more about its involvement in image influence.

BW versus BI/BE

A primary question has to do with the ways in which BW differs from BI and BE and how they each develop over time. A recent examination of these questions, based on seven annual assessments of adolescent smoking and drinking and their antecedents (Reis-Bergan et al., 2001) indicated that the BW and BI/BE trajectories tend to converge over time, but remain distinct at least into late adolescence. For example, at age 14, BW to smoke correlates highly with BI, but exceeds it by a fair amount and is a much better predictor of subsequent smoking behavior. That changes by age 17, when BI has almost caught up with BW in absolute terms and is a better predictor. By young adulthood, when substance use habits are pretty much determined, the predictive power of BW has given way to that of BI/BE, which, in turn, is largely a reflection of previous behavior (Stacy et al., 1990). To distinguish between BW and BI/BE effectively, it is best to conduct research at a time in life when they are more distinct.

Conclusion

There are risky behaviors that occur with some frequency among both young and older adults that seldom are intentional – driving under the influence, for example. And there are behaviors, such as tax evasion, that are largely willingness based even among adults. There are also behaviors that are less common, but are usually "social reactions" *any* time they occur. A prime example of this would be adultery, which is frequently unplanned and/or unintentional, at least initially (Corey, 1989). The P/W model should be effective at predicting these kinds of risk actions in adults. Generally speaking, however, the evidence suggests that the P/W model is less applicable and less useful vis-à-vis adult behavior. The primary reason is that after years of experience, adults have a much better idea than do adolescents or college students of what they will and will not do, and so reasoned or rational models are going to be more successful at predicting their behavior. Nonetheless, one of the best predictors of health problems in adulthood is risky patterns of behavior in adolescence (US Department of Health and Human Services, 1994), and so models that focus on this stage of life are useful. There are many such models (see Conner and Norman, 1996; Norman et al., 2000), but few of them are based in social psychology theory, and even fewer include relevant cognitive mediators. These health cognitions – risk perceptions, attitudes, images – are the "remote link" between family and social life during adolescence, and health behavior throughout life. For this reason, we join others (Beyth-Marom and Fischoff, 1997; Salovey et al., 1998) in calling for an empirical focus in this area that is more socio-psychological and more cognitive in its orientation. We believe such models have considerable potential.

Notes

1. In fact, there is a long history in health psychology of a relatively small number of social psychologists having a major impact on the development of the area, beginning with the pioneering work (in the 1950s) of Hochbaum, Rosenstock, Leventhal, and Kegeles. As members of the Public Health Service, they developed what was arguably the most influential theory in health psychology prior to reasoned action, and that was the health belief model. This trend continued in the 70s with Triandis's (1979) theory of social behavior (although a model of general social behavior, it was a precursor to reasoned action theory and to the current P/W model and did have an impact on health psychology), into more recent times, with the highly visible work of Richard Jessor, Richard Evans, and Thomas Wills.
2. The original theory of reasoned action included motivation to comply with the perceived wishes and desires of significant others (injunctive norms) as part of the subjective norm construct. This element of the construct has suffered from low predictive validity, however, and more recent versions of the theory have omitted it (Reinecke et al., 1997).
3. Both the BW and risk image constructs (aggregates) have been shown to have good reliability – internal (alphas > 0.70), as well as test-retest (e.g., one-year stability > 0.50).
4. In order to make comparisons across behaviors and across samples, we have usually used the same basic set of adjectives (e.g., smart, popular, careless, inconsiderate) for all prototypes and, in this study, for the self- and ideal self-descriptions as well. Undoubtedly, risk images differ on different dimensions; nonetheless, the overall favorability of the image appears to be the best predictor of risk behavior, which suggests "tailoring" of adjective lists for different images, while informative, is not necessary.
5. The fact that the negative (risk) image had more impact than the positive (non-risk) image is consistent with the P/W model's contention that health images have primarily an inhibiting effect on behavior; i.e., the motive to avoid a negative image is greater than the motive to acquire a positive one (cf. Kahnemann and Tversky's, 1979, prospect theory).
6. Increases were also reported by participants in the prototype condition who were low in CFC. The reader is referred to Ouellette et al. (2002) for a discussion of this finding, which is beyond the scope of this chapter.

References

Ajzen, I. (1991). The theory of planned behavior. *Organizational Behavior and Human Decision Processes*, 50, 179–211.

Ajzen, I. (1985). From intentions to actions: A theory of planned behavior. In J. Kuhl and J. Beckman (Eds.), *Action Control from Cognition to Behavior* (pp. 11–39). New York: Springer-Verlag.

Ajzen, I. (1999). Dual-mode processing in the pursuit of insight is no vice. *Psychological Inquiry*, 10(2), 110–12.

Albarracin, D., Johnson, B. T., Fishbein, M., and Muellereile, P. A. (2001). Theories of reasoned action and planned behavior as models of condom use: A meta-analysis. *Psychological Bulletin*, 127, 142–61.

Aloise-Young, P. A., and Hennigan, K. M. (1996). Self-image, the smoker stereotype and cigarette smoking: Developmental patterns from fifth through eighth grade. *Journal of Adolescence*, 19, 163–77.

Armitage, C. J., and Conner, M. (2001). Efficacy of the theory of planned behavior: A meta-analytic review. *British Journal of Social Psychology*, 40(4), 471–99.

Baer, J. S., Stacy, A., and Larimer, M. (1991). Biases in the perception of drinking norms among college students. *Journal of Studies on Alcohol*, 52, 580–6.

Bagozzi, R. P. (1992). The self-regulation of attitudes, intentions, and behavior. *Social Psychology Quarterly*, 55(2), 355–9.

Bagozzi, R. P., and Yi, Y. (1989). The degree of intention formation as a moderator of the attitude-behavior relationship. *Social Psychology Quarterly*, 52, 266–79.

Baldwin, A. L., Baldwin, C., and Cole, R. E. (1990). Stress-resistant families and stress-resistant children. In J. Rolf, A. S. Masten, D. Cochetti, K. H. Nuechterlein, and S. Weintraub (Eds.), *Risk and Protective Factors in the Development of Psychopathology* (pp. 257–80). New York: Cambridge University Press.

Beck, L., and Ajzen, I. (1991). Predicting dishonest actions using the theory of planned behavior. *Journal of Research in Personality*, 25, 285–301.

Beyth-Marom, R., Austin, L., Fischoff, B., Palmgren, C., and Jacobs-Quadrel, M. (1993). Perceived consequences of risky behaviors: Adults and adolescents. *Development Psychology*, 29, 549–63.

Beyth-Marom, R., and Fischoff, B. (1997). Adolescents' decisions about risks: A cognitive perspective. In J. Schulenberg and J. L. Maggs (Eds.), *Health Risks and Developmental Transitions during Adolescence* (pp. 110–35). New York: Cambridge University Press.

Blanton, H., Gibbons, F. X., Gerrard, M., Conger, K. J., and Smith, G. E. (1997). Development of health risk prototypes during adolescence: Family and peer influence. *Journal of Family Psychology*, 11, 271–88.

Blanton, H., VandenEijnden, R. J. J. M., Buunk, B. P., Gibbons, F. X., Gerrard, M., and Bakker, A. (2001). Accentuate the negative: Social images in the prediction and promotion of condom use. *Journal of Applied Social Psychology*, 31(2), 274–95.

Brandt, A. M. (1997). Behavior, disease, and health in the twentieth-century United States: The moral valence of individual risk. In A. M. Brandt and P. Rozin (Eds.), *Morality and Health* (pp. 53–77). Florence, KY: Taylor & Francis/Routledge.

Brooks-Gunn, J., and Furstenburg, F. F. (1989). Adolescent sexual behavior. *American Psychologist*, 44, 249–57.

Brown, S. A., Christianson, B. A., and Goldman, M. S. (1987). The Alcohol Expectancy Questionnaire: An instrument for the assessment of adolescent and adult alcohol expectancies. *Journal of Studies on Alcohol*, 48, 483–91.

Burton, D., Sussman, S., Hansen, W. B., Johnson, C. A., and Flay, B. R. (1989). Image attributions and smoking intentions among seventh grade students. *Journal of Applied Social Psychology*, 19, 656–64.

Cantor, N., and Mischel, W. (1979). Prototypicality and personality: Effects on free recall and personality impressions. *Journal of Research in Personality*, 13, 187–205.

Carroll, A., Durkin, K., Hattie, J., and Houghton, S. (1997). Goal setting among adolescents: A comparison of delinquent, at-risk, and not-at-risk youth. *Journal of Educational Psychology*, 89(3), 441–50.

Chassin, L., Presson, C. C., Sherman, S. J., Corty, E., Olshavsky, R. W. (1981). Self-images and cigarette smoking in adolescence. *Personality and Social Psychology Bulletin*, 7, 670–6.

Chassin, L., Presson, C. C., Sherman, S. J., and Curran, P. J. (1992). Social psychological factors in adolescent substance use and abuse. In F. J. Medaway and T. P. Cafferty (Eds.), *School Psychology: A Social Psychological Perspective* (pp. 397–424). Hillsdale, NJ: Lawrence Erlbaum.

Chassin, L., Tetzloff, C., and Hershey, M. (1985). Self-image and social-image factors in adolescent alcohol use. *Journal of Studies on Alcohol*, 46, 39–47.

Chen, S., and Chaiken, S. (1999). The heuristic-systematic model in its broader context. In S. Chaiken and Y. Trope (Eds.), *Dual-process Theories in Social Psychology* (pp. 73–96). New York: Guilford Press.

Chilman, C. S. (1983). The development of adolescent sexuality. *Journal of Research and Development in Education*, 16, 16–26.

Cho, Y., Keller, L. R., and Cooper, M. L. (1999). Applying decision-making approaches to health risk-taking behaviors: Progress and remaining challenges. *Journal of Mathematical Psychology*, 43, 261–85.

Cobliner, W. G. (1974). Pregnancy in the single adolescent girl: The role of cognitive functions. *Journal of Youth and Adolescence*, 3, 17–29.

Conner, M., and Norman, P. (1996). The role of social cognition in health behaviors. In M. Conner, P. Norman et al. (Eds.), *Predicting Health Behavior: Research and Practice with Social Cognition Models* (pp. 1–22). Buckingham, England: The Open University.

Corey, M. A. (1989). *Why Men Cheat!: Psychological Profiles of the Adulterous Male*. Springfield, IL: Charles C. Thomas.

Covington, M. V., and Omelich, C. L. (1988). I can resist anything but temptation: Adolescent expectations for smoking cigarettes. *Journal of Applied Social Psychology*, 18, 203–27.

Deutsch, M., and Gerard, H. B. (1955). A study of normative and informational influences upon individual judgment. *Journal of Abnormal and Social Psychology*, 51, 629–36.

Donaldson, S. I., Graham, J. W., Piccinin, A. N., and Hansen, W. B. (1995). Resistance-skills training and onset of alcohol use: Evidence for beneficial and potentially harmful effects in public schools and in private Catholic schools. *Health Psychology*, 14, 291–300.

Eagly, A. H., and Chaiken, S. (1993). *The Psychology of Attitudes*. Fort Worth, TX: Harcourt Brace Jovanovich College Publishers.

Eggleston, T. J. H. (1997). Altering sexual prototypes via prevalence information: An experimental analogue to a sexual intervention program. Unpublished doctoral dissertation.

Eiser, J. R., Eiser, C., and Pauwels, C. (1993). Skin cancer: Assessing perceived risk and behavioral attitudes. *Psychology and Health*, 8, 393–404.

Elkind, D. (1978). Understanding the young adolescent. *Adolescence*, 8, 127–34.

Epstein, S. (1990). Cognitive-experimental self-theory. In L. A. Pervin (Ed.), *Handbook of Personality: Theory and Research* (pp. 165–91). New York Guildford Press.

Epstein, S. (1994). Integration of the cognitive and the psychodynamic unconscious. *American Psychologist*, 49, 709–24.

Epstein, S., and Pacini, R. (1999). Some basic issues regarding dual-process theories from the perspective of cognitive-experiential self-theory. In S. Chaiken and

Y. Trope (Eds.), *Dual-process Theories in Social Psychology* (pp. 462–82). New York: Guilford Press.

Eysenck, S. B. G., and Eysenck, H. J. (1977). The place of impulsiveness in a dimensional system of personality description. *British Journal of Social and Clinical Psychology,* 16, 57–68.

Fazio, R. H. (1990). Multiple processes by which attitudes guide behavior. The MODE model as an integrative framework. In M. P. Zanna (Ed.), *Advances in Experimental Social Psychology* (Vol. 23, pp. 75–109). San Diego, CA: Academic Press.

Fazio, R. H., Sherman, S. J., and Herr, P. M. (1982). The feature-positive effect in the self-perception process: Does not doing matter as much as doing? *Journal of Personality and Social Psychology,* 42, 404–11.

Fishbein, M., and Ajzen, I. (1975). *Belief, Attitude, Intention, and Behavior: An Introduction to Theory and Research.* Reading, MA: Addison-Wesley.

Fulton, J. E. (1997). Utilizing the ultraviolet (UV detect) camera to enhance the appearance of photo damage and other skin conditions. *Dermatologic Surgery,* 23, 163–9.

Gerrard, M., Gibbons, F. X., Benthin, A. C., and Hessling, R. M. (1996). The reciprocal nature of risk behaviors and cognitions: What you think shapes what you do and vice versa. *Health Psychology,* 15, 344–54.

Gerrard, M., Gibbons, F. X., Reis-Bergan, M., Trudeau, L., Vande Lune, L. S., and Buunk, B. P. (2002). Inhibitory effects of drinker and nondrinker prototypes on adolescent alcohol consumption. *Health Psychology,* 21(6), 601–9.

Gerrard, M., Gibbons, F. X., Zhao, L., Russell, D. W., and Reis-Bergan, M. (1999). The effects of peers' alcohol consumption on parental influence: A cognitive mediational model. *Journal of Studies on Alcohol,* 13, 32–44.

Gibbons, F. X., and Buunk, B. P. (1999). Individual differences in social comparison: Development and validation of a measure of social comparison orientation. *Journal of Personality and Social Psychology,* 76, 129–42.

Gibbons, F. X., and Eggleston, T. J. (1996). Smoker networks and the "typical smoker": A prospective analysis of smoking cessation. *Health Psychology,* 15, 469–76.

Gibbons, F. X., and Gerrard, M. (1995). Predicting young adults' health risk behavior. *Journal of Personality and Social Psychology,* 69(3), 505–17.

Gibbons, F. X., and Gerrard, M. (1997). Health images and their effects on health behavior. In B. P. Buunk and F. X. Gibbons (Eds.), *Health, Coping, and Well-being: Perspectives from Social Comparison Theory* (pp. 63–94). Mahwah, NJ: Lawrence Erlbaum Associates.

Gibbons, F. X., Gerrard, M., Blanton, H., and Russell, D. W. (1998a). Reasoned action and social reaction: Willingness and intention as independent predictors of health risk. *Journal of Personality and Social Psychology,* 74, 1164–81.

Gibbons, F. X., Gerrard, M., and Boney-McCoy, S. (1995a). Prototype perception predicts (lack of) pregnancy prevention. *Personality and Social Psychology Bulletin,* 21, 85–93.

Gibbons, F. X., Gerrard, M., Lane, D. J., Mahler, H. I. M., and Kulik, J. (2002a). UV photography significantly reduces tanning booth use. Manuscript submitted for publication.

Gibbons, F. X., Gerrard, M., Ouellette, J. A., and Burzette, R. (1998b). Cognitive antecedents to adolescent health risk: Discriminating between behavioral intention and behavior willingness. *Psychology and Health,* 13, 319–39.

Gibbons, F. X., Gerrard, M., Wills, T. A. et al. (2002b). The effects of parenting and context on substance use images and willingness in African-American adolescents. Manuscript submitted for publication.

Gibbons, F. X., Helweg-Larson, M., and Gerrard, M. (1995b). Prevalence estimates and adolescent risk behavior: Cross-cultural differences in social influence. *Journal of Applied Psychology*, 80(1), 107–21.

Gibbons, F. X., Lane, D. J., Eggleston, T. J., Gerrard, M., and Reis-Bergan, M. (2002c). Image manipulation as a means of reducing risk willingness. Manuscript in preparation.

Gilbert, D. T. (1991). How mental systems believe. *American Psychologist*, 46, 107–19.

Goethals, G. R., and Darley, J. M. (1977). Related attributes and social comparison. In J. Suls and R. Miller (Eds.), *Social Comparison Theory* (pp. 259–78). Washington, DC: Hemisphere.

Gollwitzer, P. M., and Bayer, U. (1999). Deliberative versus implemental mindsets in the control of action. In S. Chaiken and Y. Trope (Eds.), *Dual-process Theories in Social Psychology* (pp. 403–22). New York: The Guilford Press.

Grube, J. (1995). Television alcohol portrayals, alcohol advertising, and alcohol expectancies among children and adolescents. *National Institute on Alcohol Abuse and Alcoholism Research Monograph 28: The Effects of the Mass Media on the Use and Abuse of Alcohol* (pp. 105–21). (National Institute of Health Publication No. 95–3743).

Hansen, W. B. (1992). School-based substance abuse prevention: A review of the state of the art in curriculum, 1980–1990. *Health Educational Research*, 7(3), 403–30.

Harms, J. B., and Wolk, J. L. (1990). Differential perception and adolescent drinking in the United States: Preliminary considerations. *Journal of Sociology and Social Welfare*, 17(4), 21–41.

Ingham, R., Woodcock, A., and Stenner, K. (1992). The limitations of rational decision-making models as applied to young people's sexual behaviour. In P. Aggleton, P. Davies, and G. Hart (Eds.), *AIDS: Rights, Risk and Reason*. London: The Falmer Press.

Jemal, A., Devessa, S. S., Fears, T. R., and Hartge, P. (2000). Cancer surveillance series: Changing patterns of cutaneous malignant melanoma mortality rates among whites in the United States. *Journal of the National Cancer Institute*, 92(10), 811–8.

Johnston, L. D., O'Malley, P. M., and Bachman, J. G. (2000). *Monitoring the Future National Survey Results on Adolescent Drug Use: Overview of Key Findings, 1999* (NIH Publication No. 00–4690). Rockville, MD: National Institute on Drug Abuse.

Kahnemann, D., and Tversky, A. (1979). Prospect theory: An analysis of decisions under risk. *Econometrica*, 47, 263–91.

Kelly, K., and Edwards, R. (1998). Image advertisements for alcohol products: is their appeal associated with adolescents' intention to consume alcohol? *Adolescence*, 33(129), 47–59.

Kippax, S., and Crawford, J. (1993). Flaws in the theory of reasoned action. In D. J. Terry, C. Gallois and M. McCamish (Eds.), *The Theory of Reasoned Action: Its Application to AIDS-preventive Behaviour* (pp. 253–69). Oxford, England: Pergamon Press.

Krosnick, L. A., and Judd, C. M. (1982). Transitions in social influence at adolescence: Who induces cigarette smoking? *Developmental Psychology*, 18, 359–68.

Landrine, H., and Klonoff, E. A. (1996). The schedule of racist events: A measure of racial discrimination and a study of its negative physical and mental health consequences. *Journal of Black Psychology*, 22, 144–68.

Leventhal, H., and Cleary, P. D. (1980). The smoking problem: A review of the research and theory in behavioral risk modification. *Psychological Bulletin*, 88, 370–405.

Linville, P. W., and Fischer, G. W. (1993). Exemplar and abstraction models of perceived group variability and stereotypicality. *Social Cognition*, 11, 92–125.

Lloyd, B., and Lucas, K. (1998). *Smoking in Adolescence: Images and Identities*. New York: Rutledge.

Lynam, D. R., Milich, R., Zimmerman, R., et al. (1999). Project Dare: No effects at 10-year follow-up. *Journal of Consulting and Clinical Psychology*, 67, 590–3.

Markus, H., and Nurius, P. (1986). Possible selves. *American Psychologist*, 41, 954–78.

McCaul, K. D., Sandgren, A. K., O'Neill, H. K., and Hinsz, V. B. (1993). The value of the theory of planned behavior, perceived control, and self-efficacy for predicting health-protective behaviors. *Basic and Applied Social Psychology*, 14(2), 231–52.

Mitchell, K., and Wellings, K. (1998). First sexual intercourse: Anticipation and communication. Interviews with young people in England. *Journal of Adolescence*, 21, 717–26.

Morojele, N. K., and Stephensen, G. M. (1994). Addictive behaviours: Predictors of abstinence intentions and expectations in the Theory of Planned Behaviour. In D. Rutter, L. Quine, et al. (Eds.), *Social Psychology and Health: European Perspectives* (pp. 47–70). Aldershot, England: Avebury/Ashgate Publishing Co.

Murry, V. M. (1994). A comparison of early versus late coital initiators. *Family Relations*, 43, 342–8.

Nisbett, R. E., and Ross, L. (1980). *Human Inference: Strategies and Shortcomings of Social Judgement*. Englewood Cliffs, NJ: Prentice-Hall.

Norman, P., Abraham, C., and Conner, M. (Eds.) (2000). *Understanding and Changing Health Behaviour: From Health Beliefs to Self-regulation*. Amsterdam: Harwood Academic Publishers.

Ouellette, J. A., Hessling, R. M., Gibbons, F. X., Reis-Bergan, M., and Gerrard, M. (2002). Using images to increase exercise behavior: Prototypes versus possible selves. Manuscript submitted for publication.

Parker, D., Manstead, A. S. R., Stradling, S. G., Reason, J. T., and Baxter, J. S. (1992). Intention to commit driving violations: An application of the theory of planned behavior. *Journal of Applied Psychology*, 77, 94–101.

Petty, R. E., and Cacioppo, J. T. (1986). *Communication and Persuasion: Central and Peripheral Routes to Attitude Change*. New York: Springer-Verlag.

Prentice, D. A., and Miller, D. T. (1993). Pluralistic ignorance and alcohol use on campus: Some consequences of misperceiving the social norm. *Journal of Personality and Social Psychology*, 64, 243–56.

Prochaska, J. O., DiClemente, C. C., and Norcross, J. C. (1992). In search of how people change: Applications to addictive behaviors. *American Psychologist*, 47, 1102–14.

Reinecke, J., Schmidt, P., and Ajzen, I. (1997). Birth control versus AIDS prevention: A hierarchical model of condom use among young people. *Journal of Applied Social Psychology*, 27, 743–59.

Reis-Bergan, M., Gibbons, F. X., and Gerrard, M. (2003). Experience as a moderator of the developmental shift from willingness to intentions. Manuscript under review.

Rothbart, M. K., and Bates, J. E. (1998). Temperament. In W. Damon (Series Ed). and N. Eisenberg (Vol. Ed.), *Handbook of Child Psychology*: Vol. 3. *Social, Emotional, and Personality Development* (5th edn, pp. 105–76). New York: Wiley.

Salovey, P., Rothman, A. J., and Rodin, J. (1998). Health behavior. In D. T. Gilbert, and S. T. Fiske (Eds.), *The Handbook of Social Psychology* (Vol. 2, 4th edn, pp. 633–83). Boston: McGraw-Hill.

Schlegel, R. P., D'Avernas, J. R., Zanna, M. P., DeCourville, N. H., and Manske, S. T. (1992). Problem drinking: A problem for the theory of reasoned action? *Journal of Applied Social Psychology*, 22, 358–85.

Schroeder, C. M., and Prentice, D. A. (1998). Exposing pluralistic ignorance to reduce alcohol use among college students. *Journal of Applied Social Psychology*, 28, 2150–80.

Setterlund, M. B., and Niedenthal, P. M. (1993). "Who am I? Why am I here?" Self-esteem self-clarity, and prototype matching. *Journal of Personality and Social Psychology*, 65(4), 769–80.

Shapiro, R., Siegel, A. M., Scovill, L. C., and Hays, J. (1998). Risk-taking patterns of female adolescents: What they do and why. *Journal of Adolescence*, 21, 143–59.

Sheeran, P., and Orbell, S. (1998). Do intentions predict condom use? Meta-analysis and examination of six moderator variables. *British Journal of Social Psychology*, 37, 231–50.

Sheppard, B. H., Hartwick, J., and Warshaw, P. R. (1988). The theory of reasoned action: A meta-analysis of past research with recommendations for modifications and future research. *Journal of Consumer Research*, 15, 325–43.

Sherif, M., and Hovland, C. I. (1961). *Social Judgment: Assimilation and Contrast Effects in Communication and Attitude Change*. New Haven, CT: Yale University Press.

Skowronski, J. J., and Carlston, D. E. (1989). Negativity and extremity biases in impression formation: A review of explanations. *Psychological Bulletin*, 105, 131–42.

Smith, E. R., and Zarate, M. A. (1992). Exemplar-based model of social judgment. *Psychological Review*, 99, 3–21.

Stacy, A. W., Bentler, P., and Flay, B. R. (1994). Attitudes and health behavior in diverse populations: Drunk driving, alcohol use, binge eating, marijuana use, and cigarette use. *Health Psychology*, 13(1), 73–85.

Stacy, A. W., Widaman, K. F., and Marlatt, G. A. (1990). Expectancy models of alcohol use. *Journal of Personality and Social Psychology*, 58, 918–28.

Strathman, A., Boninger, D. S., Gleicher, F., and Baker, S. M. (1994). Constructing the future with present behavior: An individual difference approach. In Z. Zaleski (Ed.), *Psychology of Future Orientation* (pp. 107–19). Lublin, Poland: Catholic University of Lublin.

Suls, J., Wan, C. K., and Sanders, G. S. (1988). False consensus and false uniqueness in estimating the prevalence of health-protective behaviors. *Journal of Applied Social Psychology*, 18(1), 66–79.

Sutton, S. (1987). Social-psychological approaches to understanding addictive behaviours: Attitude-behaviour and decision making models. *British Journal of Addiction*, 82, 355–70.

Thornton, B., Gibbons, F. X., and Gerrard, M. (2002). Risk perception and prototype perception: Independent processes predicting risk behavior. *Personality and Social Psychology Bulletin*, 28, 986–99.

Tobler, N. S., and Stratton, H. H. (1998). Effectiveness of school-based drug prevention programs: A meta-analysis of the research. *The Journal of Primary Prevention*, 18, 71–128.

Triandis, H. C. (1979). Values, attitudes and interpersonal behavior. In H. E. Howe, Jr. and M. M. Page (Eds.), *Nebraska Symposium on Motivation* (Vol. 27, pp. 195–259). Lincoln, NE: University of Nebraska Press.

US Department of Health and Human Services (1994). *Preventing Tobacco Use among Young People: A Report of the Surgeon General*. Atlanta Georgia: US Department of Health and Human Services, Public Health Service, Centers for Disease Control and Prevention.

Van den Putte, B. (1993). On the theory of reasoned action. Unpublished doctoral dissertation. University of Amsterdam.

Weinstein, N. D. (1984). Why it won't happen to me: Perceptions of risk factors and illness susceptibility. *Health Psychology*, 3, 431–57.

Weinstein, N. D. (1988). The precaution adoption process. *Health Psychology*, 7, 355–86.

Weinstein, N. D., Rothman, A. J., and Sutton, S. R. (1998). Stage theories of health behavior: Conceptual and methodological issues. *Health Psychology*, 17, 290–9.

Wills, T. A., Gibbons, F. X., Gerrard, M., and Brody, G. H. (2000). Protection and vulnerability processes relevant for early onset of substance use: A test among African American children. *Health Psychology*, 19, 253–63.

Wills, T. A., Gibbons, F. X., Gerrard, M., Murry, V. M., and Brody, G. H. (in press). Family communication and religiosity related to substance use and sexual behaviour in early adolescents: A test for pathways through self-control and prototype perceptions. *Psychology of Addictive Behaviors*.

Wills, T. A., Sandy, J. M., Shinar, O., and Yaeger, A. (1999). Contributions of positive and negative affect to adolescent substance use: Test of a bidimensional model in a longitudinal study. *Psychology of Addictive Behaviors*, 13, 327–38.

Zelnick, M., and Shah, F. K. (1983). First intercourse among young Americans. *Family Planning Perspectives*, 15(2), 64–70.

CHAPTER 6

Affect, Thought, and Self-protective Health Behavior: The Case of Worry and Cancer Screening

Kevin D. McCaul and Amy B. Mullens

North Dakota State University

Introduction

John Smith, a 30-year old Californian in the software industry, lies awake in his bed. It is near midnight, and he senses his wife's soft breathing, as she sleeps deeply by his side. In contrast, John shuts his eyes tightly but worries. For what seems like the hundredth time, he tried to quit smoking this week but failed again. Now he wonders about the effects of continued smoking on his health. An image of a diseased lung pops into his mind, and he has a brief moment of fear, further inhibiting his attempt to drift off. He ruminates about how embarrassing it is to creep outside his office building to the smoker's area. As John worries into the night, he resolves again to do something about his habit. I will try to quit again tomorrow, he thinks, and sleep finally overtakes him.

In this hypothetical vignette, John is trying to protect his health by quitting smoking. The story includes many elements of the social psychological models that researchers have used to help us understand why people engage in health-protective behaviors. John thinks about his risk, for example, and the thoughts that people have – their beliefs – are included in virtually all social psychological models. The social aspects of health behavior are also apparent in this vignette, as John considers how self-conscious he feels when he smokes in public. Smoking is a habitual behavior, and habits are part of some social psychological models. Finally, John's *feelings* seem to be at least partly responsible for his difficulty in getting to sleep. Put simply, John is worried. John's worrying seems to influence both his ability to achieve sleep but also his plans for making another attempt to quit smoking.

The focus of this chapter is on how affect – and in particular worry – may be important in guiding health-protective actions. The chapter is organized into four sections. First, we briefly review the most popular social psychological theories relevant to health-protective behaviors, with an eye toward their use of affective variables as model components. Second, we discuss the construct of worry, drawing on the existing literature to ask what worry is, what people worry about, and the functions that worry serves. Third, we ask whether worry influences health-protective behaviors, relying primarily on the extant literature on breast cancer screening. Finally, we discuss the implications of this last literature for social psychological theorizing.

It is perhaps worth noting that the significance of worry has been a thread running through much of the first author's work. He first thought about the concept of worry as a graduate student at the University of Kansas. His advisor, Michael Storms, asked him to assist on a paper concerning the application of attribution theories to dysfunctional emotional behavior (Storms and McCaul, 1976). They argued in that chapter that worry might exacerbate and maintain behaviors directly affected by rumination, such as stuttering and insomnia. In the health area, McCaul's initial research interest as a beginning assistant professor was the initiation of smoking behavior among adolescents. He believed that concern about consequences – whether those consequences were "short term" (e.g., social disapproval) or "long term" (health consequences) – would strengthen intentions to avoid smoking cigarettes (Glasgow et al., 1981).

The adolescent smoking research was concerned with prevention, but McCaul also surmised that worry might be important in habit cessation. In searching for a health behavior for which he would feel comfortable manipulating beliefs and affect, he selected flossing behavior. Flossing can be important for people at risk of periodontal (gum) disease. One of the anecdotal discoveries made in this dental research was that persons who were experienced with periodontal disease and its sequelae were much more likely to adhere to a daily prevention regimen. That is, persons who *knew* that they were vulnerable to the disease and had experienced the negative consequences were more likely to engage in the health behaviors that would help prevent periodontal disease in the future.

This finding, together with theoretical reasoning (e.g., Leventhal, 1970) persuaded McCaul that engaging in health-protective behavior was at least partially caused by a sense of personal risk or vulnerability supported by concern about one's risk status. Although this simple notion makes sense intuitively, it is actually still a controversial idea (cf. Aspinwall, 1999). At the beginning of this decade, McCaul wanted to test whether he could *persuade* people to change their self-protective behavior by creating a sense of personal vulnerability. Given that research goal, he also wanted to select a health-protective behavior that was of obvious value. Thus, he shifted his research focus to mammography screening. That research will form the basis of much of the third section of this chapter.

Social Psychological Theories and Affect

In this section, we consider six models frequently used to understand health-protective behaviors and the role that they reserve for affect. As you will see, with a few exceptions, that role is minimal.

Health Belief Model

The Health Belief Model (HBM) is over 40 years old and was probably the first formal model purporting to explain health behaviors (Rosenstock, 1960). It is one of several models generally based on an expectancy X value formulation (Weinstein, 1993). The expectancy/value approach suggests that health behaviors are determined by the value of a particular outcome (e.g., cancer) and the expectation that a behavior (e.g., smoking) will contribute to or allow one to avoid that outcome (e.g., smoking cessation). Over time, however, additional variables have been added to the model, making it more comprehensive but also less clear about causal relationships among model elements (Strecher et al., 1997).

Table 6.1 lists the social psychological models and the variables that each model emphasizes. Strecher et al. (1997) provide a straightforward list of variables that are included in the HBM. As befits its name, the HBM emphasizes health beliefs. Five of the listed variables are cognitions: beliefs about (1) whether one is susceptible to illness, (2) how severe or serious the illness might be in terms of its consequences, (3) the perceived benefits of engaging

Table 6.1 List of models and variables that predict health-protective behaviors

Model	Variables
Health Belief Model	Susceptibility, Severity, Benefits, Barriers, Self-efficacy, Cues to Action, "Other variables" (e.g., demographic differences)
Theory of Planned Behavior	Beliefs, Attitude, Subjective Norm, Perceived Control, Intentions
Protection Motivation Theory	Environmental and Interpersonal sources of information, Intrinsic/Extrinsic Rewards, Severity/ Vulnerability, Threat Appraisal, Response/ Self-efficacy, Response Costs
Precaution Adoption Process	Communication about Hazard, Experience with Hazard, Risk Factor Information, Seriousness Beliefs, Precaution Beliefs, Costs of Precaution
Parallel Process Model	Vulnerability, Response Efficacy, Self-efficacy, Fear
Cognitive Response Theory	Listener Involvement, Message Strength, Heuristic Cues (e.g., Source Credibility; Emotional Potential of Message)

in a health-protective behavior, (4) barriers or the negative aspects associated with a health-protective action, and (5) whether one is able to competently perform the health-protective behavior (self-efficacy). The one prominent model component that is not a belief per se is "cues to action," the concept of environmental events that might trigger behavior.

Another observation should be clear upon perusing the variable list from the HBM. *Affect* is missing. Some beliefs such as illness severity may be affectively laden, but the model does not address that possibility. If feelings and emotion have anything to do with health-protective actions, one would not know it from the HBM.

Theory of Planned Behavior

The HBM was created explicitly to explain health behavior. The Theory of Planned Behavior (TPB; Ajzen, 1991), a revision of the Theory of Reasoned Action (Fishbein and Ajzen, 1975), was developed to explain a broad range of intentions and behaviors. The theory relies on a relatively small set of variables, as shown in Table 6.1. The theory also specifies precise causal sequences. For example, one's evaluation of an action (attitude), perception of the wishes of others (subjective norm), and perceived control over the action are all assumed to independently create intentions. Intentions, together with actual control over the action, predict behavior. Similar to the HBM, affect is not a part of the TPB nor was it part of the Theory of Reasoned Action. Although attitude toward the act is measured with semantic differential scales (e.g., pleasant versus unpleasant), it is clear that attitude is an evaluative judgment – cognition, not feeling (cf. Richard et al., 1996).

Protection-motivation Theory

The next model is the third in a line of expectancy X value models. Rogers introduced protection-motivation theory specifically to improve our understanding of the effects of threatening information on attitude and behavior change (Rippetoe and Rogers, 1987; Rogers and Prentice-Dunn, 1997). The theory is similar to the HBM in its comprehensive list of variables, including distal or background elements (e.g., observational learning, prior experience, personality). However, the theory clearly focuses on a few cognitive mediating processes and proposes a summative model for how these variables combine to predict action or action inhibition. Moreover, the theory is intended to explain responses to a threatening communication as opposed to static beliefs (Rogers and Prentice-Dunn, 1997).

Table 6.1 lists the elements of Protection Motivation Theory, all of which are beliefs and judgments or are related to them. This theory also describes how these variables combine to predict behavior. For example, persons may consider adopting a "maladaptive" action (e.g., ignoring a cancer screening) in response to a health threat (e.g., symptoms associated with cancer). Persons will then consider the rewards of obtaining a screening but also their vulnerability to cancer and the severity of cancer. This process results in a threat appraisal. Importantly, the decision process can also elicit the emotion of *fear*. In theory, fear arousal is produced by the difference between the perceived severity of the health threat and one's perceived vulnerability to the health threat. However, Rogers does not enter fear arousal into any behavioral prediction; instead, it is an inert by-product of the two cognitive variables. Fear is simply there (or not). In this model, fear does nothing by itself to energize protective behavior. Indeed, in a recent quantitative meta-analysis of variables in the theoretical model, the authors did not even include fear (Floyd et al., 2000).

Precaution Adoption Process

Recently, some theorists have suggested that persons making a decision about whether to adopt a health-protective behavior often move through a series of qualitatively distinct stages. The best known of these theories is probably the Transtheoretical Model (DiClemente et al., 1991), but Weinstein (1988) also introduced a stage theory that he termed the Precaution Adoption Process. Weinstein's model relies heavily on cognitive variables, but it departs from the expectancy X value models described thus far. As he explains, "Those models treat beliefs about costs and benefits as continuous dimensions and assume that progress from ignorance to action is adequately explained by quantitative differences in the value of the decision equation. The alternative approach . . . is to represent the precaution adoption process as a series of distinct stages" (Weinstein 1988: 358).

   In the present context, the stages themselves (e.g., contemplating behavior change versus preparing for action) are less important than the variables that supposedly influence people in the different stages and that may need to change before people adopt a new health-protective action. Weinstein (1988) identified several major determinants of stage change, variables that could be important in the process of shifting from one stage to another (see Table 6.1). It is important to note that some of these determinants (e.g., experience with the hazard) can effectively motivate stage movement from more than one stage. Further, listing the variables does a disservice to the stage model, which posits interesting and testable combination rules that are meaningfully different from those used by the creators of the expectancy/value models. Nonetheless, the list also leads to an additional point most relevant to the present discussion: none of these variables addresses affect in any direct or a priori way. Weinstein (1988) suggests that emotional variables such as worry and fear have effects primarily through other, more rational variables (e.g., increasing personal vulnerability), although he acknowledges that fear may occasionally have a direct effect on behavior.

Parallel Processing Model

Only one social psychological theory explicitly addresses the role of emotion as a predictor of health-protective behavior in and of itself – Leventhal's self-regulation theory of illness cognition (Cameron, 1997; Leventhal, 1970).[1] Leventhal proposes that a health threat prompts parallel motives to cope with the threat itself and to cope with the emotional arousal caused by the threat. Thus, emotion is *motivating*. To the extent that one has an available behavioral option that will both negate the threat and relieve negative emotion, Leventhal proposes that people are likely to adopt that behavior (Leventhal et al., 1984).

Witte (1998) has expanded Leventhal's ideas in an "Extended" Parallel Process Model that borrows concepts from some of the other models shown in Table 6.1. The extended model begins with the appraisal of threat. If a person can perform a response to reduce the threat, they will do so, engaging in protection motivation. If such a response is unavailable, however, they will experience fear and engage in defensive motivation to reduce the fear. Thus, fear in the extended model is relevant only for fear control, not danger control responses. Leventhal is the only one of these theorists to suggest that emotion in and of itself has direct effects on behavior. Shortly, we will see whether the data bear him out.

Cognitive Response Theory

Before taking an empirical look at the emotion and breast cancer screening literature, we should mention one other important social psychological model of how people react to persuasive attempts – Petty and Cacioppo's (1981) Elaboration Likelihood Model. Petty and Cacioppo propose that attitudes can be formed thoughtfully, with effort – an approach to attitude change they labeled the "central route." Alternatively, attitudes can be formed or changed less thoughtfully, through short-cuts (heuristics) – an approach to attitude change they named the "peripheral route." When persons are motivated to process thoughtfully, their cognitive responses to the message content become important. Agreement with a persuasive message would produce attitude change in the direction of the communication; counter-arguing would min-imize change or even produce a boomerang effect.

How does affect enter into this process? Petty et al. (1991) lay out several possibilities. Specifically, affect could (1) serve as a persuasive argument (e.g., "if I am afraid of breast cancer, it must be a serious thing"), (2) serve as a peripheral cue (e.g., "if I feel fear it must be a good argument"), or (3) influence the extent or direction of argument processing (e.g., "if this message makes me feel afraid, I'm not going to pay careful attention to it"; cf. Jepson and Chaiken, 1990). Note that all of these examples are ways by which affect may influence attitude formation and change, but in each instance affect is important only insofar as it influences other variables – beliefs about the argument and motivation to pay attention, for example. Affect has no direct effects of its own. It is also important to note, though, that Petty and Cacioppo directed their theoretical efforts to understanding attitude change – not necessarily behavior change. In contrast, the focus of this chapter is on self-protective health *behaviors*. Attitude would typically be seen as only one variable that might be important in influencing behavioral outcomes.

In summary, the models most frequently used to explain health-protective behaviors include many variables. Table 6.1 lists six models and nearly 20 different variables hypothesized to predict health-protective behavior. With the exception of the parallel process model, however, the models essentially ignore affect. And only one of those 20 variables is explicitly affective in character. However, one might ask, "why not?" One of our colleagues suggested that our summary of the models could merely reflect the possibility that many bright minds, working independently, have come to recognize the limits of considering affect! Is emotion an important predictor of health behaviors? We believe that at least one affectively laden construct, worry, does influence health-protective actions. Before turning to the literature supporting that contention, we shall discuss the concept of worry itself.

The Concept of Worry

What Is Worry?

Historically, no clear definitions of worry in the literature have distinguished the concept from other similar ideas (Levy and Guttman, 1976). Indeed, worry has only emerged as a research interest within the last few decades, and we are still learning much about what is essentially a private phenomenon (MacLeod et al., 1991; Pruzinsky and Borkovec, 1990). Worry has been conventionally defined as a chain of thoughts and images, which are negatively affect-laden and relatively uncontrollable (Borkovec et al., 1983). Mathews (1990) has more recently defined worry as the constant rehearsal of a threatening outcome or threat scenario that may hinder successful problem solving. It is interesting that this definition includes an outcome of the worry process – poorer decision making. Worry has also been defined as unwanted cognitive activity that controls unwanted somatic experience (Roemer and Borkovec, 1993). An individual's apparent lack of control over their thoughts may be the most central feature of worry (Borkovec et al., 1994). All of the definitions, however, also emphasize negative, unwanted feelings.

Not all theorists, even today, believe that worry is emotionally important. Boehnke et al. (1998), for example, view worry as a relatively insignificant cognitive correlate of anxiety rather than as a distinct psychological phenomenon. Similarly, Deffenbacher (1980) thought that worry is the cognitive piece of anxiety as measured by intrusive and uncontrollable thoughts, rather than the somatic aspects of anxiety such as muscle tension and an upset stomach. Reports of the percentage of time spent worrying each day are significantly associated with trait and state anxiety (Borkovec et al., 1983; Metzger et al., 1990). In addition, scores on worry inventories correlate with indices of anxiety, depression and psychosomatic symptoms (Boehnke et al., 1998). However, despite the empirical connections between worry and other constructs, most theorists agree that worry is a unique phenomenon (Davey et al., 1992).

Although worry is an important concept in its own right, we would not classify it as an emotion. Russell and Barrett (1999) recently drew a distinction between emotional episodes and core affect. Fear would be an example of the former, a complex dynamic process that has a specific cause and sub-events (e.g., physiological and affective changes; a behavioral response). Worry is not an emotional episode. In contrast to an emotional episode, core affect refers to consciously felt affect, which has many causes, and is constantly present. Russell and Barrett included examples of core affect such as pleasure/displeasure and tension/relaxation. Worry is probably closer to core affect than to emotional episodes, although worry may have a specific cause, as shown next.

What Do People Worry About?

Individuals worry about specific things. Wisocki and colleagues (1986) characterized worry into the domains of finances, health, and social relationships. Among clients with Generalized Anxiety Disorder (GAD), the most common worries were related to family; illness worries were least common (Sanderson and Barlow, 1990). Stalker and colleagues (1989) found that 200 survivors of various types of cancer worried about the following topics: general health or disease recurrence, ability to plan for their future, finances, and general frame of mind. Persons in the general population typically worry about interpersonal, academic, financial, social-relationship, and health concerns (Borkovec et al., 1994). Craske et al. (1989) compared GAD patients to controls, with the latter group comprised of friends of the clients who had never been treated for psychological problems. GAD patients worried most about illness, health and injury, whereas controls worried most about issues surrounding work and school. Although worry topics may differ among different groups, health concerns are an important topic of worry for both anxious and non-anxious persons.

What Functions Does Worry Serve?

Davey et al. (1996) propose that worry can serve to both inhibit and facilitate problem solving. "Worry conveys both an adaptive, constructive problem solving process (showing concern or worry about test or environmental problems) or alternatively, an unwanted pathological state of mind (e.g., reporting uncontrollable, intrusive thoughts)" (Davey, 1993: 52). Thus, worry can disrupt effective performance, exaggerate a problem situation, and create emotional discomfort, but it can also motivate behavior and facilitate analytic thinking (Davey et al., 1996). Worry may serve as a form of problem-focused coping, and it may promote information seeking and monitoring coping strategies, all of which can be adaptive (Davey et al., 1992). Worry is correlated with variables associated with poor psychological functioning (e.g., trait anxiety, avoidant coping; Davey et al., 1992). When trait anxiety is controlled for, however, worry is highly correlated with constructive psychological factors such as problem-focused coping and information seeking (Davey, 1993).

In summary, worry is best thought of as unwanted, and perhaps uncontrollable, thoughts about a threatening outcome. Although worry is not a negative emotion, it is clear that people do not *like* to worry; it carries with it negative feelings. People worry about many outcomes, but health concern is a prevalent one. Finally, worry may cause coping problems, but it may also motivate adaptive problem solving. Of course, the question for us now is whether worry has any effects at all. Is worry related to health-protective behavior?

Does Worry Matter? Worry and Breast Cancer Screening

Cancer is perhaps the most feared disease (Murray and McMillan, 1993), and it is thus not surprising that people worry about cancer, especially those at higher risk of experiencing the disease in their lifetimes (McCaul et al., 1998). Given that people occasionally worry about cancer, it makes sense to ask whether that affect is associated with cancer-related behaviors. Researchers have examined the relationships of worry, anxiety, and fear with cancer screening behaviors such as breast self-examination (BSE), mammography, and clinical (physician) examinations. We will pay attention in this review to the distinction between different measures of worry and anxiety. However, the data ultimately show that these different measures tend to produce similar effects on screening.

Writers and researchers have proposed three possible relationships between worry and cancer screening. Some authors suggest that worry about cancer prompts denial of vulnerability and avoidance of thinking about cancer, thus serving as a barrier to engaging in self-protective behaviors (e.g., Cameron, 1997; Kash, 1995; Strax, 1989). A second possible relationship is a direct positive one, the hypothesis that brief, emotional moments of fear will serve to motivate self-protective behavior (McCaul et al., 1996a; 1996b). Finally, researchers have sometimes proposed a curvilinear hypothesis (Hailey, 1991; Marcus, 1999; Miller et al., 1996). Miller et al. suggest that activating high levels of negative affect and anxious arousal prompts maladaptive avoidant ideation – avoidant thinking that reduces intentions to perform the self-protective behavior. More modest levels of worry may promote adaptive self-protective behaviors, at least if people who worry occasionally are compared to those who are completely unconcerned about cancer.

What does the evidence suggest? We divided studies concerning worry and breast cancer screening into three groups. Most studies present a retrospective look at worry and screening. Importantly, these studies typically ask women about their current negative affect concerning the disease while measuring past screening behavior. Thus, while attempting to predict screening from worry, the measurement interval actually reverses this sequence. A few studies do present prospective correlational data, and we describe those second. Not surprisingly, no existing experiments include explicit manipulations of worry with screening as an outcome. However, the results of several studies of variables – some of which were manipulated – other than worry can possibly be explained by referring to worry. Those studies comprise the third group.

Retrospective Data

Most studies connecting emotion and screening are retrospective. A few of these studies provide data to support the first hypothesized relationship: the idea that worry or fear inhibits protective screening behavior. Lerman et al. (1993), for example, interviewed first-degree relatives of breast cancer patients. Thirty percent of the sample reported that their breast cancer worries interfered with their daily functioning either "a little" or "much", and fewer of these women (59 percent) had a recent mammogram than another group of women who reported that their worries had no impact on their daily functioning (83 percent). Lower screening levels were also associated with more frequent intrusive thoughts and with an item asking whether women "felt blue". Lerman et al. concluded that "Breast cancer worries may pose a barrier to mammography adherence among high-risk women . . ." (1993: 1074).

Using a similar sample, Kash et al. (1992) collected multiple measures of anxiety and asked about several cancer screening methods, including mammography, clinical breast examination, and BSE. The results were slightly different across the screening measures. For mammography (in which 94 percent of the women adhered to regularly scheduled mammograms), the authors reported that women with higher trait anxiety were less likely to have their mammogram on time. For clinical exams, women who scored higher on a cancer anxiety and helplessness scale were less likely to attend their physician screenings. For BSE, women with higher trait anxiety performed the self-examination less frequently. Kash et al. concluded that some women at high risk may be so immobilized by their anxiety that they fail to protect their health, a conclusion later echoed in Kash et al. (1995).

Schwartz et al. (1999b) recently reported a negative relationship between "distress" and mammography screening among a subset of women with a family history of breast cancer. The researchers measured distress using a scale of intrusive thoughts (Horowitz et al., 1979). They also measured the personality dimension of conscientiousness. Among low conscientious women, those reporting higher intrusion scores were significantly less likely (63 percent) to have had a recent mammogram than those reporting fewer intrusions (82 percent). It is worth re-emphasizing here the causal caveat concerning retrospective studies, especially given the measures that Schwartz et al. used. The researchers proposed that intrusive thoughts served as a screening barrier for the low conscientious women. But the relationship may go the other way.

It is entirely plausible that women who had not had their mammogram were thinking and worrying about cancer more than those who had been screened.

For every study reporting a negative relationship between worry and screening, one can also find a study reporting the opposite relationship. McCaul et al. (1996a), for example, interviewed over 800 women across the state of North Dakota. They found positive relationships between self-reported worry and mammography and BSE screening and intentions, with no hint of a decline in screening behavior at the highest worry levels. Such positive worry-screening relationships also appear in women at higher risk. Stefanek and Wilcox (1991) asked first-degree female relatives of breast cancer patients how much they worried about developing breast cancer. Among women 50 and over, the worry responses correlated significantly with whether women had ever had a mammogram ($r = 0.45$) and whether they had a mammogram during the previous year ($r = 0.26$) but not with BSE frequency. After examining the first set of studies cited in this section, one might be tempted to suggest that negative relationships will be obtained primarily with at-risk samples, but such is not always the case.

Other investigators have reported similar, positive worry-screening relationships. Using a community sample, Harris et al. (1991) found that greater worry was associated both with a higher frequency of prior mammograms and stronger intentions to obtain a future mammogram. Swanson et al. (1996) assessed worry and BSE among patients from general physician practices in the United Kingdom. They reported a positive linear relationship, with the percentage of women answering affirmatively to the screening question lowest among those who did not worry (66 percent), higher among those who worried "slightly" (71 percent), and higher still among those who were either "quite" or "very" worried (74 percent; see similar findings in Hailey, 1986). Bober et al. (2000) asked women to reflect on their experiences following counseling for breast/ovarian cancer risk. Women who said that they worried more about breast cancer after counseling also increased their BSE frequency ($r = 0.32$). Finally, Lerman et al. (1991b) asked women who had recent mammograms about their worry levels. Both frequency and intensity of worry positively predicted stronger intentions to obtain a mammogram in the future.

Two studies revealed positive worry-screening relationships but also suggested that negative emotionality can produce excessive health protective behaviors. Lerman et al. (1994) reported that a subset of their sample of younger women (those younger than 50) with a family history of breast cancer examined their breasts more than once a month rather than the recommended once/monthly. These women also reported a high level of breast cancer worry, as measured by intrusive thoughts. Epstein et al. (1997) uncovered similar data for high-risk women. A small group (8 percent) reported examining their breasts daily, and these same women were also more likely to say that "thinking about breast cancer negatively affects my mood" – one of the items used to measure worry. Daily performance of BSE seems obsessive, and it is worth noting that worry – at least when it is chronic – is similar, although not identical to obsessions (see Coles et al., 2001). On the other hand, the women themselves may not have felt that they were engaged in excessive testing. Indeed, these women reported being more confident that they were protecting their health and doing something about their breast cancer worries.

Brain et al. (1999) reviewed some of the studies that we have discussed and reasoned that "general" anxiety and "specific" worry would be associated differently with BSE. They suggested that general anxiety represents more serious psychological dysfunction and would thus be on the high side of an anxiety continuum that would produce avoidance (the descending side of the inverted-U shape relationship). Worry specific to breast cancer was expected to represent a more moderate level of emotion and thus should motivate screening behavior. Brain et al. studied women with a family history of breast cancer, dividing their sample into women who did BSE infrequently (less than 4 times a year), appropriately (monthly or every other week), and excessively (weekly or daily/more often). The means for these three groups generally showed that more frequent health-protective behaviors were associated with more negative affect, regardless of whether affect was measured as general anxiety or specific worry. Thus, for example, the group doing BSE excessively reported the most anxiety and the highest level of breast cancer worries. In a similar study, Erblich et al. (2000a) interviewed women with and without a family history of breast cancer and examined associations between several affective measures and BSE under- and over-performance (defined as more than once/month). Intrusive cancer thoughts were associated with over-performing BSE, although in this case, general negative affect was not.

The third possible relationship between worry and screening is a curvilinear one, with increasing levels of worry predicting higher screening levels up to a point and then tailing off when worry gets too high. Many authors have proposed such a relationship, but most empirical papers simply show a positive worry/screening relationship. On the other hand, many of the latter studies present only a Pearson correlation, which is insufficient to test for a curvilinear relationship. At minimum, one must examine the scatter plots of bivariate relationships; better still would be to conduct quadratic tests or at least test several levels of worry. Lerman et al. (1991a) conducted one such study. The authors interviewed women who had mammograms within the previous three months. Different worry levels were positively related to mammography intentions, but worry was associated in a curvilinear fashion to current BSE frequency. BSE rates were 3.78 (on a 1–4 scale) for women who were "not at all" worried, 3.93 for women who worried "sometimes" or "often" and 3.36 for women who worried "almost all the time." These data could be used to suggest that worry has different effects on a behavior that should be performed frequently such as BSE versus an infrequent behavior such as annual or biennial mammograms. However, this conclusion would be confounded by an alternative explanation – the timeframe of the measurement intervals. BSE was measured concurrently with worry, whereas mammography was measured in a future sense (intentions). Interestingly, one could even argue that failing to perform BSE often enough was creating worry that was motivating intentions to perform mammography!

In summary, worry and similar feelings like anxiety are clearly related to screening behavior, although some uncertainty still exists about the strength and direction of the association. Most studies reveal a positive linear relationship: more worry predicts more screening; perhaps at the highest levels, more worry even predicts excessive BSE screening. But the issue of whether worry causes women to engage in screening activities cannot be answered with retrospective data. Prospective studies provide a better, though still imperfect handle on likely causality. Only a few prospective studies exist, but they produce more consistent findings than the retrospective studies.

Prospective Data

In one of the earliest mammography studies, Calnan (1984) invited women between the ages of 45 and 64 to attend a breast cancer screening clinic in the United Kingdom. Calnan interviewed these women a month before the invitation was delivered. He discovered that women who reported being more concerned about breast cancer were also more likely to attend the mammography screening clinic.

McCaul et al. (1996b; 1998) conducted two studies examining connections between worry and later screening behavior. In one study (McCaul et al., 1996b), the researchers surveyed 353 women and asked how often they worried about breast cancer, how much they worried, and whether breast cancer "makes me feel upset and frightened." A scale composed of these items was used to predict screening behaviors over the following year. For all three screening behaviors, mammography, BSE, and clinical examinations, McCaul et al. discovered a linear relationship between worry and screening such that higher levels of worry predicted the highest rates of screening. In the second study (McCaul et al., 1998), the researchers asked 135 women to self-monitor their worries daily for a one-week period and, one year later, they measured BSE reports. Several worry measures (including trait anxiety) were used. For example, the women recorded every time they thought about breast cancer and indicated how "bothersome" the thought was. Then, at the end of each day, they reported whether they felt distress during the day because of breast cancer thoughts, how much worry affected their mood, and whether worry interfered with their ability to perform daily activities. The number of thoughts per day and how bothersome those thoughts were did not correlate significantly with later BSE ($rs = 0.17$ and 0.10), but the worry judgments did correlate reliably ($r = 0.31$). Trait anxiety was unrelated to BSE ($r = 0.05$).

Diefenbach et al. (1999) obtained similar data in a one-year prospective study of approximately 200 women with a strong family history of breast cancer, ovarian cancer, or both. Worry was measured with a single item addressing frequency of worries about risk: "how often have you worried about your own chances of developing breast cancer?" and "general distress" was measured with the anxiety-tension subscale from the Profile of Mood States (McNair et al., 1971). The effects of worry were tested in a prospective logistic regression after entering prior mammography use, perceived vulnerability, and general distress into the equation. Worry remained a significant, positive predictor of obtaining a mammogram. Anxiety was unrelated to obtaining a mammogram.

Rather than measuring "static" worries, Lerman et al. (1991b) interviewed women following a mammogram and asked whether they now felt better or worse about breast cancer. One might predict that women who felt relief and fewer worries would find the mammography experience reinforcing and be more likely to return for a follow-up exam. However, just the opposite was true. Lerman et al. found that women whose concerns about breast cancer decreased after the initial mammography were less likely to return for a subsequent screening compared to women who continued to be concerned.

Rather than measuring behavior, authors of the next two studies in this section asked about future intentions to be screened. Lerman et al. (1991a), interviewed women after a mammogram to ask them whether they still worried about breast cancer. Women who said that they were relieved following their mammogram were also less likely to plan to obtain a future mammogram. Clemow et al. (2000) used the Precaution Adoption Process model to categorize women according to their plans to obtain a mammogram (not planning, thinking about, definitely planning). Breast cancer worry was significantly and linearly associated with mammography intentions. Thus, those definitely planning were more worried than the other two groups; those not planning a mammogram at all were also the least worried. These last two studies rely on intentions to act in the future. Intentions are certainly not identical to behavior, so we should be cautious about the findings. On the other hand, it is worth noting that four of the studies mentioned in the section on retrospective reporting also measured future intentions. In every case, screening intentions were positively associated with worry, revealing a strong consistency across studies. Indeed, every prospective study shows a positive relationship between worry and screening.

Changes in Variables

An ideal experiment to test the hypothesized relationship between worry and breast cancer screening would be one in which women are randomly assigned to a condition in which we "make" them worry more. Alternatively, of course, we could randomly assign some "worrying" women to a condition in which we induce them to worry less. No studies of either kind exist. Instead, the experiments in this section typically examine screening behavior as a function of other variables that *change*. We suggest that some of those changing variables may also cause changes in worry.

For example, Lerman et al. (1991b) wondered about the consequences that an abnormal mammogram would have for subsequent screening. The researchers discovered that abnormal mammograms increased anxiety that (mildly) in turn increased mammography adherence during the subsequent year. Two other studies have also shown that false-positive mammogram results produce increases in subsequent mammogram levels (Burman et al.,

1999; Pisano et al., 1998). Neither of the latter studies measured worry, but other data have shown a clear connection between false positive results and increases in worry and/or anxiety (e.g., Cunningham et al., 1998). Indeed, Aro et al. (2000) discovered that false positive, compared to negative mammography results, were associated with increased risk perceptions, worry, and BSE frequency.

The data suggest that false positive screenings increase worry and motivate future screenings. Two studies suggest that, for genetic screening, negative results may do just the opposite. Bellg et al. (1999) asked a small group of women what they would do if they were tested for breast cancer genes and received a negative result. It is reasonable to speculate that receiving a negative result would reduce worrying, although Bellg et al. did not ask about worry. In any case, a strong minority of these women said they would reduce the frequency of BSEs or mammography screening in response to a negative test. The authors suggested that negative genetic tests might have the unintended consequence of becoming "a barrier factor to regular screening."

Bellg et al.'s study asked women to speculate about their likely behavior. Schwartz et al. (1999a) recently reported that the speculation tracks reality. Half of the women in their experiment learned that they were overestimating their risk of breast cancer, causing them to lower their risk estimates (and perhaps their worry as well). Some of these women (those with less education) subsequently reduced their mammography screening behavior. Although a similar study failed to show a reduction in screening intentions (Bowen et al., 1998), the Schwartz et al. study is the only one to report actual behavior.

Finally, Cameron et al. (1998) observed that changes in symptoms were associated with better BSE adherence for some women. Cameron et al. were studying the effects of tamoxifen, a drug that helps prevent cancer recurrence among breast cancer patients. High-anxiety women on tamoxifen were more adherent to BSE guidelines. Tamoxifen produces some side effects experienced by women on the drug, and the authors speculated that the women used their symptoms as cues to prompt BSE. This study is another example of how anxiety (in addition to worry) is associated with greater adherence.

Other Cognitions

Worry probably increases self-protective behaviors in the context of breast cancer screening. Evidence for the opposite effect comes exclusively from retrospective studies in which the negative affect is actually measured after women have either engaged in screening activities at some level or not. Moreover, the positive worry/screening relationship holds for both high-risk women and women who are not high risk. It may hold for other forms of negative affect besides worry, including anxiety. So here we have an important variable that apparently influences an important health-protective behavior. However, worry is almost completely ignored by models purporting to explain health-protective behaviors. On the other hand, perhaps one can account for worry effects by taking into account other cognitions.

A few studies have addressed this last issue by contrasting worry with perceived risk, an important belief in all the models discussed earlier and portrayed in Table 6.1. It is clear that risk cognitions and affect are correlated. In the breast cancer literature, in particular, perceived risk is associated with worry. So, for example, Champion (1984) correlated a single worry item with different susceptibility items, producing a correlation of $r = 0.44$. Women with a family history of breast cancer know that they are at higher risk and express greater distress than those not at risk, especially if they had a parent die of cancer (Erblich et al., 2000b; Zakowski et al., 1997). In general, people who report experiencing more anxiety also see themselves as more at risk of negative events, perhaps because negative information is more accessible from memory in anxious persons (Butler and Mathews, 1987).

Only a few studies have explicitly tested the relative contributions of cognition and affect to health-protective behaviors. We have examined judgments of perceived risk, self-efficacy, and worry in two studies. McCaul et al. (1996a) used regression analyses to test relationships between worry and screening after controlling for perceived risk. The data showed that worry was an independent predictor of screening behaviors. The opposite was also true: risk was an independent predictor of screening after controlling for worry. Taken together, these data suggest that both risk perceptions and worry may contribute independently to health behavior. This position would align well with Leventhal's suggestion that cognition and affect predict behavior along parallel paths.

The independent effects of worry on screening have been shown·in several other studies. McCaul et al. (1996b) used the same methodology as McCaul et al. (1996a) to predict screening behaviors prospectively. Worry was a significant predictor of screening after controlling for risk perceptions. Schwartz et al. (1995) showed that both family history (which could be seen as a proxy measure of perceived risk), and worry predicted screening for ovarian cancer with the other variable controlled. And Diefenbach et al. (1999) found that worry was a reliable prospective predictor of mammography screening after controlling for perceived vulnerability.

It is important to know that worry predicts variability in screening unexplained by risk perceptions. However, other data are needed to cement the case that worry operates independently of cognition. A stronger argument could be made by manipulating affect while leaving cognitions unchanged. We are unaware of any experiments of this type, a deficit that may spring partly from hesitance in making people worry. However, it is also true that a pure worry manipulation is difficult to achieve. The easiest way to manipulate worry is probably to provide people with different beliefs about their risk or about the severity of a negative outcome, but such manipulations would be likely to influence other risk cognitions as well as worry. In struggling with this issue, we recently devised a simple but potentially better way of manipulating worry: reminding people about potentially negative outcomes of their behavior (McCaul et al., 2001). The study was conducted with college smokers rather than persons possibly interested in cancer screening. The data nevertheless bear directly on the present discussion.

Daily smokers ($N = 84$) were recruited from the student population at North Dakota State University and randomly assigned to one of three conditions. In each group, smokers were given a signal watch and a set of nine small cards. The watch was programmed to sound four times a day at random intervals between 10.00 a.m. and 10.00 p.m. When participants heard the alarm, we asked them to select one of their nine cards, "think about it," and return the card to the bottom of the stack. The students performed this task four times every day for one week. In sum, then, this procedure encouraged smokers simply to think about the cards at random intervals, similar to what persons who worry naturally might experience when they have intrusive thoughts.

The manipulation of the content of smokers' intrusive thoughts was accomplished by changing the message on the cards. Some smokers read about the effects of studying more (control condition), some read brief statements about the effects of smoking (smoking causes lung cancer), and some looked at graphic pictures (e.g., a blackened lung) accompanied by a statement about smoking effects (see Figure 6.1). The smoking statements were not

SMOKING CAN CREATE SORES ON THE
LIP AND STAINED TEETH

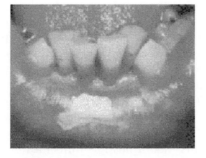

SMOKING CAN CREATE SORES ON
THE LIP AND STAINED TEETH

Figure 6.1 Cue cards for the text and image conditions.

particularly novel – smokers certainly know that their behavior can cause lung cancer. Our plan was to avoid providing new information that might change beliefs; instead, we were simply reminding people about a negative consequence of their behavior of which they were well aware.

The results were interesting. At the end of the week, the smokers returned to the lab to complete written measures. The manipulation produced strong differences on reports of intrusive thoughts during the previous week, with students in both smoking conditions ($M = 9.06$ for the picture condition; 8.24 for the text condition) reporting more intrusive thoughts about smoking than those who read the studying cards ($M = 5.75$). Importantly, no differences emerged on several measures of the perceived risk of smoking. Thus, the manipulation seemed to produce more negative thoughts without changing any beliefs about the consequences of smoking.

Researchers have defined scores from the intrusions scale we used as an indication of worry per se. However, the effect for intrusions in this study could result directly from the manipulation – one could argue that we were in a sense *making* participants experience intrusions about smoking. More important were the reported worry differences. Both smoking groups (M's $= 2.60$ for the picture condition; 2.64 for the text condition on a 1–5 scale) said that they worried more during the previous week than the studying group ($M = 2.21$; overall $p = 0.01$). Similar to the worry-screening relationship documented above, we also discovered that worry about smoking was significantly correlated with a health-protective behavior: the motivation to quit smoking cigarettes ($r = 0.50$). Although the overall between-groups effect was not significant ($p = 0.09$), the motivation to quit means for the smoking groups were similar to each other and higher than those obtained in the control condition.

One more interesting finding from this study bears mentioning. At baseline, participants completed the Penn State Worry Questionnaire (Molina and Borkovec, 1994), a trait measure of worrying. Using the median, we divided participants into high and low worriers and re-examined the reported intrusive thoughts for the week. Figure 6.2 displays the outcome of this analysis. As noted earlier, intrusive thoughts were higher for persons in the smoking text and smoking pictures conditions than for controls. The analysis also showed a main effect for worrying, with worriers reporting more intrusive thoughts compared to non-worriers (M's $= 8.86$ and 6.53, $p = 0.02$). Finally, as Figure 6.2 reveals, we also observed an interaction ($p = 0.057$). Worriers seemed more influenced by the images than smokers who were non-worriers. These data deserve further exploration in terms of how to persuade others using affect rather than cognition.

The data from McCaul et al. (2001) suggest that asking smokers merely to "think negative thoughts" about possible outcomes of their behavior leads to increased worrying. This increased worrying is unrelated to belief changes. Nevertheless, the worrying tends to enhance motivation for self-protective behavior – in this case, smoking cessation.

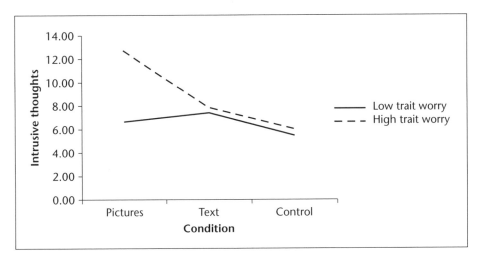

Figure 6.2 Worry manipulation × trait worry interaction.

Worry and Other Health-protective Behaviors

Thus far, our discussion of worry and health-protective behaviors has relied primarily on breast cancer screening. Given the fear that people have about cancer, it would be reasonable to suggest that the worry findings are limited to breast cancer or cancer more generally. However, we would argue that whenever people worry about their health, if a behavioral option for reducing worry is available, we should observe increases in the relevant action. Consider the following examples of behaviors other than breast cancer screening:

- Lauver (1994) found that higher levels of anxiety were associated with a shorter delay in seeking care for breast cancer symptoms for patients without an identified practitioner. We do not have enough comparative data to know whether worry and anxiety are similarly related to health-protective behaviors, but the data generally suggest that they are.
- Schwartz et al. (1995) studied an ultrasound test that serves as a screening tool to detect ovarian cancer. Higher levels of worry predicted increased test uptake. It is worth noting that the test for ovarian cancer may be of little value, so here is an instance, similar to excessive BSE, in which selecting the behavioral option may be to the detriment of the patient.
- Croyle and Lerman (1999) suggest that worry drives women to seek genetic testing for breast cancer and colon cancer. In line with this suggestion, Codori et al. (1999) reported that high cancer risk predicted genetic testing *only* among individuals who were also worried about cancer. Lerman et al. (1997) found that intrusions predicted requests for genetic testing for breast cancer whereas depression was not associated with testing uptake.

- Weinstein and Sandman (1992) found that fear predicts whether people will seek out radon testing.
- Mermelstein et al. (1999) discovered that worry about skin cancer was a significant predictor of whether sunbathers took a coupon for sunscreen. Using a completely different dependent measure, De Rooij et al. (1997) reported a similar finding: The fear of having skin cancer was an important reason given for attending a screening clinic for melanoma.
- Cuite et al. (2000) reported on the first wave of a longitudinal study predicting whether persons in a high risk area in the northeastern part of the United States obtained vaccinations for Lyme disease. Worry about getting Lyme disease in the future was a strong predictor of intentions to obtain the vaccine, with each step increase in worry associated with a similar increase in intentions. Moreover, worry was a strong predictor of intentions after controlling for cognitions such as perceived vulnerability and severity.
- Sutton and Eiser (1990), using path analyses, found that fear aroused by a videotaped message had a direct effect on intentions to use car safety belts. This finding echoed an earlier one showing direct effects of fear on intentions to quit smoking, and the authors suggested that models of health-protective behaviors need to incorporate emotional mediating processes (Sutton and Eiser, 1984).
- Van der Pligt et al. (1993) showed that increased fear was positively related to the willingness to engage in protective actions related to sex (safe sex techniques and/or using a condom). In a meta-analysis of studies concerning condom use, Sheeran et al. (1999) observed a significant, though small, positive effect size of worry on condom use.
- Stefanek et al. (1999) studied the predicted decisions of high-risk women to undergo bilateral prophylactic mastectomy to prevent breast cancer. Women read a vignette about a high-risk woman and selected standard care (e.g., mammography) versus mastectomy. The best predictor of the preventive (rather than screening) tactic was worry about breast cancer as a problem.

In summary, worry predicts improved health-protective behaviors in response to a variety of health threats besides breast cancer. Worry predicts screening for ovarian cancer, a shorter delay in responding to symptoms of cancer, seeking genetic tests for cancer, obtaining a radon test, and the use of sunscreen for cancer protection. The relationship is also observed for health behaviors having nothing to do with cancer, including vaccination for Lyme disease, protection from severe weather, seat belt use, and protection from sexually transmitted diseases. Worry is important across a broad range of health-protective actions.

Implications

The literature on worry and breast cancer screening has more general implications for our theoretical understanding of health-protective behaviors. Before turning to those suggestions, however, we must address two other issues. First, it is fair to ask a theoretical question about worry itself. To wit: *why* does worry influence health protective behaviors? Second, we should mention limitations in the strength of worry/behavior relationships and, in so doing, connect the worry data to other concepts in health and social psychology.

Why Would Worry Affect Behavior?

We see at least the following three possible explanations. First, the experience of worry may add a cognition to one's storehouse of reasons to take health-protective action. This notion fits with Petty and Cacioppo's ideas and essentially turns affect into cognition (see Petty et al., 1988). Leventhal et al. (1983) relied on a similar rationale to suggest why fear communications can continue to have effects over time even though the fear produced by the communication itself decays rapidly. Leventhal et al. proposed that the *memory* of the threat as frightening might persist and sustain actions over the long run. Of course, to the extent that the memory was actually accompanied by negative affect, then what Leventhal et al. described could be similar to what we mean by worry.

A second reason that worry may promote health-protective actions is also cognitive rather than affective. Specifically, worrying may keep an issue salient. It can thus serve as an internal reminder about things one needs to do. This suggestion, incidentally, does not jibe easily with some theorists' beliefs about worry. Aspinwall and Taylor (1997), for example, suggest that worriers always engage in avoidant coping, which would dispense with an issue rather than keeping it in mind. In contrast, McCaul et al. (1998) proposed that the frequent experience of what they called emotional "moments" – brief periods of worry and negative feelings – serve as a continual cue to action.

The third explanation relies on the cue to action notion. We suggest that the emotional arousal of worry directly promotes coping (Easterling and Leventhal, 1989). People want to manage worry because worry is aversive. And one way to control worry is to do something about the threat that is causing worry. Thus, if he or she is worrying, a woman may make her mammogram appointment, a writer may complete his chapter, a student may begin studying, and a person who needs to travel during bad weather may search for alternative routes. All of these seemingly different examples are instances in which worry may promote activity intended to manage the negative affect. Worry could thus promote coping "in advance" or what Aspinwall and Taylor (1997) call "proactive coping."

Caveats and Connections

We need to explicitly state that our concern throughout this chapter has been worry about disease. This focus, however, is somewhat simplistic. People may worry about many topics related to cancer and screening. They could, for example, worry about the costs of screening, express concern about their ability to accomplish the screening behavior (especially true of BSE), or ruminate about negative outcomes of the screening event itself. All of these other kinds of worries would likely hinder protective actions. Certainly negative affect surrounding screening itself inhibits adoption of the behavior. Millar and Millar (1995), for example, showed that thinking about disease detection can create a negative mood, and they propose that persons will avoid the detection behavior to avoid the negative feelings associated with it. Many studies in the breast cancer literature show that concern about breast cancer screening itself inhibits performing the behavior (e.g., Clemow et al., 2000).

The notion that people may worry about things other than disease connects well with a classic theoretical perspective from the stress and coping literature. Specifically, Janis (1958a; 1958b) discussed a process he called the "work of worrying." When facing a stressful event (e.g., surgery; military combat; separation from a loved one), people may engage in mental rehearsal of what is likely to take place when they actually experience the event. Such preparatory worry should, according to Janis, minimize reactions to the stressor, strengthening reality-based expectations about how to cope with the danger and plans for taking protective actions during the event. Moreover, Janis proposed a curvilinear hypothesis concerning worry and outcomes, suggesting that a moderate amount of worry worked best. Janis was concerned about reactions to stress, and he conceived of "the work of worrying as increasing a person's level of tolerance for subsequent stress stimuli" (Janis 1958a: 376). The present emphasis, in contrast, is on worry as a motivator of health-protective behaviors that might prevent stressful events. Nevertheless, the parallels are evident and Janis' theorizing predates but fits with the present emphasis on the value of worrying.

Our discussion of worry and motivation also shares some similarities with a more recent literature on defensive pessimism (Cantor and Norem, 1989; Showers, 1992). People sometimes adopt this strategy to deal with anxiety about an upcoming performance opportunity. They appear to reflect on possible outcomes, especially negative ones, and set low expectations – a process that returns a feeling of control and reduces negative affect. Moreover, defensive pessimists are motivated to work hard even though they have low expectations (Norem and Illingworth, 1993). We suspect that defensive pessimists, by thinking about negative performance outcomes and setting low expectations, are setting themselves up to worry more than optimists. It could very well be this worry that prompts work to improve outcomes. As far as we are aware, researchers studying the phenomenon of defensive pessimism have not measured worry per se (although individual differences in worrying scores and optimism-pessimism are correlated; see Thompson et al., 1999).

A thread that runs through all of the concepts we have been discussing – worry, the work of worrying, and defensive pessimism – is *control*. We noted earlier that uncontrollable thoughts might be the central feature of what we mean by worrying. Janis felt that the work of worrying would provide a sense of perceived and perhaps actual control to those who engaged in such effort. For post-surgery patients, for example, thinking about the event might inform the person about active things he or she could do to minimize aches and pains and make decisions. Defensive pessimists set their low expectations when they are concerned about whether they can control their outcomes; without concerns about such control, they do not engage in the pessimistic behavior. Research has clearly demonstrated that persons prefer to have control when they can and that control perceptions are related to health outcomes (see Wallston, 2001). Indeed, an internal locus of control predicts some types of protective behaviors related to breast cancer, including BSE and attention to health-related information (Bundek et al., 1993). One might also argue that restoring a sense of control over outcomes, via a variety of coping strategies, is crucial to ridding oneself of worrying thoughts. In short, control is a concept that may be important for understanding why worry is aversive and why and how people seek to cope with the events creating their worry.

Revising the Models

We have presented data showing that worry predicts screening behavior. Moreover, worry appears to be important independently of risk judgments. Thus, health researchers and theorists should pay more attention to the worry construct, advice that repeats what others have said about affect more generally. Salovey et al. (1999), for example, recently suggested that emotions are important in persuasion. Donovan and Henley (1997) describe the use of emotional content in social marketing campaigns, noting that a number of emotions besides fear (e.g., guilt, annoyance) are found in advertising content. Allen et al. (1992) proposed that emotion would predict behavior independently of attitudes, and they tested this notion in the context of whether persons would donate blood. Emotion was measured by asking participants to think retrospectively about the emotions they experienced before, during, and after giving blood. Emotions (e.g., sadness, joy, fear) were better behavioral predictors than attitude for relatively inexperienced and very experienced donators. Attitudes were better predictors only for moderately experienced donators. Overall, Allen et al. suggested that emotional reports can directly influence behavior independently of attitudinal judgments.

Richard et al. (1996) tested the Theory of Planned Behavior with an added construct: anticipated affective reactions to performing the behavior. Participants in their study were asked how they expected to *feel* when eating junk food, using soft drugs, going out late and drinking alcohol, and studying hard. Feelings such as worry and regret were important predictors of these behaviors, measured one month later, and feelings predicted variance in behavior beyond that accounted for by the standard model components.

When affect does not directly influence behavior, it may moderate the effects of other factors. Leventhal's model, for example, suggests that action is affected by beliefs about the possibilities of self-protection. Thus, worry may motivate action only if the action is seen as doable and valuable. Other relevant variables include a time line of the disease and if the self-protective behaviors are seen as related to the perceived cause (Leventhal et al., 1999).

Miller et al. (1996) explicitly include both cognition and affect in their model of applying cognitive-social theory to health-protective behaviors. Their emphasis is on stable individual differences (monitoring-blunting) concerning how people deal with health threats, and they propose that how monitors and blunters deal with affect will moderate the effect of interventions intended to motivate health-protective behaviors.

Although worry is an important variable in the health context, we would not argue that any of the models discussed at the chapter outset should necessarily be changed. In fact, once models in social psychology are constructed, they seem relatively impervious to change. The only formal change in 30 years of research on the Theory of Reasoned Action, for example, has been the addition of a self-efficacy variable and extension of the model to behaviors that vary in their controllability (Ajzen and the Theory of Planned Behavior, 1991). After 40 years, the Health Belief Model has changed little, in terms of the beliefs it emphasizes, although many moderating variables have been added (and self-efficacy expectations received separate and focused attention now as opposed to serving as only one of a long list of possible barriers).

We are not suggesting that the worry data presented here demand that any of the models necessarily need changing. In particular, models that are more general are intended to predict behaviors across many domains – not just health. Although we suspect that affect may be more important as a predictor of behavior in other domains than it is given credit for, the data in this chapter simply suggest that worry may be an important determinant of health-protective behaviors. What we would propose is that researchers should begin paying a great deal more attention to affect, especially worry, a strategy that has probably already been adopted by researchers in the cancer arena.

Cognition and Affect

Throughout this chapter, we have emphasized a distinction between affect and emotion. This divergence has been drawn before. Some time ago, Zajonc (1980) argued that affect is important in decision making. More recently, Cacioppo et al. (1999: 840) agreed with Zajonc, pointing to the value of studying affect in its own right and stating that affect "directs attention, guides decision making, stimulates learning, and triggers behavior." Some theorists write about the dichotomy as a literal one, suggesting that persons use two modes of processing, of thinking, of realizing the world. Epstein's (1994) cognitive experiential self-theory, for example, focuses on this dichotomy. He proposes that people have two fundamentally different ways of knowing, one associated with feelings (experiential) and the other with intellect (rational). The two systems differ on a number of dimensions. For example, the experiential (versus rational) system is holistic (versus analytic), automatic (versus intentional), and affective (versus logical). In line with our argument that worry may directly guide decision making and action, Epstein suggests that people often find the outcomes of their experiential processing more compelling than decisions resulting from rational processing (Epstein et al.,

1999). He also suggests that affect will often override cognition. Perhaps that is why smokers continue to smoke even though they know that it will kill them. As Epstein (1994: 721) noted, "Try as we may to be rationale, our rationality will be undermined by our inherently experiential nature. Cultivating them both, we may be able to achieve greater wisdom . . ."

Conclusions

Most models of health-protective behavior ignore affect as a determinant of such behaviors. The case of breast cancer screening, however, suggests that at least one affective variable – worry – is strongly related to whether women take action to protect their health. For the most part, the data point to a direct, linear relationship between greater worry and higher screening levels. Data from a variety of other health realms are consistent with the screening data. These data are also consistent with theoretical positions emphasizing the dual nature of consciousness and the importance of both cognition and affect as behavioral determinants. We suggest that the addition of affect to health models might improve their power to predict behavior. We leave the reader with the statement of Damasio (1994: xii) concerning the value of affect:

> "reason may not be as pure as most of us think it is or wish it were; emotions and feelings may not be intruders in the bastion of reason at all: They may be enmeshed in its networks, for worse and for better. The strategies of human reason probably did not develop, in either evolution or any single individual, without the guiding force of the mechanisms of biological regulation, of which emotion and feelings are notable expressions."

Acknowledgments

Preparation of this chapter was supported in part by NIH Grant CA77756. We would like to thank Kathryn B. Quinlan for helping with the literature review and Verlin Hinsz and the editors of this volume for providing helpful comments on a manuscript draft.

Correspondence concerning this chapter should be directed to: Kevin McCaul, Department of Psychology, PO Box 5057, North Dakota State University, Fargo, ND 58105-5057, USA; e-mail: Kevin.mccaul@ndsu.nodak.edu

Note

1. As with many strong statements in social psychology, the idea that Leventhal's model is the "only" social psychological theory to address emotion is an overstatement. At least two other theoretical approaches, neither of which is used frequently in health psychology, also deal with affect. First, to explain social behaviors, Triandis (1977) included a variable termed "affect toward the act," and suggested measuring the variable using strong affectively laden terms (e.g., enjoyable versus

nauseating). However, even though the anchors are emotion terms, it is neverthe-less doubtful whether this variable is any different than a *judgment* about affect, similar to Fishbein's procedure. Second, Janis and Mann (1977) developed a conflict-theory model of decision making. Although they did not include an affective element in their flow sheet, they clearly believed that emotion – especially fear – influenced decision making. That belief was partly responsible for their development of the technique of emotional role playing to promote smoking cessation.

References

Ajzen, I. (1991). The theory of planned behavior. *Organizational Behavior and Human Decision Processes*, 50, 179–211.

Allen, C. T., Machleit, K. A., and Kleine, S. S. (1992). *Journal of Consumer Research*, 18, 493–504.

Aro, A. R., Absetz, S. P., van Elderen, T. M., van der Ploeg, E., and van der Kamp, L. J. Th. (2000). False-positive findings in mammography screening induces short-term distress – breast cancer-specific concern prevails longer. *European Journal of Cancer*, 36, 1089–97.

Aspinwall, L. G. (1999). Persuasion for the purpose of cancer risk reduction: Under-standing responses to risk communications. *Monographs of the National Cancer Institute*, 25, 88–93.

Aspinwall, L. G., and Taylor, S. E. (1997). A stitch in time: Self-regulation and proactive coping. *Psychological Bulletin*, 121, 417–36.

Bellg, A. J., Matthews, A. K., and Smith, K. C. (1999). False reassurance from genetic testing for breast cancer risk. Paper presented at the Society of Behavioral Medicine Annual Meeting, San Diego.

Bober, S. L., Hoke, L. A., Tung, N. M., and Duda, R. B. (2000). Women's perceptions of worry, behavior change, and satisfaction after attending breast/ovarian cancer risk counseling. Paper presented at the Society of Behavioral Medicine Annual Meeting, Nashville.

Boehnke, K., Schwartz, S., Stromberg, C., and Sagiv, L. (1998). The structure and dynamics of worry: Theory, measurement, and cross-national replication. *Journal of Personality*, 66, 745–82.

Borkovec, T. D., Robinson, E., Pruzinsky, T., and Dupree, J. A. (1983). Preliminary exploration of worry: Some characteristics and processes. *Behaviour Research and Therapy*, 23, 481–2.

Borkovec, T. D., Shadick, R. N., and Hopkins, M. (1994). The nature of normal and pathological worry. In R. M. Rapee and D. H. Barlow (Eds.), *Chronic Anxiety: Gener-alized Anxiety Disorder and Mixed Anxiety-Depression.* New York: The Guilford Press.

Bowen, D. J., Christensen, C. L., Powers, D., Graves, D. R., and Anderson, C. A. M. (1998). Effects of counseling and ethnic identify on perceived risk and cancer worry in African American women. *Journal of Clinical Psychology in Medical Settings*, 5, 365–79.

Brain, K., Norman, P., Gray, J., and Mansel, R. (1999). Anxiety and adherence to breast self-examination in women with a family history of breast cancer. *Psycho-somatic Medicine*, 61, 181–7.

Bundek, N. I., Marks, G., and Richardson, J. L. (1993). Role of health locus of control beliefs in cancer screening of elderly Hispanic women. *Health Psychology*, 12, 193–9.

Burman, M. L., Taplin, S. H., Herta, D. F., and Elmore, J. G. (1999). *Annals of Internal Medicine*, 131, 1–6.

Butler, G., and Mathews, A. (1987). Anticipatory anxiety and risk perception. *Cognitive Therapy and Research*, 11, 551–65.

Cacioppo, J. T., Gardner, W. L., and Berntson, G. G. (1999). The affect system has parallel and integrative processing components: Form follows function. *Journal of Personality and Social Psychology*, 76, 839–55.

Calnan, M. (1984). The health belief model and participation in programmes for the early detection of breast cancer: A comparative analysis. *Social Science and Medicine*, 19, 823–30.

Cameron, L. D. (1997). Screening for cancer: Illness perceptions and illness worry. In K. J. Petrie and J. A. Weinman (Eds.), *Perceptions of Health and Illness: Current Research and Applications* (pp. 291–322). Amsterdam: Harwood Academic Publishers.

Cameron, L. D., Leventhal, H., and Love, R. R. (1998). Trait anxiety, symptom perceptions, and illness-related responses among women with breast cancer in remission during a tamoxifen clinical trial. *Health Psychology*, 17, 459–69.

Cantor, N., and Norem, J. K. (1989). Defensive pessimism and stress and coping. *Social Cognition*, 7, 92–112.

Champion, V. L. (1984). Instrument development for health belief model constructs. *Advances in Nursing Science*, 6, 73–86.

Clemow, L., Costanza, M. E., Haddad, W. P., Luckmann, R., White, M. J., Klaus, D., and Stoddard, A. M. (2000). Underutilizers of mammography screening today: characterisites of women planning, undecided about, and not planning a mammogram. *Annals of Behavioral Medicine*, 22, 1–9.

Codori, A. M., Petersen, G. M., Miglioretti, D. L. et al. (1999). Attitudes toward colon cancer gene testing: factors predicting test uptake. *Cancer Epidemiology and Biomarkers Prevention*, 8, 345–52.

Coles, M. E., Mennin, D. S., and Heimberg, R. G. (2001). Distinguishing obsessive features and worries: the role of thought-action fusion. *Behaviour Research and Therapy*, 39, 947–59.

Craske, M. G., Rapee, R. M., Jackel, L., and Barlow, D. H. (1989). Qualitative dimensions of worry in DSM-III – R generalized anxiety disorder subjects and nonanxious controls. *Behaviour Research and Therapy*, 27, 397–402.

Croyle, R. T., and Lerman, C. (1999). Risk communication in genetic testing for cancer susceptibility. *Journal of the National Cancer Institute Monographs*, No. 25, 59–66.

Cuite, C. L., Brewer, N., Weinstein, N., Herrington, J., and Hayes, N. (2000). Illness-specific worry as a predictor of intentions to vaccinate against Lyme disease. *Annals of Behavioral Medicine*, 22, S12.

Cunningham, L. L., Andrykowski, M. A., Wilson, J. F., McGrath, P. C., Sloan, D. A., and Kenady, D. E. (1998). *Health Psychology*, 17, 471–5.

Damasio, A. R. (1994). *Descartes' Error*. New York; G.P. Putnam's Sons.

Davey, G. C. (1993). A comparison of three cognitive appraisal strategies: The role of threat in devaluation of problem-focused coping. *Personality and Individual Differences*, 14, 535–46.

Davey, G. C. L., Hampton, J., Farrell, J., and Davidson, S. (1992). Some characteristics of worrying: Evidence for worrying and anxiety as separate constructs. *Personality and Individual Differences*, 13, 133–47.

Davey, G. C. L., Tallis, F., and Capuzzo, N. (1996). Beliefs about the consequences of worrying. *Cognitive Therapy and Research*, 20, 499–520.

Deffenbacher, J. L. (1980). Worry, emotionality, and task-generated interference in test anxiety. In I. G. Sarason (Ed.), *Test Anxiety: Theory, Research, and Applications*. Hillsdale, NJ: Erlbaum.

De Rooij, M. J., Rampen, F. H., Schouten, L. J., and Neumann, H. A. (1997). Factors influencing participation among melanoma screening attenders. *Acta Dermogoloy Venereology*, 77, 467–70.

DiClemente, C. C., Prochaska, J. O., Fairhurst, S. K., Velicer, W. F., Velasquez, M. M., and Rossi, J. S. (1991). The process of smoking cessation: An analysis of precontemplation, contemplation, and preparation stages of change. *Journal of Consulting and Clinical Psychology*, 59, 295–304.

Diefenbach, M. A., Miller, S. M., and Daly, M. B. (1999). Specific worry about breast cancer predicts mammography use in women at risk for breast and ovarian cancer. *Health Psychology*, 18, 532–6.

Donovan, R. J., and Henley, N. (1997). Negative outcomes, threats and threat appeals: Widening the conceptual framework for the study of fear and other emotions in social marketing communications. *Social Marketing Quarterly*, 4, 56–67.

Easterling, D. V., and Leventhal, H. (1989). Contribution of concrete cognition to emotion: neutral symptoms as elicitors of worry about cancer. *Journal of Applied Psychology*, 74, 787–96.

Epstein, S. (1994). An integration of the cognitive and psychodynamic unconscious. *American Psychologist*, 49, 709–24.

Epstein, S., Donovan, S., and Denes-Raj, V. (1999). The missing link in the paradox of the Linda conjunction problem: Beyond knowing and thinking of the conjunction rule, the intrinsic appeal of heuristic processing. *Personality and Social Psychology Bulletin*, 25, 204–14.

Epstein, S. A., Lin, T. H., Audrain, J., Stefanek, M., and Rimer, B., and Lerman, C. (1997). Excessive breast self-examination among first-degree relatives of newly diagnosed breast cancer patients. *Psychosomatics*, 38, 253–61.

Erblich, J., Bovbjerg, D. H., and Valdimarsdottir, H. B. (2000a). Psychological distress, health beliefs, and frequency of breast self-examination. *Journal of Behavioral Medicine*, 23, 277–92.

Erblich, J., Bovbjerg, D. H., and Valdimarsdottir, H. B. (2000b). Looking forward and back: distress among women at familial risk for breast cancer. *Annals of Behavioral Medicine*, 22, 53–9.

Fishbein, M., and Ajzen, I. (1975). *Belief, Attitude, Intention, and Behavior: An Introduction to Theory and Research*. Reading, MA: Addison-Wesley.

Floyd, D. L., Prentice-Dunn, S., and Rogers, R. W. (2000). A meta-analysis of research on protection motivation theory. *Journal of Applied Social Psychology*, 30, 407–29.

Glasgow, R. E., McCaul, K. D., Freeborn, V. B., and O'Neill, H. K. Immediate and long term health consequences information in the prevention of adolescent smoking. *The Behavior Therapist*, 4, 15–16.

Hailey, B. J. (1986). Breast self-examination among college females. *Women and Health*, 11, 55–65.

Hailey, B. J. (1991). Family history of breast cancer and screening behavior: An inverted U-shaped curve? *Medical Hypotheses*, 36, 397–403.

Harris, R. P., Fletcher, S. W., Gonzalez, J. J. et al. (1991). Mammography and age: Are we targeting the wrong women? *Cancer*, 67, 2010–14.

Horowitz, M. J., Wilner, N., and Alverez, W. (1979). Impact of event scale: A measure of subjective stress. *Psychosomatic Medicine*, 41, 209–18.

Janis, I. L. (1958a). *Psychological Stress*. John Wiley and Sons: New York.

Janis, I. L. (1958b). Emotional inoculation: theory and research on the effectiveness of preparatory communications. In W. Muensterberger and S. Axelrad (Eds.), *Psychoanalysis and the Social Sciences*. International Universities Press: New York.

Janis, I. L., and Mann, L. (1977). *Decision Making: A Psychological Analysis of Conflict, Choice, and Commitment*. New York: The Free Press.

Jepson, C., and Chaiken, S. (1990). Chronic issue-specific fear inhibits systematic processing of persuasive communication. *Journal of Social Behavior and Personality*, 5, 61–84.

Kash, K. M. (1995). Psychosocial and ethical implications of defining genetic risk for cancers. *Annals of the New York Academy of Sciences*, 768, 41–52.

Kash, K. M., Holland, J. C., Halper, M. S., and Miller, D. G. (1992). Psychological distress and surveillance behaviors of women with a family history of breast cancer. *Journal of the National Cancer Institute*, 84, 24–30.

Kash, K. M., Holland, J. C., Osborne, M. P., and Miller, D. G. (1995). Psychological counseling strategies for women at risk of breast cancer. *Journal of the National Cancer Institute Monographs*, No. 17, 73–9.

Lauver, D. (1994). Care-seeking behavior with breast cancer symptoms in Caucasian and African-American Women. *Research in Nursing and Health*, 17, 421–31.

Lerman, C., Daly, M., Sands, C. et al. (1993). Mammography adherence and psychological distress among women at risk for breast cancer. *Journal of the National Cancer Institute*, 85, 1074–80.

Lerman, C., Kash, K., and Stefanek, M. (1994). Younger women at increased risk for breast cancer: perceived risk, psychological well-being, and surveillance behavior. *Monographs of the National Cancer Institute*, 16, 171–6.

Lerman, C., Schwartz, M. D., Lin, T. H., Hughes, C., Narod, S., and Lynch, H. T. (1997). The influence of psychological distress on use of genetic testing for cancer risk. *Journal of Consulting and Clinical Psychology*, 65, 414–20.

Lerman, C., Trock, B., Rimer, B., Jepson, C., Brody, D., and Boyce, A. (1991a). Psychological side effects of breast cancer screening. *Health Psychology*, 10, 259–67.

Lerman, C., Trock, B., Rimer, B. K., Boyce, A., Jepson, C., and Engstrom, P. F. (1991b). Psychological and behavioral implications of abnormal mammograms. *Annals of Internal Medicine*, 114, 657–61.

Leventhal, H. (1970). Findings and theory in the study of fear communications. In L. Berkowitz (Ed.), *Advances in Experimental Social Psychology* (Vol. 3, pp. 119–86). New York: Academic Press.

Leventhal, H., Kelly, K., and Leventhal, E. A. (1999). Population risk, actual risk, perceived risk, and cancer control: a discussion. *Journal of the National Cancer Institute Monographs*, No. 25, 81–5.

Leventhal, H., Nerenz, D. R., and Steele, D. J. (1984). Illness representations and coping with health threats. In A. Baum, S. E. Taylor, and J. E. Singer (Eds.), *Handbook of Psychology and Health* (Vol. 4). Hillsdale, NJ: Lawrence Erlbaum Associates.

Leventhal, H., Safer, M. A., and Panagis, D. M. (1983). The impact of communications on the self-regulation of health beliefs, decisions, and behavior. *Health Education Quarterly*, 10, 3–29,

Levy, S., and Guttman, L. (1976). Worry, fear, and concern differentiated. *Israel Annals of Psychiatry and Related Disciplines*, 14, 211–28.

MacLeod, A. K., Williams, M. G., and Bekerian, D. A. (1991). Worry is reasonable: The role of explanations in pessimism about future personal events. *Journal of Abnormal Psychology*, 100, 478–86.

Marcus, A. C. (1999). New directions for risk communication research: a discussion with additional suggestions. *Monographs of the Journal of the National Cancer Institute*: Cancer risk communication: What we know and we need to learn, 35–42.

Mathews, A. (1990). Why worry? The cognitive structure of anxiety. *Behaviour Research and Therapy*, 28, 455–68.

McCaul, K. D., Branstetter, A. D., O'Donnell, S. M., Jacobson, K., and Quinlan, K. B. (1998). A descriptive study of breast cancer worry. *Journal of Behavioral Medicine*, 21, 565–79.

McCaul, K. D., Mullens, A. B., and Romanek, K. (2001). Creating worry by encouraging intrusive thoughts about smoking. Unpublished manuscript, North Dakota State University.

McCaul, K. D., Reid, P. A., Rathge, R. W., and Martinson, B. (1996a). Does concern about breast cancer inhibit or promote breast cancer screening? *Basic and Applied Social Psychology*, 18, 183–94.

McCaul, K. D., Schroeder, D. M., and Reid, P. A. (1996b). Breast cancer worry and screening: Some prospective data. *Health Psychology*, 15, 430–3.

McNair, D. M., Lorr, M., and Droppleman, L. F. (1971). *Manual for the Profile of Mood States*. San Diego, CA: Educational Industrial Testing Services.

Mermelstein, R., Weeks, K., Turner, L., and Cobb, J. (1999). When tailored feedback backfires: A skin cancer prevention intervention for adolescents. *Cancer Research Therapy and Control*, 8, 69–79.

Metzger, R. L., Miller, M., Cohen, M., Sofka, M., and Borkovec, T. D. (1990). Worry changes decision making: The effect of negative thoughts on cognitive processing. *Journal of Clinical Psychology*, 46, 78–88.

Millar, M. G., and Millar, K. (1995). Negative affective consequences of thinking about disease detection behaviors. *Health Psychology*, 14, 141–6.

Miller, S. M., Shoda, Y., and Hurley, K. (1996). Applying cognitive-social theory to health-protective behavior: Breast self-examination in cancer screening. *Psychological Bulletin*, 119, 70–94.

Molina, S., and Borkovec, T. D. (1994). The Penn State Worry Questionnaire: Psychometric properties and associated characteristics. In G. C. L. Davey and F. Tallis (Eds.), *Worrying: Perspectives on Theory, Assessment and Treatment*. Chichester, England: John Wiley.

Murray, J., and McMillan, C. L. (1993). Gender differences in perceptions of cancer. *Journal of Cancer Education*, 8, 53–62.

Norem, J. K., and Illingworth, K. S. S. (1993). Strategy-dependent effects of reflecting on self and tasks: Some implications of optimism and defensive pessimism. *Journal of Personality and Social Psychology*, 65, 822–35.

Petty, R. E., and Cacioppo, J. T. (1981). *Attitudes and Persuasion: Classic and Contemporary Approaches*. Dubuque, IA: Wm. C. Brown.

Petty, R. E., Cacioppo, J. T., Sedikides, C., and Strathman, A. J. (1988). Affect and persuasion: A contemporary perspective. *American Behavioral Scientist*, 31, 355–71.

Petty, R. E., Gleicher, F., and Baker, S. M. (1991). Multiple roles for affect in persuasion. In J. D. Forgas (Ed.), *Emotion and Social Judgments*. Oxford: Pergamon Press.

Pisano, E. D., Earp, J., Schell, M., Vokaty, K., and Denham, A. (1998). Screening behavior of women after a false-positive mammogram. *Radiology*, 208, 245–9.

Pruzinsky, T., and Borkovec, T. D. (1990). Cognitive and personality characteristics of worriers. *Behavior Research and Therapy*, 28, 507–12.

Richard, R., van der Pligt, J., and de Vries, N. (1996). Anticipated affect and behavioral choice. *Basic and Applied Social Psychology*, 18, 111–29.

Rippetoe, P. A., and Rogers, R. W. (1987). Effects of components of protection-motivation theory on adaptive and maladaptive coping with a health threat. *Journal of Personality and Social Psychology*, 52, 596–604.

Roemer, L., and Borkovec, T. D. (1993). Worry: Unwanted cognitive activity that controls unwanted somatic experience. In D. M. Wegner and J. W. Pennebaker (Eds.), *Handbook of Mental Control*. Englewood Cliffs, NJ: Prentice-Hall.

Rogers, R. W., and Prentice-Dunn, S. (1997). Protection motivation theory. In David S. Gochman (Ed.), *Handbook of Health Behavior Research* (Vol. 1, pp. 113–32). New York: Plenum Press.

Rosenstock, I. M. (1960). What research in motivation suggests for public health. *American Journal of Public Health*, 50, 295–301.

Russell, J. A., and Barrett, L. F. (1999). Core affect, prototypical emotional episodes, and other things called *emotion*: Dissecting the elephant. *Journal of Personality and Social Psychology*, 76, 805–19.

Salovey, P., Schneider, T. R., and Apanovitch, A. M. (1999). Persuasion for the purpose of cancer risk reduction: A discussion. *Journal of the National Cancer Institute Monographs*, No. 25, 119–22.

Sanderson, W. C., and Barlow, D. H. (1990). A description of patients diagnosed with DSM-III – R generalized anxiety disorder. *Journal of Nervous and Mental Disease*, 178, 588–91.

Schwartz, M., Lerman, C., Daly, M., Audrain, J., Masny, A., and Griffith, K. (1995). *Cancer Epidemiology, Biomarkers and Prevention*, 4, 269–73.

Schwartz, M., Rimer, B., Daly, M., Sands, C., and Lerman, C. (1999a). A randomized trial of breast cancer risk counseling: The impact of self-reported mammography use. *American Journal of Public Health*, 89, 924–6.

Schwartz, M. D., Taylor, K. L., Willard, K. S., Siegel, J. E., Lamdan, R. M., and Moran, K. (1999b). Distress, personality, and mammography utilization among women with a family history of breast cancer. *Health Psychology*, 18, 327–32.

Sheeran, P., Abraham, C., and Orbell, S. (1999). Psychosocial correlates of heterosexual condom use: A meta-analysis. *Psychological Bulletin*, 125, 90–132.

Showers, C. (1992). The motivational and emotional consequences of considering positive or negative possibilities for an upcoming event. *Journal of Personality and Social Psychology*, 63, 474–83.

Stalker, M. Z., Johnson, P. S., and Cimma, C. (1989). Supportive activities requested by survivors of cancer. *Journal of Psychosocial Oncology*, 7, 21–31.

Stefanek, M. E., Enger, C., Benkendorf, J., Flamm-Honig, S., and Lerman, C. (1999). Bilateral prophylactic mastectomy decision making: A vignette study. *Preventive Medicine*, 29, 216–21.

Stefanek, M. E., and Wilcox, P. (1991). First degree relatives of breast cancer patients: Screening practices and provision of risk information. *Journal of Cancer Detection and Prevention*, 15, 379–84.

Storms, M. D., and McCaul, K. D. (1976). Attribution processes and emotional exacerbation of dysfunctional behavior. In J. H. Harvey, W. J. Ickes, and R. F. Kidd, (Eds.), *New Directions in Attribution Research* (Vol. 1). Hillsdale, NJ: Lawrence Erlbaum Associates.

Strax, P. (1989). *Make Sure You Do Not Have Breast Cancer*. New York: St. Martin's Press.

Strecher, V. J., Champion, V. L. and Rosenstock, I. W. (1997). In D. S. Gochman (Ed.), *Handbook of Health Behavior Research I: Personal and Social Determinants* (pp. 71–91). New York: Plenum Press.

Sutton, S. R., and Eiser, J. R. (1984). The effect of fear-arousing communications on cigarette smoking: An expectancy-value approach. *Journal of Behavioral Medicine*, 7, 13–33.

Sutton, S. R., and Eiser, J. R. (1990). The decision to wear a seat belt: The role of cognitive factors, fear and prior behavior. *Psychology and Health*, 4, 111–23.

Swanson, V., McIntosh, I. B., Power, K. G., and Dobson, H. (1996). The psychological effects of breast screening in terms of patients' perceived health anxieties. *British Journal of Clinical Psychology*, 50, 129–35.

Thompson, T., Mason, B., and Montgomery, I. (1999). Worry and defensive pessimism: A test of two intervention strategies. *Behaviour Change*, 16, 246–58.

Triandis, H. C. (1977). *Interpersonal Behavior*. Monterey, CA: Brooks/Cole Publishing Company.

Van der Plight, J., Otten, W., Richard, R., and van der Velde, F. W. (1993). Perceived risk of AIDS: Unrealistic optimism and self-protective action. In J. B. Prior and G. D. Reeder (Eds.), *The Social Psychology of HIV Infection* (pp. 39–58). Hillsdale, NJ: Erlbaum.

Wallston, K. A. (2001). Conceptualization and operationalization of perceived control. In A. Baum, T. A. Revenson, and J. E. Singer (Eds.), *Handbook of Health Psychology* (pp. 49–58). Mahwah, NJ: Lawrence Erlbaum Associates.

Weinstein, N. D. (1988). The precaution adoption process. *Health Psychology*, 7, 355–86.

Weinstein, N. D. (1993). Testing four competing theories of health-protective behavior. *Health Psychology*, 12, 324–33.

Weinstein, N. D., and Sandman, P. M. (1992). A model of the precaution adoption process: Evidence from home radon testing. *Health Psychology*, 11, 170–80.

Wisocki, P. A., Handen, B., and Morse, C. K. (1986). The Worry Scale as a measure of anxiety among homebound and community active elderly. *Behavior Therapist*, 5, 91–5.

Witte, K. (1998). Fear as motivator, fear as inhibitor: Using the extended parallel process model to explain fear appeal successes and failures. In P. A. Anderson and L. K. Guerrero (Eds.), *Handbook of Communication and Emotion: Research, Theory Applications, and Contexts* (pp. 423–50). New York: Academic Press.

Zajonc, R. B. (1980). Feeling and thinking: Preferences need no inferences. *American Psychologist*, 35, 157–93.

Zakowski, S. G., Valdimarsdottir, H. B., Bovbjerg, D. H., et al. (1997). Predictors of intrusive thoughts and avoidance in women with family histories of breast cancer. *Annals of Behavioral Medicine*, 19, 362–9.

CHAPTER 7

Social-cognitive Factors in Health Behavior Change

Britta Renner

Ernst-Moritz-Arndt Universität Greifswald

and

Ralf Schwarzer

Freie Universität Berlin

Introduction

Risk communication and resource communication are two basic approaches to motivate health behavior change. Risk information, as provided in the media, is more complex than it appears. A ratio or percentage is usually based on a selected time window, a specific population, exposure rates, etc. that are hard to communicate and even harder to understand. Single exposure and cumulative exposure over various time periods result in different risk estimates. Joint exposure to a number of risks might involve synergistic effects that an individual cannot grasp. Thus, misjudging given risk information is normal, whereas the accurate understanding of risks is the exception. Moreover, even when a risk for a certain population or reference group is well understood, this does not imply that the individual would believe him or herself to be personally at risk. Defensive optimism moves people away from reality and inhibits them from preventive action. Since risk perception sets the stage for health protection motivation, it is essential to learn more about these mechanisms.

The present chapter describes risk perception biases and other variables and processes that have been found pertinent in the adoption and maintenance of health behaviors. First, one section deals with various reasons why published risk data are not accurately perceived by the public. Another section examines the optimistic bias, a particular distortion to serve self-enhancement when it comes to face severe health threats. Second, two further sections distinguish between continuum models and stage models of health behavior change. One such model, the Health Action Process Approach, is based on the assumption that there are at least two distinct phases, one that leads to a behavioral intention and another that leads to actual health behavior. Within both phases, different patterns of social-cognitive predictors may emerge, with perceived self-efficacy as the only one that remains a stable predictor. It is argued that, in designing interventions, one needs to identify whether people are pre-intentional or post-intentional before tailoring interventions to different target groups. Resource communication is seen as essential when people have set themselves a goal to change their lives, whereas risk communication is regarded as part of an early stage intervention when people are not yet motivated to set a particular goal.

Misjudging Risk Information

Many health conditions are caused by risk behaviors such as problem drinking, substance abuse, smoking, reckless driving, overeating, or unprotected sexual intercourse. Fortunately, human beings have, in principle, control over their conduct. Health-compromising behaviors can be eliminated by self-regulatory interventions, and health-enhancing behaviors such as physical exercise, smoking cessation, weight control, preventive nutrition, dental hygiene, condom use, or accident precautions, can be adopted instead. Given that most preventable diseases are rooted in lifestyle factors, health professionals are concerned with changing health risk behavior through interventions.

A necessary first step in changing health behavior is to become aware of the connections between behavior and health. Motivating people to engage in preventive nutrition demands that, for example, they are made aware of the role of dietary-intake in health. Therefore, most intervention programs provide information about health risks and hazards to improve knowledge about causes of health and illness. Since the late 1970s, for instance, numerous public health campaigns have focused on cardiovascular disease risk factors in order to inform the public about preventive behaviors. Frank et al. (1993) reported that between 1979 and 1990 general knowledge about what a person can do to keep from having a heart attack or a stroke improved significantly. Especially, cholesterol-related knowledge showed particularly marked improvements (see also Fortmann et al., 1993). This and other studies, such as the Pawtucket Heart Health Program (Niknian et al., 1991), support the notion that moving individuals from the stage of being unaware that a threat exists, to acknowledging a threat, is a necessary first step in the process of changing health behavior.

It is certainly advantageous for the message to come from someone who is perceived as a trustworthy expert (Siegrist and Cvetkovich, 2000). However, the general question – how do we change individuals' health behaviors? – is not satisfactorily answered merely by making information available. This does not by itself allow people to make informed judgments and decisions because information can be easily misinterpreted. This is particularly apparent in the way that laypersons process health risk information.

A significant part of public health campaigns is *risk communication*, which means increasing knowledge about the nature, magnitude, and significance of health risks. The underlying assumption is that people can only make appropriate decisions about preventive actions if they perceive risk accurately. Information about risks is communicated through a variety of channels such as brochures, pamphlets, newspapers, television, and the World Wide Web. Jimison and Sher (2000) reported that there are more than 40,000 producers of risk information in the United States. In spite of the expanding public information about risks, government officials and scientists often complain about the public's limited ability to evaluate and interpret risk information (Covello, 1992). Factual risk or objective risk is defined by technical experts as annual injury, fatality rates, accident probabilities, or the mean loss of life expectancy. For example, in Western countries, diseases take significantly more lives per year than accidents. Consequently, diseases represent a greater factual risk than accidents. However, Lichtenstein et al. (1978) showed that laypersons believed that accidents caused as many deaths as diseases, whereas in fact, in the United States in the late 1970s, diseases actually took about 16 times as many lives as accidents. In general, laypeople tend to overestimate rare causes of death, while underestimating common causes of death.

The study by Lichtenstein et al. (1978) stimulated numerous experiments devoted to judgmental biases in the processing of risk information (for overviews see Chapman and Elstein, 2000; Slovic et al., 1987; Yates, 1992). These studies showed that both laypersons and health providers do not calculate risk in the same "rational" manner as technical experts to determine the magnitude of risk. In contrast, Schneiderman and Kaplan (1992) demonstrated evidence for irrational behaviors in response to lethal diseases. They reported that health care providers, who are at risk of infection resulting from accidental exposure to blood, such as injury from a hypodermic needle, took only few precautions to prevent a hepatitis B infection, but they took exceptional precautions when treating patients who were HIV infected. In regard to the normative model, one can argue that this is irrational because the probability of death from both diseases is virtually the same (about 1 percent). However, these diseases differ with respect to the chance of infection following accidental exposure (hepatitis B: 25 percent versus HIV: 1 percent) and the chance of dying once one has become infected (hepatitis B: 5 percent versus HIV: 100 percent). The authors suggest that individuals take more effort to avoid an HIV infection in comparison to hepatitis B infections because they fear the certainty of death, even though the probability of an HIV infection is very low. This study makes it obvious that laypeople calculate the overall risk posed by a certain disease in a different way than risk experts do. Instead of multiplying the chance of infection by the chance of dying, which results in an overall risk of 1 percent for both diseases, people focused their judgments on the lethal consequences, while ignoring the probability of infection.

The phenomenon "fear of certainty of death" described above may apply in the case of HIV infection due to high levels of stress and anxiety, no matter how unwarranted, but on the other hand it may also lead to a greater use of protective measures. More alarming for health educators is the fact that the risk of other contagious diseases might be underestimated, since death is not perceived as a certain outcome once one has become infected, which might result in a failure to take necessary precautions. One could further reason that new and more efficient therapies not only lessen suffering, but might also lead to an unwarranted decline in perceived threat and protective behavior. For instance, since 1995, the number of new AIDS cases has declined in most Western countries (Robert Koch Institut, 2000). This is not due to a decline in the newly infected rate, but rather to the treatment of HIV infections with anti-retroviral drugs that considerably delay the onset of AIDS. Some researchers expressed their concern that the more efficient treatments will encourage risk behavior. In line with this assumption, a recent survey in Germany showed that in some sub-populations, protective behavior is in fact decreasing (Bochow, 2000).

For optimizing health promotion efforts, it is especially important to understand *how* individuals construe the risk of a certain health threat. According to most current theories of health behavior, risk perception has two aspects: perceived *severity* of a health condition, and personal *vulnerability* toward it. The first refers to the amount of harm that could occur, and the second pertains to the subjective probability that one could fall victim to that condition.

Theoretically, the relationship of these two variables has been described by a simple probability by severity interaction, which can be understood as a "normative" or "rational" principle. This means, for instance, that if the personal vulnerability or likelihood of the event is zero, the resulting perceived risk should also be zero, regardless of how serious the event may be.

Conversely, Weinstein (2000) has demonstrated that interest in obtaining protection is not always a function of severity and likelihood. The type of the relationship among severity, likelihood, and motivation to act varied with the severity and likelihood of the hazard. For serious, low-probability events, an interaction could be observed which represents this assumed synergism between the two variables. In contrast, individuals showed insensitivity to variations in likelihood once likelihood had reached the threshold of a 50–50 chance.

Weinstein (2000) suggests that people make finer distinctions at the low end of the likelihood scale than at the high end. Therefore, individuals confronted with a hazard with a 50 percent chance of occurring may display the same reaction as individuals who are confronted with a hazard with an 80 percent chance of occurring. This could explain why, for instance, many individuals view smoking and high cholesterol as cardiovascular risk factors of similar magnitude, although smoking is far more dangerous. Therefore, risk communication must supply information about the relative risks of acquiring one disease versus another to help people anchor the likelihood of occurrence and severity in appropriate ways. Otherwise, individuals may ignore considerable differences and consequently fail to take appropriate measures to protect themselves.

One could reasonably argue that the discrepancy between actual responses and those advocated by normative models or risk experts is not necessarily indicative for human irrationality, since laypeople may just have another, albeit consistent, view about risk. Slovic et al. (1987) demonstrated that laypeople's judgments of risk are sensitive, for example, to the controllability of the risk, its familiarity, and its catastrophic potential, as well as to the length of time before severe consequences will emerge. However, recent studies show more straightforwardly that laypeople not only use other conceptions about risk than experts, but that they also show clear inconsistencies and misconceptions about risk.

Many risks have a relatively low probability for any single exposure. However, these small probabilities add up over repeated exposures to create a substantial overall risk. Even if people are accurately aware that a certain behavior increases the risk of becoming ill, and that risk increases with greater exposure, they fail to apply appropriate rules when estimating the danger of increasing exposure to certain risks. For example, Sastre et al. (1999) asked 155 French adults to estimate the risk of developing lung cancer for certain smoking habits. They found that all participants, smokers as well as non-smokers, believed that the risk of lung cancer increases as the number of consumed cigarettes increases. Nevertheless, the estimated strength of this dose–response effect was negatively accelerated. After surpassing a threshold of 15 cigarettes per day, an increase in consumption led only to a small rise in perceived risk. However, the actual relationship between smoked cigarettes per day and lung cancer risk is at least proportional. Misjudging the cumulative risk of increasing exposure to risks could jeopardize appropriate behaviors, and in the worst case encourage extensive risk behaviors.

Unfortunately, not only the implications of repeated risk behavior can be misunderstood, but also the long-term effectiveness of precautions could be misconstrued. Birth control, for example, needs a continuing process of risk management. The risk of conception is relatively low on a single occasion of sexual intercourse, but accumulates over repeated occasions. Imagine a contraceptive method with a one-year reliability of 0.98. Of 100 women who apply this method, 2 will become pregnant during one year of use. This outcome appears reassuring. However, with each additional year, the number of unwanted pregnancies will further increase. After a ten-year period, 20 percent of the same group of women will be pregnant, although they might still perceive their risk as 2 percent. Therefore, individuals need to understand how the risk of conception accumulates over repeated exposure, and to what degree this could be reduced through the use of contraceptive methods.

Shaklee and Fischhoff (1990) showed that most laypersons do not realize that contraceptive effectiveness declines over time. Thus, a short-term perspective on effectiveness may promote unrealistically optimistic estimations about long-term outcomes, since individuals are not aware how rapidly small risks add up. Since most effectiveness information about birth control methods is only presented for one year of use, individuals may have too much confidence in their precautions. Hence, from a health-educational perspective, contraceptive effectiveness information should be presented for short as well as long time periods to assist people in making informed choices.

The importance of "complete" risk information becomes particularly relevant in the case of HIV prevention. Linville et al. (1993) asked male college students to rate the probability of an HIV transmission from male to female in one case and in 100 cases of *protected* sex. On average, the one-case probability of an HIV infection was overestimated, while the mean estimate for 100 cases was highly underestimated. Accordingly, public risk communication which does not emphasize how the risk of an HIV infection accumulates over repeated exposures, even for protected intercourse, could give recipients a dangerously wrong impression about their safety. To prevent a faulty understanding of cumulative risks and effectiveness, public health campaigns are needed that explicitly inform the public about how risk accumulates in the long run. Alternatively, as Shaklee and Fischhoff (1990) suggest, effectiveness estimates should be presented for all the time periods that are relevant to people's decisions.

Estimating a health risk becomes even more complex when multiple risks are considered. Certain risk behaviors, such as smoking and alcohol consumption, result in a combined risk that is greater than the sum of the single risks. However, empirical evidence shows that people have problems in understanding such synergistic relations. Hermand et al. (1997) demonstrated that study participants believed that engaging in only one risk behavior (heavy alcohol consumption or heavy smoking) results in the same risk as engaging in both at the same time. Hence, the two risks have been considered as disjunctive instead of synergistic. Hermand et al.'s (1997) research makes evident that communication about harmful effects of hazards should include information about potential synergistic or additional effects, as otherwise people might seriously misconstrue their overall risk.

In sum, providing information is a necessary first step in the process of changing health behaviors. However, the processing of health-related information could be a complex task for recipients, which may result in severe pitfalls. Individuals might harbor erroneous beliefs about health risks, which could be due to missing information, misinformation, or inadequate or biased processing. Therefore, educational efforts must be sensitive to the psychology of people's decision making. To facilitate the understanding of risks, different information must be supplied, such as (a) the relative risks of acquiring one disease versus another, (b) how risk increases over time and how precaution effectiveness declines over time, and (c) how different risk factors cumulate to provide the overall risk.

Underestimating Self-relevant Risk

At first glance, perceiving a health threat seems to be the most obvious prerequisite for the motivation to remove a risk behavior. Consequently, a central task for health communication is not only to provide information about the existence and magnitude of a certain risk, but also to increase the subjective relevance of a health issue to focus individuals' attention on information pertaining directly to their own risk. However, general perceptions of risk (e.g., "Smoking is dangerous") and personal perceptions of risk (e.g., "I am at risk because I am a smoker") often differ to a great extent. Individuals could be well informed about general aspects of certain risks and precautions (e.g., most smokers acknowledge that smoking can cause diseases), but, nevertheless, many might not feel personally at risk (Weinstein, 1998).

Especially when it comes to a comparison with similar others (for an overview of social comparison mechanisms, see Suls and Wheeler, 2000), one's view of the risk is somewhat distorted. On average, individuals tend to see themselves as being less likely than others to experience health problems in the future. For example, when asked how they judge their risk of becoming HIV-infected compared to an average peer of the same sex and age (the "average risk"), participants typically give a below-average estimate (e.g., Hahn and Renner, 1998). This bias in direct comparative risk perception, that has been coined "unrealistic optimism" or "optimistic bias" (Perloff and Fetzer, 1986; Weinstein, 1980; this volume), reflects the difference between the perceived risk for oneself and that for others, and belongs to the broader construct of defensive optimism (Schwarzer, 1994).

Similarly, Thompson et al. (1996) showed that individuals are prone to an "illusion of safety in a risky world." The authors asked undergraduates to list factors that make it less likely to become infected by HIV in comparison to an average student at their college. Despite being well informed about HIV, participants discounted their risk in terms of irrelevant factors. For example, 30 percent stated that they were less at risk than an average student because they were monogamous. These empirical findings are particularly disturbing because the majority of college students are only serially monogamous, which means that one monogamous relationship is followed by another. Hence, people may acknowledge a certain risk for others, but are reluctant to admit that they are at risk themselves.

This phenomenon becomes even more obvious in the study conducted by Hahn and Renner (1998). They asked smokers to characterize the typical smoking behavior that is necessary to be at a high risk for lung cancer in terms of the number of years of smoking, the daily amount of cigarettes consumed, and the cigarettes' nicotine content. These subjective estimates for the "risk prototype" were compared with participants' own smoking behavior. Results showed that smokers estimated their lung cancer risk only as being average when their own behavior was equivalent to that of the risk stereotype. Or, to put this effect more bluntly, even smokers who demonstrated a smoking behavior that they themselves judged as highly risky nonetheless viewed their own personal risk as only average.

Unrealistic optimism could be an important barrier for convincing people to change their health habits because optimistic bias may function to dissuade them from engaging in protective health actions. However, optimistic bias is a matter of degree. Individuals do not distort reality completely. This becomes most obvious when they are asked to estimate the absolute risk for themselves and for the average peer, as opposed to a direct comparison. Renner et al. (2000) showed that absolute risk perceptions reveal relative accuracy, since older participants perceived their risk for cardiovascular diseases as

Perceived risk for cardiovascular diseases

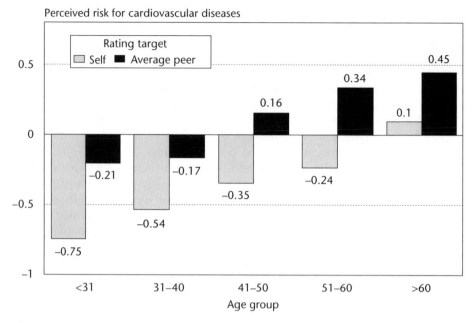

Figure 7.1 Mean absolute risk judgments for self and an average peer to cardiovascular diseases as a function of age.

being higher than younger ones did. Nevertheless, they still assumed that they were less vulnerable than their peers (see Figure 7.1).

The observed effect of aging on perceived risk leads to the conclusion that people acknowledge a higher risk with increasing age and declining health, but that aging did not curb unrealistic comparative risk perceptions. Further, these results suggest that defensive optimism is determined by the tendency to see others as more at risk from negative events than oneself. The fact that individuals harbor pessimistic biases for others may represent a mechanism by which they maintain a comparatively optimistic outlook for themselves, despite realizing that health-related risks do increase with age. This might satisfy a need for accuracy by acknowledging more objective risk at an absolute level, while also serving self-protective needs by maintaining a pessimistic view of others at the same time (Armor and Taylor, 1998; Taylor and Shepperd, 1998; Whitley and Hern, 1991).

This leads to the question about how health promotion campaigns should communicate information about risks in order to reduce unrealistic optimistic risk perceptions. The guiding principles proposed by health campaigns for risk reductions usually only list risk factors impersonally, or show high-risk persons. This may lead to an underestimation of personal risk because individuals may think that a number of risk factors do not apply to them by fostering a risk stereotype which is perceived as dissimilar (Hahn and Renner, 1998; Weinstein and Klein, 1995). Consequently, risk communication that provides only information about general risk may make people aware of a risk ("Smoking causes coronary heart disease"), but at the same time it may foster an underestimation of the magnitude of the risk for oneself ("It is unlikely that this will happen to me"). One possibility to reduce unrealistic optimism is to provide additional information about the risk faced by an average peer. Lachendro and Weinstein (1982), for instance, asked participants to come up with a number of possible risk-reducing factors that typical peers might list. This experimental intervention resulted in lower unrealistic optimism since the participants were encouraged to explicitly consider moderating factors in other persons that they usually only found in themselves. Weinstein (this volume) proposes that we are unrealistically optimistic because we do not think carefully about the target under comparison.

Such additional information may help people locate their risk status more accurately and become motivated to change risky behaviors. This type of message establishes more clearly who is likely to be affected, but it is still ambiguous since recipients have to infer the magnitude of their personal risk. In order to reduce this ambiguity, people should be informed about the existence of a health risk in a *personalized* manner to enhance self-relevance, and, furthermore, they should imagine themselves as possible victims, unless they take the necessary precautions to overcome a tendency to deny that the advice applies to them.

One frequently used method for communicating personalized health risk is to assess individuals' risk status by either self-administered questionnaires or biomedical measures. From these data, and from epidemiological statistics, estimates of individuals' morbidity or mortality risk are calculated and given as feedback (e.g., "Your actual age is 55 years, but your risk age is 61 years. If you quit smoking, you can add 5 years to your present life expectancy"). This method is called "health risk appraisal" (Strecher and Kreuter, 1995).

However, empirical studies have shown that individuals process and respond to feedback about their personal health risk in a self-defensive manner. Jemmott et al. (1986) invented an experimental procedure to study judgments about favorable and unfavorable medical information. An often-replicated finding is that participants who were made to believe that they suffer from (hypothetical) thiamine acetylase (TAA) deficiency perceived their test result as less accurate and rated TAA deficiency as a less serious threat to their health than their experimental counterparts, who were made to believe that they did not have a TAA deficiency. Similar results were found in experimental studies of appraisals of cholesterol and blood pressure test results (Croyle, 1990; Croyle et al., 1993), gum disease test results (McCaul et al., 1992), and a hypothetical bacterial condition (Cioffi, 1991). Croyle et al. (1997) interpreted these findings as evidence for motivated reasoning, arguing that people who are informed that they have an elevated risk of disease minimize the seriousness of the health threat posed by the risk factor and derogate the validity of the risk factor test in order to maintain a favorable sense of their health.

Does this mean that even individualized risk communication is ineffective in motivating people to change their behavior? People do not indiscriminately derogate or deny unfavorable risk information. Croyle and Sande (1988) reported that individuals who believed that they suffered from a TAA deficiency showed evidence for denial, but they also recalled more diagnosis-consistent symptoms and risk-increasing behaviors (e.g., use of aspirin or Tylenol, getting less than seven hours of sleep, skipping a meal) than individuals who considered themselves to be on the safe side. More interestingly, the higher the consistency with which an individual could recall symptoms, the less they denigrated the validity of the diagnostic test.

Accordingly, participants minimized the implications of the diagnosis, while simultaneously searching for diagnosis-confirming evidence. Ditto and Croyle (1995) explained these conflicting results by suggesting that minimizing the threat serves primarily to reduce negative affect. This need not necessarily conflict with instrumental coping behavior. Ditto et al. (1988) further observed that unfavorable medical feedback causes prominent denial only when recipients believed that they had no possibility of reducing the threat by modifying their behavior.

This makes obvious that the adoption of health behaviors could not be viewed simplistically as a response to a health threat. Risk information alone does not help people to change risky behaviors because it does not provide meaningful information about how to manage behavioral changes. Initial risk perception seems to be advantageous to help people become motivated to change, but later on other factors are more influential in the self-regulation process. This state of affairs has encouraged health psychologists to design more complex models that include an integrated pattern of determinants and processes of change.

Forming an Intention to Change: Continuum Models of Health Behavior

Most health behavior theories concentrate on the process leading to the formation of an explicit intention (e.g., "I intend to quit smoking this weekend") because they propose that a person's behavior is the outcome of conscious intentions. The *intention strength* is assumed to be the key indicator of cognitive preparedness for action (Abraham and Sheeran, 2000). In line with this assumption, Godin and Kok (1996), who examined 19 studies, found a mean correlation of 0.46 between intention and health behavior, such as exercise, screening attendance, and addictions. In general, Abraham and Sheeran (2000) expect behavioral intention measures to account for 20–25 percent of the variance[1] in health behavior measures.

The process of intention formation is in turn assumed to be determined by certain beliefs and attitudes. Therefore, in the past, the focus of such models has been on identifying a parsimonious set of predictors that included constructs such as perceived barriers, social norms, disease severity, personal vulnerability, perceived self-efficacy, etc. These are then combined into a single prediction equation for explaining behavioral intention and individual health behavior change (Weinstein et al., 1998b). Since this implies that the way in which these predictors combine to influence actions is expected to be the same for everyone, these models are called continuum models.

The most prominent approaches are the Theory of Reasoned Action, the Theory of Planned Behavior, and the Protection Motivation Theory (for an overview and critique of these and other models, see Abraham and Sheeran, 2000; Armitage and Conner, 2000; Conner and Norman, 1996; Schwarzer, 1992; Wallston and Armstrong, 2002; Weinstein, 1993). The current revised versions of these continuum health behavior models share several common predictors. Two other variables beside risk perception are considered to play a major role in this process: (a) outcome expectancies, and (b) perceived self-efficacy (Bandura, 1997; 2000; Schwarzer, 1992; Weinstein, 1993). The wording of these determinants differs in different theories, but their meaning is about the same. For example, behavioral beliefs (as precursors of attitudes) can be equated to outcome expectancies, and behavioral control can be more or less matched to perceived self-efficacy (see also Wallston, 2001).

Outcome Expectancies

According to these theories, people not only need to be aware of a health threat, they also need enough knowledge about how to regulate their behavior. They need to understand the links between their actions and subsequent outcomes. These *outcome expectancies* can be the most influential beliefs in the motivation to change. A smoker may find more good reasons to quit than good reasons to continue smoking ("If I quit smoking then my friend will like me much more"), and while this imbalance may not lead directly to action, it can help to generate the intention to quit. Many of those cognitions represent social outcome expectancies by pertaining to the social consequences of a particular behavior. The pros and cons that are typical in rational decision making represent positive and negative outcome expectancies. However, such contingencies between actions and outcomes need not be explicitly worded and evaluated, they can also be rather diffuse mental representations, loaded with emotions. Outcome expectancies can also be understood as methods, or means-ends relationships, indicating that people know proper strategies to produce the desired effects.

Perceived Self-efficacy

The efficacy of a method has to be distinguished from the belief in one's personal efficacy to apply the method. *Perceived self-efficacy* portrays individuals' beliefs in their capabilities to exercise control over challenging demands and over their own functioning (Bandura, 1997; 2000). According to Bandura (1997; 2000) perceived self-efficacy involves the regulation of thought processes, affective states, motivation, behavior, or changing environmental conditions. These beliefs are critical in approaching novel or difficult situations, or in adopting a strenuous self-regimen. People make an internal attribution in terms of personal competence when forecasting their behavior (e.g., "I am certain that I can quit smoking even if my friend continues to smoke."). Such optimistic self-beliefs influence the goals people set for themselves, what courses of action they choose to pursue, how much effort they invest in given endeavors, and how long they persevere in the face of barriers and setbacks. Some people harbor self-doubts and cannot motivate themselves. They see little point in even setting a goal if they believe they do not have what it takes to succeed. Thus, the intention to change a habit that affects health is to some degree dependent on a firm belief in one's capability to exercise control over that habit.

Perceived self-efficacy operates in concert with risk perception, outcome expectancies, and other factors when it comes to motivation to change. There is a large body of evidence documenting the influence of these three predictors on forming an intention. Unfortunately, self-efficacy research that employs behavioral intentions as the criterion variable is more frequent than research that addresses actual behaviors (for reviews see Bandura, 1997; Schwarzer and Fuchs, 1995; 1996). This may be partly due to methodological difficulties in health behavior assessment (Renner, 2001). Additionally, although continuum models assume an underlying process towards behavior change, most empirical studies are limited to cross-sectional designs where criterion variables (intentions and self-reported behaviors) are assessed at the same time as predictor variables (risk perception, outcome expectancies, and self-efficacy). Therefore, only little is known about the causal sequence and interplay of these factors. It is assumed that initial risk perception sets the stage, whereas outcome expectancies and perceived self-efficacy may emerge later. At the point in time when the behavioral intention is measured, the latter two emanate as the major predictors, whereas the former is often insubstantial (Schwarzer and Renner, 2000).

Apart from limitations at the empirical level, researchers have suggested two major theoretical deficiencies. First, a single prediction rule for describing behavior change implies that cognitive and behavioral change occur in a linear fashion, and that a "one-size-fits-all" intervention approach (Winders et al., 1999) is suitable for all individuals engaging in unhealthy behaviors. Consequently, it excludes qualitative changes during the course of time, such as stage transitions or recycling through phases. Weinstein et al. (1998a) noted that, according to continuum models, it is not important whether an intervention approach is targeted towards changing perceived vulnerability, perceived consequences, or perceived self-efficacy first. Hence, interventions are not required to be progressed in a certain sequence. Rather, they could be applied in any order, or even simultaneously.

Second, none of these models account for the post-intentional phase where goals are translated into action. The segment between intentions and behaviors is a black box. Theorizing about health behavior change, then, is reduced to the motivation phase only, while omitting the decisive action phase.

Different Processes at Different Stages:
Dynamic Models of Health Behavior Change

The Transtheoretical Model of Behavior Change

To overcome these limitations, stage theorists have made an attempt to consider process characteristics by proposing a number of qualitative stages. The *Transtheoretical Model of Behavior Change* (TTM) (e.g., DiClemente and Prochaska, 1982; Prochaska et al., 1992; 1998), for example, has become the most popular stage model. Its main feature is the implication that different types of cognitions may be important at different stages of the health behavior change process. The most common version of the TTM includes five discrete stages of health behavior change that are defined in terms of one's past behavior and future plans (pre-contemplation, contemplation, preparation, action, maintenance). For example, at the *pre-contemplation stage*, a problem drinker has no intention of stopping in the future. At the *contemplation stage*, he or she reflects about quitting sometime within the next six months, but does not make any specific plans for behavior change. At the *preparation stage*, the problem drinker resolves to quit within the next six months. The *action stage* includes individuals who have taken successful action for any period of time. If this abstinence has lasted for more than six months, the person is categorized as being in the *maintenance stage*. The five stages are expected to be mutually exclusive and qualitatively different. People could make multiple attempts to progress from pre-action stages to action. However, relapses could occur anytime, resulting in a spiral-like progression through the behavior-change process.

In addition to the described basic stages of change, the TTM also includes ten processes of change, the perceived pros and cons of changing, perceived self-efficacy and temptation. These additional constructs are conceptualized as causes for the transitions between the stages, whereby it is assumed that different factors influence different stage transitions.

The TTM has received a lot of attention, since its "practicability" for educational interventions is very appealing. However, the TTM has also been seriously criticized by several researchers. Bandura (2000) argued that different qualitative stages necessarily imply that individuals cannot move back in the transitions of stages (irreversibility), and they cannot progress from one stage to another while passing over another one (invariance). This requirement might be too conservative, but there are other significant disadvantages. Weinstein et al. (1998b) and Sutton (2000; 2001) argued that the notion of stages might be flawed or circular, in that the stages are not genuinely qualitative, but are rather arbitrary distinctions within a continuous process. In particular, the proposed time frame for distinguishing between different qualitative stages is not conclusive. Furthermore, different studies have referred to different time frames for operational stage definitions. For instance, Velicer et al. (1985) defined contemplation as the time in which individuals seriously think about changing behavior within the next year, whereas Prochaska et al. (1994) defined contemplation as thinking about changing within the next six months. Why should individuals who intend to quit within the next six months (contemplators) be in a different qualitative stage of action-readiness than individuals who intend to quit within the next five months (preparers)? In line with this reasoning, Kraft et al. (1999) demonstrated within a sample of 421 Norwegian daily smokers, that pre-contemplators, contemplators, and preparers were not at different qualitative stages rather than at different places along an underlying continuum. Similarly, Courneya et al. (2000) reported that continuous measures of intention explained more variance in exercise behavior than the stage algorithm proposed by the TTM. Other researchers have examined the TTM and found that processes of change did not predict smoking stage movements (Herzog et al., 1999), and that stage-matched and stage-mismatched interventions with young adult smokers did not yield the hypothesized results (Quinlan and McCaul, 2000). Stages of change did not predict success in weight control in adult women, either (Jeffery et al., 1999). In sum, the TTM has received only weak support to date, which led Abraham et al. (2000) to conclude that TTM stage classifications are questionable.

Hence, these "stages" might be better understood as "process heuristics" to underscore the nature of the entire model. That is, the TTM can serve as a useful heuristic that describes a health behavior change process, which has not been the major focus of health behavior theories so far. In contrast to continuum models, stage models such as the transtheoretical model assume that factors producing movement toward action differ in respect to a person's stage. The identification of stages could bear important implications for intervention and treatment because it can be used to match stage position or readiness of change of the target group with particular intervention strategies (Oldenburg et al., 1999).

The Precaution Adoption Process Mode

In redirecting attention to a self-regulatory process, the transtheoretical model has served an important purpose for applied settings. However, the number of stages and how these stages should be defined is a major challenge for further research. The more recent Precaution Adoption Process Model (PAPM; Weinstein, 1988; this volume; Weinstein and Sandman, 1992) does not involve past behavior or any particular time frame in classification, and identifies people at seven stages: (1) unaware of the health action, (2) aware but not personally engaged, (3) engaged and trying to decide what to do, (4) decided not to act, (5) decided to act but not yet having acted, (6) acting, and (7) maintaining the new adopted health behavior. Hence, the PAPM extends the TTM by further differentiating the first two stages of the transtheoretical model: it distinguishes between people who are unaware of an issue (Stage 1), and people who are aware but not personally engaged (Stage 2). Second, it discriminates people who are engaged and considering their action (Stage 3) from those who decided not to act (Stage 4). Similarly to the TTM, the PAPM proposes certain factors that influence different stage transitions. Perceived vulnerability is assumed to be the necessary essence to move individuals from being aware to deciding to take action. Situational barriers determine whether individuals progress from the intention to act to actually implementing the behavior.

This model has been applied to home testing for radon (Weinstein et al., 1998a; for further details see also Chapter 2, this volume). The focus of this experimental study was on two different transitions: from being undecided about testing one's home (Stage 3), to deciding to test (Stage 5), and from this stage to actually ordering the test (Stage 6).

As expected, the results show that stage-matched interventions were more effective than stage-mismatched ones. However, the combination of both treatments was at least as effective as the stage-matched single treatments for undecided participants or decided-to-act participants. The combined treatment, for instance, prompted 54 percent of the participants to form an intention to test amongst the undecided group, whereas the matched vulnerability treatment encouraged only 42 percent to develop a decision to act. This result suggests that administrating matched treatments is not necessarily the most productive approach to encourage health behavior change – combination treatments might be even more successful. In terms of utility, Abraham et al. (2000) argued that as long as targeting stage-defined audiences is problematic and causes additional costs, investment in stage-specific interventions is not justified. Combining interventions that are designed to promote a variety of cognitive changes might be less expensive, since this does not require prior screening for action preparedness within the audience, and above all they might be even more successful. Nonetheless, it would be premature to conclude that stage-tailored interventions are not useful since they can only be as good as the underlying stage definitions. Refining stage definitions or different stage conceptions might generate stronger support for the stage framework.

The Health Action Process Approach

Another more parsimonious model is the *Health Action Process Approach* (HAPA; Schwarzer, 1992; 1999; Schwarzer and Fuchs, 1995; 1996). This health behavior change model is regarded as a heuristic to better understand the complex mechanisms that operate when people become motivated to change, and when they attempt to resist temptations. It applies to all health-compromising and health-enhancing behaviors and pays particular attention to post-intentional mechanisms, and it conveys an explicit self-regulation perspective. It suggests a distinction between (a) pre-intentional motivation processes that lead to a behavioral intention, and (b) post-intentional volition processes that lead to actual health behavior. Within both phases, different patterns of social-cognitive predictors may emerge (see Figure 7.2).

Pre-intentional Motivation Processes
In the initial *motivation phase*, a person develops an intention to act. In this phase, *risk perception* ("I have a high risk of suffering a heart attack because of my high cholesterol level and body weight") is merely seen as a distal

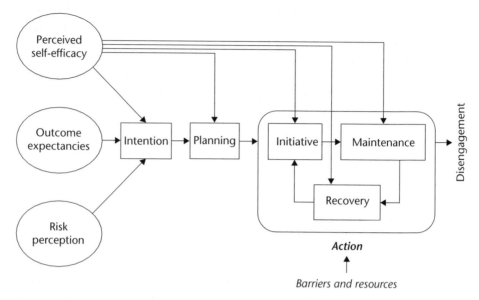

Figure 7.2   The Health Action Process Approach.

antecedent within the motivation phase. It may include not only the perceived severity of possible health threats, but also one's personal vulnerability
to fall prey to them. Risk perception in itself is insufficient to enable a person
to form an intention. Rather, it sets the stage for a contemplation process
and further elaboration of thoughts about consequences and competencies.
Similarly, *outcome expectancies* ("If I eat healthful foods, I will reduce my cardiovascular risk") are chiefly seen as being important in the motivation phase,
when a person balances the pros and cons of certain behavior consequences.
Further, one needs to believe in one's capability to perform a desired action
("I am capable of controlling my healthy diet in spite of sweet temptations"),
otherwise one will fail to initiate action. Outcome expectancies operate in
concert with *perceived self-efficacy*, both of which contribute substantially to the
forming of an intention (Schwarzer and Renner, 2000). Both resources are
needed, especially for implementing difficult or complex behaviors, such as
body weight control (Bagozzi and Edwards, 1999).

Post-intentional Volition Processes
After a person develops an inclination towards a particular health behavior,
the "good intention" has to be transformed into detailed instructions on how
to perform the desired action. The importance of *planning* has been emphasized by Gollwitzer (1999), who reviews research on what he calls "implementation intentions" (see also Gollwitzer and Oettingen, 2000). These plans
specify the *when*, *where*, and *how* of a desired action and carry the structure of
"When situation S arises, I will perform response R." Consequently, situational
circumstances or opportunities are cognitively linked to one's goal behavior.
It is argued that goals do not induce actions directly; rather, they need to

be mediated by highly specific plans (Taylor et al., 1998). For example, the pursuit of health promotion goals such as strenuous physical exercise, and disease-prevention goals such as cancer screening are facilitated by mental process simulation. Sheeran and Orbell (2000) asked women who were due for a cervical smear test to write down when, where, and how they will make an appointment. These women were more likely to actually attend for screening compared with controls who were equally motivated to attend, but who did not specify their implementation intention. Thus, a global intention can be specified by a set of subordinate intentions and action plans that contain proximal goals and algorithms of action sequences.

The volition process may be influenced by outcome expectancies, but it is more strongly affected by self-efficacy because the number and quality of action plans depend on one's perceived competence and experience. Self-efficacy beliefs influence the cognitive construction of specific action plans, for example by visualizing scenarios that may guide goal attainment (Bandura, 1997). These post-decisional, pre-actional cognitions are necessary for successful action because otherwise the person would act impulsively in a trial-and-error fashion, not knowing where to allocate the available resources.

If the appropriate opportunity for a desired action is clearly defined in terms of when, where, and how, the probability for procrastination is reduced. People take *initiative* when the critical situation arises and give it a try. This requires a firm self-belief in being capable of performing the action. People who do not hold such beliefs see little point in even trying.

Once an action has been initiated, it has to be controlled by cognitions in order to be *maintained* (unless it is purely habitual, e.g., brushing teeth). This is not achieved through a single act of will, but involves the development of self-regulatory skills and strategies. It embraces various means to influence one's own motivation and behaviors, such as the setting of attainable, proximal subgoals, creating incentives, drawing from an array of coping options, and mobilizing social support. The action has to be protected from being interrupted and abandoned prematurely due to incompatible competing intentions that may dominate an ongoing behavior. Meta-cognitive activity (e.g., monitoring one's self-regulatory strategies) is needed in order to complete the primary action and to suppress distracting secondary action tendencies. Daily physical exercise, for example, requires self-regulatory processes in order to secure effort, and persistence to keep adverse motivational tendencies at bay (such as the desire to eat, socialize, or sleep) until these tendencies are allowed to prevail for the required time period (see also Carver and Scheier, 1996; 1998). Perceived *self-efficacy* determines the amount of effort invested and the perseverance. People who harbor self-doubts are more inclined to anticipate failure scenarios, worry about possible performance deficiencies, and abort their attempts prematurely. Those with an optimistic sense of self-efficacy, on the other hand, visualize success scenarios that guide the action and let them persevere even in the face of obstacles. They recover quickly when running into unforeseen difficulties.

Adherence to a self-imposed health behavior is difficult because of fluctuations in performance such as improvements, plateaus, setbacks, and failures.

Hence, competent *relapse management* is needed to recover from setbacks. Some people rapidly abandon their newly adopted behavior when they fail to get quick results. When they enter high-risk situations (e.g., a bar where others smoke), they cannot resist due to a lack of self-efficacy. At this point, a belief in one's capability to recover is needed. In studying addictive behaviors, Marlatt et al. (1995) have suggested distinguishing between recovery self-efficacy, action self-efficacy, and coping self-efficacy. The authors argue that the competence to recover is different from the competence enlisted to commence an action. Restoration, harm reduction, and renewal of motivation are serviceable strategies within the context of health self-regulation.

Disengagement from the goal before achieving it can be evidence for lack of persistence and, thus, an indication of self-regulatory failure. In the case of repeated failures, disengagement or scaling back the goal becomes an option, which may be adaptive. For example, if the goal was set too high or if the situation has changed and becomes more difficult than before, it is seldom worthwhile to continue the struggle. In the case of health-compromising behaviors, giving up is not a tenable option. Better self-regulatory skills have to be developed and unique approaches to the problem need to be taken. The experience of failure can be a useful learning experience to build up more competence, under the condition that the individual makes a beneficial causal attribution of the episode and practices constructive self-talk to renew the motivation.

Phase-specific Self-efficacy: When Beliefs Make a Difference
Optimistic self-beliefs may be phase-specific within a self-regulatory cycle. For example, some people may have high confidence in their ability to set ambitious goals and to take initiative, but little confidence in their ability to maintain the desired behaviors. In contrast, others may have high confidence in their ability to resist temptation and to recover from setbacks, but little confidence in getting started. Thus, perceived self-efficacy is seen as functional at different levels and at different points in time within a self-regulatory goal attainment process. It might be useful to subdivide the construct in a phase-specific manner in order to characterize these functions (Dijkstra and de Vries, 2000; Marlatt et al., 1995). *Action self-efficacy* makes a difference in the pre-intentional phase. Individuals high in self-efficacy imagine success scenarios, anticipate potential outcomes of diverse strategies, and take the initiative in trying to adopt a new behavior (Bagozzi and Edwards, 2000). People with less self-efficacy, on the other hand, imagine failure scenarios, harbor self-doubts, and procrastinate. Those with high action self-efficacy choose to perform more challenging tasks (Bandura, 1997). They set higher goals for themselves and take the initiative more easily. *Coping self-efficacy*, on the other hand, describes optimistic beliefs about one's capability to deal with barriers that arise during the postintentional phase. A new health behavior might turn out to be much more difficult to adhere to than expected, but a self-efficacious person responds confidently with better strategies, more effort, and prolonged persistence to overcome such hurdles. Once an action has been taken, high coping self-efficacious persons invest more effort and persist

longer than those who are low in self-efficacy. When setbacks occur, they recover more quickly and maintain the commitment to their goals.

In order to examine the effects of social-cognitive factors on nutrition behaviors and corresponding behavioral intentions, a study was launched with 524 men and women with an average age of 43 years (Schwarzer and Renner, 2000). The study does not allow an experimental test of the HAPA model, but it does include some crucial variables, and, therefore, it permits the exploration of some of the proposed relationships and helps to establish empirically the conceptual distinction between action self-efficacy and coping self-efficacy. The study covers the three predictors within the pre-intentional phase (risk perception, outcome expectancies, and action self-efficacy) and the intention phase to adopt a healthy diet at Wave 1. The study also includes coping self-efficacy in the post-intentional phase half a year later, covering two preventive nutrition behaviors. It is assumed that behavioral intention and coping self-efficacy served as mediators linking the three predictors with two self-reported nutrition behaviors, namely low-fat and high-fiber dietary intake, six months later, at Wave 2. The questions are, in particular, how strong the associations will be and what kind of prediction pattern will emerge.

A set of 22 questionnaire items related to nutrition was designed to assess seven constructs, four at Time 1 and three at Time 2. Risk perception, outcome expectancies, action self-efficacy, and intentions were measured first, whereas coping self-efficacy, low-fat diet, and high-fiber diet were measured half a year later.

For the assessment of *comparative risk perception*, respondents were asked to estimate their risk for heart disease, high blood pressure, and a stroke. Responses were given on seven-point scales anchored at *much below average* (−3) and *much above average* (+3).

Outcome expectancies were measured by three items. Participants were asked, "What do you think will be the personal consequences for yourself if you adopt a low-fat, high-fiber diet?" After this header, responses were elicited to three specific questions: "If I stick to a low-fat, high-fiber diet, then . . . (a) I would feel physically more attractive, (b) mentally I would feel better, and (c) I would have no (or fewer) body weight problems."

The general stem for all perceived self-efficacy items was "How certain are you that you could overcome the following barriers?" *Action self-efficacy* consisted of two indicators: "I can manage to stick to healthful food, (a) . . . even if I have to make a detailed plan, (b) . . . even if I have to rethink my entire way of nutrition." *Coping self-efficacy* consisted of three indicators: "I can manage to stick to healthful food, (a) . . . even if I have to try several times until it works, (b) . . . even if I need a long time to develop the necessary routines, (c) . . . even if I do not receive a great deal of support from others when making my first attempts."

The *intention to adopt preventive nutrition habits* was assessed with four items: "I intend to eat only a very small amount of fat (such as saturated fat, cheese, butter) over the next months," "I intend to live a healthier life," "I intend to eat healthful foods over the next months," and "I intend to invest more into my health."

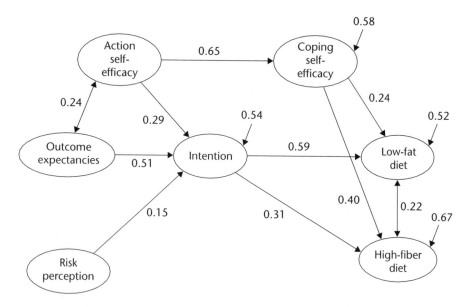

Figure 7.3 Causal model predicting preventive nutrition by phase-specific self-efficacy.

There were two dimensions of *nutrition behavior* half a year later. One related to a high-fiber diet with three items: "I eat a lot of fresh fruit and vegetables," "I observe a high vitamin diet," and "I stick to a balanced diet." The other dimension, related to a low-fat diet, contained four items: "I follow a low-fat diet," "When I eat milk products or drink milk, I choose low-fat products (such as low-fat milk or yogurt)," "I avoid foods with cholesterol," and "I am aware of my calorie intake."

To examine the associations between the variables, a structural equations approach was chosen. The model fit was good with $GFI = 0.98$, $RMR = 0.051$, $RMSEA = 0.038$ ($p = 0.73$), and $\chi^2 = 348.93$ ($df = 197$; $p < 0.001$) (Figure 7.3).

In the prediction of the intention, the hypothesized rank order was confirmed: (a) outcome expectancies (0.50), (b) self-efficacy (0.28), and (c) risk perception (0.15). The relationship between action self-efficacy (Time 1) and coping self-efficacy (Time 2) was 0.62. The latter, in conjunction with the intention, predicted the two behavior dimensions very well. Of the low-fat diet variation, 48 percent was accounted for, whereas of the high-fiber diet variation, 33 percent was accounted for by intention and coping self-efficacy. Low-fat diet was better predicted by the intention, whereas high-fiber diet was better predicted by coping self-efficacy.

All current popular health behavior theories suggest that an intention to change is probably the best predictor of subsequent behavior, unless unexpected barriers make the adoption of a health behavior unlikely. The present study has confirmed this assumption. The two nutrition behaviors were well predicted by the behavioral intention that the research participants had expressed half a year before.

A second assumption, based on the HAPA model, was the differential prediction within both the motivation phase and the volition phase. In the pre-intentional phase a weaker influence of perceived action self-efficacy on intentions was expected, compared to the influence of outcome expectancies. In the post-intentional phase, however, a stronger influence of perceived coping self-efficacy on behavior compared to that of outcome expectancies was assumed. Self-efficacious individuals are expected to develop more optimistic success scenarios for behavioral change, enhanced initiative, superior resistance in the face of temptation, and improved recovery after setbacks. Outcome expectancies, on the other hand, lose their importance at later stages of behavioral change, as confirmed by the present data.

Conclusions

Risk Communication or Resource Communication?

This chapter has described some social-cognitive factors that inhibit or promote individual health behavior change. Knowledge is certainly a precondition for health behavior change. In general, there is a great public interest in health-related information. Internet users, for example, who were asked about the future activities they intend to focus on, mentioned "health and medicine" as one of the top five areas (Brown, 1996). However, regardless of the vast amount of available information and attention it receives, appropriate health behavior change can only emerge if the information presented is processed accurately. Particular risk information can be multifaceted and complex, causing diverse misapprehension in the audience. To support comprehension, the public should be informed of the relative risk of acquiring one disease versus another, the relative impact of various risk factors over time, and the benefits derived from changing a targeted behavior.

To enhance perceived self-relevance of risk information, and in order to decrease defensive optimism, recipients should be informed about their risk relative to similar others, or, even better, should receive personalized risk information. Risk communicators could achieve quite different effects if they choose to describe the risk of one exposure in comparison to cumulative exposure. They could cast more or less favorable light on health-related behaviors, depending on the chosen length of the communicated time horizon. Considering the lifetime-cumulative risk of experiencing a stroke raises the perceived probability of disease and susceptibility, as opposed to only considering the risk over a five-year period. In view of that, the detrimental *effects of risk factors* could be emphasized by communicating the magnitude of harm in the long run. In contrast, the *effectiveness of protective measures* could be better communicated by using a shorter time frame. Becoming aware of one's own risk is indeed a necessary prerequisite, but by no means a sufficient one to motivate health behavior change. Following initial risk communication, it is mandatory to make people aware of their coping resources, such as their capability to change a refractory behavior. *Resource communication* is recommended at advanced stages of change. It shifts the focus towards the actual means and opportunities of behavior change as well as the optimistic beliefs of being competent to handle challenging risk situations. When people have reached a post-intentional stage, they need not be scared but rather encouraged to master their health goals.

Considering Stages of Health Behavioral Change

Interventions need to be theory-based and require scientific evaluation. Otherwise, the outcomes cannot be explained and accurately assessed in terms of those factors that may allow generalizations and could be adopted by others. Much progress has been achieved in the last decade. The ongoing debate on continuum models and stage models of health behavior change has sparked a great deal of good research and theoretical elaboration (for an overview see Armitage and Conner, 2000; Sutton, 2000; Wallston and Armstrong, 2002). The two major continuum models, the Protection Motivation Theory (PMT) and the Theory of Reasoned Action (TRA) or its variant Theory of Planned Behavior (TPB), are "intention models." They are designed to "predict" intentions, and they do this well. However, practically, this is mostly done in cross-sectional correlation studies. The models do not consider post-intentional processes, which can be seen as the main shortcoming (see Schwarzer, 1992). Stage models, in contrast, emphasize pre-intentional as well as post-intentional processes.

Stage models assume that behavior change involves movement through a sequence of discrete, qualitatively distinct, stages. Different patterns of predictors are believed to be relevant at different stages. Hence, people at one stage may require different interventions than people at another stage. The *transtheoretical model* (TTM; Prochaska et al., 1992; 1994; 1998) is the earliest and most popular of the stage models. It includes 15 constructs drawn from different theories. Thus, it is not parsimonious, and it suffers from a number of further problems, such as lack of standardized instruments, particularly for the five stages of change, logical flaws in the staging algorithms, poor specification of the causal relationships among the constructs, frequent misinterpretation of cross-sectional data on stages of change, and confusion about the nature of stage models and how they should be tested (Sutton, 2000; 2001).

The *precaution adoption process model* (PAPM; Weinstein, 1988; 1993; 2000; this volume) is a well-founded stage model that defeats the shortcomings of the TTM. So far, two of its stages have been experimentally confirmed (Weinstein et al., 1998a).

The *health action process approach* (HAPA; Schwarzer, 1992; 1999) is a hybrid model. It is conceptualized as two stages: the first one is a continuum phase, incorporating, more or less, the PMT and TPB constructs, and the second one a logical sequence of post-intentional processes. The idea was to adopt the strongest parts from earlier theories and arrive at a fruitful integration, conceptually based on Bandura's (1997) social-cognitive theory.

There is a large extent of similarity and overlap among constructs and among models, but there are also distinct features with clear strengths and weaknesses. It is of note that some parts of old theories can be converted into better founded and more recent constructs. Resolution of controversies requires clearer definitions of constructs and a more thorough examination of the validity of those constructs.

Stage models bear the potential of creating a rationale for stage-matched treatments that encourage or help individuals to get on track or master a difficult course of action. *Interventions* should be tailored to fit the needs of the recipients. According to the HAPA model, at least two different phases should be distinguished: a motivational or pre-intentional phase that results in intention formation, and a volitional or post-decisional phase that refers to the actual adoption and maintenance of a health behavior. For people who are in the pre-intentional phase, enhancing perceived vulnerability would be the first step, followed by improving outcome expectancies and action self-efficacy. For their counterparts in the post-intentional phase, it would be more suitable to enhance goal prioritization, implementation intentions, and action plans. Persons who are ready to act should be encouraged to form plans which specify when, where and how a desired action is to be undertaken. Forming plans depends to a large extent on action self-efficacy, since the latter establishes how challenging the chosen action will be, how much effort someone needs to invest, and how much persistence is necessary. People will not even try to enact behaviors they do not feel capable of performing. Resource communication, therefore, should lead to greater confidence in one's capability to control health-related behavior. This also applies to relapse management, after people have failed to maintain their desired health behaviors. Recovery self-efficacy is a valuable resource that needs to be developed and cultivated, particularly in those who strive to overcome their personal shortcomings, such as being dependent on addictive substances.

Acknowledgments

We would like to thank Kenneth Wallston and Jerry Suls for their helpful comments. We would also like to thank Tony Arthur, Judith Bäßler and Mary Wegner for their advice and support throughout the stages of drafting and editing.

The research was partly supported by the Deutsche Forschungsgemeinschaft (Grant Schw 208/11-01-03).

Correspondence concerning this chapter should be sent to: Brita Renner, Department of Psychologie, Ernst-Moritz-Arndt-Universität Greifswald, Franz-Mehringstr. 47, 17487 Greifswald, Germany; e-mail: renner@uni-greifswald.de

Note

1. Abraham and Sheeran (2000) based their calculation on different empirical studies. The explained variance in health behavior measures is calculated by squaring the correlation between behavioral intention and behavior and multiplying the sum by 100. For example, a correlation of 0.46 accounts for 21 percent of the variation.

References

Abraham, C., Norman, P., and Conner, M. (2000). Towards a psychology of health-related behavior change. In P. Norman, C. Abraham, and M. Conner (Eds.), *Understanding and Changing Health Behavior* (pp. 343–69). Amsterdam: Harwood Academic Publishers.

Abraham, C., and Sheeran, P. (2000). Understanding and changing health behavior: From health beliefs to self-regulation. In P. Norman, C. Abraham, and M. Conner (Eds.), *Understanding and Changing Health Behavior* (pp. 3–24). Amsterdam: Harwood Academic Publishers.

Armitage, C. J., and Conner, M. (2000). Social cognition models and health behaviour. *Psychology and Health*, 15, 173–89.

Armor, D. A., and Taylor, S. E. (1998). Situated optimism: Specific outcome expectancies and self-regulation. In M. P. Zanna (Ed.), *Advances in Experimental Social Psychology* (Vol. 30, pp. 309–79). New York: Academic Press.

Bagozzi, R. P., and Edwards, E. A. (1999). Goal-striving and the implementation of goal intentions in the regulation of body weight. *Psychology and Health*, 13, 593–621.

Bagozzi, R. P., and Edwards, E. A. (2000). Goal setting and goal pursuit in the regulation of body weight. In P. Norman, C. Abraham, and M. Conner (Eds.), *Understanding and Changing Health Behavior* (pp. 261–97). Amsterdam: Harwood Academic Publishers.

Bandura, A. (1997). *Self-efficacy: The Exercise of Control*. New York: Freeman.

Bandura, A. (2000). Health promotion from the perspective of social cognitive theory. In P. Norman, C. Abraham, and M. Conner (Eds.), *Understanding and Changing Health Behavior* (pp. 299–339). Amsterdam: Harwood Academic Publishers.

Bochow, M. (2000). Wie leben schwule Männer heute? [How do gay men live today?] *Bundesgesundheitsblatt, Gesundheitsforschung, Gesundheitsschutz*, 43, 677–82.

Brown, M. S. (1996). Polish and glitz aside, net resources fall short on the content yardstick. *Medicine on the Net*, 2, 7–8.

Carver, C. S., and Scheier, M. F. (1996). Self-regulation and its failures. *Psychological Inquiry*, 7, 32–40.

Carver, C. S., and Scheier, M. F. (1998). *On the Self-regulation of Behavior*. New York: Cambridge University Press.

Chapman, G. B., and Elstein, A. S. (2000). Cognitive processes and biases in medical decision making. In G. B. Chapman and F. A. Sonnenberg (Eds.), *Decision Making in Health Care* (pp. 183–210). Cambridge: Cambridge University Press.

Cioffi, D. (1991). Asymmetry of doubt in medical self-diagnosis: The ambiguity of "uncertain wellness". *Journal of Personality and Social Psychology*, 61, 969–80.

Conner, M., and Norman, P. (Eds.). (1996). *Predicting Health Behavior: Research and Practice with Social Cognition Models*. Buckingham, UK: Open University Press.

Courneya, K. S., Nigg, C. R., and Estabrooks, P. A. (2000). Relationships among the theory of planned behavior, stages of change, and exercise behavior in older persons over a three year period. In P. Norman, C. Abraham, and M. Conner (Eds.), *Understanding and Changing Health Behavior* (pp. 189–206). Amsterdam: Harwood Academic Publishers.

Covello, V. T. (1992). Risk communication: An emerging area of health communication research. In S. A. Deetz (Ed.), *Communication Yearbook* (Vol. 15, pp. 359–73). Newbury Park, CA: Sage.

Croyle, R. T. (1990). Biased appraisal of high blood pressure. *Preventive Medicine*, 19, 40–4.

Croyle, R. T., and Sande, G. N. (1988). Denial and confirmatory search: Paradoxical consequences of medical diagnosis. *Journal of Applied Social Psychology*, 18, 473–90.

Croyle, R. T., Sun, Y. C., and Hart, M. (1997). Processing risk factor information: Defensive biases in health-related judgments and memory. In K. J. Petrie, and J. A. Weinman (Eds.), *Perceptions of Health and Illness: Current Research and Applications* (pp. 267–90). Singapore: Harwood Academic Publishers.

Croyle, R. T., Sun, Y. C., and Louie, D. H. (1993). Psychological minimization of cholesterol test results: Moderators of appraisal in college students and community residents. *Health Psychology*, 12, 1–5.

DiClemente, C. C., and Prochaska, J. O. (1982). Self-change and therapy change of smoking behavior: A comparison of processes of change in cessation and maintenance. *Addictive Behaviors*, 7, 133–42.

Dijkstra, A., and De Vries, H. (2000). Self-efficacy expectations with regard to different tasks in smoking cessation. *Psychology and Health*, 15, 501–11.

Ditto, P. H., and Croyle, R. T. (1995). Understanding the impact of risk factor test results: Insights from a basic research program. In R. T. Croyle (Ed.), *Psychological Effects of Screening for Disease Prevention and Detection* (pp. 144–81). New York: Oxford University Press.

Ditto, P. H., Jemmott, J. B. III, and Darley, J. M. (1988). Appraising the threat of illness: A mental representational approach. *Health Psychology*, 7, 183–201.

Fortmann, S. P., Taylor, C. B., Flora, J. A., and Winkleby, M. A. (1993). Effects of community health education on plasma cholesterol levels and diet: The Stanford Five-City Project. *American Journal of Epidemiology*, 137, 1039–55.

Frank, E., Winkleby, M., Fortmann, S., and Farquhar, J. W. (1993). Cardiovascular disease risk factors: Improvements in knowledge and behavior in the 1980s. *American Journal of Public Health*, 83, 590–3.

Godin, G., and Kok, G. (1996). The theory of planned behavior: A review of its applications to health-related behaviors. *American Journal of Health Promotion*, 11, 87–97.

Gollwitzer, P. M. (1999). Implementation intentions: Strong effects of simple plans. *American Psychologist*, 54, 493–503.

Gollwitzer, P. M., and Oettingen, G. (2000). The emergence and implementation of health goals. In P. Norman, C. Abraham, and M. Conner (Eds.), *Understanding and Changing Health Behavior* (pp. 229–60). Amsterdam: Harwood Academic Publishers.

Hahn, A., and Renner, B. (1998). Perception of health risks: How smoker status affects defensive optimism. *Anxiety, Stress, and Coping*, 11, 93–112.

Hermand, D., Mullet, E., and Lavieville, S. (1997). Perception of the combined effects of smoking and alcohol on cancer risks in never smokers and heavy smokers. *Journal of Health Psychology*, 2, 481–91.

Herzog, T. A., Abrams, D. B., Emmons, K. M., Linnan, L. A., and Shadel, W. G. (1999). Do processes of change predict smoking stage movements? A prospective analysis of the transtheoretical model. *Health Psychology*, 18, 369–75.

Jeffery, R. W., French, S. A., and Rothman, A. J. (1999). Stage of change as a predictor of success in weight control in adult women. *Health Psychology*, 18, 543–6.

Jemmott, J. B., Ditto, P. H., and Croyle, R. T. (1986). Judging health status: Effects of perceived prevalence and personal relevance. *Journal of Personality and Social Psychology*, 50, 899–905.

Jimison, H. B., and Sher, P. (2000). Advances in presenting health information to patients. In G. B. Chapman and F. A. Sonnenberg (Eds.), *Decision Making in Health Care* (pp. 334–61). Cambridge, England: Cambridge University Press.

Kraft, P., Sutton, S. R., and McCreath-Reynolds, H. (1999). The transtheoretical model of behaviour change: Are the stages qualitatively different? *Psychology and Health*, 14, 433–50.

Lachendro, E., and Weinstein, N. D. (1982). Egocentrism as a source of unrealistic optimism. *Personality and Social Psychology Bulletin*, 8, 195–200.

Lichtenstein, S., Slovic, P., Fischhoff, B., Layman, M., and Combs, B. (1978). Judged frequency of lethal events. *Journal of Experimental Psychology: Human Learning and Memory*, 4, 551–78.

Linville, P. W., Fischer, G. W., and Fischhoff, B. (1993). AIDS risk perceptions and decision biases. In J. B. Pryor and G. D. Reeder (Eds.), *The Social Psychology of HIV Infection* (pp. 5–38). Hillsdale, NJ: Erlbaum.

Marlatt, G. A., Baer, J. S., and Quigley, L. A. (1995). Self-efficacy and addictive behavior. In A. Bandura (Ed.), *Self-efficacy in Changing Societies* (pp. 289–315). New York: Cambridge University Press.

McCaul, K. D., Thiesse-Duffy, E., and Wilson, P. (1992). Coping with medical diagnosis: The effects of at-risk versus disease labels over time. *Journal of Applied Social Psychology*, 22, 1340–55.

Niknian, M., Lefebvre, R. C., and Carleton, R. A. (1991). Are people more health conscious? A longitudinal study of one community. *American Journal of Public Health*, 81, 203–5.

Oldenburg, B., Glanz, K., and French, M. (1999). The application of staging models to the understanding of health behaviour change and the promotion of health. *Psychology and Health*, 14, 503–16.

Perloff, L. S., and Fetzer, B. K. (1986). Self-other judgments and perceived vulnerability to victimization. *Journal of Personality and Social Psychology*, 50, 502–10.

Prochaska, J. O., DiClemente, C. C., and Norcross, J. C. (1992). In the search of how people change: Applications to addictive behaviors. *American Psychologist*, 47, 1102–14.

Prochaska, J. O., Johnson, S., and Lee, P. (1998). The transtheoretical model of behavior change. In S. A. Shumacker, E. B. Schron, J. K. Ockene, and W. L. McBee (Eds.), *The Handbook of Health Behavior Change* (pp. 59–84). New York: Springer.

Prochaska, J. O., Velicer, W. F., Rossi, J. S. et al. (1994). Stages of change and decisional balance for 12 problem behaviors. *Health Psychology*, 13, 39–46.

Quinlan, K. B., and McCaul, K. D. (2000). Matched and mismatched interventions with young adult smokers: Testing a stage theory. *Health Psychology*, 19, 165–71.

Renner, B. (2001). Health behavior assessment. In N. J. Smelser and P. B. Baltes (Eds.), *The International Encyclopedia of the Social and Behavioral Sciences* (Vol. 10, pp. 6512–15). Oxford, England: Elsevier.

Renner, B., Knoll, N., and Schwarzer, R. (2000). Age and body weight make a difference in optimistic health beliefs and nutrition behaviors. *International Journal of Behavioral Medicine*, 7, 143–59.

Robert Koch Institut (2000). Sexuelles Risikoverhalten bei homosexuellen Männern in Deutschland [Sexual risk behavior among gay men in Germany]. *Epidemiologisches Bulletin*, 48, 379–86.

Sastre, M. T. M., Mullet, E., and Sorum, P. C. (1999). Relationship between cigarette dose and perceived risk of lung cancer. *Preventive Medicine: An International Journal Devoted to Practice and Theory*, 28, 566–71.

Schneiderman, L. J., and Kaplan, R. M. (1992). Fear of dying and HIV infection vs. hepatitis B infection. *American Journal of Public Health*, 82, 584–6.

Schwarzer, R. (1992). Self-efficacy in the adoption and maintenance of health behaviors: Theoretical approaches and a new model. In Schwarzer, R. (Ed.), *Self-efficacy: Thought Control of Action* (pp. 217–43). Washington, DC: Hemisphere.

Schwarzer, R. (1994). Optimism, vulnerability, and self-beliefs as health-related cognitions: A systematic overview. *Psychology and Health*, 9, 161–80.

Schwarzer, R. (1999). Self-regulatory processes in the adoption and maintenance of health behaviors. The role of optimism, goals, and threats. *Journal of Health Psychology*, 4, 115–27.

Schwarzer, R., and Fuchs, R. (1995). Changing risk behaviors and adopting health behaviors: The role of self-efficacy beliefs. In A. Bandura (Ed.), *Self-efficacy in Changing Societies* (pp. 259–88). New York: Cambridge University Press.

Schwarzer, R., and Fuchs, R. (1996). Self-efficacy and health behaviors. In M. Conner and P. Norman (Eds.), *Predicting Health Behaviour: Research and Practice with Social Cognition Models* (pp. 163–96). Buckingham, UK: Open University Press.

Schwarzer, R., and Renner, B. (2000). Social-cognitive predictors of health behavior: Action self-efficacy and coping self-efficacy, *Health Psychology*, 19, 487–95.

Shaklee, H., and Fischhoff, B. (1990). The psychology of contraceptive surprises: Cumulative risk and contraceptive effectiveness. *Journal of Applied Social Psychology*, 20, 385–403.

Sheeran, P., and Orbell, S. (2000). Using implementation intentions to increase attendance for cervical cancer screening. *Health Psychology*, 19, 283–9.

Siegrist, M., and Cvetkovich, G. (2000). Perceptions of hazards: The role of trust and knowledge. *Risk Analysis*, 20, 713–19.

Slovic, P., Fischhoff, B., and Lichtenstein, S. (1987). Behavioral decision theory perspectives on protective behavior. In N. D. Weinstein (Ed.), *Taking Care: Understanding and Encouraging Self-protective Behavior* (pp. 14–41). Cambridge, England: Cambridge University Press.

Strecher, V. J., and Kreuter, M. W. (1995). The psychological and behavioral impact of health risk appraisals. In R. T. Croyle (Ed.), *Psychological Effects of Screening for Disease Prevention and Detection* (pp. 126–43). New York: Oxford University Press.

Suls, J., and Wheeler, L. (2000). *Handbook of Social Comparison*. New York: Kluwer.

Sutton, S. R. (2000). A critical review of the transtheoretical model applied to smoking cessation. In P. Norman, C. Abraham, and M. Conner (Eds.), *Understanding and Changing Health Behavior* (pp. 207–25). Amsterdam: Harwood Academic Publishers.

Sutton, S. R. (2001). Health behavior, psychosocial theories of. In N. J. Smelser and P. B. Baltes (Eds.), *The International Encyclopedia of the Social and Behavioral Sciences* (Vol. 10, pp. 6499–6506). Oxford, England: Elsevier.

Taylor, K. M., and Shepperd, J. A. (1998). Bracing for the worst: Severity, testing, and feedback timing as moderators of the optimistic bias. *Personality and Social Psychology Bulletin*, 24, 915–26.

Taylor, S. E., Pham, L. B., Rivkin, I. D., and Armor, D. A. (1998). Harnessing the imagination: Mental stimulation, self-regulation, and coping. *American Psychologist*, 53, 429–39.

Thompson, S. C., Anderson, K., Freedman, D., and Swan, J. (1996). Illusions of safety in a risky world: A study of college students' condom use. *Journal of Applied Social Psychology*, 26, 189–210.

Velicer, W. F., DiClemente, C. C., Prochaska, J. O., and Brandenburg, N. (1985). Decisional balance measure for assessing and predicting smoking status. *Journal of Personality and Social Psychology*, 48, 1279–89.

Wallston, K. A. (2001). Control beliefs. In N. J. Smelser and P. B. Baltes (Eds.), *The International Encyclopedia of the Social and Behavioral Sciences* (Vol. 10, pp. 2724–26). Oxford, England: Elsevier.

Wallston, K., and Armstrong, C. (2002). Theoretically-based strategies for health behavior change. In M. P. O'Donnell (Ed.), *Health Promotion in the Workplace* (3rd edn., pp. 182–201). Albany, NY: Delmar.

Weinstein, N. D. (1980). Unrealistic optimism about future life events. *Journal of Personality and Social Psychology*, 39, 806–20.

Weinstein, N. D. (1988). The precaution adoption process. *Health Psychology*, 7, 355–86.

Weinstein, N. D. (1993). Testing four competing theories of health-protective behavior. *Health Psychology*, 12, 324–33.

Weinstein, N. D. (1998). Accuracy of smokers' risk perceptions. *Annals of Behavioral Medicine*, 20, 135–40.

Weinstein, N. D. (2000). Perceived probability, perceived severity, and health-protective behavior. *Health Psychology*, 19, 65–74.

Weinstein, N. D., and Klein, W. M. (1995). Resistance of personal risk perceptions to debiasing interventions. *Health Psychology*, 14, 132–40.

Weinstein, N. D., Lyon, J. E., Sandman, P. M., and Cuite, C. L. (1998a). Experimental evidence for stages of health behavior change: The precaution adoption process model applied to home radon testing. *Health Psychology*, 17, 445–53.

Weinstein, N. D., Rothman, A. J., and Sutton, S. R. (1998b). Stage theories of health behavior: Conceptual and methodological issues, *Health Psychology*, 17, 290–9.

Weinstein, N. D., and Sandman, P. M. (1992). A model of the precaution adoption process: Evidence from home radon testing. *Health Psychology*, 11, 170–80.

Whitley, B. E., and Hern, A. L. (1991). Perceptions of vulnerability to pregnancy and the use of effective contraception. *Personality and Social Psychology Bulletin*, 17, 104–10.

Winders, S. E., Kohler, C. L., Grimley, D. M., and Gallagher, E. A. (1999). Tobacco use prevention and cessation. In J. M. Raczynski and R. J. DiClemente (Eds.), *Handbook of Health Promotion and Disease Prevention.* (pp. 149–69). New York: Kluwer Academic Plenum Publishers.

Yates, J. F. (Ed.). (1992). *Risk-taking Behavior.* New York: Wiley.

PART II

Social-cognitive Processes in Health

CHAPTER 8

Common Sense Models of Illness: Implications for Symptom Perception and Health-related Behaviors

René Martin, Nan Rothrock,

University of Iowa

Howard Leventhal

Rutgers University

and

Elaine Leventhal

University of Medicine and Dentistry of New Jersey

Introduction

A large national survey recently found that more than 90 percent of women suffering from ovarian cancer had experienced symptoms prior to diagnosis (Goff et al., 2000). The survey results were startling to health care providers, who typically are taught that ovarian carcinoma is asymptomatic until very late in its progression (e.g., American College of Obstetricians and Gynecologists, 1999; Clement and Connor, 1998; Ihde and Longo, 1998; Young, 1998). As behavioral medicine researchers, the survey captured our attention because 70 percent of the respondents described experiencing symptoms for three months or longer, with 15 percent enduring symptoms for more than a year. In addition, a substantial proportion of the women reported that they had ignored their symptoms. The self-referral delay described by these patients is particularly troublesome, because survival rates decline precipitously as ovarian carcinoma advances (Boring et al., 1993).

Why would a woman suffering ovarian carcinoma delay in seeking medical intervention? The answer to this question is likely to be found in her common sense model of her symptoms; that is, in how she perceived and interpreted her symptoms, as well as in her emotional response to the symptom experience. Common sense models of illness involve a variety of processes, including cognitive representations, affective reactions, and contextual factors. This chapter will review what social and health psychologists know about how common sense models of health and illness influence symptom perception, illness self-management, and the utilization of health care services. We will begin by discussing the self-referral delay period and psychological processes in symptom perception. We will then turn our attention to Leventhal's Common Sense Model (CSM) of health and illness behavior (Brownlee et al., 2000; H. Leventhal, 1970; H. Leventhal and Diefenbach, 1991) as a framework for describing how cognitive and affective processes shape health and illness behaviors. Some of the processes we address initially may seem fairly asocial in nature. However, as the chapter progresses, it will become increasingly apparent that social psychological variables are extremely important in understanding how common sense models shape health and illness behaviors.

Self-referral Delay: The Layperson as Diagnostician

Let us return to the question of why so many of Goff et al.'s (2000) survey respondents were slow in seeking medical care. In discussing this question, it is helpful to begin by considering what happens during self-referral delay – that is, during the period of time between the onset of symptoms and the receipt of medical care. For the symptomatic individual, the self-referral delay period is not a time of passive waiting. Instead, it is characterized by active problem-solving behaviors. Three issues are addressed during self-referral delay (Safer et al., 1979). The first involves the appraisal of untoward somatic sensations. In other words, the initial question to be answered is, "Do these symptoms mean that I am ill?" For the typical respondent in Goff et al.'s (2000) study, the appraisal phase involved determining whether sensations such as abdominal bloating, discomfort, and indigestion implied the presence of some sort of dysfunction or disease. Given the ambiguous nature of many abdominal and gastrointestinal symptoms, it seems very likely that some of the survey respondents initially concluded that their symptoms did not necessarily mean that they were ill. This preliminary conclusion undoubtedly delayed their entry into the health care delivery system.

Even those women who realized that their symptoms reflected some sort of illness may have continued to delay before seeing a physician. Experience teaches us that that not every illness warrants medical attention. Medical visits are expensive, time-consuming and potentially painful or embarrassing.

Thus, the second issue to be addressed during the self-referral delay period is whether a perceived illness requires the services of a health care provider. More simply stated, "Given that I seem to be sick, do I need to see a doctor?" Alternatively, "Can I manage these symptoms on my own?" For some symptoms, the answer to such illness evaluation questions will be straightforward. If the jagged edge of a broken bone is protruding through the skin, the merits of expert intervention will seem obvious. However, for many symptoms, it may be challenging to identify the behavioral response that will be most effective in maintaining daily function. Often, the layperson may need to revisit or revise her understanding of the symptoms and her coping strategies multiple times before finding a satisfactory resolution. Thus, the illness evaluation phase can proceed quickly or slowly, depending on the circumstances.

If medical care is deemed appropriate, the final segment of self-referral delay involves making arrangements to actually receive health care. This would include activities such as scheduling an office visit or dialing "911" for an ambulance. Although there can be exceptions, especially in the context of socioeconomic barriers, the delay related to accessing medical care usually is small relative to the time invested in symptom appraisal and illness evaluation. For example, among victims of acute myocardial infarction (MI or heart attack), transportation to the hospital accounts for only a small proportion of the elapsed time between symptom onset and arrival in a hospital emergency room (Dracup and Moser, 1997). Along similar lines, only a very small proportion of the ovarian cancer patients in Goff et al.'s (2000) sample identified difficulty in scheduling a medical appointment as a contributory factor to diagnostic delay.

It should be apparent in our characterization of the activities that comprise the self-referral delay period, that the symptomatic layperson undergoes a sort of self-diagnostic process before ever coming into contact with a health care provider. The intellectual origins of this perspective can be found in Heider's (1958) naive epistemology. Just as Heider spoke of the "lay scientist," ordinary people can be said to function as "lay physicians." Much like a highly trained health care provider, laypeople notice and collect data regarding symptom onset, duration, and intensity. They also observe patterns of covariation that are used in attributing symptoms to possible causal forces. Just as a doctor might prescribe a drug or a surgical procedure for a patient, laypeople prescribe all sorts of treatments for themselves (e.g., tolerating uncomfortable sensations, self-medication, the use of hot or cold packs). The purpose of these self-care strategies is to maintain function and equilibrium in daily life. Finally, laypeople frequently speak to family members and friends about symptoms. In these lay consultations, ordinary people seek information, comparison opportunities and social support, much as would a trained physician who confers with her expert colleagues. Overall, the lay response to symptoms can be viewed as a self-regulatory process (Cameron et al., 1993; H. Leventhal, 1970; H. Leventhal and Diefenbach, 1991; H. Leventhal et al., 1980), directed toward the maintenance or restoration of function.

In appreciating the behaviors of the lay physician, it becomes apparent that, in many ways, the most interesting aspects of symptom interpretation and management occur *outside* the context of the health care delivery system. For example, abdominal distress and bloating might suggest any number of inter- pretations, including the transient effects of a stressful day, intolerance for foods containing lactose, infection by a microorganism or a toxin from tainted food, hormonal fluctuations, or – as was the case for Goff et al.'s respondents – even an ovarian tumor. The meaning attached to abdominal symptoms by any given individual will be determined, in large part, by the social and environmental context in which those symptoms occur. Professional health care providers become involved in the process only when the symptoms are understood by laypeople in a manner that is consistent with assuming the role of patient. Once expert treatment has been sought, the views and values of ordinary people will continue to be critical in determining treatment implementation, compliance and outcome.

Fundamental Psychological Processes in Symptom Perception

As described above, the early phase of self-referral delay is characterized by the appraisal of symptoms. Before proceeding further, we should consider how psychological processes influence the perception of symptoms. When someone complains about a disruptive somatic sensation, they are commun- icating information about a symptom (Cameron et al., 1993). For example, an elderly woman might complain of breathlessness. Her perception of this symptom originates with the detection of sensory information related to the presence of fluid in the alveoli of her lungs; her central nervous system will integrate and organize this sensory input. Sensation is a data driven phenom- enon and it represents a bottom-up process in symptom perception. However, as we will see, top-down processes (e.g., attention, expectations) also make important contributions to the perception of symptoms (Bishop, 1991; Brownlee et al., 2000).

Daily life bombards us with sensory input, including ongoing informa- tion about the position and status of our bodies. We are fortunate that not every somatic sensation is interpreted to be a symptom. Stable and repetitive somatic sensations, such as the movement of air through the nostrils and the expansion of the chest cavity with every breath, are unlikely to be perceived as symptoms unless they present with novel features. If that is the case, the sensations will attract attention and be further processed at the cortical level. For the elderly woman in our example, breathlessness primarily is of concern because it is disruptive. Shortness of breath may prevent her from climbing a flight of stairs or from sleeping comfortably. Breathlessness also may elicit feelings of anxiety, making it difficult for her to concentrate on daily activities.

The disruptive nature of symptoms means that they function as a sort of early warning system for the body. The perception of symptoms raises the specter that something is amiss in the body's function. It is notable that the absence of symptoms can be devastating (e.g., people who lack pain sensation easily develop severe injuries). Symptoms consequently play a prominent role in our conceptualizations of both health and illness. In lay definitions, to be sick *is* to experience symptoms (Borawski et al., 1996; Idler et al., 1999; Lau, 1997; Lau et al., 1989). In contrast, healthy people are thought of as symptom-free by both laypeople and medical care practitioners (Bauman, 1961; Laffrey, 1986; Natapoff, 1978), although as we discuss later, this is not always the case. Lay descriptions of symptoms and illness tend to be dominated by physical maladies. However, laypeople also treat disruptive psychological phenomena, such as anhedonia or hallucinations, as symptoms (Lau, 1997; Lau et al., 1989).

Another critical aspect of the symptom construct is that symptom reports convey fundamentally subjective information. If our elderly woman seeks medical attention for her breathlessness, an emergency room nurse might measure her blood pressure and auscultate rales in the lower lobes of her lungs. In this example, only the report of breathlessness is a symptom. The blood pressure reading and abnormal breath sounds instead represent signs. Signs are objective indices of pathology and health care professionals are expert observers and interpreters of signs. Signs are present or absent and subsequent trained observers can verify the identification of a sign. Symptoms, on the other hand, reflect subjective perceptions. Thus, the only available expert who can speak to our elderly woman's breathlessness is the woman herself (Marchant-Haycox and Salmon, 1997; Shorter, 1992; 1995). Her perception of breathlessness is meaningful, even if the health care provider's assessment ultimately fails to identify any abnormal signs.

Although symptoms are grounded in somatic sensations, the salience of symptoms varies as a function of the situation. In his competition-of-cues model, Pennebaker (1982) proposed that somatic sensations are less likely to be noticed and reported in engaging environments. This has been tested in the laboratory by manipulating attentional focus. Subjects report more symptoms when instructed to focus on internal sensations, such as breathing, than when asked to attend to the external environment (Fillingim and Fine, 1986; Padgett and Hill, 1989; Pennebaker and Lightner, 1980; Watson and Pennebaker, 1991). The competition-of-cues effect is not limited to the laboratory; dull occupational and residential environments also are associated with increased symptom reports (Moos and VanDort, 1977; National Center for Health Statistics, 1980; Wan, 1976). The competition-of-cues model illustrates how attention functions as a top-down process in symptom perception. Variations in the availability of attentional resources can mean that the same symptom that attracts considerable attention in a non-demanding environment might go unnoticed in a busier context. The effect of attention on the prominence of symptoms also means that manipulating cognitive load (e.g., through distraction) can be a useful tool for symptom management.

Symptom complaints are a hallmark of health care visits. Almost all patients who seek medical attention report suffering symptoms (Berkanovic et al.,

1981; Cameron et al., 1993; Costa and McCrae, 1980; E. Leventhal et al., 1996; Stoller, 1997). Yet, health care providers evaluate only a small proportion of symptomatic people. Ostensibly healthy people commonly report a wide variety of symptoms (Bishop, 1984; Kutner and Gordon, 1961; Pennebaker, 1982; Safer et al., 1979). Although these symptoms sometimes cause substantial discomfort and disruption, it appears that less than half of symptom episodes lead to self-referral behavior (Scambler et al., 1981; Sorofman et al., 1990).

Symptoms can be unreliable indicators of the need for medical attention. Symptom intensity often is a poor predictor of either the presence or severity of pathology. For example, a number of sexually transmitted infections, such as chlamydia, have few symptoms. Similarly, initial infection with HIV typically is symptom free. On the other hand, a sinus headache may be brutally painful, but unrelated to serious pathology.

Consequently, it is difficult for laypeople to identify which symptoms demand medical attention. Errors in self-referral judgment are common. Although laypeople cope with many, if not most, symptoms independently and effectively (Hannay and Maddox, 1976; Ingham and Miller, 1979; Schober and Lacroix, 1991; White et al., 1961), symptoms sometimes trigger unnecessary medical care visits. For example, a significant number of patients seek care for minor complaints that would have been more appropriately managed at home (National Center for Health Statistics, 1980). In addition, it often is not possible for physicians to identify any veridical pathology underlying patients' symptoms (Backett et al., 1954; Barsky, 1981; Kroenke and Mangelsdorff, 1989). To borrow the language of signal detection theory (Green and Swets, 1974), the costs of such "false alarms" are high. Unnecessary medical visits drain time, effort, and financial resources and needlessly place patients at risk of iatrogenic complications (Peters et al., 1998).

To continue with our analogy to signal detection theory, "misses" also occur when ordinary people evaluate symptoms. That is, laypeople often delay in seeking medical care – or even fail entirely to seek medical attention for symptoms that reflect serious pathology. For example, Ingham and Miller (1979) found that a remarkable proportion of people neglected to seek care for serious symptoms that would have benefited from medical attention. Heart attack victims provide another excellent example of "misses" in the lay evaluation of symptoms. The average layperson is fluent in identifying symptoms of a heart attack (Goff et al., 1998), yet a substantial proportion of myocardial infarction victims delay several hours or longer after the onset of acute symptoms before seeking potentially life-saving medical intervention (Goff et al., 1995). Along similar lines, many of the ovarian cancer patients described in our opening example reported ignoring symptoms for some period of time prior to seeking medical evaluation (Goff et al., 2000). To summarize, the association between symptoms and seeking medical attention is complex. Important symptoms sometimes are overlooked, whereas resources often are invested unnecessarily in the evaluation and management of trivial symptoms.

The Common Sense Model (CSM) of Health and Illness Behavior

According to the CSM, two systems – cognitive and affective – make independent and potentially interactive contributions to health and illness behavior (Brownlee et al., 2000; H. Leventhal, 1970; H. Leventhal and Diefenbach, 1991). In discussing the role of cognition in determining health behaviors, we will address the content and decision-making implications of illness representations. We also will consider the roles of fear and negative mood states as affective processes that influence health and illness behaviors.

The Role of Illness Representations in Common Sense Models of Illness

Cameron et al. (1993) provide an excellent example of how symptom representations determine health care seeking behavior. In a large sample of community-residing adults, participants who sought medical care were interviewed regarding their symptoms, moods, and illness representations. Care-seekers were matched on age, sex, and health status to other adults who had not sought care. Care-seekers consistently reported symptoms; however, many control participants reported symptoms as well. Thus, the mere presence of symptoms was not sufficient to provoke self-referral behavior. A number of differences emerged when Cameron et al. compared the illness representations of care-seekers versus controls. A strong predictor of self-referral behavior was perceived seriousness of the symptoms, a finding that also has been observed by others (Janz and Becker, 1984; Mora et al., 2002). Cameron et al. additionally found that the cognitive representations of care-seekers were more detailed than those held by their symptomatic, but non-care-seeking counterparts. Care-seekers described their symptoms as more uncomfortable and disruptive than did symptomatic controls. Care-seekers further seemed to have devoted more thought to the potential consequences of their symptoms. Care-seekers reported engaging in more symptom self-care behavior than did controls. Perhaps not surprisingly, they were dissatisfied with the outcome of these self-care activities. E. Leventhal and Crouch (1997) also found that unsatisfactory self-care outcomes were related to seeking medical care, as was the inability to generate a meaningful label for the symptoms.

Mora et al.'s (2002) recent findings add to our understanding of illness representations and care-seeking behavior. These researchers considered how two stable attributes of the self, trait negative affect (NA) and self-assessed health (SAH), were related to self-referral behavior. Four features of the illness episode were related to care-seeking: symptom severity, novelty, duration, and symptom-related worry. What is especially important about Mora et al.'s findings is that self-referral primarily was driven by participants' understanding of features of the current illness episode. Trait NA was unrelated to care-seeking for both acute and chronic illnesses (and we will have more to say about trait NA below). SAH did predict care-seeking for chronic problems, but its effects were more modest than those observed for representational factors (i.e., the perceived severity, novelty and duration of symptoms).

Components of Illness Representations

The variables associated with care-seeking all reflect dimensions of lay illness representations. In broad terms, illness representations typically incorporate five types of information, including symptom labels, causal attributions, perceived consequences, temporal expectations, and symptom management beliefs (Baumann et al., 1989; Lau, 1997; Meyer et al., 1985; Scharloo and Kaptein, 1997; Skelton and Croyle, 1991). The tangible, sensory experience of a symptom is named or labeled. The symptom label itself provides an abstract, symbolic representation that is useful for communicating symptom information to others. Symptom labels are derived, at least in part, from prototypes based upon past experiences with the manifestations of various disorders (Bishop, 1991; Bishop et al., 1987; Bishop and Converse, 1986).

Causal attributions represent the layperson's assessment of the likely origin of the symptoms. As previously described, patterns of covariation in the environment can provide salient cues for the layperson struggling to explain a symptom experience. Perceived consequences reflect lay beliefs about what is likely to happen if the symptoms are left unchecked, in both the short and long term. Illness representations also include a temporal component, such as how long it takes to develop a disease, how long a symptom episode is likely to last, and how long it should take for self-care or medical treatment to produce a change. Finally, people also hold beliefs about strategies likely to yield symptom relief or even cure. Biomedical treatments typically are viewed as most acceptable in industrialized nations (Peters et al., 1998). However, the popularity of complimentary and alternative medicine treatments (e.g., chiropractic, relaxation, imagery, herbal supplements) has risen dramatically in recent years in both the United States and European countries (Eisenberg et al., 1993; Spencer and Jacobs, 1999). As will be discussed at greater length, culture plays an important role in determining the strategies people view to be appropriate for symptom management.

Behavioral Implications of Illness Representations

The five components of illness representations are interrelated and function as implicit hypotheses with behavioral implications. These associations can be thought of as "if-then" rules (Anderson, 1983, 1990; Anderson and Lebiere, 1998). In this view, the illness representation provides a prominent goal (the "if" dimension of the equation), which is addressed by the ensuing behavioral response (the "then" dimension). "If-then" rules connect symptom representations to plans for performing specific procedures in the individual's current environment. For example, if dizziness and muscle weakness are attributed to the fatigue of moving heavy boxes, the sufferer may anticipate that the discomfort will resolve with fluids and a good night of sleep. If the dizziness and weakness are still present the following morning, it probably will be necessary to reevaluate the symptom label and attribution. If the same dizziness and weakness are attributed to a possible stroke, then seeking medical care becomes an urgent priority. The victim now will perceive the symptoms to be life threatening. The "if-then" conceptualization is useful in illustrating how expectancy violations lead to health care seeking behavior. For example, self-referral is extremely likely for symptoms that exceed their expected duration; in other words (Mora et al., 2002), "*if* these symptoms last too long, *then* I will call a doctor." As another example, Johnson and King (1995) found that myocardial infarctions were particularly likely to delay in seeking medical care if their cardiac symptoms deviated from their expectations about the typical heart attack (e.g., "*If* I don't have crushing pain in the middle of my chest, *then* this must not be a heart attack."). Johnson and King's findings illustrate how laypeople sometimes have well-developed schemas about particular illnesses – unfortunately these schemas can actually reduce the likelihood of self-referral if personal symptoms are schema-inconsistent.

Sometimes people fail to connect symptoms to labels or to elaborate upon the likely cause or consequences of symptoms. If the representation of a disease threat is fuzzy or incoherent, there will be no motivation to select or perform any procedure directed at symptom or disease management. This is well illustrated by patients who fail to adhere to treatments during the symptom-free episodes of chronic conditions, such as asthma or congestive heart failure. Both conditions produce an ongoing array of low level and seemingly unchanging symptoms that may fly below the patient's "symptom radar." In other words, baseline symptoms may go largely unnoticed or unlabeled. The net result is that the patient fails to generate or implement plans for chronic disease management; instead, plans focus on seeking emergency intervention for severe disease exacerbations.

From the perspective of a health care provider, a layperson's interpretation of symptoms might be grossly inaccurate. Yet, distortions do not render lay health beliefs obsolete. Illness representations determine the response to symptoms, even when those naive theories are idiosyncratic or downright peculiar. For example, as a child, one of the authors was told by a pastor's wife that the psychological disorders suffered by the residents of a local mental health institution represented punishments sent by God. A psychiatrist or other health care provider would have found the woman's common sense model to be seriously flawed. Nonetheless, her naive theory of mental illness dictated that the institution's residents required prayer and self-discipline, rather than medications or psychotherapy.

Problems may arise when there is a mismatch between a patient's representation of his or her illness and the illness conceptualization held by the relevant health care providers. For example, during one of her first days as a cardiology nurse, one of the authors was dismayed to discover that a patient had been having anginal discomfort for an hour or more, even though he had answered "no" when asked if he was having any "chest pain." Once his discomfort had been relieved by nitroglycerine, the author asked the patient why he had not spoken up earlier. The bewildered patient answered that "it wasn't pain; it was more of a squeezing." The author quickly learned to initiate conversations with patients that elicited their personal labels for their cardiac pain, as well as explaining that the nurses and doctors tended to use the words "chest pain" as a generic phrase covering a broad array of cardiac symptoms. Although few studies speak to the issue of fit between the illness representations held by patients versus health care providers, there is suggestive evidence that a disjunction in symptom or illness models can have consequences for the patients' well-being. For example, Cohen et al. (1994) compared the explanatory models held by diabetics and their health care practitioners. Significant differences were found, especially with regard to disease etiology, pathophysiology, severity, and symptom presentations, and there was a trend for better patient/practitioner model congruence to be related to normal serum glucose levels.

The failure to integrate symptoms into illness representations may help explain why seemingly important symptoms sometimes are ignored. In a sense, these symptoms are "un-interpreted." That is, they are not linked to an illness label or integrated into a meaningful naive theory. To return to our discussion of women with ovarian cancer, many of the symptoms they recalled were troublesome in that they were so very ordinary. People suffering congestive heart failure (CHF) are in a similar problematic situation because the most salient symptoms are either routine in daily life (e.g., fatigue) or slow to change (e.g., increasing pedal edema) and less easily linked to a disease episode. Without labels and meaningful interpretations, the symptoms are disregarded and go unmanaged – even though these same people effectively manage other symptoms which have been labeled and linked to effective control procedures.

The Symmetry Hypothesis

It seems quite straightforward that symptom perception leads to evaluation and decision-making within the context of illness representations. It may seem more surprising, however, that illness representations can provide the basis for the perception of symptoms per se. In other words, illness representations can generate the expectation that symptoms *should* be perceived in certain situations. The symmetry hypothesis captures this reciprocal association between illness representations and symptoms. For example, a hyperlipidemic patient with a new prescription for atorvastatin (a cholesterol-lowering agent) might look up information about the new medication on the Internet. There he will learn that muscle weakness and pain can be a side effect of the drug, albeit uncommon. This knowledge may cause him to be unusually vigilant in monitoring the state of his muscles and minor sensations that previously would have gone unnoticed now may be more likely to be labeled as "weakness" or "pain." Along similar lines, hypertensives routinely report symptoms such as face flushing and headache – even though these symptoms are uncorrelated with blood pressure fluctuations and hypertension is known to be an asymptomatic disorder (Baumann and Leventhal, 1985; Meyer et al., 1985). This suggests that the idea that illnesses are reflected in symptoms is so strongly engrained in our common sense models, that it is difficult for laypeople to understand asymptomatic disease states. We appear to manufacture symptoms consistent with our understanding of the disease label. This phenomenon also has been demonstrated in the laboratory. Bauman et al. (1989) provided research participants with (bogus) elevated blood pressure readings. The participants subsequently reported symptoms they believed to be indicative of hypertension.

Decision Rules in the Evaluation of Symptoms

Some of the most interesting research about common sense models of illness has demonstrated how laypeople appear to use heuristics or decision rules to evaluate symptoms more quickly and efficiently. This work underscores two fundamental ideas. First, we use cognitive resources strategically whenever possible (Fiske and Taylor, 1991). Second, we reason about health and illness very much as we process information and make judgments in other domains. This similarity, however, should not obscure the fact that the content and procedures of illness cognition are shaped by the disease experienced, the physiological operation of the body in response to pathogens, and the socio-cultural myths and institutions that have been created over the centuries to manage these biological threats.

Several illness-related decision rules have been identified. These decision rules function as rules of thumb or heuristics that increase the speed and efficiency of symptom evaluation. For example, when mild symptoms develop gradually, laypeople tend to explain those symptoms in terms of normal aging rather than illness (the *age-illness rule*; Prohaska et al., 1987). The *prevalence rule* describes how people tend to assume that common health threats are fairly minor, whereas rare ailments are judged to be more serious (Ditto and Jemmott, 1989). The *stress-illness rule* reflects the classic discounting effect from attribution theory (Kelley, 1967). That is, if symptoms co-vary with troublesome life events, the symptoms tend to be attributed to stress, rather than to illness. Laypeople are especially likely to use the stress-illness rule when explaining the recent onset of ambiguous symptoms (Cameron et al., 1995).

People sometimes wish to avoid the effortful evaluation of ambiguous symptoms entirely. For example, older adults may entrust the responsibility for symptom evaluation and decision-making to health care providers, rather than straining their own more limited cognitive and physical energies (the *conservation rule*); as a consequence, their use of medical care is swift in comparison to that of middle-aged adults and less likely to be deterred by the fear of receiving a threatening diagnosis (E. Leventhal and Crouch, 1997; E. Leventhal et al., 1993). Conservation-related beliefs also may shape other health-related behaviors. For example, a cardiac patient who believes that strenuous activity or emotion will trigger an anginal episode is likely to conserve energy by avoiding exercise and excitement.

The decision rules described above usually generate reasonable lay diagnoses and self-management strategies. However, as with any heuristic processing, the age-illness, prevalence, stress-illness, and conservation rules can contribute either to prolonged self-referral delay or the unnecessary utilization of health care services. Along similar lines, a self-imposed invalidism in response to symptoms is likely to inhibit finding suitable replacements for activities abandoned due to illness and add to the risk of progressive disease (Zimmer et al., 1997; Duke et al., 2001).

The Role of Affect in Common Sense Models of Illness

Thus far, we have emphasized cognitive processes in the lay evaluation of symptoms. However, symptoms are accompanied by affective responses as well. Symptoms may elicit fear, anxiety, discouragement, annoyance, or a host of other emotional states. In addition to implementing action plans intended to relieve the symptoms themselves, the symptomatic layperson also will be motivated to moderate his or her emotional distress. For example, women with moderate levels of worry about developing breast cancer are more likely to engage in breast self-examination and to receive mammography screenings than those who are unconcerned (Diefenbach et al., 1999; McCaul et al., 1998). In addition to facilitating early detection of pathology, these behavioral strategies also serve to regulate the women's worry and anxiety.

As noted previously, the CSM proposes that affect and cognition can have independent effects on health and illness behaviors. Therefore, affective and cognitive responses to symptoms may or may not be compatible. For example, a person might intellectually understand that a symptom (e.g., bloody stools or a suspicious lump) could have serious consequences if left untreated. This belief might motivate care-seeking in the interests of early detection (as in the McCaul et al. study described above). However, for some people, the fear of potentially receiving an ominous diagnosis (e.g., cancer) actually might inhibit self-referral behavior. Research on the effects of emotion on symptom perception and illness behaviors has emphasized the roles of fear and negative affect.

Using Fear to Motivate Health-related Behaviors

It is extremely tempting for health care providers to use fear in an attempt to motivate their patients, providing detailed information about gum disease, lung cancer, and an endless array of other dire consequences. Fear-related messages are a potentially useful tool. Early research on the fear-drive model taught us two important lessons (Dollard and Miller, 1950; Miller, 1951).

First, fear responses can be classically conditioned to environmental stimuli. Second, fear acts as a drive state and energizes behaviors oriented toward fear reduction, which then are reinforced and learned through operant conditioning processes. However, simply eliciting fear, in and of itself, is unlikely to be effective in triggering health-related behaviors.

Research on the effects of fear communications has determined that effective messages must include two components (Leventhal et al., 1965; 1967). As an initial step, the message must present a threat to health that is viewed as personally relevant by the recipient. This component of the message typically is the source of fear and the fear must be linked (i.e., conditioned) to the threat. The message also must include a tangible plan of action that provides an effective avenue for fear management. For example, a dentist might show a patient graphic photographs of gums ravaged by gingivitis and resulting tooth loss. If the message stops at this point, the patient simply will be afraid and perhaps repulsed by the illustrations. But, if the dentist makes it clear that feelings of fear (and perhaps disgust and other negative emotions) are indeed reasonable reactions to gingivitis, that gingivitis is the appropriate source of fear, and follows this association with a simple action plan of tooth brushing and flossing to avoid gingivitis, that patient may very well be motivated to adopt these inexpensive, modest effort procedures. The failure to link the negative emotional response to a specific, avoidable outcome and the failure to combine this association with an action plan for threat management leaves the patient open to a wide range of alternatives for ameliorating his or her distress – including avoiding future interactions with the dentist. Thus, fear messages are most effective in motivation health behaviors when the fear is linked to an appropriate cognition and combined with a clear action plan. Free-floating fear that is unattached to a source of danger and or linked to appropriate avoidance behaviors is of little benefit for motivating health behaviors.

Negative Emotions and Common Sense Models of Illness

Fears of gingivitis or other threatening health outcomes are linked to specific sources and differ therefore from other "person-based" measures of fear, such as neuroticism and NA. NA is a broad construct that incorporates specific types of related emotions, such as sadness, anger, anxiety, and fear (Watson and Clark, 1992). NA can be experienced either at the state or trait level. "Trait NA" and "neuroticism" are used interchangeably as labels for stable individual differences in the propensity to experience negative emotional states. From the CSM perspective, individual difference measures, such as NA, are important inasmuch as they influence the effects of affective processes in health and illness behavior.

Certain studies have reported a seemingly paradoxical pattern of findings with regard to NA and health-related variables. In these studies, trait NA or neuroticism is positively correlated with subjective symptom complaints, but unrelated to objective markers of health (Costa and McCrae, 1980; 1985;

1987; Pennebaker, 1982; Watson and Pennebaker, 1989; 1991). This series of findings led to the formulation of the symptom perception hypothesis, which proposes that highly neurotic people either exaggerate the importance or intensity of their somatic sensations or perhaps even offer bogus symptom complaints (Watson and Pennebaker, 1989; 1991). The over-reporting of symptoms by negatively affective people may reflect a tendency among these individuals to be internally focused and highly attuned to somatic sensations. In addition, high NA individuals chronically monitor the environment for potential problems (Cloninger, 1987; Gray, 1982; 1985; Pennebaker, 1989; Tellegen, 1985) and thus may be inclined to interpret ambiguous stimuli, such as somatic sensations, as threatening (Barsky and Klerman, 1983; Costa and McCrae, 1985; Watson and Clark, 1984; Watson and Pennebaker, 1991). The symptom perception hypothesis has had at least two important effects on health psychology research. First, the hypothesis implies that studies of the relationship between stress and illness should control for NA as a nuisance variable (Davison and Pennebaker, 1996; Watson and Pennebaker, 1991). In addition, the symptom perception hypothesis highlighted the importance of using objective indices to assess health, rather than merely self-report variables.

There are several lines of evidence that suggest that the relationship between NA and symptom perception is more complex than initially conceptualized. First, some investigators do find that NA predicts objective health outcomes. For example, a number of studies have reported that anxiety, which can be thought of as a dimension of NA, increases the risk of heart disease (see review by Kubzansky et al., 1998). Depression, another component of NA, also has been found to predict disease longitudinally (Aneshensel et al., 1984). Level of NA predicted nasal congestion and sneezing in a study by Cohen et al., (1995), in which subjects were experimentally exposed to viruses in a "cold laboratory." Finally, E. Leventhal et al. (1996) found that state negative mood predicted longitudinal symptom complaints in two samples of elderly adults, even after controlling for baseline symptoms. They proposed that state NA might be related to reductions in immune resistance, thus generating increased symptom complaints over time.

Second, trait NA is not always positively correlated with symptom complaints. For example, in the longitudinal study of elderly adults described above, Leventhal et al. (1996) found no association between trait NA and prospective symptom reports. Instead, symptoms complaints sometimes are found to be more closely related to veridical pathology than to trait NA. Along these lines, Smith et al. (1995) found that disease severity was a better predictor of discomfort and impairment among persons with rheumatoid arthritis than was trait NA. Diefenbach et al. (1996) similarly found that trait NA was unrelated to longitudinal complaints of flu-like symptoms among adults who recently had received inoculations. In an ongoing project by one of the authors, trait NA shows no association with the number or severity of symptoms reported by myocardial infarction patients.

It is not entirely clear how to resolve these divergent bodies of evidence. However, it seems possible that extant measures of trait NA may be capturing at least two rather different and independent processes. First, NA may act as a sort of interpretive filter for the processing of somatic information. Second, NA may be associated with physiologic hyper-reactivity. In certain low-level situations – such as cross-sectional, retrospective accounts of ambiguous symptoms among healthy subjects – NA acts as a filter, which directs attention to, memory for, and labeling of somatic experience. For the subjects, there is nothing about this low-level scenario that provokes physiologic reactivity and so NA is unrelated to more objective indices of health. This characterization of NA is consistent with Watson and Pennebaker's symptom perception hypothesis.

However, other situations involve a challenge (e.g., undergoing a medical procedure), which elicits high levels of physiologic reactivity among negatively affective individuals (e.g., Suls et al., 1998; Thayer et al., 1996). As a function of hyper-reactivity, high NA subjects will actually experience more somatic sensations and symptoms than their low NA counterparts. In addition, the physiologic consequences of reactivity on the immune and cardiovascular systems may engender pathology (and associated symptoms) for those with high NA. As an example of a mid-level medical stressor, women high in trait NA showed more physiological responses and reported more symptoms in response to tamoxifen (a single hormonal agent) administration then did low NA women (Cameron et al., 1998). It should be noted that the interpretive filter of NA could operate as well in this situation, accentuating symptom perception and labeling.

Finally, both the filtering and reactivity dimensions of NA may be undetectable in instances of severe pathology, such as a myocardial infarction or rheumatoid arthritis. In this scenario, variability is reduced and research subjects are at the ceiling of somatic experience. For example, an extremely powerful intervention, such as the four and five drug infusions used in cancer chemotherapy, may override any individual differences in reporting chemotherapeutic side effects because both low and high NA patients will respond maximally to the challenge (Rabin et al., 2001).

To summarize, it seems plausible that, depending on the situation, (1) trait NA may predict symptom reports but not objective health indices; (2) trait NA may predict both symptom reports and physiologic responses; and (3) trait NA may not predict either symptom reports or physiologic outcomes. This suggests that the effects of NA on health can only be understood with an eye toward the context in which both health-related stressors and data collection occur. In further assessing the role of NA, future researchers should strive to parse the effects of somatic filtering from those of physiologic reactivity.

Social Context and Common Sense Models of Illness

In teaching an introductory course in social psychology, one of the authors frequently uses an example of symptom perception to illustrate how social processes influence the self-regulation of behavior. Students initially find the example to be an odd choice, because they assume that symptom perception is an asocial undertaking involving the individual and his or her somatic sensations. However, as Dewey observed, "the non-social individual is an abstraction arrived at by imagining what man would be if all his human qualities were taken away. Society, as a real whole, is the normal order, and the mass as an aggregate of isolated units is the fiction" (as cited by Menand, 2001: 304–5) As applied to health psychology, Dewey's observation conveys how the lay interpretation of symptoms is a function of the social context in which those symptoms are experienced. We will discuss how aspects of the social environment, such as stereotypes, the lay referral network, media, and culture act as moderating variables in the effects of common sense models on health and illness behaviors.

Social Identity and Stereotypes

One important factor that influences the response to symptoms is the identity of the sufferer. Stereotypes about disease vulnerability and typical victims have implications for symptom labels and attributions. Martin et al. (1998) observed that victim gender influenced how participants responded to information about symptoms and stressors in a series of experiments using diverse samples. Participants read brief vignettes that described someone experiencing chest pain, shortness of breath, and sweating (i.e., symptoms of a heart attack or myocardial infarction). The sex of the target and recent stressors (high versus low) were manipulated and subjects were asked to indicate the likelihood that the victim's symptoms were due to a heart-related problem. Martin et al. found that subjects applied the *stress-illness rule*, but only for female targets. In other words, cardiac attributions were significantly lower when a female target experienced high versus low concomitant stressors. However, the manipulation of stressors had no effects on symptom attributions for male targets. Subjects persisted in discounting the symptoms of the female/high stress victim even when her age placed her at high risk of myocardial infarction and when her symptoms were highly indicative of an acute cardiac event (e.g., crushing chest pain). Martin and her colleagues reported two further studies suggesting that laypeople hold stereotypic assumptions associating vulnerability to heart disease with male, rather than female gender. These findings suggest that the same pattern of symptoms that suggests the label "heart attack" for a male victim are likely to be misunderstood or misattributed when the victim is female.

The experiments reported by Martin et al. informed our understanding of naive theories of heart disease. In addition, their findings also suggested that laypeople view women as more likely than men to report symptoms in the context of stressors. Subsequent research by Martin and Lemos (2002) found evidence that laypeople expect women to somatize; participants were significantly less likely to recommend medical intervention for a female (versus male) high stress target suffering heart attack, gallstone, and melanoma symptoms.

Martin's (2000) ongoing research follows up on the idea that lay expectations about heart disease vulnerability have self-referral implications for female victims. A small sample of heart attack patients were interviewed about their symptoms and self-referral behaviors, with the interviews focusing on events and perceptions that occurred prior to the receipt of medical treatment. Female myocardial infarction victims were found to have been significantly less likely than their male counterparts to attribute their initial symptoms to cardiac causes. Family members and friends (i.e., support providers) also were less likely to articulate a cardiac symptom attribution for female versus male victims. Finally, support providers were less likely to recommend that the woman needed to seek medical care.

The Lay Referral Network

It is very common for laypeople to consult family members and friends – that is, members of the lay referral network – in evaluating symptoms (Friedson, 1961; Suls et al., 1997). The lay referral network serves several functions, including the provision of social support, opportunities for social comparison, and sharing information and advice. Suls et al. (1997) observed three ways in which the lay support network influences symptom perception and self-referral behavior.

First, others can help the sufferer understand the meaning of a symptom. Lay conversations about symptoms typically focus on finding an appropriate label, identifying a plausible cause, and soliciting advice regarding comfort or cure (Suls et al., 1997). Not every person can be equally helpful in helping intuit the meaning of symptoms. For example, if someone suspects that the oysters he consumed at a new restaurant gave him food poisoning, he will gain useful information from comparing his symptoms to those of the co-worker who joined him for lunch. However, if the same fellow is worried that his symptoms might be due to cancer, he will be more likely to share his concerns with a loved one who is likely to be most reassuring (H. Leventhal et al., 1997).

Second, exposure to others who are ill can prime the perception of symptoms. For example, sitting next to a sniffling, sneezing stranger on a crowded airplane will prompt several days of self-monitoring for respiratory symptoms. Exposure to the contagious other also may generate self-protective behaviors, such as the use of zinc lozenges to ward off infection. Exposure to ill others can influence symptom perception, even when the illness in question is known not to be contagious. Turk and colleagues (1985) found that self-referral behavior increases when people recall that a family member has a history of being treated for similar symptoms. In this case, the salience of the family member's illness lends special meaning to one's own somatic sensations.

Finally, the scenarios described above involved situations where others in the social environment suffer veridical ailments; however, others' illness-related behaviors can influence the perception of symptoms, even in the absence of objective pathology (Colligan et al., 1982). The "June-bug" episode, reported by Kerckhoff and Back (1968), provides a classic example of this phenomenon. Kerckhoff and Back described the experiences of factory workers during a particularly busy season. One day, many employees reported fever and nausea, which they attributed to insect bites. So many workers were ill that it was necessary to close the factory and call in the Centers for Disease Control (CDC). Despite a thorough investigation, the CDC found no objective evidence of disease in any of the workers, nor did they find evidence of insect infestation in the working environment. The "June-Bug" episode instead appears to have been an episode of mass psychogenic illness.

It is important to keep in mind that the workers who were stricken by the "June-Bug" epidemic were not attempting to deceive their employer in any explicit manner. What probably happened instead was that the workers, who were working unusually long, stressful hours, experienced ambiguous somatic sensations (e.g., feeling warm, flushed and nauseated). It is one thing to feel a bit off-color oneself. It is quite another to discover that neighboring workers on the assembly line also feel overheated and a bit queasy. One worker spoke to the next and the next – and a psychogenic episode soon was underway. Through the process of social interaction, the workers first identified that many of them felt unwell and together they generated a plausible explanation (bug bites) for their symptoms.

The lay network performs a variety of other functions, as well (Zola, 1973). Consultations with the lay network can help reduce the symptomatic individual's feelings of isolation and threat (Cameron et al., 1993; H. Leventhal et al., 1997). We encourage loved ones to seek medical care (Cameron et al., 1993; Oberlander et al., 1993; Sanders, 1982). We sanction or punish loved ones as needed to force them to take good care of themselves (e.g., nagging) and facilitate their health behaviors (e.g., pointedly handing out bottles of sunscreen or stocking the refrigerator with healthy snacks). We also may seek medical care ourselves in order to be sure that we can continue to meet our family and work responsibilities (Apple, 1960; Zola, 1973).

Although lay influence may be well intentioned, its effects are not uniformly positive. Patients with chronic illnesses report that loved ones and health care providers sometimes offer support that is perceived to be unhelpful (Dakof and Taylor, 1990; Martin et al., 1994; Revenson et al., 1991; Rook, 1984). For example, in the study of symptom perception among heart attack victims described previously, family members and friends sometimes offered poor advice, especially to the women in the sample. Interestingly, people with strong social networks often tend to be slow in seeking medical care (Berkanovic et al., 1981; Granovetter, 1978; Liu and Duff, 1972). On the surface, this seems surprising. It would seem that a large and loving network ought to encourage taking care of oneself. However, there are several ways in which the social network can delay or circumvent entry into the medical care system. For example, some social networks may generally distrust doctors and, thus, discourage seeking medical intervention (Suls and Goodkin, 1994). In addition, the presence of others often reduces anxiety and keeps us active and busy – factors which may further delay entry into the medical care system. Even when friends and family members do encourage their loved one to visit a health care provider, lay consultations consume time (Suls et al., 1997). If advice to seek care is perceived to be nagging, the ill individual may respond with psychological reactance and avoid visiting a physician despite the potential benefits of medical care.

It also is important to note that illness representations can be irrelevant to action when the individual's behavior is regulated by social rules. For example, one of the authors knew an elderly woman who understood virtually nothing about her CHF. Ordinarily, this would be a patient who would lack the skills to care effectively for herself. However, she did very well because her son was a cardiologist and called frequently to monitor her progress and activities. She followed his daily rules faithfully, despite possessing an impoverished illness representation of her condition.

The media and Internet represent relatively new sources of social influence on the content of illness representations. These mass communication outlets now provide laypeople with health-related information that traditionally was available only through the auspices of a physician (Shorter, 1992, 1995). For example, Brody (1999) described how press reports about a study published in the *New England Journal of Medicine* (Lagergren et al., 1999) prompted thousands of chronic heartburn patients to schedule appointments with their physicians. What is most interesting about this example is that the vast majority of these people already were being treated for heartburn and their symptoms had not altered. What had changed was the way in which they understood their familiar heartburn symptoms. The realization that chronic heartburn is related to the development of esophageal cancer transformed an annoying symptom into a potentially life-threatening concern.

Culture Shapes the Content of Illness Representations

Medical anthropology tells us that knowledge about illness is organized or meaningfully structured across cultures (Helman, 1985). Although the literature is small, it probably is reasonable to assume that basic cognitive and affective processes function similarly across cultural contexts (Lau, 1997; Weller, 1984). However, the content of illness representations and their implications for action vary as a function of culture, ethnicity, and locale (Brownlee et al., 2000; Lau, 1997; Pachter, 1994; Weller, 1984). For example, a Latino might label a particular set of somatic symptoms as "*ataques de vervios susto*" (meaning an attack of nerves or emotional turmoil; Penn et al., 2000), whereas someone of European origin might label the same symptoms as "depression." The depressed European might consult a psychiatrist regarding his condition and accept a psychotropic medication as an appropriate treatment. In contrast, the Latino suffering *ataques de vervios susto* might be more likely to consult a primary care physician or a clergy member (Giachello, 1996; Guarnaccia, 1997; Penn et al., 2000) for advice and might believe that medications would exacerbate, rather than relieve the problem (Hosch et al., 1995; Penn et al., 2000). Western samples undoubtedly have been over-studied. As a consequence, the literature on common sense models of illness probably devotes inordinate attention to the role played by concepts such as contagion and physiology in illness representations.

Conclusion

To return to our opening example of women struggling to interpret the often ambiguous symptoms of ovarian cancer, expanding our understanding of how common sense models of symptoms and illness influence treatment seeking represents a critical step in the development of programmatic interventions targeted at facilitating early detection and treatment. Along similar lines, common sense models of illness also have the potential to elucidate why some individuals use health care resources unnecessarily. This chapter illustrates that the factors that lead people to believe that they are ill or that they need to seek medical care are not simply determined by the presence or absence of pathology or injury. Instead, symptom perception and related behaviors represent a complex configuration of somatic sensations, attributional rules, affective reactions, and sociocultural situational factors. The CSM view of ordinary people as "lay physicians" offers much to both health care practitioners and behavioral medicine researchers in understanding health and illness behaviors.

Authors' Note

Correspondence concerning this chapter should be addressed to René Martin, Department of Psychology, 11 Seashore Hall E, University of Iowa, Iowa City, IA 52242-1407, USA; e-mail: rene-martin@uiowa.edu.

References

American College of Obstetricians and Gynecologists (1999). Ovarian Cancer. ACOG educational bulletin number 250. In *Compendium of Selected Publications* (pp. 665–73). Washington, DC: American College of Obstetricians and Gynecologists.

Anderson, J. R. (1983). *The Architecture of Cognition*. Cambridge, MA: Harvard University Press.

Anderson, J. R. (1990). *The Adaptive Character of Thought*. Hillsdale, NJ: Erlbaum.

Anderson, J. R., and Lebiere, C. (1998). *The Atomic Components of Thought*. Mahwah, NJ: Erlbaum.

Aneshensel, C. S., Frerichs, R. R., and Huba, G. J. (1984). Depression and physical illness: A multiwave, nonrecursive causal model. *Journal of Health and Social Behavior*, 25, 350–71.

Apple, D. (1960). How laymen define illness. *Journal of Health and Social Behavior*, 13, 219–28.

Backett, E. M., Heady, J. A., and Evans, J. C. (1954). Studies of a general practice. II. The doctor's job in an urban area. *British Medical Journal*, 1, 109–23.

Barsky, A. (1981). Hidden reasons some patients visit doctors. *Annals of Internal Medicine*, 94, 492–7.

Barsky, A. J., and Klerman, G. L. (1983). Overview: Hypochondriasis, bodily complaints, and somatic symptoms. *Psychosomatic Medicine*, 50, 510–19.

Bauman, B. (1961). Diversities in conceptions of health and physical fitness. *Journal of Health and Human Behavior*, 2, 39–46.

Baumann, L. J., Cameron, L. D., Zimmerman, R. S., and Leventhal, H. (1989). Illness representations and matching labels with symptoms. *Health Psychology*, 8, 449–69.

Baumann, L. J., and Leventhal, H. (1985). "I can tell when my blood pressure is up, can't I?" *Health Psychology*, 4, 203–18.

Berkanovic, E., Telesky, C., and Reeder, S. (1981). Structural and social psychological factors in the decision to seek medical care for symptoms. *Medical Care*, 19, 693–709.

Bishop, G. D. (1984). Gender, role, and illness behavior in a military population. *Health Psychology*, 3, 519–34.

Bishop, G. D. (1991). Understanding the understanding of illness: Lay disease representations. In J. A. Skelton and R. T. Croyle (Eds.), *Mental Representations in Health and Illness* (pp. 32–59). New York: Springer-Verlag.

Bishop, G. D., Briede, C., Cavazos, L., Grotzinger, R., and McMahon, S. (1987). Processing illness information: The role of disease prototypes. *Basic and Applied Social Psychology*, 8, 21–43.

Bishop, G. D., and Converse, S. A. (1986). Illness representations: A prototype approach. *Health Psychology*, 5, 95–114.

Borawski, E., Kinney, J. and Kahana, E. (1996). The meaning of older adults health appraisals: Congruence with health status and determinant of mortality. *Journal of Gerontology: Social Sciences*, 51B, S157–70.

Boring, C. C., Squires, T. S., and Tong, T. (1993). Cancer statistics. *Ca: A Cancer Journal for Clinicians*, 43, 7–26.

Brody, J. E. (1999). Chronic heartburn, an ominous warning. *The New York Times*, April 27, p. D6.

Brownlee, S., Leventhal, H., and Leventhal, E. A. (2000). Regulation, self-regulation and construction of the self in the maintenance of physical health. In M. Boekaerts, P. Pintrich, and M. Zeidner (Eds.), *Handbook of Self-regulation* (pp. 369–415). San Diego, CA: Academic Press.

Cameron, L., Leventhal, E. A., and Leventhal, H. (1993). Symptom representation and affect as determinants of care seeking in a community-dwelling, adult sample population. *Health Psychology*, 12, 171–9.

Cameron, L., Leventhal, E. A., and Leventhal, H. (1995). Seeking medical care in response to symptoms and life stress. *Psychosomatic Medicine*, 57, 37–47.

Cameron, L., Leventhal, H., and Love, R. R. (1998). Trait anxiety, symptom perceptions, and illness-related responses among women in a Tamoxifen clinical trial. *Health Psychology*, 17, 459–69.

Clement, K. D., and Connor, P. D. (1998). Tumors of the female reproductive organs. In R. B. Taylor (Ed.), *Family Medicine: Principles and Practice* (5th edn, pp. 916–24). New York: Springer-Verlag.

Cloninger, C. R. (1987). Neurogenetic adaptive mechanism in alcoholism. *Science*, 236, 410–16.

Cohen, M. Z., Tripp-Reimer, T., Smith, C., Sorofman, B., and Lively, S. (1994). Explanatory models of diabetes: Patient practitioner variation. *Social Science and Medicine*, 38, 59–66.

Cohen, S., Doyle, W. J., Skoner, D. P., Fireman, P., Gwaltney, J. M., and Newsom, J. T. (1995). State and trait negative affect as predictors of objective and subjective symptoms of respiratory viral infections. *Journal of Personality and Social Psychology*, 68, 159–69.

Colligan, M., Pennebaker, J. W., and Murphy, L. (Eds.). (1982). *Mass Psychogenic Illness: A Social Psychological Perspective*. Hillsdale, NJ: Erlbaum.

Costa, P. T., Jr., and McCrae, R. R. (1980). Somatic complaints in males as a function of age and neuroticism: A longitudinal analysis. *Journal of Behavioral Medicine*, 3, 245–57.

Costa, P. T., Jr., and McCrae, R. R. (1985). Hypochondriasis, neuroticism, and aging: When are somatic complaints unfounded? *American Psychologist*, 40, 19–28.

Costa, P. T., Jr., and McCrae, R. R. (1987). Neuroticism, somatic complaints, and disease: Is the bark worse than the bite? *Journal of Personality*, 55, 299–316.

Dakof, G. A., and Taylor, S. E. (1990). Victims' perceptions of social support: What is helpful from whom? *Journal of Personality and Social Psychology*, 58, 80–9.

Davison, K. P., and Pennebaker, J. W. (1996). Social psychosomatics. In E. T. Higgins and A. W. Kruglanski (Eds.), *Social Psychology: Handbook of Basic Principles* (pp. 102–30). New York: Guilford.

Diefenbach, M. A., Leventhal, E. A., Leventhal, H., and Patrick-Miller, L. (1996). Negative affect relates to cross-sectional but not longitudinal symptom reporting: Data from elderly adults. *Health Psychology*, 15, 282–8.

Diefenbach, M. A., Miller, S. M., and Daly, M. B. (1999). Specific worry about breast cancer predicts mammography use in women at risk for breast and ovarian cancer. *Health Psychology*, 18, 532–6.

Ditto, P. H., and Jemmott, J. B., III. (1989). From rarity to evaluative extremity: Effects of prevalence information on evaluations of positive and negative characteristics. *Journal of Personality and Social Psychology*, 57, 16–26.

Dollard, J., and Miller, N. E. (1950). *Personality and Psychotherapy*. New York: McGraw Hill.

Dracup, K., and Moser, D. K. (1997). Beyond sociodemographics: Factors influencing the decision to seek treatment for symptoms of acute myocardial infarction. *Heart and Lung*, 26, 253–62.

Duke, J., Leventhal, H., Brownlee, S., and Leventhal, E. A. (2001). Given up and replacing activities in response to illness. Manuscript submitted for publication.

Eisenberg, D. M., Kessler, R. C., Foster, C., Norlock, F. E., Calkins, D. R., and Delbanco, T. L. (1993). Unconventional medicine in the United States: Prevalence, costs and patterns of use. *New England Journal of Medicine*, 328, 246–52.

Fillingim, R. B., and Fine, M. A. (1986). The effects of internal versus external information processing on symptom perception in an exercise setting. *Health Psychology*, 5, 115–23.

Fiske, S. T., and Taylor, S. E. (1991). *Social Cognition*. New York: McGraw Hill.

Friedson, E. (1961). *Patients' Views of Medical Practice*. New York: Russell Sage.

Giachello, A. L. (1996). Latino women. In M. Bayne-Smith (Ed.), *Race, Gender, and Health* (pp. 121–71). Thousand Oaks, CA: Sage.

Goff, B. A., Mandel, L., Muntz, H. G., and Melancon, C. H. (2000). Ovarian carcinoma diagnosis: Results of a national ovarian cancer survey. *Cancer*, 89, 2068–75.

Goff, D. C., Nichaman, M. Z., Ramsey, D. J., Meyer, P. S., and Labarthe, D. R. (1995). A population-based assessment of the use and effectiveness of thrombolytic therapy: The Corpus Christi Hearty Project. *Annals of Epidemiology*, 5, 171–8.

Goff, D. C., Sellers, D. E., McGovern, P. G., et al., for the REACT Study Group. (1998). Knowledge of heart attack symptoms in a population survey in the United States. *Archives of Internal Medicine*, 158, 2329–38.

Granovetter, M. S. (1978). The strength of weak ties. *American Journal of Sociology*, 31, 1360–9.

Gray, J. A. (1982). *The Neuropsychology of Anxiety: An Enquiry into the Functions of the Septo-hippocampal System*. New York: Oxford University Press.

Gray, J. A. (1985). Issues in the neuropsychology of anxiety. In A. H. Tuma and J. D. Maser (Eds.), *Anxiety and the Anxiety Disorders* (pp. 5–25). Hillsdale, NJ: Erlbaum.

Green, D. M., and Swets, J. A. (1974). *Signal Detection Theory and Psychophysics*. New York: Krieger.

Guarnaccia, P. J. (1997). Social stress and psychological distress among Latinos in the United States. In I. Al-Issa and M. Tousignant (Eds.), *Ethnicity, Immigration, and Psychopathology* (pp. 71–94). New York: Plenum.

Hannay, D. R., and Maddox, E. J. (1976). Symptom prevalence and referral behavior in Glasgow. *Social Science and Medicine*, 10, 185–9.

Heider, F. (1958). *The Psychology of Interpersonal Relations*. New York: Wiley.

Helman, C. G. (1985). Psyche, soma, and society: The social construction of psychosomatic disorders. *Culture and Medicine in Psychiatry*, 9, 1–26.

Hosch, H. M., Barrientos, G. A., Fierro, C., Ramirez, J. I., Pelaez, M. P., Cedillos, A. M., Meyer, L. D., and Prez, Y. (1995). Predicting adherence to medications by Hispanics with schizophrenia. *Hispanic Journal of Behavioral Sciences*, 17, 320–33.

Idler, E. L., Hudson, S. V., and Leventhal, H. (1999). The meanings of self-ratings of health: A qualitative and quantitative approach. *Research on Aging*, 21, 458–76.

Ihde, D. C., and Longo, D. L. (1998). Presentations of the patient with cancer: Solid tumors in adults. In A. S. Fauci, E. Braunwald, K. J. Isselbacher, J. D. Wilson, J. B. Martin, and D. L. Kasper (Eds.), *Harrison's Principles of Internal Medicine* (14th edn, pp. 360–2). New York: McGraw Hill.

Ingham, I., and Miller, P. (1979). Symptom prevalence and severity in a general practice. *Journal of Epidemiology and Community Health*, 33, 191–8.

Janz, N., and Becker, M. (1984). The health belief model: A decade later. *Health Education Quarterly*, 2, 1–47.

Johnson, J. A., and King, K. B. (1995). Influence of expectations about symptoms on delay in seeking treatment during a myocardial infarction. *American Journal of Critical Care*, 4, 29–35.

Kelley, H. H. (1967). Attribution theory in social psychology. In D. Levine (Ed.), *Nebraska Symposium on Motivation* (Vol. 15, pp. 192–240). Lincoln: University of Nebraska Press.

Kerckhoff, A. C., and Back, K. W. (1968). *The June Bug: A Study of Hysterical Contagion*. New York: Appleton-Century-Crofts.

Kroenke, K., and Mangelsdorff, A. D. (1989). Common symptoms in ambulatory care: Incidence, evaluation, therapy, and outcome. *American Journal of Medicine*, 86, 262–6.

Kubzansky, L. D., Kawachi, I., Weiss, S. T., and Sparrow, D. (1998). Anxiety and coronary heart disease: A synthesis of epidemiological, psychological, and experimental evidence. *Annals of Behavioral Medicine*, 20, 47–58.

Kutner, B., and Gordon, G. (1961). Seeking care for cancer. *Journal of Health and Human Behavior*, 2, 171–8.

Laffrey, S. C. (1986). Development of a health conception scale. *Research in Nursing and Health*, 9, 107–13.

Lagergren, J., Bergström, R., Lindgren, A., and Nyrén, O. (1999). Symptomatic gastroesophageal reflux as a risk factor for esophageal adenocarcinoma. *New England Journal of Medicine*, 340, 825–31.

Lau, R. R. (1997). Cognitive representations of health and illness. In D. S. Gochman (Ed.), *Handbook of Health Behavior Research. I: Personal and Social Determinants* (pp. 51–69). New York: Plenum.

Lau, R. R., Bernard, T. M., and Hartmann, K. A. (1989). Further explorations of common-sense representations of common illnesses. *Health Psychology*, 8, 195–219.

Leventhal, E. A., and Crouch, M. (1997). Are there differences in perceptions of illness across the lifespan? In K. J. Petrie and J. A. Weinman (Eds.), *Perceptions of Health and Illness: Current Research and Applications* (pp. 77–102). London: Harwood Academic Press.

Leventhal, E. A., Hansell, S., Diefenbach, M., Leventhal, H., and Glass, D. C. (1996). Negative affect and self-report of physical symptoms: Two longitudinal studies of older adults. *Health Psychology*, 15, 192–9.

Leventhal, E. A., Leventhal, H., Schaefer, P., and Easterling, D. (1993). Conservation of energy, uncertainty reduction and swift utilization of medical care among the elderly. *Journal of Gerontology: Psychological Sciences*, 48, 78–86.

Leventhal, H. (1970). Findings and theory in the study of fear communications. In L. Berkowitz (Ed.), *Advances in Experimental Social Psychology* (Vol. 5, pp. 119–86). San Diego, CA: Academic Press.

Leventhal, H., and Diefenbach, M. (1991). The active side of illness cognition. In J. A. Skelton and R. T. Croyle (Eds.), *Mental Representation in Health and Illness* (pp. 247–72). New York: Springer-Verlag.

Leventhal, H., Hudson, S., and Robitaille, C. (1997). Social comparison and health: A process model. In B. Buunk and F. X. Gibbons (Eds.), *Health, Coping and Well Being: Perspectives from Social Comparison Theory* (pp. 411–32). Hillsdale, NJ: Erlbaum.

Leventhal, H., Meyer, D., and Nerenz, D. (1980). The common sense representation of illness danger. In S. Rachman (Ed.), *Contributions to Medical Psychology* (Vol. 2, pp. 7–30). New York: Pergamon Press.

Leventhal, H., Singer, R., and Jones, S. (1965). Effects of fear and specificity of recommendations upon attitudes and behavior. *Journal of Personality and Social Psychology*, 2, 20–9.

Leventhal, H., Watts, J. C., and Pagano, F. (1967). Effects of fear and instructions on how to cope with danger. *Journal of Personality and Social Psychology*, 6, 313–21.

Liu, W. T., and Duff, R. W. (1972). The strength in weak ties. *Public Opinion Quarterly*, 42, 361–7.

Marchant-Haycox, S., and Salmon, P. (1997). Patients' and doctors' strategies in consultations with unexplained symptoms: Interactions of gynecologists with women presenting menstrual problems. *Psychosomatics*, 38, 440–50.

Martin, R. (2000). Gender disparities in symptom attribution and referral patterns. Presented at the annual meeting of the Academy of Behavioral Medicine Research, June 10, 2000, Mont Tremblant, Quebec.

Martin, R., Davis, G. M., Baron, R. S., Suls, J., and Blanchard, E. B. (1994). Specificity in social support: Perceptions of helpful and unhelpful provider behaviors among irritable bowel syndrome, headache, and cancer patients. *Health Psychology*, 13, 432–9.

Martin, R., Gordon, E. E. I., and Lounsbury, P. (1998). Gender disparities in the interpretation of cardiac-related symptoms: The contribution of common sense models of illness. *Health Psychology*, 17, 346–57.

Martin, R., and Lemos, K. (2002). From heart attacks to melanoma: Do common sense models of somatization influence symptom interpretation for female victims? *Health Psychology*, 21, 25–32.

McCaul, K. D., Braastetter, A. D., O'Donnell, S. M., Jacobson, K., and Quinlan, K. B. (1998). A descriptive study of breast cancer worry. *Journal of Behavioral Medicine*, 21, 565–79.

Menand, L. (2001). *The Metaphysical Club*. New York: Farrar, Straus, and Giroux.

Meyer, D., Leventhal, H., and Gutmann, M. (1985). Common-sense models of illness: The example of hypertension. *Health Psychology*, 4, 115–35.

Miller, N. E. (1951). Learnable drives and rewards. In S. S. Stevens (Ed.) *Handbook of Experimental Psychology* (pp. 435–72). New York: Wiley.

Moos, R., and Van Dort, B. (1977). Physical and emotional symptoms and campus health center utilization. *Social Psychiatry*, 12, 107–15.

Mora, P., Robitaille, C., Leventhal, H., Swigar, M., and Leventhal, E. A. (2002). Trait negative affect relates to prior week symptoms, but not to reports of illness episodes, illness symptoms, or care seeking. *Psychosomatic Medicine*, 64, 436–49.

Natapoff, J. N. (1978). Children's views of health: A developmental study. *American Journal of Public Health*, 68, 995–9.

National Center for Health Statistics (1980). *Geographic Patterns in the Risk of Dying and Associated Factors Ages 35–74 Years* (Series 3, No. 18). Washington, DC: US Government Printing Office.

Oberlander, T. F., Pless, I. B., and Dougherty, G. E. (1993). Advice seeking and appropriate use of a pediatric emergency department. *American Journal of Developmental Care*, 147, 863–7.

Pachter, L. M. (1994). Culture and clinical care: Folk illness beliefs and behaviors and their implications for health care delivery. *Journal of the American Medical Association*, 271, 690–4.

Padgett, V. R., and Hill, A. K. (1989). Maximizing athletic performance in endurance events: A comparison of coping strategies. *Journal of Applied Social Psychology*, 19, 331–40.

Penn, N. E., Kramer, J., Skinner, J. F. et al. (2000). Health practices and health-care systems among cultural groups. In R. M. Eisler and M. Hersen (Eds.), *Handbook of Gender, Culture, and Health*, (pp. 105–37). Mahwah, NJ: Erlbaum.

Pennebaker, J. W. (1982). *The Psychology of Physical Symptoms*. New York: Springer-Verlag.

Pennebaker, J. W. (1989). Confession, inhibition, and disease. In L. Berkowitz (Ed.), *Advances in Experimental Social Psychology* (Vol. 22, pp. 211–44). Orlando, FL: Academic Press.

Pennebaker, J. W., and Lightner, J. M. (1980). Competition of internal and external information in an exercise setting. *Journal of Personality and Social Psychology*, 39, 165–74.

Peters, S., Stanley, I., Rose, M., and Salmon, P. (1998). Patients with medically unexplained symptoms: Sources of patients' authority and implications for demands on medical care. *Social Science and Medicine*, 46, 559–65.

Prohaska, T. R., Keller, M. L., Leventhal, E. A., and Leventhal, H. (1987). Impact of symptoms and aging attribution on emotions and coping. *Health Psychology*, 6, 495–514.

Rabin, C., Ward, S., Leventhal, H., and Schmitz, M. (2001). Explaining retrospective reports of symptoms: Anxiety, initial symptom experience, and post-treatment symptoms. *Health Psychology*, 20, 91–8.

Revenson, T. A., Schiaffino, K. M., Majerovitz, S. D., and Gibofsky, A. (1991). Social support as a double-edged sword: The relation of positive and problematic support to depression among rheumatoid arthritis patients. *Social Science and Medicine*, 7, 807–13.

Rook, K. S. (1984). The negative side of social interaction: Impact on psychological well-being. *Journal of Personality and Social Psychology*, 46, 1097–108.

Safer, M., Tharps, D., Jackson, T., and Leventhal, H. (1979). Determinants of three stages of delay in seeking care at a medical clinic. *Medical Care*, 17, 11–29.

Sanders, G. S. (1982). Social comparison and perceptions of health and illness. In G. S. Sanders and J. Suls (Eds.), *Social Psychology of Health and Illness* (pp. 129–57). Hillsdale, NJ: Erlbaum.

Scambler, A., Scambler, G., and Craig, D. (1981). Kinship and friendship networks and women's demand for primary care. *Journal of the Royal College of General Practitioners*, 26, 746–50.

Scharloo, M., and Kaptein, A. (1997). Measurement of illness perceptions in patients with chronic somatic illness: A review. In K. J. Petrie and J. A. Weinman (Eds.), *Perceptions of Health and Illness: Current Research and Applications* (pp. 103–54). London: Harwood Academic Press.

Schober, R., and Lacroix, J. M. (1991). Lay illness models in the enlightenment and the 20th century: Some historical lessons. In J. A. Skelton and R. T. Croyle (Eds.), *Mental Representations in Health and Illness* (pp. 10–31). New York: Springer-Verlag.

Shorter, E. (1992). *From Paralysis to Fatigue: A History of Psychosomatic Illness.* New York: Free Press.

Shorter, E. (1995). Sucker-punched again! Physicians meet the disease-of-the-month syndrome. *Journal of Psychosomatic Research, 39,* 115–18.

Skelton, J. A., and Croyle, R. T. (1991). Mental representation, health, and illness: An introduction. In J. A. Skelton and R. T. Croyle (Eds.), *Mental Representations in Health and Illness* (pp. 1–9). New York: Springer-Verlag.

Smith, C. A., Wallston, K. A., and Dwyer, K. A. (1995). On babies and bathwater: Disease impact and negative affectivity in the self-reports of persons with rheumatoid arthritis. *Heath Psychology, 14,* 64–73.

Sorofman, B., Tripp-Reimer, T., Lauer, G. M., and Martin, M. E. (1990). Symptom self-care. *Holistic Nursing Practice, 4,* 45–55.

Spencer, J. W., and Jacobs, J. J. (1999). *Complementary/Alternative Medicine: An Evidence-based Approach.* St. Louis, MO: Mosby.

Stoller, E. P. (1997). Medical self care: Lay management of symptoms by elderly people. M. G. Ory and G. DeFries (Eds.), *Self-care in Later Life: Research, Program, and Policy Issues* (pp. 24–61). New York: Springer.

Suls, J. and Goodkin, F. (1994). Medical gossip and rumor: Their role in the lay referral system. In R. F. Goodman and A. Ben-Zeev (Eds.), *Good Gossip* (pp. 169–79). Lawrence, KS: University Press of Kansas.

Suls, J., Green, P., and Hillis, S. (1998). Emotional reactivity to everyday problems, affective inertia, and neuroticism. *Personality and Social Psychology Bulletin, 24,* 127–36.

Suls, J., Martin, R., and Leventhal, H. (1997). Social comparison, lay referral, and the decision to seek medical care. In B. P. Buunk and F. X. Gibbons (Eds.), *Health, Coping, and Well-being: Perspectives from Social Comparison Theory* (pp. 195–226). Mahwah, NJ: Erlbaum.

Tellegen, A. (1985). Structures of mood and personality and their relevance to assessing anxiety, with an emphasis on self-report. In H. H. Tuma and J. D. Maser (Eds.), *Anxiety and the Anxiety Disorders* (pp. 681–706). Hillsdale, NJ: Erlbaum.

Thayer, J. F., Friedman, B. H., Borkovek, T. D. (1996). Autonomic characteristics of generalized anxiety disorder and worry. *Biological Psychiatry, 39,* 255–66.

Turk, D. C., Litt, M. D., Salovey, P., and Walker, J. (1985). Seeking urgent pediatric treatment: Factors contributing to frequency, delay, and appropriateness. *Health Psychology, 4,* 43–59.

Wan, T. (1976). Predicting self-assessed health status: A multivariate approach. *Health Services Research, 11,* 464–77.

Watson, D., and Clark, L. A. (1984). Negative affectivity: The disposition to experience aversive emotional states. *Psychological Bulletin, 96,* 465–90.

Watson, D., and Clark, L. A. (1992). Affects separable and inseparable: On the hierarchical arrangement of negative affect. *Journal of Personality and Social Psychology, 62,* 489–505.

Watson, D., and Pennebaker, J. W. (1989). Health complaints, stress, and disease: Exploring the central role of negative affectivity. *Psychological Review, 96,* 234–54.

Watson, D., and Pennebaker, J. W. (1991). Situational, dispositional, and genetic bases of symptom reporting. In J. A. Skelton and R. T. Croyle (Eds.), *Mental Representations in Health and Illness* (pp. 60–84). New York: Springer-Verlag.

Weller, S. S. (1984). Cross cultural concepts of illness: Variables and validation. *American Anthropologist*, 86, 341–51.

White, K. L., Williams, T. F., and Greenberg, B. G. (1961). The ecology of medical care. *New England Journal of Medicine*, 265, 885–92.

Young, R. C. (1998). Gynecologic malignancies. In A. S. Fauci, E. Braunwald, K. J., Isselbacher, J. D. Wilson, J. B. Martin, and D. L. Kasper (Eds.), *Harrison's Principles of Internal Medicine* (14th edn, pp. 605–11). New York: McGraw Hill.

Zimmer, Z., Hickey, T., and Searle, M. S. (1997). The pattern of change in leisure activity behavior among older adults with arthritis. *The Gerontologist*, 37, 384–92.

Zola, I. (1973). Pathways to the doctor: From person to patient. *Social Science and Medicine*, 7, 677–89.

CHAPTER 9

Contributions of Social Comparison to Physical Illness and Well-being

Jerry Suls

University of Iowa

Introduction

The three following examples introduce the topic of this chapter. Example 1: When a disaster strikes, such as an earthquake, a war, or a terrorist attack, people tend to openly talk about the event in the first two weeks, even with complete strangers (Pennebaker and Harber, 1993). Example 2: A teenage girl who is sexually active rarely takes safe-sex precautions but she sometimes worries about the health risks. She puts aside the worries, however, because she assumes that most of her peers also rarely take precautions. Example 3: A patient who had coronary bypass surgery four weeks earlier is waiting for an appointment with her cardiologist. She notices another patient who also had a recent bypass who appears to be experiencing a lot more pain and requires more help from her husband. The first patient concludes that she, herself, is doing pretty well.

These three examples all involve social comparison. In the first, persons experiencing an upheaval felt the need to talk and compare reactions to gauge their feelings. The teenager in the second example uses her projected estimate about the comparison norm to support her behavior. In the third, a patient who is adapting to a serious chronic illness feels better about her own recovery as a result of seeing someone who is worse off. Although casual observation may not suggest that comparisons with other people play a significant role in physical health and illness, this chapter will attempt to demonstrate that social comparisons are integral to almost every element of physical health.

A brief description of early social comparison theory and research will be followed by coverage of subsequent conceptual and empirical developments with particular relevance for health and medical care seeking. The contribution of comparisons to disease etiology, prevention, health behavior, and adaptation to illness will then be discussed.

Early History

Festinger (1954) provided the first systematic theory of social comparison processes. He noted that people have the need to know whether their opinions are correct and what their abilities allow them to do. When it is not feasible to test these opinions or abilities directly in the environment or when objective standards are unavailable, people evaluate their opinions and abilities by comparisons with others. Festinger thought that people preferred to compare themselves with others who were similar. For opinions, agreement with others should make us feel more confident in our opinions. In the case of abilities, observing those with similar abilities allows us to know what our own possibilities for action are.

Shortly thereafter, Schachter (1959) conducted a series of experiments on the effects of fear on affiliation. His major finding was that research subjects who were waiting to receive painful electric shocks expressed the desire to affiliate with other subjects also expecting to participate in the shock experiment. Schachter thought that the need for social comparison furnished an explanation for why subjects wanted to wait with others expecting the same experience ("Misery doesn't love just any company, it loves only similar company," p. 24): subjects hoped to evaluate the appropriateness of their feelings via emotional social comparison. Schachter's research had at least two important consequences – it showed that social comparisons also extended to emotional states and set the stage for other researchers to examine how social support and affiliation help people cope with stressful situations, still an active topic receiving the attention of health psychologists. For example, Pennebaker and Harber (1993) found immediately after the Loma Prieta earthquake and the Persian Gulf War that individuals openly talked about the event for about two weeks, presumably as a way to sort out their feelings (see Pennebaker's chapter in this volume).

Schachter, however, extended his research by reasoning that if people are emotionally aroused, but are not sure what they are feeling, they will look for cues in the environment, including the behavior of other people (i.e., social comparison) that will shape the emotions they are experiencing. According to Festinger (1954), other people facing the same situations that we face should be the most appropriate for labeling our ambiguous reactions. In a classic experiment (Schachter and Singer, 1962), subjects were given injections of epinephrine that makes people feel physiologically aroused. Some subjects were informed of the drug's effects; they were told that they would experience an increase in heart rate, a flushed face and occasional trembling. Because they already had an explanation for what they would experience later, Schachter hypothesized they should not need to compare their reactions with others to figure out what they were feeling (see also Schachter and Wheeler, 1962). Other subjects were misinformed; they were told that they would experience headaches or numb feet. Still other subjects were uninformed about possible side effects of the injection. The misinformed and uninformed subjects would need an explanation for the unexpected effects of the epinephrine injection. After receiving the drug and being informed, misinformed, or given no information, the subjects were asked to wait with another person who supposedly also had had the same injection. The other person was an accomplice of the experimenter (a "stooge"), who, in one set of conditions, had been trained to act euphorically. In a second set of conditions, the subject was with a stooge trained to act angry. After a few minutes, the experimenter returned and asked the subject to complete a questionnaire about his/her feelings.

The results of this experiment by Schachter and Singer indicated that subjects took on the mood of the confederate when they received an epinephrine injection and were either misinformed or uninformed of its effects. Thus, unexpected and unexplainable arousal motivated social comparisons that prompted the person to label their ambiguous physiological arousal with the emotion that was made salient by the accomplices. In control conditions, where subjects were injected with a saline placebo which did not produce arousal or were injected with epinephrine but told about the symptoms that they would experience, the confederate's angry or euphoric behavior had no impact on the subject's mood or emotion. These results suggested that external cues, such as social comparison information, can significantly influence emotional states when experiencing unexpected or ambiguous internal cues.

In subsequent research, Schachter (1971) and his students explored the idea that some people are more predisposed to give weight to the external cues, such as comparisons with others, than internal physical signs, when labeling their thoughts and feelings. In particular, Schachter speculated that obesity may, in part, be a consequence of over-reliance on external cues. This was suggested by the fact that, compared to normal weight individuals, obese people are more sensitive to food-related cues in the environment. For example, the obese eat more than normal weight people do when food tastes good, but less when it tastes bad. This means that the obese may be more susceptible to a waitress's sales pitch for a rich dessert (Herman et al., 1983) and consume more food in the company of hungry people. Indeed, a variety of forms of empirical evidence collected by Schachter and his associates supported the idea that the eating behavior of obese persons is influenced more by external than internal cues. Of course, social comparison is only one form of external cue; Schachter's subsequent research on obesity (Schachter and Rodin, 1974) and smoking (Schachter et al., 1977) emphasized the complex interactions between environmental cues, other than social comparisons, and biological determinants. Nonetheless, he opened the way for other researchers to look for additional ways that social comparisons influence physical health.

Direct Implications for Physical Health

The implications of Schachter's ideas about emotions for physical symptom interpretation and medical health-seeking were quickly recognized by David Mechanic (1972), a medical sociologist. Because people's access to and awareness of internal states is indirect and many symptoms are ambiguous, situational factors, such as social comparisons, may influence whether a person notices symptoms and how they label them. For example, people may be experiencing anxiety and subsequently learn that a flu has been reported by members of the community. The stress and anxiety may be labeled as symptoms of incipient flu and provoke a health-care visit. Hence, ambiguous states are susceptible to interpretations consistent with illness reports of comparison others.

The phenomenon known as "mass psychogenic illness" is a good example of this process. Episodes of mass psychogenic illness involve widespread symptom perception among a group of individuals, even though there is no objective evidence of physical illness based on medical tests. Such episodes tend to occur most commonly during stressful periods in places like factories, schools, and military bases. Typically, the "illness" spreads among people with whom one works closely or knows personally (Colligan et al., 1982). The classic case is the so-called "June Bug" episode studied by Kerckhoff and Back (1968) that occurred in an industrial plant. Victims (about one-quarter of the employees) reported nausea and feverishness, which sent some to the hospital although no objective evidence of illness was found. The conclusion of health inspectors (and Kerckhoff and Back) was that the people who became "ill" showed a pattern of hysterical contagion in which psychosomatic symptoms of stress were mislabeled as markers of physical illness.

The general pattern in psychogenic episodes is that people are already fatigued, anxious, and experiencing ambiguous symptoms (e.g., the June Bug episode occurred during a busy time at the plant). If others claim to have contracted a flu or been bitten by a bug, this becomes a plausible illness label for the ambiguous state. Similarity of environment and exposure of the comparison other with the "illness" are critical. Further, if the other persons have similar constitutional attributes this probably facilitates the attribution of illness in oneself because similarity may suggest a comparable level of vulnerability. Indeed, available evidence suggests that mass psychogenic illness tends to occur among persons who share personal attributes (Stahl and Lebedun, 1974).

The preceding discussion illustrates how thinking and research about social comparison in the 1950–60s initially was applied to a medical problem such as symptom interpretation (see Martin et al.'s chapter in this volume for further discussion of social factors influencing symptom interpretation). Since then, basic comparison research has been applied to several areas of health psychology. But first, I will describe some conceptual innovations that provided the context for the developments in health psychology.

Theoretical Developments in Social Comparison after Festinger and Schachter

From the late 1970s to the present time, social comparison research has seen refinements and extensions with respect to the motives underlying comparisons, opinion and ability assessment, the use of comparison as a coping strategy, and the perception of social norms that support and motivate behavior (Suls and Wills, 1991). In the next sections, capsule summaries of these developments are provided to serve as a framework for the specific applications in health psychology described later.

Self-evaluation

Festinger (1954) hypothesized that similar persons serve as the most useful comparisons for self-evaluation, but he was ambiguous about the ways in which others needed to be similar. In the attributional reformulation of comparison theory, Goethals and Darley (1977) proposed that comparisons are preferred with others who are similar by virtue of sharing background attributes that are thought to be related to performance on the ability or opinion under evaluation (i.e., related attributes). For example, to gauge whether I am as good as I ought to be at swimming, comparison with someone who is similar in body build, swimming experience, and level of motivation should be most informative (Zanna et al., 1975). This kind of comparison addresses general self-evaluations of ability.

A different kind of self-evaluation concerns predictions about future performance. This is addressed by the Proxy model of ability social comparison (Wheeler et al., 1997). To accurately predict whether she will be able to achieve a given performance ("Can I do X?"), a person might try to learn whether someone else who already attempted "X" succeeded or failed. Such a person can be considered a "proxy," but not all persons who have attempted the task previously are equally appropriate. A good proxy is someone else who has already attempted the same task and who has performed comparably to oneself in the past on a similar task (assuming the proxy exerted her maximum effort; Wheeler et al., 1997). If information about whether the proxy made a maximum effort in the past is unavailable, however, then similarity on related attributes with the proxy can signal whether one will perform as the proxy did (Martin et al., 2002).

Festinger's formulation for opinion comparison also has received revisions. Following and extending the attributional reformulation, Suls et al.'s (2000) Triadic model distinguishes among three types of opinions: preferences, beliefs, and preference predictions. Preference, or value-type opinions, are personally relevant and lack an objectively correct answer. "Do I like my family physician?" and "Do I hate the taste of this medicine?" are examples of preference-type opinions. Because of their personal relevance, the views of others who share our general perspective or background (i.e., related attributes) are most useful.

Beliefs refer to empirically verifiable facts. An example in the health domain is "Am I in control of my health?" In this case, persons who have expertise provide more meaningful information. However, according to the Triadic model, not all experts are highly preferred; someone's greater knowledge is credible only when that person shares the same basic values. Turner (1991: 165) observed, "One takes advice from a medical doctor, for example, because he or she has been socially designated as an acceptable representative of modern, scientific medicine, an institution defined by social values one shares (such as the belief in science and its normative procedures)." The "similar expert" idea seems persuasive if we consider the example of a physician with prestigious credentials who performs or recommends euthanasia. Such a physician is probably not considered a credible source of any kind of medical information by someone who holds strong values about the sanctity of life.

The third kind of opinion evaluation concerns personal predictions about likely affective responses to an anticipated or possible situation (e.g., "Will I like the new physician assigned to my case?"). The dynamics of the comparison process for this type of opinion follow a form similar to that advanced in the Proxy model described earlier. Predictions concerning whether self will like or dislike "X" are facilitated by learning about the response of a proxy who has already experienced X. The utility of the proxy depends on similarity to oneself either in terms of related attributes or agreement about previous likes and dislikes. If the proxy in the past tended to like physicians who are very directive, but I prefer physicians who have a more client-centered orientation, then the proxy's experience with the new physician is unlikely to be relevant for me.

Self-enhancement and Self-improvement

Thus far, we have considered social comparisons motivated by the need for *self-evaluation*, that is, the accurate rendering of abilities or opinions, because there will be situations where holding the "correct" opinion or knowing one's capabilities are essential for survival. But comparisons also might be made strategically to make oneself feel better. Evidence for *self-enhancing* comparisons was reviewed by Wills (1981) who proposed that people who experience threats to self-esteem tend to compare with others who were worse off (i.e., downward comparisons) to increase their self-esteem. Shortly afterward, a pioneering study in health psychology was reported by Wood et al. (1985) who conducted lengthy interviews with a sample of breast cancer patients. Analysis of the transcripts showed that a majority of the spontaneously reported comparisons were with patients who were less fortunate. In some cases, these comparisons seemed to be with actual people, but in others they seemed to be manufactured. A self-enhancing coping function for social comparison was thus identified (Gibbons and Gerrard, 1991; Wills, 1987) and led to considerable research on the role of downward social comparisons in eating disorders, chronic pain, infertility, smoking cessation and depression (e.g., Blalock et al., 1989; Buunk and Gibbons, 1997). The intuitively plausible conclusion was that downward comparisons make people feel better; conversely, upward comparisons should make them feel worse.

However, certain developments suggest a reconsideration about upward comparison being aversive. Collins (2000) reviewed research showing that people intentionally compare with superior others and that such comparisons can produce self-views that are more positive. This is because people want to believe they have positive characteristics, and their expectations drive construals such that they perceive similarity with upward sources to indicate "that they are among the better ones" (Collins, 2000, p. 170; see also Wheeler, 1966).

Also, a third motive for comparison, *self-improvement*, was proposed (Wood, 1989). Comparisons with persons who are doing better (i.e., upward comparisons) can inspire hope or provide information to improve oneself (Lockwood and Kunda, 1997; Taylor and Lobel, 1989). For example, Molleman et al. (1986) reported that medical patients under threat appeared to desire affiliation with patients doing better than themselves rather than patients doing worse, contrary to the downward comparison prediction. In another study, college students aspiring to be teachers who were exposed to a superstar high school teacher made more positive self-evaluations, presumably because they used the superstar's success as potentially attainable for themselves (Lockwood and Kunda, 1997).

Adding to the complications, in later research both upward and downward comparisons were found to be capable of producing positive and negative consequences. As some researchers concluded, "each direction has its ups and downs" (Buunk et al., 1990). Hence, the self-evaluative consequences of social comparison appear to depend less on its direction than on the manner of its use. Recent research and theorizing helps to provide some resolution of these complexities. How these developments bear on the adaptation of medical patients to physical disease will be considered in a later section of this chapter.

Constructive Social Comparisons

To this point, we described actual comparisons made with other individuals and groups, but people also hold implicit ideas about the distribution of opinions, emotions, and personal attributes among their peers and the population at large (Goethals et al., 1991; Suls, 1986). Asked about how many of their peers smoke, college students may assume 35 percent; or asked about how many use condoms, perhaps only 20 percent. These "in the head" norms are based on some combination of memory, guesswork, projection, and reconstruction. Constructing these "norms" may have to suffice because it is impossible for the individual (short of systematic polling) to gather all of the necessary information to obtain an accurate estimate. Such constructions also may be biased in self-enhancing directions since they carry fewer constraints of reality. Regardless of how these norms are derived, they appear to have a self-perpetuating nature, and people may treat the constructed norms as veridical and behave in accord with them.

Four types of constructive comparisons have been identified. (A fifth type, health prototypes, is the subject of the chapter by Gibbons et al. in this volume.) The *false consensus effect* (FCE) refers to the tendency to attribute one's own opinion or behavior to others (e.g., Ross et al., 1977). For example, marijuana smokers report that a higher proportion of people smoke marijuana than do persons who do not smoke marijuana.

A second constructive comparison is the *better than average effect*, the tendency for a majority of people to rate themselves as higher on positive attributes and lower on negative attributes than their peers. A closely related phenomenon is *unrealistic optimism*, whereby people estimate that they are less likely to succumb to negative life events, such as automobile accidents or heart attacks, than their peers (Weinstein, 1980; Klein and Weinstein, 1997; see also Weinstein's chapter in this volume). These constructed norms appear to be self-enhancing or self-protective. Thinking that one shares significant attributes and behaviors with other people, that is, FCE, provides social validation. Believing one stands above one's peers on desirable attributes and is less likely to experience a serious accident or disease may provide reassurance and hope.

A third type of constructive comparison is *false uniqueness*. This phenomenon refers to people underestimating (compared to the actual sample norms) how many of their peers share their assets but overestimating the number of peers who share their flaws (Goethals et al., 1991; Suls and Wan, 1987). This kind of constructed norm also seems to serve a self-enhancing function. (False uniqueness may seem contradictory to the FCE, but keep in mind that the latter concerns the relative proportion of people seen as sharing versus not sharing one's attributes. A person who practices safe-sex might estimate that 55 percent of his peers also practice safe sex compared to a non-practicer estimating only 30 percent of peers, but the first estimate still might be an underestimate of the actual number).

A fourth type of constructive comparison, *pluralistic ignorance*, is different from the others because it does not seem to reflect positively on the self. Pluralistic ignorance is a psychological state characterized by the belief that one's private attitudes and judgments are different from those of others, even though one's public behavior is identical (Allport, 1924; Miller and McFarland, 1987). In essence, most people take a public position on a social issue that misrepresents their private position. A classic case of pluralistic ignorance is described by Schanck (1932) who studied a small rural community in which virtually all of the members condemned use of alcohol and card playing publicly because it was part of church dogma, but did not hold such extreme views privately. Public behavior was used by members of the community to identify the social norm, but because everyone mistakenly assumed that public behavior reflected private sentiment and underestimated how much fear of disapproval or embarrassment was responsible for the public behavior, they drew incorrect conclusions about others' feelings. Interestingly, because of pluralistic ignorance, the status quo is perpetuated because "even if no one believes ... everyone believes that everyone else believes" (Miller and McFarland, 1991: 287–8).

While the FCE, the better-than-average effect, unrealistic optimism and false uniqueness may bolster the ego, pluralistic ignorance should emphasize a person's distinctiveness and even alienation from others. It apparently persists because people are reluctant to let down their public façade.

In sum, several key concepts and developments in social comparison theory have been introduced. How these concepts shed light on key issues in health psychology is described below.

Can Social Comparisons Make People Sick?

People recognize that too little food, water, sleep and/or activity can make them more susceptible to physical illness. Certain kinds of social comparisons also can be harmful to one's health. In fact, the author of this chapter initially became interested in health psychology because of some intriguing connections between comparison behavior and physical health.

Type A Behavior

In the late 1970s, I read Meyer Friedman and Ray Rosenman's (1974) popular book on *Type A and Your Heart*. The Type A behavior pattern represents tendencies to exhibit exaggerated achievement-striving, competitiveness, impatience, and hostility (see T. Smith et al., Chapter 13 in this volume). The highly stressful Type A life-style has been associated with a two-fold increase in risk of coronary disease compared to individuals who do not exhibit these behaviors, called "Type Bs," even after controlling for traditional risk factors (Rosenman et al., 1975). What is striking about Friedman and Rosenman's description of Type As is their active and indiscriminate engagement in social comparisons. This, of course, is already implied by their extreme competitiveness, but Friedman and Rosenman's clinical examples suggested that Type As compete and compare with everyone, even with others who are not really appropriate because they are already so advantaged. Nonetheless, Type As seem to engage in a relentless struggle to attain their status or best them. These observations suggested to me that persons with the coronary-prone behavior pattern not only exhibit a high need for social comparison but also they are not selective in their choices. Consequently they set goals and choose competitors when their chances of success are low.

Dembroski and MacDougall (1978) provided the initial evidence in a study which recruited Type A and Type B subjects for a stressful work situation, which in some conditions purportedly involved the receipt of electric shock. As in Schachter's (1959) affiliation research, subjects were given the opportunity to wait with others or alone. Consistent with the idea that Type As display more social comparison tendencies, they indicated a stronger desire to wait with others. Suls et al. (1981) administered a paper-and-pencil measure of the Type A behavior pattern along with a series of other questionnaires including items about the frequency with which the respondents compared their academic, athletic and social accomplishments with other peoples' accomplishments. Persons who were higher in Type A reported more interest in social comparison information and also reported being upset for a longer time following a poor school performance, although not being happier for a longer time following a successful performance.

Gastorf et al. (1980) tested whether Type As, because of their responsiveness to social comparison, would be more sensitive to the presence of co-workers and indiscriminate in their competitive tendencies. Some subjects worked at a task in the presence of co-workers who had been given practice previously and who, therefore, should have performed much better. Other subjects had co-workers with the same lack of experience as themselves. We predicted that Type A subjects, because of their ambiguous and vague goals, would even be competitive with co-workers who were clearly at an advantage. Further, this would lead the Type As to be distracted by wanting to see how their competitors were doing and would influence their performance. Consistent with these predictions, Type A's performance was affected both by the presence of similar and superior co-workers. Their Type B counterparts were only weakly effected by the presence of co-workers and only in the presence of similar co-workers. The implication of this research is that Type As, by making inappropriate comparisons, may create struggles and stress for themselves that over time may take a serious toll on their physical health.

Neuroticism

Evidence also has emerged that persons predisposed to experience chronically high levels of anxiety, tension, guilt and anger are at greater risk of morbidity and mortality (Kubzansky and Kawachi, 2000; also see T. Smith et al.'s and Friedman's chapters in this volume). Neuroticism is related to increases in blood pressure (Markovitz et al., 1993) and premature death from heart disease (Barefoot and Schroll, 1996). Explanations for this relationship include more pronounced increases in negative emotions to stressful events with corresponding effects of pathophysiology, such as atherosclerosis, cardiac arrhythmias and suppression of immune system function. Neuroticism also is related to unhealthy practices such as reduced exercise, poor diet, smoking, alcohol consumption and poor self-care (e.g., Booth-Kewley and Vickers, 1994).

One stressor for neurotic persons may be social comparison; for example, learning that others are doing better. In fact, some evidence finds that neurotic individuals actively engage in more comparison than non-neurotic persons (e.g., Gibbons and Buunk, 1999; van der Zee et al., 1996). The initial interest in comparison may be a function of their low self-esteem and uncertainty which create a need to find social validation. But this pursuit may result in neurotics learning about status differences with other people that only intensify their negative emotions. There also is the possibility that neurotics become more upset upon learning that others are doing worse because they identify with the downward comparison target. Buunk et al. (2001) had nurses read a bogus interview with another nurse who was either coping very well with her job or coping poorly. Nurses high in neuroticism responded less positively to a nurse who was doing better than themselves. Further, these same nurses identified more with the nurse who was described as coping poorly. By this account, neurotics experience more negative consequences than non-neurotic persons whether they compare up or down.

In sum, neurotic individuals may create more intense stress for themselves by actively seeking out social comparisons and then responding in an exaggerated fashion. Aversive psychophysiological reactions may, in turn, be produced that increase the probability of pathophysiology and subsequent physical disease.

Socioeconomic Status and Dominance Hierarchies

Individuals who rank higher in the social hierarchy typically enjoy better health than do those who are below. In fact, there are differences in socioeconomic status for rates of morbidity and mortality from almost every disease and physical condition (Adler et al., 1994). For studies that contrast the health of individuals at the bottom of the SES hierarchy with those above the poverty level or with those at the top of the hierarchy, the apparent role of poor nutrition, crowding, and inadequate medical care seems obvious. However, evidence indicates an association between SES and health outcomes at every level of the SES hierarchy, not simply below the threshold of poverty. For example, individuals at the highest level of the SES hierarchy enjoy better health than do those *just* below (Marmot et al., 1991). This suggests that factors responsible for health differences at the upper levels are not likely to be the same as those at the lower levels and that social ranking is important to health not only for those in poverty.

In addition to differences in the physical and social environment across SES levels, hierarchical position, apart from its material implications, may affect the risk of disease. Wilkinson (1992) has shown that the effects of SES hierarchies are stronger within than across countries, suggesting that relative status rather than absolute status may be the most critical variable.

Dominance hierarchies emerge in virtually all human social groups and among subprimates. Interestingly, even in artificially constructed hierarchies in laboratory settings, health effects according to dominance can be observed. Animal research shows that subordinate animals have lower levels of protective cholesterol (HDCL) (Sapolsky and Mott, 1987), higher levels of cortisol, and more central fat than dominant animals, characteristics which increase the risk of cardiac disease (Sapolsky, 1982). Manuck et al. (1983) found that dominant macaques have less atherosclerosis under stable social conditions. However, under unstable conditions (created by introducing unfamiliar animals to the group) that presented recurrent threats to dominant status, dominant animals actually showed more atherosclerosis than did submissive animals. This damage is reversed when a beta antagonist is provided to the dominant animals implying that unstable social conditions create stress which, in turn, produces heightened cardiovascular reactivity.

Adler et al. (2000) examined associations between objective (education, income and occupation) and subjective socioeconomic status (i.e., a single scale where respondents were asked to use a simple drawing of a 10-step ladder on which individuals place themselves in terms of where they stand in society) with psychological and physiological variables in a sample of 157 healthy white women who had completed at least a high school education. The subjective indicator of status was more consistently related than the objective status index to psychological functioning and health-related factors, such as self-reported health, heart rate, sleep latency, body fat distribution and cortisol habituation to repeated stress. Furthermore, most of these associated remained significant even after controlling for objective social status. These results suggest that low subjective standing is associated with greater stress and perhaps contributes to disease processes.

Subjective social standing, of course, is a kind of social comparison. The fact that it does not correspond all that highly (an r of about 0.4) with objective indicators of standing indicates there is a substantial psychological component to the subjective ranking.

Links also have been found among SES, hostility, and health outcomes. High hostility has been found to be consistently associated with higher risk of coronary disease and also associated with low SES, as measured by income, occupation and education (Barefoot et al., 1991; Scherwitz et al., 1991). It is not too big a leap to suggest that hostility, which may arise in part from the perception of social status inequities, contributes to increased risk of premature mortality. For example, Williams et al. (1995) found that US cities with higher death rates had higher hostility scores even after controlling for traditional risk factors of the sample.

Summary

In this section, I reviewed evidence suggesting that social comparisons may be one pathway to illness. Certain types of people – Type As and neurotics – may engage in invidious comparisons that exacerbate their drive to excel, in the former case, or reinforce their negative perceptions of themselves, in the latter case. Such experiences may increase stress and negative health behaviors and may potentiate pathogenic processes that increase the risk of disease. More generally, the struggle to attain dominant status or finding oneself chronically outperformed may lead to feelings and behaviors that eventuate in poorer health.

Role of Comparisons in Prevention and Health Behaviors

Research has substantiated that a wide-range of life-style behaviors, such as smoking, alcohol, overeating and lack of physical exercise are associated with early mortality and morbidity. Considerable resources have been devoted to prevention and interventions to promote healthy behaviors and discourage unhealthy ones.

Virtually all theoretical accounts of health-related practices posit that normative expectations about specific practices are important. Ajzen and Fishbein's (1980) very influential Theory of Reasoned Action (TRA), posits that behavior is a function of the person's attitudes about the behavior and their perceptions of the subjective norm, that is, others' opinions regarding the appropriateness of the behavior.

With regard to social influences on health behaviors, one of the most consistent predictors of alcohol and cigarette use among high school and college students is the student's perception of alcohol and cigarette use by his or her peers (e.g., Graham et al., 1991; Kandel, 1980; Stein et al., 1987). Experimental and field studies indicate that people move closer to the group's consensual position when they note a discrepancy between themselves and the group (Asch, 1956; Crandall, 1988; Schachter, 1951). For social influence to occur, of course, the individual must have identified (or think they have identified) the social norm. Although the general sentiment of society about a specific practice (e.g., smoking) may be easily discerned from casual observation or mass media sources, details regarding normative practices may be harder for the layperson to ascertain. Contemporary society does not condone heavy drinking of alcohol, but there is no readily available definition of "drinking to excess." Percentage alcohol content in the blood may be used by the police and the courts to decide whether someone has been driving while intoxicated. However, this is not an index commonly available to most people. In the absence of comprehensive information about the average and range of use, it is virtually impossible for the individual to obtain a precise idea of how much drinking other people, besides their closest companions, do. We only have available a thin slice of the population from which to infer the norms of the larger group. These considerations make identification of health behavior norms difficult. For these reasons, people probably use their constructed comparisons as defaults for the actual norms.

False Consensus Effect and Health Behavior

People depend on simpler rules of thumb, or heuristics, when confronted with complex patterns of information. One rule of thumb is the availability heuristic (Kahneman and Tversky, 1973); if a behavior is easy to recall, it tends to be perceived as common. Thus, particularly memorable or accessible instances of a behavior tend to inflate estimates of the general probability of such behavior. Because one's own behavior is probably most available or accessible (Krueger, 2000), people are likely to distort the norm in the direction of their own behavior. This is demonstrated by the classic FCE (Ross et al., 1977), described earlier.

The FCE represents a constructed social comparison norm, as described in the introduction to this chapter. A byproduct of such egocentric perceptions is justification for one's own behavior. The FCE has been reported for a wide range of health-relevant behaviors. For example, Chassin and her associates (1984) found that adolescents' ratings of their friends' use of alcohol, cigarettes, and marijuana were positively correlated with their own current use. Suls et al. (1988) found the FCE for a wide range of health-relevant practices (e.g., substance use, seat belts, etc.) among college students. For example, smokers believed that more of their peers smoked cigarettes than did the non-smokers. Suls and Green (1996) found that students who tended not to practice safe sex estimated there was a higher proportion of other students like themselves than did respondents who consistently practiced safe sex.

A particularly interesting application of the FCE concerns perceptions of the prevalence of symptoms and diseases. Jemmott et al. (1988) had college students and practicing physicians indicate whether they had a history of various physical conditions, such as migraine headache or viral pneumonia, and then estimate their prevalence in the population. Both laypeople and physicians with a history of a particular condition gave higher estimates of its prevalence. For example, those physicians who had once had viral pneumonia estimated that 32 percent of the population had the health disturbance while physicians who had not had pneumonia estimated only 13 percent. Even though physicians should have expertise about these matters, their personal experience appeared to produce egocentric perceptions. This may have important implications for medical diagnosis because medical textbooks advise using medical prevalence as a guide for diagnosis. However, if physicians' ideas of prevalence are based on their own experience, they may not as readily diagnose conditions that they have not personally experienced.

Better than Average Effect and Unrealistic Optimism

Smokers think that there are more smokers than do non-smokers (i.e., FCE). However, estimating that friends and peers abuse alcohol and cigarettes more than oneself is a highly reliable finding among high school students (Graham et al., 1991; Hansen and Graham, 1991), college students, and community-residing adults (Suls and Green, in press). In essence, people report that they engage less in unhealthy practices, which represents a case of the "better than average effect." As mentioned earlier, this has a parallel in unrealistic optimism; by believing that personal risk of incurring health problems and accidents is lower than one's peers, the "illusion of invulnerability" can be maintained. (This phenomenon is not discussed at length here because it receives considerable attention in Weinstein's chapter in this volume.)

False Uniqueness

If a person practices a healthy behavior regularly and is asked to estimate the percentage of peers who also do the behavior, his/her estimate will tend to be lower than the actual number. That is, there is an *underestimate* of the number who engage in healthy practices (Suls and Wan, 1987; Suls et al., 1988). In contrast, the estimate of someone who engages regularly in an unhealthy practice will typically be higher than the actual sample mean. In other words, people tend to see themselves as more unique with respect to good practices, but more like everyone else for bad practices.

This pattern of perceptions has a strong self-protective quality and probably represents the results of motivated distortion. By seeing oneself as more unique in the practice of acting responsibly, self-esteem is bolstered. Perceiving that many other people act as irresponsibly as oneself with respect to other practices follows a different route but leads to a similar self-protective conclusion. Such constructed norms may undermine prevention efforts and reinforce existing unhealthy patterns of behavior.

Providing information about the actual social norms might appear to be an appropriate remedy to correct these misconceptions. Prevention researchers have developed school interventions that attempt to correct erroneous normative perceptions about prevalence and acceptability of drug use among peers. For example, Hansen and Graham (1991) found that normative education, which tried to correct the mis-estimation of drug use norms among junior high-school students, was effective in reducing alcohol, marijuana, and tobacco use over a year's time. In contrast, a treatment involving resistance training to peer influence (i.e., teaching children how to decline cigarettes or alcoholic beverages) was ineffective. Hansen and Graham suggested that resistance training fails because instruction in techniques to resist peer pressure communicates first that peer pressure exists and implies that most adolescents perceive substance use as common and acceptable. The efficacy of Hansen and Graham's (1991) normative education about actual rates of peer smoking is encouraging, but may, however, provide only a partial solution because some public behaviors may not reflect the person's actual feelings or inclinations (see next section).

Pluralistic Ignorance and Health-relevant Behaviors

The failure to realize that other members of the group also may be experiencing a discrepancy between how they behave in public and how they feel personally appears to play a role in college drinking practices. Excessive alcohol use by college students has become a major concern of parents, college administrators, and health officials because of its prevalence on many college campuses (Wechsler et al., 1994), with such consequences as low academic performance, legal infractions and injuries. Transition to college appears to be associated with an increase in alcohol consumption (Friend and Koushki, 1984), which decreases after graduation. What accounts for the apparent peer support for excessive rather than moderate drinking on campus?

There are strong public norms favoring alcohol at colleges and universities; indeed, drinking seems to play an important role in campus social life. Prentice and Miller (1993), however, observed that students *privately* may hold misgivings about alcohol practices as they obtain first-hand exposure to sick roommates and inappropriate behavior associated with drinking. These private misgivings may remain hidden, however, because nearly everyone's public behavior appears to support the alcohol norms and perpetuates the status quo.

Evidence of pluralistic ignorance concerning campus alcohol practices comes from several sources. For example, Princeton students consistently reported being less comfortable with campus drinking practices than their peers (Prentice and Miller, 1993). Because the majority of people cannot be less comfortable than their peers, these results confirm that students' comfort with alcohol on campus manifests the classic characteristics of pluralistic ignorance – divergence of private attitudes and the social norm.

Pluralistic ignorance on campus is not restricted to alcohol. In several studies at a large Midwestern university, Suls and Green (1996) examined the degree to which college students were personally concerned and how much they thought other college students were concerned about alcohol use, driving under the influence, safe-sex precautions, cigarette smoking, and marijuana use. Across all practices, most students thought that others were less concerned than they were. It follows that persons who feel their personal attitudes are discrepant with the majority may bring their behavior in line with the (erroneous) norm.

Gender, Pluralistic Ignorance and Alcohol

Our research group has followed up on an interesting finding that men shifted their private attitudes closer to the perceived norm and also reported more episodes of excessive drinking than did the women over the course of the semester. The suggestion was that pluralistic ignorance may operate differently for men than women.

Indeed, several survey studies (Suls and Green, in press) indicated that college men believe that they personally were more uncomfortable with campus alcohol practices than other males, and actually closer in sentiment to females. Females believed that their personal attitudes were not shared with other women or with men (although the discrepancy with members of the same-sex was smaller than with members of the opposite sex). The fact that men did not identify their personal attitudes with same-sex peers may create a particular sex-role conflict for them. In addition, men may be especially reluctant to communicate concerns about alcohol, which may be seen as incompatible with a masculine image. The result is a strong disjunction between their privately held beliefs and their observable behavior. In attempting to maintain a "macho" image, male students may behave in ways to reduce the (erroneous) discrepancy they perceive between themselves and their same-sex peers. Such a dynamic may explain why campus males have been found to shift their attitudes in the direction of the perceived norm.

An important question is why female students do not show this shift; after all, they also report feeling alienated from both other women and male students who drink too much. The answer may lie in two observations: (1) drinking is associated more with male than female campus life; in addition, (2) the stigma for not conforming to the norm may be considered more severe for men. Consistent with this idea, Suls and Green (in press) found that men who voice significant concerns about alcohol practices are perceived by other students to encounter more difficulties fitting in on campus than do women voicing the same concerns.

Reducing Pluralistic Ignorance

Conventional prevention programs with youth provide important information about health risks and resistance skills for risky practices. Education about relevant group norms, such as those of Hanson and Graham (1991), also has become popular. However, if pluralistic ignorance underlies the performance of certain health practices then something more will be required because private attitudes may be changed without affecting (perceived) social norms and public behaviors.

In an attempt to dispel pluralistic ignorance, Schroeder and Prentice (1998) have implemented peer-oriented discussion groups in which students are encouraged to speak openly about their private attitudes. In one study, the researchers provided information about pluralistic ignorance and had facilitators talk about their experience of personally feeling negatively about excessive drinking but feeling uncomfortable about disclosing their misgivings to their friends. The effectiveness of this intervention was compared to a more conventional individually oriented discussion emphasizing the risks of excessive drinking. Educating students about pluralistic ignorance was associated with a larger reduction in the impact of perceived public norms on drinking, especially for students who were highly concerned about being negatively evaluated by peers. Interestingly, there also were larger shifts in attitudes among men than women.

Alcohol appears to be associated with different normative perceptions and meanings for the campus social lives of men and women. Consequently, the development of special interventions may be required to address these different social dynamics.

The Similar Expert and Health Behavior

The study of comparison processes also lends insights about who should be most effective as a source of health messages. Conventional wisdom in prevention research recommends that individuals with expertise should be used. However, such experts as physicians or public health specialists are not always persuasive because the information they provide is viewed as inaccurate, a manifestation of social control, irrelevant, or not yet substantiated by adequate evidence (see Barr et al., 1992; Herek and Capitanio, 1994; Misovich et al., 1997). The Triadic model of opinion comparison also posits that expertise by itself is not sufficient to be persuasive. Even issues of fact or belief presuppose certain value assumptions. The Triadic model (Suls et al., 2000) posits that "similar experts" are most effective in such cases. Such persons are considered opinion leaders because they are more knowledgeable but share underlying values with their audience that are related to the area of belief. Two empirical demonstrations will be described briefly.

The Aromatherapy Experiment

To assess the role of similar experts, our research group (Suls et al., 2002) created a description of aromatherapy, an alternative medicine treatment, sometimes used for headache and stress reduction, that was delivered to a sample of college students. Approximately, one-half of these participants identified themselves as "traditionalists" and the other half as "unconventional and willing to try new things." Some of the subjects were asked to judge the effectiveness of aromatherapy (belief) while others were asked how much they thought they would enjoy it (preference prediction). Then all participants were given the opportunity to learn about the opinion of physicians (presumed experts) or other college students who were either traditional or unconventional in orientation. Consistent with the Triadic model, experts (i.e., physicians) were selected if the opinion issue concerned a belief; however, traditional students preferred a traditional physician while unconventional students preferred an unconventional physician. For the preference issue, however, participants, regardless of their own orientation, selected a person with an unconventional orientation when deciding whether they would enjoy aromatherapy. Such an individual is more likely than a traditionalist to have tried aromatherapy, so participants appeared to select an appropriate (or experienced) proxy.

The HIV Field Experiment
AIDS prevention researchers have observed that certain high risk groups are highly mistrustful of mass media suggestions and expert sources with respect to safe-sex practices. To create a credible and persuasive intervention for a high-risk gay population, Kelly et al. (1991) recruited well-respected, popular persons from the gay community who were then trained to be very knowledgeable about HIV, AIDS, and safe-sex practices. These persons were then deployed to disseminate accurate information in real-world settings, such as gay bars. The effectiveness of this intervention was associated with a significant increase in safe-sex practices in comparison to a more conventional educational program. This research and related efforts with at-risk youth, drug users, etc. (e.g., Kalichman and Hunter, 1992) indicates that interventions can create experts who are similar to the target audience and who can be highly effective persuasion agents.

Summary
In this section, I have considered the role of constructive comparisons in health behavior adoption and maintenance and social comparison on the reception of health messages. In each case, I have tried to illustrate how basic research and theory have informed practical knowledge about ways to encourage health-promotive practices.

Social Comparison and Patients' Adaptation to Illness

Social comparison can play a significant role in adaptation to physical illness. I begin by reviewing research among hospital patients coping with acute medical threats, such as surgery, followed by discussion of comparison processes among persons coping with chronic illness.

Patients Coping with Acute Medical Threats

In the last three decades, health psychologists and medical practitioners have learned that patients adapt better to stressful medical procedures if they are provided beforehand with information about the sensations and procedures that they are likely to experience (Johnson, 1973; Leventhal et al., 1989). Are there other things that can be done for patients to ameliorate distress and discomfort during preparation and recovery from surgery? Schachter's (1959) research that was described earlier suggests that affiliating with other patients, particularly ones also waiting for surgery, might be helpful. In this way, patients may be able to engage in emotional comparison to assess the appropriateness of their feelings about the upcoming stressor.

Recent research conducted by Kulik, Mahler and their colleagues (Kulik and Mahler, 1997) has shed new light on this matter. Schachter focused on the comparison and appraisal of emotion although he acknowledged that people also might want cognitive clarity (i.e., concrete details) about the impending threat to reduce uncertainty about the nature and dangers associated with the situation. But he discounted seeking cognitive clarity as an explanation for the affiliative tendency among his high-fear subjects because in conditions where subjects were prohibited from talking (and presumably could not gain cognitive clarity), the affiliative tendency still was exhibited (see also Zimbardo and Formica, 1963). Emotional comparison could still occur even when speaking was prohibited.

Kulik and Mahler (1997) observed that among patients waiting for surgery, verbal communication would be possible and cognitive clarity might be an important motive. But would such patients prefer to affiliate with others patients also waiting for surgery? Classic comparison theory postulates a preference for similar others, but the kind of concerns on the minds of patients anticipating surgery are likely to be of the sort, "Can I do X?" or "Will I like this?" In such cases, the Proxy model seems relevant. Pre-operative patients want to know what they will experience. Greater cognitive clarity should be obtained by talking to others who had more experience with the threat. In other words, post-operative patients should be the best proxies, rather than patients who also are awaiting the stressor.

To test this idea, Kulik and Mahler (1989) asked men hospitalized for coronary bypass procedures whether they would prefer assignment to a roommate who was awaiting bypass surgery (like themselves), a roommate who was back on the main ward recovering after bypass surgery, or whether they had no preference. Contrary to the emotional comparison notion but consistent with cognitive clarity and the Proxy model, patients most often preferred a roommate who was already recovering from the surgery. Indeed, comments from patients confirmed this interpretation – "It's more helpful for me to talk to someone who's already had it, because the guy that's waiting doesn't know anything about it, only what he's told" (Kulik and Mahler, 1997: 231).

A most important empirical demonstration was reported by Kulik et al. (1996) who studied comparison processes among hospitalized patients awaiting open-heart bypass surgery. Preoperative patients were randomly assigned either to roommates who had previously undergone cardiac surgery or roommates with non-cardiac diagnoses. Consistent with the idea that affiliative tendencies are strongly motivated by the need for cognitive clarity, preoperative patients who roomed with a postoperative patient actively sought information regarding the bypass surgery. There were also indications that exposure to an experienced proxy provided beneficial opportunities to gain information and reduce anticipatory anxiety. Patients who had postoperative roommates ambulated more quickly following surgery, had shorter hospital stays, and reported level anxiety.

There was also some evidence for emotional comparison, such as roommates discussing feelings prior to surgery, but it was not the predominant topic that Schachter's theory would predict and did not vary as a function of the type of surgery, a finding contrary to the emotional comparison hypothesis. Patients, interestingly, became more alike in their level of anxiety regardless of the similarity of the roommates' problem (Kulik et al., 1993) which may represent evidence for a form of primitive emotional contagion (Hatfield et al., 1993). Although this contagion could be the result of comparison, it may also reflect a more general mimicry of facial expressions, vocalizations, posture, and body movements.

These extensions of Schachter's original affiliation research refine understanding about patient's responses to acute medical threats and provide independent support for recent conceptual models in social comparison. In addition, this research indicates that roommate assignment offers a simple and potentially cost-effective measure to facilitate comparison, cognitive clarity and encourage adjustment in hospital.

Patient Coping with Chronic Medical Illness

The Wood et al. (1985) study with breast cancer patients discussed earlier provided some of the earliest evidence of downward comparison among medical patients. Eighty percent of those interviewed, even those who by available evidence were not doing well, reported adjusting somewhat better or much better than other patients. This evidence seemed supportive of downward comparison as a coping strategy. Indeed, reports of downward comparison are common among many different types of medical populations (see Buunk and Gibbons, 1997; Helgeson and Taylor, 1993).

Problems with this conception have surfaced, however. First, although persons experiencing the greatest threat are hypothesized to make more downward comparisons in an attempt to increase subjective well-being (Wills, 1981), often the reverse is seen: people in a good mood report making downward comparisons while those in a bad mood report more upward comparisons

(Wheeler and Miyake, 1992). Also, upward comparison has been associated, at least for some individuals, with benefits (Taylor and Lobel, 1989). Finally, some researchers have noted that the correlational evidence for downward comparison as an effortful coping strategy is ambiguous. Tennen and Affleck (1997) observed that what is taken as evidence of the effects of comparison as a coping strategy may merely be an inference or conclusion. Unfortunately, much of the available correlational evidence does not distinguish between using comparison as an effortful strategy versus as a conclusion or belief that may simply be wishful thinking or reflect actual status. In the absence of naturalistic studies that track changes in comparison activity among medical patents, it remains unclear how frequently medical patients actually engage in upward and downward comparison as a coping strategy. Fortunately, however, there are experimental studies assessing the impact of upward and downward comparison on affect in medical patients and these yield more consistent conclusions.

For example, Stanton et al. (1999) randomly assigned Stage I or II breast cancer patients who had been diagnosed within the past 5 years to listen to an audiotaped interview in which the target's adjustment and prognosis were manipulated to reflect good, poor or unspecified psychological and physical health status. They were then asked to indicate their desire for affiliation with the target and also completed ratings about their prognosis and coping. Patients were more likely to want support from a target exhibiting good adjustment compared to a less well-adjusted target, supporting the assertion that patients prefer upward contacts (e.g., Taylor and Lobel, 1989). However, patients who were exposed to the poorly adjusted target rated their own coping and prognosis as better than those exposed to the well-adjusted target, indicating that comparing with worse-off others can be beneficial. But even those patients who were exposed to a high-functioning target (i.e., upward target) evaluated their own adjustment and prognosis as better than those of the target. Further, patients reported that the audio interview, regardless of whether it involved a high- or low-functioning target, made them feel better about their own prognosis and treatment. Hence, patients appeared to be able to find positive meaning in either direction. Stanton et al. (1999: 155) noted some of the ways their patients were able to "preserve salutary self-evaluations." For example, some patients "noted that the well-functioning target was 'too good to be true,' that she must be engaging in denial, and that they therefore were adjusting more positively" (ibid.).

The preceding study shows that upward and downward comparison can offer psychological benefits to patients, but it is limited to a breast cancer sample diagnosed on average 2 years earlier. Whether women just diagnosed or those with terminal illness respond in the same way is unclear. With regard to a chronic but less severe disorder, rheumatoid arthritis, DeVellis et al. (1991) also found that patients were able to extract self-enhancing information even when exposed to a superior comparison target. The generalizability of these results to other chronic diseases is unknown but research is ongoing.

Individual Differences in Response to Upward and Downward Comparisons

By virtue of temperament, people probably vary in their responses to upward and downward comparisons. Van der Zee et al. (1998b) provided patients who were being treated for cancer with a special computer program which enabled them to access information about fellow patients' disease-related experiences. The participants also completed a measure of neuroticism. Overall, patients selected more interviews with more fortunate others and showed more positive reactions to such information. Consistent with findings discussed earlier, neuroticism was associated with greater interest in social comparison but with less favorable reactions whether with upward or downward sources (see Van der Zee et al., 1998a for another replication.).

Some individuals by virtue of their temperament are less able to obtain salutary benefits from either upward or downward comparisons. Neuroticism, of course, does not exhaust the individual differences that may moderate comparison effects. For example, Gibbons and Buunk (1999) have identified differences in the predisposition to make social comparisons with the Iowa-Netherlands Comparison Orientation Measure. This measure, independent of neuroticism, was associated with more negative reactions to downward comparisons (Buunk et al., 2001).

Integrative Concepts

Available evidence indicates that comparisons with better- and worse-functioning patients can yield both positive and negative outcomes. But if the effects of comparison are not intrinsic to their direction, then what accounts for different responses? Answering this question is important for the successful implementation of informational and social support interventions with patients with chronic illnesses where comparisons undoubtedly occur. At least two general conceptions have been advanced.

Expectancies about Prognosis
Wood and van der Zee (1997) propose that preferences for and reactions to comparison depend on whether people believe their standing will change (see also Major et al., 1991). If people think that their status will improve, upward comparison or contact should produce positive affect, but if improvement seems unlikely to them, then upward comparison should be associated with negative affect. Conversely, if patients do not expect to decline in condition, comparison with persons worse off should be self-enhancing, but if patients believe that they may personally decline, downward comparisons should be threatening. Thus, the main moderating factor, according to Wood and van der Zee (1997), is the person's beliefs about improvement or decline. Although Lockwood and Kunda's (1997) research involved college students,

the finding that a superstar inspired subjects when they either had enough time to achieve comparable success or believed their own abilities could improve over time, is certainly consistent with Wood and Van der Zee's proposal.

Assimilation and Contrast

Historically, research on the effects of social comparisons has tended to emphasize contrastive effects – others worse off generating positive feelings and others better off generating negative affect (e.g., Morse and Gergen, 1969). But comparisons also might lead to assimilative tendencies, in which a person might see their own performance as comparable to "one of the better ones" (Wheeler, 1966; Collins, 1996) or a proxy's performance may signal that one will perform similarly on a future task (Martin et al., 2002).

Stapel and Koomen (2000; 2001) proposed that assimilation occurs when information about a comparison target is used as an interpretation frame; contrast is more likely when information is used as a comparison standard. In the former case, if information about the target activated during social comparison is diffuse such information "can spill over onto unrelated stimuli" (Murphy and Zajonc, 1993: 736). Thus, similarities between the self and the comparison target are accentuated, especially if the self-attribute is perceived as mutable. When the comparison target is perceived as distinct – for example, a particular person (Betty Ford or Nancy Reagan) – then the target produces contrast because the target serves as an anchor.

In several recent experiments testing this general model, Stapel and Koomen (2001) had participants work on a proofreading task that made salient either the personal ("Circle first-person pronouns") or the social self ("Circle 'we' or 'us'"). Previous experiments have demonstrated that the latter type of priming activates social self-construals ("we"), while the former activates personal self-construals ("I"). Subsequently, participants were exposed to descriptions of either a highly successful (upward) or very unsuccessful (downward) comparison target and then made a series of self-ratings. Self-descriptions were more similar to the upward or downward comparison targets when previously primed for social construals. However, after personal ("I") priming, participants described themselves as less like the respective upward or downward targets. Thus, assimilation occurred when aspects of the self-reflecting integration and inclusion in the group were cognitively activated. Contrast occurred when the personal self, one's unique attributes (the "I"), was activated.

The idea that assimilation-contrast depends on the interpretative set of the individual and mutability of one's status (a concept shared with Wood and van der Zee) has not been directly tested on medical patients. However, this general approach offers an intriguing perspective that integrates research on social comparison and social cognition. Moreover, it offers some suggestions for how social support groups might facilitate information exchange and patient coping by emphasizing personal versus communal construal and by alerting patients to things about their physical condition that are mutable versus those that are not.

Conclusion

The seventeenth-century English monarch Charles I is said to have announced 12 "good rules," one of which was "Make no comparisons." Charles was known to be physically unattractive so this strategy may reflect his personal self-protective strategy or his appreciation that social comparisons can lead to envy and frustration, emotions about which monarchs need to be concerned. As we have seen, however, matters are more complicated than that in the domain of health and illness. Comparisons with other people, for example, can aid in the interpretation of physical symptoms, provide social validation for personal health practices and facilitate adaptation to health threats. These comparisons do not even need to be with actual people; they may be fabricated. Social comparisons also have the potential to do harm. Certain kinds of motivated comparisons can provide validation and apparent support for unhealthy "health" practices, create unrealistically optimistic expectations, and provide discouragement to those grappling with serious illness. By researching the role of social comparisons in the health domain, the opportunity to exploit their benefits and reduce the mischief they can do is increased. Hopefully, this chapter has made a persuasive case for the worth of social comparison study, its relevance for physical health, and prospects for its application.

Acknowledgments

Some of the author's research reported here and preparation of the chapter was facilitated by National Science Foundation grant BCS-99-10592. Ken Wallston and Renny Martin provided useful criticism of a prior draft.

Correspondence should be addressed to: Jerry Suls, PhD, Department of Psychology E-11 SSH, University of Iowa, Iowa City, Iowa 52245, USA; e-mail: Jerry-suls@uiowa.edu

References

Adler, N., Boyce, T., Chesney, M. et al. (1994). Socioeconomic status and health: The challenge of the gradient. *American Psychologist*, 49, 15–24.

Adler, N., Epel, E., Castellazzo, G., and Ickovics, J. (2000). Relationship of subjective and objective social status with psychological and physiological functioning: Preliminary data in healthy, white women. *Health Psychology*, 19, 586–92.

Affleck, G., and Tennen, H. (1991). Social comparison and coping with major medical disorders. In J. Suls and T. A. Wills (Eds.), *Social Comparison: Contemporary Theory and Research* (pp. 369–93). Hillsdale, NJ: Lawrence Erlbaum.

Ajzen, I., and Fishbein, M. (1980). *Understanding Attitudes and Predicting Social Behavior*. Englewood Cliffs, NJ: Prentice-Hall.

Allport, F. H. (1924). *Social Psychology*. Boston: Houghton Mifflin.

Asch, S. (1956). Studies in independence and conformity: A minority of one against a unanimous majority. *Psychological Monographs*, 70, 1–70.

Barefoot, J., Peterson, B., Dahlstrom, W., Siegler, I., Anderson, N., and Williams, R. (1991). Hostility patterns and health implications: Correlates of Cook-Medley Hostility scale scores in a national survey. *Health Psychology*, 10, 18–24.

Barefoot, J., and Schroll, M. (1996). Symptoms of depression, acute myocardial infarction, and total mortality in a community sample. *Circulation*, 93, 1976–80.

Barr, J., Waring, J., and Warshaw, L. (1992). Knowledge and attitudes about AIDS among corporate and public service employees. *American Journal of Public Health*, 82, 225–8.

Blalock, S. J., DeVellis, B. M., and DeVellis, R. F. (1989). Social comparison among individuals with rheumatoid arthritis. *Journal of Applied Social Psychology*, 19, 665–80.

Booth-Kewley, S., and Vickers, R. (1994). Associations between major domains of personality and health behavior. *Journal of Personality*, 62, 281–98.

Buunk, B. P., Collins, R. L., Taylor, S. E., Van Yperen, N., and Dakof, G. A. (1990). The affective consequences of social comparison: Either direction has its ups and downs. *Journal of Personality and Social Psychology*, 59, 1238–49.

Buunk, B., and Gibbons, F. X. (Eds.) (1997). *Health and Coping: Perspectives from Social Comparison Theory*. Mahwah, NJ: Lawrence Erlbaum.

Buunk, B., van der Zee, K., and VanYperen, N. (2001). Neuroticism and social comparison orientation as moderators of affective responses to social comparison at work. *Journal of Personality*, 69, 745–64.

Chassin, L., Presson, C., Sherman, J., Corty, E., and Olshavsky, R. (1984). Predicting the onset of cigarette smoking in adolescents: A longitudinal study. *Journal of Applied Social Psychology*, 14, 224–43.

Colligan, M., Pennebaker, J., and Murphy, L. (Eds.) (1982). *Mass Psychogenic Illess: A Social Psychological Analysis*. Hillsdale, NJ: Erlbaum.

Collins, R. L. (1996). For better or worse: The impact of upward comparisons on self-evaluations. *Psychological Bulletin*, 119, 51–69.

Collins, R. L. (2000). Among the better ones: Upward assimilation in social comparison. In J. Suls and L. Wheeler (Eds.), *Handbook of Social Comparison* (pp. 159–72). New York: Kluwer Academic/Plenum.

Crandall, C. S. (1988). Social contagion of binge eating. *Journal of Personality and Social Psychology*, 55, 588–98.

Dembroski, T., and MacDougall, J. (1978). Stress effects on affiliation preferences among subjects possessing the Type A coronary-prone behavior pattern. *Journal of Personality and Social Psychology*, 36, 23–33.

DeVellis, R., Blalock, S., Holt, K., Renner, B., Blanchard, L., and Klotz, M. (1991). Arthritis patients' reactions to unavoidable social comparisons. *Personality and Social Psychology Bulletin*, 17, 392–9.

Festinger, L. (1954). A theory of social comparison processes. *Human Relations*, 7, 117–40.

Friedman, M., and Rosenman, R. (1974). *Type A and Your Heart*. New York: Knopf.

Friend, K. E., and Koushki, P. A. (1984). Student substance abuse: Stability and change across college years. *Public Opinion Quarterly*, 40, 427–48.

Gastorf, J., Suls, J., and Sanders, G. S. (1980). Type A Coronary-Prone Behavior Pattern and social facilitation. *Journal of Personality and Social Psychology*, 38, 773–80.

Gibbons, F. X., and Buunk, B. (1999). Individual differences in social comparison: Development of a scale of social comparison orientation. *Journal of Personality and Social Psychology*, 76, 129–42.

Gibbons, F. X., and Gerrard, M. (1991). Downward comparison and coping with threat. In J. Suls and T. A. Wills (Eds.), *Social Comparison: Contemporary Theory and Research* (pp. 317–46). Hillsdale, NJ: Lawrence Erlbaum.

Gibbons, F. X., Gerrard, M., Lando, H., and McGovern, P. G. (1991). Social comparison and smoking cesssation: The role of the "typical smoker." *Journal of Experimental Social Psychology*, 27, 239–58.

Goethals, G. R., and Darley, J. (1977). Social comparison theory: An attributional approach. In J. Suls and R. L. Miller (Eds.), *Social Comparison Processes: Theoretical and Empirical Perspectives* (pp. 259–78). Washington, DC: Hemisphere Publishing Company.

Goethals, G. R., Messick, D. M., and Allison, S. T. (1991). The uniqueness bias: Studies of constructive social comparison. In J. Suls and T. A. Wills (Eds.), *Social Comparison: Contemporary Theory and Research* (pp. 317–46). Hillsdale, NJ: Lawrence Erlbaum.

Graham, J. W., Marks, G., and Hansen, W. B. (1991). Social influence processes affecting adolescent substance use. *Journal of Applied Psychology*, 76, 291–8.

Hansen, W. B., and Graham, J. W. (1991). Preventing alcohol, marijuana and cigarette use among adolescents: Peer resistance training versus establishing conservative norms. *Preventative Medicine*, 20, 414–30.

Hatfield, E., Cacioppo, J. T., and Rapson, R. L. (1993). Emotional contagion. *Current Directions in Psychological Science*, 2, 96–9.

Helgeson, V. S., and Taylor, S. E. (1993). Social comparisons and adjustment among cardiac patients. *Journal of Applied Social Psychology*, 23, 1171–95.

Herek, G., and Capitanio, J. (1994). Conspiracies, contagion and compassion: Trust and public reactions to AIDS. *AIDS Education and Prevention*, 6, 365–75.

Herman, C. P., Olmstead, M., and Polivy, J. (1983). Obesity, externality and social influence: An integrated analysis. *Journal of Personality and Social Psychology*, 45, 926–34.

Jemmott, J., Croyle, R., and Ditto, P. (1988). Commonsense epidemiology: Self-based judgments from laypersons and physicians. *Health Psychology*, 7, 55–74.

Johnson, J. (1973). Effects of accurate expectations about sensations on the sensory and affective components of pain. *Journal of Personality and Social Psychology*, 27, 261–75.

Kahneman, D., and Tversky, A. (1973). On the psychology of prediction. *Psychological Review*, 80, 237–51.

Kalichman, S., and Hunter, T. (1992). The disclosure of celebrity HIV infection: Its effects on public attitudes. *American Journal of Public Health*, 82, 1374–6.

Kandel, D. B. (1980). Drug and drinking behavior among youth. *Annual Review of Sociology*, 6, 235–85.

Kelly, J. A., St. Lawrence, J., Diaz, Y. et al. (1991). HIV risk behavior reduction following intervention with key opinion leaders of the population: An experimental analysis. *American Journal of Public Health*, 81, 168–71.

Kerckhoff, A. C., and Back, K. W. (1968). *The June Bug: A Study of Hysterical Contagion*. New York: Appleton-Century-Crofts.

Klein, W., and Weinstein, N. (1997). Social comparison and unrealistic optimism about personal risk. In B. Buunk, and F. X. Gibbons (Eds.), *Health and Coping: Perspectives from Social Comparison Theory* (pp. 25–61). Mahwah, NJ: Lawrence Erlbaum.

Krueger, J. (2000). The projective perception of the social world: A building block of social comparison processes. In J. Suls and L. Wheeler (Eds.), *Handbook of Social Comparison* (pp. 323–52). New York: Kluwer Academic/Plenum Publishers.

Kubzansky, L., and Kawachi, I. (2000). Going to the heart of the matter: Do negative emotions cause coronary heart disease? *Journal of Psychosomatic Research*, 48, 323–37.

Kulik, J. A., and Mahler, H. L. (1987). Effects of preoperative roommate assignment on preoperative anxiety and postoperative recovery from coronary bypass surgery. *Health Psychology*, 6, 525–43.

Kulik, J. A., and Mahler, H. L. (1989). Stress and affiliation in a hospital setting: Preoperative roommate preferences. *Personality and Social Psychology Bulletin*, 15, 183–93.

Kulik, J. A., and Mahler, H. L. (1997). Social comparison, affiliation, and coping with acute medical threats. In B. P. Buunk and F. X. Gibbons (Eds.), *Health and Coping: Perspectives from Social Comparison Theory* (pp. 227–61). Mahwah, NJ: Lawrence Erlbaum.

Kulik, J. A., Mahler, H. L., and Moore, P. (1996). Social comparison and affiliation under threat: Effects on recovery from major surgery. *Journal of Personality and Social Psychology*, 71, 967–79.

Kulik, J. A., Moore, P., and Mahler, H. L. (1993). Stress and affiliation: Hospital roommate effects on preoperative anxiety and social interaction. *Health Psychology*, 12, 119–25.

Leventhal, H., Leventhal, E., Shacham, S., and Easterling, D. (1989). Active coping reduces reports of pain from childbirth. *Journal of Consulting and Clinical Psychology*, 57, 365–72.

Lockwood, P., and Kunda, Z. (1997). Superstars and me: Predicting the impact of role models on the self. *Journal of Personality and Social Psychology*, 73, 91–103.

Major, B., Testa, M., and Bylsma, W. (1991). Responses to upward and downward social comparisons: The impact of esteem-relevance and perceived control. In J. Suls, and T. Wills (Eds.), *Social Comparison: Contemporary Theory and Research* (pp. 237–60). Hillsdale. NJ: Erlbaum.

Manuck, S., Kaplan, J., and Clarkson, T. (1983). Social instability and coronary artery atherosclerosis in cynomolgus monkeys. *Neuroscience and Biobehavioral Reviews*, 7, 485–91.

Marmot, M., Smith, G., Stansfeld, S. et al. (1991). Health inequalities among British civil servants: The Whitehall II study. *Lancet*, 337, 1387–93.

Markovitz, J., Matthews, K., Kannel, W. et al. (1993). Psychological predictors of hypertension in the Framingham study: Is there tension in hypertension? *Journal of the American Medical Association*, 270, 2439–43.

Martin, R., Suls, J., and Wheeler, L. (2002). Ability evaluation by proxy: Role of maximum performance and related attributes. *Journal of Personality and Social Psychology: Interpersonal Relations and Group Processes*, 82, 781–92.

Mechanic, D. (1972). Social psychological factors affecting the presentation of bodily complaints. *New England Journal of Medicine*, 286, 1132–9.

Miller, D. T., and McFarland, C. (1987). Pluralistic ignorance: When similarity is interpreted as dissimilarity. *Journal of Personality and Social Psychology*, 53, 298–305.

Miller, D. T., and McFarland, C. (1991). When social comparison goes awry: The case of pluralistic ignorance. In J. Suls and T. A. Wills (Eds.), *Social Comparison: Contemporary Theory and Research* (pp. 287–313). Hillsdale, NJ: Lawrence Erlbaum.

Misovich, S., Fisher, J., and Fisher, W. (1997). Social comparison processes and AIDS risk and AIDS prevention behavior. In B. Buunk, and F. X. Gibbons (Eds.), *Health and Coping: Perspectives from Social Comparison Theory* (pp. 95–123). Mahwah, NJ: Lawrence Erlbaum.

Molleman, E., Pruyn, J., and van Knippenberg, A. (1986). Social comparison processes among cancer patients. *British Journal of Social Psychology*, 25, 1–13.

Morse, S., and Gergen, K. E. (1969). Social comparison, self-consistency and the concept of the self. *Journal of Personality and Social Psychology*, 16, 148–56.

Murphy, S., and Zajonc, R. (1993). Affect, cognition, and awareness: Affective priming with optimal and suboptimal stimulus exposures. *Journal of Personality and Social Psychology*, 64, 723–39.

Pennebaker, J., and Harber, K. (1993). A social stage model of collective coping: The Loma Prieta earthquake and the Persian Gulf War. *Journal of Social Issues*, 49, 125–42.

Prentice, D. A., and Miller, D. T. (1993). Pluralistic ignorance and alcohol use on campus: Some consequences of misperceiving the social norm. *Journal of Personality and Social Psychology*, 64, 243–56.

Rosenman, R., Brand, R., Jenkins, C., Friedman, M., Straus, R., and Wurm, M. (1975). Coronary heart disease in the Western Collaborative Group Study: Final follow-up experience of 8^1/2 years. *Journal of American Medical Association*, 233, 872–7.

Ross, L., Greene, and House, P. (1977). The "false consensus effect": An egocentric bias in social perception and attributional processes. *Journal of Experimental Social Psychology*, 13, 279–301.

Sanders, G. S. (1982). Social comparison and perceptions of health and illness. In G. S. Sanders and J. Suls (Eds.), *Social Psychology of Health and Illness* (pp. 129–57). Hillsdale, NJ: Lawrence Erlbaum Associates.

Sapolsky, R. (1982). The endocrine stress-response. *Hormones and Behavior*, 16, 279–92.

Sapolsky, R., and Mott, G. (1987). Social subordination in wild baboons is associated with suppressed high density lipoprotein-cholesterol concentrations: The possible role of chronic social stress. *Endocrinology*, 121, 1605–10.

Schachter, S. (1951). Deviation, rejection, and communication. *Journal of Abnormal and Social Psychology*, 46, 190–207.

Schachter, S. (1959). *The Psychology of Affiliation*. Stanford, CA: Stanford University Press.

Schachter, S. (1971). Some extraordinary facts about obese humans and rats. *American Psychologist*, 45, 1263–6.

Schachter, S., and Rodin, J. (1974). *Obese Humans and Rats*. Potomac, MD: Erlbaum.

Schachter, S., Silverstein, B., Kozlowski, L., Perlick, D., Herman, C. P., and Liebling, B. (1977). Studies of the interaction of psychological and pharmacological determinants of smoking. *Journal of Experimental Psychology: General*, 106, 3–40.

Schachter, S., and Singer, J. E. (1962). Cognitive, social, and physiological determinants of emotional state. *Psychological Review*, 69, 379–99.

Schachter, S., and Wheeler, L. (1962). Epinephrine, chlorpromazine, and amusement. *Journal of Abnormal and Social Psychology*, 65, 121–8.

Schanck, R. L. (1932). A study of community and its group institutions conceived of as behavior of individuals. *Psychological Monographs*, 43 (2), 1–133.

Scherwitz, L., Perkins, K., Chesney, M., and Hughes, G. (1991). Cook-Medley Hostility and subsets: Relationship to demographic and psychosocial characteristics in young adults in the CARDIA study. *Psychosomatic Medicine*, 53, 36–49.

Schroeder, C. M., and Prentice, D. A. (1998). Exposing pluralistic ignorance to reduce alcohol use among college students. *Journal of Applied Social Psychology*, 28, 2150–80.

Stahl, S. M., and Lebedun, M. (1974). Mystery gas: An analysis of mass hysteria. *Journal of Health and Social Behavior*, 15, 44–50.

Stanton, A., Danoff-Burg, S., Cameron, C., Snider, P., and Kirk, S. (1999). Social comparison and adjustment to breast cancer: An experimental examination of upward affiliation and downward evaluation. *Health Psychology*, 18, 151–8.

Stapel, D., and Koomen, W. (2000). Distinctness of others, mutability of selves: Their impact on self-evaluations. *Journal of Personality and Social Psychology*, 79, 1068–87.

Stapel, D., and Koomen, W. (2001). I, we and the effects of others on me: How self-construal level moderates social comparison effects. *Journal of Personality and Social Psychology*, 80, 766–81.

Stein, J. A., Newcomb, M. D., and Bentler, P. M. (1987). An 8-year study of multiple influences on drug use and drug use consequences. *Journal of Personality and Social Psychology*, 53, 1094–105.

Suls, J. (1986). Notes on the occasion of social comparison theory's thirtieth birthday. *Personality and Social Psychology Bulletin*, 12, 289–96.

Suls, J., Becker, M. A., and Mullen, B. (1981). Coronary-prone behavior, social insecurity and stress among college-aged adults. *Journal of Human Stress*, 7, 27–34.

Suls, J., and Green, P. (1996) Misconstrual of social norms about health-relevant practices in college students: False consensus, pluralistic ignorance, and the above-average effect. Unpublished manuscript, University of Iowa.

Suls, J., and Green, P. (in press). Pluralistic ignorance and college student perceptions of gender-specific alcohol norms. *Health Psychology*.

Suls, J., Martin, R., and Wheeler (2000). Three kinds of opinion comparison: The Triadic Model. *Personality and Social Psychology Review*, 4, 219–37.

Suls, J., Martin, R., Wheeler, L., Wallio, S., Bobier, D., and Lemos, K. (2002). The similar expert: Two tests of the Triadic opinion comparison model. Poster presented at Society for Personality and Social Psychology annual meeting, Savannah, Georgia.

Suls, J., and Wan, C. K. (1987). In search of the false uniqueness phenomenon: fear and estimates of social consensus. *Journal of Personality and Social Psychology*, 52, 211–17.

Suls, J., Wan, C., and Sanders, G. (1988). False consensus and false uniqueness in estimating the prevalence of health-protective behaviors. *Journal of Applied Social Psychology*, 18, 66–79.

Suls, J., and Wills, T. A. (Eds.) (1991). *Social Comparison: Contemporary Theory and Research*. Hillsdale, NJ: Erlbaum.

Taylor, S. E., and Brown, J. D. (1988). Illusion and mental health: A social psychological perspective. *Psychological Bulletin*, 103, 193–210.

Taylor, S. E., and Lobel, M. (1989). Social comparison activity under threat: Downward evaluation and upward contacts. *Psychological Review*, 96, 569–75.

Tennen, H., and Affleck, G. (1997). Social comparison as a coping process: A critical review and application to chronic pain disorders. In B. Buunk and F. X. Gibbons (Eds.), *Health and Coping: Perspectives from Social Comparison Theory* (pp. 263–98). Mahwah, NJ: Lawrence Erlbaum.

Turner, J. (1991). *Social Influence*. Pacific Grove, CA: Brooks/Cole Publishing Company.

van der Zee, K., Buunk, B., and Sanderman, R. (1996). The relationship between social comparison and personality. *Personality and Individual Differences*, 20, 551–65.

van der Zee, K., Buunk, B., and Sandersman, R. (1998a). Neuroticism and reactions to social comparison information among cancer patients. *Journal of Personality*, 66, 175–94.

van der Zee, K., Oldersma, F., Buunk, B., and Bos, D. (1998b). Social comparison preferences among cancer patients as related to neuroticism and social comparison orientation. *Journal of Personality and Social Psychology*, 75, 801–10.

Wechsler, H., Davenport, A., Dowdall, G., Moeykens, B., and Castillo, S. (1994). Health and behavioral consequences of binge drinking in college. *Journal of the American Medical Association*, 272, 1672–7.

Weinstein, N. (1980). Unrealistic optimism about future life events. *Journal of Personality and Social Psychology*, 39, 806–20.

Weinstein, N. (1982). Unrealistic optimism about susceptibility to health problems: Future life events. *Journal of Behavioral Medicine*, 5, 441–60.

Wheeler, L. (1966). Motivation as a determinant of upward comparison. *Journal of Experimental Social Psychology*, 2 (Suppl. 1), 27–31.

Wheeler, L., Martin, R., and Suls, J. (1997). The Proxy social comparison model for self-assessment of ability. *Personality and Social Psychology Review*, 1, 54–61.

Wheeler, L., and Miyake, K. (1992). Social comparisons in everyday life. *Journal of Personality and Social Psychology*, 62, 760–73.

Wilkinson, R. (1992). Income distribution and life expectancy. *British Medical Journal*, 304, 165–8.

Williams, R., Feaganes, J., and Barefoot, J. (1995). Hostility and death rates in ten US cities (Abstract). *Psychosomatic Medicine*, 57, 94.

Wills, T. A. (1981). Downward comparison principles in social psychology. *Psychological Bulletin*, 90, 245–71.

Wills, T. A. (1987). Downward comparison as a coping mechanism. In C. R. Snyder and C. E. Ford (Eds.), *Coping with Negative Life Events: Clinical and Social Psychological Perspectives* (pp. 243–68). New York: Plenum.

Wood, J. V. (1989). Theory and research concerning social comparisons of personal attributes. *Psychological Bulletin*, 106, 231–48.

Wood, J. V., Taylor, S. E., and Lichtman, R. (1985). Social comparison in adjustment to breast cancer. *Journal of Personality and Social Psychology*, 49, 1169–83.

Wood, J. V., and van der Zee, K. (1997). Social comparison among cancer patients: Under what conditions are comparisons upward or downward? In B. P. Buunk and F. X. Gibbons (Eds.), *Health and Coping: Perspectives from Social Comparison Theory* (pp. 299–328). Mahwah, NJ: Lawrence Erlbaum.

Zanna, M., Goethals, G., and Hill, S. (1975). Evaluating sex-related ability: Social comparison with similar others and standard setters. *Journal of Experimental Social Psychology*, 11, 86–93.

Zimbardo, P., and Formica, R. (1963). Emotional comparison and self-esteem as determinants of affiliation. *Journal of Personality*, 31, 141–62.

CHAPTER 10

Interpersonal Emotional Processes in Adjustment to Chronic Illness

Robert F. DeVellis, Megan A. Lewis, and Katherine Regan Sterba

University of North Carolina at Chapel Hill

Introduction

The goal of this chapter is to introduce readers to a variety of perspectives that have not been widely applied to understanding the impact of interpersonal emotional factors in adjustment to chronic illness. More specifically, we present theories and models derived from the field of relationship science (Ryff and Singer, 2000), which has a tradition of studying dyadic relationships and their connection to emotions and adjustment. In addition, we apply concepts and ideas from fields related to emotional management that have focused on understanding how people manage their moods from both an intra- and interpersonal perspective. Most of these theories and models, however, have not been systematically applied or studied in health-related contexts. The main goal of this chapter is to bring together these largely independent lines of research and hopefully to spur social psychologists interested in health outcomes to think about interpersonal emotional processes in new ways.

Why a New Perspective Is Needed

We view this subject as distinct from social support, which has traditionally been studied in health-related contexts, because the methods and models that have been applied to dyadic relationships are different from those applied to support more generally. Moreover, in contrast to social support, theory and research in the area of relationship science and close relationships has been largely overlooked by health psychologists. Also, because of the nature of *close* interpersonal relationships, the discussion that follows necessarily includes interpersonal emotional processes. Indeed, it is probably the nature of emotional exchanges between individuals that make an interpersonal relationship *close*, as most people understand that term.

Although social support has been linked with a variety of health outcomes including health-related behaviors, emotional well-being, immunological and cardiovascular functioning and mortality risk (House et al., 1988), translation of research to intervention has been largely unsuccessful. Given the extensive correlational data linking social support with better health, many psychosocial and behavior change interventions have been designed to include spouses in the intervention effort. By including spouses, these interventions attempted to capitalize on the benefits of social relationships in changing behaviors related to chronic disease risk, including smoking cessation, dietary changes, reductions in weight, and physical activity. These interventions are typically guided by the assumption that involving the spouse in the process of change enhances social support for behavior change attempts.

For example, a meta-analysis of couple interventions focused on weight loss indicate that couple interventions are more successful than individual treatment, but the effect is very small and, at best, the superiority only lasts for two to three months post-program (Black et al., 1990). There are other explanations for these intervention failures, such as poor conceptualization, implementation, and evaluation (Glass, 2000). One analysis suggests, however, that support interventions that are more "relational" than individually focused are more successful (Lassner, 1991). That is, programs that take into account how spouses interact and communicate as well as capitalizing on how their relationship may facilitate change are more successful than interventions that do not account for the relational aspects of change. We hope that the perspectives we integrate in this chapter will lead to a better understanding of exactly how spouses interact and communicate regarding adjustment to chronic illness.

Because it is still unclear exactly how support provides benefits (Heller et al., 1986; Cohen, 1988), a number of authors have argued that social support needs to be "disaggregated into a number of component parts" (Lieberman, 1986: 464). In this chapter, we promote research to examine the mechanisms underlying the concept of social support in an effort to better understand how these processes work. The ultimate goal of this line of inquiry is an increased understanding of how support works in interpersonal relationships so that interventions can be developed to help couples cope with the ongoing challenges of having a chronic illness.

Understanding social mechanisms may be especially important for older married couples. Older spouses rate their partner, compared to other social network members, as closer, and exchange support more frequently with their partner (Akiyama et al., 1996). Further, older couples tend to be "socially isolated," meaning when illness develops they are more likely to rely on one another and not other people (Johnson, 1985). Developing a better understanding of how interpersonal factors contribute to the variability in disease management is important because the burden of chronic illness on middle-aged and older adults is large, and initiating disease management behaviors can stem disease progression.

Although there are many forms of close interpersonal relationships, we focus primarily on marriage and similar partnerships. At times, we will use marriage as a term of convenience to embrace a range of close, dyadic relationships involving emotion and mutual obligation, such as on-going gay or lesbian relationships. Relationships of this type may or may not have distinct features that bear consideration but we suspect that much of the discussion that follows is applicable beyond a narrow definition of marriage. Marriage has been the focus of the bulk of research in this area and may be an especially significant relationship for matters related to health and illness (Burman and Margolin, 1992). We believe this is so because marriage relationships are often very interdependent, emotionally close, endure for a considerable period of time, and extend across a portion of the life-span during which both prevention of and adaptation to chronic illness may take place. Although we focus on the marriage relationship, we recognize that there are several other potentially equally important dyadic relationships including parents and children, siblings, and close friends. We discuss these briefly later in the chapter. Regrettably, social psychologists have studied these less intensively than the marriage dyad.

Chapter Overview

We begin with a historical perspective on close relationships and the emotions they engender. That section briefly surveys how the status of feelings and emotional closeness has varied over time, as revealed in works of historians and philosophers. Capturing all the nuances of well-elaborated philosophies or social systems in a few sentences is impossible. It is possible, however, to examine in broad strokes some streams of Western thought and culture to get a sense of how emotions, close relationships, and health were or were not linked to one another. Thus, although this treatment is selective rather than exhaustive, we believe it gives a sense of how the nature of dyadic relationships and the attention paid to emotion has waxed and waned in various periods. Following the historical overview, we describe theoretical perspectives from the areas of relationship science and emotional regulation. Next, we provide examples of contemporary work in which we have translated these theories and concepts to examine adjustment in the context of chronic illness. Additionally, we summarize the implications of this previous work for future research on interpersonal emotional factors and adjustment. Finally, we conclude by noting some further technical issues that may be pertinent to future research.

We believe that using new perspectives and methodologies, like those used in the field of close relationships, will help social psychologists build explanatory bridges between the social epidemiological work that documents the consequential role of marriage in health (e.g. House et al., 1988; Seeman, 1996), and the emerging literature that focuses on interpersonal flourishing (e.g. Ryff and Singer, 2000). If we can better understand the positive qualities of interpersonal relationships and the social mechanisms underlying the exchange and regulation of moods between partners in such relationships, we can think about "build[ing] the factors that allow [couples] to flourish" (Seligman and Csikszentmihalyi, 2000: 13) in the context of adjustment.

Historical Perspectives on Dyadic Relationships, Emotions, and Health

In the opening years of the twenty-first century, the idea that emotions associated with close personal relationships may have relevance to health does not seem radical. Today, even in popular song, love and marriage are intimately linked and love is a healing force. The equation of love and marriage and the potential impact of close relationships on health, however, have not always been as apparent as they now seem.

Acknowledging and attempting to understand emotion, within and outside of close relationships, have a long history in Western thought. Feelings and relationships to others are inescapable features of human existence. The formal incorporation of emotion and interpersonal relationships into the scholarly discussions of health, however, is a more recent phenomenon. As Reis (2001: 82) has stated, "The tantalizing notion that social relations are fundamental to human health and well-being has been a central element of folk wisdom for centuries, in nearly all recorded human societies and cultures. Behavioral science research has, however, been slow to pick up on this scheme and begin the arduous but critical task of putting empirical flesh and scholarly meat on this skeletal notion."

Emotion as Seen by Early Writers

Although classical *mythology* is replete with amorous romps, the scholarly writing of the period assigns far less significance to either inter- or intra-personal feelings and concentrates more on *reason*. Plato at least acknowledged emotions when he classified the mind into three components, one of which was the spirited-affective (thumoeides) (Fecteau, n.d.). Aristotle, according to Solomon (2000), saw emotions, once properly channeled by reason, giving rise to virtues (such as anger leading to courage) and, thus, as essential and valuable, if in a somewhat paradoxical way. Galen, the second-century philosopher and personal physician to Marcus Aurelius, linked emotional dispositions to biological underpinnings. He arguably developed the first theory of personality by ascribing four temperaments (sanguine or cheerful, melancholy or sad, choleric or quick-tempered, and phlegmatic or indifferent) to corresponding bodily humors (blood, black bile, yellow bile, and phlegm, respectively) that had been described centuries earlier by Hippocrates (who related them to the four elements: earth, air, fire, and water). For the most part, these classical philosophers saw emotions as stirring impulsive and irrational actions and, thus, as forces that reason had to contain or redirect.

There is little mention in classical sources of relationships as contributing to health or well-being. There are some isolated recommendations that familiar others provide care to those in need. Plato, for example, asserted that insanity should be treated by members of the family (Fecteau, n.d.). And Homer's *Iliad* observes that wounded soldiers were treated primarily by being given comfort from comrades rather than by active medical intervention (Demand, 1997). In a similar vein, the Roman historian Tacitus (109 AD) observed of the Germans that, "they take their injuries to their mothers and wives, who do not fear to examine and treat their wounds" suggesting at least that one's close female relatives were consulted in health matters (Mayeaux, 2000). But these instances do not imply a belief that interaction with comrades or family members is particularly beneficial to health so much as it is socially convenient.

In his *Confessions*, Augustine recounts unsuccessful attempts at subduing his passions as a young man. The often-cited quote is, "Give me chastity and continency, only not yet!" (*Confessions*, 406 AD, cited by Watson, 1963: 89). For Augustine, pleasures of the flesh (and, presumably the emotions associated with them) were impulses to be subdued by faith. If there is any implication that love has the power to heal, it is love of God rather than of another mortal.

Descartes, in the seventeenth century, identified six primary passions: wonder, love, hatred, desire, joy, and sadness. Reminiscent of Galen, he saw these as having a strong physiological basis (i.e., as being of the body) but interacting with intellectual processes (i.e., the mind) at the pineal body. Unlike his intellectual predecessors, Descartes saw both the mental and bodily (including emotions) capacities as equally important (Watson, 1963). David Hume, in the eighteenth century, gave still greater prominence to emotions and their critical role in motivating either good or evil action (Solomon, 2000).

In each of these philosophical systems, emotions are seen in some sense as contrasting with reason or some other mental faculty such as will. Moreover, they are largely intra-individual rather than interpersonal phenomena. Typically, emotions are not expressly linked to health any more than to other possible consequences of behavior. Galen seems to be an early exception (Watson, 1963). His work draws a connection between states of well-being and temperament. But the correlation is spurious in that each of these outcomes is the result of a "third variable," that is, the status of bodily humors. Thus, temperament may be a *sign* of health but is not a fundamental *determinant or consequence* of it.

Emotion as Seen by Behavioral Scientists

Psychological discussions of emotions, moods, feelings, and affect (terms that have useful distinctions in certain contexts but that we use more-or-less interchangeably here), although evident from an early date, were largely fragmentary until quite recently (Izard, 1991). The first notable exception is the work of Sigmund Freud (e.g., 1938). Psychoanalysis (e.g., Freud, 1938) gives emotions a prominent position, focuses explicitly on their role in inter-personal transactions ranging from mother–child attraction to transference, and champions their relevance to well-being. Despite this emotion-friendly stance, psychoanalysis may have had an adverse impact on how psychologists viewed emotional and interpersonal processes as they relate to health and well-being. This may be so because of the backlash that the psychoanalysis's non-empirical approach evoked, at least among American behaviorists. The subsequent flowering of cognitive models demonstrated that internal states could be examined in a rigorous fashion. This did not lead immediately to an acknowledgment of emotion as an equally suitable focus for psychological inquiry. Indeed, as alternatives to strictly behavioral models emerged, they tended to include cognitive rather than emotional elements. Examples of this include the various forms of expectancy-value theories (e.g., Bandura and Walters, 1963; Rotter, 1954), which incorporated essentially cognitive features such as outcome expectations.

More recently, emotions and the interpersonal situations in which they occur have occupied a position of higher visibility in psychological inquiry. This may be due in part to the recognition that emotions are not isolated experiences but are an integral part of human psychology. Lazarus (1991: 4) has commented that, "It is inconceivable to me that there could be an approach to the mind, or to human and animal adaptation, in which emotions are not a key component. The failure to give emotion a central role puts theoretical and research psychology out of step with human preoccupations from the beginning of recorded time." He notes that separating emotions from behavior and cognition may be a largely artificial exercise. The neurophysiology of emotions has been yet another source lending legitimacy to the topic. Pro-cesses that have long existed only in the subjective experience of an individual can now be observed in brain activity (Damasio, 1994). Thus, while emotion has always been there as an inseparable component of human experience and an undeniable factor in human psychology, it has only more recently become a topic of both extensive and systematic study in psychology.

Lazarus (1991) notes that the emotions that most easily gained admission to the psychological literature were negative. This too has changed, how-ever. "Positive psychology" has received considerable theoretical and empirical attention in the last few years (e.g., Seligman and Csikszentmihalyi, 2000; Frederickson, 2000; 2001).

The availability of a growing literature describing emotional processes is essentially a "supply side" explanation of the topic's increased popularity. That is, the availability of more information about emotion makes it easy to incorporate into new activities. Another factor has been the increased demand from various sectors for a clearer understanding of emotion. One such sector is health care. Issues such as satisfaction with care and quality of life often include elements of emotion. Also, individuals involved in outcomes research recognize that transitory mood states can play a part in how respondents assess a variety of relevant variables such as well-being and perceived risk of contracting a given health problem (Jobe, 2000; Kihlstrom et al., 2000). The increasing visibility and legitimacy of alternative health care suggests that there is also demand from consumers for health approaches that embrace the human experience more fully.

Anecdotal observation also suggests that emotions and personal relationships are an important part of consumers' beliefs about what contributes to their health and well-being. The best-seller status of Daniel Goleman's (1995) *Emotional Intelligence* is testimony to public interest in psychological research pertaining to emotions. Goleman devotes an entire chapter to mind and medicine and a subsection of that chapter to the medical value of relationships. Thus, there is a readiness among scientists and the lay public to embrace a more comprehensive understanding of how issues related to emotions and relationships affect and interact with other variables in the health domain.

As work related to emotion becomes more strongly identified with health on the one hand and close personal relationships on the other, it provides a common ground for health psychology and social psychology. A melding of interests across these specialty areas thus becomes an attractive inevitability. In the following pages, we provide selected examples of how this melding can occur. The social psychological constructs we have selected have been largely overlooked by health researchers. And yet, we believe they hold substantial promise for increasing our understanding of adaptation to chronic illness and the inextricable linkages between social psychology and health psychology.

Theoretical Perspectives on Close Relationships and Emotional Regulation

In the section that follows, we describe two categories of psychological perspectives that are central to the topic of this chapter: close relationship perspectives and emotional regulation perspectives. We also provide an overview followed by a discussion of each perspective's potential relevance to health. After examining both close relationship and emotional regulation perspectives in this way, we describe some of our efforts to translate these perspectives into health-related research.

Overview of Close Relationship Perspectives

Past research examining interpersonal emotional processes and adjustment to chronic illness has typically been guided by individual level conceptual models that lead to examining a person's report of his or her own interpersonal and emotional experiences, but tell us little about the reciprocal and joint influence marital partners exert on each other's adjustment. This research has yielded a large literature of important and meaningful information about the significance of interpersonal and emotional experiences as they affect chronic illness adjustment. For example, marital quality predicts psychological adjustment to heart disease (Brecht et al., 1994), relationship closeness predicts the experience of less angina and an easier return to normal activities after heart bypass surgery (King et al., 1993), and emotional social support has been established as an independent predictor of six-month mortality after heart attack (Berkman et al., 1992). In patients with arthritis, social support has been linked to less subsequent pain (DeVellis et al., 1986), better family role functioning (Goodenow et al., 1990), and enhanced psychological well-being (Fitzpatrick et al., 1988).

While these findings have advanced our understanding of adjustment to chronic illness, they open the door to many questions related to the interpersonal emotional nature of adjustment to chronic illness. For example, they do not elucidate the mediational mechanisms that help explain how interactions with a spouse can change the course of illness and adaptation. The limitations of past research relate to a common bias, termed pseudounilaterality (Duncan et al., 1984). This bias is prevalent in social psychological research examining interpersonal phenomena. Pseudounilaterality refers to problems that stem from continually examining only one side of two-sided interactions. Much of what we know about interpersonal phenomena is only from one perspective, rather than from the dual perspective of both participants during personal interaction. This results from examining the individual as the unit of analysis, when examining the dyad or couple would be more appropriate. Figure 10.1 depicts a simple dyadic model showing the types of effects that can be examined when one thinks about the interpersonal emotional consequences of social interaction from a dyadic rather than individual point of view. This conceptual model highlights the interdependence of interacting partners' outcomes (Lewis and Butterfield, 1998a; 1998b). Each spouse's thoughts, emotions, and behaviors depend partly on their partner (see Figure 10.1).

Interdependence theory is commonly used to guide research related to close dyadic relationships, although the outcomes commonly studied in this literature are relationship maintenance or dissolution (Rusbult and Van Lange, 1996). Compared to other relationships, the unique quality of close on-going relationships is the interdependence between partners' emotions, beliefs, and behaviors. Interdependence refers to the process by which people influence each other's experiences or the effects an individual exerts on another's

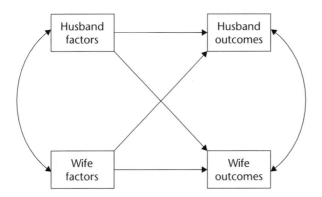

Figure 10.1   Interdependence model of couple adjustment.

motives, preferences, behavior, and outcomes (Rusbult and Van Lange, 1996). Relationship interdependence arises from structural characteristics of the relationship that bring people closer together and/or drive them apart. Interdependence theory suggests that relationship characteristics that bring people together such as closeness, quality, or equality should facilitate the effects interacting partners have on each other's preferences and behavior and, of most relevance to the focus of the present chapter, adaptation or adjustment to chronic illness. Conversely, relationship characteristics that drive people apart, such as conflict or disagreement, should impede adaptation or adjustment. Relationship interdependence is the amalgam of these push-pull forces in relationships.

In addition to the influence of interdependence structures in the relationship, interdependence theory suggests that individual-level factors that occur in response to social interaction, or reflect patterns of response over the history of the relationship, are another way in which involvement in close on-going relationships may influence emotions, behaviors, or adjustment. The theory proposes that accommodation and change in the context of close relationships is understood via a process termed "transformation of motivation" (Yovetich and Rusbult, 1994). Transformation of motivation occurs when an individual internalizes social interactions from another person, and thus acts in pro-relationship, health-enhancing ways rather than acting in a purely self-interested manner. It can be described as a shift from an "I" or "you" to a "we" orientation. This transformation is thought to be facilitated by proximal factors to interaction (such as attributions for and emotional reactions to spousal behavior, or taking the perspective of one's spouse) as well as distal factors to the interaction (such as long-term relationship goals, relationship roles, and norms). The theory suggests that these determinants of transformation of motivation should facilitate spousal interactions focused on adjustment to chronic illness, whether adjustment entails emotional coping or behavioral adaptations and changes. Transformation of motivation is thought to be the combination of cognitive, normative, and affective factors that facilitate or impede the internalization of different types of social interaction.

Interdependence and transformation of motivation are thought to facilitate accommodation to the beliefs, circumstances, and behavior of one's partner (Bissonnette et al., 1997). Accommodation between partners is believed to be a fundamental process in close relationships. Interdependence researchers commonly study the process of accommodation by examining how partners react when one acts "badly" toward the other by expressing criticism, hostility, or otherwise threatening the relationship in some way. In the context of the present chapter, the accommodation between partners could be the choices each make when one expresses negative emotions, or the behavioral choices each make when one partner is diagnosed with a chronic health condition. For example, does the husband choose to quit smoking along with his wife when she is diagnosed with heart disease? That is, does the husband accommodate to his wife's circumstance, even though he hasn't been diagnosed with the condition, and he may enjoy smoking? How married partners accommodate to each other in such circumstances could depend on the level of interdependence or the process of transformation of motivation.

Several theorists have suggested examining relationship interdependence in the context of health and behavior, particularly with regard to adaptation to chronic illness such as heart disease (Coyne et al., 1990) and behavior change after a heart attack (Ewart and Fitzgerald, 1994). These calls for research are consistent with: (a) qualitative data indicating that successful marriages among older couples are distinguished by their interdependence when faced with recovery and adaptation to chronic illness; and (b) theorists who contend that an increasingly important developmental task in adulthood is interdependence between partners (Veroff and Veroff, 1980; Baltes and Silverberg, 1994).

There are two reasons why this theoretical approach has not been used more extensively. First, interdependence theory is complex, and translation for use in more applied research contexts has not taken place. Second, this theory specifies dyads as the basic unit of analysis; such data pose methodological and statistical challenges. Most methods and analytic procedures assume that data points are independent of each other, and violation of this assumption leads to biases in statistical tests (Kenny and Judd, 1986). This poses a significant challenge for researchers, because it is precisely this interdependence between data points (i.e., patient-spouse or husband-wife) that we need to maintain to test certain relational explanations. Recent advances in estimating and testing statistical models that use dyadic data should help researchers advance our understanding of the role of relationship interdependence in adjustment (e.g., Kenny, 1996; Kashy and Kenny, 2000; Judd et al., 2001). These recent advances may herald a change in perspective from more individually focused to more couples-focused research approaches – a transition evident in the work we discuss below.

Potential Relevance of Close Relationship Perspectives to Health

Relationship interdependence, transformation of motivation, and accommodation may influence how successfully couples adjust to chronic illness. Those theorists that have suggested examining relationship interdependence in the context of health and behavior have found that patient self-efficacy is jointly determined by both patient and spouse variables (Coyne et al., 1990). Successful adjustment involves a variety of cognitive, emotional and behavioral tasks on both the part of the person who is diagnosed and the spouse. The couple's level of interdependence (i.e. the pushes and pulls on their relationship) could facilitate adjustment or make it more difficult. Transformation of motivation could help explain why some partners accommodate more easily than other partners when a spouse is diagnosed with a condition that involves a great deal of change. A husband who takes into account the roles, norms, and long-term relationship goals of a partnership might be more likely to eat a low fat diet, or start exercising with his wife when she is diagnosed with diabetes. Understanding how interdependence and transformation of motivation influence the choices partners make in a relationship can help shed light on the mechanisms by which social interactions within the couple lead to better or poorer adjustment to chronic illness.

In a later section of this chapter, we will discuss how we are translating these theoretical concepts from close relationship perspectives to studying adaptation to chronic illness. But first we will summarize our second major category of perspectives, emotion management.

Overview of Emotion Management Perspectives

In the following paragraphs, we briefly describe three largely separate emotion management perspectives: emotional intelligence, empathic accuracy, and emotional contagion. Following these descriptions, we examine their potential relevance to health.

Overview of Emotional Intelligence Perspective

Emotional intelligence was first introduced to the general public in 1995 (Goleman, 1995), and has been defined as, "the subset of social intelligence that involves the *ability to monitor one's own and others' feelings and emotions, to discriminate among them and to use this information to guide one's thinking and actions*" (Salovey and Mayer, 1990: 189; emphasis in original). More recently, there has been a flurry of empirical and theoretical activity related to emotional intelligence and the definition of emotional intelligence has varied over time (see the volume edited by Bar-On and Parker, 2000, for several examples). Our own thinking has been influenced primarily by the model first described by Salovey and Mayer (1990).

According to this view, people who are emotionally intelligent should be better equipped to manage their lives in a way that optimizes their own positive feelings and the positive feelings of others with whom they interact (Mayer and Salovey, 1995). Studies of emotional intelligence have emphasized the importance of several skills related to regulating one's own and other people's moods. Mayer and Gaschke (1988) have described meta-mood as the awareness of how one manages emotional states. Their original work concerned transient meta-mood experiences. More recently, Salovey and colleagues have developed a measure of *trait* meta-mood (Salovey et al., 1995), which taps the awareness of emotional management as a relatively stable trait rather than a transient state. Their description identifies three key elements of emotional management: attention to moods, mood clarity, and mood maintenance and repair. *Attention to moods* refers to an awareness that oneself or someone else is experiencing some mood state. *Mood clarity* is the self-perceived ability to identify correctly the mood that oneself or someone else is experiencing. *Mood maintenance and repair* is the self-perceived ability to regulate one's own or someone else's mood state so as to maintain positive moods or disrupt negative moods. As with other emotional intelligence constructs, these meta-mood experiences concern both intra-and interpersonal contexts.

Overview of Empathic Accuracy Perspective

The ability to spot, correctly identify, and regulate moods in another individual requires an awareness of that person's emotional state, even when he or she does not divulge it directly. This awareness has been termed "empathic accuracy" (for an excellent overview, see the volume edited by Ickes, 1997). Although bearing a superficial resemblance to concepts such as perspective taking or general empathy, empathic accuracy is distinct in two important respects. First, as the name of the construct suggests, it is concerned with the *accuracy of judgments* about another person's thoughts and feelings and not merely with the extent of feeling for others. Measures of perspective taking, for example, typically assess the respondent's tendency to pick up on others' feelings, understand their moods, or take their points of view into consideration. Such measures concern *whether* or *how much* rather than *how well* someone attends to another person's moods. Ickes (1997) describes the act of noticing another person's feelings as empathic inference. Empathic accuracy, in contrast, focuses specifically on *how well* one reads another person's thoughts and feelings, that is, the correctness of those inferences. It is, "the measure of one's skill in empathic inference," (Ickes, 1997: 2). Individuals who possess a high level of that skill should enjoy greater success in their interpersonal dealings. Thomas and Fletcher (1997: 195) point out that, "empathic accuracy should not be confused with definitions that assert that the sharing of affect between empathizer and target is a primary component of empathy." Thus, empathic accuracy is more directly about correctly understanding or recognizing rather than feeling what another person is experiencing.

Although conceptual distinctions between empathic accuracy and related constructs such as perspective taking are important, the second, and even more significant, difference between empathic accuracy and other indicators of empathy is the way that the former is assessed: it is performance-based rather than self-reported. The methodology used is the Dyadic Interaction Paradigm (Ickes et al., 1990). This involves videotaping interactions between two individuals (e.g., husbands and wives) and then having each view the video twice. The viewing process occurs with each member of the couple separated from their partner, who is in a different location taking part in an exactly parallel set of procedures with another member of the investigative team. Each person functions first as a target, that is, disclosing thoughts and feelings the first time through the tape, and then as the observer, that is, inferring the other partner's thoughts and feelings the second time through the tape. For clarity, we will describe this process from the perspective of the wife. Keep in mind, however, that her husband simultaneously participates in a parallel sequence of events. During the first viewing, the wife stops the tape at each point where she had a thought or feeling that was not expressed openly during the preceding interaction. She is asked, at each of these points, to describe her unexpressed thought or feeling. Her description is written down. During the second viewing, the investigator stops the tape at points where the husband indicated an unexpressed thought or feeling and prompts the wife to describe what she believes her husband was thinking or feeling. Her description of her husband's thoughts and feelings is also written down.

For the couple jointly, this procedure results in two descriptions of each occasion of an unexpressed thought or feeling, for example, the wife's description of her own thoughts and her husband's inferences about those thoughts. Descriptions subsequently are compared by trained observers who see the written statements on either side of a split-screen display. On one side is a self-description by one partner and on the other side is an inference by the other partner. The raters' task is to judge the similarity of the thought or feeling described by the statements on the two sides of the screen. The two statements displayed may either be a self-description for one partner and inference from the other concerning the same moment in time (e.g., the wife's description of her first unexpressed thought or feeling on the tape and her husband's inference about what she was thinking and feeling at that moment) or randomly paired descriptions of different moments from the initial interaction (e.g., the wife's self-description of an unexpressed thought or feeling paired with her husband's inference about a different unexpressed thought or feeling of hers). The coders have no contact with the couples and often are not even aware of the nature of the research questions being asked. Multiple raters, often as many as five, evaluate the statement pairs independently with a final score based on an average of their individual similarity assessments.

Overview of Emotional Contagion Perspective
The sharing of emotions can be a major component of close personal relationships. Empathic accuracy, as we have noted, involves making accurate inferences about another person's feelings. Does understanding another's feelings cause one to feel the same way? Emotional contagion, the transmission of moods from one person to another, is one of the most elemental forms of empathic responding (Davis, 1994). Primitive emotional contagion is the tendency to automatically mimic and synchronize facial expressions, vocalizations, postures, and movements with those of another person and, consequently, to converge emotionally (Hatfield et al., 1994). The transfer of moods can be explained as a process where an individual mimics another and falls into a synchrony of movements and vocalizations. Emotional experience is affected by the feedback from this mimicry process and a "convergence of emotions" among participants can result. A close interpersonal relationship, such as marriage, provides many opportunities for emotional experiences to converge. Emotional contagion, then, is relevant to close personal relationships, coming directly from the interactions between partners.

The way that emotional contagion manifests itself is through a reciprocal coordination developing between people as they interact. In couples that are "in tune" with each other's emotions, their facial expressions, postures, and vocal inflections, as well as their subjective mood states, become coordinated. Such couples can come to resemble mirror images of one another over the course of a brief dialogue, for example, smiling and nodding in unison, manifesting simultaneous facial changes such as raising of eyebrows or furrowing of the brow, leaning toward or away from each other at the same moments, sitting in similar positions, and manifesting coordinated changes in vocal inflection and pacing (cf., Kendon, 1970). Researchers in fields including psychotherapy, social psychology, and communication have identified this type of emotional synchronicity as indicative of empathic contact. Evidence indicates that interactions are more successful in several respects when the linking of emotional responses characteristic of emotional contagion occurs between people (Hatfield et al., 1993). These overt manifestations of synchronicity that develop during emotional contagion are accompanied by coordinated subjective (e.g., self-reported mood) and objective (e.g., changes in electrophysiological indicators of emotional arousal such as heart rate and skin conductance) states in the participants. Thus, emotional contagion entails not merely superficial mimicry but a true transmission of emotional states between people (Davis, 1994).

Several mechanisms have been implicated in mediating emotional contagion. Clearly, seeing another's emotional reactions frequently produces similar emotions in an observer. The imitative synchronization of posture and facial expressions noted by Hatfield et al. (1992; 1993) is an important element. Darwin (1965) suggested that subjective emotions were influenced by facial expressions. A substantial body of more recent evidence supports that assertion. A variety of studies consistently reveal that individuals who are asked to assume facial expressions report feeling the emotional states associated with those expressions (see Hatfield et al., 1992 for a review). This is even true when the facial expression (e.g., a frown or smile) is induced without reference to mood by asking people to relax and contract specific groups of facial muscles (e.g., Strack et al., 1988). Goleman (1995) describes studies that involved depressed women and their romantic partners. In those investigations, the men were more likely to "catch" their partners' negative moods when the couple manifested a high degree of non-verbal synchronicity – a finding consistent with the mediating role of non-verbal processes. But other mechanisms also play a role.

Social comparison (Festinger, 1954) is a process by which people take stock of their own situation by comparing themselves with others in similar circumstances. Wrightsman (1960) argued that social comparison processes were responsible for the emotional convergence he observed between experimental participants who interacted briefly and believed themselves to be facing the same situation (an experimental task). As a consequence of doing this, according to Wrightsman (1960), these individuals also "caught" each other's feelings. As predicted by social comparison theory (Festinger, 1954), no such convergence was observed between pairs of people who believed themselves to be facing unrelated situations.

Various aspects of personality have also been implicated in how people acquire moods. Larsen and Ketelaar (1991) identified extroversion and neuroticism as related to susceptibility to mood acquisition. They report that people scoring high on scales of extroversion and neuroticism were more susceptible to acquiring, respectively, positive and negative affective states. Friedman and Riggio (1981), on the other hand, found that emotional contagion was influenced by individual differences in expressive styles. Specifically, they observed that more emotionally expressive people tended to influence the moods of others.

Sullins (1991) found support for both the social comparison and emotional expressiveness processes. However, the strongest instances of emotional contagion in her study occurred when strongly expressive people were paired with relatively less expressive partners; the latter tended to acquire the emotions of the former. She interpreted this pattern of results as suggesting that (a) emotionally expressive people give off strong emotional cues and (b) emotionally unexpressive people may rely more on external cues as a means of defining their personal mood states. Sullins also reported that contagion was stronger for negative than positive moods. Collectively, these and similar studies suggest that (a) spontaneous facial and postural mimicry, (b) social circumstances such as a perceived commonality of interests, (c) individual differences in emotional expressiveness, and (d) the valence (i.e. positive or negative) of the emotions in question all contribute to emotional contagion.

Potential Relevance of Emotion Management Perspectives to Health

Emotional intelligence, empathic accuracy, and emotional contagion may each contribute to how successfully couples can adapt to a chronic illness in one or both partners. Dealing with chronic illness necessarily involves confronting and solving a variety of problems. For example, making sense of information about one's illness, seeking out appropriate sources of care, and adjusting to changes imposed by health problems are common challenges to which individuals with chronic conditions must seek solutions. Arguably, emotional intelligence may facilitate finding suitable solutions. Help from one's partner can play a vital role in the adaptation process. Logically, a greater degree of empathic accuracy between partners should facilitate this process. For example, a husband who correctly identifies his wife's thoughts and feelings should be more able to respond in a helpful fashion. Likewise, examining patterns of emotional contagion between husbands and wives may reveal important aspects of the interpersonal processes involved in dealing with stressors. For example, moods can influence how people interpret and respond to chronic illness. Since chronic health issues can place special emotional strains, needs, and expectations on couples, the transfer of moods between partners may be particularly important in the context of coping with illness. The experience of emotional contagion between partners facing an illness may be an important determinant of whether the relationship with one's spouse promotes or undermines adjustment.

Translation from Theory to Research

We have translated the ideas and concepts discussed above, and applied them to studying interpersonal emotional factors in adjustment to chronic illness. This section describes a series of studies that build on each previous one and adopt a progressively more dyadic focus. We hope that a review of these studies will provide a better understanding of the mechanisms/processes under-lying interpersonal interactions in the face of chronic illness.

Translating Emotional Management Perspectives to Research on Adjustment

In a series of independent studies, DeVellis and colleagues examined how specific emotional management skills derived from emotional intelligence theory related to other variables among people who either had arthritis or whose spouses had arthritis. This work began with an examination of the original Trait Meta-Mood Scale (TMMS; Salovey et al., 1991; 1995) men-tioned earlier. DeVellis (1993) has developed a modified version of the ori-ginal scale. In their first description of the trait meta mood scale, Salovey and colleagues (1991) reported some difficulty in obtaining a desirable factor struc-ture among their items. Initial factor analyses conducted by DeVellis (1993) on data collected from individuals with arthritis similarly failed to identify a suitable factor solution. The number of factors underlying the original item set could not be ascertained unambiguously. Consequently, several alterna-tive factor solutions were examined. In addition, items that loaded on multiple factors were eliminated in an attempt to approximate simple structure. This process resulted in two acceptable factor solutions, one entailing three and the other four factors. We chose to use the scales obtained from the three-factor solution based on the fact that Salovey et al. (1991) had originally classified their items into three factors. Scale scores for each of the three item sets were correlated with other selected variables as a means of gauging the construct validity of the modified scales. Our validation strategy involved examining simple correlations between each of the modified scales and a variety of other indicators.

Based on our understanding of the constructs represented by the scales, we predicted which of the other variables would or would not correlate with them. For example, we predicted significant correlations between mood clarity and affect variables such as the CES-D (Radloff, 1977) and a measure of anxiety. In contrast, we predicted no correlations between the modified TMMS scales and indicators of arthritis-relevant symptoms such as mobility or dexterity. Thus, while not definitive, the observed pattern of correlations suggested acceptable convergent and discriminant validity.

Having derived acceptable measures of the meta-mood experience for use with arthritis patients, the next step in this line of inquiry examined their relationships to other variables of interest. Salovey and colleagues (1991; 1995), in their original reports of the TMMS, observed that mood clarity predicted how people recovered baseline affect following a mood induction. We conceptually replicated this study on a sample of 90 people with osteoarthritis (OA) (DeVellis et al., 1998). In Salovey et al.'s (1991; 1995) study, high mood clarity was associated with greater recovery of baseline mood following exposure to affectively negative information (a stressful movie). In our study, we induced negative mood not by means of a movie but by asking participants to recall a time in their recent past when things had gone poorly for them. We also assessed transient mood states differently than Salovey et al. by means of a brief checklist on which participants could indicate whether they were or were not experiencing each of several moods. Positive and negative moods were scored separately, whereas in the Salovey et al. (1991; 1995) study mood valence was scored on a single dimension from positive to negative.

Our analyses revealed that, for positive moods, clarity played an interesting and potentially important role. Individuals scoring relatively high on mood clarity (combined unidimensional measure) were able to maintain higher levels of positive affect following a negative mood induction than were low scorers. Both groups showed increases in negative affect. That is, for low-clarity individuals, as negative mood increased following the mood induction, positive mood decreased. In contrast, among high scorers, the mood induction elevated negative moods (as it did for low clarity people) but there was significantly less reduction in positive affect. This pattern suggests that people who report being high in mood clarity demonstrate a more differentiated response to affectively negative material than do low-clarity individuals.

We subsequently attempted to replicate these findings on a separate sample of people with rheumatoid arthritis (RA), once again computing scores for three components of meta mood: attention to feelings, mood clarity, and mood maintenance and repair. Our initial analyses failed to replicate the effect. When we examined the factor structure of the items we were using to assess meta mood, our results slightly favored four rather than three factors. As with the four-factor solution obtained from our earlier data set, this analysis yielded two separate factors corresponding to mood clarity and mood confusion rather than a combined factor comprising both positive and negative items.

To obtain a clearer sense of the structure underlying these items, we combined data from OA and RA samples and performed another factor analysis on the combined group of approximately 400 individuals. These results unambiguously supported a four-factor solution. The two separate clarity factors (representing mood clarity versus mood confusion) correlated −0.30, which supported maintaining them as separate factors. In addition, a separate factor analysis performed only on the clarity and confusion items yielded two factors rather than one. Finally, correlations between each of the two scales (i.e. mood clarity and mood confusion) and other variables supported their discriminant validity. For example, correlations between positive affect as measured by the Positive and Negative Affect Schedule (PANAS; Watson et al., 1988) with the mood clarity and mood confusion scales, respectively, were $r = 0.32$ and $r = 0.01$. The overall pattern of correlations suggested that mood clarity shared more variance with affective state then did mood confusion.

In another, independent sample of 90 people with OA, we examined the relationship of mood clarity to satisfaction with medical care. We hypothesized that greater mood clarity should enable patients with arthritis to communicate their feelings to their physicians with less ambiguity and to differentiate between negative affect arising from the illness itself versus from their interactions with their physicians. As expected, we observed that patients with higher mood clarity scores reported higher satisfaction with medical care (as measured by the affective items of a modified version of the Medical Interview Satisfaction Scale (Wolf et al., 1978). A more recent replication of that study conducted by Cowhig (2001) reveals a somewhat more complex pattern of results, varying by gender, among a sample of patients with RA. For males, both high mood clarity and low mood confusion were independently related to satisfaction with medical care (controlling for arthritis symptoms, age, depressive symptoms, and experiences of positive and negative affect). This relationship was not evident among females, however, leaving unresolved gender differences in this area of research. It is unclear whether these findings represent a true gender difference or merely an isolated failure to detect an effect among females.

These various studies suggested the potential relevance of mood-related processes to two potentially important circumstances faced by people with arthritis, that is, dealing with affectively negative information and feeling satisfied with the medical care one receives. Exposure to affectively negative information can certainly occur in an intimate relationship and the patient-provider dyad is inherently interpersonal. But these investigations did not directly examine processes unambiguously arising from close relationships. The study described next did.

Translating Empathic Accuracy Perspective to Research on Adjustment

We have used the Dyadic Interaction Paradigm (Ickes et al., 1990) to study the relationship of empathic accuracy to psychological adjustment among people with rheumatoid arthritis and their spouses. Cross-sectional analyses underscore the potential importance of empathic accuracy (DeVellis, 1998). Our most striking finding is that women with RA whose husbands achieve high empathic accuracy scores have better psychological adjustment, as assessed by a composite based on depressive symptoms, positive and negative affect, and optimism/pessimism. This relationship holds when measures of arthritis severity, and both spouses' meta-mood variables are controlled. Moreover, the relationship persists prospectively so that empathic accuracy predicts psychological adjustment assessed three months later, controlling for initial adjustment and the other variables controlled in cross-sectional analyses (DeVellis, 1999). Again, husbands' higher accuracy scores predict better adjustment. These findings are unusual in an important respect: many findings linking personal attributes to health-related outcomes are difficult to interpret causally because they involve self-reports of variables collected from a single individual cross-sectionally. These findings, in contrast, involve a performance-based assessment of one partner predicting an outcome in the other partner measured three months later.

We are presently launching a study (funded by the National Institute of Arthritis, Musculoskeletal, and Skin Diseases) examining how perceived control and social support mediate between illness severity and psychological adjustment in small vessel vasculitis, a rare and potentially fatal auto-immune disease. Both perceived control and social support are operationalized in ways that reflect the more specific, dyad-focused, process-oriented perspective we have advocated in this chapter. Empathic accuracy and transformation of motivation will be assessed as specific elements of social support. Indicators of perceived control will include a measure of dyadic efficacy intended to assess the extent to which couples believe that they can accomplish various actions related to illness management as a team. A secondary aim of this five-year investigation is to explore whether a more convenient means of assessing empathic accuracy can be devised and validated, using the dyadic interaction paradigm as a criterion.

Currently, we are also testing the feasibility of using the empathic accuracy paradigm to assess persuasive communication and the concomitant perceptions of thoughts and feelings, and accuracy of these thoughts and feelings among couples in which one partner has been recently diagnosed with heart disease or Type 2 diabetes. Emerging evidence indicates that close others can be effective in influencing and persuading social network members to change health-related behaviors. While health behavior change may be positive on one hand, this persuasive influence comes with a cost, namely psychological distress (Lewis and Rook, 1999). The empathic accuracy paradigm provides the unique opportunity to examine when persuasion and influence may result in positive or negative emotions, as well as thoughts such as intention to change a behavior. In addition, the accuracy with which a spouse perceives these emotions and intentions can be measured. Learning when persuasive communication can facilitate adaptation while minimizing distress could provide valuable information to interventions that attempt to involve spouses in the behavior change process.

Translating Emotional Contagion to Research on Adjustment

One of our current studies, funded by the Arthritis Foundation, is exploring patterns of emotional contagion in couples where one partner has osteoarthritis. The goals of the study are to characterize the patterns of emotional contagion that occur between spouses dealing with a chronic illness and to determine whether certain patterns are associated with perceptions of spousal support, marital satisfaction, and psychological adjustment. Several different patterns of emotional contagion may arise with important implications for coping with chronic illness. For example, both members of a couple may be insensitive to emotional cues and fail to manifest the emotional synchronicity that characterizes contagion. This lack of sensitivity may indicate a less supportive relationship. An alternative pattern that may arise is one where one partner tends to dominate with respect to emotional contagion resulting in one-directional contagion. In this scenario, if the person with arthritis is the dominating spouse, then he or she may guide the emotions of the couple based on the emotional challenges of the arthritis. On the other hand, if the well spouse is the dominating partner, he or she may be able to suppress manifestations of negative emotions related to the arthritis. Mutual contagion may be another pattern where an averaging of two individuals' emotional states occurs. When partners are experiencing emotions of opposite valences, a neutralization of each partner's mood could occur in this pattern, resulting in the partners meeting emotionally somewhere in the middle. Finally, contagion may be mood-driven. In this scenario, a negative or positive mood will always prevail. Each of these potential patterns has different consequences for partners coping with arthritis.

Learning about different patterns of contagion may inform interventions to help couples manage emotions. Because emotional contagion involves the actions and responses of two individuals, there may potentially be several points for intervention. Individuals may be able to learn about the benefits and harms of specific patterns of contagion in order to avoid or embrace them. Individuals may also be able to better monitor and manage moods. The possibility of making people more sensitive to contagion or building a resistance to contagion could be explored.

Implications and Speculations Concerning Future Research on Interpersonal Emotional Processes in Adjustment

The preceding discussion highlights selected examples that integrate theory and research from the fields of relationship science and emotion management, and suggests how this convergence can be applied to study interpersonal emotional processes in the context of adaptation to chronic illness in couples. Recognizing that the hallmark experience of close relationships is the interdependence between individuals can lead researchers to think about emotional management and adjustment in new ways.

One new way is to acknowledge that the interdependence between couples in later years can be a double-edged sword in terms of adjustment to chronic illness (Revenson et al., 1991). In later years, when couples experience chronic illness, partners tend to rely more on each other for assistance in coping and adjustment than relying on other family members (Johnson, 1985). Lyons et al. (1995) argue that this communal coping orientation could have both positive and negative consequences. On the positive side, viewing the problem from the perspective of "we," versus "I" or "you," redistributes the responsibility of support and coping to one that is more shared rather than private. This shared responsibility could decrease the stress associated with adjustment to chronic illness for both spouses. On the negative side, however, viewing the problem communally could increase the ill partner's expectations for social support, and foster feelings of dissatisfaction with the support that is actually provided by the other partner (Lam and Power, 1991). Thus, the heightened interdependence that may come with chronic illness confers both risk and protection for the couple, and research that can clarify how to maximize protection while minimizing risk is needed.

A second new way to think about interpersonal emotional factors and adjustment is to recognize that interpersonal processes are temporal in nature. Reis et al. (2000) have argued that influence is the defining characteristic of relationships, because each partner affects the other, and that these interactions affect subsequent interactions and behavior, with this process continuing over time. Thus, to recognize the impact of close on-going relationships requires acknowledging their temporal nature. Thomas and Fletcher (1997) affirm this temporality and note that, typically, empathic accuracy may actually peak relatively early in a relationship and that complacency and familiarity over time may lessen accuracy. Although emotional transactions may become routinized over time within well couples, the diagnosis of a chronic health condition may substantially alter pre-existing patterns of interdependence or interpersonal emotional functioning, such that diagnosis becomes a window of opportunity to leverage interventions. That is, the adjustments required by the emergence of a chronic illness may jar couples out of their complacency and create new opportunities for enhancing empathic accuracy skills.

A third new way to think about interpersonal factors and adjustment to illness is to explore interconnections among concepts. This last point – that exploring plausible but thus far undocumented linkages among variables can offer new insights into how people adjust to illness – is considered more fully below. Specifically, in the following paragraphs, we briefly review potential linkages among the variables we have discussed earlier in this chapter and between those concepts and emerging ideas in the field of positive psychology.

Interconnections

Close Relationships and Positive Psychology
A theme running through the material we have reviewed thus far is a focus on how interpersonal relationships can facilitate more positive emotional states and how they, in turn, can contribute to optimal adjustment to chronic illness. This perspective is highly consistent with recent work described under the rubric of positive psychology. Fredrickson (1998; 2001) has recently presented a broaden-and-build model of positive emotions that emphasizes how positive mood states influence information processing, behavior, and even physiological responding. She describes several lines of research suggesting that positive emotional states expand individuals' thought-action repertoires and build their enduring personal resources (physical, social, intellectual, and physiological) (Fredrickson, 2001). Negative emotions, in contrast, promote a narrowing of attention, selective focus on sources of threat, and preparation for fight or flight.

In a recent review of the broaden-and-build model, Fredrickson (2001) summarizes several of the key features of positive emotions. Among these are (a) undoing lingering negative emotions, (b) promoting psychological resiliency, and (c) triggering upward spirals in which positive feelings engender further positive states, progressing toward emotional well-being. Elsewhere,

Fredrickson (2000) has discussed positive emotions specifically in the context of relationships. She argues that, while unhappy couples tend to interact in a more rigid and repetitive way, happy couples are more imaginative and innovative in their interactions. The broaden-and-build model suggests that a positive frame of mind is conducive to effective problem solving. Furthermore, she cites work suggesting that happy couples can actually accumulate a reserve of positive feelings for one another that can be drawn upon during more difficult periods in the relationship. A consequence of this reserve of goodwill is that happy couples are less likely to exacerbate one another's negative feelings in the face of hardship or disagreement. Thus, a potentially fruitful line of inquiry is to assess to what extent the processes comprising the broaden-and-build model mediate the relationship between close personal relationships and successful adjustment to chronic illness.

Interdependence and Emotional Contagion
Increases in interdependence between partners may enhance contagion processes. Strong emotional bonds facilitate contagion (Hatfield et al., 1992). As a result, couples in close, ongoing relationships may become more susceptible to emotional contagion over time as their emotional bonds strengthen. Mood contagion may induce positive or negative affective states that, in turn, predispose individuals to an expansion or restriction of their perspectives as the broaden-and-build model suggests. Levenson et al. (1993) found among older couples in dissatisfying marriages that there was greater reciprocity of negative affect while engaged in conversations about problem areas during lab-based videotaped conversations. This may indicate that catching a negative mood could constrict problem-solving abilities while catching a positive mood may enhance receptivity to problem solving through the mechanism of broadening one's momentary thought-action repertoire. Through contagion, one partner's mood could influence the other's. If the partner with a chronic health problem is more likely to experience negative affect due to the challenges of the illness, then the well spouse may be at a greater risk of catching that negative affect and thus, may be less equipped to provide effective aid or support. This potentially could create a negative spiral toward poorer functioning for both individuals. This reasoning suggests a second potentially fruitful line of inquiry that includes contagion as an additional mediator between close relationship factors and the components of the broaden-and-build model.

Empathic Accuracy and Transformation of Motivation
Bissonnette et al. (1997) have suggested that empathic accuracy facilitates better analysis of the meaning of thoughts, emotions, and behaviors within couples as well as more adaptive transformation of motivation. Their study of newly married couples supports this proposition. During discussions that involve disagreements, partners who are better at empathically assessing a spouse's thoughts and feelings display more accommodation when discussing disagreements than partners who are less empathically accurate (Bissonnette et al., 1997). This accommodation is viewed as a sign of adaptive transformation

of motivation, that is, being able to act in pro-relationship rather than self-interested ways, in the context of conflict, disagreement or stress. Better or more accurate analysis of thoughts, emotions, and behaviors among partners could result in better social support for coping with a chronic illness diagnosis as well as adjustment in terms of changing health-related behaviors. This underscores the potential value of research examining empathic accuracy and transformation of motivation.

Protective buffering, the intentional withholding of one's concerns in order to protect another person from worry, may also be relevant. Suls et al. (1997) found that for both patient and spouse, not disclosing concerns and emotions about the patient's medical problem (heart attack) was associated with more distress for the non-discloser but not the other partner. That is, spouse protective buffering was associated with spouse distress but not patient distress, and patient protective buffering was associated with patient distress but not spouse distress. This appears to be a case in which non-disclosure is motivated by a concern for one's partner, and thus appears initially to be consistent with transformation of motivation, but inhibits a true sharing of concerns that transformation of motivation implies.

Empathic Accuracy and Meta-mood Variables
Eisenberg et al. (1997) suggested that the ability to decode emotional information emerges progressively during childhood and lays a foundation for empathic accuracy. At first blush, there may appear to be an obvious connection between empathic accuracy and meta-mood variables such as clarity and confusion. Achieving high scores on empathic accuracy seems to imply that one is clear about partner moods. Clarity might thus seem to be a necessary prerequisite for empathic accuracy. This may not automatically be the case, however, because of the way in which these variables are assessed. Clarity and confusion, as meta-mood constructs, are assessed by self-report. In essence, the resulting measurements reflect the individual's belief in his or her own perceptive skill with respect to moods. Although some of our findings, such as the more differentiated responses to negative information manifested by people who score higher on clarity or lower on confusion, suggest that these self-perceptions may be fairly accurate, there is no logical necessity that this be so. Therefore, people could have a high score on the meta-mood measure of clarity, but actually score poorly on a behavioral measure of empathic accuracy. A person high on empathic accuracy, on the other hand, may not be aware of his or her perceptive accuracy. In fact, self-reports of empathic accuracy tend not to converge with behavioral demonstrations of the phenomenon. As Thomas and Fletcher (1997: 196) have noted, "judges' estimates of their own levels of empathic accuracy generally fail to predict their actual performance on empathic accuracy tasks." So, people's actual empathic accuracy skill might not correspond to their beliefs (and self-reports) about how skillfully they can judge others' thoughts or feelings. Thus, skills in perceiving other people's emotions may exist in the absence of an awareness of those skills or people might believe that they possess such skills when that is not the case. The nature of the relationship between actual clarity and confusion on

the one hand and empathic accuracy on the other is not well documented. It may, in fact, prove to be substantial. Ability-based measures of emotional intelligence, such as those described by Mayer et al. (2000) tapping emotional perception, facilitation, understanding, and management may thus play an important role in clarifying the relationships among variables. Were clarity measured as an actual ability rather than as a self-rating, one might expect a positive association. But there is certainly no necessity of that being the case for a self-report measure of clarity.

Positive affect may be conducive to the accurate appraisal of others' emotional states. This is consistent with Fredrickson's (2000) "broaden-and-build" model, which suggests that positive affective states promote attentiveness, openness, and receptivity to new information. These in turn should facilitate paying greater attention to moods and making more perceptive distinctions among them. Thus, positive affect should enhance empathic accuracy, although negative affect (e.g. neuroticism and anxiety) appears unrelated to empathic accuracy (Davis and Kraus, 1997). To the extent that meta-mood variables reflect actual behavior, self-perceived attention to moods and mood clarity should also increase in the face of positive emotions. Negative affect, on the other hand, should constrict the intake of new information and thus interfere with accurate assessments of other people's emotional states (Frederickson, 2000). To our knowledge, these hypotheses have not been tested empirically. One potential research implication of these points is the need to assess the relationship between empathic accuracy and clarity and whether positive affect plays a mediating role.

Emotional Contagion and Meta-mood Variables
One might expect increased attention to moods to facilitate emotional contagion. As we have noted earlier, the foundation of emotional contagion is that observing another person's emotional state induces that emotional state in the observer (e.g., Hatfield et al., 1994). To the extent that an individual is generally attentive to emotional information, opportunities for contagion should be enhanced. Furthermore, being able to differentiate emotions might also contribute to emotional contagion (e.g. Eisenberg et al., 1997). That is, someone who is more able to differentiate emotional states with clarity may take on an emotion that matches more precisely that of the person observed. Self-report measures of meta-mood may not fully capture these relationships, however, if they do not represent actual skills. For the same reasons noted in the preceding section, positive affect might enhance receptivity to emotional cues. This in turn, might increase emotional contagion. Thus, it might be useful to study the relationships of attention to moods and mood clarity with emotional contagion.

Further Complexities

Three other issues related to applying emotional and interpersonal concepts in health psychology merit discussion. These are (a) measurement, (b) close personal relationships other than marriage, and (c) the potential importance of variables at other levels of specificity than the individual or dyad.

The processes we have discussed vary with respect to ease of measurement. Meta-mood variables are reflective observations of one's own activities or processes. The individual's perception is the variable of interest. Thus, it is less surprising that these variables have been measured successfully by means of questionnaires. Mayer et al. (2000) now favor greater reliance on performance-based measures of emotional intelligence constructs. Although there seems to be conceptual overlap between the earlier meta-mood variables and specific components (e.g., Emotional Perception and Emotional Understanding) of the more recent measures of emotional intelligence, they do not appear to be identical. These new measures, should further work support their validity, are potentially attractive because they can be administered in a paper and pencil format.

Empathic accuracy can only be assessed at the present time by performance-based methods such as the dyadic interaction paradigm. This is a labor-intensive procedure that poses a substantial obstacle for many studies not specifically concerned with dyadic relationships. As a result, the potential importance of empathic accuracy may be largely overlooked. A more convenient means of assessment would be very attractive, but this may be difficult to achieve. Thomas and Fletcher (1997) note that self-report measures of empathic accuracy have not succeeded, in part because of social desirability bias and also because individuals simply cannot estimate their empathic accuracy with an acceptable degree of precision. Other conceptual problems plague attempts to develop self-report measures of empathic accuracy. If one were to use questionnaire methodology, for example, to whom would the questions be administered? Stated somewhat differently, is empathic accuracy something that we should perceive in ourselves or that others should see in us? Or, is it a fundamentally interpersonal process that cannot be assessed from the perspective of either member of the dyad singly? Empathic accuracy may entail the interaction of one partner's skill in transmitting and the other's in receiving relevant cues. In support of this view, Noller (1981) observed that members of unhappy couples had more difficulty assessing the thoughts and feelings of their spouses than those of strangers. One possible interpretation for such a pattern of findings is that while one spouse was capable of receiving relevant cues, the other failed to transmit them clearly. Thus, when paired with a less inept transmitter, perhaps, the performance of the successful receiver would improve. Finally, if empathic accuracy is truly a skill (or set of skills), perhaps only actual performance is a credible indicator. Some of the same issues might also pertain to the ability-based measurement of emotional intelligence, despite the apparent success of a paper and pencil measure such as the Mayer, Salovey and Caruso Emotional Intelligence Test (MSCEIT; Mayer et al., 1999; 2000).

Although we have focused primarily on married couples, there are other interesting and potentially important dyadic relationships to which the same theories and methods may apply. In the course of our research, for example, we have observed that many mature women with chronic illnesses rely primarily on their adult daughters as sources of support. In cases where a woman's husband is deceased, the mother–daughter relationship may be even more important. To our knowledge, this relationship has received relatively little attention from health psychologists. Although such a relationship might not entail the same forms of interdependence as marriage, empathic accuracy and emotional contagion may still be important elements of the emotional communications surrounding a chronic illness. Other non-marital close relationships may be similarly important. Enduring friendships, loving relationships between members of gay and lesbian couples, and interactions among blood relatives other than mothers and daughters (e.g., siblings) may all influence adaptation to chronic illness and serve as arenas in which the interpersonal processes we have been discussing are transacted. An important relationship of a very different sort is that between patient and provider. Here too, a sense of mutual commitment to common goals, clarity in communicating about emotions, and empathic skills may influence adjustment to chronic illness. These factors may also lessen the burden on the person in the helping role, either professional or non-professional.

In all of these examples, as in the work with married couples, it is essential to recognize the two-way nature of dyadic communication and interaction and to avoid the pseudounilaterality bias (Duncan et al., 1984). Although interpersonal processes may not be perfectly symmetrical, it may not be one's role as patient that determines what skills will yield benefits to whom. In our past work, husbands' empathic accuracy seemed to benefit their wives irrespective of which partner was the person with the chronic illness. Expectations for mutual benefit, no doubt, are different in patient–provider relationships (Lewis et al., 2002), for example, but this does not imply that only one member of the dyad need have skills in emotional management.

Throughout this chapter we have argued that dyadic relationships are important and provide insights not necessarily obtainable from studies focused at the individual level. This principle can be extended both to *more general and more specific levels of analysis*. Health problems have a fundamental biological component and occur in the context of societies and cultures. Ultimately, a full understanding of health and illness requires examination at all levels. The variables and processes we have discussed do not exist solely at the individual or dyadic level. Mood processes have physiological underpinnings and social consequences. The rash of recent violence in schools, in some cases apparently stemming from interpersonal antipathies, exemplifies the latter. Processes such as emotional contagion have been described in terms of their biological adaptive value on the one hand and are manifested in the actions of mobs, on the other. Taylor and colleagues (2000) recently have suggested that affiliation in response to stress may have a biological foundation. Thus, it seems appropriate to view the variables we have discussed at the individual and dyadic levels as having meaningful analogs at both lower and higher levels of analysis. A biopsychosocial model, as described by Engel (1977) may be necessary to embrace all of the features that have a bearing on interpersonal emotional processes in adjustment to chronic illness. Within the arthritis research community, the need to enhance both professional and public understanding of the biopsychosocial aspects of the illness and its management has been formally stated (Parker et al., 1993). Scientific disciplines whose subspecialties span multiple levels, such as psychology and public health, may be in a critical position to play an important and active role in broadening public and scientific awareness of the multi-level determinants and consequences of health and illness.

We have provided some selective examples of how specific social psychological perspectives can be applied to understanding adaptation to chronic illness. We chose work related to interdependence theory and emotional management because we believe that these areas may be especially well-suited for addressing certain research questions of interest to health psychology. Moreover, instances in which theoretical and empirical work from these areas has been applied to questions of health and illness remain scarce. We hope that by drawing the attention of health psychologists to the potential importance of this work, these theoretical approaches will be used more widely. Ultimately, we believe that the type of work we have described will also serve as a basis for interventions aimed at couples confronting chronic illness. Applying concepts from relationship science and mood management perspectives to research and applications in health psychology may pose substantial conceptual and methodological challenges. We view these not so much as barriers to further progress but as opportunities for the continued development of our understanding of emotional and interpersonal processes and their role in health and illness.

Acknowledgments

The authors wish to thank the Arthritis Foundation; National Institute of Arthritis, Musculoskeletal, and Skin Diseases; and University Research Council of the University of North Carolina at Chapel Hill for their support of the first author's work described in this chapter and the National Institute of Health Clinical Research Unit Pilot Feasibility Program for their support of the second author's work described in this chapter. We would also like to thank Brenda M. DeVellis for her helpful comments on an earlier version of this manuscript.

Correspondence concerning this chapter should be directed to: Robert F. DeVellis, Department of Health Behavior and Health Education, University of North Carolina, Chapel Hill, NC 27599-7330, USA; e-mail: Bob_devellis@unc.edu

References

Akiyama, H., Elliott, K., and Antonucci, T. C. (1996). Same-sex and cross-sex relationships. *Journals of Gerontology: Psychological Sciences*, 51B, P374–P382.
Augustine (406 AD). The confessions. In R. I. Watson (1963). *The Great Psychologists: From Aristotle to Freud*. Philadelphia: J. B. Lipincott Company.

Baltes, M., and Silverberg, S. B. (1994). The dynamics between dependency and autonomy: Illustrations across the life span. In D. L. Featherman, R. M. Lerner, and M. Perlmutter (Eds.), *Life-span Development and Behavior* (pp. 41–90). Hillsdale, NJ: Jossey-Bass.

Bandura, A., and Walters, R. H. (1963). *Social Learning and Personality Development.* New York: Holt, Rinehart and Winston.

Bar-On, R., and Parker, J. D. A. (Eds.) (2000). *The Handbook of Emotional Intelligence: Theory, Development, Assessment, and Application at Home, School, and in the Workplace.* San Francisco: Jossey-Bass.

Berkman, L. F., Leo-Summers, L., and Horwitz, R. I. (1992). Emotional support and survival after myocardial infarction. *Annals of Internal Medicine,* 117, 1003–9.

Bissonnette, V. L., Rusbult, C. E., and Kilpatrick, S. D. (1997). Empathic accuracy and marital conflict resolution. In W. Ickes (Ed.), *Empathic Accuracy* (pp. 251–81). New York: The Guilford Press.

Black, D. R., Gleser, L. J., and Kooyers, K. J. (1990). A meta-analytic evaluation of weight-loss programs. *Health Psychology,* 9, 330–347.

Brecht, M., Dracup, K., Moser, D. K., and Reigel, B. (1994). The relationship of marital quality and psychological adjustment to heart disease. *Journal of Cardiovascular Nursing,* 9, 74–85.

Burman, B., and Margolin, G. (1992). Analysis of the association between marital relationships and health problems: An interactional perspective. *Psychological Bulletin,* 112, 39–63.

Cohen, S. (1988). Psychosocial models of the role of social support in the etiology of physical disease. *Health Psychology,* 7(3), 269–97.

Cowhig, R. A. (2001). The relationship between emotional management and satisfaction with medical care in individuals with arthritis. (Advisor, Robert DeVellis). Master's paper at the University of North Carolina-Chapel Hill School of Public Health.

Coyne, J. C., Ellard, J. H., and Smith, D. A. (1990). Social support, interdependence, and the dilemmas of helping. In B. R. Sarason, I. G. Sarason, and G. R. Pierce (Eds.), *Social Support: An Interactional View* (pp. 129–49). New York: Wiley.

Damasio, A. R. (1994). *Descartes' Error: Emotion, Reason, and the Human Brain.* New York: Avon Books, Inc.

Darwin, C. (1965). *The Expression of the Emotions in Man and Animals.* Chicago: University of Chicago Press. (Original work published in 1872).

Davis, M. H. (1994). *Empathy: A Social Psychological Approach.* Madison, WI: Brown and Benchmark Publishers.

Davis, M. H., and Kraus, L. A. (1997). Personality and empathic accuracy. In W. Ickes (Ed.) *Empathic Accuracy,* (pp. 144–68). New York: Guilford.

Demand, N. (1997). Medicine in Homer [WWW document]. URL http://www.indiana.edu/χancmed/Homer.htm, The Trustees of Indiana University. Last updated: May 19, 2000.

DeVellis, R. F. (1993). Factor analysis of Trait Meta-Mood Scale. Unpublished raw data.

DeVellis, R. F. (1998). The role of cognitive and emotional skills in spousal social support for Arthritis: I. Invited paper presented at the meeting of the Association of Rheumatology Health Professionals, San Diego, CA, November, 1998.

DeVellis, R. F. (1999). The role of cognitive and emotional skills in spousal social support for Arthritis: II. Invited paper presented at the meeting of the Association of Rheumatology Health Professionals, Boston, MA, November, 1999.

DeVellis, R. F., Carl, K., DeVellis, B. M., Blalock, S. J., and Patterson, C. C. (1998). Correlates of changes in mood following a mood induction in osteoarthritis patients. *Arthritis Care and Research,* 11, 234–42.

DeVellis, R. F., DeVellis, B. M., Sauter, S. V. H., Harring, K., and Cohen, J. L. (1986). Predictors of pain and functioning in arthritis. *Health Education Research: Theory and Practice*, 1, 61–7.

Duncan, S., Kanki, B. G., Mokros, H., and Fiske, D. (1984). Pseudounilaterality, simple-rate variables, and other ills to which interaction research is heir. *Journal of Personality and Social Psychology*, 46, 1335–48.

Eisenberg, N., Murphy, B. C., and Shepard, S. (1997). The development of empathic accuracy. In W. Ickes (Ed.), *Empathic Accuracy* (pp. 73–116). New York: Guilford.

Engel, G. L. (1977). The need for a new medical model: A challenge for biomedicine. *Science*, 196, 129–36.

Ewart, C. K., and Fitzgerald, S. T. (1994). Changing behavior and promoting well-being after heart attack: A social action theory approach. *The Irish Journal of Psychology*, 15, 219–41.

Fecteau, J. (n.d./2001). The ancients: Theories and therapies for psychopathology. [WWW document]. URL http://library.scar.utoronto.ca/ClassicsC42/Fecteau/WEBPAGE/PSYCH.HTM#plato

Festinger, L. (1954). A theory of social comparison processes. *Human Relations*, 7, 114–40.

Fitzpatrick, R., Newman, S., Lamb, R., and Shipley, M. (1988). Social relationships and psychological well-being in rheumatoid arthritis. *Social Science and Medicine*, 9, 399–403.

Fredrickson, B. L. (1998). What good are positive emotions? *Review of General Psychology*, 2, 300–19.

Fredrickson, B. L. (2000). Cultivating research on positive emotions. *Prevention and Treatment*, 3(7), posted March 7, 2000 by the American Psychological Association (http://journals.apa.org/prevention/volume 3/pre0030007r.html).

Fredrickson, B. L. (2001). The role of positive emotions in positive psychology: The broaden-and-build theory of positive emotions. *American Psychologist*, 56, 218–26.

Friedman, H. S., and Riggio, R. E. (1981). Effect of individual differences in nonverbal expressiveness on transmission of emotion. *Journal of Nonverbal Behavior*, 7, 114–40.

Freud, S. (1938). The history of the psychoanalytic movement. In A. A. Brill (Ed.), *The Basic Writing of Sigmund Freud* (pp. 933–77). New York: Random House.

Glass, T. A. (2000). Psychosocial intervention. In L.F. Berkman and I. Kawachi (Eds.), *Social Epidemiology* (pp. 267–305). New York: Oxford University Press.

Goleman, D. (1995). *Emotional Intelligence: Why Can It Matter More Than IQ?* New York: Bantam Books.

Goodenow, C., Reisine, S. T., and Grady, K. E. (1990). Quality of social support and associated social and psychological functioning in women with rheumatoid arthritis. *Health Psychology*, 9, 266–84.

Hatfield, E., Cacioppo, J. T., and Rapson, R. L. (1992). Primitive emotional contagion. In M. S. Clark (Ed.). *Emotion and Social Behavior* (pp. 151–77). Newbury Park: Sage Publications.

Hatfield, E., Cacioppo, J. T., and Rapson, R. L. (1993). Emotional contagion. *Current Directions in Psychological Science*, 2, 96–9.

Hatfield, E., Cacioppo, J. T., and Rapson, R. L. (1994). *Emotional Contagion*. Paris: Cambridge University Press.

Heller, K., Swindle, R. W., Jr., and Dusenbury, L. (1986). Component social support processes: comments and integration. *Journal of Consulting and Clinical Psychology*, 54, 466–70.

House, J. S., Landis, K. R., and Umberson, D. (1988). Social relationships and health. *Science*, 241, 540–5.

Hull, C. L. (1943). *Principles of Behavior*. New York: Appleton-Century-Crofts.

Hume, D. (1748). The enquiry concerning human understanding. In R. Ackerman (1965). *Theories of Knowledge: A Critical Introduction* (pp. 191–213). New York: McGraw-Hill Book Company.

Ickes, W. (1993). Empathic accuracy. *Journal of Personality*, 61, 587–610.

Ickes, W. (Ed.) (1997). *Empathic Accuracy*. New York: The Guilford Press.

Ickes, W., Bissonnette, V., Garcia, S., and Stinson, L. L. (1990). Implementing and using the dyadic interaction paradigm. In C. Hendrick and M. S. Clark (Eds.), *Research Methods in Personality and Social Psychology* (pp. 16–44). Newbury Park, CA: Sage Publications.

Izard, C. E. (1991). *The Psychology of Emotions*. New York: Plenum Press.

Jobe, J. B. (2000). Cognitive processes in self-report. In A. A. Stone, J. S. Turkkan, C. A. Bachrach, J. B. Jobe, H. S. Kurtzman, and V. S. Cain (Eds.), *The Science of Self Report: Implications for Research and Practice* (pp. 25–8). Mahwah, NJ: Lawrence Erlbaum Associates.

Johnson, C. L. (1985). The impact of illness on late-life marriage. *Journal of Marriage and the Family, February*, 165–72.

Judd, C. M., Kenny, D. A., and McClelland, G. H. (2001). Estimating and testing mediation and moderation in within-participant designs. *Psychological Methods*, 6, 115–34.

Kashy, D. A., and Kenny, D. A. (2000). The analysis of data from dyads and groups. In H. T. Reis and C. M. Judd (Eds.), *Handbook of Research Methods in Social and Personality Psychology* (pp. 451–77). Cambridge, UK: Cambridge University Press.

Kendon, A. (1970). Movement coordination and in social interaction: Some examples described. *Acta Psychologica*, 32, 1–25.

Kenny, D. A. (1996). Models of interdependence in dyadic research. *Journal of Social and Personal Relationships*, 13, 279–94.

Kenny, D. A., and Judd, C. M. (1986). The consequences of violating the independence assumption in analysis of variance. *Psychological Bulletin*, 99, 422–31.

Kihlstrom, J. F., Eich, E., Sandbrand, D., and Tobias, B. A. (2000). Emotion and memory: implications for self-report. In A. A. Stone, J. S. Turkkan, C. A. Bachrach, J. B. Jobe, H. S. Kurtzman, and V. S. Cain (Eds.), *The Science of Self Report: Implications for Research and Practice* (pp. 81–100). Mahwah, NJ: Lawrence Erlbaum Associates.

King, K. B., Reis, H. T., Porter, L. A., and Norsen, L. H. (1993). Social support and long-term recovery from coronary artery disease: Effects on patients and spouses. *Health Psychology*, 12, 56–63.

Lam, D. H., and Power, M. J. (1991). Social support in a general practice elderly sample. *International Journal of Geriatric Psychology*, 6, 89–93.

Larsen, R. J., and Ketelaar, T. (1991). Personality and susceptibility to positive and negative emotional states. *Journal of Personality and Social Psychology* 61, 132–40.

Lassner, J. B. (1991). Does social support aid in weight loss and smoking interventions? Reply from a family systems perspective. *Annals of Behavioral Medicine*, 13, 66–72.

Lazarus, R. S. (1991). *Emotion and Adaptation*. New York: Oxford University Press.

Levenson, R. W., Carstensen, L. L., and Gottman, J. M. (1993). Long-term marriage: Age, gender, and satisfaction. *Psychology and Aging*, 8, 301–13.

Lewis, M. A., and Butterfield, R. (1998a). Social influence tactics and health behavior change. Paper presented at the annual meeting of the American Psychological Association, San Francisco.

Lewis, M. A., and Butterfield, R. (1998b). Social control, relationship functioning, and health behavior change. Paper presented at the biennial meeting of the International Society for the Study of Personal Relationships, Saratoga Springs.

Lewis, M. A., DeVellis, B. M., and Sleath, B. (2002). Interpersonal communication and social influence. In K. Glanz, F. Lewis, and B. Rimer (Eds.), *Health Behavior and Health Education: Theory, Research and Practice* (3rd edn, pp. 363–402). San Francisco: Jossey Bass.

Lewis, M. A., and Rook, K. S. (1999). Social control in personal relationships: Impact on health behaviors and psychological distress. *Health Psychology*, 18, 63–71.

Lieberman, M. A. (1986). Social supports – the consequences of psychologizing: A commentary. *Journal of Consulting and Clinical Psychology*, 54, 461–5.

Lyons R. F., Sullivan, M. J. L., and Ritvo, P. G. (Eds.) (1995). *Relationships in Chronic Illness and Disability*. Thousand Oaks, CA: Sage Publications.

Mayeaux, E. J. (2000). A history of western medicine and surgery. [WWW document]. URL http://lib-sh.lsumc.edu/fammed/grounds/history.html, Louisiana State University Medical Center Shreveport, Louisiana, Grand Rounds Lecture Handouts.

Mayer, J. D., and Gaschke, Y. N. (1988). The experience and meta-experience of mood. *Journal of Personality and Social Psychology*, 55, 102–11.

Mayer, J. D., and Salovey, P. (1995). Emotional intelligence and the construction and regulation of feelings. *Applied and Preventive Psychology*, 4, 197–208.

Mayer, J. D., Salovey, P., and Caruso, D. R. (1999a). MSCEIT Item Booklet (Research Version 1.1) Toronto, CA: Multi-Health Systems.

Mayer, J. D., Salovey, P., and Caruso, D. R. (2000). Emotional intelligence as zeitgeist, as personality, and as mental ability. In R. Bar-On and J. D. A. Parker (Eds.), *The Handbook of Emotional Intelligence: Theory, Development, Assessment, and Application at Home, School, and in the Workplace* (pp. 18–135). San Francisco: Jossey-Bass.

Noller, P. (1981). Gender and marital adjustment level differences in decoding messages from spouses and strangers. *Journal of Personality and Social Psychology*, 41, 272–8.

Parker, J. C., Bradley, L. A., DeVellis, R. F. et al. (1993). Biopsychosocial contributions to the management of arthritis disability: Blueprints from an NIDRR-sponsored conference. *Arthritis and Rheumatism*, 36, 885–9.

Radloff, L. S. (1977). The CESD scale: A self-report depression scale for research in the general population. *Applied Psychology Measurement*, 1, 385–401.

Reis, H. T. (2001). Relationship experiences and emotional well-being. In C. D. Ryff and B. H. Singer (Eds.), *Emotion, Social Relationships, and Health* (pp. 57–86). New York: Oxford University Press.

Reis, H. T., Collins, W. A., and Berscheid, E. (2000). The relationship context of human behavior and development. *Psychological Bulletin*, 126, 844–72.

Revenson, T. A., Schiaffino, K. M., Majerovitz, S. D., and Gibofsky, A. (1991). Social support as a double-edged sword: the relation of positive and problematic support to depression among rheumatoid arthritis patients. *Social Science and Medicine*, 33, 801–13.

Rotter, J. B. (1954). *Social Learning and Clinical Psychology*. Engelwood-Cliffs: Prentice Hall.

Rusbult, C. E., and VanLange, P. A. M. (1996). Interdependence processes. In E. T. Higgins and A. W. Kruglanski (Eds.), *Social Psychology: Handbook of Basic Principles* (pp. 564–96). New York: Guilford.

Ryff, C., and Singer, B. (2000). Interpersonal flourishing: A positive health agenda for the new millennium. *Personality and Social Psychology Review*, 4, 30–44.

Salovey, P. S., and Mayer, J. D. (1990). Emotional intelligence. *Imagination, Cognition and Personality*, 9, 185–211.

Salovey, P., Mayer, J. D., Goldman, S., Turvey, C., and Palfai, T. P. (1991). The trait meta-mood scale and emotional intelligence: Measuring attention to, clarity, and maintenance/repair of mood. Unpublished manuscript, Yale University.

Salovey, P., Mayer, J. D., Goldman, S., Turvey, C., and Palfai, T. P. (1995). Emotional attention, clarity, repair: Exploring emotional intelligence using the trait meta-mood scale. In J. W. Pennebaker (Ed.), *Emotion, Disclosure, and Health* (pp. 125–54). Washington DC: American Psychological Association.

Seeman, T. E. (1996). Social ties and health: The benefits of social integration. *Annals of Epidemiology*, 6, 442–51.

Seligman, E. P., and Csikszentmihalyi, M. (2000). Positive psychology: an introduction. *American Psychologist*, 55, 5–14.

Solomon, R. C. (2000). The philosophy of emotions. In M. Lewis and J. M. Haviland-Jones (Eds.), *Handbook of Emotions* (pp. 3–15). New York: The Guilford Press.

Strack, F., Martin, L. L., and Stepper, S. (1988). Inhibiting and facilitating conditions of facial expressions: A non-obtrusive test of the facial feedback hypothesis. *Journal of Personality and Social Psychology*, 54, 768–76.

Sullins, E. S. (1991). Emotional contagion revisited: Effects of social comparison and expressive style on mood convergence. *Personality and Social Psychology Bulletin*, 7, 166–74.

Suls, J., Green, P., Rose, G., Lounsbury, P., and Gordon, E. (1997). Hiding worries from one's spouse: Associations between coping via protective buffering and distress in male post-myocardial infarction patients and their wives. *Journal of Behavioral Medicine*, 20, 333–49.

Taylor, S. E., Klein, L. C., Lewis, B. P., Gruenewald, T. L., Gurung, R. A. R., and Updegraff, J. A. (2000). Biobehavioral responses to stress in females: Tend-and-befriend, not fight-or-flight. *Psychological Review*, 107, 411–29.

Thomas, G., and Fletcher, G. J. O. (1997). Empathic accuracy in close relationships. In W. Ickes (Ed.), *Empathic Accuracy* (pp. 194–217). New York: The Guilford Press.

Veroff, J., and Veroff, J. B. (1980). *Social Incentives: A Life-span Developmental Approach*. New York: Academic Press.

Watson, R. I. (1963). *The Great Psychologists: From Aristotle to Freud*. Philadelphia: J. B. Lipincott Company.

Watson, D., Clark, L. A., and Tellegen, A. (1988). Development and validation of brief measures of positive and negative affect: The PANAS scales. *Journal of Personality and Social Psychology*, 54, 1063–70.

Wolf, M. H., Putnam, S. M., James, S. A., and Stiles, W. B. (1978). The medical interview satisfaction scale: Development of a scale to measure patient perceptions of physician behavior. *Journal of Behavioral Medicine*, 1, 391–401.

Wrightsman, L. (1960). Effects of waiting with others on changes in level of felt anxiety. *Journal of Abnormal and Social Psychology*, 61, 216–22.

Yovetich, N. A., and Rusbult, C. E. (1994). Accommodative behavior in close relationships: Exploring transformation of motivation. *Journal of Experimental Social Psychology*, 30, 138–64.

CHAPTER 11

The Social, Linguistic, and Health Consequences of Emotional Disclosure

James W. Pennebaker

The University of Texas at Austin

Introduction

Writing or talking about upsetting emotional experiences is associated with improvements in mental and physical health. The goal of this paper is to explore the social, linguistic, physiological, and personality correlates of this phenomenon. Central to this work is the idea that writing brings about greater social integration which, in addition to the cognitive and emotional changes, is associated with better health. To what degree does writing about an emotional event bring about changes in peoples' social worlds? To what degree is it possible to identify who is most likely to benefit from writing about emotional topics? How do individuals talk, interact, and move about in the natural environment and what do these patterns tell us about their potential health?

Research surrounding the effects of writing about emotional experiences has progressed at a remarkable rate (Lepore and Smyth, 2002). Work from multiple labs, including our own, has repeatedly demonstrated that translating experiences into language can influence health in several ways. Studies have demonstrated that writing benefits samples of both healthy and unhealthy participants. Particularly important, a number of projects are beginning to demonstrate some of the cognitive and linguistic bases of the benefits of writing. Below, some of the more promising findings are mentioned.

A Brief History of the Writing Paradigm

The basic writing paradigm developed in our labs in the mid-1980s required individuals to write for 3–4 consecutive days about traumatic or emotional experiences or to write about non-emotional control topics (Pennebaker and Beall, 1986). The primary finding has been that emotional writing is associated with improved physical health, as measured by drops in physician visits, reductions in self-reported physical symptoms, and enhanced biological functioning (as measured by various immune and autonomic measures). Smyth (1998), in a meta-analysis of the writing paradigm drawing on 13 studies from five labs, reported that disclosive compared with control writing was associated with improved physical and mental health, including drops in doctor visits ($d = 0.42$), changes in physiological functioning, including improved immune and hormonal function ($d = 0.68$), and reports of better psychological well-being ($d = 0.66$).

Since the submission of Smyth's paper, dozens of additional studies have been published, accepted for publication, or submitted that further demonstrate the effects of writing. Although the majority of replications and extensions have been conducted with college students, others have found that writing about emotional topics is associated with reductions in pain behavior (Kelley et al., 1997) and medication use among chronic pain sufferers, fewer health visits to the infirmary of maximum security psychiatric prisoners (Richards et al., 2000), reduced rates of depression among victims of crime (Schoutrop et al., 1997), and better health and adjustment of women following the birth of a child (Rimé et al., 1998). In two recent studies, Smyth et al. (1999) report that writing about emotional topics relative to superficial ones is associated with better clinical prognoses (as rated by blind physicians), including greater lung capacity among asthmatics and better mobility scores among arthritics. The disclosure effect holds up across cultures, age, and social class (see Pennebaker and Graybeal, 2001; Lepore and Smyth, 2002).

Expanding the Domain of Outcome Measures

In the late 1980s and early 1990s, the writing paradigm consistently demonstrated positive effects for objective health outcome measures, such as health center visits, medication use, medical costs, and various immune markers. Soon, an increasing number of experiments began demonstrating that writing about emotional topics could potentially affect non-health measures. For example, three studies have found that students who write about coming to college subsequently evidence improved grades. Men laid off from their jobs who wrote about this experience found jobs more quickly than controls who either didn't write or who wrote about time management (Spera et al., 1994). The writing paradigm, then, has proven to be a powerful technique to bring about behavioral changes.

More complex has been the ability of disclosive writing to bring about changes in self-reports of distress. Smyth (1998) reports that immediately after writing about emotional topics people report feeling more distressed than controls. However, follow-ups at least one month after the writing studies indicate that self-reported distress is lower among experimentals than controls. The self-reports, however, vary most extremely from study to study – with approximately half of the studies finding no long term self-report effects and the other half finding rather large effects. Interestingly, some studies measuring more extreme distress – such as post-traumatic stress disorder (PTSD) symptoms (Schoutrop et al., 1997) or depression or rumination about a specific event (Lepore, 1997) have found writing to be more beneficial than labs relying on general negative affect. Indeed, Lepore's studies indicate that the actual levels of intrusive thoughts about the writing topic may not drop, but the degree to which the thoughts are disturbing is much lower.

Of particular relevance is the fact that studies have not found consistent changes in any self-reports of overt behaviors following writing. In other words, emotion writing participants go to the doctor less and are in better objective physical condition after emotional writing even though they report no differences in sleep or eating patterns, dietary or exercise habits. Similarly, in three studies where college grades were measured, disclosive writing participants' grades improved even though their self-reports of studying, class attendance, or any other school-related behaviors did not change. Finally, even though experimental participants are able to land jobs based on their job interviews compared to controls, the two groups do not differ on any self-reports of social behaviors, including number of heart-to-heart discussions with others, social participation with others, or comfort in talking with others. In short, self-reports of social and psychological factors appear to be virtually independent of the more objective variables that they should mirror. As will be apparent, this probably reflects shortcomings in the nature of self-reports rather than an absence of true behavioral change.

Developing New Theoretical Conceptions

The evidence is now fairly solid that translating emotional experiences into language can be healthy. The explanations for the phenomenon are still in dispute. Further, the writing-health link appears to influence individuals along multiple levels. To further complicate the picture, a number of intriguing and oftentimes unexpected findings are emerging from multiple labs.

Inhibitory Processes
One of the first hypotheses to explain the effectiveness of disclosure dealt with inhibition. Specifically, it was proposed that not talking about emotional upheavals was a form of inhibition. That is, actively holding back thoughts, feelings, or emotions was a form of stress that exacerbated a number of adverse biological processes – such as increased cortisol production and immune suppression. According to this inhibition model, the act of writing about an emotional topic would allow individuals to organize and assimilate the event which would bypass the need for further inhibition (Pennebaker, 1989). Indeed, several correlational studies hinted that such processes may be at work (e.g., Cole et al., 1996a; 1996b; Major et al., 1998; Gross and Levenson, 1997). Note that these ideas are consistent with Wegner's (1994) work on thought suppression and ironic processing. That is, by attempting to control ongoing thoughts, individuals are ultimately monitoring more information at higher rates which could help to explain the apparent work of inhibition.

Despite the promise of inhibition models, direct tests of changes in inhibition among people who write about emotional topics have yielded disappointing results. For example, no differences in health outcomes have been found between participants who claim that they have not previously disclosed traumas versus those who have disclosed their traumas (Greenberg and Stone, 1992). Similarly, individuals are not able to report (or even understand) questions that ask them the degree to which they are actively inhibiting or holding back their thoughts, emotions, or behaviors (Pennebaker et al., 1988). At this point, then, the inhibition hypothesis would have to be considered as unproven and still not adequately tested.

Cognitive Integration Ideas

A number of labs, including ours, have been working on the assumption that writing about an upsetting topic helps to organize and/or assimilate the complex features of traumatic experience. The various explicit and implicit cognitive models have focused on different facets of cognitive organization and narrative construction. Smyth and his colleagues (1999), for example, have assumed that writing fundamentally organizes an upsetting experience. As an indirect test of this, the authors had people either write about a trauma in an organized or fragmented way. Only doing so in an organized way was associated with health and mood improvements. Williams-Avery (1998) reported similar effects such that writing instructions that stressed organization provided better outcomes than those that did not. Using a different analysis strategy of looking directly at the ways individuals write about emotional topics, several labs are now finding support for the idea that constructing a narrative over the course of writing helps the individuals to integrate the experience. Specifically, by looking at word usage (e.g., an increasing use of specific cognitive words over the days of writing), health improvements are efficiently predicted. These word patterns have now been reported by Pennebaker and Francis (1996), Pennebaker et al. (1997), Keough et al (1998), Petrie et al. (1998), and Klein and Boals (2001).

Using techniques that focus more on the direct cognitive effects of emotional writing, Klein and Boals (2001) have recently found that a task that measures working memory shows differential effects from before to after writing as a function of emotional writing. That is, participants who wrote about traumatic experiences evidenced greater working memory in the weeks after writing in comparison with those who wrote about superficial topics.

Finally, Taylor and her colleagues (1998) have reported that individuals who are asked to visualize an emotionally upsetting experience show mood and self-reported health effects consistent with writing about an upsetting experience. Based on Taylor and Schneider's (1989) mental simulation model, the act of carefully thinking through an event may help the individual to find meaning to the event and, at the same time, help them adopt more efficient coping strategies. What is particularly intriguing about this approach is that the mental simulation exercise is not requiring participants to use language as a mental simulation tool. Indeed, it would be instructive to learn the degree to which people are using language automatically within the paradigm.

Other Explanatory Models

It is tempting to consider each of the above models as mutually exclusive. Indeed, one problem is that many of these approaches are examining the disclosure/health link from different levels of analysis. Hence several models could all be true. In addition to the inhibitory and cognitive approaches, a number of additional explanatory schemes have been suggested in recent years.

1. *Habituation.* Greenberg et al. (1996) reported the results of a fascinating project wherein previously traumatized students wrote about either their own personal trauma or about someone else's trauma as though it were their own or, in a third group, about superficial topics. The authors found that writing about an imaginary trauma was as effective as writing about one's own trauma. They argue that the mere writing of an emotional topic helps to habituate the person to the emotions aroused by the topic (cf., Mendolia and Kleck, 1993). Note that the important work of Foa and Meadows (1997) is consistent with this habituation explanation. That is, when individuals must actively confront an emotional topic on multiple occasions, the magnitude of anxiety ratings and ANS activity drops.

2. *Individual differences.* An ongoing debate in the writing-health research area concerns the degree to which individual differences may moderate the benefits of translating experiences into words. Most studies drawing on normal populations have failed to find consistent personality markers. However, studies drawing extreme samples of high and low hostility (Christensen and Smith, 1993) and alexithymia (Paez et al., 1999) suggest that those naturally more hostile and unable to verbalize their feelings may benefit more than low hostile or alexithymic individuals. Similarly, Smyth's meta-analysis indicates that males may benefit more from writing than females.

3. *Mapping the social dynamics of disclosure.* Rimé (1995) argues that disclosure of emotional topics is essentially a social act. His work on social sharing has roots in the self-disclosure literature (e.g., Jourard, 1971; Derlega et al., 1993). He is finding that well over 90 percent of emotional experiences are shared with others. Further, social sharing in the first few days after an event is correlated with improved health. Continued social sharing several weeks or months after an experience both reflects and, perhaps, exacerbates negative emotions (cf., Bonanno et al., 1995). Much like Stiles et al.'s (1992) fever model of disclosure, social sharing both reflects emotional turmoil and indicates movement towards improved health. Consistent with much of the social support literature, Rimé (1995) argues that disclosure in the first days or weeks after a trauma ultimately changes the quality of a person's social network by bringing people closer together. Disclosure, then, serves as a force of social integration. Interestingly, Rimé suggests that even private disclosure (as with writing) helps free the person from the stress of the non-disclosed event which ultimately allows for greater social integration.

Rimé's work, as well as some of our own, is also consistent with many of the social integration ideas first suggested by Durkheim (1951) wherein mental health was viewed as the result of the relationship between individuals and their social worlds. Durkheim, and, more recently, a growing number of social support researchers (e.g., Cohen et al., 2000; Cutrona, 1989; Pierce et al., 1992), have argued that individuals' relations with others must be viewed from both the individuals' own needs as well as those of their potential social network. Unfortunately, with a few notable exceptions (e.g., Bradbury and Fincham, 1992; Dunkel-Schetter et al., 1992), most work that attempts to look at social support and integration has relied exclusively on self-reports rather than on objective changes in peoples' social interactions or relationships.

A number of investigators have reported findings that support the idea that either inhibiting a secret or an emotion can disrupt social processes or, conversely, that disclosure can facilitate social dynamics. Finkenauer (1998) conducted an experiment wherein individuals were asked to sit in a room and talk with another participant. For half of the dyads, one member was told a secret that they were not supposed to tell the other person. For the remaining dyads, the person was told the same information but it was not conveyed as a secret. Self-reports of the quality of the subsequent interaction (from both parties) indicated that the secret-shrouded interaction was viewed as less satisfying than the non-secret condition. Similarly, a recent study by Richards and Gross (1999) employed a similar paradigm wherein two people watched a disturbing film. For half the dyads, one of the members was instructed to suppress emotional feelings. In those dyads where emotional suppression had taken place, the subsequent "free" interactions were shorter and less satisfying for both parties. Finally, Lepore and Greenberg (in press) have found that individuals who had recently broken up with a loved one were more likely to return to their old relationship if they were randomly assigned to write about the relationship than about a control topic.

Summary

Writing about emotional topics exerts a powerful influence on mental and physical health. Across multiple labs, there is now sufficient evidence to indicate that the systematic writing (or talking) about emotional events is a therapeutic tool with clinically significant medical and social effects. Although there are overlapping explanations for the effect, most either directly or indirectly indicate that the translation of emotional events into a linguistic format is sufficient, and perhaps necessary, for long-term effects to accrue.

Explorations into Language

Language, by its very nature and evolution, is a social tool. Many of the behavioral effects associated with writing – better grades, fewer illnesses, ability to get better jobs, etc – are indirectly and directly social. What many of these studies are now indicating is that the cognitive changes that may result from writing change the writers' relationships with others in their social worlds. Whereas the immediate effects of writing is to change how the individual thinks and, perhaps, is able to move past the trauma, the salutary effects are likely to be the social changes that result from these cognitive changes.

Development and Use of a Language Analysis Technique: LIWC

One of the biggest barriers to studying the role of language in a social context is in deciding which dimensions of language to explore. More importantly, any measurement strategy must be relatively simple and, at the same time, capture language on a rather broad level. One of the first goals in our own language work was to further develop a computerized text analysis program, Linguistic Inquiry and Word Count, or LIWC (Pennebaker et al., 2001). The original LIWC program was developed without a general sense of how individuals naturally use language and, therefore, was largely deduced from ongoing theories in psychology. Over its years of development, the basic structure of the program was changed to include categories that were often used by writers and speakers. For most common (i.e., not technical) text files of written or spoken transcripts, the LIWC program now captures approximately 80 percent of words. Cosmetically, the program was updated by making it compatible with most desktop computers, including PCs and Macintosh. The current version of the program is user friendly and fast.

Although a number of validity studies have been conducted using LIWC (see below), most have compared LIWC categories against self-report measures or judges' ratings. An inherent difficulty of LIWC is that it is a conceptually crude program. That is, word count programs fail to correct for context, synonyms, irony, metaphor, etc. In addition, they are unable to assess co-occurrence of words or phrases. Higher-order concepts such as text coherence are simply not computed. An important goal for future research is to compare LIWC results with those of more traditional discourse strategies. Further, it is imperative that we link strategies such as LIWC with more sophisticated strategies such as Latent Semantic Analysis (LSA).

Language and Disclosure

Why does writing or talking about emotional upheavals affect physical and psychological health? This question, of course, goes beyond the writing paradigm and addresses the broader question of why psychotherapy itself is effective. At least two strong possibilities exist. The first deals with the construction of a narrative. That is, individuals who write about traumas naturally come to a coherent understanding of the event. Further, this understanding is thought to be inherent in the cognitive language of their disclosure. A parallel argument suggests that translating emotional experiences into words is ultimately a labeling phenomenon. That is, by merely attaching a linguistic label to an inchoate feeling, the person would be less autonomically aroused due to increased certainty, which would help the person to better construct a narrative about their experience.

Use of Cognitive and Emotion Words

One of the primary motivations for developing the LIWC program was to learn if the language individuals used while disclosing emotional topics would predict long-term health changes. Based on the Pennebaker and Francis (1996) pilot study, we found that a particular linguistic "fingerprint" was associated with reductions in physician visits following participation in the disclosive writing. Those who wrote about traumas were more likely to benefit if, over the three days of writing, they used a high number of positive emotion words, a moderate number of negative emotion words, and, most important, an increasing number of cognitive (i.e., causal and insight) words from the beginning to the last day of writing.

We were able to apply this model to six writing studies in a more systematic way (see Pennebaker et al., 1997). Again, the same linguistic pattern predicted improved health. The implications of these findings are intriguing. First, use of emotion terms is moderately important. Counter to our earlier predictions, positive emotion words are linearly related to health while negative emotion words are curvilinearly related (an inverse-U function). These findings support current views on the value of optimism (e.g., Scheier and Carver, 1985; Peterson et al., 1988). At the same time, the negative emotion findings are consistent with the repressive coping literature (Jamner et al., 1988) in that those people who do not use negative emotion words in describing traumatic events are at greater risk for subsequent health problems than those who use at least some negative emotion words.

Most striking, however, are the relative effect sizes of cognitive change words. An increasing use of cognitive words accounted for far more variance in health improvement than did emotion words. These data, as noted below, indicate that the construction of a story or narrative concerning an emotional upheaval is essential to coping. Particularly exciting is that this pattern of effects has now been reported by two independent labs. Keough et al. (1998) found that cognitive change over a 2-week diary writing period was linked to health improvements. Klein and Boals (2001) have reported that an increase in cognitive word use over the days of writing is linked to measures of greater working memory up to 12 weeks after the study.

References to Self and Others: Pronouns and Perspectives

An alternative computer-based approach to linguistic analysis relies on more inductive ways of establishing the pattern of word use. One particularly promising strategy is Latent Semantic Analysis, or LSA (e.g., Landauer and Dumais, 1997). A technique such as LSA is akin to a factor analysis of individual words. By establishing the factor structure of a large number of writing samples, it is possible to learn how any new writing samples are similar to one another. Traditionally, this technique has been used to determine the degree to which any two texts are similar in terms of their content – almost a proxy of text coherence. In theory, then, one might predict that the more similar the content of trauma essays over the 3–4 days of writing, the more the person's health would improve. If one made such a prediction, however, one would be wrong. LSA analyses of three writing studies failed to uncover any relationship between linguistic content and health.

An alternative way to think about writing is to focus on writing style as opposed to writing content. Style is, to a large extent, determined by "junk" words – pronouns, articles, conjunctions, prepositions, and auxiliary verbs. These style-related words are variously referred to as closed-class words, function words, or particles (Miller, 1995). Interestingly, most LSA techniques routinely throw out these particles since they do not carry the same information as more content-heavy nouns and verbs.

Across a series of style-based LSA analyses, we have recently discovered that particles in general and pronouns in particular have been found to correlate highly with health improvements. Basically, the more that individuals shift in their use of pronouns from day to day in writing, the more their health improves. Indeed, across three separate studies, pronoun shifts among trauma writers correlated between 0.3 and 0.5 with changes in physician visits (Campbell and Pennebaker, 2002). Closer inspection of these data suggest that healthy writing is associated with a relatively high number of self-references on some days but not others. Alternatively, people who always write in a particular voice – such as first person singular – simply don't improve.

Although our LSA studies are still in the early stages, they are suggesting that the ability to change perspective in dealing with an emotional upheaval may be critically important. The data also indicate that pronouns may be an overlooked linguistic dimension that could have important meaning for researchers in health and social psychology. After all, pronouns are markers of self- versus group-identity (e.g., I versus we) as well as the degree to which people are focused on or are relating to others. As discussed below, pronouns may provide insight into people's level of social integration as well as self-focus.

Emotion Labeling

Concurrent with the language and disclosure project, it is important to know if the mere act of labeling an emotion can help to reduce its adverse effects. To explore this possibility, Hayward (1997) conducted an emotion labeling study where 77 college students saw two 5-minute movie clips that aroused sadness or anger. After viewing each clip, subjects wrote a description of the movie "as though you were describing it to a friend." Skin conductance level (SCL) and heart rate (HR) were recorded every 20 seconds over the course of the experiment. After the second movie (which was counterbalanced), the primary manipulation was introduced: half of the participants were asked to list the emotions they were currently feeling; the remaining were asked to list objects in the room. Ratings of the narrative by the independent judges indicated that those who labeled their emotions wrote "better" narratives about the second movie than those who listed objects in the room. Unexpectedly, emotion labeling was associated with immediate increases in both SCL and HR compared to object labeling. Better narratives, then, may have been motivated by the forced awareness of how people were feeling. That is, if individuals are required to acknowledge how they feel, they may be more invested in analyzing why they feel the way they do.

Inhibition and Immune Function

An explanatory scheme that has not been tested well concerns inhibition. Originally it was argued that non-disclosed traumatic experiences increased illness rates because of the physiological work of inhibition. To directly explore the links between inhibition and immune markers, we conducted a 2 (emotional versus control writing for 3 days) × 2 (suppression versus non-suppression) × 2 (pre versus post) between-within experiment on 40 medical students to learn if (a) writing about traumatic experiences could bring about immediate change in immune markers, and (b) if suppressing thoughts about the writing topics would be associated with immune suppression (Petrie et al., 1998). Participants wrote for 3 consecutive days, 15 minutes per day. After each day's writing, participants were told to sit quietly for 5 minutes and either think about anything (no suppression) or to think about anything except their writing topic (suppression). Blood was drawn before writing and after the 5-minute thinking period each day. Blood counts of lymphocytes (e.g., t-helper, t-suppressor, and NK cells) were assayed.

Two important effects emerged. First, lymphocyte counts were affected by the manipulations in the predicted directions. That is, emotion writing was associated with higher lymphocyte counts than control writing; suppression manipulations were linked to lower lymphocyte counts. More intriguing were the correlations between the lymphocyte changes and language use over the course of writing. Congruent with the original LIWC-disclosure findings, the more that individuals' cognitive word counts increased over the 3 days of writing, the greater the lymphocyte counts after each day after writing. In other words, those who are constructing a story or working through their traumas are the same subjects who show the most pronounced immune change each day. A third finding is also notable. These trends in the suppression condition failed to show consistent language-immune correlations. Indeed, all indications suggest that suppression after writing may block the normal assimilation process.

Writing Among Unique Samples

Part of the disclosure-health project has been devoted to learning the boundary conditions of writing. Are there some groups for which writing is not beneficial? Are certain classes of instructions more efficient than others? How flexible can the writing instructions and context be? Among the samples that we have been studying include stigmatized members of the university community, those most stigmatized within a psychiatric prison population, and workers in an unstable city bureaucracy under stress from both their clients and their employer.

In the last few years, social psychologists have conducted some intriguing studies that indicate people who are members of stigmatized groups (e.g., ethnic minorities) underperform in stereotype relevant domains if they are reminded of the stereotype or their membership in that group. For example, Steele and Aronson (1995) report that if African Americans are given a standardized test and, at the beginning of the test they are asked to report their race, they subsequently perform more poorly than if they don't first report their race. Similarly, Brown and Josephs (1999) find that women do more poorly on standardized math tests if they initially report their sex than if they don't. Interestingly, feelings of being stigmatized are also associated with poorer general physical health, even after age, sex, social class, etc. are statistically controlled (Williams, 1997). Would writing about one's stigmatized status help to resolve issues about this stigma and be associated with improved health?

As a pilot test of this, we selected a sample of approximately 60 students who claimed to be a member of a group of people who, from society's view, were seen in a negative light, including ethnic minorities, gays/lesbians, and so on (Pennebaker and Seagal, 1999). Participants wrote either about being a member of the stigmatized group or about being a member of the general university community. A third control group wrote about superficial topics. Approximately one month after writing, the students were again contacted and asked the degree to which they identified with their stigmatized group and with the university in general. Those who wrote about being a member of a stigmatized group reported higher levels of collective self-esteem at the one-month follow-up than those who wrote about being a member of the university community. Levels of reported campus activity did not change as a function of writing topic. When the data were analyzed looking at the visibility of the stigma, a writing condition by visibility interaction was revealed. Those writing about being a member of the university community who had a visible identity (e.g., race) and those writing about being a member of a stigmatized group who had a non-visible identity (e.g., sexual orientation) reported the highest levels of collective self-esteem a month after writing. Although not statistically significant ($p < 0.12$), health center effects were in the same direction. That is, people with visible identities benefited from trying to come to terms with the general university community whereas those with secret identities – such as lesbians and gay men – benefited more in trying to come to terms with their secrets.

Applying the logic of the stigma project, we re-analyzed data from an earlier study among psychiatric prison inmates at a maximum security unit in Illinois. Going on the assumption that sex offenders were the most stigmatized of all prisoners in both the other prisoners' and the guards' eyes, we predicted that sex offenders would benefit most from writing. Indeed, in a study of almost 100 prisoners who were randomly assigned to write about trauma, about a control topic, or a no-writing control for three days, we found that the stigmatized sex offenders evidenced much greater health (as measured by drops in prison infirmary visits) after emotional writing than any other group or condition (see Richards et al., 2000).

In Search of Cognitive Measures

A continuing frustration has been that participants in our writing studies tell us that writing or talking about traumas profoundly change the ways they think about them. Self-reports asking people how much they think about the topics fail to yield meaningful results. Our attempts at finding meaningful cognitive markers of change have simply not panned out. Despite these failures in self-reports and cognitive markers of change, it is inconceivable that cognitive and/or social changes are not occurring. This assumption is based on the objective facts that writing produces clinically and statistically meaningful changes in health behavior, physiological activity, study behavior, etc. – effects that are clear to the participants and researchers.

One of our attempts to better tag cognitive changes from before to after writing was a variation of the beeper strategy. The basic idea was that participants were given a tape recorder and a beeper. Whenever they were beeped (actually "vibrated" since the beep mode was turned off), they were to quietly talk into the tape recorder about what they were thinking as they were paged. As an initial test of this procedure, a group of 15 undergraduates, graduates, and the author were paged, on average, every 12 minutes (plus or minus 8 minutes) for two consecutive days. Although the technique itself was workable – albeit rather annoying – we discovered some interesting problems in the study of spontaneous thoughts. For example, on most beeping occasions, people were not thinking – or at least they weren't aware that they were thinking. Indeed, thinking was most likely to be reported when people were disengaged from their environment (alone driving, in an unpleasant group setting, exercising alone). If they were engaged in a conversation, watching television, listening to music, or reading, most respondents noted that they were not thinking. Their entries on the tape recorder reflected this. Examples of "thoughts" include: watching the Simpsons on television, talking to mother about clothes, not thinking about anything.

In addition, there were large individual differences. Even with extensive training on the nature of thoughts and how to record them, some people had virtually no thoughts at all (approximately 1 percent of all their recording entries); others were as high as 80 percent. Even among those with high rates of reported thoughts, many later reported during debriefing that they made up thoughts based on the context of being beeped. For example, one person who was driving when he was beeped said he was thinking about how his cat was doing. During debriefing, he admitted that he was thinking about his cat because the beeper's vibrations reminded him of his cat's purring.

Although the thought sampling idea was appealing, it simply didn't work. In fact, the failure of the beeper technique led us into a far more promising direction that involved the random sampling of language and social behavior. Indeed, our recent findings from our language sampling has opened up new vistas in trying to understand language, cognition, social behaviors, and health.

Summary

Although there appear to be cognitive changes resulting from the writing, these changes are not immediately measurable using self-reports or cognitive measures of accessibility or semantic networks based on self-reports. Further, self-reports of behaviors following writing typically fail to yield consistent effects as a function of condition. It is critical to explore alternative measurement strategies – ideally some which serve as reliable proxies for cognitive activity (e.g., naturalistic language) and for real world behaviors.

The awareness and labeling of one's emotions may contribute to health and behavior change. The awareness of negative emotions above some minimal threshold may be necessary for health improvements but excessive awareness and/or expression may be counter-productive. The awareness/expression of positive emotions exert a positive effect on health. Ultimately, however, the effect size of using emotion words in writing about an event is relatively small. Emotion awareness, then, rather than expression per se appears to be an important factor in writing about emotional topics and subsequent health.

Through all of this research on word use, it is easy to lose sight of a central fact: Language is ultimately a social act. Our ability to express ourselves in words evolved so that we could convey thoughts and perceptions to others. The various linguistic analyses suggest that certain ways of using language in writing may explain why the use of cognitive words and pronouns may be particularly important in predicting health changes. Changes in causal and insight words serve as markers of how individuals change in the ways they are organizing and representing complex emotional or traumatic experiences. At the same time, pronouns reflect how people are thinking about themselves relative to other people. The stigma data further point to the role of social factors in both the inhibition and expression of emotional topics. As outlined below, the understanding of linguistic changes associated with writing *must* be looked at within the context of the participants' social worlds.

Towards a Theory of Social Integration

Much of our earlier work has suggested that there is a need for greater examination of the social dynamics surrounding the disclosure processes. Through a number of unexpected findings and the unforeseen power of the LIWC and LSA methodologies, we have embarked on several studies that directly examine some of the social and language changes surrounding writing, talking, and health. Three research projects have been particularly promising: the development of environmental monitoring, the study of natural conversation on the Internet (specifically, the ways people talked following the death of Princess Diana), and the study of support groups. From these studies, we have been developing a general theoretical perspective dealing with social integration.

Recording Natural Language in the Environment

For the last few years, we have become intrigued with the idea of capturing what people are naturally saying and doing in their worlds. Recall that we had originally attempted to use a thought sampling methodology using the beeper strategy as a way of learning how people changed in the ways they thought from before to after writing. As we learned, any beeper system is inherently invasive and ultimately relies on individuals' self-reports of their environments. As an alternative, we designed a tape-recording system that remains off for a specified number of minutes and then records for a set amount of time before turning itself off and starting the cycle over again. The most recent version of the system relies on a digital recorder and microphone that fit easily into a jogging pouch or a person's pocket which can comfortably be worn for up to four days. The current system, which we call an Electronically Activated Recorder (EAR), records for 30 seconds and is off for 12 minutes. This 12.5 minute cycle is repeated during the participants' waking hours for two days. The advantage of the EAR over a beeper system is that the participant never knows when the system is on. At the end of the recording period – which currently lasts two days – the participant is given the opportunity to listen to the digital files and to erase any parts of the files that he/she finds embarrassing or private. See Mehl et al. (2001) for a description of the EAR system.

We have conducted one large-scale pilot study with 52 subjects. The basic methodology is this: 2 days of EAR recordings are measured at Time 1 and again at Time 2, which are separated by 4–5 weeks. Midway between the recording periods, students are asked to write about either traumatic or superficial topics for 3 consecutive days. The EAR recordings are both transcribed and rated by raters. In addition, participants complete a battery of questionnaires and physiological markers both before and after each 2-day EAR recording period. The basic findings are as follows:

- The quality of the recordings are good, allowing for the reliable transcribing of the person's conversations and the ratings of the setting of the participant during each period. Three independent raters agreed on all of the major categories for three separate tapes, including whether the participant was talking, on the phone, studying, in class, in transit, watching TV, etc. (mean inter-judge ratings for all categories was 0.80 or higher). Self-ratings of the perceived invasiveness of the system were uniformly low (see Mehl et al., 2001).

- The reliability of people's social and daily activities across the two time periods was remarkably high. That is, the degree to which people talk, are on the phone, watch television, study, etc. are generally highly correlated across the two time periods (rs range from 0.3 to 0.8). Similarly, their basic language use (e.g., self-references, cognitive word use, articles, etc.) is consistent over time, ranging from 0.2 to 0.6. In other words, people exhibit consistent social and linguistic behaviors, interact in similar ways, and seek out similar settings over a 1-month interval (Mehl and Pennebaker, in press).
- Writing about traumas versus superficial topics produced measurable changes in social behavior. In general, experimental participants interacted more with others after writing than controls; those in the experimental condition also used more positive emotion words and laughed more than control participants after writing. Unexpectedly, we are also finding impressive sex differences as a function of condition. That is, after emotional writing, men drop in their use of first person singular (I, me, my) and increase in their first person plural pronouns (we, us, our); women do just the opposite. It is almost as if the writing paradigm is getting participants to behave in non-sex role stereotyped ways.
- Blood pressure changes from before to after writing were correlated with changes in social behaviors. That is, the more that people's diastolic blood pressure dropped from before to after writing (measured at the time of the EAR recordings), the more their social behaviors increased, $r(16) = -0.44$, $p = 0.05$. This preliminary finding is extremely encouraging and points to the possible mediating effects of social changes on health.

Taken together, the preliminary data offer a fascinating glimpse into people's social worlds. Writing about emotional topics is bringing about significant shifts in people's social behaviors. Ironically, individuals don't see these shifts through their own self-reports. Further, these shifts appear to underlie changes in long-term stress markers, such as blood pressure. Most intriguing is that these effects are consistent with our thinking about social integration. That is, people who write about emotional topics now talk more with others, use more positive emotion words, laugh more, and, in their interactions, talk more in the present tense and not reliving past experiences.

Talking about Shared Traumatic Experiences: The Princess Diana Project

The disclosure research is premised on the assumption that the failure to talk about traumatic experience distances individuals from their social group and, at the same time, does not allow them to integrate the experience on a cognitive level. In recent years, we have been perplexed by the ways individuals abruptly stop talking about major psychological upheavals (e.g., Loma Prieta earthquake, Persian Gulf War) about two weeks after their occurrence (Pennebaker and Harber, 1993). Again, these trauma studies are all based on self-reports. In order to begin to understand naturalistic talking, we have begun a series of projects looking at how people talk to one another on the Internet – in both bulletin boards and in the chat rooms on commercial servers, such as America Online (AOL).

Immediately after the announcement of Princess Diana's death, we began downloading ongoing chat on AOL 4–8 times per day, at least 10 minutes per time for four weeks (see Stone and Pennebaker, 2002). The rates at which people talked about the death and Diana were remarkably high during the first three days and then dropped over the next week and a half. By two weeks after the death, the references to Diana and the royal family were extremely low. Using daily LIWC analyses as well as ratings by judges, we were able to see how some of the social dynamics of talking about this emotional experience evolve over time. Whereas in the first 10 days after the death people were compassionate about Diana's death, expressed concern for her family, and were likely to approach the topic in a collective manner (high use of first person plural as opposed to first person singular), this pattern changed markedly two weeks after the death. Indeed, two weeks later the dominant comments about Diana and her death were caustic humor or hostile attacks. Most expressions of compassion were followed by social punishment. To our knowledge, this is the first study to actually capture the social dynamics of inhibition in relatively natural social encounters. This strategy also helps us to see the way emotions and self-views are expressed and how they evolve over time.

Social Dynamics of Support Groups

In 1995, my wife was diagnosed with breast cancer. Being a writer, she told her story of the diagnosis in her column in the local newspaper, the *Dallas Morning News*. Within days, she was contacted by a number of friends and acquaintances whom we both had known for years who told her that they, too, had been diagnosed with and treated for breast cancer. Even though we had seen them during their treatment (which often involved surgery, chemotherapy, and/or radiation), they had not told any of their friends. Not only had these women been profoundly affected by the experience, but their decision not to tell others did not allow them to integrate their experience with others in their social network. This led my students, colleagues, and me to begin studying who seeks and who avoids discussion of massively traumatic personal upheavals, including the diagnosis of disease (e.g., Davison and Pennebaker, 1997; Davison, et al., 2000).

Our first task was simply to learn the degree to which people sought support and/or made posts on the various bulletin boards for 20 of the most prevalent diseases that strike individuals between the ages of 15 and about 70. We were also interested in how individuals with selected diseases (breast cancer, prostate cancer, lung cancer, heart disease, arthritis, diabetes, and chronic fatigue syndrome) talked about their diseases on the bulletin boards. First, there were large and systematic differences in the number of posts as a function of disease. For example, the number of posts per day was almost 10 times higher for breast cancer than for coronary heart disease (CHD), even though the base rates for the two disorders are much higher for CHD. Second, the ways people talked, via analyses using the LIWC program, were strikingly and significantly different.

Based on the initial findings, we extended the project to determine the number of real support groups for each of the 20 diseases in four metropolitan areas in the USA – Los Angeles, Chicago, New York City, and Dallas. The raw numbers and adjusted prevalence of support groups were highly correlated across towns and were correlated with the rates of bulletin board support. Independent judges then rated all 20 diseases along multiple psychological dimensions. The number and prevalence of support groups for diseases are most highly correlated with how stigmatizing the disease is seen. Hence, real and bulletin board support groups are most likely to exist for AIDS, alcoholism, breast and prostate cancer, and least likely to exist for heart disease, stroke, headache, etc. Group formation and use, then, are unrelated to cost of disease, age of onset, life expectancy, degree of pain, sex ratio of disease, or virtually any other dimension. These data square particularly well with Festinger's (1954) original conception of social comparison theory. Contrary to Sarnoff and Zimbardo's (1961) highly controlled laboratory study where embarrassing, anxiety-provoking experiences were not talked about, the support group findings indicate that such experiences can lead to the greatest need for social comparison in real world, life-threatening situations.

Summary

There is a dynamic interaction between individuals and their social worlds. The decision to talk or not talk about a traumatic experience depends both on the individuals' needs to talk and the social world's ability to listen. The more potentially stigmatizing a disorder – especially if it is a secret – the more motivated people are to talk with others who share the problem. If it is a secret, however, the difficulty is often in finding others to talk to about the problem. As our data suggest, the social environment can subtly encourage or discourage talking about emotional topics. There is also an inherent series of questions about the links between a person's social and emotional needs and the needs of those around them. Our various studies dealing with social processes raise a number of important questions that have direct and indirect bearing on social behavior and health:

- To what degree do individuals maintain a linguistic niche that reflects the way they think and talk? If, after disclosing and coming to terms with important psychological events, to what degree does their social niche change? Does a mismatch between one's linguistic proclivities and those of their social world produce stress and predict illness? To what degree are individuals aware of shifts in their social worlds?
- Do people's worlds differ in the degree to which they are inherently coherent, organized, or lend themselves to potential structure? By social coherence, we mean the degree to which the person's daily activities and

discussions are organized as opposed to random and chaotic. Is social coherence a function of the person's psychological state? That is, does disclosure, such as in the writing paradigm, increase social coherence?

Individual Differences

From the first studies dealing with disclosure, researchers have been consumed with finding individual differences that would demonstrate that certain types of people would benefit more from disclosive writing than others. In the Smyth meta-analysis, there was some evidence that males benefited more from disclosive writing than females. Similarly, Christensen and Smith (1993) found that people high in hostility benefited more from writing than those low in hostility and Paez et al. (1999) reported that those high in alexithymia showed greater improvement than those low. We have examined a number of individual difference measures including self-esteem, self-deception, social desirability, positive and negative affect, and all of the Big 5 personality factors – all without success. With the development of LIWC, however, we have come to think about the definition and measurement of personality in a different light.

Linguistic Styles: Language Use as Personality

In a recent multi-study paper, we have proposed that the ways people use language has the psychometric markings of a stable individual difference measure (Pennebaker and King, 1999). In several studies, we applied the LIWC program to 10–18 separate writing samples of varying numbers of writers: inpatients in a drug rehabilitation program who wrote in diaries for 18 consecutive days; students in a health psychology summer school class who turned in 10 writing assignments during the course on different topics; and 15 journal abstracts from each of 40 social psychologists who were members of the elite group Society for Experimental Social Psychology (SESP). Approximately half of the 72 language dimensions evidenced at least modest internal consistency (Cronbach alphas of 0.60 or greater) averaging across the three samples. A separate study, involving over 800 introductory psychology students who wrote on four occasions over the course of a semester, found that the most reliable language dimensions from the first studies showed acceptable factor structure. Further, we were able to demonstrate that these primary dimensions were modestly correlated with self-reports of personality (correlations were generally in the 0.10 to 0.25 range).

   The net effects of the linguistic styles paper is that language use is reliable over time and topic and has some degree of factor structure. More intriguing, however, is that language factors bear no relationship to the structure of self-reported personality (i.e., five-factor model). Further, the language-self-report correlations are fascinatingly low. For example, use of negative emotion words across essays, although highly reliable, is correlated with self-ratings of Negative

Affectivity (from Watson et al.'s 1989 Positive Affect and Negative Affect Scale – PANAS) or Neuroticism (from the five-factor inventory of John et al., 1991) on the order of 0.11. Use of self-references is uncorrelated with self-esteem (0.00); general emotion word use is actually positively correlated with alexithymia (0.11), etc. Of particular relevance is that the language factors generally accounted for more variance than the five-factor model in predicting alcohol and cigarette use, days restricted activity due to illness and health center visits for illness.

One can't help but look at these data and begin to question what the gold standard of personality might be. Should we trust who people say they are (i.e., the five-factor approach) or infer who they are by looking at how they portray themselves through the use of language? What, then, do these linguistic variables reflect? Note that these questions have been part of the personality literature since Allport's (1961) discussions of individual difference styles or even Rosenberg et al.'s (1990) attempts to understand the Thematic Apperception Test (TAT).

Language Use as a Predictor or Reflection of Suicide Proneness

If certain writing styles are associated with improved health within the disclosure paradigm, it is not unreasonable to assume that there may be characteristic writing styles for individuals either suffering from or prone to significant mood or thought disorders. Indeed, Rosenberg et al. (1990) have successfully used the General Inquirer text analysis program that was pioneered in the 1960s and 1970s to distinguish among inpatients suffering from depression, schizophrenia, and somatization disorders. In an extension of this idea, we sought to learn if it would be possible to distinguish suicidal from non-suicidal poets based on the corpus of their work over their career. A minimum of five poems from each of three periods in the lives of nine suicidal poets and matched controls were selected for analysis by LIWC. Drawing on two theories of suicide based on social integration and hopelessness, specific text dimensions were used to examine both chronic word usage over the course of the poets' entire careers as well as shifts in usage. Overall, we found evidence for social integration theory – that is, suicidal poets were chronically more self-obsessed (usage of first person singular and lower usage of first person plural), made fewer references to other people, and used more words associated with death (Stirman and Pennebaker, 2001). Although a speculative study, this project points to the potential value of examining lifetime usage of patterns of words to predict risk behaviors.

Summary

The personality projects raise the distinct possibility that the ways people write and/or talk can be used as stable trait markers. Whether linguistic styles are best thought of as true personality measures or merely as stable reflections of how people communicate is not yet clear. The data from the LIWC analyses hint that there may well be an individual difference associated with people's needs to find meaning. This need for finding meaning is not related to self-reported needs for finding meaning as measured by Cacioppo and Petty's (1982) need for cognition scale. Perhaps the underlying dimension is a need/drive/proclivity for constructing stories. Taken together, however, the studies suggest that those individuals who seek to construct stories about important emotional topics are able to do so and, after disclosive writing, evidence improved health. Further, it may well be that the same types of individuals who are given essentially meaningless tasks continue to try to construct stories from them which may be impossible and, conceivably, unhealthy.

General Summary and Theoretical/ Practical Implications

A number of significant advances in our understanding of disclosure have occurred. Some of the findings in our lab have been particularly promising in pointing to the social, linguistic, personality, and even physiological mechanisms that may underlie the power of disclosure in improving physical health. Based on the current state of our knowledge on disclosure and health, we think the following areas are particularly promising.

Moving Beyond Self-reports: Social and Linguistic Markers in the Real World

Human beings certainly have the native abilities to use questionnaires to define their thoughts, feelings, and personalities. A long line of research in social and personality psychology, including our own, continues to demonstrate that self-reports are of limited utility in predicting behaviors such as illness episodes, immune function, depression, alcohol and tobacco use, and performance at school or work. The preliminary findings concerning LIWC and the EAR recording system suggest new methodological approaches that move far beyond self-reports. Language use, as measured by word count systems such as LIWC, has proven to be a reliable predictor and correlate of a variety of health-relevant behaviors. The EAR system indicates that it is possible to capture ongoing social, linguistic, and other contextual aspects of people's lives with minimal interference. With further development, the EAR system will give us a glimpse into the ways individuals naturally communicate with others and when and how they choose the environments they move to.

Towards a Theory of Social Integration and Coherence

Almost by definition, a traumatic experience partially disintegrates one's social world. For example, if I have a personal trauma, my experiences will be unique and I will be motivated to seek out others to get social comparison information and perhaps social support. At the same time, it will be important to continue to update my social network about my psychological/emotional status concerning the trauma. In this way, they will know how to understand me and I will know how to understand them. This work of social sharing, then, will help to maintain our shared beliefs and perceptions of the world. Indeed, this same process should occur in the case of a shared trauma – such as the death of Princess Diana or the attacks on the World Trade Center and Pentagon. The degree to which I am socially integrated with others, then, should be correlated with markers of physical and mental health (cf., Brissette et al., 2000).

The difficulties arise when traumas impede natural social integration processes. Consider what happens if I have been diagnosed with a stigmatizing disease or have faced a trauma that I am unable or unwilling to talk with others about. In this case, I may be motivated to maintain my social relationships while, at the same time, dealing with the personal upheaval of a trauma (see also Gross, 1999). Not only will I get no social support or comparison information from my friends, but I will become isolated from them in a remarkably subtle way. I will know about my trauma but they won't. They will assume all is normal while I work to deal with my own turmoil. When we are together, I will be a poor listener to their issues and will be emotionally unavailable to them. Similarly, they will find my contributions to their social and emotional lives wanting. As in the Finkenauer (1998) and Richards and Gross (1999) studies, we will find our interactions less satisfying and will be less motivated to talk in the future.

Taken together, our work suggests that disclosing and coming to terms with emotional upheavals promotes a more integrated and coherent social world. Further, it suggests that we should be focusing on models of social integration and coherence in far greater detail. By social integration, we propose that persons are able to talk more openly with others about their thoughts and feelings, spend more time with others, use more positive and negative emotion words, and laugh more with one another on a daily basis. Further, we suspect that people who are socially integrated are also able to remain on various daily and life tasks in a more focused way, and are able to construct more coherent stories about their experiences. This approach to social integration is much more active and dynamic than traditional views of social support. In line with Durkheim (1951) and, more recently, Carstensen (1995) and others, we assume that the traumatized individuals are active in selecting and using their social worlds.

Using the EAR system, we seek to establish baseline markers of social integration by measuring social and linguistic behaviors among individuals over several weeks or months. To what degree are people's lives reliable from day to day? Does stability predict health? It is hoped that future research will begin to learn how traumatic experiences alter the social world. Eventually, future research must capitalize on emotional upheavals – either personal (e.g., death of a friend, divorce, or even something positive) or socially shared (e.g., death of a very famous person, natural disaster). Tracking how people naturally talk and behave in quiescent and tumultuous times will provide insights into real world disclosure processes and long-term health and well-being.

Acknowledgments

Preparation of this manuscript was made possible by a grant from the National Institutes of Health (MH59321).

Correspondence should be sent to James W. Pennebaker, Department of Psychology, The University of Texas, Austin, TX 78712 USA; e-mail: Pennebaker@psy.utexas.edu.

References

Allport, G. W. (1961). *Pattern and Growth in Personality*. New York: Holt, Rinehart and Winston.

Bonanno, G. A., Keltner, D., Holen, A., and Horowitz, M. J. (1995). When avoiding unpleasant emotions might not be such a bad thing: Verbal-autonomic response dissociation and midlife conjugal bereavement. *Journal of Personality and Social Psychology*, 69, 975–89.

Bradbury, T. N., and Fincham, E. D. (1992). Attributions and behavior in marital interaction. *Journal of Personality and Social Psychology*, 63, 613–28.

Brissette, I., Cohen, S., and Seeman, T. E. (2000). Measuring social integration and social networks. In S. Cohen, L. G. Underwood, and B. H. Gottlieb (Eds.), *Social Support Measurement and Intervention: A Guide for Health and Social Scientists* (pp. 53–85). New York: Oxford University Press.

Brown, R. P., and Josephs, R. A. (1999). A burden of proof: Stereotype relevance and gender differences in math performance. *Journal of Personality and Social Psychology*, 76, 246–57.

Cacciopo, J. T., and Petty, R. E. (1982). The need for cognition. *Journal of Personality and Social Psychology*, 42, 116–31.

Campbell, R. S., and Pennebaker, J. W. (2003). The secret life of pronouns: Flexibility in writing style and physical health. *Psychological Science*, 14, 60–5.

Carstensen, L. L. (1995). Evidence for a life-span theory of socioemotional selectivity. *Current Directions in Psychological Science*, 4, 151–6.

Christensen, A. J., and Smith, T. W. (1993). Cynical hostility and cardiovascular reactivity during self-disclosure. *Psychosomatic Medicine*, 55, 193–202.

Cohen, S., Underwood, L. G., and Gottlieb, B. H. (Eds.) (2000). *Social Support Measurement and Intervention: A Guide for Health and Social Scientists*. New York: Oxford University Press.

Cole, S. W., Kemeny, M. E., Taylor, S. E., and Visscher, B. R. (1996a). Elevated physical health risk among gay men who conceal their homosexual identity. *Health Psychology*, 15, 243–51.

Cole, S. W., Kemeny, M. E., Taylor, S. E., Visscher, B. R., and Fahey, J. L. (1996b). Accelerated course of human immunodeficiency virus infection in gay men who conceal their homosexual identity. *Psychosomatic Medicine*, 58, 219–31.

Cutrona, C. E. (1989). Ratings of social support by adolescents and adult informants: Degree of correspondence and prediction of depressive symptoms. *Journal of Personality and Social Psychology*, 57, 723–30.

Davison, K. P., and Pennebaker, J. W. (1997). Virtual narratives: Illness representations in online support groups. In K. J. Petrie and J. Weinman (Eds.), *Perceptions of Health and Illness: Current Research and Applications.* London: Harwood Academic Press.

Davison, K. P., Pennebaker, J. W., and Dickerson, S. S. (2000). Who talks: The social psychology of illness support groups. *American Psychologist*, 55, 205–17.

Derlega, V. J., Metts, S., Petronio, S., and Margulis, S. T. (1993). *Self-disclosure.* Thousand Oaks, CA: Sage.

Dunkel-Schetter, C., Blasband, D. E., Feinstein, L. G., and Herbert, T. B. (1992). Elements of supportive interactions: When are attempts to help effective? In S. Spacapan and S. Oskamp (Eds.), *Helping and Being Helped in the Real World* (pp. 83–114). Newbury Park, CA: Sage.

Durkheim, E. (1951). *Suicide.* New York: Free Press.

Festinger, L. A. (1954). A theory of social comparison processes. *Human Relations*, 7, 117–40.

Finkenauer, C. (1998). Secrets: Types, Determinants, Functions, and Consequences. Unpublished doctoral dissertation, Catholic University of Louvain, Louvain-la-Neuve, Belgium.

Foa, E. B., and Meadows, E. A. (1997). Psychosocial treatments for post-traumatic stress disorder: A critical review. *Annual Review of Psychology*, 48, 449–80.

Gidron, Y., Peri, T., Connolly, J. F., and Shalev, A. Y. (1996). Written disclosure in post-traumatic stress disorder: Is it beneficial for the patient? *Journal of Nervous and Mental Disease*, 184, 505–7.

Greenberg, M. A., and Stone, A. A. (1992). Emotional disclosure about traumas and its relation to health: Effects of previous disclosure and trauma severity. *Journal of Personality and Social Psychology*, 63, 75–84.

Greenberg, M. A., Stone, A. A., and Wortman, C. B. (1996). Health and psychological effects of emotional disclosure: A test of the inhibition-confrontation approach. *Journal of Personality and Social Psychology*, 71, 588–602.

Gross, J. J. (1999). Emotion suppression: There's more to it than meets the eye. Paper presented at the American Psychological Society annual meeting, Denver, CO.

Gross, J. J., and Levenson, R. W. (1997). Hiding feelings: The acute effects of inhibiting negative and positive emotion. *Journal of Abnormal Psychology*, 106, 95–103.

Hayward, M. S. (1997). The effect of emotion labeling on physiology, emotions, and narrative style. Unpublished master's thesis, Southern Methodist University, Dallas.

Jamner, L. D., Schwartz, G. E., and Leigh, H. (1988). The relationship between repressive and defensive coping styles and monocyte, eosinophile, and serum glucose levels: Support for the opioid peptide hypothesis of repression. *Psychosomatic Medicine*, 50, 567–75.

John, O. P., Donahue, E. M., and Kentle, R. L. (1991). *The Big Five Inventory, Versions 4a and 4b.* Technical Report, Institute for Personality and Social Research. University of California, Berkeley, CA.

Jourard, S. M. (1971). *Self-disclosure: An Experimental Analysis of the Transparent Self.* New York: Wiley.

Kelley, J. E., Lumley, M. A., and Leisen, J. C. (1997). Health effects of emotional disclosure in rheumatoid arthritis patients. *Health Psychology*, 16, 331–40.

Keough, K. A., Garcia, J., and Steele, C. M. (1998). Reducing stress and illness by affirming the self. Unpublished manuscript.

Klein, K., and Boals, A. (2001). Expressive writing can increase working memory capacity. *Journal of Experimental Psychology: General*, 130, 520–33.

Landauer, T. K. and Dumais, S. T. (1997). A solution to Plato's problem: The latent semantic analysis theory of acquisition, induction, and representation of knowledge. *Psychological Review*, 104, 211–40.

Lepore, S. J. (1997). Expressive writing moderates the relation between intrusive thoughts and depressive symptoms. *Journal of Personality and Social Psychology*, 73, 1030–7.

Lepore, S. J., and Greenberg, M. A. (2002). Mending broken hearts: Effects of expressive writing on mood, cognitive processing, social adjustment and health following a relationship breakup. *Psychology and Health*, 17, 547–60.

Lepore, S. J., and Smyth, J. (2002). *The Writing Cure*. Washington, DC: American Psychological Association.

Major, B., and Gramzow, R. (1999). Abortion as stigma: Cognitive and emotional implications of concealment. *Journal of Personality and Social Psychology* 77, 735–45.

Major, B., Richards, C., Cooper, M. L., Cozzarelli, C., and Zubek, J. (1998). Personal resilience, cognitive appraisals, and coping: An integrative model of adjustment to abortion. *Journal of Personality and Social Psychology*, 74, 735–52.

Mehl, M. R., and Pennebaker, J. W. (in press). The sounds of social life: A psychometric analysis of students' daily social environments and natural conversations. *Journal of Personality and Social Psychology*.

Mehl, M. R., Pennebaker, J. W., Crow, D. M., Dabbs, J., and Price, J. (2001). The Electronically-Activated Recorder (EAR): A device for sampling naturalistic daily activities and conversations. *Behavior Research Methods, Instruments, and Computers*, 33, 517–23.

Mendolia, M., and Kleck, R. E. (1993). Effects of talking about a stressful event on arousal: Does what we talk about make a difference? *Journal of Personality and Social Psychology*, 64, 283–92.

Miller, G. (1995). *The Science of Words*. New York: Scientific American Library.

Paez, D., Velasco, C., and Gonzales, J. L. (1999). Alexithymia as dispositional deficit in self-disclosure and cognitive assimilation of emotional events. *Journal of Personality and Social Psychology*, 77, 630–41.

Pennebaker, J. W. (1989). Confession, inhibition, and disease. In L. Berkowitz (Ed.), *Advances in Experimental Social Psychology* (Vol. 22, pp. 211–44). San Diego: Academic Press.

Pennebaker, J. W. (1997). Writing about emotional experiences as a therapeutic process. *Psychological Science*, 8, 162–6.

Pennebaker, J. W., and Beall, S. K. (1986). Confronting a traumatic event: Toward an understanding of inhibition and disease. *Journal of Abnormal Psychology*, 95, 274–81.

Pennebaker, J. W., and Francis, M. E. (1996). Cognitive, emotional, and language processes in disclosure. *Cognition and Emotion*, 10, 601–26.

Pennebaker, J. W., Francis, M. E., and Booth, R. J. (2001). *Linguistic Inquiry and Word Count (LIWC)*. Mahwah, NJ: Erlbaum Publishers.

Pennebaker, J. W., and Graybeal, A. (2001). Patterns of natural language use: Disclosure, personality, and social integration. *Current Directions in Psychological Science*, 10, 90–3.

Pennebaker, J. W., and Harber, K. D. (1993). A social stage model of collective coping: The Persian Gulf War and other natural disasters. *Journal of Social Issues*, 49, 125–45.

Pennebaker, J. W., Kiecolt-Glaser, J. K., and Glaser, R. (1988). Disclosure of traumas and immune function: Health implications for psychotherapy. *Journal of Consulting and Clinical Psychology*, 56, 239–45.

Pennebaker, J. W., and King, L. A. (1999). Linguistic styles: Language use as an individual difference. *Journal of Personality and Social Psychology*, 77, 1296–1312.

Pennebaker, J. W., Mayne, T. J., and Francis, M. E. (1997). Linguistic predictors of adaptive bereavement. *Journal of Personality and Social Psychology*, 72, 863–71.

Pennebaker, J. W., and Seagal, J. D. (1999). Forming a story: The health benefits of narrative. *Journal of Clinical Psychology*, 55, 1243–54.

Peterson, C., Seligman, M. E. P., and Vaillant, G. E. (1988). Pessimistic explanatory style is a risk factor for physical illness: A thirty-five-year longitudinal study. *Journal of Personality and Social Psychology*, 55, 23–7.

Petrie, K. P., Booth, R. J., and Pennebaker, J. W. (1998). The immunological effects of thought suppression. *Journal of Personality and Social Psychology*, 75, 1264–72.

Pierce, G. R., Sarason, B. R., and Sarason, I. G. (1992). General and specific support expectations and stress as predictors of perceived supportiveness: An experimental study. *Journal of Personality and Social Psychology*, 63, 297–307.

Richards, J. M., Beal, W. E., Seagal, J. D., and Pennebaker, J. W. (2000). The disclosure of traumatic events and illness behavior among psychiatric prison inmates. *Journal of Abnormal Psychology*, 109, 156–60.

Richards, J. M., and Gross, J. J. (1999). Emotion suppression and social behavior. Data presented by J.J. Gross in Keynote Address of The (Non)Expression of Emotions in Health and Disease conference, June 10, 1999, Tilburg, The Netherlands.

Rimé, B. (1995). Mental rumination, social sharing, and the recovery from emotional exposure. In J. Pennebaker (Ed.), *Emotion, Disclosure, and Health* (pp. 271–91). Washington, DC: American Psychological Association.

Rimé, B., Finkenauer, C., Luminet, O., Zech, E., and Philippot, P. (1998). Social sharing of emotion: New evidence and new questions. In W. Stroebe and M. Hewstone (Eds.), *European Review of Social Psychology* (Vol. 9, pp. 145–89). Chichester: Wiley.

Rosenberg, S. D., Schnurr, P. P., and Oxman, T. E. (1990). Content analysis: A comparison of manual and computerized systems. *Journal of Personality Assessment*, 54, 298–310.

Sarnoff, I., and Zimbardo, P. G. (1961). Anxiety, fear, and social facilitation. *Journal of Abnormal and Social Psychology*, 62, 597–605.

Scheier, M., and Carver, C. S. (1985). Optimism, coping and health: Assessment and implications of generalized outcome expectancies. *Health Psychology*, 4, 219–47.

Schoutrop, M. J. A., Lange, A., Brosschot, J., and Everaerd, W. (1997). Overcoming traumatic events by means of writing assignments. In A. Vingerhoets, F. van Bussel, and J. Boelhouwer (Eds.), *The (Non)expression of Emotions in Health and Disease* (pp. 279–89). Tilburg, The Netherlands: Tilburg University Press.

Smyth, J. M. (1998). Written emotional expression: Effect sizes, outcome types, and moderating variables. *Journal of Consulting and Clinical Psychology*, 66, 174–84.

Smyth, J. M., Stone, A. A., Hurewitz, A., and Kaell, A. (1999). Effects of writing about stressful experiences on symptom reduction in patients with asthma or rheumatoid arthritis: A randomized trial. *Journal of the American Medical Association*, 281, 1304–9.

Spera, S. P., Buhrfeind, E. D., and Pennebaker, J. W. (1994). Expressive writing and coping with job loss. *Academy of Management Journal*, 37, 722–33.

Steele, C. M., and Aronson, J. (1995). Stereotype threat and the intellectual test performance of African Americans. *Journal of Personality and Social Psychology*, 69, 797–811.

Stiles, W. B., Shuster, P. L., and Harrigan, J. A. (1992). Disclosure and anxiety: A test of the fever model. *Journal of Personality and Social Psychology*, 63, 980–8.

Stirman, S., and Pennebaker, J. W. (2001). Word use in the poetry of suicidal and non-suicidal poets. *Psychosomatic Medicine*, 63, 517–22.

Stone, L. D., and Pennebaker, J. W. (2002). Trauma in real time: Talking and avoiding online conversations about the death of Princess Diana. *Basic and Applied Social Psychology*, 24, 172–82.

Taylor, S. E., and Schneider, S. K. (1989). Coping and the simulation of events. *Social Cognition*, 7, 174–94.

Taylor, S. E., Pham, L. B., Rivkin, I. D., and Armor, D. A. (1998). Harnessing the imagination: Mental simulation, self-regulation, and coping. *American Psychologist*, 53, 429–39.

Watson, D., Clark, L. A., and Tellegen, A. (1989). Development and validation of brief measures of positive and negative affect: The PANAS scales. *Journal of Personality and Social Psychology*, 54, 1063–70.

Wegner, D. M. (1994). Ironic process of mental control. *Psychological Review*, 101, 34–52.

Williams, D. R. (1997). Race and health: basic questions, emerging directions. *Annals of Epidemiology*, 7, 322–33.

Williams-Avery, R. (1998). Cognitive processing: Linking disclosure, inhibition and health. Paper presented at the meeting of the Society of Behavioral Medicine, New Orleans, March.

CHAPTER 12

Affiliation, Social Support, and Biobehavioral Responses to Stress

Shelley E. Taylor

University of California, Los Angeles

Laura C. Klein

Pennsylvania State University

Tara L. Gruenewald

University of California, Los Angeles

Regan A. R. Gurung

University of Wisconsin

and

Sara Fernandes-Taylor

University of California, Los Angeles

Introduction

The term "stress" was once little more than a colloquialism for feelings of pressure or agitation in response to the demands of daily living. As research on responses to stress has progressed, however, it has become clear that chronic and acute stress are implicated in adverse physiological and neuroendocrine changes, health-compromising behavior changes such as substance abuse and homicide, and risk for mortality from a variety of stress-related disorders (Taylor, 1999). As the significance of the health risks of stress have become known, the study of how people cope with stress, especially how they cope with stress successfully, has taken on scientific and clinical urgency. In particular, research efforts have focused on the ways of coping and personal resources that may mute the adverse behavioral, physiological, and neuro-endocrine consequences of stress.

One way that people cope with stress is by turning to others. Living in social groups is thought to be an evolutionary adaptation that has survival value for humans (Caporael, 1997; Dunbar, 1996). Groups provide more eyes for the detection of predators, and most predators are reluctant to attack potential prey if they believe there are others who might come to the rescue. Because human beings lack so many of the "weapons" that are beneficial to other species, such as sharp teeth, claws, and substantial size, as well as defensive resources, such as thick skin, thick fur, and speed, group living may be one of the most significant evolutionary strategies by which human beings have survived.

Affiliation with others appears to be especially common under stress. A large literature reveals that people who are going through stressful events turn to others to help them deal with those events or to provide them with solace (Bachrach and Zautra, 1985; Ferraro et al., 1984). Psychologists refer to this tendency and the benefits it provides as social support. Social support has been defined as information from others that one is loved and cared for, esteemed and valued, and part of a network of communication and mutual obligation (Cobb, 1976). Such support can come from a partner, other relatives, friends, and social or community ties.

Research on social support indicates that turning to others in stressful circumstances provides a variety of benefits, such as appraisal support, tangible assistance, information, and emotional support (e.g., Cohen, 1988; Schwarzer and Leppin, 1991). *Appraisal support* is help from another person that improves one's understanding of a stressful event and the resources and coping strategies that may be mustered to deal with it. Through the exchange of appraisals, a person facing a stressful event can determine how threatening the stressful event is likely to be and can reduce uncertainty about the nature of the stressor. *Tangible assistance* involves the provision of material support, such as services, financial assistance, or goods that may ameliorate a stressful event. For example, the gifts of food that often arrive after a death in the family means that bereaved family members will not have to perform certain routine chores at a time when their energy and enthusiasm for such tasks may be low. Other people can provide *informational support* about stressful events. For example, a person having a problem on the job may get information from coworkers about how best to manage time or delegate tasks appropriately, or about how to approach a supervisor about restructuring the job. During stressful times, people often suffer emotionally and may experience bouts of sadness, depression, anxiety, or loss of self-esteem. Supportive friends, family, and acquaintances can provide *emotional support* by reassuring a person under stress that he or she is a valued individual who is cared for and esteemed. The warmth and nurturance provided by other people can enable a person under stress to approach that event with greater assurance. Networks of potentially supportive friends, acquaintances, and relatives are not always supportive, it should be noted (e.g., Dakof and Taylor, 1990; Coyne et al., 1988), but on balance social networks are more likely to ameliorate than exacerbate psychological distress during stressful times.

Potentially, then, there is a broad array of functions that turning to others can provide during times of stress, ranging from increasing the likelihood of survival to ameliorating the distress that may occur in response to stress. What is the evidence that affiliation under stress and the support it provides can be beneficial to human psychological and physical functioning?

The Psychology of Affiliation

In 1959, Stanley Schachter conducted the first experiments on affiliation in response to stress. At the time, it was not his intention to study stress responses, but rather to demonstrate that under anxiety-arousing circumstances, people choose to affiliate with others for the purpose of evaluating their emotional experience. Nonetheless, the paradigm he adopted approximates what is now termed the experimental acute stress paradigm. Schachter recruited undergraduate women to participate in his experiments and scheduled them to arrive at his laboratory in small groups. In what he termed the "high anxiety condition," the women were met by a white-coated scientist who informed them that each woman would receive a series of electric shocks that would hurt and be painful, but that would do no permanent damage. In the "low-anxiety condition," the women were told that the shocks would be very mild, resembling a tingle or tickle rather than an unpleasant sensation. All the women were then told that they would need to wait their turn and were asked whether they preferred to wait alone or with others. In a now commonly replicated effect, Schachter found that the women in the high-anxiety condition were significantly more likely to want to wait with other women anticipating the same fate, whereas those in the low-anxiety condition typically indicated that they did not care whether they were together with the other women or alone.

Subsequent studies revealed that the desire to affiliate with others under stress is not as general as had originally been thought. First, the effects were found primarily with female participants; indeed, after some unsuccessful pilot work, Schachter never recruited male participants again. The desire to affiliate was also confined to wanting to be with women anticipating the same fate. When the opportunity was provided to wait with other people anticipating a different experiment, most women preferred to wait alone. The desire to affiliate with others was present only when the women were given the opportunity to talk about the stressful event, and not when they were allowed only to talk about irrelevant topics. Finally, the effect appeared to be considerably stronger for women who were firstborn members of their family than later-born. Despite these qualifications, research on affiliation and social support proliferated in subsequent decades and, increasingly, the beneficial effects of the companionship of others under stress have been clarified.

Benefits of Social Support

Research consistently demonstrates that social support effectively reduces distress during times of stress (Cohen and Wills, 1985; Kessler and McLeod, 1985; Wallston et al., 1983). Studies attesting to this important role of social support have ranged from laboratory investigations similar to those conducted by Schachter and his students, to naturalistic studies of neighborhoods coping with a trauma such as the Three-Mile Island nuclear accident (Fleming et al., 1982), soldiers in combat, and individuals coping with personal tragedies, such as bereavement (Dunkel-Schetter and Wortman, 1981) or adverse changes in health (House et al., 1988). This last literature on the relation of social support to health has most clearly confirmed the apparent beneficial physiological consequences of social support. That is, in addition to providing psychosocial benefits, social support also appears to lower the likelihood of illness, to speed recovery from illness when it does occur, and to reduce the likelihood of mortality due to serious disease (House et al., 1988; Kulik and Mahler, 1989; Wallston et al., 1983).

An example of the significance of social support for combating the threat of illness comes from a classic study of adults in Alameda County, California, conducted in 1979 (Berkman and Syme, 1979). Approximately 7,000 people were asked about their social and community ties, and their death rate was tracked over a nine-year period. The study showed that people who had fewer social and community ties were more likely to die during this period than were people with many such ties. Having social contact appeared to give women an average of 2.8 years of longer life, and men, an average of 2.3 years of longer life. These differences could not be explained by socioeconomic status, health differences at the beginning of the study, or the practice of health habits.

Since that time, numerous studies have shown that social support is associated with better health. People with high levels of social support have fewer complications during pregnancy and childbirth (Collins et al., 1993), less susceptibility to herpes attacks (VanderPlate et al., 1988), and lower rates of myocardial infarction (Bruhn, 1965). Social support promotes better adjustment to and/or faster recovery from coronary artery surgery (King et al., 1993; Kulik and Mahler, 1993), rheumatoid arthritis (Goodenow et al., 1990), kidney disease (Dimond, 1979), childhood leukemia (Magni et al., 1988), and stroke (Robertson and Suinn, 1968); it has been tied to a reduced likelihood of mortality from myocardial infarction (Wiklund et al., 1988), better diabetes control (Marteau et al., 1987), and less pain among arthritis patients (DeVellis et al., 1986). This consistent evidence showing the apparent health benefits of social support has increasingly led to a search for physiological and neuro-endocrine mechanisms whereby social support may exert these effects.

Physiologic and Neuroendocrine Studies of Acute Stress

Stress is known to produce a variety of short-term and long-term physio-logical and neuroendocrine responses, and so it is likely that social support exerts its protective effects, in part, by moderating some of these responses. Most research on human stress has focused on the fight-or-flight response, which involves the release of the catecholamines, epinephrine and nore-pinephrine, and concomitant sympathetic nervous system (SNS) arousal, and/or HPA (hypothalamic-pituitary-adrenocortical) activation, involving the release of corticosteroids, especially cortisol. Although these responses have short-term protective functions under stressful circumstances, with chronic or recurrent activation, they are associated with deleterious long-term effects.

Specifically, excessive or repeated discharge of epinephrine or norepinephrine is believed to lead to the suppression of cellular immune function, produce hemodynamic changes such as increased blood pressure and heart rate, pro-voke abnormal heart rhythms such as ventricular arrhythmias, and produce neuro-chemical imbalances that may relate to the development of psychiatric disorders (McEwen and Stellar, 1993). Enhanced physiological reactivity in the form of intense, rapid, and/or long-lasting sympathetic responses to repeated stress or challenge have been implicated in the development of hypertension and coronary heart disease (see Fredrickson and Matthews, 1990; Krantz and Manuck, 1984).

Corticosteroids have immunosuppressive effects, and increases in cortisol have been related both to decreased lymphocyte responsivity to mitogenic stimulation and to decreased lymphocyte cytotoxicity (e.g., Cunningham, 1981). Such immunosuppressive changes may be associated with increased suscep-tibility to infectious diseases, among other adverse health outcomes. Pro-longed cortisol secretion has been related to the destruction of neurons in the hippocampus, which is believed to underlie problems in memory and con-centration, particularly in older age (McEwen and Sapolsky, 1995; Sapolsky, 1996; Seeman and Robbins, 1994). Pronounced HPA activation has also been associated with depression (Sapolsky, 1996). Links between HPA axis activity and sympathetic nervous system activity (SNS) suggest that increased activa-tion of the HPA axis could potentiate overactivation of sympathetic function-ing (Chrousos and Gold, 1992). Indeed, the combination of catecholamine and cortisol hypersecretion is thought to increase the likelihood of coronary atherosclerosis and acute coronary events (Krantz and Manuck, 1984). Given this broad range of adverse effects, it comes as no surprise that researchers have increasingly turned their attention to the ways in which social support may attenuate SNS and HPA stress responses.

Studies of Responses to Acute Stress

The effort to identify the beneficial effects of social support on physiologic and neuroendocrine responses to stress has utilized an experimental paradigm very much like that of the original Schachter affiliation studies. In a typical investigation, participants are brought into the laboratory and asked to engage in a stressful experience either alone or in the presence of a supportive other person. The stressful tasks range from immersing one's hand in ice water for several minutes (the cold pressor test), receiving electric shock, preparing a speech to give to a panel of judges, or performing stressful cognitive tasks, such as difficult memory tasks, arithmetic, counting backwards by threes or sevens, or completing the Stroop color-naming task (in which participants must identify the color of the ink in which the name of a color has been written (e.g., saying "green" in response to the word "purple" written in green ink). Blood pressure and heart rate are typically monitored before, during, and after the stressor, selected neuroendocrine responses are sometimes assessed, and participants complete questionnaires assessing their anxiety and other emotional responses to the stressful task. Because blood pressure and heart rate typically increase during the performance of a stress-inducing task, relative to baseline, this paradigm has been especially used to study cardiovascular reactions to stress.

Consistent with the health studies on social support, a substantial literature suggests that the presence of a supportive person during a stressful task, whether friend or stranger, can reduce cardiovascular and HPA reactivity to stress (Christenfeld et al., 1997; Gerin et al., 1992; 1995; Kamarck et al., 1990; Kors et al., 1997; Lepore et al., 1993; Sheffield and Carroll, 1994). In addition to reducing heart rate, blood pressure, and cortisol, the presence of others also typically reduces feelings of arousal and anxiety in response to stress, although psychological and physiological changes are typically only moderately correlated with each other.

Despite the converging evidence from these studies, some ambiguities remain. First, the paradigm in acute stress studies departs in an important way from that initially developed by Schachter. Schachter's original investigations manipulated the presence of potentially supportive others during the waiting period, but not during the stressful event itself. Indeed, Schachter's participants never went through an actual stressful event; they anticipated but did not actually experience electric shock. Subsequent studies have typically had the supportive stranger or friend present before the stressor, during the stressful event, and afterwards. As noted, in most studies, the presence of a supportive stranger or friend is typically stress-reducing, lowering cardiovascular responses to stress during the stressor itself (Christenfeld et al., 1997; Edens et al., 1992; Gerin et al., 1992; Kamarck et al., 1995), but sometimes the presence of a friend or stranger can actually increase sympathetic reactivity (Allen et al., 1991; Mullen et al., 1997). For example, Allen et al. (1991) found that, relative to a control condition in which they remained alone, women who completed a stress task in the presence of a female friend showed higher physiological reactivity and poorer performance. Kirschbaum et al. (1995) and Smith et al. (1998) found that women, but not men, showed enhanced physiological reactivity to a stressful task performed in the presence of the partner, as opposed to when they completed the stressful task alone.

Research has yet to systematically sort out the effects of affiliation and support at these different times. It is possible that affiliation is more consistently helpful before and after a stressful event than it is during a stressful event. Indeed, the original Schachter paradigm may more properly reflect the kind of social support that people typically receive from others during times of stress. Under many stressful circumstances (such as going through noxious medical procedures or taking tests), people typically receive support from family and friends before they go through the stressful event, or after it has occurred, but not necessarily during the event itself. Indeed, when others are present during the stressful event, often they are experiencing the same stressor. More research will be needed to identify those factors that influence when affiliation during a stressful event is stress-reducing or not.

A second ambiguity concerns what constitutes support in a situation of acute stress. When other people are physically present during a stressful event but do not offer any support, electrodermal responses in particular and, in some cases, cardiovascular responses, may actually increase rather than decrease (Mullen et al., 1997). In addition, when support is provided by a confederate or a friend during a stressful event, friends appear to reduce cardiovascular reactions to stress better than do supportive strangers (e.g., Christenfeld et al., 1997; Edens et al., 1992; Kamarck et al., 1990; 1995). The studies showing the beneficial effects of friends involve disproportionately female participants, however, which may represent a qualification to these findings.

Gender, Affiliation, and Stress Responses

An additional unresolved issue concerns who seeks and who benefits from social support under stress: men or women, or both. Perhaps because the emphasis of acute stress studies has been on cardiovascular responses to stress, males have been over-represented in these studies, relative to females (men are vulnerable to cardiovascular disease at earlier ages than are women). Of 196 experimental investigations of responses to stress over a 15-year period from 1984 to 1998 involving 14,131 participants, 65.8 percent of the participants were male, and only 34.2 percent were female (Gruenewald et al., 1998). However, as was true in Schachter's studies, when the acute stress paradigm has been used to study the effects of affiliation in response to stress, females are over-represented. Five of 31 acute stress studies during the 1984–98 time period involving all female participants examined affiliative reactions to stress, whereas none of 96 all-male investigations examined affiliation. Unhappily, this over-representation of women in studies of affiliative responses to stress renders gender comparisons difficult. Nonetheless, women's greater preference to affiliate under stress is well established in the non-experimental literature.

Reviews of the stress literature consistently reveal evidence of women's higher investment in the creation and maintenance of social networks relative to men's (e.g., Belle, 1987). This is one of the most robust gender differences in adult human behavior, and it is the primary gender difference in adult human behavioral responses to stress (Belle, 1987; Luckow et al., 1998). Across the entire life cycle, girls and women are more likely to mobilize social support, especially from other females, in times of stress. They seek it out more, they receive more, and they are more satisfied with the support that they receive (Belle, 1987; Copeland and Hess, 1995; McDonald and Korabik, 1991; Ogus et al., 1990; Ptacek et al., 1992; Wethington et al., 1987). In a survey study, Veroff et al. (1981) found that women were 30 percent more likely than men to have provided some type of social support in response to a stressor in their social network. Thus, for example, women are much more likely to provide transportation, food, child care, or even just a willing ear to friends and relatives going through stressful events, including job loss, divorce, bereavement, and natural disasters. Moreover, these findings have substantial cross-cultural generalizability. In a study of six cultures, Whiting and Whiting (1975) found that women and girls sought more help and gave more help to others than males in stressful times, and Edwards (1993) found similar sex differences across 12 additional cultures.

Despite the fact that women seek social support under stress more than men, they do not seem to profit from it more. Both men and women show psychological and health benefits in response to stress (e.g., Berkman and Syme, 1979; Unger et al., 1999), but men seem to show somewhat greater benefits (Barer, 1994; House et al., 1982; Seeman et al., 1994; Umberson et al., 1992; but see Tower and Kasl, 1996). All the reasons for this gender difference are not yet known, and the difference may be more apparent than real. For example, many of these studies use mortality as an endpoint, and because women die at later ages than men, the beneficial effects of social support may be less evident for women, given little variance in the outcome (i.e., fewer women die). Paradoxically, then, social relationships may lengthen women's lives, but appear less effective precisely because they help to lower mortality. Alternatively, the gender difference in social support favoring men may be real. Men most often report receiving their social support from women (especially their mothers and wives) who are more likely to provide support than men (Wethington et al., 1987). Women find their husbands' efforts to provide support to be less supportive than men find their wives' efforts to be (Gurung et al., 2001), and so the quality of support received by men may be somewhat higher than that received by women. In addition, women appear to be more vulnerable than men to negative events in their social networks which may erase some of the benefits that social ties would otherwise provide (Schuster et al., 1990). For example, women are more likely than men to be the caregivers for elderly or infirmed relatives and are more likely to provide housekeeping services or child care during acutely stressful events, efforts which may tax their time and emotional and physical resources.

In summary, women seek and give more social support under stress, men may get more and better social support under stress, but both genders are psychologically and physically benefited by higher levels of social support under stress. How are we to understand this unusual pattern? Turning to the biology of stress responses and sex differences in those biological responses may provide some answers.

Gender, Affiliation, and Neuroendocrine Responses

Recent experimental evidence from animal studies yields a model that may provide a biobehavioral account of sex differences in the likelihood of and the effects of affiliation under stress. This model, which remains somewhat speculative with respect to humans, implicates oxytocin in the modulation of sympathetic and HPA responses to stress, in emotional responses to stress, and in affiliative behavior under stress.

Both sexes experience a cascade of hormonal responses to stress that mobilizes the organism to respond to threat, the so-called "fight-or-flight" response. Yet within this neuroendocrine response may be the basis of a counter-regulatory response that reduces the arousal and anxiety that typically accompanies stress, instead helping to promote relaxation and affiliation.

A substantial animal literature reveals that oxytocin downregulates sympathetic and HPA activity. McCarthy (1995) has suggested that, among animals in the natural environment who face a constant barrage of stress, oxytocin is associated with parasympathetic (vagal) functioning that plays a counter-regulatory role in fear responses to stress (Dreifuss et al., 1992; Sawchenko and Swanson, 1982; Swanson and Sawchenko, 1980). Oxytocin is known to be released early on in the neuroendocrine stress response (Sapolsky, 1992). In experimental studies, oxytocin has been found to enhance sedation and relaxation, reduce anxiety, and decrease sympathetic activity (Altemus et al., 1995; Uvnas-Moberg, 1997). The exogenous administration of oxytocin in rats results in decreases in blood pressure, pain sensitivity, and corticosteroid levels, among other findings indicative of a reduced stress response (Uvnas-Moberg, 1997). Oxytocin appears to inhibit the secretion of adrenocorticotrophin hormone (ACTH) and cortisol in humans (Chiodera and Legros, 1981; Legros et al., 1985). The relation of oxytocin to reduced anxiety under stressful conditions is thought to be one reason why female rats reliably show indications of reduced fear in stressful circumstances (such as less freezing and more exploration in open-field tests) than is true of male rats (see McCarthy, 1995). Thus, oxytocin-mediated reductions in anxiety under stress may have beneficial effects on an organism, especially one that is repeatedly exposed to stressful circumstances, by muting sympathetic and HPA responses to stress.

A growing literature suggests that oxytocin increases affiliative behavior as well. Social contact is enhanced and aggression is diminished following central oxytocin treatment in estrogen-treated prairie voles (Witt et al., 1990), and experimental studies with female rats have found that the administration of oxytocin causes an increase in social contact and in grooming (Argiolas and Gessa, 1991; Carter et al., 1995; Witt et al., 1992). It is important to note that this relationship appears to be bidirectional; that is, oxytocin enhances affiliation, and affiliation, particularly of an affectionate nature, enhances the flow of oxytocin which, in turn, downregulates neuroendocrine stress responses. Because social groups are protective against certain forms of stress (such as attack by predators), and because such protection may be especially helpful to females nurturing young infants, oxytocin-facilitated affiliative responses to stress are thought to represent an adaptive response to stressful circumstances (Drago et al., 1986; Fahrbach et al., 1985; McCarthy, 1995). In summary, animal data suggest that oxytocin induces a state of mild sedation and relaxation, reduces anxiety, decreases sympathetic and HPA activity, and promotes affiliative and prosocial behavior under stressful conditions, which may, in turn, enhance the secretion of oxytocin, downregulating stress responses.

The effects of oxytocin on anxiety and social behavior in response to stress appear to be different for males and females. The effects of oxytocin are believed to be particularly important for females, because they may enhance the affiliative and protective behaviors essential for the care of offspring (McCarthy, 1995). For example, oxytocin is known to promote maternal and other forms of affiliative behavior in rats (McCarthy, 1995), and it is believed to be a neurochemical underpinning of mother-infant bonding (Keverne et al., 1997; Mendoza and Mason, 1997). In rodents, the effects of oxytocin in reducing anxiety, decreasing sympathetic activity, and enhancing social activity are greater for females than for males, first, because oxytocin release in response to stress appears to be greater in females than in males (Jezova et al., 1996); second, because androgens appear to inhibit oxytocin release under conditions of stress (Jezova et al., 1996); and, third, because the effects of oxytocin are strongly enhanced by estrogen (McCarthy, 1995). Thus, there is a robust sex difference in affiliative responses to stress in rodents, such that females seek more such contact.

Carter (1998) reviewed evidence that oxytocin may be at the core of many forms of human social attachment, including caregiver–infant attachments, adult pair bonds, and other forms of affiliative behavior (Carter and Altemus, 1997). For example, Uvnas-Moberg (1996) found that women who were breastfeeding (and therefore very high in plasma oxytocin concentration) perceived themselves to be calmer and rated themselves as more social on personality inventories than age-matched women who were not breastfeeding or pregnant. Moreover, the level of plasma oxytocin in these women correlated strongly with the level of calm reported, and oxytocin pulsatility was significantly correlated with self-reported sociability (Uvnas-Moberg, 1996). Virden (1988) found that breastfeeding mothers one month post-partum were less anxious than bottle-feeding mothers, and women who used both feeding methods reported less anxiety, less depression, and less stress after breastfeeding than after bottle feeding (Modahl and Newton, 1979; Heck and deCastro, 1993), presumably because breastfeeding is a potent elicitor of oxytocin release. Breastfeeding also has been found to suppress cortisol responses in women (Amico et al., 1994). Oxytocin may be related either to enhanced perceptions of one's sociability and the positivity of one's social relationships or to behavioral tendencies that lead to more prosocial activity or both.

Oxytocin has also been related to lower neuroendocrine responses to stress. Light and her colleagues (2000) examined the relation of oxytocin responsivity to blood pressure changes in women in response to a stress task. The women, who were either breastfeeding or bottle-feeding their newborns, completed the task on two successive days, once with their baby and once without. Greater oxytocin responsivity was seen among women who were breastfeeders and during baby contact days. Those women who showed oxytocin increases in response to stress had lower blood pressure responses. Heinrichs (2000) enrolled lactating mothers in a stress study, half of whom breastfed their infants just before the task, the other half of whom merely held their infants. Those who had breastfed their infants, and who presumably had higher levels of oxytocin as a result, had significantly lower plasma cortisol levels at all points during the stress task. Altemus and colleagues (1995) compared the stress responses of breastfeeding and non-breastfeeding women in response to an exercise stressor and found similar effects.

Although we have argued that the effects of oxytocin on men may be less than is the case with women (either because they may produce less oxytocin in response to stress or because its effects may be antagonized by androgens), there is, nonetheless, intriguing evidence to suggest an impact of oxytocin in men similar to that in women, when it is administered exogenously. Pitman et al. (1993) administered an internasal solution of either oxytocin, vasopressin, or a placebo and observed effects on heart rate, skin conductance, and EMG responses of 43 male Vietnam veterans with post-traumatic stress disorders (PTSD). Those receiving OT showed the lowest activation on these measures.

To summarize, consistent evidence from animal studies and suggestive data from humans leads to the hypotheses that oxytocin may be associated with enhanced affiliative behavior, reduced anxiety, and reduced neuroendocrine and physiological responses to stress. These effects may be more pronounced in females than in males, although the requisite comparative studies have not yet been done.

Taken together, evidence from studies of affiliation, social support, and neuroendocrine studies of stress responses in rats and humans suggest the following testable model of human affiliative behavior under stress. In response to the perception of stress or threat, neuroendocrine hormones are secreted that prepare the body for fight-or-flight. Simultaneously, however, oxytocin is secreted, which may lead to a desire to affiliate, especially among females, because estrogen is believed to enhance the behavioral effects of oxytocin, especially its effects on affiliation and/on relaxation. This biobehavioral response may damp down adverse physiological and behavioral reactions to at least some types of stress by reducing anxiety and arousal and increasing prosocial tendencies, especially in females.

There may be long-term benefits of these responses to stress as well. To the extent that this is a reliable response that occurs to a broad array of chronic and recurring acute stressors, females may suffer fewer of the cumulative adverse effects of stress. For example, women are less vulnerable to cardiovascular disorders and to behavioral effects of stress that may be anxiety-related, such as aggression and substance abuse. Sex differences in affiliative and neuroendocrine responses to stress may provide a partial explanation for these patterns.

Whether oxytocin confers behavioral and neuroendocrine protection in human females as it seems to do in female rodents remains to be seen. The fact that human females show more preference for affiliation under conditions of stress than men and the fact that their stress responses appear to be downregulated as a result is tantalizingly consistent with the above-described animal model. Nonetheless, these links remain speculative, requiring more evidence from studies with humans.

Conclusion

The preference to be with other people appears to be a robust characteristic of human beings (Baumeister and Leary, 1995). Although both men and women appear to benefit psychologically and physiologically from social support, the desire for social support under conditions of stress and the provision of social support to others appear to be more characteristic of women than men. These findings may have relevance to understanding sex differences in health and health-related behavior. Women live longer than men in all developed nations. Women show fewer behavioral disruptions in response to stress than men, in the form of fewer health-compromising behaviors (such as smoking or drinking to excess) and aggression and its behavioral concomitants (such as fighting, homicide, and suicide) (Verbrugge, 1989a; 1989b; Waldron and Johnston, 1976; Wingard, 1982). Neuroendocrine reactions to stress may be implicated in some of these gender patterns. As we have noted, animal data and modest data from humans suggest that oxytocin may downregulate sympathetic and hypothalamic-pituitary-adrenocortical (HPA) responses to stress by leading to a preference to affiliate, by lowering anxiety and arousal in response to stress, and by reducing the likelihood of stress-related behavior indicative of arousal or anxiety.

In closing, we point out the advantages of an approach to affiliation and social support in response to stress that draws on contributions from social psychology, from health psychology, and from studies of neuroendocrine responses to stress. This area is well suited to such an integrative analysis. Although the oxytocin-based model proposed here remains speculative and warrants continued examination, especially in humans, it nonetheless provides a potentially viable biobehavioral account of the affiliative processes for coping with stress uncovered by Stanley Schachter more than 40 years ago.

Acknowledgments

Preparation of this manuscript was supported by a grant from the National Science Foundation (SBR9905157), by a grant from the National Institute of Mental Health (MH 056880) and by funds from the MacArthur Foundation's SES and Health Network.

Correspondence concerning this chapter should be directed to: Shelley Taylor, Department of Psychology, University of California Los Angeles, Los Angeles, CA 90095, USA; e-mail: taylors@psych.ucla.edu

References

Allen, K. M., Blascovich, J., Tomaka, J., and Kelsey, R. M. (1991). Presence of human friends and pet dogs as moderators of autonomic responses to stress in women. *Journal of Personality and Social Psychology*, 61, 582–9.

Altemus, M., Deuster, P. A., Galliven, E., Carter, C. S., and Gold, P. W. (1995). Suppression of hypothalamic-pituitary-adrenal axis responses to stress in lactating women. *Journal of Clinical Endocrinology and Metabolism*, 80, 2954–9.

Amico, J. A., Johnston, J. M., and Vagnucci, A. H. (1994). Suckling induced attenuation of plasma cortisol in postpartum lactating women. *Endocrinology Research*, 20, 79–87.

Argiolas, A., and Gessa, G. L. (1991). Central functions of oxytocin. *Neuroscience and Biobehavioral Reviews*, 15, 217–31.

Bachrach, K. M., and Zautra, A. J. (1985). Coping with a community stressor: The threat of a hazardous waste facility. *Journal of Health and Social Behavior*, 26, 127–41.

Barer, B. M. (1994). Men and women aging differently. *International Journal of Aging and Human Development*, 38, 29–40.

Baumeister, R., and Leary, M. (1995). The need to belong: Desire for interpersonal attachments as a fundamental human motivation. *Psychological Bulletin*, 117, 497–529.

Belle, D. (1987). Gender differences in the social moderators of stress. In R. C. Barnett, L. Biener, and G. K. Baruch (Eds.), *Gender and Stress* (pp. 257–77). New York: The Free Press.

Berkman, L. F., and Syme, S. L. (1979). Social networks, host resistance, and mortality: A nine-year followup study of the Alameda County residents. *American Journal of Epidemiology*, 109, 186–204.

Bruhn, J. G. (1965). An epidemiological study of myocardial infarction in an Italian-American community. *Journal of Chronic Diseases*, 18, 326–38.

Caporael, L. R. (1997). The evolution of truly social cognition: The core configurations model. *Personality and Social Psychology Review*, 1, 276–89.

Carter, C. S. (1998). Neuroendocrine perspectives on social attachment and love. *Psychoneuroendocrinology*, 23, 779–818.

Carter, C. S., and Altemus, M. (1997). Integrative functions of lactational hormones in social behavior and stress management. In C. S. Carter, I. I. Lederhendler, and B. Kirkpatrick (Eds.), *The Integrative Neurobiology of Affiliation* (Vol. 807, pp. 164–74). New York: Annals of the New York Academy of Sciences.

Carter, C. S., DeVries, A. C., and Getz, L. L. (1995). Physiological substrates of mammalian monogamy: The prairie vole model. *Neuroscience and Biobehavioral Reviews*, 19, 303–14.

Chiodera, P., and Legros, J. J. (1981). L'injection intraveineuse d'osytocine entraine une diminution de la concentration plasmatique de cortisol chez l'homme normal. *C. R. Soc. Bio. (Paris)*, 175, 546.

Christenfeld, N., Gerin, W., Lindon, W. et al. (1997). Social support effects on cardiovascular reactivity: Is a stranger effective as a friend? *Psychosomatic Medicine*, 59, 388–98.

Chrousos, G. P., and Gold, P. W. (1992). The concepts of stress and stress system disorders: Overview of physical and behavioral homeostasis. *Journal of the American Medical Association*, 267(9), 1244–52.

Cobb, S. (1976). Social support as a moderator of life stress. *Psychosomatic Medicine*, 38, 300–14.

Cohen, S. (1988). Psychosocial models of the role of social support in the etiology of physical disease. *Health Psychology*, 7, 269–97.

Cohen, S., and Wills, T. A. (1985). Stress, social support, and the buffering hypothesis. *Psychological Bulletin*, 98, 310–57.

Collins, N. L., Dunkel-Schetter, C., Lobel, M., and Scrimshaw, S. L. M. (1993). Social support in pregnancy: Psychosocial correlates of birth outcomes and postpartum depression. *Journal of Personality and Social Psychology*, 6, 1243–58.

Copeland, E. P., and Hess, R. S. (1995). Differences in young adolescents' coping strategies based on gender and ethnicity. *Journal of Early Adolescence*, 15, 203–19.

Coyne, J., Wortman, C., and Lehman, D. (1988). The other side of support: Emotional overinvolvement and miscarried helping. In B. H. Gottlieb (Ed.), *Marshaling Social Support: Formats, Processes, and Effects* (pp. 305–30). Thousand Oaks, CA: Sage Publications.

Cunningham, A. J. (1981). Mind, body, and immune response. In R. Adler (Ed.), *Psychoneuroimmunology* (pp. 609–17). New York: Academic Press.

Dakof, G. A., and Taylor, S. E. (1990). Victims' perceptions of social support: What is helpful from whom? *Journal of Personality and Social Psychology*, 58, 80–9.

DeVellis, R. F., DeVellis, B. M., Sauter, S. V. H., and Cohen, J. L. (1986). Predictors of pain and functioning in arthritis. *Health Education Research*, 1, 61–7.

Dimond, M. (1979). Social support and adaptation to chronic illness: The case of maintenance hemodialysis. *Research in Nursing and Health*, 2, 101–8.

Drago, F., Pederson, C. A., Caldwell, J. D., and Prange, A. J., Jr. (1986). Oxytocin potently enhances novelty-induced grooming behavior in the rat. *Brain Research*, 368, 287–95.

Dreifuss, J. J., Dubois-Dauphin, M., Widmer, H., and Raggenbass, M. (1992). Electrophysiology of oxytocin actions on central neurons. *Annals of the New York Academy of Science*, 652, 46–57.

Dunbar, R. (1996). *Grooming, Gossip, and the Evolution of Language*. Cambridge, MA: Harvard University Press.

Dunkel-Schetter, C., and Wortman, C. B. (1981). Dilemmas of social support: Parallels between victimization and aging. In S. B. Kiesler, J. N., Morgan, and V. K. Oppenheimer (Eds.), *Aging: Social Change* (pp. 349–81). New York: Academic Press.

Edens, J. L., Larkin, K. T., and Abel, J. L. (1992). The effect of social support and physical touch on cardiovascular reactions to mental stress. *Journal of Psychosomatic Research*, 36, 371–81.

Edwards, C. P. (1993). Behavioral sex differences in children of diverse cultures: The case of nurturance to infants. In M. E. Pereira and L. A. Fairbanks (Eds.), *Juvenile Primates: Life History, Development, and Behavior* (pp. 327–38). New York: Oxford University Press.

Fahrbach, S. E., Morrell, J. I., and Pfaff, D. W. (1985). Possible role for endogenous oxytocin in estrogen-facilitated maternal behavior in rats. *Neuroendocrinology*, 40, 526–32.

Ferraro, K. F., Mutran, E., and Barresi, C. M. (1984). Widowhood, health, and friendship support in later life. *Journal of Health and Social Behavior*, 25, 245–59.

Fleming, R., Baum, A., Gisriel, M. M., and Gatchel, R. J. (1982). Mediating influences of social support on stress at Three-Mile Island. *Journal of Human Stress*, September, 14–23.

Fredrickson, M., and Matthews, K. A. (1990). Cardiovascular responses to behavioral stress and hypertension: A meta-analytic review. *Annals of Behavioral Medicine*, 12, 30–9.

Gerin, M., Milner, D., Chawla, S., et al. (1995). Social support as a moderator of cardiovascular reactivity: A test of the direct effects and buffering hypothesis. *Psychosomatic Medicine*, 57, 16–22.

Gerin, M., Pieper, C., Levy, R., and Pickering, T. G. (1992). Social support in social interaction: A moderator of cardiovascular reactivity. *Psychosomatic Medicine*, 54, 324–36.

Goodenow, C., Reisine, S. T., and Grady, K. E. (1990). Quality of social support and associated social and psychological functioning in women with rheumatoid arthritis. *Health Psychology*, 9, 266–84.

Gruenewald, T. L., Taylor, S. E., Klein, L. C., and Seeman, T. E. (1998). Gender disparities in acute stress research [Abstract]. *Proceedings of the Society of Behavioral Medicine's 20th Annual Meeting: Annals of Behavioral Medicine*, 21 (Suppl.), S141.

Gurung, R. A. R., Seeman, T. E., and Taylor, S. E. (2001). Social support in older adults: What helped in ages past my help for years to come. Manuscript under review.

Heck, H., and deCastro, J. M. (1993). The caloric demand of lactation does not alter spontaneous meal patterns, nutrient intakes, or moods of women. *Physiology and Behavior*, 54, 641–8.

Heinrichs, M. (2000). *Oxytocin and Behavior*. Gottingen: Cuvillier Verlag.

House, J. S., Robbins, C., and Metzner, H. L. (1982). The association of social relationships and activities with mortality: Prospective evidence from the Tecumseh Community Health Study. *American Journal of Epidemiology*, 116, 123–40.

House, J. S., Umberson, D., and Landis, K. R. (1988). Structures and processes of social support. *American Review of Sociology*, 14, 293–318.

Jezova, D., Jurankova, E., Mosnarova, A., Kriska, M., and Skultetyova, I. (1996). Neuroendocrine response during stress with relation to gender differences. *Acta Neurobiologae Experimentalis*, 56, 779–85.

Kamarck, T. W., Annunziato, B., and Amateau, L. M. (1995). Affiliations moderate the effect of social threat on stress-related cardiovascular responses: Boundary conditions for a laboratory model of social support. *Psychosomatic Medicine*, 57, 183–94.

Kamarck, T. W., Manuck, S. B., and Jennings, J. R. (1990). Social support reduces cardiovascular reactivity to psychological challenge: A laboratory model. *Psychosomatic Medicine*, 52, 42–58.

Kessler, R. C., and McLeod, J. D. (1985). Social support and mental health in community samples. In S. Cohen and S. L. Syme (Eds.), *Social Support and Health* (pp. 219–40). Orlando, FL: Academic Press.

Keverne, E. B., Nevison, C. M., and Martel, F. L. (1997). Early learning and the social bond. In C. S. Carter, I. I. Lederhendler, and B. Kirkpatrick (Eds.), *The Integrative Neurobiology of Affiliation* (Vol. 807, pp. 329–339). New York: Annals of the New York Academy of Sciences.

King, K. B., Reis, H. T., Porter, L. A., and Norsen, L. H. (1993). Social support and long-term recovery from coronary artery surgery: Effects on patients and spouses. *Health Psychology*, 12, 56–63.

Kirschbaum, C., Klauer, T., Filipp, S. H., and Hellhammer, D. H. (1995). Sex-specific effects of social support on cortisol and subjective responses to acute psychological stress. *Psychosomatic Medicine*, 57, 23–31.

Kors, D., Linden, W., and Gerin, W. (1997). Evaluation interferes with social support: Effects on cardiovascular stress reactivity. *Journal of Social and Clinical Psychology*, 16, 1–23.

Krantz, D. S., and Manuck, S. B. (1984). Acute psychophysiologic reactivity and risk of cardiovascular disease: A review and methodologic critique. *Psychological Bulletin*, 96, 435–64.

Kulik, J. A., and Mahler, H. I. M. (1989). Social support and recovery from surgery. *Health Psychology*, 8, 221–38.

Kulik, J. A., and Mahler, H. I. M. (1993). Emotional support as a mediator of adjustment and compliance after coronary artery bypass surgery: A longitudinal study. *Journal of Behavioral Medicine*, 16, 45–64.

Legros, J. J., Chiodera, P., and Demy-Ponsart, E. (1982). Inhibitory influence of exogenous oxytocin on adrenocorticotrophin secretion in normal human subjects. *Journal of Clinical Endocrinology and Metabolism*, 55, 1035–9.

Lepore, S. J., Allen, K. A. M., and Evans, G. W. (1993). Social support lowers cardiovascular reactivity to an acute stress. *Psychosomatic Medicine*, 55, 518–24.

Light, K. C., Smith, T. E., Johns, J. M., Brownley, K. A., Hofheimer, J. A., and Amico, J. A. (2000). Oxytocin responsivity in mothers of infants: A preliminary study of relationships with blood pressure during laboratory stress and normal ambulatory activity. *Health Psychology*, 19, 560–7.

Luckow, A., Reifman, A., and McIntosh, D. N. (1998). Gender differences in coping: A meta-analysis. Poster session presented at the 106th Annual Convention of the American Psychological Association, San Francisco, CA, August.

Magni, G., Silvestro, A., Tamiello, M., Zanesco, L., and Carl, M. (1988). An integrated approach to the assessment of family adjustment to acute lymphocytic leukemia in children. *Acta Psychiatrica Scandinavia*, 78, 639–42.

Marteau, T. M., Bloch, S., and Baum, J. D. (1987). Family life and diabetic control. *Journal of Child Psychology and Psychiatry*, 28, 823–33.

McCarthy, M. M. (1995). Estrogen modulation of oxytocin and its relation to behavior. In R. Ivell and J. Russell (Eds.), *Oxytocin: Cellular and Molecular Approaches in Medicine and Research* (pp. 235–42). New York: Plenum Press.

McDonald, L. M., and Korabik, K. (1991). Sources of stress and ways of coping among male and female managers. *Journal of Social Behavior and Personality*, 6, 185–98.

McEwen, B. S., and Sapolsky, R. M. (1995). Stress and cognitive function. *Current Opinion in Neurobiology*, 5, 205–16.

McEwen, B. S., and Stellar, E. (1993). Stress and the individual: Mechanisms leading to disease. *Archives of Internal Medicine*, 153, 2093–101.

Mendoza, S. P., and Mason, W. A. (1997). Attachment relationships in New World primates. In C. S. Carter, I. I. Lederhendler, and B. Kirkpatrick (Eds.), *The Integrative Neurobiology of Affiliation* (Vol. 807, pp. 203–9). New York: Annals of the New York Academy of Sciences.

Modahl, C., and Newton, N. (1979). Mood state difference between breast and bottle feeding mothers. In L. Carenza and L. Zinchella (Eds.), *Emotion and Reproduction: Proceedings of the Serrano Symposium* (Vol. 20B, pp. 819–22). New York: Academic Press.

Mullen, B., Bryant, B., and Driskell, J. E. (1997). Presence of others and arousal: An integration. *Group Dynamics: Theory, Research, and Practice*, 1, 52–64.

Ogus, E. D., Greenglass, E. R., and Burke, R. J. (1990). Gender-role differences, work stress and depersonalization. *Journal of Social Behavior and Personality*, 5, 387–98.

Pitman, R. K., Orr, S. P., and Lasko, N. B. (1993). Effects of intranasal vasopressin and oxytocin on physiologic responding during personal combat imagery in Vietnam veterans with posttraumatic stress disorder. *Psychiatry Research*, 48, 107–17.

Ptacek, J. T., Smith, R. E., and Zanas, J. (1992). Gender, appraisal, and coping: A longitudinal analysis. *Journal of Personality*, 60, 747–70.

Robertson, E. K., and Suinn, R. M. (1968). The determination of rate of progress of stroke patients through empathy measures of patient and family. *Journal of Psychosomatic Research*, 12, 189–91.

Sapolsky, R. M. (1992). *Stress, the Aging Brain, and the Mechanisms of Neuron Death.* Cambridge, MA: MIT Press.

Sapolsky, R. M. (1996). Why stress is bad for your brain. *Science*, 273, 749–50.

Sawchenko, P. E., and Swanson, L. W. (1982). Immunohistochemical identification of neurons in the paraventricular nucleus of the hypothalamus that project to the medulla or to the spinal cord in the rat. *Journal of Comparative Neurology*, 205, 260–72.

Schachter, S. (1959). *The Psychology of Affiliation.* Stanford, CA: Stanford University Press.

Schuster, T. L., Kessler, R. C., and Aseltine, R. H., Jr. (1990). Supportive interactions, negative interactions, and depressed mood. *American Journal of Community Psychology*, 18, 423–38.

Schwarzer, R., and Leppin, A. (1991). Social support and health: A theoretical and empirical overview. *Journal of Social and Personal Relationships*, 8, 99–127.

Seeman, T. E., Berkman, L. F., Blazer, D., and Rowe, J. W. (1994). Social ties and support and neuroendocrine function: The MacArthur studies on successful aging. *Annals of Behavioral Medicine*, 16, 95–106.

Seeman, T. E., and Robbins, R. J. (1994). Aging and hypothalamic-pituitary-adrenal response to challenge in humans. *Endocrinology Review*, 15, 233–60.

Sheffield, D., and Carroll, D. (1994). Social support and cardiovascular reactions to active laboratory stressors. *Psychology and Health*, 9, 305–16.

Smith, T. L., Gallo, L. C., Goble, L., Ngu, L. Q., and Stark, K. A. (1998). Agency, communion, and cardiovascular reactivity during marital interaction. *Health Psychology*, 17, 537–45.

Swanson, L. W., and Sawchenko, P. E. (1980). Paraventricular nucleus: A site for the integration of neuroendocrine and autonomic mechanisms. *Neuroendocrinology*, 31, 410–17.

Taylor, S. E. (1999). *Health Psychology* (4th edn.). New York: McGraw-Hill.

Tower, R. B., and Kasl, S. V. (1996). Gender, marital closeness, and depressive symptoms in elderly couples. *Journals of Gerontology Series B: Psychological Sciences and Social Sciences*, 51, P115–29.

Umberson, D., Wortman, C. B., and Kessler, R. C. (1992). Widowhood and depression: Explaining long-term gender differences in vulnerability. *Journal of Health and Social Behavior*, 33, 10–24.

Unger, J., McAvay, G., Bruce, M. L., Berkman, L. F., and Seeman, T. E. (1999). Variation in the impact of social network characteristics on physical functioning in elderly persons: MacArthur Studies of Successful Aging. *Journal of Gerontology: Social Science*, 54B, S245–52.

Uvnas-Moberg, K. (1996). Neuroendocrinology of the mother-child interaction. *Trends in Endocrinology and Metabolism*, 7, 126–31.

Uvnas-Moberg, K. (1997). Oxytocin linked antistress effects: the relaxation and growth response. *Acta Psychologica Scandinavica (Supplementum)*, 640, 38–42.

VanderPlate, C., Aral, S. O., and Magder, L. (1988). The relationship among genital herpes simplex virus, stress, and social support. *Health Psychology*, 7, 159–68.

Verbrugge, L. M. (1989a). Multiple roles and physical health of women and men. *Journal of Health and Social Behavior*, 24, 16–30.

Verbrugge, L. M. (1989b). The twain meet: Empirical explanations of sex differences in health and mortality. *Journal of Health and Social Behavior*, 30, 282–304.

Verbrugge, L. M. (1990). Pathways of health and death. In R. D. Apple (Ed.), *Women, health, and medicine in America: A historical handbook* (pp. 41–79). New York: Garland.

Veroff, J., Kulka, R., and Douvan, E. (1981). *Mental Health in America: Patterns of Help-seeking from 1957 to 1976*. New York: Basic Books.

Virden, S. F. (1988). The relationship between infant feeding method and maternal role adjustment. *Journal of Nurse Midwifery*, 33, 31–5.

Waldron, I., and Johnston, S. (1976). Why do women live longer than men? Part 2. *Journal of Human Stress*, 2, 19–30.

Wallston, B. S., Alagna, S. W., DeVellis, B. M., and DeVellis, R. F. (1983). Social support and physical health. *Health Psychology*, 2, 367–91.

Wethington, E., McLeod, J. D., and Kessler, R. C. (1987). The importance of life events for explaining sex differences in psychological distress. In R. C. Barnett, L. Biener, and G. K. Baruch (Eds.), *Gender and Stress* (pp. 144–56). New York: The Free Press.

Whiting, B., and Whiting, J. (1975). *Children of Six Cultures*. Cambridge, MA: Harvard University Press.

Wiklund, I., Oden, A., Sanne, H., Ulvenstam, G., Wilhemsson, C., and Wilhemsen, L. (1988). Prognostic importance of somatic and psychosocial variables after a first myocardial infarction. *American Journal of Epidemiology*, 128, 786–95.

Wingard, D. L. (1982). The sex differential in mortality rates: Demographic and behavioral factors. *American Journal of Epidemiology*, 115, 205–16.

Witt, D. M., Carter, C. S., and Walton, D. (1990). Central and peripheral effects of oxytocin administration in prairie voles (*Microtus ochrogaster*). *Pharmacology, Biochemistry, and Behavior*, 37, 63–9.

Witt, D. M., Winslow, J. T., and Insel, T. R. (1992). Enhanced social interactions in rats following chronic, centrally infused oxytocin. *Pharmacology, Biochemistry, and Behavior*, 43, 855–86.

PART III

Personality and Health

CHAPTER 13

Toward a Social Psychophysiology of Cardiovascular Reactivity: Interpersonal Concepts and Methods in the Study of Stress and Coronary Disease

Timothy W. Smith

University of Utah

Linda C. Gallo

San Diego State University

and

John M. Ruiz

University of Pittsburgh School of Medicine

Introduction

Each year in the United States, 1,000,000 persons suffer a coronary event, including 450,000 deaths (American Heart Association, 2001). Well-known risk factors (e.g., cholesterol, smoking) guide prevention efforts, but provide an incomplete account of the causes of coronary heart disease (CHD). Medical and behavioral scientists have long suspected that psychological stress, personality traits, and the social environment influence CHD, and mounting evidence supports this view (Rozanski et al., 1999). Current psychosocial research on CHD addresses three goals. First, epidemiological and clinical research examines the association of personality traits, emotions, and aspects of the social environment with the development and course of CHD. Second, psychophysiological research examines mechanisms underlying these associations. Third, once psychosocial risk factors and mechanisms are identified, risk-reducing interventions can be evaluated in a theory-driven manner.

Despite notable advances, major challenges remain in each area. A diverse set of personality traits and aspects of the social environment complicates the development of a comprehensive and integrated account of psychosocial influences on CHD. Further, these characteristics are typically studied separately, even though they are often highly correlated, perhaps obscuring basic dimensions of psychosocial risk. Similarly, the lack of an overarching conceptual framework impedes the development of an integrated view of the association between dimensions of psychosocial risk and psychophysiological mechanisms linking them to disease. To develop a more complete account of the associations among characteristics of people, social environments, and physiological responses, a common conceptual and methodological framework for the study of personality and interpersonal processes is needed.

In this chapter, we argue that the concepts and methods of the interpersonal tradition (Kiesler, 1996) in personality and social psychology can facilitate progress toward each goal of psychosocial research on CHD. Through an established dimensional model of personality and social behavior (i.e., the *interpersonal circumplex*), this perspective provides an integrative framework. Through a related model of personality and social interaction (i.e., the *transactional cycle*), it suggests a new approach to interrelated risk factors. This tradition also includes methodological tools to model associations between psychosocial risk factors and psychophysiological mechanisms. Finally, this perspective could guide the refinement of interventions. A full presentation of these implications is beyond our present scope. Instead, we discuss these concepts and methods in studies of a primary mechanism in models of psychosocial influences on CHD – cardiovascular reactivity (CVR) – changes in blood pressure, heart rate, and other variables in response to stressful stimuli. In our view, the sophistication of research on the nature and health consequences of CVR (Brownley et al., 2000; Rozanski et al., 1999) has not been matched by refinements in the study of its psychosocial determinants, though there are notable exceptions. The interpersonal perspective is particularly valuable in this regard. Before presenting our interpersonal approach to CVR, we review three essential topics – the role of CVR in CHD pathophysiology, interpersonal concepts and methods, and research on psychosocial risk factors.

Cardiovascular Reactivity and the Development of Coronary Heart Disease

The development of CHD is a complex, decades-long process with diverse endpoints. Angina pectoris (i.e., chest pain from myocardial ischemia), myocardial infarction (MI; ischemic death of heart muscle), and sudden coronary death (SCD; death within hours of symptom onset) are primary manifestations, but each stems from coronary artery disease (CAD). Microscopic accumulations of lipids and related cells within arterial walls progress to visible "fatty streaks" as early as childhood (Strong et al., 1999), reflecting cellular responses to plasma-derived lipoproteins and injuries to the inner lining (i.e., endothelium) of the arteries. At these sites, reparative and inflammatory responses promote deposition of lipoproteins in cellular structures within artery walls. Later, extracellular lipids accumulate within thickened arterial walls. Eventually, lesions include fibrous tissues and calcium deposits, and encroach into artery openings. Blood flow, and as a result oxygen supply to myocardial tissues is impeded. Advanced lesions are sometimes observed in adolescence and become increasingly common with age (Tuzcu et al., 2001).

In severe CAD, heightened oxygen demand during physical exertion or mental stress can exceed the impaired supply, resulting in ischemia. The calcified, fibrous plaque may rupture or break, and resulting blood clots (i.e., thrombus) further obstruct blood flow. Portions of clots may be dislodged and carried to narrower artery sections (i.e., embolus). Thrombi and emboli can abruptly cause severe disruptions of blood supply, resulting in unstable angina or MI. Ischemia also renders the myocardium susceptible to disturbances in rhythm. SCD is caused by a severe rhythm disturbance – ventricular fibrillation – in which pump function is lost.

Cardiovascular Reactivity as a Mechanism

Statistical associations between psychosocial characteristics and later cardiac outcomes could reflect effects on one or more of the multiple processes involved in the initiation and progression of CAD and emergence of CHD (Cohen et al., 1994). Psychosocial risk factors have been linked to stress-induced changes in several mechanisms, including blood lipids, circulating neuro-endocrine levels (e.g., cortisol, catecholamines), parasympathetic tone, and the readiness with which blood coagulates (Von Kanel et al., 2001; Rozanski et al., 1999). However, the largest body of research concerns CVR. The general model holds that increased magnitude, duration, and frequency of episodes of CVR promote the initiation and progression of CAD and the emergence of CHD (Rozanski et al., 1999).

Several types of studies suggest that CVR influences multiple disease stages. CVR in response to mental stressors predicts the extent and progression of carotid artery atherosclerosis in otherwise healthy persons (Barnett et al., 1997; Matthews et al., 1998). Carotid atherosclerosis contributes to stroke, but is also associated with the presence of CAD. Current models suggest that CVR fosters damage to the coronary endothelium, rendering arteries more susceptible to inflammation and lipid deposition. Animal research supports this view. In non-human primates, animals displaying the largest heart rate responses to stressors also display more severe CAD. Chronic stress promotes microscopic endothelial injury in these animals, as well as the development of CAD. Importantly, these effects can be eliminated by the administration of drugs that block sympathetically mediated CVR (Kaplan and Manuck, 1998;

Skantze et al., 1998). In CHD patients, CVR in response to mental stress is associated with susceptibility to myocardial ischemia (Krantz et al., 1991). Greater rate and force of heart contractions increase myocardial oxygen demand, contributing to ischemia. Further, increased hemodynamic force (e.g., blood pressure, turbulence, sheer stress) promotes plaque rupture. Hence, CVR may contribute to both the development of CAD and later emergence of CHD.

There are a variety of important issues in CVR research. First, some studies have not found the expected association with later disease (Rozanski et al., 1999). Second, these responses involve multiple physiologic mechanisms. Heart rate reactivity can reflect increased sympathetic activation of the heart and/or decreased parasympathetic input, whereas blood pressure reactivity can reflect increases in cardiac output and/or peripheral resistance (Brownley et al., 2000). Similar levels of CVR could be due to different underlying determinants and these patterns may be differentially related to atherogenesis and ischemia (e.g., Goldberg et al., 1996). Hence, studies increasingly incorporate methods to examine both the magnitude and determinants of CVR. Finally, the concept of CVR is used in two very different ways. It is seen as an *individual difference* dimension that is stable across time and situations (Kamarck et al., 2000) and confers risk of CHD. In a different model, CVR *mediates* the effects of psychosocial risk factors on CAD and CHD. For example, socially isolated or chronically hostile persons may be prone to larger, more frequent, and/or more enduring increases in heart rate and blood pressure, accounting for their greater risk of disease. The interpersonal approach is relevant to individual differences, but primarily informs research on the mediational model.

Psychosocial Risk Factors for Coronary Heart Disease

Many characteristics of individuals and their social circumstances predict CHD. Until recently, Type A behavior was the best known, but inconsistent results led researchers to examine its components. Hostility has emerged as particularly important in this regard (Miller et al., 1996). Social isolation (i.e., low social support) also predicts the development and course of CHD (Berkman, 1995). The interpersonal perspective is well suited to these risk factors. However, it is also relevant to a recently emerging cluster of risk factors – depression and other negative affects (Smith and Gallo, 2001).

Hostility, Anger, and Aggressiveness

Hostility is a multi-dimensional construct (Smith, 1994). The emotional component comprises feelings of anger and resentment. Hostile behavior refers to verbal and physical aggressive actions intended to inflict harm. The term hostility most accurately refers to a cognitive style of cynicism, mistrust, and other negative beliefs about others. Considerable epidemiological and clinical research demonstrates that hostility predicts the development and course of CHD (Miller et al., 1996). For example, behavioral ratings of hostility predict incident CHD in longitudinal research (Dembroski et al., 1989; Hecker et al., 1988). In several prospective studies, self-reports of hostile cognition predict new CHD (Barefoot et al., 1983; Everson et al., 1997b), as does trait anger (Kawachi et al., 1996; Williams et al., 2000).

Hostility predicts the severity and progression of atherosclerosis among persons without CHD (Iribarren et al., 2000; Whiteman et al., 2000) and restenosis following angioplasty (Goodman et al., 1996). It also predicts susceptibility to ischemia among persons with established CHD (Helmers et al., 1993). Anger inductions can evoke ischemia in both human (Ironson et al., 1992) and animal laboratory models (Verrier et al., 1987), and anger is associated with ischemia during ambulatory monitoring (Gullette et al., 1997). In case-crossover studies, episodes of anger increase the risk of acute MI (e.g., Möller et al., 1999). Despite some conflicting findings, hostility is an important CHD risk factor (Miller et al., 1996) that apparently influences the development of CAD and later CHD manifestations.

Dominance as Coronary-prone Behavior

Social dominance is a second element of the Type A pattern. In analyses of behavioral ratings, hostility and social dominance emerge as independent predictors of CHD and mortality (Houston et al., 1997). In this case, social dominance refers to a set of controlling behaviors including vigorous speech and a tendency to "cut off" and "talk over" an interviewer. Cross-sectional studies also find that behavioral ratings of dominance and hostility are independently related to CHD (Siegman et al., 2000b). Prospective studies using self-reports of dominance have replicated the association with CHD (Siegman et al., 2000a). These findings have an intriguing parallel in non-human primate research. Socially dominant male macaques develop CAD when exposed to the chronic stress of unstable housing conditions. When required to re-establish their social status on a regular basis they develop more severe CAD, as compared to dominant animals in stable social conditions or subordinate animals regardless of social conditions (Kaplan and Manuck, 1998). This effect can be prevented by drugs that attenuate sympathetically mediated CVR, suggesting that recurring efforts to assert dominance promote CAD through this mechanism.

Social Support, Integration, and Conflict

Characteristics of the social environment have been studied extensively as CHD risk factors (Berkman, 1995), especially structural aspects of one's social network (i.e., marital status) and qualitative appraisals (i.e., perceptions of support; Sarason et al., 1990). In prospective studies, social isolation and qualitative aspects of support predict CHD morbidity and mortality in initially healthy populations (e.g., House et al., 1988; Orth-Gomer et al., 1993). Markers of social integration (e.g., living alone) predict death or recurrent events in CHD patients (e.g., Case et al., 1992; Jenkinson et al., 1993). Perception of emotional support has a strong protective effect after coronary events (Horsten et al., 2000; Welin et al., 2000). Animal research supports these findings, as monkeys housed in isolation develop more severe coronary atherosclerosis than do those housed in groups (Shively et al., 1989). Some studies have examined the health consequences of negative social characteristics. For example, women reporting marital distress were nearly three times as likely to suffer a recurrent coronary event following admission for CHD than were their married but non-distressed counterparts (Orth-Gomer et al., 2000). As noted above, social conflict promotes endothelial injuries and atherosclerosis in animal models (Skantze et al., 1998).

Depression, Anxiety, and Negative Affectivity

For decades, individual differences in negative affect and related traits have been discussed as a cause of CHD. These characteristics can be grouped under the labels "negative affectivity" (Watson and Clark, 1984) or "neuroticism" (Costa and McCrae, 1987). The studies include self-reports of symptoms, as well as clinically diagnosed emotional disorders. Measures of various negative emotions and related characteristics are often so highly correlated as to be statistically indistinguishable (Watson et al., 1994). Further, despite important distinctions between emotional symptoms and emotional disorders (e.g., Santor and Coyne, 2001), individuals with such disorders score high on the personality and symptom measures (Clark et al., 1994). Hence, the effects of specific emotions, personality characteristics, and related disorders on CHD are difficult to distinguish.

Mounting evidence suggests that depression, anxiety, and related characteristics confer risk for the development and progression of CHD (Rozanski et al., 1999). Depression, anxiety and hopelessness increase the risk of future coronary events in studies of initially healthy community populations (e.g., Ford et al., 1998; Penninx et al., 2001), and predict poor prognosis in established CHD (Frasure-Smith et al., 1999; Pennix et al., 2001). One study found that hopelessness predicted the progression of atherosclerosis (Everson et al., 1997a). Thus, despite some negative findings (Mayou et al., 2000), negative emotionality confers risk of CHD.

Conclusions Regarding Psychosocial Risk

Individual differences in hostility, dominance, social support, social conflict, and negative affect predict the development and course of CHD. These risk factors can extend our understanding of causes of CHD, and suggest directions in prevention and management. However, they are typically studied separately, thereby impeding an integrated view of psychosocial influences on CHD. Given its relevance to a broad range of personality and social phenomenon, the interpersonal perspective can facilitate a comprehensive approach.

A Primer of Interpersonal Theory and Methods

Sullivan (1953: 111) defined personality as, "the relatively enduring pattern of recurrent interpersonal situations which characterize a human life". The statement conveys the underpinnings of the interpersonal approach, and suggests why it is conducive to integrative research on risk factors. Because it views social experiences and personality characteristics as a single phenomenon, the perspective provides a general framework for conceptualizing a wide variety of risk factors. Sullivan's words also challenge the field's habit of parsing risk factors into characteristics of people and characteristics of their social context.

The Interpersonal Circumplex

Since Leary's (1957) pioneering work, two broad dimensions of the interpersonal circumplex can describe social behavior – friendliness (or warmth) versus hostility (or coldness), and dominance (or control) versus submissiveness (or passivity) (Figure 13.1). These coordinates can characterize specific social stimuli, social responses, individual differences in social behavior (i.e., personality traits), and stable features of social environments. Several authors (e.g., Wiggins and Trapnell, 1996) suggest that interpersonal interactions represent exchanges of two social resources – status (i.e., esteem or regard), corresponding to the vertical circumplex axis, and love (i.e., acceptance or liking), corresponding to the horizontal axis. Hence, motivations underlying interpersonal behavior involve efforts to obtain or retain status and acceptance. Wiggins and Trapnell (1996) also interpret the affiliation and control dimensions as broad motivational complexes. *Communion* involves interest in being part of a larger social group, with associated strivings for intimacy and the maintenance of relationships. *Agency* involves concerns with separateness, associated strivings for achievement, and power. This view converges with discussions of sex differences in stress vulnerability. Helgeson (1994) suggests that the masculine/agency and feminine/communion sex roles provide conceptual coordinates for examining classes of stressors and traits that differentially render men and women susceptible to the effects of stress on health.

Two circumplex assessments have featured prominently in our work. Wiggins' Interpersonal Adjectives Scales (revised form, IAS-R; Wiggins et al., 1988) consist of adjectives corresponding to eight points around the circumplex (i.e., octants). Octant scores, as well as friendliness and dominance composites,

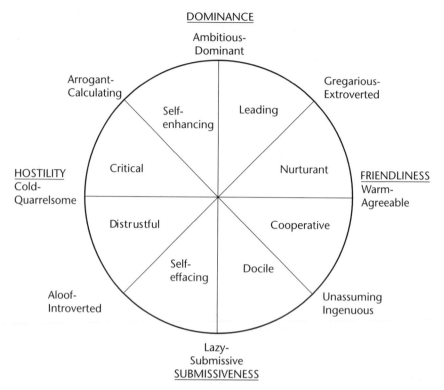

Figure 13.1   The interpersonal circumplex.

provide self-descriptions or ratings of others. An important extension (Trapnell and Wiggins, 1990) adds three additional scales – neuroticism, conscientious-ness, and openness to experience – to assess the five-factor model (FFM) of personality (McCrae and John, 1992), substituting the circumplex axes for extroversion and agreeableness. The FFM can compare, contrast, and integrate personality characteristics studied as risk factors (Smith and Williams, 1992). The circumplex version can also integrate personality and social behavior. We have used this version of the IAS-R to compare measures of trait hostility (Gallo and Smith, 1998) and the regular IAS-R to assess social context in CVR studies. Example items are listed in Table 13.1. We have also used the Impact Message Inventory (IMI-C; Kiesler et al., 1997) to assess responses to social interactions. Respondents describe the impact a particular target produced in him or her during a specific interaction, or during their prior relationship. As with the IAS-R, octant and dimension scores are derived. Example items are also presented in Table 13.1. We have used the IMI-C to assess interactions manipulated in the laboratory and interaction patterns of previously acquainted persons. A variety of other circumplex-based assessments are available (Kiesler, 1996). Further, methods for evaluating and utilizing such measures are well established (Gurtman, 1997).

Table 13.1 Octants and selected items for the Interpersonal Adjectives Scales (revised form, IAS-R) and the Impact Message Inventory (IMI)

	IAS-R	IMI
Dominance	Assertive Dominant	When I am with this person, he/she makes me feel bossed around.
Hostile dominance	Boastful Cocky	When I am with this person, he/she makes me feel that they think it's every person for him or herself.
Hostility	Cruel Coldhearted	When I am with this person, he/she makes me feel distant from them.
Hostile submissiveness	Distant Introverted	When I am with this person, he/she makes me feel that they think they're inadequate.
Submissiveness	Timid Meek	When I am with this person, he/she makes me feel in charge.
Friendly submissiveness	Boastless Undemanding	When I am with this person, he/she makes me feel that they would accept whatever I said.
Friendliness	Sympathetic Kind	When I am with this person, he/she makes me feel appreciated by them.
Friendly dominance	Extroverted Enthusiastic	When I am with this person, he/she makes me feel that they want to be the charming one.

The Transactional Cycle

The interpersonal perspective construes personality characteristics and social contexts too as aspects of one process, formally represented as the *transactional cycle* (Kiesler, 1996), depicted in Figure 13.2. As in other contemporary views (Mischel and Shoda, 1999), personality and social context are seen as reciprocally determined. Individuals both shape and are shaped by their social experiences. Through the situations and relationships they choose to enter or avoid, expectations, appraisals of others, goals they pursue, tactics they employ in pursuit of goals, and their expressive behavior, people influence others' internal and subsequent overt responses. These selected, evoked, and intentionally manipulated responses of others, in turn, tend to maintain the individual's characteristic interpersonal style.

Transactional cycles consist of cognitive structures (e.g., self and other schemas or "personifications"), cognitive processes (e.g., construal; distortion), emotional responses, and communications. In Figure 13.2, we also include other constructs from cognitive-social approaches to personality (Mischel and Shoda, 1999). One key aspect of the cycle is the covert experience of interaction partners – or the "impact message" (Kiesler, 1996). The individual's

INDIVIDUAL

Covert experience

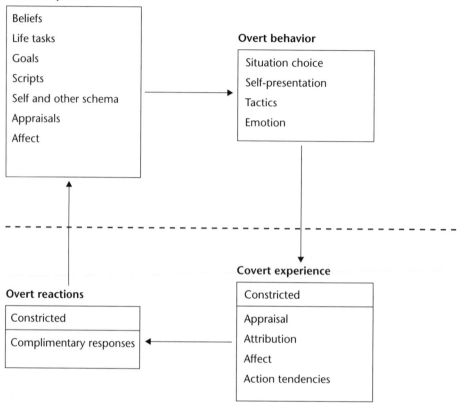

Figure 13.2 The transactional cycle (Smith and Gallo, 1998).

characteristic behaviors (e.g., warmth) tend to constrict the covert reactions from others. These evoked reactions, in turn, prompt overt responses from interaction partners that complement the original actor's response, thereby sustaining his or her interpersonal style. In the circumplex model, complementarity of social behavior involves similarity of affiliation (i.e., hostility evokes hostility; friendliness evokes friendliness) and reciprocity of control (i.e., dominance evokes submissiveness, and vice versa). Most would agree that personality and social context are reciprocally related, but patterns of complementarity are the subject of considerable debate and research (Gurtman, 2001). Nonetheless, the transactional cycle provides an account of correlations between personality characteristics and aspects of the social environment studied as risk factors. This model also suggests that mechanisms through which risk factors affect CHD involve a dynamic process in which individuals shape and are shaped by the social environment.

Personality and Social Environment across Time

The transactional cycle in Figure 13.2 depicts a brief interaction. When repeated over time and across contexts, it describes continuities in development and maintenance of personality characteristics, relationships, and social environments. That is, recurring cycles contribute to longer-term development and stability and coherence of personality (Caspi and Roberts, 1999; Cervone and Shoda, 1999). This longer-term process produces health-relevant psychosocial *trajectories*. For example, warm and agreeable persons – through their thoughts and actions and the social experiences they create – experience an accumulation of exposure to health-promoting social contexts. Greater exposure to friendly, health-promoting contexts, in turn, facilitates the continuation of an agreeable style. In contrast, cold and antagonistic persons tend to create conflict and undermine support, thereby increasing their cumulative exposure to unhealthy contexts. Further, healthy and unhealthy social contexts – regardless of whether they reflect self-fulfilling expectancies or "imposed" social conditions – foster adaptive (i.e., healthy) or maladaptive transactional cycles, thereby sustaining health-relevant trajectories.

The interpersonal perspective emphasizes transactions with family (e.g., parents) and peers in personality and social development. Further, current family and close relationships are important recurring transactions or contexts, given their frequency and disproportionate impact on stress and emotion. Other contexts, such as work and the local community can be seen as both components of recurring cycles and as contexts fostering either health promoting or health damaging transactions, thereby permitting the integration of personality and interpersonal influences on health with broader social and socio-economic influences.

Circumplex Concepts and Methods in Reactivity Research

Of the interpersonal concepts and methods, the circumplex is the most immediately relevant to CVR research. To varying degrees, risk factors can be located in the circumplex. Trait hostility is clearly related to the horizontal axis, but various aspects of hostility have different placements. Verbal aggressiveness corresponds to hostile dominance, whereas cynicism and mistrust reflect hostile submissiveness (Gallo and Smith, 1998). Trait dominance, of course, reflects the vertical axis. Conceptual and empirical analyses place social support along the horizontal axis, but with varying degrees of dominance (Trobst, 2000). For example, giving advice is more dominant than expressing affection and respect. Social conflict can be located at the unfriendly pole of horizontal axis. The circumplex location of negative affectivity is less obvious, as it is typically conceptualized as an intra-individual phenomenon. However, social isolation and conflict are both causes and consequences of depression (Joiner and Coyne, 1999), and depressive symptoms correlate with self-reports of unfriendly submissiveness in the circumplex (Ruiz et al., 2001).

In the social psychophysiology of CVR, we consider four circumplexes: (a) transient social stimuli; (b) transient expressions of social behavior; (c) stable individual differences in social behavior; and (d) stable social situations or environments. In this way, circumplex concepts and methods address four distinct psychophysiological questions. First, what are the effects on CVR of *exposure* to social stimuli (e.g., behavior of interaction partners) varying in dominance and friendliness? Second, what are the effects on CVR of *expression* of social behavior (e.g., toward an interaction partner) varying in dominance and friendliness? Third, what are the associations between *individual differences* in dominance and friendliness (i.e., personality traits) and CVR? Finally, what are the associations between CVR and *stable characteristics of the social environment* (e.g., degree of marital discord) varying in friendliness and dominance? Additional questions combine these circumplexes (e.g., interactive effects of individual differences and manipulated social stimuli).

Circumplex-based measures are useful in these efforts. In construct validation of individual difference measures, well-developed methods can describe the extent to which a personality trait involves interpersonal processes and its circumplex location (Gurtman, 1997). When manipulating social stimuli or social behavior, circumplex measures can determine whether or not specific constructs of interest have been manipulated. Finally, these measures are useful in assessing the association of CVR with more enduring features of the social environment, as when partners (e.g., spouses, friends) describe personal relationships. The use of a common set of conceptual coordinates and standardized information about the extent of a specific interpersonal behavior facilitate integration of research findings.

The Horizontal Axis

Given that many psychosocial risk factors fall along the horizontal circumplex axis, it is not surprising that much of the research on social aspects of CVR does as well. All four types of effects (i.e., social stimuli; social responses; individual differences; stable aspects of context) and combinations (e.g., person by situation interactive effects) have been examined.

Hostile and Supportive Social Stimuli
Hostile or unfriendly social stimuli – such as harassment or criticism during a laboratory stressor – heighten CVR relative to neutral social stimuli. For example, Powch and Houston (1996) examined cardiovascular responses of young women to a discussion task. In a low stress condition, participants discussed an unimportant issue with a confederate who politely agreed. In the high stress condition, participants discussed an issue on which they held strong views with a confederate who expressed the opposite opinion in a condescending manner. The latter condition elicited greater BP and HR reactivity, as well as angry affect and hostile behavior. Other studies have shown that

participants harassed during laboratory tasks (e.g., solving anagrams, Suarez et al., 1998; mental arithmetic, Bongard et al., 1997; current events speech, Gallo et al., 2000) exhibit increased CVR compared with those completing the same tasks under neutral conditions. These findings likely reflect the effects of state anger on CVR. The specific manipulations reflect hostile-dominant social stimuli (e.g., criticism, etc.), but without circumplex measures it is not certain. Further, either the implied threat of loss of status or acceptance could affect CVR.

Supportive gestures or the presence of a supportive companion while experiencing stress attenuate cardiovascular reactivity (Kamarck et al., 1998; Lepore, 1998). For example, in a study by Gerin and colleagues (1992), participants engaged in a discussion task with three confederates, two of whom argued against the participant's views. In a support condition, the third confederate spoke in defense of the participant; in the neutral condition this confederate was silent. Participants in the support condition displayed smaller HR and BP responses during the task. Uchino and Garvey (1997) found that simply informing participants that support would be available during a speech task, if needed, attenuated CVR. The mere presence of a stranger or friend can also attenuate CVR, compared to conditions where participants undergo a stressful task alone (e.g., Christenfeld et al., 1997; Fontana et al., 1999; Gerin et al., 1995). However, other studies found no effects (Sheffield and Carroll, 1994) or even heightened reactivity in friend versus alone conditions (Allen et al., 1991). These discrepancies may reflect factors that alter the interpersonal meaning of support manipulations. Social support usually conveys acceptance, but it can also pose a threat to status by implying an evaluation of competence or a judgment that the recipient is not capable (Trobst, 2000). Studies where support providers are in a position to evaluate recipients do not find beneficial effects on CVR (e.g., Allen et al., 1991), whereas studies that minimize potential evaluation do find such effects (e.g., Fontana et al., 1999; Kors, Linden, and Gerin, 1997). Closer, more supportive friends produce larger reductions in CVR (Fontana et al., 1999; Kors et al., 1997), perhaps because they are less likely to pose evaluative threats.

In studies of critical or supportive social stimuli, the interpersonal meaning or "impact message" (Kiesler, 1996) is a key determinant of CVR, as illustrated by two recent studies in our laboratory that used circumplex assessments. In the first (Gallo et al., 2000), young women performed a stressful speaking task and received supportive, neutral, or hostile comments from the experimenter. On the IAS-R scales, women rated the supportive experimenter as clearly friendly and significantly more so than the neutral experimenter; they rated the hostile experimenter as quite hostile and much more so (and somewhat more dominant) than the neutral one. The hostile experimenter produced greater CVR, as compared to the neutral condition. Further, appraisals of the experimenter's friendliness versus hostility (but not dominance versus submissiveness) mediated (Baron and Kenny, 1986) these effects. Compared to the neutral experimenter, the supportive stimulus attenuated electrodermal response (i.e., skin conductance) but not CVR, and appraisals of the experimenter's friendliness (but not dominance) again accounted for these effects.

The IAS-R ratings were useful in verifying the effectiveness and specificity of the social manipulations, and the mediational analyses provided information as to which aspects of the social stimuli were responsible for the physiological effects.

In the second study (Smith et al., 2001), we examined mental representations of support. From several perspectives (Lakey and Drew, 1997), support can reduce stress not only through actual transactions but also through activation of its internal representations. That is, activated support schema should also attenuate CVR. Therefore, we asked participants to write about and then contemplate their interactions with either a casual acquaintance or a close and supportive friend or family member. After completing IMI-C ratings of the targets, they underwent an evaluative speech stressor. As expected, participants rated supportive ties as much friendlier and slightly less dominant than acquaintances. Prior activation of supportive ties attenuated CVR during the stressor. However, IMI ratings of the target did not mediate the effects of support. Instead, effects of support on anxiety during the stressor accounted for effects on CVR. Hence, beneficial effects of support on CVR can occur through internal representations of affiliative ties.

Hostile and Supportive Social Behavior
Expressions of social behavior along the horizontal axis also affect CVR. However, anger expression has produced inconsistent results. For example, participants who described previous anger-arousing events in a mood-congruent manner (i.e., vehemently) displayed greater CVR than those in a mood-incongruent manner (i.e., quietly) or those who simply reviewed the event silently (Siegman and Snow, 1997). However, in another recent study, participants who described anger-provoking incidents in mood-congruent speech (i.e., loud and rapid) displayed *less* CVR than those who described them in a mood incongruent manner (i.e., soft and slow; Drummond and Quah, 2001). Similarly, Anderson and Lawler (1995) found that women who recalled an anger-provoking experience and expressed anger assertively displayed less CVR than those who suppressed anger. As we discuss below, some of these inconsistencies may be due to the interpersonal meaning of anger expression and the match (or mismatch) between expression and the individuals' preferred response to anger (i.e., anger-in versus anger-out). Further, some research indicates that anger expression promotes faster recovery from CVR, suggesting that the expression and inhibition of angry behaviors could have differing effects over time (Brosschot and Thayer, 1998).

The effects of expressions of friendliness have received far less attention. In one study (Nealey et al., 1998), we assigned women to one of three interactions with a video-taped partner. In a control condition, they took turns describing their daily schedule. Other participants provided support (e.g., expressions of empathy) to a partner who described a problem (i.e., recent breakup of a relationship). In the third, participants debated the partner. Relative to controls, the support task evoked greater sympathetic cardiac activation (i.e., reductions in pre-ejection period). Compared to debate, providing support evoked larger increases in cardiac output and smaller increases in peripheral resistance. This pattern of CVR converges with participants' ratings of the support task as challenging as opposed to threatening (Blascovich and Tomaka, 1996), and therefore may not be unhealthy. However, recurring efforts to provide support could be physiologically taxing, perhaps contributing to the negative health effects of caregiving (Schulz and Beach, 1999).

Individual Differences in Hostility and Friendliness

Interpersonal traits along the horizontal axis have been studied frequently. Individual differences in perceived support can be seen as a personality characteristic (Pierce, et al., 1997), but this trait has been examined less frequently in relation to CVR than have experimentally manipulated supportive stimuli. Broadwell and Light (1999) found that participants reporting high family support displayed less CVR during stressful marital interactions than did those with low support. Uchino et al. (1992) found that age and social support interacted to affect CVR, such that individuals low in support evidenced greater age-related increases in reactivity. However, other studies report more complex effects. We found that the effects of individual differences in perceived support varied across social contexts (Gallo et al., 2000). Compared to women with lower perceived support, those with higher support showed attenuated CVR to stress in a supportive context (i.e., a friendly experimenter), but trait support was associated with heightened reactivity in a provoking context.

Numerous studies find that individuals with high levels of trait hostility exhibit heightened CV and neuroendocrine responses to social but not non-social stressors (see Smith and Gallo, 2001, for a review). This effect occurs in men (e.g., Suarez et al., 1998) and women (e.g., Suarez et al., 1993). The specific social stimuli evoking greater CVR in hostile persons include harassment (e.g., Powch and Houston, 1996), social conflicts (Hardy and Smith, 1988) and disagreement (Smith and Allred, 1989). Hostility is associated with CVR during marital interactions, but more so for men than women (Smith and Brown, 1991). For example, we found that hostile husbands engaged in a current events discussion under conditions of high (but not low) evaluative threat displayed larger increases in systolic blood pressure (Smith and Gallo, 1999). Wives' IAS-R ratings of their husbands' dominance during the interaction followed a similar pattern; in the high (but not low) threat condition wives rated hostile husbands as asserting more dominance than low hostile husbands. Perhaps hostile husbands responded to this agency stressor with an effortful assertion of their status, with corresponding effects on CVR.

Hostility is also associated with heightened CVR in response to less antagonistic social stressors, such as self-disclosure to a confederate (Christensen and Smith, 1993), perhaps because of perceived vulnerability and threat of embarrassment. Finally, two studies evaluating the joint effects of trait hostility and manipulations of support showed that hostile individuals did not show reduced CVR when strangers (Lepore, 1995) or friends (Smith et al., 2000b) provided social support during a laboratory stress task, whereas non-hostile persons did display this beneficial effect. Hence, hostility may promote CVR not only by potentiating responses to stressful social stimuli, but also by undermining the effects of support.

Other research has focused on individual differences in the tendency to suppress versus express anger. Studies of simple associations of "anger-in" and "anger-out" with CVR have produced inconsistent results. Sometimes anger-out is associated with increased CVR (e.g., Burns and Katkin, 1993), whereas in other studies anger suppression is associated with greater reactivity (Vogele et al., 1997). These inconsistencies could be due to the use of tasks that are not conceptually related to anger expression (e.g., mental arithmetic without harassment). In studies with more relevant stressors, variations in the specific social context may be important. For example, Engebretson et al. (1989) found that mismatches between individual differences in anger expression and situational requirements for aggressive responding were associated with heightened CVR. We recently found that individual differences in anger expression (i.e., "anger-out") are associated with self-reports of hostile dominance in the circumplex, whereas anger suppression (i.e., "anger-in") is associated with hostile submissiveness. The general association of these styles with CVR could be due to the fact that they are both associated with unfriendliness and the tendency to become angry. The situational differences in their association with CVR could reflect the moderating impact of dominant versus submissive social styles. Individuals may find it more difficult or unpleasant to behave in a manner that is inconsistent with their typical interpersonal style. Conceptualization and assessment of both the individual differences and aspects of the evoking situation in the circumplex framework could reconcile some of these inconsistent findings.

Stable Social Situations Differing in Hostility versus Friendliness

Stable aspects of social situations also affect CVR, especially in close relationships. Spouses in marriages high in conflict or low in satisfaction display heightened CVR during marital interaction (e.g., Broadwell and Light, 1999; Ewart et al., 1991). Marital conflict may be especially problematic for women, who tend to display larger physiological stress responses than men (Ewart et al., 1991). In two studies (Smith and Brown, 1991; Smith and Gallo, 1999), we found that wives disagreeing with husbands who were high in trait hostility displayed greater CVR than did wives with low hostile husbands. Thus, individuals in marriages high in conflict may be more vulnerable to CHD through the experience of more frequent and severe CVR, and sex differences in this response might explain the fact that marriage confers a smaller reduction in CHD risk for women than for men (Kiecolt-Glaser and Newton, 2001).

Summary

Social stimuli, behavior, individual differences, and stable situations related to the horizontal axis of the circumplex affect CVR. A consistent pattern emerges; the right pole of the horizontal axis is associated with reduced reactivity and the left pole with heightened CVR. Contradictory findings likely reflect moderating variables or procedural factors that produce complex or unintended social manipulations. Circumplex assessments of social behavior and context could help to reconcile the conflicting findings.

The Vertical Axis

Compared to CVR effects of the affiliation axis, there is far less research on the dominance circumplex axis. Yet, as noted above, human and animal studies suggest this dimension of social interaction influences CHD. The available studies of dominance suggest that this dimension is important in the social psychophysiology of CVR, as well.

Dominant and Submissive Social Stimuli

Some studies indicate that the dominance versus submissiveness of interaction partners influences CVR. Interactions with high status experimenters evoke greater CVR than do equal status experimenters (Kleinke and Williams, 1994). Newton et al. (1999) found that participants interacting with previously unacquainted partners who scored high in trait dominance (i.e., agency) displayed greater CVR than did those interacting with submissive partners. To confirm this apparent effect of dominant social stimuli, we asked participants to engage in a role-played interaction in which they attempted to return a recently purchased defective item. They responded to a pre-recorded audiotape of either a submissive or dominant sales person. Participants' IAS-R ratings of the clerk confirmed the effectiveness of the manipulation. Further, interactions with the dominant partner evoked greater blood pressure reactivity than did the submissive partner (Burgess et al., 2001). Several factors could account for effects of dominant social stimuli on CVR. For example, interactions with dominant partners could be more difficult or more threatening.

Competitive tasks have implications for gaining and losing status and can be placed along the vertical axis. Competitive games – compared to non-competitive tasks – evoke greater CVR (e.g., Harrison et al., 2001; Van Egeren, 1979). Similarly, evaluative threat – such as expectations that important competencies will be tested – involves status motivations, and hence this social stimulus falls on the vertical axis. Compared to non-evaluative conditions, evaluative threat also evokes greater CVR (e.g., Kelsey et al., 2000; Smith et al., 1997).

Expressions of Dominance during Social Interaction

Impressed by atherogenic effects of asserting dominance in primate research, several years ago we began studying effortful attempts to influence others. The basic paradigm manipulates incentives to influence an interaction partner. In the first study (Smith et al., 1989), we asked pairs of previously unacquainted male undergraduates to take opposite sides in a current events discussion. Unbeknownst to secondary participants, primary participants were told (1) that the number of times their name was entered in a lottery drawing would be determined by chance or (2) that their lottery chances would be determined by their success in persuading their partner (i.e., his pre to post-discussion attitude change). Participants attempting to persuade displayed greater CVR than did those in the simple discussion. In subsequent studies, we demonstrated this effect in men and women, and while participants silently prepared and actively engaged in influence attempts (Smith et al., 1989; 1990; 1997; 2000a). Further, the magnitude of this effect varies positively with incentive magnitude (Smith et al., 1989), and as a curvilinear function of the difficulty of influence (Smith et al., 1990). These effects of incentive magnitude and task difficulty are well established in the traditional non-social literature on CVR.

To test these effects in established relationships, we assigned married couples to a condition where their odds in a lottery would be determined by chance (discussion condition) or to one in which both spouses were told that their chances would depend on the extent to which they persuaded their partner (influence condition) (Brown and Smith, 1992). Circumplex-based behavioral ratings (Benjamin, 1974) confirmed that husbands and wives in the influence condition displayed more controlling behavior than in the discussion condition, but only husbands displayed greater CVR while they prepared and delivered their influence attempt. Because efforts to exert influence heightened CVR in men and women equally in our prior studies, we concluded that the marital context had attenuated the effect in women.

We recently used impedance cardiography to assess determinants of CVR evoked during influence attempts (Smith et al., 2000a). As depicted in Figure 13.3, incentives to influence a discussion partner increased CVR both before and during the interaction. Efforts to exert influence also increased cardiac output and reduced pre-ejection period, reflecting heightened sympathetic activation of the heart. As noted above, this mechanism has been implicated in the non-human primate model of social dominance and CAD. Interestingly, efforts to exert influence also decreased parasympathetic activity (i.e., respiratory sinus arrhythmia – RSA).

Individual Differences in Dominance
The few studies of the relationship between the personality trait of dominance versus submissiveness and CVR find significant associations. Newton et al. (1999) found that individual differences in agency were positively associated with CVR during social interactions. Harrison et al. (2001) similarly found that individual differences in competitiveness were positively associated with CVR during a car racing game. This latter finding is consistent with studies in which Type A behavior predicts CVR during challenging tasks (Houston, 1988), as competitiveness is a central element of the pattern.

Dominance versus Submissiveness as Social Context
In analyses of our study of influence in married couples (Brown et al., 1998), we used husbands' and wives' responses to circumplex-based scales to assess dominance and submissiveness as an element of social context – in this case their roles in the relationship. Husbands' and wives' independent ratings of relative dominance in the relationship converged significantly. Further, we found a curvilinear association between an index of "relative spouse dominance" and CVR during the interaction task. Spouses who were either clearly dominant or submissive displayed smaller increases in blood pressure than did those at intermediate levels. We interpreted these results as reflecting

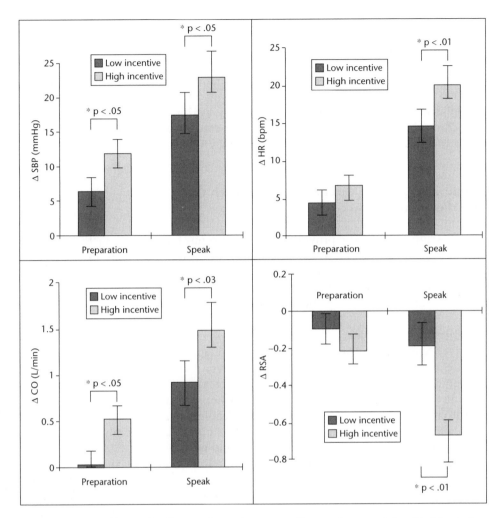

Figure 13.3   Effects of influence incentive on cardiovascular reactivity (Smith et al., 2000).

the impact of perceived difficulty of asserting oneself. That is, dominant spouses likely find asserting an opinion relatively easy, whereas submissive spouses find it more difficult. On the basis of prior research (e.g., Smith et al., 1990), we expected that very low and very high levels of difficulty would evoke smaller increases in blood pressure than would intermediate levels. Increasing levels of task difficulty require more effort (and as a result, produce more CVR), up until the point that the task is seen as so difficult that success is unlikely and additional effort not justified. The reduced effort expenditure evokes lower levels of CVR (Wright and Kirby, 2001). However, we did not measure perceived difficulty and effort. Nonetheless, the vertical axis of the circumplex is apparently an important contextual influence on CVR.

Summary of the Vertical Axis Findings
The dominance versus submissiveness dimension is clearly related to CVR, consistent with the role of dominance as a CHD risk factor. Expressing dominance evokes heightened CVR, and dominant individuals tend to display greater reactivity. Interactions with dominant individuals, competition, and social evaluation evoke heightened reactivity, perhaps because of activation of concerns about status. Finally, dominance versus submissiveness as a characteristic of relationships may also influence CVR.

Limitations of the Circumplex Approach to Cardiovascular Reactivity

The circumplex clearly provides useful concepts for organizing the diverse literature on the social psychophysiology of CVR, as well as methods for difficult but essential aspects of this research. However, the approach has limitations. One lies outside of the interpersonal perspective, whereas the other involves one of its major assumptions.

Alternatives to the Primary Axes
In the circumplex, hostility and friendliness are opposite ends of one continuum, as are dominance and submissiveness. However, Uchino and colleagues (2001) suggest that positivity (i.e., friendliness, support) and negativity (i.e., hostility, conflict) are separate relationship dimensions. Further, co-occurrence of positivity and negativity – a constellation labeled *ambivalence* – may be independently associated with CVR and risk. In an ambulatory study, interactions with partners rated high in both positivity and negativity were associated with the highest levels of systolic blood pressure (Holt-Lunstad et al., 2000). Similarly, Benjamin (1974) suggests that the opposite of expressing dominance or control is not submission but granting autonomy to others; the opposite of submission is not dominance, but asserting one's own autonomy. Dominance and submissiveness may both be more physiologically taxing than autonomy, as they reflect engagement in potentially stressful interpersonal processes. Hence, the psychophysiological correlates of two additional interpersonal concepts – ambivalence and autonomy – require further research.

Reactivity versus Exposure
Finally, most studies of social determinants of CVR examine responses to a single stressor. Some models of stress and the interpersonal perspective itself suggest that this focus is too narrow. Bolger and Zuckerman (1995) have shown that *reactivity* to stressors and the degree of *exposure* to stressors are independent mechanisms through which personality traits (e.g., negative affectivity) determine adjustment. Negative emotion in daily life is influenced by the degree of both reactivity and exposure to stressors, and neuroticism influences both processes. The transactional cycle suggests that personality characteristics influence not only the degree of CVR to stressors but also the

frequency and severity of exposure. Hence, studies of reactivity to controlled experimental stressors address only one way in which psychosocial characteristics impact CVR and risk.

These effects are illustrated in Figure 13.4. Individuals with hostile-dominant and friendly interpersonal styles are depicted in the upper and lower portions of the figure. In the laboratory (left side), a hostile-dominant person displays greater CVR than a friendly person to a controlled stressor

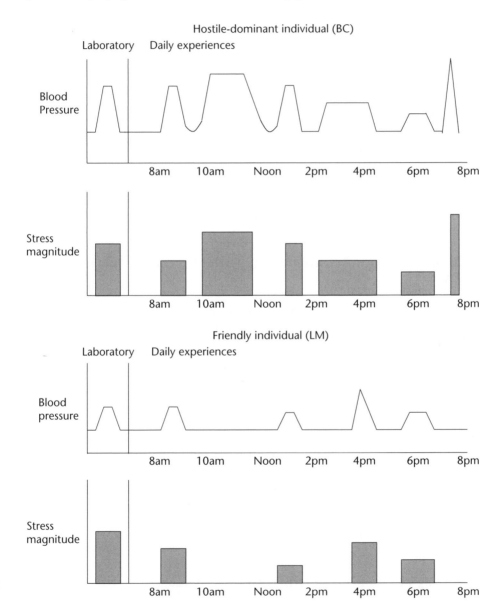

Figure 13.4   Stress reactivity and exposure as determinants of cardiovascular response (adapted from Smith and Rhodewalt, 1986).

(e.g., conflict). Once outside the laboratory, the hostile-dominant person again responds with greater CVR than the agreeable person when they face the same stressor, such as the unpleasantries of heavy morning traffic. However, overall CVR displayed during daily activities is greater for the hostile-dominant individual not only because of this greater response to equivalent stressors, but also because of exposure to more frequent, severe, and prolonged stressors. Through appraisals of ambiguous social stimuli as challenges or threats, selection of more confrontational situations, and aggressive responses, the hostile-dominant person likely creates increased exposure to physiologically taxing events. Hence, models of social determinants of CVR must include processes underlying exposure to interpersonal stressors (Friedman, Chapter 1 of this volume; Suls and Sanders, 1989).

Future Directions

These limitations suggest avenues for research. Exploring effects on CVR of distinctions within the control and affiliation dimensions, and assessing stress exposure and CVR in daily life will contribute to a more complete view of how this mechanism links psychosocial characteristics and CHD. There are other implications of the interpersonal perspective.

A Guide to Future Research on the Social Psychophysiology of CVR

The four circumplexes – social stimuli, social behaviors, individual differences, and stable social environments – as well as combinations (e.g., individual difference by social stimuli designs) provide a taxonomy of interpersonal determinants of CVR. Placing the available research in this framework identifies areas where little prior work (e.g., effects of providing support), or methodological limitations and inconsistent findings (e.g., effects of anger expression) create a need for additional studies. In such efforts, circumplex-based assessments will be useful. In the often-neglected task of construct validation of psychosocial risk factor assessments, well-validated circumplex measures can facilitate an integrated literature on their similarities and differences. The circumplex model is a unique resource, as it provides a common framework for characteristics of persons and social environments. Further, when modeling the associations among social stimuli, social responses and CVR, circumplex assessments offer standardized tests of the effectiveness and specificity of manipulations (Smith et al., 1996; 1998).

Modeling Mechanisms in Other Risk Factors

The interpersonal view is useful in examining mechanisms underlying risk factors that are not typically thought to involve social processes. For example, individual differences in optimism versus pessimism and the related construct of hopelessness predict the development and course of CHD (Everson et al., 1996; Scheier et al., 1999). These traits are generally conceptualized as intra-individual, self-regulatory variables. However, we found that optimism was correlated with IAS-R self-ratings of friendly dominance. Further, optimists reported lower levels of social stressors (e.g., marital conflict), and wives of optimistic husbands displayed less CVR during a marital conflict discussion than did wives of pessimists (Smith and Ruiz, 2000). Hence, interpersonal consequences of optimism may contribute to its salubrious effects.

Jobs with high demand and low control and those involving an asymmetry between personal efforts and rewards confer increased CHD risk (Peter and Siegrist, 2000). Conceptually, these work experiences can be located in the circumplex. As aspects of job stress, support from supervisors, colleagues, or inherent in the general work environment falls on the horizontal axis. Low control and decision latitude implies a subordinate position in a hierarchical relationship and can be placed on the vertical axis. Recently, we asked a sample of 80 working adults to complete an IMI-C about their co-workers. Well-validated measures of job stress were associated with perceiving co-workers as controlling and unfriendly. Thus, the circumplex provides a nomological net for understanding job characteristics and CHD risk.

Socioeconomic status (SES) is a multi-dimensional construct variably defined according to resources or prestige in relation to others (Krieger et al., 1997). SES can be measured at the level of individuals, households, or communities (Krieger et al., 1997) and each appears to influence health (e.g., Diez-Roux et al., 1997; Lynch, et al., 2000), especially the development and course of CHD (Gonzalez et al., 1998; Kaplan and Keil, 1993). SES shapes social experiences in ways that affect health. Low SES is associated with social experiences related to the horizontal circumplex axis, such as a less affiliative interpersonal style (e.g., Barefoot et al., 1991) and less perceived support and social integration (Bosma et al., 1999). On the vertical axis, low SES persons may be placed in low status positions relative to others, perhaps prompting feelings of inferiority and difficult efforts to assert status. These experiences likely begin early in development and recur across the life-span. Therefore, the low SES context or environments could shape repeating interpersonal cycles that contribute to high-risk psychosocial trajectories (c.f., Singer and Ryff, 1999). Further, interpersonal experiences and their physiological consequences may account for some of the effect of SES on CHD (Anderson and Armstead, 1995).

Comprehensive views of psychosocial influences on CHD and the mechanisms underlying their effects must attend to and integrate the multiple levels of the biopsychosocial model (Engel, 1977). The concepts and methods of the interpersonal perspective are useful in organizing, directing, and strengthening research on the connections between psychosocial processes and physiological mechanisms. This approach may also be useful in describing the co-occurrence of personality and social risk factors (Gallo and Smith, 1999), and in articulating the interpersonal experiences through which broader social-economic and cultural risk factors come to affect the physiology of individuals.

Authors' Note

Correspondence concerning this chapter should be sent to: Timothy W. Smith, PhD, Department of Psychology, University of Utah, 390 South 1530 East (Rm 502), Salt Lake City, UT 84112, USA; e-mail: tim.smith@psych.utah.edu

References

Allen, K. M., Blascovich, J., Tomaka, J., and Kelsey, R. M. (1991). Presence of human friends and pet dogs as moderators of autonomic responses to stress in women. *Journal of Personality and Social Psychology*, 61, 582–9.

American Heart Association (2001). *2001 Heart and Stroke Statistical Update*. Dallas, TX: American Heart Association.

Andersen, N. B., and Armstead, C. A. (1995). Toward understanding the association of socioeconomic status and health: A new challenge for the biopsychosocial approach. *Psychosomatic Medicine*, 57, 213–25.

Anderson, S. F., and Lawler, K. A. (1995). The anger recall interview and cardiovascular reactivity in women: An examination of context and experience. *Journal of Psychosomatic Research*, 39, 335–43.

Barefoot, J. C., Dahlstrom, G., and Williams, R. B. (1983). Hostility, CHD incidence, and total mortality: A 25-year follow-up study of 255 physicians. *Psychosomatic Medicine*, 45, 59–63.

Barefoot, J. C., Peterson, B. L., Dahlstrom, W. G., Siegler, I. C., Anderson, N. B., Williams, R. B. Jr. (1991). Hostility patterns and health implications: correlates of Cook-Medley Hostility Scale scores in a national survey. *Health Psychology*, 10, 18–24.

Barnett, P. A., Spence, J. D., Manuck, S. B., and Jennings, J. R. (1997). Psychological stress and the progression of carotid artery disease. *Journal of Hypertension*, 15, 49–55.

Baron, R. M., and Kenney, D. A. (1986). The moderator-mediator variable distinction in social psychological research: Conceptual, strategic, and statistical considerations. *Journal of Personality and Social Psychology*, 51, 1173–82.

Benjamin, L. S. (1974). Structural analysis of social behavior. *Psychological Review*, 81, 392–425.

Berkman, L. F. (1995). The role of social relations in health promotion. *Psychosomatic Medicine*, 57, 245–54.

Blascovich, J., and Tomaka, J. (1996). The biopsychosocial model of arousal regulation. *Advances in Experimental Social Psychology*, 28, 1–51.

Bolger, N., and Zuckerman, A. (1995). A framework for studying personality in the stress process. *Journal of Personality and Social Psychology*, 69, 890–902.

Bongard, S., Pfeiffer, J. S., al'Absi, M., Hodapp, V., and Linenkemper, G. (1997). Cardiovascular responses during effortful active coping and acute experience of anger in women. *Psychophysiology*, 34, 459–66.

Bosma, H., van de Mheen, H. D., and Mackenbach, J. P. (1999). Social class in childhood and general health in adulthood: Questionnaire study of contribution of psychological attributes. *British Medical Journal*, 318, 18–22.

Broadwell, S. D., and Light, K. C. (1999). Family support and cardiovascular responses in married couples during conflict and other interactions. *International Journal of Behavioral Medicine*, 6, 40–63.

Brosschot, J. F., and Thayer, J. F. (1998). Anger inhibition, cardiovascular recovery, and vagal function: A model of the link between hostility and cardiovascular disease. *Annals of Behavioral Medicine*, 20, 326–32.

Brown, P. C., and Smith, T. W. (1992). Social influence, marriage, and the heart: Cardiovascular consequences of interpersonal control in husbands and wives. *Health Psychology*, 11, 88–96.

Brown, P. C., Smith, T. W., and Benjamin, L. S. (1998). Perceptions of spouse dominance predict blood pressure reactivity during marital interactions. *Annals of Behavioral Medicine*, 20, 286–93.

Brownley, K. A., Hurwitz, B. E., and Schneiderman, N. (2000). Cardiovascular psychophysiology. In J. T. Cacioppo, L. G. Tassinary, and G. G. Berntson (Eds.), *Handbook of Psychophysiology* (2nd edn., pp. 224–64). Cambridge: Cambridge University Press.

Burgess, L. M., Smith, T. W., and Henry, W. P. (2001). Interpersonal determinants of cardiovascular reactivity: Effects of partner dominance and trait agency on women's response during social interaction. Manuscript under review.

Burns, J. W., and Katkin, E. S. (1993). Psychological, situational, and gender predictors of cardiovascular reactivity to stress: A multivariate approach. *Journal of Behavioral Medicine*, 16, 445–65.

Case, R. B., Moss, A. J., Case, N., McDermott, M., and Eberly, S. (1992). Living alone after myocardial infarction: impact on prognosis. *Journal of the American Medical Association*, 267, 515–19.

Caspi, A., and Roberts, B. W. (1999). Personality continuity and change across the life course. In L. A. Pervin and O. P. John (Eds.), *Handbook of Personality: Theory and Research* (2nd edn., pp. 300–26). New York: Guilford.

Cervone, D., and Shoda, Y. (1999). *The Coherence of Personality: Social-cognitive Bases of Consistency, Variability, and Organization*. New York: Guilford Press.

Christenfeld, N., Gerin, W., Linden, W., et al. (1997). Social support effects on cardiovascular reactivity: Is a stranger as effective as a friend? *Psychosomatic Medicine*, 59, 388–98.

Christensen, A. J., and Smith, T. W. (1993). Cynical hostility and cardiovascular reactivity during self-disclosure. *Psychosomatic Medicine*, 55, 193–202.

Clark, L. A., Watson, D., and Mineka, S. (1994). Temperament, personality, and the mood and anxiety disorders. *Journal of Abnormal Psychology*, 103, 103–16.

Cohen, S., Kaplan, J., and Manuck, S. (1994). Social support and coronary heart disease: Underlying psychological and biological mechanisms. In S. A. Shumaker and S. M. Czajkowski (Eds.), *Social Support and Cardiovascular Disease* (pp. 195–222). New York: Plenum.

Costa, P. T., Jr., and McCrae, R. R. (1987). Neuroticism, somatic complaints and disease: Is the bark worse than the bite? *Journal of Personality*, 55, 299–316.

Dembroski, T. M., MacDougall, J. M., Costa, P. T., Jr., and Grandits, G. A. (1989). Components of hostility as predictors of sudden death and myocardial infarction in the Multiple Risk Factor Intervention Trial. *Psychosomatic Medicine*, 51, 514–22.

Diez-Roux, A., Nieto, F. J., Muntaner, C., et al. (1997). Neighborhood environments and coronary heart disease: a multilevel analysis. *American Journal of Epidemiology*, 146, 48–63.

Drummond, P. D., and Quah, S. H. (2001). The effect of expressing anger on cardiovascular and facial blood flow in Chinese and Caucasians. *Psychophysiology*, 38, 190–6.

Engebretson, T. O., Matthews, K. A., and Scheier, M. F. (1989). Relations between anger expression and cardiovascular reactivity: Reconciling inconsistent findings through a matching hypothesis. *Journal of Personality and Social Psychology*, 57, 513–21.

Engel, G. L. (1977). The need for a new medical model: A challenge for biomedicine. *Science*, 196, 129–36.

Everson, S. A., Goldberg, D. E., Kaplan, G. A., et al. (1996). Hopelessness and risk of mortality and incidence of myocardial infarction and cancer. *Psychosomatic Medicine*, 58, 113–21.

Everson, S. A., Kaplan, G. A., Goldberg, D. E., Salonen, R., and Salonen, J. T. (1997a). Hopelessness and 4-year progression of carotid atherosclerosis. *Arteriosclerosis, Thrombosis, and Vascular Biology*, 17, 1490–5.

Everson, S. A., Kauhanen, J., Kaplan, G. A., et al. (1997b). Hostility and increased risk of mortality and myocardial infarction: The mediating role of behavioral risk factors. *American Journal of Epidemiology*, 146, 142–52.

Ewart, C. K., Taylor, C. B., Kraemer, H. C., and Agras, W. S. (1991). High blood pressure and marital discord: Not being nasty matters more than being nice. *Health Psychology*, 10, 155–63.

Fontana, A. M., Diegman, T., Villeneuve, A., and Lepore, S. J. (1999). Nonevaluative social support reduces cardiovascular reactivity in young women during acutely stressful performance situations. *Journal of Behavioral Medicine*, 22, 75–91.

Ford, D. E., Mead, L. A., Chang, P. P., Cooper-Patrick, L., Wang, N., and Klag, M. J. (1998). Depression is a risk factor for coronary artery disease in men. *Archives of Internal Medicine*, 158, 1422–6.

Frasure-Smith, N., Lespérance, F., Juneau, M., Talajic, M., and Bourassa, M. G. (1999). Gender, depression, and one-year prognosis after myocardial infarction. *Psychosomatic Medicine*, 61, 26–37.

Gallo, L. C., and Smith, T. W. (1998). Construct validation of health-relevant personality traits: Interpersonal circumplex and five-factor model analyses of the Aggression Questionnaire. *International Journal of Behavioral Medicine*, 5, 129–47.

Gallo, L. C., and Smith, T. W. (1999). Patterns of hostility and social support: Conceptualizing psychosocial risk factors as a characteristic of the person and the environment. *Journal of Research in Personality*, 33, 281–310.

Gallo, L. C., Smith, T. W., and Kircher, J. C. (2000). Cardiovascular and electrodermal responses to support and provocation: Interpersonal methods in the study of psychophysiological reactivity. *Psychophysiology*, 37, 289–301.

Gerin, W., Milner, D., Chawla, S., and Pickering, T. G. (1995). Social support as a moderator of cardiovascular reactivity in women: A test of the direct effects and buffering hypotheses. *Psychosomatic Medicine*, 57, 16–22.

Gerin, W., Pieper, C., Levy, R., and Pickering, T. G. (1992). Social support in social interaction: A moderator of cardiovascular reactivity. *Psychosomatic Medicine*, 54, 324–36.

Goldberg, A. D., Becker, L. C., Bonsall, R., et al. (1996). Ischemic, hemodynamic, and neurohormonal responses to mental and exercise stress: Experience from the psychophysiological investigations of myocardial ischemia study (PIMI). *Circulation*, 94, 2402–9.

Gonzalez, M. A., Rodriguez, A. F., and Calero, J. R. (1998). Relationship between socioeconomic status and ischaemic heart disease in cohort and case-control studies: 1960–1993. *International Journal of Epidemiology*, 27, 350–8.

Goodman, M., Quigley, J., Moran, G., Meilman, H., and Sherman, M. (1996). Hostility predicts Restenosis after percutaneous transluminal coronary angioplasty. *Mayo Clinic Proceedings*, 71, 729–34.

Gullette, E., Blumenthal, J., and Babyak, M. (1997). Mental stress triggers myocardial ischemia during daily life. *Journal of the American Medical Association*, 277, 1521–6.

Gurtman, M. B. (1997). Studying personality traits: The circular way. In R. Plutchik and H. R. Conte (Eds.), *Circumplex Models of Personality and Emotions* (pp. 81–102). Washington, DC: American Psychological Association.

Gurtman, M. B. (2001). Interpersonal complimentarity: Integrating interpersonal measurement with interpersonal models. *Journal of Counseling Psychology*, 48, 97–110.

Hardy, J. D., and Smith, T. W. (1988). Cynical hostility and vulnerability to disease: Social support, life stress, and physiological response to conflict. *Health Psychology*, 7, 447–59.

Harrison, L. K., Denning, S., Easton, H. L., et al. (2001). The effects of competition and competitiveness on cardiovascular activity. *Psychophysiology*, 38, 601–6.

Hecker, M. H. L., Chesney, M. A., Black, G. W., and Frautchi, N. (1988). Coronary-prone behaviors in the Western Collaborative Group Study. *Psychosomatic Medicine*, 50, 153–64.

Helgeson, V. S. (1994). Relation of agency and communion to well-being: Evidence and potential explanations. *Psychological Bulletin*, 116, 412–28.

Helmers, K. F., Krantz, D. S., Howell, R., Klein, J., Bairey, N., and Rozanski, A. (1993). Hostility and myocardial ischemia in coronary artery disease patients: Evaluation by gender and ischemic index. *Psychosomatic Medicine*, 50, 29–36.

Holt-Lunstad, J., Uchino, B. N., and Smith, T. W. (2000). *Relationship Quality Predicts Ambulatory Blood Pressure during Social Interactions*. Society for Psychophysiological Research.

Horsten, M., Mittleman, M. A., Wamala, S. P., Schenck-Gustafsson, K., and Orth-Gomer, K. (2000). Depressive symptoms and lack of social integration in relation to prognosis of CHD in middle-aged women. The Stockholm Female Coronary Risk Study. *European Heart Journal*, 21, 1072–80.

House, J. S., Umberson, D., and Landis, K. R. (1988). Structures and processes of social support. *American Review of Sociology*, 14, 293–318.

Houston, B. K. (1988). Cardiovascular and neuroendocrine reactivity, global Type A, and components of Type A behavior. In B. K. Houston and C. R. Snyder (Eds.), *Type A Behavior Pattern: Research, Theory, and Intervention* (pp. 212–53). New York: Wiley.

Houston, B. K., Babyak, M. A., Chesney, M. A., Black, G., and Ragland, D. R. (1997). Social dominance and 22-year all-cause mortality in men. *Psychosomatic Medicine*, 59, 5–12.

Iribarren, C., Sidney, S., Bild, D. E., et al. (2000). Association of hostility with coronary artery calcification in young adults: The CARDIA study. *Journal of the American Medical Association*, 283, 2546–51.

Ironson, G., Taylor, C. B., Boltwood, M., et al. (1992). Effects of anger on left ventricular ejection fraction in coronary disease. *American Journal of Cardiology*, 70, 281–5.

Jenkinson, C. M., Madeley, R. J., Mitchell, J. R. A., and Turner, I. D. (1993). The influence of psychosocial function on survival after myocardial infarction. *Public Health*, 107, 305–17.

Joiner, T., and Coyne, J. C. (1999). *The Interactional Nature of Depression: Advances in Interpersonal Approaches*. Washington, DC: American Psychological Association.

Kamarck, T. W., Debski, T. T., and Manuck, S. B. (2000). Enhancing the laboratory-to-life generalizability of cardiovascular reactivity using multiple occasions of measurement. *Psychophysiology*, 37, 533–42.

Kamarck, T. W., Peterman, A. H., and Raynor, D. A. (1998). The effects of the social environment on stress-related cardiovascular activation: Current findings, prospects, and implications. *Annals of Behavioral Medicine*, 20, 247–25.

Kaplan, G. A., and Keil, J. E. (1993). Socioeconomic factors and cardiovascular disease: A review of the literature. *Circulation*, 88, 1973–98.

Kaplan, J. R., and Manuck, S. B. (1998). Monkeys, aggression, and the pathobiology of atherosclerosis. *Aggressive Behavior*, 24, 323–34.

Kawachi, I., Sparrow, D., Spiro, A., Vokonas, P., and Weiss, S. T. (1996). A prospective study of anger and coronary heart disease. The Normative Aging Study. *Circulation*, 94, 2090–5.

Kelsey, R. M., Blascovich, J., Leitten, C. L., Schneider, T. R., Tomaka, J., and Weins, S. (2000). Cardiovascular reactivity and adaptation to recurrent psychological stress: Moderating effects of evaluative observation. *Psychophysiology*, 37, 748–56.

Kiecolt-Glaser, J. K., and Newton, T. L. (2001). Marriage and health: His and hers. *Psychological Bulletin*, 127, 472–503.

Kiesler, D. J. (1996). *Contemporary Interpersonal Theory and Research: Personality, Psychopathology, and Psychotherapy*. New York: John Wiley and Sons.

Kiesler, D. J., Schmidt, J. A., and Wagner, C. C. (1997). A circumplex inventory of impact messages: An operational bridge between emotion and interpersonal behavior. In R. Plutchik and H. R. Conte (Eds.), *Circumplex Models of Personality and Emotions* (pp. 221–44). Washington, DC: American Psychological Association.

Kleinke, C. L., and Williams, G. (1994). Effects of interviewer status, touch, and gender on cardiovascular reactivity. *Journal of Social Psychology*, 134, 247–9.

Kors, D. J., Linden, W., and Gerin, W. (1997). Evaluation interferes with social support: Effects on cardiovascular stress reactivity in women. *Journal of Social and Clinical Psychology*. 16, 1–23.

Krantz, D. S., Helmers, K. F., Bairey, C. N., Nebel, L. E., Hedges, S. M., and Rosanski, A. (1991). Cardiovascular reactivity and mental stress-induced myocardial ischemia in patients with coronary artery disease. *Psychosomatic Medicine*, 53, 1–12.

Krieger, N., Williams, D. R., and Moss, N. E. (1997). Measuring social class in US public health research: Concepts, methodologies, and guidelines. *Annual Review of Public Health*, 18, 341–78.

Lakey, B., and Drew, J. B. (1997). A social-cognitive perspective on social support. In G. R. Pierce, B. Lakey, I. G. Sarason, and B. R. Sarason (Eds.), *Sourcebook of Social Support and Personality* (pp. 107–40). New York: Plenum Press.

Leary, T. (1957). *Interpersonal Diagnosis of Personality*. New York: Ronald.

Lepore, S. J. (1995). Cynicism, social support, and cardiovascular reactivity. *Health Psychology*, 14, 210–16.

Lepore, S. J. (1998). Problems and prospects for the social support-reactivity hypothesis. *Annals of Behavioral Medicine*, 20, 257–69.

Lynch, J. W., Smith, G. D., Kaplan, G. A., and House, J. S. (2000). Income inequality and mortality: importance to health of individual income, psychosocial environment, or material conditions. *British Medical Journal*, 320, 1200–4.

Matthews, K. A., Owens, J. F., Kuller, L. H., Sutton-Tyrell, K., Lassila, H. C., and Wolfson, S. K. (1998). Stress-induced pulse-pressure changes predict women's carotid atherosclerosis. *Stroke*, 29, 1525–30.

Mayou, R. A., Gill, D., Thompson, D. R., Day, A., Hicks, N., and Volmink, J. (2000). Depression and anxiety as predictors of outcome after myocardial infarction. *Psychosomatic Medicine*, 62, 212–19.

McCrae, R. R., and John, O. P. (1992). An introduction to the Five-Factor Model and its applications. *Journal of Personality*, 60, 175–216.

Miller, T. Q., Smith, T. W., Turner, C. W., Guijarro, M. L., and Hallet, A. J. (1996). A meta-analytic review of research on hostility and physical health. *Psychological Bulletin*, 119, 322–48.

Mischel, W., and Shoda, Y. (1999). Integrating dispositions and processing dynamics within a unified theory of personality: The cognitive-affective personality system. In

L. A. Pervin and O. P. John (Eds.), *Handbook of Personality: Theory and Research* (2nd edn., pp. 197–218). New York: Guilford Press.

Möller, J., Hallqvist, J., Diderichsen, F., Theorell, T., Reuterwall, C., and Ahlbom, A. (1999). Do episodes of anger trigger myocardial infarction? A case-crossover analysis in the Stockholm Heart Epidemiology Program (SHEEP). *Psychosomatic Medicine*, 61, 842–9.

Nealey, J. B., Smith, T. W., and Uchino, B. N. (2002). Cardiovascular responses to agency and communion stressors in young women. *Journal of Research in Personality*, 36, 395–418.

Newton, T. L., Bane, C. M., Flores, A., and Greenfield, J. (1999). Dominance, gender, and cardiovascular reactivity during social interaction. *Psychophysiology*, 36, 245–52.

Orth-Gomer, K., Rosengren, A., and Wilhelmsen, L. (1993). Lack of social support and incidence of coronary heart disease in middle-aged Swedish men. *Psychosomatic Medicine*, 55, 37–43.

Orth-Gomer, K., Wamala, S. P., Horsten, M., Schenck-Gustafsson, K., Schneiderman, N., and Mittleman, M. A. (2000). Marital stress worsens prognosis in women with coronary heart disease: The Stockholm Female Coronary Risk Study. *Journal of the American Medical Association*, 284, 3008–14.

Penninx, B. W. J. H., Beekman, A. T. F., Honig, A., et al. (2001). Depression and cardiac mortality: Results from a community-based longitudinal study. *Archives of General Psychiatry*, 58, 221–7.

Peter, R., and Siegrist, J. (2000). Psychosocial work environment and the risk of coronary heart disease *International Archives of Occupational and Environmental Health*, 73, S41–5.

Pierce, G. R., Lakey, B., Sarason, I., Sarason, B., and Joseph, H. (1997). Personality and social support processes: A conceptual overview. In G. R. Pierce, B. Lakey, I. Sarason, and B. Sarason (Eds.), *Sourcebook of Social Support and Personality* (pp. 19–47). New York: Plenum.

Powch, I. G., and Houston, B. K. (1996). Hostility, anger-in, and cardiovascular re-activity in white women. *Health Psychology*, 15, 200–8.

Rozanski, A., Blumenthal, J. A., and Kaplan, J. (1999). Impact of psychological factors on the pathogenesis of cardiovascular disease and implications for therapy. *Circulation*, 99, 2192–2217.

Ruiz, J. M., Smith, T. W., Nealey, J. B., Hawkins, M., Uno, D., and Uchino, B. N. (2001). *From Seeing Red to Feeling Blue: Differentiating Negative Affects in Interpersonal Contexts*. Paper presented at the meeting of the Society for Personality and Social Psychology, San Antonio.

Santor, D. A., and Coyne, J. C. (2001). Evaluating the continuity of symptomatology between depressed and nondepressed individuals. *Journal of Abnormal Psychology*, 110, 216–25.

Sarason, B. R., Sarason, I. G., and Pierce, G. R. (1990). Traditional views of social support and their impact on assessment. In idem. (Eds.), *Social Support: An Interactional View* (pp. 9–25). New York: John Wiley and Sons.

Scheier, M. F., Matthews, K. A., Owens, J. F., et al. (1999). Optimism and rehospit-alization after coronary artery bypass graft surgery. *Archives of Internal Medicine*, 159, 829–33.

Schulz, R., and Beach, S. R. (1999). Caregiving as a risk factor for mortality: The care-giver health effects study. *Journal of the American Medical Association*, 282, 2215–19.

Sheffield, D., and Carroll, D. (1994). Social support and cardiovascular reactions to active laboratory stressors. *Psychology and Health*, 9, 305–16.

Shively, C. A., Clarkson, T. B., and Kaplan, J. R. (1989). Social deprivation and coronary artery atherosclerosis in female cynomolgus monkeys. *Atherosclerosis*, 77, 69–76.

Siegman, A. W., Kubzansky, L. D., Kawachi, I., Boyle, S., Vokonas, P. S., and Sparrow, D. (2000a). A prospective study of dominance and coronary heart disease in the normative aging study. *American Journal of Cardiology*, 86, 145–9.

Siegman, A. W., and Snow, S. C. (1997). The outward expression of anger, the inward experience of anger and CVR: The role of vocal expression. *Journal of Behavioral Medicine*, 20, 29–45.

Siegman, A. W., Townsend, S. T., Civelek, A. C., and Blumenthal, R. S. (2000b). Antagonistic behavior, dominance, hostility, and coronary heart disease. *Psychosomatic Medicine*, 62, 248–57.

Singer, B., and Ryff, C. D. (1999). Hierarchies of life histories and associated health risks. *Annals of the New York Academy of Sciences*, 896, 96–115.

Skantze, H. B., Kaplan, J., Pettersson, K., et al. (1998). Psychosocial stress causes endothelial injury in cynomolgus monkeys via B1-adrenoceptor activation. *Atherosclerosis*, 136, 153–61.

Smith, T. W. (1994). Concepts and methods in the study of anger, hostility, and health. In A. W. Siegman and T. W. Smith (Eds.), *Anger, Hostility and the Heart* (pp. 23–42). Hillsdale, NJ: Lawrence Erlbaum.

Smith, T. W., and Allred, K. D. (1989). Blood pressure responses during social interaction in high and low cynically hostile males. *Journal of Behavioral Medicine*, 12, 135–43.

Smith, T. W., Allred, K. D., Morrison, C. A., and Carlson, S. D. (1989). Cardiovascular reactivity and interpersonal influence: Active coping in a social context. *Journal of Personality and Social Psychology*, 56, 209–18.

Smith, T. W., Baldwin, M., and Christensen, A. J. (1990). Interpersonal influence as active coping: Effects of task difficulty on cardiovascular reactivity. *Psychophysiology*, 27, 429–37.

Smith, T. W., and Brown, P. W. (1991). Cynical hostility, attempts to exert social control, and cardiovascular reactivity in married couples. *Journal of Behavioral Medicine*, 14, 581–92.

Smith, T. W., and Gallo, L. C. (1999). Hostility and cardiovascular reactivity during marital interaction. *Psychosomatic Medicine*, 61, 436–45.

Smith, T. W., and Gallo, L. C. (2001). Personality traits as risk factors for physical illness. In A. Baum, T. Revenson and J. Singer (Eds.), *Handbook of Health Psychology* (pp. 139–72). Hillsdale, NJ: Lawrence Erlbaum.

Smith, T. W., Gallo, L. C., Goble, L., Ngu, L. Q., and Stark, K. A. (1998). Agency, communion, and cardiovascular reactivity during marital interaction. *Health Psychology*, 17, 537–45.

Smith, T. W., Limon, J. P., Gallo, L. C., and Ngu, L. Q. (1996). Interpersonal control and cardiovascular reactivity: Goals, behavioral expression, and the moderating effects of sex. *Journal of Personality and Social Psychology*, 70, 1012–24.

Smith, T. W., Nealey, J. B., Kircher, J. C., and Limon, J. P. (1997). Social determinants of cardiovascular reactivity: Effects of incentive to exert influence and evaluative threat. *Psychophysiology*, 34, 65–73.

Smith, T. W., and Rhodewalt, F. (1986). On states, traits, and processes: A transactional alternative to individual difference assumptions in Type A behavior and physiological reactivity. *Journal of Research in Personality*, 20, 229–51.

Smith, T. W., and Ruiz, J. M. (2000). *On the Bright Side of Love and Work: Optimism in Social Context*. Paper presented at the meeting of the Society of Personality and Social Psychology, San Antonio.

Smith, T. W., Ruiz, J. M., and Uchino, B. N. (2000a). Vigilance, active coping, and cardiovascular reactivity during social interaction in young men. *Health Psychology*, 19, 382–92.

Smith, T. W., Ruiz, J. M., and Uchino, B. N. (2001). Mental activation of supportive ties reduces blood pressure reactivity to stress. Presented at the Annual Meeting of the American Psychosomatic Society, Monterey, CA, March 7–10, 2001. *Psychosomatic Medicine*, 63, 114.

Smith, T. W., Uno, D., Uchino, B. N. and Ruiz, J. M. (2000b). *Hostility, Social Support from Friends, and Blood Pressure Reactivity in Young Women.* Society for Psychophysiological Research.

Smith, T. W., and Williams, P. G. (1992). Personality and health: Advantages and limitations of the five factor model. *Journal of Personality*, 60, 395–423.

Strong, J. P., Malcom, G. T., McMahan, C. A., et al. (1999). Prevalence and extent of atherosclerosis in adolescents and young adults: Implications for prevention from the pathobiological determinants of atherosclerosis in youth study. *Journal of the American Medical Association*, 281, 727–35.

Suarez, E. C., Harlan, E., Peoples, M. C., and Williams, R. B. (1993). Cardiovascular and emotional responses in women: The role of hostility and harassment. *Health Psychology*, 12, 459–68.

Suarez, E. C., Kuhn, C. M., Schanberg, S. M., Williams, R. B., and Zimmermann, E. A. (1998). Neuroendocrine, cardiovascular, and emotional responses of hostile men: The role of interpersonal challenge. *Psychosomatic Medicine*, 60, 78–88.

Sullivan, H. S. (1953). *The Interpersonal Theory of Psychiatry.* New York: Norton.

Suls, J., and Sanders, G. (1989). Why do some behavioral styles place people at coronary risk? In A. W. Siegman and T. M. Dembroski (Eds.), *In Search of Coronary-prone Behavior: Beyond Type A* (pp. 1–20). Hillsdale, NJ: Lawrence Erlbaum.

Trapnell, P. D., and Wiggins, J. S. (1990). Extension of the Interpersonal Adjective Scales to include the big five dimensions of personality. *Journal of Personality and Social Psychology*, 59, 781–90.

Trobst, K. (2000). An interpersonal conceptualization and quantification of social support transactions. *Personality and Social Psychology Bulletin*, 26, 971–86.

Tuzcu, E. M., Kapadia, S. R., Tutar, E., et al. (2001). High prevalence of coronary atherosclerosis in asymptomatic teenagers and young adults: Evidence from intravascular ultrasound. *Circulation*, 103, 2705–10.

Uchino, B. N., Kiecolt-Glaser, J., and Cacioppo, J. T. (1992). Age-related changes in cardiovascular response as a function of a chronic stressor and social support. *Journal of Personality and Social Psychology*, 63, 839–46.

Uchino, B. N., and Garvey, T. S. (1997). The availability of social support reduces cardiovascular reactivity to acute psychological stress. *Journal of Behavioral Medicine*, 20, 15–26.

Uchino, B. N., Holt-Lunstead, J., Uno, D., and Flinders, J. B. (2001). Heterogeneity in the social networks of young and older adults: Prediction of mental health and cardiovascular reactivity during acute stress. *Journal of Behavioral Medicine*, 24, 361–82.

Van Egeren, L. F. (1979). Cardiovascular changes during social competition in a mixed-motive game. *Journal of Personality and Social Psychology*, 37, 858–64.

Verrier, R. L., Hagestad, E. L., and Lown, B., (1987). Delayed myocardial ischemia induced by anger. *Circulation*, 75, 249–54.

Vogele, C., Jarvis, A., and Cheeseman, K. (1997). Anger suppression, reactivity, and hypertension risk: Gender makes a difference. *Annals of Behavioral Medicine*, 19, 61–9.

Von Kanel, R., Mills, P. J., Fainman, C., and Dimsdale, J. E. (2001). Effects of psychological stress and psychiatric disorders on blood coagulation and fibrinolysis: A biobehavioral pathway to coronary artery disease? *Psychosomatic Medicine*, 63, 531–44.

Watson, D., Clark, L. A., and Harkness, A. R. (1994). Structures of personality and their relevance to psychopathology. *Journal of Abnormal Psychology*, 103, 18–31.

Watson, D., and Clark, L. A. (1984). Negative affectivity: The disposition to experience aversive emotional states. *Psychological Bulletin*, 96, 465–90.

Welin, C., Lappas, G., and Wilhelmsen, L. (2000). Independent importance of psychosocial factors for prognosis after myocardial infarction. *Journal of Internal Medicine*, 247, 629–39.

Whiteman, M. C., Dreary, I. J., and Fowkes, G. R. (2000). Personality and social predictors of atherosclerotic progression: Edinburgh Artery Study. *Psychosomatic Medicine*, 62, 703–14.

Wiggins, J. S., Trapnell, P., and Philips, N. (1988). Psychometric and geometric characteristics of the revised Interpersonal Adjective Scales (IAS-R). *Multivariate Behavioral Research*, 23, 517–30.

Wiggins, J. S., and Trapnell, P. D. (1996). A dyadic-interactional perspective on the five-factor model. In J. S. Wiggins (Ed.), *The Five-factor Model of Personality* (pp. 88–162). New York: Guilford Press.

Williams, J. E., Paton, C. C., Siegler, I. C., Eigenbrodt, M. L., Nieto, F. J., and Tyroler, H. A. (2000). Anger proneness predicts coronary heart disease risk: Prospective analysis from the Atherosclerosis Risk in Communities (ARIC) study. *Circulation*, 101, 2034–9.

Wright, R. A., and Kirby, L. D. (2001). Effort determination of cardiovascular response: An integrative analysis with application in social psychology. In M. Zanna (Ed.), *Advances in Experimental Social Psychology*. San Diego, CA: Academic Press.

CHAPTER 14

Gender-related Traits and Health

Vicki S. Helgeson

Carnegie Mellon University

Introduction

Sex differences in cognitive domains, such as mathematical ability, and social domains, such as moral development, continue to be hotly debated, but there is widespread agreement that there are sex differences in health and that the size of these differences are substantive. To start with, women live longer than men (Hoyert et al., 1999). In fact, men are more likely than women to die of each of the ten leading causes of death, which include heart disease, cancer, accidents, and stroke (Hoyert et al., 1999). However, while living, women's health appears to be worse than that of men. Women suffer from more acute illnesses and more nonfatal chronic illnesses compared to men (Verbrugge, 1989). Thus, at any given point in time, women are more likely than men to be ill and to be living with a chronic disease. Women report more disability than men – more days spent in bed due to illness and more days in which they restrict their activities due to illness compared to men (Cleary et al., 1982; Kandrack et al., 1991; Verbrugge, 1989). Women also suffer from more painful disorders compared to men (Berkley, 1997; Macintyre et al., 1996; Unruh, 1996), and women perceive their health to be worse than men (Arber and Ginn, 1993; Cleary et al., 1982; Denton and Walters, 1999). Women suffer twice the rate of depression as men (Culbertson, 1997; Nolen-Hoeksema, 1987), yet men are roughly four times as likely as women to commit suicide (US Department of Justice, 1998).

There are numerous explanations for these differences in men's and women's health. Because many of these sex differences either emerge during the course of development, as in the case of depression, or have emerged over the course of the twentieth century, as in the case of the widening sex difference in longevity, genetic or other biological factors have limited explanatory power. Thus, investigators have turned to social and cultural explanations. One appealing social explanation is gender-role socialization – the idea that men and women have been socialized in different ways which then impacts on their health.

One way that gender role socialization has been studied is by focusing on traits that are more common in one sex than the other. These gender-related traits have historically been referred to as psychological masculinity and femininity. The measurement of psychological masculinity and femininity has a century-long history but two of the most widely-used instruments were developed in the 1970s and are still commonly used today – the Bem Sex Role Inventory (BSRI; Bem, 1974) and the Personal Attributes Questionnaire (PAQ; Spence et al., 1974). These are self-report inventories in which people rate the extent to which a number of personality traits characterize themselves. More recently researchers have realized that masculinity and femininity are multidimensional constructs and that these instruments only tap one aspect of masculinity and femininity, namely agency or instrumentality and communion or expressivity (Spence, 1984).

Agency and communion are two fundamental ways of relating to the world. These constructs were first discussed by Bakan (1966) in his book, *The Duality of Human Existence*. Agency reflects one's existence as an individual, and communion reflects the participation of the individual in a larger organism of which the individual is a part. Agency includes self-protection, self-assertion, self-expansion, self-control, and self-direction and emphasizes the forming of separations. Communion includes group participation, cooperation, attachment, and connections and emphasizes the creation of unions. More succinctly, agency represents a focus on the self and separation, whereas communion represents a focus on others and connection. Bakan also linked these two principles to gender. He stated that both agency and communion are present in men and women but that agency is more characteristic of men and communion is more characteristic of women: "I propose for consideration that what we have been referring to as agency is more characteristically masculine, and what we have been referring to as communion is more characteristically feminine" (Bakan, 1966: 110). There is empirical evidence that Bakan's assertion is correct. Sex differences on measures of agency and communion are quite consistent (Bem, 1974; Spence and Helmreich, 1978). Men tend to score higher than women on measures of agency, and women tend to score higher than men on measures of communion. These differences hold across cultures (e.g., Ajdukovic and Kljaic, 1984; Runge et al., 1981).

Sex differences in agency and communion are supported by other work that has shown men and women have different ways of construing themselves. Men are more likely to describe themselves in terms of their independence from others (e.g., emphasizing personal attributes and skills), whereas women are more likely to describe themselves in terms of their connection to others (e.g., emphasizing roles and relationships to others; Cross and Madson, 1997). Men maintain an independent sense of self that is separate from others, whereas women maintain an interdependent sense of self in which others are integrated into the self (Clancy and Dollinger, 1993; Cross and Madson, 1997). There also is evidence that men's self-esteem is linked to independence and differentiation from others, whereas women's self-esteem is linked to their connections with others (Josephs et al., 1992; Stein et al., 1992). Thus, there is substantive reason to believe that men are more likely than women to be characterized by an agentic orientation and women are more likely than men to be characterized by a communal orientation.

Alice Eagly (1987) argues that sex differences in agency and communion stem from the traditional social roles that men and women hold in society. Women's social roles are primarily nurturant or communal roles, as women take care of and raise children. Men's social roles are primarily agentic or instrumental in that they are the primary breadwinners of families. Eagly argues that it is this division of labor in society that is responsible for linking agency to men and communion to women. In fact, Eagly argues that when men's and women's roles are more similar, sex differences in agency and communion are minimized. In one study, homemakers – regardless of whether they were male or female – were perceived to be more communal and less agentic than people who held full-time jobs outside the home (Eagly and Steffen, 1984).

Agency and communion, however, do little to explain sex differences in health. The agency (formerly known as masculinity) scale of the PAQ consists of traits such as independence, persistence, competitiveness, and self-confidence. The communion (formerly known as femininity) scale of the PAQ consists of traits such as warm in relations with others, helpful, and emotional. These are socially desirable dimensions of gender roles that are unrelated to indicators of poor health. Agency reflects a positive orientation toward the self, and communion reflects a positive orientation toward others.

Communion, in particular, is virtually unrelated to any health outcome. One meta-analytic review of the literature showed that communion was un-related to indicators of mental health (Bassoff and Glass, 1982), whereas another showed that communion had a small *positive* relation to psychological well-being (Whitley, 1984). In more recent studies, communion has been unrelated to psychological or physical functioning in studies of adolescents (Horwitz and White, 1987), college students (Aube et al., 1995), cardiac patients (Fritz, 2000; Helgeson, 1993), women with breast cancer (Helgeson, 2000; Piro, 1998), women with rheumatoid arthritis (Trudeau et al., 1999), and adolescents with diabetes (Helgeson and Fritz, 1996). Thus, communion cannot explain women's greater health problems than men, in particular why women are more depressed than men.

Agency is associated with health but in a positive direction. Agency is consistently associated with high self-esteem (Helgeson and Fritz, 1999; see Whitley, 1983, for a review), positive mental health (Aube et al., 1995; Berg et al., 1991; Bowers, 1999; see Helgeson, 1994, for a review; Horwitz and White, 1987; Saragovi et al., 1997; Trudeau et al., 1999), and fewer physical symptoms (Heiser and Gannon, 1984; Robbins et al., 1991). Agency also has been associated with positive adjustment to illnesses, such as prostate cancer (Helgeson and Lepore, 1997), breast cancer (Piro, 1998), heart disease (Helgeson, 1993; Fritz, 2000), and rheumatoid arthritis (Trudeau et al., 1999). Thus, agency cannot explain any of men's poor health outcomes.

I have argued that agency and communion are broad personality traits that do little to explain men's and women's health difficulties. I have also argued that agency and communion share some overlap with two other traits – unmitigated agency and unmitigated communion – which are more useful when studying health (Helgeson, 1994; Helgeson and Fritz, 1998; 1999). Unmitigated agency is a form of agency, in that there is some shared focus on the self. But the unmitigated agency individual's focus on the self is unhealthy in that it reflects self-absorption. Unmitigated agency, unlike agency, lacks a focus on others. Unmitigated agency is explicitly defined as a focus on the self to the exclusion of others. Unmitigated communion is a form of communion, in that there is some shared focus on others. But the unmitigated communion individual's focus on others is unhealthy because it stems from a need for self-esteem rather than from a genuine concern about others' welfare. The focus on others leads to self-neglect for the unmitigated communion individual. Unmitigated communion is explicitly defined as a focus on others to the exclusion of the self. Both orientations reflect the result of the extreme of one orientation gone awry. Unmitigated agency and un-mitigated communion are measured by self-report inventories. Unmitigated agency consists of a set of 8 bipolar scales that contain personality traits. Unmitigated communion consists of 9 statements with which respondents agree or disagree.

Although agency and communion are independent constructs that are em-pirically uncorrelated (Spence and Helmreich, 1978), unmitigated agency and unmitigated communion reveal predictable relations to both agency and com-munion. Unmitigated agency reveals a small positive correlation with agency, reflecting the self-focus, but an inverse association with communion, reflect-ing the absence of a focus on others (Helgeson and Fritz, 1998; Piro, 1998; Willard, 1996). Unmitigated communion reveals a positive correlation with communion, reflecting the focus on others, but an inverse correlation with agency, reflecting the absence of a focus on the self (Helgeson and Fritz, 1998; Piro, 1998; Willard, 1996).

Despite the fact that unmitigated agency and unmitigated communion are associated with agency and communion, unmitigated agency and unmitigated communion cannot be defined by or reduced to some combination of agency and communion scores. Unmitigated agency and unmitigated communion are much more narrow constructs than agency and communion. They only tap the essence of agency and communion. The person characterized by unmitig-ated agency is hostile, cynical, and self-absorbed. This person has a negative view of others and the world. Someone who is high in an agentic trait, such as self-confidence, and low on a communal trait, such as helpfulness is not *necessarily* characterized by unmitigated agency. The person characterized by unmitigated communion becomes overly involved in others' problems to the neglect of the self. Someone who is high on a communal trait, such as warm in relations with others, and low on an agentic trait, such as making decisions easily, is not *necessarily* characterized by unmitigated communion. Aside from this conceptual point, there also is empirical evidence that unmitigated agency and unmitigated communion cannot be reduced to some combination of agency and communion when predicting health outcomes (Helgeson and Fritz, 1999).

Like agency and communion, it is certainly possible that Eagly's (1987) social role theory has implications for the development of unmitigated agency and unmitigated communion. There are many social roles that women inhabit that involve caretaking. Women are not only primary caretakers of children but they also take care of elderly parents and other ill family members. Many of women's common positions of employment – nurse, teacher, social workers – are also communal roles. Exposure to multiple caretaking roles in society and reinforcement of these roles could certainly lead to the overly nurturant orientation that underlies unmitigated communion.

Many of men's social roles in society involve leadership, dominance, and even aggression. The military role was a position that used to be limited to men. More aggressive sports are exclusively male. Among positions of paid employment, men are more likely than women to hold leadership positions and positions of power, as evidenced by the fact that 996 of the top 1,000 corporations in the United States were headed by men in 1996 (Valian, 1998). It is certainly possible that preparation for these kinds of roles can lead to the development of traits such as aggression, emotional inhibition, self-focus, and preservation of the self that characterizes unmitigated agency.

The goal of this chapter is two-fold: (1) to link unmitigated communion and unmitigated agency to health outcomes, and (2) to examine mechanisms that might explain these associations.

Unmitigated Communion and Health

Evidence

Unmitigated communion has been linked to depressive symptoms among college students (Fritz and Helgeson, 1998), healthy adults (Fritz and Helgeson, 1998), cardiac patients (Fritz, 2000; Helgeson, 1993; Helgeson and Fritz, 1999), women with breast cancer (Helgeson, 2000), women with rheumatoid arthritis (Trudeau et al., 1999), healthy adolescents (Fritz and Helgeson, 1998), and adolescents with diabetes (Helgeson and Fritz, 1996). Recall that communion is unrelated to depression. Thus, it is not merely orienting oneself toward others that is unhealthy; it is a particular orientation – an orientation that places others' needs before those of the self.

Unmitigated communion also has been linked to indices of poor adjustment to illness, such as greater functional disability in women with rheumatoid arthritis (Trudeau et al., 1999), greater anxiety, lower well-being, and poor mental functioning among cardiac patients (Fritz, 2000; Helgeson, 1993; Helgeson and Fritz, 1999), poor mental and physical functioning among women with breast cancer (Helgeson, 2000), and poor psychological and physical adjustment to diabetes (Helgeson and Fritz, 1996). In longitudinal studies, un-mitigated communion has predicted an increase in depression, anxiety, and physical symptoms over time among cardiac patients (Fritz, 2000; Helgeson,

1993), an increase in depression and worsening of metabolic control among adolescents with diabetes (Helgeson and Fritz, 1996), and a decline in mental health among women with breast cancer (Helgeson, 2000). Unmitigated communion also is a better predictor of these outcomes than sex alone. For example, in a study of adolescents with diabetes, sex differences in depression disappeared when unmitigated communion was entered into the equation (Helgeson and Fritz, 1996).

Explanations for Unmitigated Communion and Poor Health

There are two sets of explanations for the link of unmitigated communion to health. The first set has to do with the unmitigated communion individual's orientation to others and the second set has to do with the unmitigated communion individual's orientation to the self. Although I discuss these two categories of explanations separately, I do so only for organizational purposes. There is a great deal of overlap between the two categories of explanations.

Orientation to Others

Many of the explanations as to why the unmitigated communion person is psychologically distressed and adjusts poorly to illness have to do with the way that a person characterized by this trait behaves in relationships with others. First, they provide support to others. Support provision is taxing for the unmitigated communion individual, partly due to the sheer amount of support provided but also due to the fact that they take on other people's problems as their own. That is, the nature of unmitigated communion may lead to both greater *exposure* to others' problems and also to greater *vulnerability* to others' problems. Second, unmitigated communion individuals behave in relationships in inappropriate ways. They are overly nurturant, intrusive and controlling. Third, despite all of the support provided to others, they do not necessarily receive support in turn. Unmitigated communion people do not perceive that others are available to meet their needs. Relationships are imbalanced. A fourth problem that the unmitigated communion person has is not seeking support. They are unlikely to ask for help from network members to cope with stressful events. This may be one reason that they do not receive support from others. Fifth, unmitigated communion individuals report higher levels of conflict in their relationships. A conceptual model that integrates the inter-relatedness of these explanations is shown in Figure 14.1.

Support Provision
Unmitigated communion is related to providing support to others. Thus, one reason for a link to poor health has to do with the mere burden of taking care of others or being exposed to others' problems. This work is reminiscent of Kessler's research on the "costs of caring" (Kessler et al., 1985) and Gove's

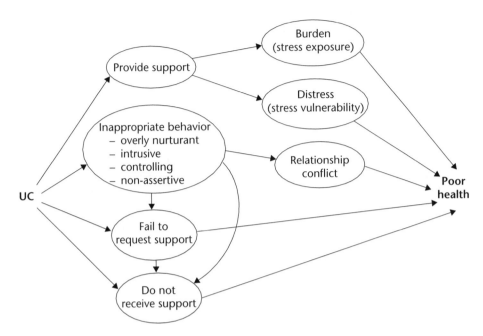

Figure 14.1   Conceptual model of the relation of unmitigated communion (UC) to problems in the "orientation to others."

"nurturant role hypothesis" (Gove, 1984; Gove and Hughes, 1979). Kessler and colleagues argued that there are costs associated with caring for other people. One cost is that taking care of others can interfere with taking care of oneself. Another cost is that becoming involved in others' problems can increase one's own distress. According to the nurturant role hypothesis, women's roles require them to attend to the needs of others, and taking care of others interferes with taking care of oneself. First, the nurturant role leads to caretaking behavior, which results in fatigue and vulnerability to illness. Second, the nurturant role leads to greater exposure to communicable disease. Finally, once sick, the nurturant role prevents one from taking care of oneself. Unmitigated communion may be a personality trait that underlies these social role explanations.

Many studies have linked unmitigated communion to support provision (see Helgeson and Fritz, 1998, for a review). Support provision was examined recently in a study of college freshmen. We examined their relationships with family and friends from home as well as the newly formed friendships at college. Unmitigated communion was associated with providing support to family and friends from home prior to college arrival and then to an increase in support provision to family and friends from home after arrival at college (Helgeson and Fritz, 2000). Unmitigated communion also was associated with an increase in providing support to friends at college over the course of the first semester.

Support provision may be especially problematic for unmitigated communion individuals in the context of a chronic illness because they are taking care of others at exactly the time when they should be attending to their own needs. Studies of patients who have sustained a cardiac event have shown that unmitigated communion is associated with providing support to network members and to an increase in support provision during the first few months after hospital discharge (Helgeson, 1993; Helgeson and Fritz, 1995).

There is evidence that providing support to others explains some of the relation of unmitigated communion to poor health outcomes. In a study of cardiac patients and spouses, providing assistance to the patient explained part of the relation of spouse unmitigated communion to spouse distress (Helgeson, 1993). In a study of freshmen college students, those who scored high on unmitigated communion reported that their efforts to help others interfered with their studies. Here it is not health that suffers but an aspect of tending to one's own needs. Unmitigated communion was linked to a decline in grades between the middle and end of the semester (Valenti, 1997). Providing support to others explained this relation.

Why is support provision hazardous for unmitigated communion individuals? One reason is that they do so much of it. This is the *exposure* explanation. Because unmitigated communion individuals seek out others to help, they may be exposed to more problems than other people. A second reason that helping others is problematic is that unmitigated communion people take on others' problems as their own. That is, unmitigated communion may be associated with being more strongly affected by other peoples' problems. This is the *vulnerability* explanation. Because unmitigated communion individuals are so involved with others, an event that occurs to someone else may be construed by the unmitigated communion individual as his or her own personal event. The exposure hypothesis suggests that unmitigated communion individuals will identify more stressful events that happen to others when asked to recall their own stressful life events. The vulnerability hypothesis suggests that unmitigated communion individuals will report being more strongly affected by stressful events that occur to others. Note that Kessler and McLeod (1984) tested whether exposure or vulnerability to relationship stressors best explained sex differences in depression. Across five epidemiologic studies, there was more support for the idea that women's vulnerability to relationship stressors rather than women's exposure to these kinds of stressors explained the sex difference in depression.

Both exposure and vulnerability ideas have received some support with respect to unmitigated communion. In one study, university staff reviewed a list of stressful life events twice, once with respect to whether the event occurred to them and once with respect to whether the event occurred to someone in their network (Helgeson and Fritz, 1998). Unmitigated communion was *not* related to the number of personal stressors but was marginally related to the number of stressful events that happened to others. This supports the exposure hypothesis. Unmitigated communion also was associated with being more strongly affected by those network events, which supports the vulnerability hypothesis. A study of adolescents with diabetes showed a link between unmitigated communion and vulnerability to interpersonal stressors (Helgeson and Fritz, 1996). Unmitigated communion was

not associated with a greater number of interpersonal stressors but was associated with being more strongly affected by relationship stressors. It is important
to point out that unmitigated communion individuals were not more strongly
affected by other categories of stressful events. The impact of relationship
stressors explained the association of unmitigated communion to depression
and poor metabolic control. Thus, one reason that unmitigated communion
individuals are distressed and may be less likely to take care of themselves is
because they are more adversely affected by stressful events that involve
relationships.

Other support for the vulnerability hypothesis comes from research that
shows unmitigated communion is associated with worrying about other people's
problems. In two laboratory studies, one person was exposed to another
person's problem. In one study, the person with the problem was a friend. In
the other study, the person with the problem was a stranger, a confederate of
the experimenter. In both studies, college women characterized by unmitigated communion who listened to the problem reported more intrusive thoughts
about the problem two days later (Fritz and Helgeson, 1998). In field studies
of non-college students, unmitigated communion also has been linked to
intrusive thoughts about other people's problems. Spouses of cardiac patients
characterized by unmitigated communion reported greater intrusive thoughts
about the patient's illness (Broge, 1998); nurses who scored high in unmitigated communion reported more intrusive thoughts about patients (Bone,
1998); and university staff characterized by unmitigated communion reported
greater intrusive thoughts about a network member's problem (Helgeson and
Fritz, 1998).

It is important to point out that the concern or worry over others does not
reflect a general tendency to worry about problems. Unmitigated communion
is not linked to intrusive thoughts about one's own problems (Helgeson and
Fritz, 1998). As you will see in a later section, unmitigated communion may
be associated with an avoidance of one's own problems.

Interpersonal Difficulties
Unmitigated communion people behave inappropriately in relationships. They
are overbearing in their attempts to help others and they do not assert their
own needs. These interpersonal problems are a reflection of the two aspects
of unmitigated communion – over-involvement in others and self-neglect.
Support for these ideas has come from studying the relation of unmitigated
communion to the circumplex scales from the Inventory for Interpersonal
Problems (IIP; Horowitz et al., 1988) derived by Alden et al. (1990). In two
studies of college students, unmitigated communion was associated with being
overly nurturant in relationships, being easily exploitable, and being non-
assertive (Helgeson and Fritz, 1999). Surprisingly, unmitigated communion
was not related to the IIP measure of intrusiveness. However, a subsequent
inspection of the scale items revealed the reason. The intrusiveness scale
reflects intruding into others' affairs as well as wanting others to become
involved in your affairs by self-disclosing too much. As will be explained in
the next section, unmitigated communion individuals are unlikely to do the

latter. When we distinguished the two sets of items, we found that unmitigated communion was only linked to the items in the intrusiveness scale that reflect being intrusive into others' problems (Helgeson and Fritz, 1999). Although unmitigated communion was unrelated to the overall dominance scale, as one would expect, we considered the possibility that unmitigated communion would be associated with a particular kind of interpersonal dominance, one that reflects wanting to change others and control others. Two items on the IIP dominance scale reflect those aspects of interpersonal control. Unmitigated communion was positively associated with that two-item index (Helgeson and Fritz, 1999).

Taken collectively, all of these problems portray a person who is overly involved in others problems, intrusive, and controlling. Yet, at the same time, the person is not behaving in a way that would elicit help from others because the person has difficulty asserting his or her own needs. Thus, it appears that unmitigated communion individuals have two primary problems in interpersonal relationships. One problem stems from their over-involvement with others (overly nurturant, intrusive) and the other problem stems from neglecting the self in relationships with others (easily exploitable, non-assertive). We computed an index of self-neglect and over-involvement with others in one study of college students and found that both interpersonal difficulties mediated the relation of unmitigated communion to depressive symptoms (Fritz and Helgeson, 1998). However, only the over-involvement factor explained the relation of unmitigated communion to intrusive thoughts about others' problems. Thus, the unmitigated communion person's distress is a product of both over-involvement in others and not attending to one's own needs. But, one particular kind of distress – worry about others – is only tied to their over-involvement in others' affairs.

Social Control

In the previous section, I linked unmitigated communion to a kind of interpersonal control. One type of control that has been examined in the context of support provision is social control. Lewis and Rook (1999: 63) define social control as "interactions between social network members that entail regulation, influence, and constraint." These regulations frequently involve health behaviors. I considered the idea that unmitigated communion might be related to social control. In a previous study of cardiac patients and their spouses, patients reported that unmitigated communion spouses were overprotective and unmitigated communion spouses themselves reported being overprotective (Helgeson, 1993). This overprotective behavior could be perceived as controlling. Unmitigated communion also was associated with reminding the patient of appropriate health behaviors. To investigate the link of unmitigated communion to social control, we asked wives of men with prostate cancer how often they "remind" or "urge" their spouse to perform a number of appropriate health behaviors, such as watching what they eat, reducing caffeine, and getting more sleep. Wives who scored high on unmitigated communion were more likely to engage in social control (DeFilippo, 1998). Social control was related to greater patient distress and greater wife distress (DeFilippo,

1998; Helgeson et al., 1999). Wives' distress mediated the relation between unmitigated communion and social control. In other words, social control may have been the result of unmitigated communion spouses' distress. If one is worried about the well-being of another, one way to reduce that worry would be to ensure that the other is taking proper care of him or herself. Social control may be a more likely response to distress for unmitigated communion individuals.

Imbalanced Relationships
Most people provide as well as receive support from network members. Although unmitigated communion individuals provide a great deal of support to others, their relationships are not reciprocal. Unmitigated communion people provide support to others but do not necessarily report receiving support, or perceive that support is available. In a longitudinal study of freshmen college students that included four waves of assessment, unmitigated communion was rarely associated with reports of support receipt (Helgeson and Fritz, 2000). Even during times of stress, unmitigated communion individuals do not report that others provide support. In a study of women with breast cancer, unmitigated communion was unrelated to the perceived availability of support shortly after diagnosis (Helgeson and Fritz, 2000) and was actually associated with a decline in perceived support over time (Helgeson, 2000). In studies of cardiac patients, unmitigated communion has been unrelated to the perceived availability of support (Helgeson, 1993; Helgeson and Fritz, 1999). Because individuals who score high on unmitigated communion provide more support than others but do not necessarily receive more support in return, their relationships may be less balanced or equitable in terms of support.

There is some evidence that unmitigated communion individuals prefer this imbalance according to their self-reports. Unmitigated communion has been associated with feeling uncomfortable receiving support and having difficulty disclosing problems (Fritz and Helgeson, 1998). Why would someone prefer one-sided relationships? First, a one-sided relationship has the potential to enhance self-esteem. By providing so much to others without asking (or accepting) anything in return, one may appear altruistic in the eyes of others. Second, unmitigated communion individuals' low self-esteem may make them feel unworthy of support from others.

Help-seeking Behavior
If unmitigated communion individuals prefer one-sided relationships, it is not a surprise that they do not seek help from others. In one study, college students were asked to indicate the reasons that they would not ask others for help when they need it (Helgeson and Fritz, 2000). Unmitigated communion was associated with believing that asking others for help imposes a burden on them, that asking others for help annoys people, and that other people do not really want to help. Thus, the unmitigated communion person had reasons that focused on their concern for others (e.g., I don't want to impose a burden) but also reasons that had to do with their perception that

others regard them unfavorably (e.g., others are annoyed and others don't want to help). The latter reason may stem from the low self-esteem of the unmitigated communion individual. A study of women with rheumatoid arthritis shows that unmitigated communion people do not turn to others for help. When asked how they cope with an interpersonal stressor, those high in unmitigated communion were *less* likely to seek emotional support during times of stress (Trudeau et al., 1999). Instead, unmitigated communion was associated with self-blame, which fits with the low self-esteem of the unmitigated communion individual, and with denial, which fits with an idea introduced later – unmitigated communion individuals avoid focusing on their own problems.

Negative Interactions
Unmitigated communion also has been associated with negative interactions with network members (Helgeson, 2000; Helgeson and Fritz, 1999; 2000). This should come as no surprise given the inappropriate ways that unmitigated communion individuals behave in relationships. One unanswered question is exactly how others view the unmitigated communion individual's support attempts. Do other people first respond positively to the unmitigated communion person's helpful overtures, but then retreat when these overtures become intrusive and controlling?

   What is the nature of these negative interactions? One study suggested that conflict could resolve around others' failures to help the unmitigated communion individual. Cardiac patients who scored high on unmitigated communion perceived that network members not only did not help but interfered with their ability to make the appropriate lifestyle changes necessary to adjust to heart disease (e.g., quit smoking, eat healthy diet, reduce stress; Fritz, 2000). And, this perception of network members' interference partly explained the relation of unmitigated communion to increased depression and increased cardiac symptoms over time. The question is whether network members actively interfered with unmitigated communion patients' attempts to practice good health behavior or whether network members did not offer *unsolicited* support. The unmitigated communion person may have high expectations of others – expectations that cannot possibly be met.

Orientation to Self

Relations of unmitigated communion to poor psychological health and poor physical health are partly explained by the fact that unmitigated communion individuals are not oriented toward themselves. First, they do not regard themselves highly. Second, they do not attend to themselves, in terms of their attentional focus or in terms of taking care of their health. These ideas are not independent of the unmitigated communion person's orientation toward others. There are many ways in which the two may be related. The focus on others may lead to the neglect of the self. The lack of a positive sense of self may lead to a focus on others as a way to enhance views of the self.

Or, a focus on others may be used as a way to relieve one from focusing on the self.

Low self-esteem
Unmitigated communion is associated with low self-esteem (Fritz and Helgeson, 1998). Thus, low self-esteem may be one basis for the link of unmitigated communion to poor psychological well-being. In one study, self-esteem mediated the relation of unmitigated communion to depressive symptoms (Fritz and Helgeson, 1998). One reason that unmitigated communion individuals have low self-esteem is that they base their view of themselves upon what others think (Fritz and Helgeson, 1998). Unmitigated communion individuals not only have low-self esteem, but they may have unstable self-esteem because their feelings about themselves change in accordance with their perception of others' attitudes towards them. Unfortunately, people high in unmitigated communion often perceive that others do not evaluate them favorably (Fritz and Helgeson, 1998). Thus, a cycle is set in motion whereby unmitigated communion individuals base their self-worth on others' perceptions, perceive that others regard them unfavorably, and subsequently perceive the self in unfavorable terms. Low self-esteem persists.

Low self-esteem not only may be an explanation for the link between unmitigated communion and poor health but also may be a motivating force behind the unmitigated communion person's behavior. In other words, the unmitigated communion individual may become overly involved in others and neglect the self *because* of low self-esteem. Unmitigated communion people may help others and become enmeshed in their affairs in order to enhance their self-worth in the eyes of others. If others need them and depend on them, perhaps others will view them more favorably. This strategy is not effective, however. Although unmitigated communion people do help others, their behavior is not always perceived as helpful and others do not grant them the esteem that they desire.

Evidence that helping is so tied to unmitigated communion individuals' self-esteem comes from findings that show unmitigated communion individuals do not respond well when others do not want, need, or reject their support attempts. Unmitigated communion individuals appear to take the rejection personally. Two studies showed that unmitigated communion individuals report feeling bad about themselves when others reject their support or advice (Helgeson and Fritz, 1998; Fritz and Helgeson, 1998). Because helping is central to the self-esteem of the unmitigated communion individual, a rejection of an attempt to help is a threat to self-esteem.

Having self-esteem so closely tied to relationships with others also suggests that low self-esteem might play a role in why unmitigated communion individuals adjust poorly following the onset of an illness. One reason that unmitigated communion individuals fare poorly in the face of a chronic illness, such as cancer, heart disease, or diabetes, is that the limitations imposed on them by the illness may interfere with their caretaking responsibilities. Because caretaking is central to the self-esteem of the unmitigated communion individual, adjustment will be difficult.

Lack self-focus

The unmitigated communion personality is partly defined by not being oriented toward or focused on oneself, but is there any evidence that unmitigated communion individuals do not reflect on themselves? A student of mine investigated this issue in a laboratory study that manipulated self-focus with a mirror (Chung, 2000). We measured private self-consciousness, which reflects thinking about the self. We also measured avoiding private self-consciousness with items such as, "I am avoiding taking a hard look at myself," and "I am trying not to think about my reasons for what I am doing." Unmitigated communion individuals did not respond to the mirror manipulation by increasing private self-consciousness. Instead, unmitigated communion was associated with the *avoidance* of thoughts about the self in the presence of the mirror. There also were indications that unmitigated communion people responded to the mirror manipulation by thinking more about other people rather than themselves. First, unmitigated communion was associated with greater intrusive thoughts about other people in the mirror condition. Second, in response to a sentence completion task that assesses attentional focus (Exner, 1973), unmitigated communion people completed sentences with greater external responses in the mirror condition. Thus, unmitigated communion individuals appear to be uncomfortable focusing on themselves and respond to a self-focusing stimulus by increasing their focus on others. This finding suggests that unmitigated communion individuals may use others' problems as a way to distract them from their own problems. Alternatively, escape from one's own problems may not be the motivator but may be a side benefit from involvement in others' problems. These ideas require empirical investigation.

Poor Health Behavior

Unmitigated communion has been linked to self-reports of poor health behavior among cardiac patients (Helgeson and Fritz, 1999) and women with breast cancer (Helgeson and Fritz, 2000). Unmitigated communion also has been linked to the failure to adhere to physicians' instructions. In a study of cardiac patients, those who scored high on unmitigated communion were less likely to reduce household activities 3 months later (Helgeson, 1993). In another study of cardiac patients, those who scored high on unmitigated communion were less likely to adhere to an exercise regimen prescribed by the physician over time (Fritz, 2000). In a study of adolescents with diabetes, unmitigated communion was not linked to health behavior per se, but it was associated with poor metabolic control (Helgeson and Fritz, 1996). That is, adolescents who scored higher on unmitigated communion had worse blood glucose levels over the past few months, and blood glucose levels are at least partly determined by health behaviors.

The poor health behavior of the unmitigated communion individual stems from a general tendency to neglect the self. Indirect evidence of self-neglect appeared in a study of healthy adolescents (Helgeson and Fritz, 1998). Physical symptoms were associated with the number of health care visits for people who scored low on unmitigated communion, but there was absolutely no relation between physical symptoms and health care visits for those who scored high on unmitigated communion. One explanation for this finding is that unmitigated communion individuals are less likely than others to respond to symptoms by seeking appropriate medical attention.

If unmitigated communion individuals neglect their health, they may neglect other aspects of self-care. In a study of college students, we reasoned that unmitigated communion people's schoolwork may suffer from helping others. We found that unmitigated communion was unrelated to general study habits but that helping others interfered with the unmitigated communion person's studies (Helgeson and Fritz, 2000). That is, the unmitigated communion person reported missing class, being late for class, and not studying for exams because they were helping friends with problems.

Why don't unmitigated communion individuals take care of themselves? They may not take care of themselves because taking care of others leaves no time to tend to their own needs. Alternatively, they may not take care of themselves because they do not regard themselves as worthy of care.

Unmitigated Agency and Health

Evidence

Unmitigated agency has been linked to poor mental and physical health outcomes. Unmitigated agency has been associated with poor mental health among college students (Holahan and Spence, 1980) and to greater pathology among male psychiatric inpatients (Evans and Dinning, 1982). Although agency is strongly linked to high self-esteem (see Whitley, 1983, for a review), the relation of unmitigated agency to self-esteem is unclear. Because unmitigated agency is partly defined by having an overly inflated view of the self (e.g., egotistical, arrogant), one might expect unmitigated agency to be related to high self-esteem. However, it is always possible that the overly inflated view of the self is defensive and stems from a low self-regard. Unmitigated agency has never been related to high self-esteem. In some studies, unmitigated agency is unrelated to self-esteem (Helgeson, 1995; Spence et al., 1979) and in other studies unmitigated agency has been associated with low self-esteem (Helgeson and Fritz, 1999; Helgeson and Lepore, 2001).

In studies of people with chronic illness, unmitigated agency has been associated with poor adjustment. Two studies of men with prostate cancer have shown that unmitigated agency is linked to poor mental and physical functioning (Helgeson and Lepore, 1997; Helgeson and Lepore, 2001). A study of women with breast cancer revealed that unmitigated agency was associated with greater tension, depression, and anger (Piro, 1998). Studies of cardiac patients have linked unmitigated agency to multiple indicators of psychological distress, including anxiety, depression, and hostility, as well as lower levels of life satisfaction and general well-being (Helgeson, 1993; 1995; Helgeson and Fritz, 1999). Unmitigated agency has been linked to an important physical health outcome, a prognostic indicator of heart attack severity (Helgeson, 1990).

This latter finding makes one wonder about the link between unmitigated agency and the Type A behavior pattern, which has been referred to as the "coronary-prone personality" due to its links to heart disease (e.g., see Matthews and Haynes, 1986, for a review). Interestingly, there is some overlap between this coronary-prone personality and the traditional male gender role. List (1967) described the coronary-prone person as hiding weaknesses, inhibiting emotional expression, lacking empathy, and being homophobic. In a study of cardiac patients, I found that unmitigated agency, but not agency, was associated with Type A behavior (Helgeson, 1990). The aspects of Type A behavior that I measured were impatience and hostility. Today, research has revealed that these are the toxic components of Type A (Williams, 1989). The specific components of hostility that predict mortality in general as well as mortality from heart disease are: cynicism (i.e., negative view of people), hostile affect (i.e., anger and impatience during interactions with others), and aggressive responding (i.e., anger as a response to a problem; Barefoot et al., 1989). In a recent study of 52 college students, unmitigated agency, but not agency, was correlated with all three aspects of hostility: cynicism ($r = 0.32$, $p < 0.05$), hostile affect ($r = 0.35$, $p < 0.05$), and aggressive responding ($r = 0.32$, $p < 0.05$).

Explanations for Unmitigated Agency and Poor Health

Like unmitigated communion, the explanations for the link between unmitigated agency and poor health can be placed into two categories: those that stem from problems in the orientation to the self and those that stem from problems in the orientation toward others. Again, the two are inter-related. If the unmitigated agency person was not so self-absorbed, maybe attention would be paid to others. However, their negative view of others makes that unlikely.

Orientation to Self

The unmitigated agency person's focus is on the self. The self-focus is extreme. Traits on the unmitigated agency scale that reflect this extreme self-focus include being greedy, arrogant, boastful, and egotistical. This overly positive view of the self may instill a sense of invulnerability. Being overly self-confident in the body's capacities could cause one to refrain from taking proper care of the self. As you will see in this section, unmitigated agency individuals not only do not take proper care of themselves but they also engage in risky behaviors.

Poor Health Behavior
Unmitigated agency, like unmitigated communion, has been associated with poor health behavior. In a study of older college students, unmitigated agency was associated with a composite index of poor health behavior (Willard, 1996).

In two studies of cardiac patients, unmitigated agency was linked to composite indices of poor health behavior (Helgeson, 1993; Helgeson and Fritz,
1999). Unmitigated agency has been associated with the failure to adhere to
physicians' instructions to reduce activities, but only certain activities – those
linked to the traditional male gender role (e.g., taking out the garbage, shoveling
snow; Helgeson, 1993). In another study of cardiac patients, unmitigated
agency predicted the failure to quit smoking within 3 months of a first coronary event (Helgeson, 1995).

Health behavior can be construed more broadly as self-care. In a study of
college students, we developed an index of studiousness that consisted of taking
notes in class, attending class, paying attention in class, being on time for class,
and turning in homework on time (Helgeson and Fritz, 2000). Unmitigated
agency was associated with a lack of studiousness. By contrast, agency was
associated with higher scores on the studiousness index. In this case, unmitigated agency was associated with not taking care of one's studies.

The unmitigated agency individual's poor health behavior, however, does
not stem from benign self-neglect, as is the case with unmitigated communion. It is purposeful. There are two reasons that the unmitigated agency
person does not practice good health behavior. First, poor health behavior can
be viewed as risky behavior. Unmitigated agency is tied to risky behavior. The
overly inflated view of the self can be tied to a sense of invulnerability which
makes risk-taking possible. Unmitigated agency also may be tied to poor
health behavior because such individuals seek to violate norms – especially
when those norms are made explicit by others. Recall that unmitigated agency
was associated with the failure to adhere to physician instructions. This failure
may be the result of psychological reactance (Brehm, 1966).

Unmitigated agency individuals have a high need for control and may be
more sensitive than other individuals to threats to control. A physician who
tries to dictate how an unmitigated agency patient should behave might arouse
psychological reactance. Anecdotally, I recall interviewing a high unmitigated
agency cardiac patient who told me 3 months after hospital discharge that
he had *increased* his intake of eggs! Did he eat more eggs to prove a sense of
invulnerability? Did he purposely defy the physician because he had such a
low regard for expert information? Or did he react against the physician's
instructions to assert control?

Other evidence that psychological reactance might explain the link of unmitigated agency to non-compliance comes from work on reflective versus
reactive autonomy (Koestner et al., 1999). Reflective autonomy involves the
careful evaluation of options and then reaching a decision on one's own.
Reactive autonomy occurs when someone is compelled to act differently from
another's advice. Unmitigated agency is similar to reactive autonomy. In fact,
the measure of reactive autonomy that Koestner et al. (1999) used included
half of the traits listed on the unmitigated agency scale. Koestner et al. (1999)
distinguished reactive autonomy and reflective autonomy in a laboratory study
in which college students were given advice from credible and non-credible
sources before placing bets on horses at a track. Reflective autonomy was
associated with bets that reflected the advice of the credible source, but that

were unrelated to the advice of the non-credible source. Reactive autonomy was related to making bets that were *opposite* of those advised by the credible source and that were unrelated to the advice of the non-credible source. That is, individuals who score high in reactive autonomy did just the opposite of what an expert advised. What is interesting about these individuals is that they did not react against the advice of the non-credible source. The authors concluded that reactive autonomy individuals are motivated to reject the advice of experts because expert advice is most likely to arouse psychological reactance. The unmitigated agency person is likely to behave in a similar way. Evidence that unmitigated agency individuals may be less likely to consider information provided by experts comes from a psychoeducational intervention for men with prostate cancer (Helgeson and Lepore, 2001). Unmitigated agency was associated with less positive evaluations of the expert speakers in each of the sessions. In a study of 68 college students, unmitigated agency was associated with a self-report measure of psychological reactance ($r = 0.36$, $p < 0.01$).

Acting Out Behavior
Another reason that unmitigated agency may be linked to poor mental and physical health is that these individuals engage in acting out behavior. Spence et al. (1979) constructed a measure of acting out behavior that included using alcohol and drugs, misdemeanors such as property destruction and shoplifting, lying, and verbal and physical fighting. Unmitigated agency was associated with this index among college students. Another study of college men found a relation of unmitigated agency to using alcohol, mind-altering drugs, and tranquilizers and sedatives, especially when under stress (Snell et al., 1987). In a study of adolescents with diabetes, unmitigated agency was associated with more stressful life events that fell into the category of delinquency (Helgeson and Fritz, 2000). These events included getting into trouble at school and with the police, as well as using drugs and alcohol. Unmitigated agency also has been directly associated with alcohol use in older students (Willard, 1996) and in men with prostate cancer (Helgeson and Lepore, 2001). The latter finding has important health implications because these men are told to avoid alcohol.

Orientation to Others

Unmitigated agency individuals have a negative view of other people and do not tend to others' needs. These two issues may be related. Unmitigated agency individuals may perceive that others are not worthy of their time and attention. Not surprisingly, unmitigated agency individuals perceive that others are not available to help them in times of need. Because people have not been treated well by the unmitigated agency individual, they may not feel the need to provide the unmitigated agency person with assistance. However, there are other reasons that unmitigated agency individuals do not have support available. They do not directly ask for help and they do not indirectly

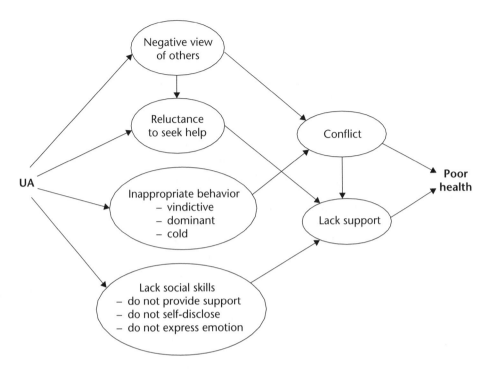

Figure 14.2 Conceptual model of the relation of unmitigated agency (UA) to problems in the "orientation to others".

ask for help by conveying concerns or distress. Thus, others may be unaware that the unmitigated agency individual needs assistance. The negative view of others and the direct disregard for others in terms of dominance and hostility also leads to conflict in relationships. A conceptual model showing unmitigated agency individuals' orientation toward others is shown in Figure 14.2.

View of Others
Unmitigated agency individuals have a negative view of other people. In a study of adolescents (described in Fritz and Helgeson, Study 1, 1998) unmitigated agency was inversely associated with Fey's (1953) Acceptance of Others Scale ($r = -0.24$, $p < 0.05$), which reflects an unfavorable view of others in general, and was also associated with a negative view of parents ($r = -0.25$, $p < 0.05$). In a study of college students (also described in Fritz and Helgeson, Study 1, 1998), unmitigated agency was associated with a negative view of others ($r = -0.54$, $p < 0.001$) as assessed by an adapted version of the Rosenberg scale (e.g., "I have a positive view of others" instead of "I have a positive view of myself"). In that same study, unmitigated agency also was inversely associated with a measure of interpersonal trust ($r = -0.35$, $p < 0.001$). These findings show that unmitigated agency individuals generally have a low opinion of other people. As previously mentioned, unmitigated agency individuals had less positive views of expert speakers in a psychoeducational intervention

for prostate cancer (Helgeson and Lepore, 2001). Interestingly, unmitigated agency was more strongly associated with negative ratings of physician presentations than other expert presentations (i.e., dietician, nurse, psychologist). This finding may reflect psychological reactance on the part of the unmitigated agency individual. Unmitigated agency people may view physicians as more credible sources and react negatively to any information that they convey.

Help-seeking

Seeking help from others is inconsistent with the hyper-independence of the unmitigated agency individual. In an ongoing study of college ($n = 150$) students, unmitigated agency individuals reported having difficulties with seeking others' help ($r = -0.17$, $p < 0.05$). In general, unmitigated agency individuals are unlikely to seek the assistance of others. In a study of freshmen college students, unmitigated agency was associated with fewer visits to the advising office during the first semester (Helgeson and Fritz, 2000). Students are expected to visit the advising office at least once to decide which classes to take the next semester. When students were asked to indicate reasons that they would not seek help in certain situations, unmitigated agency individuals were likely to say that asking others for help is a sign of weakness and that other people can't help anyway.

There are times, however, when the assistance of others is needed. Seeking medical attention for a significant health problem is one such occasion. In a study of cardiac patients, unmitigated agency was associated with longer delays between the onset of symptoms and seeking medical attention for a heart attack (Helgeson, 1990). The long delay could stem from a sense of invulnerability, a belief that symptoms could be "conquered" on one's own. Or, the long delay could stem from the unwillingness to believe that others are capable of helping.

Thus, there are two reasons that unmitigated agency individuals do not seek help. The first has to do with the orientation to the self. They view themselves as strong, self-reliant, and not in need of others. The second has to do with the orientation toward others. They view others negatively – as incapable of helping.

Problematic Social Relationships

Like the unmitigated communion individual, the unmitigated agency individual has interpersonal difficulties. As evidenced by the Inventory for Interpersonal Problems (Horowitz et al., 1988), those difficulties differ vastly from those of the unmitigated communion individual. Unmitigated agency has been linked to being vindictive, domineering, and cold in relationships with others (Helgeson and Fritz, 1999). Buss (1990) found that unmitigated agency was associated with dominant behaviors motivated by self-interest, such as manipulating others for selfish ends, refusing requests, and ordering others. Given these associations, it is not surprising that the unmitigated agency individual does not have high quality relationships.

This person has two primary problems with relationships. First, he or she is likely to lack supportive relationships. In a study of freshmen college students, unmitigated agency was associated with a decrease in perceived support from family and friends at home over time (Helgeson and Fritz, 2000). A lack of support may be especially problematic during times of stress. A study of women with breast cancer showed that unmitigated agency was associated with the perception that support was unavailable (Helgeson and Fritz, 2000). In a study of men and women with heart disease, unmitigated agency was associated with a decrease in perceived availability of support within 3 months of hospital discharge (Helgeson, 1993). In a psychoeducational intervention study for men with prostate cancer, men who scored high in unmitigated agency reported less support from family/friends and also less support from peers in the intervention group (Helgeson and Lepore, 2001). Unmitigated agency was associated with reports of receiving less encouragement and less advice during group discussions and with less satisfaction with the support received during group discussions.

The second problem that unmitigated agency individuals have with relationships is that their hostile behavior and negative view of others leads to conflict during social interactions. There is a large literature on the interpersonal consequences of a hostile personality and those consequences are negative (Smith, 1992). Unmitigated agency has been associated with negative interactions with network members in a study of women with breast cancer (Helgeson and Fritz, 2000) and in studies of cardiac patients and their spouses (Helgeson, 1993; 1995; Helgeson and Fritz, 1999). In one of those studies, negative interactions explained part of the relation between unmitigated agency and greater distress (Helgeson, 1993). In a study of women with breast cancer, unmitigated agency was associated with an index of poor interpersonal functioning, which meant problematic relationships with family, friends, and health care professionals (Piro, 1998). In a study of newly diagnosed men with prostate cancer, unmitigated agency was associated with an increase in family conflict over the first 4 months following treatment (Helgeson and Lepore, 2001).

Lack of Social Skills
Why don't unmitigated agency individuals receive support from others or perceive it to be available, and instead face social conflict? One reason is that unmitigated agency individuals lack the social skills necessary to elicit support and negotiate successful social interactions. For example, unmitigated agency individuals are not responsive to others' needs by their own admission. In an ongoing study of college students, the first wave of data collection showed that unmitigated agency is inversely associated with helping others ($r = -0.26$, $p < 0.01$). Unmitigated agency individuals also reported that they do not enjoy hearing others' problems ($r = -0.45$, $p < 0.001$), that they have difficulty providing emotional support to others ($r = -0.30$, $p < 0.001$), and that – not surprisingly – others do not disclose problems to them ($r = -0.27$, $p < 0.001$). There is other evidence that unmitigated agency people do not provide assistance to others, even when needed. In a study of cardiac spouses, those who were high in unmitigated agency were less likely to assist patients with household chores and withdrew from patients (Helgeson, 1993). Unmitigated agency persons are uncomfortable in situations where others are distressed. In a

laboratory study of problem disclosure, unmitigated agency was associated with a lack of interest in the other person's problem ($r = -0.34$, $p < 0.05$) and feeling uncomfortable listening to the problem ($r = 0.29$, $p < 0.06$; study described in Fritz and Helgeson, Study 3, 1998). There also is more objective evidence that unmitigated agency individuals do not provide support to others. In a laboratory study, one friend disclosed a problem to another friend who was provided with the opportunity to respond to the problem. Listeners who scored high in unmitigated agency were less likely to provide emotional support as indicated by objective coders who read transcripts of the conversation (Fritz et al., in press).

Another interpersonal skill required to elicit support is the disclosing of problems. In the ongoing study of college students, unmitigated agency is associated with having difficulties disclosing problems ($r = -0.17$, $p < 0.05$). In a study of cardiac patients, those who scored high in unmitigated agency were less likely to discuss their heart problem with family members (Helgeson, 1995). In a psychoeducational intervention for men with prostate cancer, men who scored high in unmitigated agency were less comfortable talking about their illness during facilitated group discussions (Helgeson and Lepore, 2001). Unmitigated agency individuals have difficulty expressing emotions. The one emotion the unmitigated agency individual does express outwardly is anger (Helgeson and Fritz, 2000), but this does not elicit support. In a study of men with prostate cancer, unmitigated agency was associated with emotional inhibition, and emotional inhibition explained most of the link of unmitigated agency to poor mental and physical functioning (Helgeson and Lepore, 1997). Network members cannot provide support to someone who is unable to communicate his or her needs.

Another issue is whether unmitigated agency individuals are unable to take advantage of support when it is available. One feature of unmitigated agency is cynicism and research has shown that cynical people do not benefit from emotional support. Lepore (1995) examined whether the presence of a supportive confederate would buffer the increase in cardiovascular reactivity that occurs in response to a stressful speech task. Support was provided by a confederate nodding and agreeing. Results showed that non-cynical people benefited from the supportive confederate but cynical people did not. The kind of support evaluated in this study was emotional support. In the prostate cancer intervention which focused primarily on education, patients who scored high on unmitigated agency seemed to benefit psychologically from the intervention compared to the control group, despite their negative evaluation of the intervention, (Helgeson and Lepore, 2001). Thus, unmitigated agency individuals may be more likely to benefit from informational than emotional support, despite their criticism of it.

Conclusions

At the beginning of this chapter, I outlined many differences between men's and women's health. The goal of this chapter was to draw the reader's attention to the possibility that traits socialized in one sex more than another might have implications for these sex differences in health. I provided evidence that unmitigated agency, more characteristic of men than women, and unmitigated communion, more characteristic of women than men, are associated with indices of poor psychological and physical well-being. I also provided a variety of explanations for these links to poor health, which can be construed as problems in one's orientation to the self and problems in one's orientation to others. The argument that I have been trying to make is that we will learn more about men's and women's health by focusing on these traits than by focusing on sex differences alone. Now it is time to examine the sex differences in health outcomes for which these traits might have implications.

The interpersonal behavior that characterizes the unmitigated communion person can be directly tied to depression. Exposure to others' problems and vulnerability to others' problems can explain the link of unmitigated communion to psychological distress. Poor health in women more generally might be tied to the fact that the unmitigated communion person has a low regard for oneself and does not take care of the self. Thus, unmitigated communion has implications for women's higher rates of depression and higher rates of morbidity, in general, compared to men.

The overly inflated view of the self and the hostile view toward the world that characterizes unmitigated agency may have implications for men's higher mortality rates compared to women. First, unmitigated agency is directly associated with behaviors that have been shown to shorten the life-span, such as using alcohol, drugs, and smoking. Unmitigated agency also is associated with risk-taking behavior in general, which could be specifically tied to men's higher mortality rates from accidents compared to women. Unmitigated agency has been linked to noncompliance, perhaps due to psychological reactance, and delays in seeking help from health care professionals, both of which might have implications for progression of disease in men. Recall that unmitigated agency was directly related to a prognostic indicator of heart attack severity (Helgeson, 1990). Second, hostility is a central feature of unmitigated agency and hostility has been strongly implicated in health, in particular heart disease (see Smith, 1992, for a review).

Obviously, it would be better for practitioners and investigators to know an individual's score on unmitigated agency and unmitigated communion rather than their sex alone when trying to identify individuals at risk for health problems. However, it is not always feasible to administer personality inventories. Sex can certainly be construed as a predisposing factor for unmitigated agency and unmitigated communion. However, it is not the case that the majority of women are high in unmitigated communion nor are the majority of men high in unmitigated agency. To the contrary, it is a minority of individuals who can be characterized by these traits. However, investigators may be sensitive to intrapersonal and interpersonal markers of the traits. A woman who has cast a wide net of caring and whose self-esteem seems to be linked to others' views of herself could be high on unmitigated communion. A man who appears to be cynical and distrusting of others, antagonistic toward advice, and overly confident in himself could be high on unmitigated agency.

In sum, there are vast differences in men's and women's health. Two traits, unmitigated agency and unmitigated communion, are differentially socialized in men and women and may explain some of these sex differences in health. Unmitigated communion is linked to an over-involvement with others to the neglect of the self which may enhance risk for depression and undermine taking care of oneself. Unmitigated agency is linked to an overly inflated view of the self and a negative view of others which may lead to risk-taking behavior, noncompliance, and a lack of supportive relationships – all of which pose serious risks to psychological and physical health.

Author's Note

Correspondence concerning this chapter should be sent to: Vicki Helgeson, Department of Psychology, Carnegie Mellon University, Pittsburgh, PA 15213, USA; e-mail: Vh2e@andrew.cmu.edu

References

Ajdukovic, D., and Kljaic, S. (1984). Personal attributes, self-esteem, and attitudes toward women: Some cross-cultural comparisons. *Studia Psychologia*, 26, 193–8.

Alden, L. E., Wiggins, J. S., and Pincus, A. L. (1990). Construction of circumplex scales for the inventory of interpersonal problems. *Journal of Personality Assessment*, 55, 521–36.

Arber, S., and Ginn, J. (1993). Gender and inequalities in health in later life. *Social Science and Medicine*, 36, 33–46.

Aube, J., Norcliffe, H., Craig, J.-A., and Koestner, R. (1995). Gender characteristics and adjustment-related outcomes: Questioning the masculinity model. *Personality and Social Psychology Bulletin*, 21, 284–95.

Bakan, D. (1966). *The Duality of Human Existence*. Chicago: Rand McNally.

Barefoot, J. C., Dodge, K. A., Peterson, B. L., Dahlstrom, W. G., and Williams, R. B. (1989). The Cook-Medley Hostility Scale: Item content and ability to predict survival. *Psychosomatic Medicine*, 51, 46–57.

Bassoff, E., and Glass, G. (1982). The relationship between sex roles and mental health: A meta-analysis of 26 studies. *The Counseling Psychologist*, 10, 105–12.

Bem, S. L. (1974). The measurement of psychological androgyny. *Journal of Consulting and Clinical Psychology*, 42(2), 155–62.

Berg, B. J., Wilson, J. F., and Weingartner, P. J. (1991). Psychological sequelae of infertility treatment: The role of gender and sex-role identification. *Social Science Medicine*, 33, 1070–80.

Berkley, K. J. (1997). Sex differences in pain. *Behavioral and Brain Sciences*, 20, 371–80.

Bone, A. D. (1998). Nurses as caregivers: Identifying some negative aspects of caregiving. Unpublished honor's thesis, Carnegie Mellon University.

Bowers, S. P. (1999). Gender role identity and the caregiving experience of widowed men. *Sex Roles*, 41, 645–55.

Brehm, J. W. (1966). *A Theory of Psychological Reactance*. New York: Academic Press.

Broge, M. M. (1998). The implications of communion and unmitigated communion for caregiver adjustment to a spouse's myocardial infarction. Unpublished honor's thesis, Carnegie Mellon University.

Buss, D. M. (1990). Unmitigated agency and unmitigated communion: An analysis of the negative components of masculinity and femininity. *Sex Roles*, 22, 555–68.

Chung, M. S. (2000). Unmitigated communion and private versus public self-consciousness: Where is the attention focused? Unpublished honor's thesis, Carnegie Mellon University.

Clancy, S. M., and Dollinger, S. J. (1993). Photographic depictions of the self: Gender and age differences in social connectedness. *Sex Roles*, 29, 477–95.

Cleary, P. D., Mechanic, D., and Greenley, J. R. (1982). Sex differences in medical care utilization: An empirical investigation. *Journal of Health and Social Behavior*, 23, 106–19.

Cross, S. E., and Madson, L. (1997). Models of the self: Self-construals and gender. *Psychological Bulletin*, 122, 5–37.

Culbertson, F. M. (1997). Depression and gender: An international review. *American Psychologist*, 52, 25–31.

DeFilippo, J. A. (1998). The effects of spouse social control on patient and spouse adjustment to prostate cancer: Who shows it and when does it help? Unpublished honor's thesis, Carnegie Mellon University.

Denton, M., and Walters, V. (1999). Gender differences in structural and behavioral determinants of health: An analysis of the social production of health. *Social Science and Medicine*, 48, 1221–35.

Eagly, A. H. (1987). *Sex Differences in Social Behavior: A Social Role Interpretation*. Hillsdale; NJ: Erlbaum.

Eagly, A. H., and Steffen, V. J. (1984). Gender stereotypes stem from the distribution of women and men into social roles. *Journal of Personality and Social Psychology*, 46, 735–54.

Evans, R. G., and Dinning, W. D. (1982). MMPI correlates of the Bem Sex Role Inventory and Extended Personal Attributes Questionnaire. *Journal of Clinical Psychology*, 38, 811–15.

Exner, J. E. (1973). The self-focus sentence completion scale: A study of egocentricity. *Journal of Personality Assessment*, 37, 437–55.

Fey, W. F. (1953). Acceptance by others and its relation to acceptance of self and others: A reevaluation. *Journal of Abnormal and Social Psychology*, 50, 274–6.

Fritz, H. L. (2000). Gender-linked personality traits predict mental health and functional status following a first coronary event. *Health Psychology*, 19, 420–8.

Fritz, H. L., and Helgeson, V. S. (1998). Distinctions of unmitigated communion from communion: Self-neglect and over involvement with others. *Journal of Personality and Social Psychology*, 75, 121–40.

Fritz, H. L., Nagurney, A., and Helgeson, V. S. (in press). The effects of partner sex, gender-related personality traits, and social support on cardiovascular reactivity during problem discourse. *Personality and Social Psychology Bulletin*.

Gove, W. R. (1984). Gender differences in mental and physical illness: The effects of fixed roles and nurturant roles. *Social Science and Medicine*, 19, 77–91.

Gove, W. R., and Hughes, M. (1979). Possible causes of the apparent sex differences in physical health: An empirical investigation. *American Sociological Review*, 44, 126–46.

Heiser, P., and Gannon, R. (1984). The relationship of sex-role stereotype to anger expression and the report of psychosomatic symptoms. *Sex Roles*, 10, 601–11.

Helgeson, V. S. (1990). The role of masculinity as a predictor of heart attack severity. *Sex Roles*, 22, 755–74.

Helgeson, V. S. (1993). Implications of agency and communion for patient and spouse adjustment to a first coronary event. *Journal of Personality and Social Psychology*, 64, 807–16.

Helgeson, V. S. (1994). Relation of agency and communion to well-being: Evidence and potential explanations. *Psychological Bulletin*, 116, 412–28.

Helgeson, V. S. (1995). Masculinity, men's roles, and coronary heart disease. In S. D. F. Gordon (Ed.), *Men's Health and Illness* (pp. 68–104). Thousand Oaks, CA: Sage Publications.

Helgeson, V. S. (2000). Psychosocial and cultural contributions to depression in women. Paper presented at the Summit on Women and Depression, Wye River Conference Center, Maryland, October.

Helgeson, V. S., and Fritz, H. L. (1995). The health consequences of an extreme "other-orientation": Unmitigated communion. Paper presented at the International Network on Personal Relationships Conference, Williamsburg, VA, June.

Helgeson, V. S., and Fritz, H. L. (1996). Implications of communion and unmitigated communion for adolescent adjustment to Type I diabetes. *Women's Health: Research on Gender, Behavior, and Policy*, 2, 169–94.

Helgeson, V. S., and Fritz, H. L. (1998). A theory of unmitigated communion. *Personality and Social Psychology Review*, 2, 173–83.

Helgeson, V. S., and Fritz, H. L. (1999). Unmitigated agency and unmitigated communion: Distinctions from agency and communion. *Journal of Research in Personality*, 33, 131–58.

Helgeson, V. S., and Fritz, H. L. (2000). The implications of unmitigated agency and unmitigated communion for domains of problem behavior. *Journal of Personality*, 68, 1031–57.

Helgeson, V. S., and Lepore, S. J. (1997). Men's adjustment to prostate cancer: The role of agency and unmitigated agency. *Sex Roles*, 37, 251–67.

Helgeson, V. S., and Lepore, S. J. (2001). Implications of unmitigated agency for support interventions for prostate cancer. Manuscript submitted for publication.

Helgeson, V. S., Lepore, S. J., and Eton, D. J. (1999). The effect of spouse social control on patient and spouse adjustment to prostate cancer. Paper presented at the Pan American Congress of Psychosocial and Behavioral Oncology, New York, October.

Holahan, C. K., and Spence, J. T. (1980). Desirable and undesirable masculine and feminine traits in counseling clients and unselected students. *Journal of Consulting and Clinical Psychology*, 48, 300–2.

Horowitz, L. M., Rosenberg, S. E., Baer, B. A., Ureno, G., and Villasenor, V. S. (1988). Inventory of Interpersonal Problems: Psychometric properties and clinical applications. *Journal of Consulting and Clinical Psychology*, 56, 885–92.

Horwitz, A. V., and White, H. R. (1987). Gender role orientations and styles of pathology among adolescents. *Journal of Health and Social Behavior*, 28, 158–70.

Hoyert, D. L., Kochanek, K. D., and Murphy, S. L. (1999). *National Vital Statistics Reports*. (Vol. 47). Washington, DC: United States Department of Health and Human Services.

Josephs, R. A., Markus, H. R., and Tafarodi, R. W. (1992). Gender and self-esteem. *Journal of Personality and Social Psychology*, 63, 391–402.

Kandrack, M. A., Grant, K. R., and Segall, A. (1991). Gender differences in health related behaviour: Some unanswered questions. *Social Science and Medicine*, 32, 579–90.

Kessler, R. C., and McLeod, J. D. (1984). Sex differences in vulnerability to undesirable life events. *American Sociological Review*, 49, 620–31.

Kessler, R. C., McLeod, J. D., and Wethington, E. (1985). The costs of caring: A perspective on the relationship between sex and psychological distress. In I. G. Sarason and B. R. Sarason (Eds.), *Social Support: Theory, Research, and Applications* (pp. 491–506). Dordrecht, The Netherlands: Martinus Nijhoff.

Koestner, R., Gingras, I., Abutaa, R., Losier, G. F., Didio, L., and Gagne, M. (1999). To follow expert advice when making a decision: An examination of reactive versus reflective autonomy. *Journal of Personality*, 67, 851–72.

Lepore, S. J. (1995). Cynicism, social support, and cardiovascular reactivity. *Health Psychology*, 14, 210–16.

Lewis, M. A., and Rook, K. S. (1999). Social control in personal relationships: Impact on health behaviors and psychological stress. *Health Psychology*, 18, 63–71.

List, J. S. (1967). *A Psychological Approach to Heart Disease*. New York: Institute of Applied Psychology.

Macintyre, S., Hunt, K., and Sweeting, H. (1996). Gender differences in health: Are things really as simple as they seem? *Social Science and Medicine*, 42, 617–24.

Matthews, K. A., and Haynes, S. G. (1986). Type A behavior pattern and coronary disease risk. *American Journal of Epidemiology*, 123, 923–60.

Nolen-Hoeksema, S. (1987). Sex differences in unipolar depression: Evidence and theory. *Psychological Bulletin*, 101, 259–82.

Piro, S. M. (1998). The relationship between agentic and communal personality traits and adjustment to breast cancer. Unpublished doctoral dissertation, Northwestern University.

Robbins, A. S., Spence, J. T., and Clark, H. (1991). Psychological determinants of health and performance: The tangled web of desirable and undesirable characteristics. *Journal of Personality and Social Psychology*, 61, 755–65.

Runge, T. E., Frey, D., Gollwitzer, P. M., Helmreich, R. L., and Spence, J. T. (1981). Masculine (instrumental) and feminine (expressive) traits: A comparison between students in the United States and West Germany. *Journal of Cross-Cultural Psychology*, 12, 142–62.

Saragovi, C., Koestner, R., Di Dio, L., and Aube, J. (1997). Agency, communion, and well-being: Extending Helgeson's (1994) model. *Journal of Personality and Social Psychology*, 73, 593–609.

Smith, T. W. (1992). Hostility and health: Current status of a psychosomatic hypothesis. *Health Psychology*, 11, 139–50.

Snell, W. E., Belk, S. S., and Hawkins, R. C. I. (1987). Alcohol and drug use in stressful times: The influence of the masculine role and sex-related personality attributes. *Sex Roles*, 16, 359–73.

Spence, J. T. (1984). Masculinity, femininity, and gender-related traits: A conceptual analysis and critique of current research. In B. A. Maher and W. B. Maher (Eds.), *Progress in Experimental Personality Research* (Vol. 13, pp. 1–97). San Diego, CA: Academic.

Spence, J. T., and Helmreich, R. (1978). *Masculinity and Femininity: Their Psychological Dimensions, Correlates, and Antecedents*. Austin, TX: University of Texas Press.

Spence, J. T., Helmreich, R. L., and Holahan, C. K. (1979). Negative and positive components of psychological masculinity and femininity and their relationship to self-reports of neurotic and acting out behaviors. *Journal of Personality and Social Psychology*, 37, 1673–82.

Spence, J. T., Helmreich, R. L., and Stapp, J. (1974). The Personal Attributes Questionnaire: A measure of sex role stereotypes and masculinity-femininity. *JSAS Catalog of Selected Documents in Psychology*, 43, Ms. no. 617.

Stein, J. A., Newcombe, M. D., and Bentler, P. M. (1992). The effect of agency and communality on self-esteem: Gender differences in longitudinal data. *Sex Roles*, 26, 465–83.

Trudeau, K. J., Danoff-Burg, S., and Revenson, T. A. (1999). Accessing agency and communion among women with rheumatoid arthritis. Paper presented at the Association of Rheumatoid Arthritis Professional, Boston, MA, November.

Unruh, A. M. (1996). Gender variations in clinical pain experience. *Pain*, 65, 123–67.

US Department of Justice, and Bureau of Justice Statistics. (1998). Table 3.142: Suicide rate (per 100,000 persons in each age group) for persons 10 years of age and older. In K. McGuire and A. L. Pastore (Eds.), *Sourcebook of Criminal Justice Statistics* (p. 299). Washington, DC: USGPO.

Valenti, M. (1997). Implications of unmitigated communion and communion for freshman adjustment to college. Unpublished honor's thesis, Carnegie Mellon University.

Valian, V. (1998). *Why So Slow?: The Advancement of Women*. Cambridge, MA: The MIT Press.

Verbrugge, L. M. (1989). The twain meet: Empirical explanations of sex differences in health and mortality. *Journal of Health and Social Behavior*, 30, 282–304.

Whitley, B. E. (1983). Sex role orientation and self-esteem: A critical meta-analytic review. *Journal of Personality and Social Psychology*, 44, 765–78.

Whitley, B. E. (1984). Sex role orientation and psychological well-being: Two meta-analyses. *Sex Roles*, 12, 207–25.

Willard, W. A. (1996). The role of unmitigated agency and unmitigated communion in physical and psychological health. Unpublished doctoral dissertation, Syracuse University.

Williams, R. (1989). *The Trusting Heart*. New York: Random House.

CHAPTER 15

Self-regulatory Processes and Responses to Health Threats: Effects of Optimism on Well-being

Michael F. Scheier

Carnegie Mellon University

and

Charles S. Carver

University of Miami

Introduction

Twenty years ago or so, we made the following statement (Carver and Scheier, 1981: 40), "Deep in his heart, one of us is a social psychologist, the other a personality psychologist." In part, we intended this statement to convey the sense that our professional lives were soundly rooted in the traditions of both experimental social psychology and personality psychology. As graduate students (and as young assistant professors), our interest was in studying the behavioral effects of self-directed attention in carefully controlled laboratory settings, and in testing the validity of the theoretical model we were trying to construct.

Two things happened as our careers unfolded. First, we came to take a broader view of the phenomena that we were trying to investigate, construing the processes influenced by self-focused attention as reflecting a broader, more general set of self-regulatory activities. Second, we developed a strong interest in applying our evolving model of behavioral self-regulation to the domain of health psychology, in order to better understand how people react to health-related threats in the manner that they do. Thus, like many of the other contributors to this volume, we began our professional lives constructing and testing mainstream social psychological theory, and then only later began applying such theory to issues involving health and well-being.

What implications do self-regulatory models have for understanding reactions to health threats? We think that the implications are many. At their core, self-regulatory models of action and experience are organized around people's efforts to attain and maintain desired conditions in their lives. These desired conditions can be relatively stable (e.g., a car that starts in the morning when you turn the ignition key, a constant body weight, good health). They can also be much more dynamic. Examples of the latter include developing a professional career, becoming involved in an interesting book, and taking a revitalizing vacation trip. Whether the person's goal is to maintain a steady state or to make something happen, the process by which the goal is realized is a process of self-regulation.

Self-regulatory efforts often run off smoothly, unimpeded by external obstructions or personal shortcomings. Sometimes, however, people encounter difficulties in doing what they want to do and being what they want to be. A younger women undergoing chemotherapy for breast cancer, for example, may lose the capacity to have a desired third child, because of the impact of the toxic chemicals on her reproductive system. A jogger diagnosed with chronic obstructive pulmonary disease may have a difficult time going on his daily 5-mile run. Self-regulatory models also address what happens in situations of this sort.

We begin this chapter by describing a set of orienting assumptions and principles embedded in models of self-regulation, placing the heaviest emphasis on our own approach. As processes and principles are described, we consider some of the implications the ideas hold for understanding physical well-being and responses to health threats. After presenting general orienting principles, we focus in depth on a set of findings involving one particular aspect of those principles, relating dispositional optimism to responses to health threats and adjustment to chronic disease.

Behavioral Self-regulation

A prevailing view among current personality theorists is that human behavior is organized around goals (Austin and Vancouver, 1996; Bandura, 1997; Cantor and Kihlstrom, 1987; Carver and Scheier, 1998; Elliott and Dweck, 1988; Emmons, 1986; Higgins, 1987; 1996; Klinger, 1975; Little, 1989; Markus and Nurius, 1986; Miller and Read, 1987; Pervin, 1982; 1989). Although the goal concept is treated differently by different theorists (for broader discussions see Austin and Vancouver, 1996; Carver and Scheier, 1998; 1999b), there are also important underlying similarities, which we choose to emphasize here. All assume that goals energize and direct activities (Pervin, 1982). Where there's a behavior, there's presumed to be a goal behind it, even if the goal is sometimes a trivial one or an implicit one. Goal theories also convey the sense that it is goals that give meaning to people's lives (Baumeister, 1989; Scheier and Carver, 2001). In each approach there's an emphasis on the idea that understanding the person means understanding the person's goals. Indeed, goal-related theories often assume that the self consists partly of the person's goals and the organization among them.

We should also reiterate that although some goals have a static quality, others are quite dynamic. The goal of taking a vacation isn't to be sitting in your driveway at the end of the two weeks, but to experience the events planned for the vacation. The goal of developing a relationship isn't just to experience one's fiftieth wedding anniversary. It is the pathway of interactive steps involved in getting there.

Goals and Feedback Processes

Clearly, people's goals wouldn't be very interesting if they were not some-how linked to their actions. But how exactly are goals used in acting? Most theorists approach this issue in terms of the decomposition of goals into subgoals. Although this is part of the answer, it is not the whole answer. Another part of the story is that goals serve as reference values for feedback processes. A feedback loop is comprised of four elements in a particular organ-ization (cf. Miller et al., 1960). The elements are an input function, a refer-ence value, a comparator, and an output function (Figure 15.1).

An input function is a sensor that brings in information about the current state of affairs. For present purposes it can be thought of as perception. The

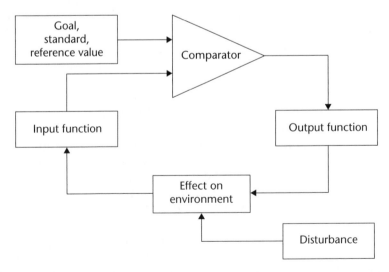

Figure 15.1 Schematic depiction of a feedback loop. In such a loop a sensed value is compared to a reference value or standard, and adjustments are made in an output function (as necessary) to shift the sensed value either in the direction of the standard or away from it, depending on whether the feedback loop is discrepancy reducing or discrepancy enlarging, respectively.

reference value serves to provide information about what is intended or desired. It provides information about the target around which the system attempts to regulate. In the kinds of feedback loops we will be discussing, reference values are roughly equivalent to goals. The comparator is a device that makes comparisons between input and reference value, yielding one of two outcomes: either the values being compared are discriminably different from one another or they're not. Comparators can vary in sensitivity, however. Some are able to detect very small discrepancies, whereas others are only able to detect discrepancies that are very large. Following the comparison is an output function. For present purposes, output is behavior, though sometimes the behavior is internal.

The nature of the output varies, depending on what kind of loop is under consideration. There are two kinds of loops, corresponding to two kinds of goals. In a discrepancy *reducing* feedback loop, the output is aimed at diminishing any discrepancy detected between input and reference value. If the comparison yields "no difference," the output function remains whatever it was. If the comparison yields "discrepancy," the output changes in a way that will diminish the discrepancy. In human behavior, discrepancy reduction (matching of input to reference value) is reflected in attempts to approach desired goals. For example, a dieter who has the goal of consuming only 1,500 calories per day will adjust his caloric intake downward, in order to minimize discrepancies between what is actually consumed each day and what is intended to be consumed each day.

The second kind of loop is a discrepancy *enlarging* feedback loop. The reference value here isn't a desirable one, leading to approach, but rather is one to avoid. It may be simplest to think of such values as "anti-goals." A discrepancy enlarging loop senses conditions, compares them to the anti-goal, and tries to enlarge any discrepancy sensed between the two. For example, the Cuban-American in Miami who wants to avoid any appearance of sympathy with Castro compares her opinions with the positions of Castro's government, and tries to make her opinions as different from those positions as she can (Carver and Humphries, 1981). An example from the health domain would be the case of a person whose goal is to avoid any symptoms of illness, or to never see a physician in her office.

Discrepancy enlarging processes are inherently unstable because they provide no clear target at which to direct the system's activities. The goal is to move away from the reference value, but movement away in one direction is as good as movement away in another. This lack of specificity is typically countered in living systems by the fact that discrepancy enlarging loops are usually constrained by discrepancy reducing loops (Carver et al., 1996; Carver and Scheier, 1998). That is, the attempt to avoid something often results in approaching something else (e.g., avoiding illness symptoms by engaging in health-promoting activities). In this chapter we focus largely on approach loops, but it should be recognized that some of the situations we describe also have aspects that can be viewed in terms of avoidance.

We should make one final point with respect to the output function, which applies to both discrepancy reducing and discrepancy enlarging systems.

Specifically, it is important to bear in mind that we are not talking here about behavior for behavior's sake, but behavior in the service of creating a certain relationship between input and reference value. That is, the value sensed by the input function depends on more than the output of the system (Figure 15.1). Disturbances from outside can change present conditions too, either increasing a discrepancy or diminishing a discrepancy. What is important is that the desired relationship between input and reference value be maintained, whether from actions of the system itself or actions and characteristics of external forces. Consider, for example, someone who has the goal of being healthy. If this person happens to have a group of co-workers who are illness free, it will be easier for the person to maintain good health, even though the success may have nothing to do with what the person has done.

Implications for Health

Feedback is essential to the functioning of self-regulating systems. Without feedback, comparisons between present state and optimal state cannot be made, and evaluation of the effects of one's self-regulatory actions would not be possible. Research from health psychology suggests that informational feedback matters so much that people will seek it out and rely on it *even when it doesn't tell them anything.* They will rely on it even when they are *told* it doesn't tell them anything. They will rely on it even though relying on it creates *problems* for their health. Under such circumstances, the feedback loop governing behavior continues to operate, continues to sense, compare, and guide behavior, but it does so in a manner that is counterproductive. In essence, the system misregulates (Carver and Scheier, 1981).

Several studies that illustrate this type of misregulation examine the behavior of people being treated for hypertension (Baumann and Leventhal, 1985; Meyer et al., 1985). Most people with hypertension have no reliable symptoms. Yet most people who enter treatment for hypertension quickly come to believe that they *can* isolate a symptom of it. Indeed, the longer they are in treatment, the more likely they are to think they can tell when their blood pressure is up. More than 90 percent of those in treatment for more than 3 months claim to be able to tell (Meyer et al., 1985).

Can they? By and large, no. In one study (Baumann and Leventhal, 1985), self-reports of elevated blood pressure were well correlated with self-reports of symptoms and (somewhat less well) with self-reported moods. Unfortunately, self-reported blood pressure elevation was virtually unrelated to actual elevation.

Why unfortunately? Because people with hypertension use their symptoms as a guide to whether their blood pressure is up (Leventhal et al., 1980). They then make important decisions on the basis of those symptoms. For example, they might use the symptom to tell them whether to take their medication. If they think their blood pressure isn't up (because the symptom isn't there), they don't take the medication. Indeed, they may even use the symptom to tell them whether or not to stay in therapy. If they stop experiencing symptoms, they may think they are cured, and drop out of treatment altogether. Alternatively, if the symptoms do *not* go away, patients might get discouraged that the treatment isn't working. The end result again might be a withdrawal from treatment. Obviously, treatment noncompliance can lead to serious medical problems – all because the people are relying on a particular kind of invalid feedback information to guide their decisions and actions.

This example also illustrates how much people rely on feedback to guide behavior. If the people with hypertension perceive a discrepancy between present state (symptom) and standard (no symptoms), they act in a way they think will reduce the discrepancy (take their medication). They are using feedback, just as the self-regulation approach suggests people do all the time. The problem is that the input channel is faulty. One interpretation of such phenomena is that people *need* feedback. The natural bias to use feedback apparently is so strong that people will continue to do so even when the feedback they are using is actually unrelated to what they are trying to control.

Hierarchical Organization among Goals

Earlier we drew a distinction between approach goals and avoidance goals. This is one way in which goals differ. Another way they differ is in level of abstraction (for broader treatment of this issue, see Carver and Scheier, 1998). For example, a man might have the goal, at a high level of abstraction, of being healthy. He may also have the goal, at a lower level of abstraction, of taking his vitamin pills on a daily basis. The first goal is to be a particular kind of *person*, the second concerns completing particular kinds of *action*. You can also imagine goals that are even more concrete than the latter one, such as the goal of removing the vitamin pills from the bottle. Such goals are closer to specifications of individual acts than were the second, which was more a summary statement about the desired outcome of intended action patterns.

These examples of concrete goals link directly to the example of an abstract goal, helping to illustrate the idea that goals can be connected hierarchically. In 1973, William Powers argued that behavior occurs via a hierarchical organization of discrepancy reducing feedback loops. Inasmuch as such loops imply goals, his argument assumed a hierarchical model of goals. He reasoned that the output of a high level system consists of resetting reference values at the next lower level. To put it differently, higher order systems "behave" by providing goals to the systems just below them. Goals are more concrete at each lower level. Control at each level regulates a quality that contributes to that controlled at the next higher level. Each level monitors input at its own level of abstraction, and each level adjusts output to minimize its discrepancies. In this manner, there is a "cascade" of control from higher order loops to lower order loops, as the constituents of the higher order goal are embodied in more and more specific pieces of action.

Powers was most interested in low levels of abstraction, but he did suggest labels for several higher level loops that control the qualities of behavior that are of interest to social, personality, and health psychologists. *Sequences* are

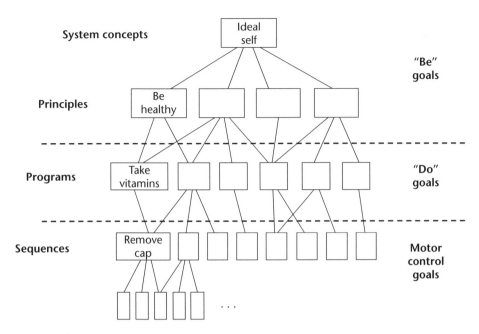

Figure 15.2 A hierarchy of goals (or of feedback loops). Lines indicate the contribution of lower level goals to specific higher level goals. They can also be read in the opposite direction, indicating that a given higher order goal specifies more-concrete goals at the next lower level. The hierarchy described in text involves goals of "being" particular ways, which are attained by "doing" particular actions. Adapted from C. S. Carver and M. F. Scheier, *On the Self-regulation of Behavior*, copyright 1998 Cambridge University Press; reprinted with permission.

sets of acts that run off directly once cued. One level up from sequences are *programs*, activities involving conscious decisions at various points. The level above programs is *principles*, qualities that are abstracted from (or implemented by) programs. These are the kinds of qualities represented by trait terms. Powers gave the name *system concepts* to the highest level he considered. Goal representations there include the idealized overall sense of self, of a close relationship, or of a group identity.

Figure 15.2 shows a simple portrayal of this hierarchy. This diagram omits the loops of feedback processes, using lines to indicate only the links among goal values. The lines imply that moving toward a particular lower goal contributes to the attainment of a higher goal (or even several at once). Multiple lines to a given goal indicates that several lower level action qualities can contribute to its attainment. As indicated previously, there are goals to "be" a particular way and goals to "do" certain things (and at lower levels, goals to create physical movement).

This hierarchical model per se has not been tested empirically. However, a similar notion of hierarchicality is embedded in Vallacher and Wegner's (1985; 1987) theory of action identification, and their theory has been tested.

Although the Vallacher and Wegner model is framed in terms of how people define their behavior, how people think about their actions is also informative about the goals that underlie those actions. Research related to action identification theory has developed considerable support for the idea that there is a hierarchicality within the flow of behavior.

Implications for Health

For several decades, Leventhal has been studying the commonsense models of illness that people hold (Leventhal et al., 1980; 2001; Leventhal and Carr, 2001). Commonsense models of illness reflect the manner in which people represent illnesses to themselves. Illness representations are thought to encompass five different domains or attributes: identity (involving a disease label and symptoms), time line (e.g., time to onset, time to cure or recovery, time to death), cause (e.g., genetic versus environmental), controllability, and consequences (see, e.g., Lau and Hartman, 1983; Leventhal et al., 1980).

What is important for present purposes is that each of the five domains of illness representation is thought to be bi-level in nature (Leventhal and Carr, 2001). That is, illness attributes are represented both at an abstract, cognitive level and at a more concrete, perceptual level (Meyer et al., 1985). Take as an example the domain of illness identity. At a concrete level, illnesses are identified by a collection of discrete symptoms and other bodily cues, biological in nature. At a more abstract level, these collections of symptoms give rise to an illness label. The collection of scratchy throat, cough, fever and stuffy nose is identified as a cold; the combination of shortness of breath accompanied by extreme pain radiating down the left arm is labeled a heart attack. It is possible to construe these two levels of illness representation as forming a simple hierarchy of feedback control (Leventhal and Carr, 2001). At the higher level, people regulate their activities so as to avoid the recognition that they have a particular illness. They do this by managing and regulating their lower level symptoms upon which the illness label depends.

Leventhal and Carr (2001) suggest that important differences can emerge depending on whether people try to regulate their symptoms or their disease, especially when the disease is chronic in nature. For example, Affleck et al. (1987) found that people with rheumatoid arthritis expressed high levels of negative affect when they perceived their coping efforts as directed toward controlling their disease. Presumably, this occurs because the symptoms of patients with a chronic disease never fully disappear, thereby reminding them that the goal of being disease free is never attained. In contrast, high levels of positive affect were reported in the Affleck et al. (1987) study by patients whose coping efforts were directed toward symptom control. Presumably, these patients were happy about being able to exert some degree of control over the symptoms they were experiencing. Based on findings such as these, Leventhal and Carr (2001) suggest that it might be quite adaptive to disconnect the built-in hierarchical arrangement between symptoms and diseases labels, that is, to cause the lower level of symptom control to become functionally superordinate, particularly when the person's self-regulatory efforts are directed at an illness that is chronic in nature.

Hierarchicality and Behavioral Complexity

Although the idea of a behavioral hierarchy is in some ways simple, it has several implications for thinking about the manner in which different levels of action are connected (see Carver and Scheier, 1998). One implication is that goals at any given level can often be achieved by a variety of means at lower levels. This fits the fact that people sometimes shift radically the manner in which they try to reach a goal, when the goal itself has not changed. For example, you can be productive (fulfilling an abstract goal) by building a house, by compiling a report from a set of records, or by thinking through a problem and describing its solution verbally. Goal substitution at a lower level can only occur, of course, if the quality that constitutes the higher order goal is manifested in several different kinds of lower order activities.

These particular examples were chosen because the first implies a good deal of physical exertion, whereas the others do not. Physical mobility is an issue that often arises in thinking about the impact of chronic illness. As these examples illustrate, having a chronic illness that impedes physical movements does not in principle remove the capacity to reach abstract goals.

Just as a given goal can be obtained via multiple pathways, so can a specific act be performed in the service of diverse goals. For example, a person might take her insulin to avoid dying, to be able to eat more of the high sugar foods that she enjoys, or to not inconvenience her family by developing medical problems as she ages. Thus, a given act can have strikingly different meanings, depending on the purpose it is intended to serve. This is an important sub-theme of a self-regulation view on action: behavior can be understood only by identifying the goals to which behavior is addressed. This idea may have important implications for designing health-related interventions. That is, interventions that take underlying purposes into account may result in more successful intervention efforts than interventions that focus only on the behavior and fail to consider why the behavior is being done.

A related point is that goals are not equal in importance (see Carver and Scheier, 1998). The higher one goes in the goal hierarchy, the more important the goals become, because the goal qualities encountered at higher levels are more fundamental to the person's overriding sense of self. Thus, goal qualities at higher levels tend to be more important, by virtue of their closer links to the core sense of self.

Goals at a given level can also vary in importance. There are two ways for importance to accrue to goals residing at the same hierarchical level (Figure 15.3). First, the more directly the attainment of a given level goal contributes to the attainment of a valued higher order goal, the more important is the given level goal. Second, a given level goal that contributes to the attainment of several higher level goals at once is more important than a given level act that contributes to the attainment of only one such goal. With respect to the significance of a person's goals, then, importance tends to accrue (a) as one considers goals higher in the hierarchy, (b) as a given level goal relates more directly to the attainment of a higher level goal, or (c) as a

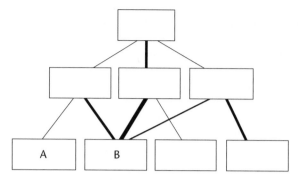

Figure 15.3   Importance accrues to a given level goal in either of two ways. The action can contribute in a major way to the attainment of a higher order goal (indicated here by a thicker line), or the action can contribute to several higher order goals at once (indicated here by a larger number of upward projections). On both of these criteria, action goal A is relatively unimportant, whereas B is more important.

given level goal represents a step toward multiple higher order goals simultaneously (see also Carver and Scheier, 1999a).

Feelings

The model described to this point addresses the control of action, but there is more to be considered. People also experience feelings during their actions. We have suggested a way of thinking about how feelings arise in the course of behavior, via the operation of a second feedback process (Carver and Scheier, 1990; 1998). This second process operates simultaneously with the behavior-guiding system and in parallel to it. One way to characterize what it does is to say it is checking on how well the behavior system is doing at carrying out its job. For discrepancy reducing behavioral loops, the perceptual input for the affect-creating loop is a representation of the *rate of discrepancy reduction in the action system over time* (we consider discrepancy enlarging loops shortly).

We find an analogy useful here. Because action implies change between behavioral states, consider behavior as analogous to distance (change from one physical position to another). If the action loop deals with distance, and if the affect loop assesses the *progress* of the action loop over time, then the affect loop is dealing with the psychological equivalent of velocity (change in physical distance over time).

We don't believe that rate of discrepancy reduction creates affect by itself, because a given rate of progress has different affective consequences under different circumstances. As in any feedback system, this input is compared against a reference value (cf. Frijda, 1986; 1988): an acceptable or desired rate of behavioral discrepancy reduction. As in other feedback loops, the comparison checks for a deviation from the standard.

We suggest that the result of the comparison process at the heart of this loop (the error signal from the comparator) is manifest phenomenologically in two ways. The first is as a hazy and nonverbal sense of confidence or doubt. The second is as affect – a sense of positiveness or negativeness. Several studies have yielded evidence that tends to support this view of the source of affect (e.g., Brunstein, 1993; Guy and Lord, 1998; Hsee and Abelson, 1991; Lawrence et al., 2002; for a more thorough discussion, see Carver and Scheier, 1998).

What about attempts to distance oneself from a point of comparison – discrepancy *enlarging* loops? The view we just described rests on the idea that positive feelings arise when an action system is doing well at *doing what it is organized to do*. Approach systems are organized to reduce discrepancies. When approach systems are making good progress toward desired goals, positive affect is experienced. When satisfactory progress is not being made, affect turns more negative. We see no obvious reason why the same principle shouldn't also apply to systems organized to increase discrepancies. Thus, if avoidance systems are doing well at what they are organized to do – distancing the person from anti-goals – positive affect should result. If they are doing poorly at what they are organized to do, the affective experience should be negative.

This much seems the same across the two types of systems. On the other hand, we do see a difference in the specific affects that are involved (Carver and Scheier, 1998). For both approach and avoidance systems there is a positive pole and a negative pole, but the positives aren't quite the same, nor are the negatives (see Figure 15.4). Our view of this difference derives partly from insights of Higgins and colleagues (1987; 1996). Following their lead, we suggest that the affect dimension relating to discrepancy reducing loops (in its

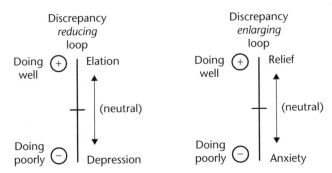

Figure 15.4 Two sorts of affect generating systems and the affective dimensions we believe arise from the functioning of each. Discrepancy reducing systems are presumed to yield affective qualities of sadness or depression when progress is below standard and happiness or elation when progress is above standard. Discrepancy enlarging systems are presumed to yield anxiety when progress is below standard and relief or contentment when progress is above standard.

From C. S. Carver and M. F. Scheier, *On the Self-regulation of Behavior*, copyright 1998 Cambridge University Press; reprinted with permission.

purest form) runs from depression to elation. The affect dimension that relates to discrepancy enlarging loops (in its purest form) runs from anxiety to relief or contentment.

Interface Between Affect and Action

We characterized the affect system as working in conjunction with and in parallel to the system guiding action. How do the two systems interface? Put differently, how does affect influence action? The answers to these questions lie in the nature of the mechanism behind the generation of affect. That is, we argued that affect is the error signal of a feedback loop. What's the *output function* of this loop? If the input function is a perception of rate of progress, then the output function must be an *adjustment* in rate of progress.

Some adjustments are straightforward – go faster. Some adjustments are less obvious. The rates of many "behaviors" (higher order activities) are not defined by the literal pace of physical action. Rather, they are defined in terms of choices among potential actions, or even potential *programs* of action. For example, increasing your rate of progress on recovering from knee surgery may mean choosing to spend more time at the gym lifting weights rather than at work. Thus, adjustment in rate must often be translated into other terms, such as concentration, or reallocation of time and effort. The action system and the rate system do work in concert, however. Both are involved in the flow of action. They influence different *aspects* of the action, but both are always involved (for a broader treatment see Carver and Scheier, 1998).

Although it may not be readily apparent, the model we have described is essentially a "cruise control" model of affect and action. The system we have described operates in much the same way as the cruise control on a car. If you are going too slowly toward some behavioral goal, negative affect arises. You respond by putting more effort into your behavior, trying to speed it up. If you are going faster than the set-point, positive affect arises, and you coast.

The car's cruise control is similar. The car comes to a hill, and starts to slow down. The cruise control responds by feeding the engine more gas, to bring the speed up to the set-point. The car crests the hill and starts rolling downhill too fast, the cruise control system reduces the flow of gas and the speed is dragged back down.

Implications for Health

To date, we are unaware of any direct attempt to apply our velocity model of affect to health-relevant activities. On the other hand, application of the model seems relatively straightforward. People recover all the time from different types of physical trauma, from different types of illnesses, and from different types of surgical procedures. People also experience affect during the course of the recovery process.

The velocity model of affect would suggest that the person's affective experience is influenced in an important way by the extent to which the person's perceived rate of progress matches, exceeds, or falls short of some desired rate of progress. To the extent that the patient's progress matches or exceeds the desired rate of progress, positive affect should result. If progress falls below some desired rate, affect should become more negative. Moreover, the model predicts that different qualities of affect will be experienced, depending on the nature of the goals that the patient is pursuing. If the goal is to *not* get worse, agitation related affects such as anxiety, fearfulness, and contentment should be involved. If the goal is to get healthy, affect should be more closely related to the qualities of elation and depression. These considerations suggest that care should be taken when prescribing recovery goals for patients, so that the recovery goals reflect a realistic appraisal of the patient's unique medical status, established in order to maximize the likelihood that the patient's desired or expected rate of progress will be within reach.

Confidence and Doubt

The foregoing account of the regulation of affect suggested that one mechanism yields two subjective readouts: affect, and a hazy sense of confidence versus doubt. We believe that the affect and expectancies that get generated "on-line" as behavior unfolds are intertwined. As affect becomes more negative, doubt tends to increase; as affect becomes more positive, hopefulness, confidence, and favorable expectations also rise. Thus, what we have said about affect applies equally well to the vague sense of confidence versus doubt that also emerges in parallel with ongoing action, as rate of progress falls above or below a desired level.

The on-line sense of confidence and doubt does not operate in a psychological vacuum, however. Although disrupted goal-attainment efforts can evoke distress emotions and doubtful feelings in an almost reflexive fashion, these initial reactions are often over-ridden by other information. We've suggested that when people experience adversity in trying to move toward their goals, they periodically interrupt their efforts and assess in a more deliberate way the likelihood of success (e.g., Carver and Scheier, 1981; 1990; 1998). In effect, people suspend the behavioral stream, step outside it, and evaluate the possibility of success in a more thoughtful way than occurs while acting (Figure 15.5).

This assessment process may happen once, or often. It may be brief or prolonged. It may occur after initial attempts at goal-attainment are underway, or before any behavior is ever begun. In conducting this outcome assessment, people presumably depend heavily on memories of prior outcomes in similar situations, and consider such things as additional resources they might bring to bear (cf. Lazarus, 1966; MacNair and Elliott, 1992) or alternative approaches to the problem. People also use social comparison information (e.g., Wills, 1981; Wood, 1989; Wood et al., 1985) and attributional analyses of prior events (Pittman and Pittman, 1980; Wong and Weiner, 1981).

How do these thoughts influence the expectancies that result? In some cases, people retrieve chronic expectancies from memory. As such, the information already *is* expectancies, summaries of products of previous behavior.

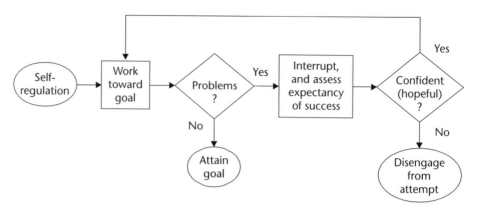

Figure 15.5 Flow-chart depiction of self-regulatory possibilities, indicating that action sometimes continues unimpeded toward goal attainment, that obstacles to goal attainment sometimes induce a sequence of evaluation and decision making, and that if expectancies for eventual success are sufficiently unfavorable the person may disengage from further effort. Adapted from C. S. Carver and M. F. Scheier, *On the Self-regulation of Behavior*, copyright 1998 Cambridge University Press; reprinted with permission.

These chronic expectancies may simply substitute for the expectancies derived from immediate experience, or they may blend with and color those immediate expectancies to a greater or lesser degree. For example, a person who routinely receives unfavorable information from doctors may find himself automatically expecting the worst as his next physical examination approaches.

In some cases, people think more expansively about how the situation might be changed. For these possibilities to influence expectancies, their consequences must be evaluated. One way to evaluate the possibilities is to play them through mentally as behavioral scenarios (cf. Taylor and Pham, 1996), allowing conclusions to be reached about potential outcomes that can influence the expectancy. For example, a cancer patient with brain metastases may play through a scenario of undergoing gamma knife radiation therapy, experiencing few side effects of treatment, and having her tumors eradicated. She may generate from that scenario a favorable expectancy about the resolution of her illness.

It seems reasonable that this mental simulation engages the same mechanism as creates the sense of affect and confidence during actual behavior. When your progress is temporarily stalled, playing through a scenario that leads to a favorable outcome yields a sense of perceived progress that is more rapid than is presently being experienced. The confidence loop thus yields a more optimistic outcome assessment than is being derived from current action. If the scenario is negative and hopeless, it indicates a further loss of progress, and the confidence loop yields further doubt. What determines whether the simulation leads to positive or negative assessments? Taylor et al. (1998) have argued that effective mental scenarios explicitly emphasize the actual behavioral processes that are needed for reaching a goal, the concrete steps that must be enacted in order to get there (see also Cameron and Nicholls, 1998). Simply imagining the goal as attained is not good enough to facilitate self-regulatory activities, and it can even be detrimental (Oettingen, 1996).

Efforts and Giving Up

Expectancies – whether generated on line or through further processing – have an important influence on behavior. If expectations are favorable, the result is renewed and continued effort to attain the goal. If doubts are strong enough, the result is an impetus to disengage from further effort, and even from the goal itself. Sometimes the disengagement is overt, as the person suspends behavioral actions directed toward goal-attainment. Disengagement can also be mental, however, reflected in off-task thinking, daydreaming, wishful thinking, self-distraction, and so on. Often mental disengagement cannot be sustained, as situational cues force the person to re-confront the problem being confronted. The resultant phenomenology in such cases may involve repetitive negative rumination, focusing on self-doubt and percep-tions of inadequacy. This cycle is both unpleasant and performance-impairing.

We have long argued that these two general classes of responses form a "psychological watershed" (Carver and Scheier, 1981; 1998). That is, one set of responses consists of continued comparisons between present state and goal, and continued efforts at movement toward desired goals. The other set consists of disengagement from comparisons, and quitting (see also Klinger, 1975; Kukla, 1972; Wortman and Brehm, 1975). Just as rainwater falling on a mountain ridge ultimately flows to one side of the ridge or the other, so do behaviors ultimately flow to one of these classes or the other. This theme – divergence in cognitive and behavioral response as a function of expectancies – is an important one, applying to a surprisingly broad range of literatures (Carver and Scheier, 1998; 1999b).

Implications for Health

How do these principles apply to illness episodes? In some respects illness is no different from any other obstacle to goal-attainment (what is labeled in Figure 15.5 as "problems"). Illness is one of a host of adversities that a person might encounter on the way to goal attainment. On the other hand, episodes of serious illness have a particularly pernicious role. Major illnesses explicitly and directly threaten the desire to stay alive and be healthy (valued goals in their own right). They also indirectly undermine other ongoing goal-pursuits. Thus, people diagnosed with a chronic, perhaps life-threatening disease suffer two sorts of disruption, potentially undermining two classes of hopes. They may lose confidence that they will continue living; they may also confront the loss of hope of achieving major life ambitions.

Negative expectations are detrimental because they tend to undermine the person's motivation to remain goal engaged. However, the loss of engagement in a goal does not necessarily lead to a vacuum of goal-lessness. Elsewhere, we've discussed the ebb and flow of engagement and disengagement in terms of competition among goals (Carver and Scheier, 1998). We suggested that disengagement from one goal may reflect a weakening of commitment to it. Because people usually have many goals at once, however, this weakening of commitment permits another goal to become prepotent and thus permits behavior to shift toward *its* pursuit. Thus, the loss of one goal is often followed directly by pursuit of another one.

Sometimes this means scaling back to a less ambitious goal in the same domain as the abandoned goal. By taking up an attainable alternative, the person remains engaged in goal pursuit and forward movement. This is particularly important when the path being blocked by the disease or illness episode concerns a value central to the self. Important goals are hard to give up. People need multiple paths to these core values (cf. Linville, 1985; 1987; Showers and Ryff, 1996; Wicklund and Gollwitzer, 1982). If one path is barricaded, people need to be able to jump to another one. Consider a breast cancer patient who has great personal investment in being a mother and raising a child. If chemotherapy destroys the ability to have children, the desire to be nurturant can be fulfilled in other ways (cf. Clark et al., 1991). If long-term career ambitions are threatened by a potentially fatal illness, those ambitions might be realized in smaller ways in the time that remains. Alternatively, the person might reprioritize various aspects of life and spend less time working and more time in close relationships.

In any case, it seems apparent that the ability to shift to a new goal, or a new path to a continuing goal, is a very important part of remaining goal-engaged. What happens if there's no alternative to take up? In such a case disengagement from an unattainable goal is not accompanied by a shift, because there's nothing to shift to. This is the worst situation, where there is nothing to pursue, nothing to take the place of what is seen as unattainable (cf. Moskowitz et al., 1996). If commitment to the unattainable goal remains, the result is considerable distress. If the commitment wanes, the result is emptiness. There is reason to suspect that such a state might also be implicated in premature death (Carver and Scheier, 1998).

Expectancies Vary in Specificity and Abstraction

The fact that goals vary in specificity suggests that people have a comparable range of variations in expectancies (Armor and Taylor, 1998; Carver and Scheier, 1998). To put it more concretely, you can be confident or doubtful about maintaining your general physical health, about getting through your daily exercise regimen successfully, or about being able to do one more sit-up.

Which of these sorts of expectancies matter? Probably all of them. Expectancy-based theories often hold that behavior is predicted best when the specificity of the expectancy matches that of the behavior. Sometimes it is argued that prediction is best when taking into account several levels of specificity. But many outcomes in life have multiple causes, people often face situations they have never experienced before, and situations unfold and change over time. It has been suggested that in circumstances such as these, generalized expectations are particularly useful in predicting behavior and emotions (Scheier and Carver, 1985).

The same principles that apply to focused confidence also apply to the generalized sense of optimism and pessimism. When researchers talk about variables such as optimism and pessimism, the sense of confidence that is at issue is simply more diffuse and broader in scope. Thus, when confronting a challenge (presumably any type of challenge), optimists should tend to take a posture of confidence and persistence, assuming the adversity can be handled successfully in one way or another. Pessimists should be more doubtful and hesitant, more ready to anticipate disaster.

Optimism as Confidence Rather Than Control

One more conceptual issue that should be addressed is the extent to which the concept of optimism overlaps with the concept of control (Thompson and Spacapan, 1991) or personal efficacy (Bandura, 1986). All these constructs have strong overtones of expecting desired outcomes to take place (cf. Carver, 1997). However, there is an important difference in the assumptions that are made (or not made) regarding how the desired outcomes are expected to come about. Self-efficacy represents a construct in which the self as a causal agent is paramount. If people have high self-efficacy expectancies, they presumably believe that their personal efforts (or personal skills) are what will determine the outcome. The same is true of the concept of control. When people perceive themselves as in control, they are assuming that the desired outcome will occur through their own personal efforts (for broader discussion see Carver et al., 2000; Carver and Scheier, 1998: 204–8).

In contrast to this emphasis, our view of the optimism construct has always been that it is broader than personal control. People who are optimistic can be optimistic because they believe they are immensely talented, because they are hard-working, because they are blessed, because they are lucky, or because they have friends in the right places, or any combination of these or other factors that produce good outcomes (cf. Murphy et al., 2000). Clearly there are some circumstances in which personal efficacy is the key determinant of a desired outcome. There are also circumstances in which the goal is explicitly to do something yourself. In the latter case, *only* a personally determined success is the desired end-point, so personal control over the outcome is critical. However, there are also many cases in which the causal determinant of the outcome is far less important than the occurrence of the outcome. We believe those cases should also be included under the umbrella of the optimism construct. Believing that one will recover from a serious illness because of the beneficial effects of the medicine that has been prescribed would seem to have very little to do with one's sense of personal agency. Yet, such a person might be highly confident about overcoming the adverse effects of the illness.

This position has sometimes caused people to question whether optimists can really be expected to exert efforts toward attainment of desired goals. That is, why should optimists not just sit quietly waiting for good things to happen to them from out of the sky? (As is described shortly, they do not appear to do this.) Our answer is that the expectation of good outcomes appears to be held contingent on remaining in pursuit of those good outcomes. It may be one's own efforts that turn the tide, or it may be that by remaining involved the person is able to take advantage of breaks that fall their way. In either case, the optimist expects the best, but also understands the need to be part of the matrix of influences on the outcome. This reasoning also helps to explain the fact that measures of optimism consistently correlate in a positive direction with measures of control and self-efficacy, but only to a moderate degree (see, e.g., Cozzarelli, 1993; Scheier and Carver, 1985).

Optimism, Pessimism, and Coping with Health Threats

We believe that many of the principles reviewed in the foregoing pages hold implications for understanding health-related behavior and feelings. In point of fact, however, most of the research spawned by the model has focused on one particular set of issues. This research has sought to determine how variations in expectations influence quality of life when people are confronted with different types of health threats. The research has also sought to identify the mediators of the relationship between expectancies and quality of life outcomes.

The rationale for this research, derived from the model just presented, runs as follows. When people confront adversity or difficulty in their lives, they experience a variety of emotions. Most common are anger, anxiety, distress, and depression. Sometimes, though, confrontations with adversity can create eagerness to combat and overcome it. The balance among these feelings should relate to the expectations people hold about likely outcomes. When people expect positive outcomes, even when things are difficult, they should experience a mix of feelings that is relatively positive. When people are more pessimistic, they should experience a stronger bias toward negative feelings (Carver and Scheier, 1998; Scheier and Carver, 1992).

Many individual difference variables might be invoked as determinants of differences such as these. Here we focus primarily on research in which expectancies were operationalized in terms of generalized optimism versus pessimism. Although expectancies are pivotal in all contemporary theories of optimism, there are at least a couple of ways to think about expectancies and how to measure them, leading to two distinct literatures. One approach measures expectancies directly, asking people to indicate the extent to which they believe that their future outcomes will be good or bad. This is the approach we've taken in our work (Scheier et al., 1994). Our own approach thus adds little further conceptual complexity to what we have said so far. Expectancies that are generalized – expectancies that pertain more or less to the person's entire life space – are what we mean when we use the terms optimism and pessimism.

In 1985 we developed a measure called the Life Orientation Test, or LOT (Scheier and Carver, 1985), to assess differences between people in optimism and pessimism. Currently we use a briefer form of the LOT, called the Life Orientation Test-Revised, or LOT-R (Scheier et al., 1994). The LOT-R has good internal consistency and relatively stable test-retest reliability. Because of the extensive item overlap between the original scale and the revised scale, correlations between the two scales are very high, often exceeding 0.90 (Scheier et al., 1994).

We should perhaps note explicitly that both the LOT and the LOT-R provide continuous distributions of scores. Although we refer throughout the chapter to optimists and pessimists as though they were distinct categories, this is a matter of descriptive convenience. People actually range from the very optimistic to the very pessimistic, with most falling somewhere in the middle.

Another approach to assessing optimism makes the assumption that people's expectancies for the future derive from their understanding of the causes of events in the past (Peterson and Seligman, 1984; Seligman, 1991). If attributions or explanations for past failures in some domain focus on causes that are stable, the person's expectancy for the future in that domain will be for bad outcomes, because the cause is seen as relatively permanent and thus likely to remain in force. If attributions for past failures focus on cases that are unstable, then the outlook for the future may be brighter, because the cause may no longer be in force. If explanations for past failures are global (apply to many aspects of life), the person's expectancy for the future across many domains will be for bad outcomes, because the causal forces are at work everywhere. If the explanations are specific, however, the outlook in other areas of life may be brighter because the causes don't apply there. It is often assumed that people have "explanatory styles," which bear on the person's whole life space. The theory that's identified with the term explanatory style holds that optimism and pessimism are defined by adaptive versus problematic patterns of explanation (Peterson and Seligman, 1984; Seligman, 1991).

These two approaches to optimism and pessimism have led to their own research literatures, each of which sheds light on the nature and function of optimism and pessimism (see also Snyder's 1994 discussion of hope, another closely related construct). In what follows, we focus mostly on optimism as operationalized by Scheier and Carver (Scheier and Carver, 1985; 1992; Scheier et al., 1994) – that is, in terms of self-reported generalized expectancies.

Over the past 15 or so years, a variety of different studies have examined the relationship between optimism and distress among people facing difficult or adverse circumstances. The stressors investigated in this research have been diverse, ranging from the experiences of students entering college (Aspinwall and Taylor, 1992) to survivors of missile attacks (Zeidner and Hammer, 1992). The bulk of this research, however, has been aimed at understanding how optimism and pessimism affect well-being in contexts that are health-related. In the following sections we review some of this research literature, focusing primarily on studies that are prospective in nature, or that examined reactions to adversity over a relatively long period of time.

Coronary Disease

One early project examined the effects of optimism and pessimism on the reactions of a group of men undergoing and recovering from coronary artery bypass graft surgery (Scheier et al., 1989). Patients completed a set of psycho-social measures the day before surgery, 6–8 days after surgery, and 6 months post-surgery. Prior to surgery, optimists reported less hostility and depression than pessimists. A week after surgery, optimists reported more relief and happiness, greater satisfaction with their medical care, and greater satisfaction with the emotional support they had received from friends. Six months after surgery, optimists reported higher quality of life than pessimists. In a follow-up of the same patients 5 years after surgery (described in Scheier and Carver, 1992), optimists continued to experience greater subjective well-being and general quality of life compared to pessimists. For example, optimists reported greater work satisfaction, satisfaction with relationships with others, and less sleep disturbances. All these differences remained significant when medical factors were statistically controlled.

Another study on optimism and quality of life after coronary artery bypass surgery (Fitzgerald et al., 1993) assessed participants 1 month before surgery and 8 months afterward. Optimism was negatively related to pre-surgical distress. Further, controlling for pre-surgical life satisfaction, optimism was positively related to post-surgical life satisfaction. Further analysis revealed that the general sense of optimism appeared to operate on feelings of life satisfaction through a more focused sense of confidence about the surgery. That is, the general sense of optimism about life was channeled into a specific optimism regarding the surgery, and from there to satisfaction with life. All of the effects involving optimism reported by Fitzgerald et al. (1993) were inde-pendent of disease severity.

Similar beneficial effects of optimism have been observed in a group of women undergoing coronary artery bypass surgery (King et al., 1998). In this study, optimism was assessed 1 week following surgery. Additional psycho-social measures were obtained at the same point in time, and again 1, 6, and 12 months post-surgery. Optimism demonstrated significant relationships with positive mood, negative mood (inversely), and satisfaction with life at all points. More importantly, optimism assessed at 1 week predicted more positive mood and less negative mood at 1 month, independent of initial levels of mood.

A final research project (Leedham et al., 1995) explored the effects of posit-ive expectations on experiences surrounding heart transplant surgery (this study did not examine optimism per se, but variables conceptually linked to optimism). Patients (and their nurses) completed questionnaires prior to sur-gery, at discharge, and at 3 and 6 months post-surgery. Initial questionnaires assessed patients' confidence about the efficacy of treatment, their expecta-tions about their future health and survival, and broader expectations for the future. Positive expectations related to higher quality of life later on, even among patients who had health setbacks.

Reproductive Medical Issues

Other research has examined the effects of optimism on emotional well-being in the context of developing postpartum depressed affect following childbirth (Carver and Gaines, 1987). Women in this study completed measures of optimism and depression in the last third of their pregnancy, and completed the depression measure again three weeks postpartum. Optimism predicted lower levels of depressed affect at baseline. More important, optimism also predicted lower levels of depressive symptoms postpartum, even when initial levels of depression were statistically controlled.

A similar point is made by two more recent studies. As did Carver and Gaines, Fontaine and Jones (1997) assessed optimism and depression before and after childbirth. Optimism was once again associated with fewer depressive symptoms, both during pregnancy and two weeks postpartum. Park et al. (1997) also examined the effects of optimism on adjustment during pregnancy. Optimism was assessed during their first prenatal clinic visit. During the last trimester of the pregnancy, the women's anxiety was assessed, as well as the extent to which they were maintaining positive states of mind. Optimism was negatively associated with anxiety and positively associated with positive states of mind.

Another reproduction-related medical situation that has been studied with respect to optimism is infertility. In vitro fertilization is one way to get around fertility problems, but it doesn't always work. Litt et al. (1992) examined reactions among people whose attempts at in vitro fertilization were unsuccessful. Optimism was assessed approximately eight weeks before the attempt, as were specific expectancies for fertilization success, coping strategies, distress levels, and the impact of the infertility on participants' lives. Two weeks after notification of a negative pregnancy test, distress was assessed again. Neither demographics, obstetric history, marital adjustment, nor the rated effect of infertility on subjects' lives predicted Time-2 distress levels – but pessimism did. Controlling for Time-1 distress, pessimism was the strongest predictor of Time-2 distress of any of the variables measured.

Yet other studies have examined the influence of optimism on adjustment to abortion. In one, Cozzarelli (1993) had women complete measures of optimism, self-esteem, self-mastery, self-efficacy, and depression one hour prior to the abortion. Depression and psychological adjustment were assessed 30 minutes after the abortion and again 3 weeks later. Optimists had less pre-abortion depression, better post-abortion adjustment, and better 3-week adjustment than did pessimists. A second study relating optimism to adjustment to abortion was conducted by Major et al. (1998), who were interested in personal resources that might protect women from distress. Optimism was identified in their research as a key component in a style of personal resilience which facilitated post-abortion adjustment.

Cancer

Optimism has also been studied in the context of adjusting to the diagnosis and treatment for cancer. One study examined the effect of optimism on psychological adaptation to treatment for early-stage breast cancer (Carver et al., 1993). Patients in this study were interviewed 6 times: at the time of diagnosis, the day before surgery, 7–10 days after surgery, and 3, 6, and 12 months later. Optimism was assessed at the time of diagnosis and was used to predict distress levels at the subsequent time points. Optimism inversely predicted distress over time, above and beyond the effect of relevant medical variables and beyond the effects of earlier distress. That is, the prediction of distress at 3, 6, and 12 months after surgery was significant even when the immediately prior level of distress was controlled. Thus, optimism predicted not just lower initial distress, but also resilience to distress during the year following surgery.

Similarly, Johnson (1996) demonstrated the beneficial effects of optimism among a group of men receiving radiation therapy for prostate cancer. Optimism was assessed prior to the first radiation treatment. Mood was assessed throughout the treatment period and 2 weeks, 1 month, and 3 months following the end of treatment. Optimism was a strong predictor of patients' emotional responses both during and after treatment, with less optimistic patients being particularly vulnerable to negative moods.

Finally, Christman (1990) examined adjustment among a group of patients undergoing radiotherapy for a variety of different kinds of cancers. Patients were enrolled into the project at one of three points in time, on the first day of treatment, on the fifteenth day of treatment, and on the last day of treatment. Multiple assessments were made on those patients who were enrolled prior to the conclusion of their treatment. Optimism was negatively related to adjustment problems at all three assessment points, as well as to illness uncertainty at the first and second assessment points.

Other Health Contexts

The majority of the research that relates optimism to psychological well-being has focused on heart disease, experiences surrounding reproductive issues, and cancer. There is also research, however, from other domains that makes similar points. For example, Taylor et al. (1992) studied optimism and psychological well-being among a cohort of gay and bisexual men at risk of developing Acquired Immunodeficiency Syndrome (AIDS). Among both seropositive (HIV+) and seronegative (HIV−) men, greater optimism was associated with lower levels of subsequent distress as measured by a composite index of negative affect and by specific worries and concerns about AIDS.

In a somewhat different medical population, Chamberlain and colleagues (1992) demonstrated the beneficial effects of optimism among a group of joint replacement patients. Data were collected before surgery, the third day following surgery, and approximately 6 weeks following surgery. Optimism assessed pre-surgically was positively associated with follow-up levels of life satisfaction and positive well-being, and negatively associated with psychological distress and pain. Finally, Smith et al. (1994) observed that optimism predicted lowered levels of negative affectivity and disease impact among a large group of persons with rheumatoid arthritis (albeit these associations were cross-sectional in nature).

Not only does optimism have a positive effect on the psychological well-being of people dealing with medical conditions, but it also has an influence on the psychological well-being of people who act as caregivers to patients. For example, Given et al. (1993) studied a group of cancer patients and their caregivers, and found that caregivers' optimism related to a number of caregiver well-being variables – i.e., lower symptoms of depression, less impact of caregiving on physical health, and less impact on caregivers' daily schedules. Caregiver optimism thus predicted caregiver reactions to the burdens of caring for a family member with cancer, and did so independent of patient variables.

Similar results have been found in research on caregivers of Alzheimer's patients (Hooker et al., 1992; Shifren and Hooker, 1995) and caregivers of patients suffering from stroke (Tompkins et al., 1988). In each case, optimism was associated with lower levels of depression and higher levels of psychological well-being.

Optimism, Pessimism, and Coping

Coping as a Mediator of Distress Effects

One conclusion seems clear from the findings described in the previous section – when experiencing a threat to their health, optimists experience less distress than do pessimists. The reasons for these differences are less apparent, however. Perhaps optimists are just more cheerful than pessimists, or have a bias to see the world in a more favorable light. Although possible, this explanation becomes less plausible in studies where differences in distress remain even when statistical controls are instituted for previous distress. Other explanations seem needed. One possibility that is gaining empirical support focuses on the idea that optimists and pessimists cope differently with adversity.

In this section we consider the strategies that optimists and pessimists use to cope with health threats, and we link those differences in coping to differences that have emerged between optimists and pessimists in levels of distress. In many ways, our discussion here represents a more detailed depiction of some of the broad behavioral tendencies described in the self-regulation portion of the chapter. An important theme introduced there was that expectations play a pivotal role in behavioral responses to adversity. People who are confident about the future exert continuing effort, even when dealing with serious adversity. People who are doubtful about the future withdraw effort. They are more likely to try to push the adversity away as though they can somehow escape its existence by wishful thinking, and they are more likely to do things that provide temporary distractions but don't help solve the problem. Sometimes they even give up completely.

A number of the studies on optimism and distress (some reviewed previously) have also contained measures of coping tendencies. This allowed those researchers to examine whether the differences they observed in well-being were mediated by differences in coping. Several of these studies examined the relationship between optimism, coping, and distress among cancer patients. One study in this group followed women undergoing breast biopsy (Stanton and Snider, 1993). Optimism, coping, and mood were assessed the day before biopsy in all women participating in the study. Women who received a cancer diagnosis were then reassessed 24 hours before surgery and 3 weeks after surgery. Women with a benign diagnosis completed a second assessment that corresponded to either the second or the third assessment of the cancer group. Pessimists used more cognitive avoidance in coping with the upcoming diagnostic procedure than did optimists. This contributed significantly to distress prior to biopsy, and also predicted post-biopsy distress among women with positive diagnoses.

Another study of cancer patients, mentioned earlier in the chapter, examined the ways women cope with treatment for early stage breast cancer during the first full year after treatment (Carver et al., 1993). Optimism, coping (with the diagnosis of cancer), and mood were assessed the day before surgery. Coping and mood were also assessed 10 days post-surgery, and at three follow-up points during the next year. Both before and after surgery, optimism was associated with a pattern of reported coping tactics that revolved around accepting the reality of the situation, placing as positive a light on the situation as possible, trying to relieve the situation with humor, and (at pre-surgery only) taking active steps to do whatever there was to be done. Pessimism related to denial and behavioral disengagement (giving up) at each measurement point.

The coping tactics that related to optimism and pessimism also related to distress. Positive reframing, acceptance, and the use of humor all related inversely to self-reported distress, both before surgery and after. Denial and behavioral disengagement related positively to distress at all measurement points. At the 6-month point a new association emerged, such that distress related positively to another kind of avoidance coping: self-distraction. Not unexpectedly, given the pattern of the correlations, further analyses revealed that the effect of optimism on distress was largely indirect through coping, particularly at post-surgery.

The fact that optimists and pessimists differed in their use of problem focused-coping at pre-surgery is entirely consistent with the self-regulation model presented earlier. Not directly predicted, however, was the fact that optimists and pessimists also differed on accepting the reality of this difficult situation. In retrospect, however, the findings fit the self-regulation framework. That is, it probably is easier to accept the reality of a bad situation if one is confident of favorable eventual outcomes. Further, acceptance of a hard situation is the first necessary step in the process of dealing with and overcoming the threat that the situation imposes.

We find it particularly noteworthy that optimists turn in part toward acceptance whereas pessimists tend toward denial. Denial (the refusal to accept the reality of the situation) means trying to adhere to a world view that is no longer valid. In contrast, acceptance implies a restructuring of one's experience to come to grips with the reality of the situation. Acceptance thus may involve a deeper set of processes, in which the person actively works through the experience, attempting to integrate it into an evolving world view (cf. Janoff-Bulman, 1992; Tedeschi and Calhoun, 1995).

The attempt to come to terms with the existence of problems may confer special benefit to acceptance as a coping response. We should be very clear, however, about what we mean. The acceptance we are stressing here is a willingness to admit that a problem exists or that an event has happened – even an event that may irrevocably alter the fabric of the person's life. We are *not* talking about a stoic resignation, a fatalistic acceptance of the negative consequences to which the problem or event might lead, no matter how likely those consequences might be. The latter response does not confer a benefit and may even be detrimental (Greer et al. 1979; 1990; Pettingale et al., 1985; Reed et al., 1994; for further discussion of this issue see Scheier and Carver, 2001).

In addition to the data on cancer, data are also available linking coping and distress among patients undergoing coronary artery bypass surgery. One study assessed the use of attentional-cognitive strategies as ways of dealing with the stress produced by the surgery and recovery (Scheier et al., 1989). Before surgery, optimists were more likely than pessimists to report that they were making plans for their future and setting goals for their recovery (remaining engaged with their personal futures). Optimists, as compared to pessimists, also tended to report being less focused on the negative aspects of their experience – their distress emotions and physical symptoms.

Once the surgery was past, optimists were more likely than pessimists to seek out and request information about what the physician would be requiring of them in the months ahead (reflecting greater engagement in the recovery process). Optimists were also less likely to report trying to suppress thoughts about their physical symptoms. Results from path analyses suggested that the positive impact of optimism on quality of life 6 months post-surgery occurred through the indirect effect of differences in coping.

Similarly, King et al. (1998) also assessed coping in their study of women undergoing coronary bypass graft surgery. In general, optimists displayed more positive thinking during the week following surgery, engaged in more attempts at finding meaning at 1 month, and employed less escapism at 12 months. Mediational analyses demonstrated that finding meaning and escapism were responsible, at least in part, for the relation observed between optimism and negative mood.

The study of adaptation to failed in vitro fertilization described earlier (Litt et al., 1992) also examined coping. Although the researchers did not find a relationship in this study between optimism and instrumental coping, they did find that pessimism related to escape as a coping strategy. Escape, in turn, related to greater distress after the fertilization failure. In addition, optimists were more likely than pessimists to report feeling that they benefited somehow from the failed fertilization experience (e.g., by becoming closer to their spouse).

Finally, in a study described earlier concerning adjustment to pregnancy (Park et al., 1997), optimistic women were more likely than pessimistic women to engage in constructive thinking (i.e., the tendency to think about and solve daily problems in an effective way). Further, as with optimism, constructive thinking also correlated negatively with later anxiety and positively with later positive states of mind. Subsequent analyses revealed that the association between optimism and each of these markers of psychological adjustment was mediated through the tendency of optimists to engage in constructive (problem-focused) thinking.

In sum, these studies indicate that optimists differ from pessimists in the kinds of coping strategies they use when confronting health threats. In general, findings from this research suggest that optimists tend to use more problem-focused coping strategies than do pessimists. When problem-focused coping is not feasible, optimists turn to adaptive emotion-focused coping strategies such as acceptance, use of humor, and positive reframing. Pessimists tend to cope through overt denial and by mentally and behaviorally disengaging from the goals with which the stressor is interfering. Moreover, these differences in coping appear to be at least partly responsible for differences between optimists and pessimists in emotional well-being. The findings thus implicate elements of self-regulation models in coping with chronic illness and other threats to physical health.

It is important to realize that the various associations that have emerged between optimism and coping do not seem to be due simply to a difference in the manner in which optimists and pessimists appraise events. For example, Chang (1998) examined the impact of optimism and appraisals on coping with an upcoming course exam. Optimists and pessimists did not differ in their primary appraisal of the event, but did differ in terms of their secondary appraisal. That is, optimists perceived the exam to be more controllable and their efforts to cope with it more effective than did pessimists. On the other hand, significant differences still emerged between optimism and several varieties of coping even after the effect of secondary appraisals on coping was statistically controlled.

Promoting Well-being

In describing how optimists and pessimists cope with health threats, several other studies are worth noting. As a group, these studies demonstrate that optimists are more likely than pessimists to engage in proactive processes that promote good health and well-being (Aspinwall, 1997; Aspinwall and Taylor, 1997). Alternatively, the behavior might be seen as attempts to move away from conditions that put the person at higher risk for disease or disease progression – escape from anti-goals.

One study looking at individual differences in health promotion followed a group of heart patients who were participating in a cardiac rehabilitation program (Shepperd et al., 1996). Optimism was related to greater success in lowering levels of saturated fat, body fat, and global coronary risk. Optimism was also related to increases in level of exercise across the rehabilitation period. Another study (cited in Scheier and Carver, 1992) investigated the lifestyles of coronary artery bypass patients 5 years after their surgery. This study found that optimists were more likely than pessimists to be taking vitamins, to be eating low-fat foods, and to be enrolled in a cardiac rehabilitation program.

Another study on bypass patients is also relevant here, as well (Scheier et al., 1999). This report focused on a medical problem that sometimes arises after bypass surgery: the need for rehospitalization, due to infection from the surgery or to complications from the underlying disease. Scheier et al. (1999) found that optimists were significantly less likely to be rehospitalized, controlling for medical variables and other personality characteristics, including trait anxiety, self-esteem, and self-mastery. It is not clear whether this effect stems from differences in the tendency to engage in proactive health behaviors following surgery (e.g., remaining active, complying more fully with medical regimens), from differences in emotional responses, or from concomitant differences in the physical processes inside the patients (e.g., immune function). Nonetheless, the finding is consistent with the notion that optimistic people are more likely than pessimistic people to engage in positive health practices that promote better recovery.

Heart disease is not the only health problem in which optimism has been linked to risk avoidance. Another obvious health risk related to people's behavior is HIV infection. By avoiding certain sexual practices (e.g., sex with unknown partners), people reduce their risk of infection. One study of HIV-negative gay men revealed that optimists reported having fewer anonymous sexual partners than did pessimists (Taylor et al., 1992). Another study found that among sexually active inner-city minority adolescents, optimists reported stronger intentions of avoiding unsafe sex (Carvajal et al., 1998). Taken together, these findings suggest that optimists were making efforts or intending to make efforts to reduce their risk, thereby safeguarding their health.

One final study is also relevant here. Friedman et al. (1995) examined health behavior and health behavior intentions among a group of hospital employees at risk for skin cancer. Optimists were more likely than pessimists to report intentions to engage in skin cancer-relevant health prevention behaviors (e.g., regular sunscreen use). In addition, among those with suspicious lesions at screening, those who were more optimistic were more likely to comply with recommended follow-up care.

Other studies have examined the health-related habits reported by groups of people with no particular salient health concerns. At least two such projects found associations such that optimists reported more health-promoting behaviors than pessimists (Robbins et al., 1991; Steptoe et al., 1994). In sum, the various studies that we have described in the preceding paragraphs suggest that optimism is associated with behaviors aimed at promoting health and reducing health risk.

Consistent with this pattern is research showing conclusively that optimists aren't simply people who stick their heads in the sand and ignore threats to their well-being. Rather, they display a pattern of attending selectively to risks – risks that both are applicable to them and also are related to serious health problems (Aspinwall and Brunhart, 1996). If the potential health problem is minor, or if it is unlikely to bear on them personally, optimists don't show this elevated vigilance. Only when the threat matters does it emerge. This fits the idea that optimists scan their surroundings for threats to their well-being, but save their active coping efforts for threats that are truly meaningful.

Concluding Comment

The purpose of this chapter was to explore the implications of self-regulatory models of human action for understanding how people react to the stress induced by illness threats. We began by describing a general model of behavioral self-regulation. We then described how aspects of that model – variations in positive and negative expectations – are reflected in a line of research on responses to several different types of health problems and illness threats.

In general, the data reviewed here showed that optimistic persons react with less distress when confronting health problems than do persons who are more pessimistic in outlook. Related data further suggested that optimists experience better psychological outcomes in part because of the manner in which they cope with their illness episodes and health problems. That is, they confront health threats with active attempts to deal with the problem at hand, doing what they can to aid their recovery and promote good health. Consistent with this problem-focused approach to coping, they are also more likely than pessimists to accept that they have a problem in the first place, and are less likely to engage in denial and other forms of avoidance coping.

Although the evidence we reviewed is quite consistent with self-regulatory models of action, it is also important to realize that testing the implications of such models is still in its infancy. For example, coping clearly explains part of the association between optimism and distress, but it does not explain all of the shared variance between the two variables. Other mechanisms are needed. Further, the majority of the research that has been conducted has explored implications for psychological well-being. Although studies are also beginning to document associations between optimism and physical well-being (e.g., Scheier et al., 1989; 1999; Schulz et al., 1996), more research on physical health outcomes is desirable.

Finally, it might be time to step back a bit from the prior research on expectancies and utilize more fully the broad heuristic value that self-regulatory models provide. Although variations in expectations, such as individual differences in optimism and pessimism, are clearly important in predicting reactions to health-related events, they are only a part of the set of variables and processes that self-regulatory models identify. Also important are variations in planning and problem solving skills – as are the need at times to reprioritize one's goals and to scale back on one's aspirations, in order to maintain a sense of engagement with life. Self-regulatory models can help us to understand when and how such variables are important. Our sense is that future research (and theorizing) would benefit by exploring the implications of self-regulatory models more fully.

Acknowledgments

Preparation of this chapter was facilitated by support from the National Cancer Institute (grants CA64710, CA64711, CA78995, and CA84944) and the National Heart, Lung, and Blood Institute (grants HL65111 and HL 65112).

Correspondence concerning this chapter should be sent to: Michael F. Scheier, Department of Psychology, Carnegie Mellon University, Pittsburgh, PA 15213, USA; e-mail: scheier@cmu.edu

References

Affleck, G., Tennen, H., Pfeiffer, C., and Fifield, J. (1987). Appraisals of control and predictability in adapting to a chronic disease. *Journal of Personality and Socal Psychology*, 53, 273–9.

Armor, D. A., and Taylor, S. E. (1998). Situated optimism: Specific outcome expectancies and self-regulation. In M. Zanna (Ed.), *Advances in Experimental Social Psychology* (Vol. 29, pp. 309–79). San Diego: Academic Press.

Aspinwall, L. G. (1997). Where planning meets coping: Proactive coping and the detection and management of potential stressors. In S. L. Friedman, and E. K. Scholnick (Eds.), *The Developmental Psychology of Planning: Why, How, and When Do We Plan?* (pp. 285–320). Mahwah, NJ: Erlbaum.

Aspinwall, L. G., and Brunhart, S. N. (1996). Distinguishing optimism from denial: Optimistic beliefs predict attention to health threats. *Personality and Social Psychology Bulletin*, 22, 993–1003.

Aspinwall, L. G., and Taylor, S. E. (1992). Modeling cognitive adaptation: A longitudinal investigation of the impact of individual differences and coping on college adjustment and performance. *Journal of Personality and Social Psychology*, 61, 755–65.

Aspinwall, L. G., and Taylor, S. E. (1997). A stitch in time: Self-regulation and proactive coping. *Psychological Bulletin*, 121, 417–36.

Austin, J. T., and Vancouver, J. B. (1996). Goal constructs in psychology: Structure, process, and content. *Psychological Bulletin*, 120, 338–75.

Bandura, A. (1986). *Social Foundations of Thought and Action: A Social Cognitive Theory*. Englewood Cliffs, NJ: Prentice-Hall.

Bandura, A. (1997). *Self-efficacy: The Exercise of Control*. New York: Freeman.

Baumeister, R. F. (1989). The problem of life's meaning. In D. M. Buss and N. Cantor (Eds.), *Personality Psychology: Recent Trends and Emerging Directions* (pp. 138–48). New York: Springer-Verlag.

Baumann, L. J., and Leventhal, H. (1985). "I can tell when my blood pressure is up, can't I?" *Health Psychologist*, 4, 203–18.

Brunstein, J. C. (1993). Personal goals and subjective well-being: A longitudinal study. *Journal of Personality and Social Psychology*, 65, 1061–70.

Cameron, L. D., and Nicholls, G. (1998). Expression of stressful experiences through writing: Effects of a self-regulation manipulation for pessimists and optimists. *Health Psychology*, 17, 84–92.

Cantor, N., and Kihlstrom, J. F. (1987). *Personality and Social Intelligence*. Englewood Cliffs, NJ: Prentice-Hall.

Carvajal, S. C., Garner, R. L., and Evans, R. I. (1998). Dispositional optimism as a protective factor in resisting HIV exposure in sexually active inner-city minority adolescents. *Journal of Applied Social Psychology*, 28, 2196–211.

Carver, C. S. (1997). The Internal–External scale confounds internal locus of control with expectancies of positive outcomes. *Personality and Social Psychology Bulletin*, 23, 580–5.

Carver, C. S., and Gaines, J. G. (1987). Optimism, pessimism, and postpartum depression. *Cognitive Therapy and Research*, 11, 449–62.

Carver, C. S., Harris, S. D., Lehman, J. M. et al. (2000). How important is the perception of personal control? Studies of early stage breast cancer patients. *Personality and Social Psychology Bulletin*, 26, 139–150.

Carver, C. S., and Humphries, C. (1981). Havana daydreaming: A study of self-consciousness and the negative reference group among Cuban Americans. *Journal of Personality and Social Psychology*, 40, 545–52.

Carver, C. S., Lawrence, J. W., and Scheier, M. F. (1999). Self-discrepancies and affect: Incorporating the role of feared selves. *Personality and Social Psychology Bulletin*, 25, 783–92.

Carver, C. S., Pozo, C., Harris, S. D. et al. (1993). How coping mediates the effect of optimism on distress: A study of women with early stage breast cancer. *Journal of Personality and Social Psychology*, 65, 375–90.

Carver, C. S., and Scheier, M. F. (1981). *Attention and Self-regulation: A Control-theory Approach to Human Behavior*. New York: Springer Verlag.

Carver, C. S., and Scheier, M. F. (1990). Origins and functions of positive and negative affect: A control-process view. *Psychological Review*, 97, 19–35.

Carver, C. S., and Scheier, M. F. (1998). *On the Self-regulation of Behavior*. New York: Cambridge University Press.

Carver, C. S., and Scheier, M. F. (1999a). A few more themes, a lot more issues: Commentary on the commentaries. In R. S. Wyer, Jr. (Ed.), *Advances in Social Cognition* (Vol. 12, pp. 261–302). Mahwah, NJ: Erlbaum.

Carver, C. S., and Scheier, M. F. (1999b). Themes and issues in the self-regulation of behavior. In R. S. Wyer, Jr., (Ed.), *Advances in Social Cognition* (Vol. 12, pp. 1–105). Mahwah, NJ: Erlbaum.

Chang, E. C. (1998). Dispositional optimism and primary and secondary appraisal of a stressor: Controlling for confounding influences and relations to coping and psychological and physical adjustment. *Journal of Personality and Social Psychology*, 74, 1109–20.

Chamberlain, K., Petrie, K., and Azaria, R. (1992). The role of optimism and sense of coherence in predicting recovery following surgery. *Psychology and Health*, 7, 301–10.

Christman, N. J. (1990). Uncertainty and adjustment during radiotherapy. *Nursing Research*, 39, 17–20, continued on 47.

Clark, L. F., Henry, S. M., and Taylor, D. M. (1991). Cognitive examination of motivation for childbearing as a factor in adjustment to infertility. In A. L. Stanton and C. Dunkel-Schetter (Eds.), *Infertility: Perspectives from Stress and Coping Research* (pp. 157–80). New York: Plenum.

Cozzarelli, C. (1993). Personality and self-efficacy as predictors of coping with abortion. *Journal of Personality and Social Psychology*, 65, 1224–36.

Elliott, E. S., and Dweck, C. S. (1988). Goals: An approach to motivation and achievement. *Journal of Personality and Social Psychology*, 54, 5–12.

Emmons, R. A. (1986). Personal strivings: An approach to personality and subjective well being. *Journal of Personality and Social Psychology*, 51, 1058–68.

Fitzgerald, T. E., Tennen, H., Affleck, G., and Pransky, G. S. (1993). The relative importance of dispositional optimism and control appraisals in quality of life after coronary artery bypass surgery. *Journal of Behavioral Medicine*, 16, 25–43.

Fontaine, K. R. and Jones, L. C. (1997). Self-esteem, optimism, and postpartum depression. *Journal of Clinical Psychology*, 53, 59–63.

Friedman, L. C., Weinberg, A. D., Webb, J. A., Cooper, H. P., and Bruce, S. (1995). Skin cancer prevention and early detection intentions and behavior. *American Journal of Preventive Medicine*, 11, 59–65.

Frijda, N. H. (1986). *The Emotions*. Cambridge: Cambridge University Press.

Frijda, N. H. (1988). The laws of emotion. *American Psychologist*, 43, 349–58.

Given, C. W., Stommel, M., Given, B., Osuch, J., Kurtz, M. E., and Kurtz, J. C. (1993). The influence of cancer patients' symptoms and functional states on patients' depression and family caregivers' reaction and depression. *Health Psychology*, 12, 277–85.

Greer, S., Morris, T., and Pettingale, K. W. (1979). Psychological response to breast cancer: Effect on outcome. *Lancet*, 2, 785–7.

Greer, S., Morris, T., Pettingale, K. W., and Haybittle, J. L. (1990). Psychological response to breast cancer and 15-year outcome. *Lancet*, 1, 49–50.

Guy, J. L., and Lord, R. G. (1998). The effects of perceived velocity on job satisfaction: An expansion of current theory. Paper presented and the 10th Annual Conference of the American Psychological Society, Washington, DC, May.

Higgins, E. T. (1987). Self-discrepancy: A theory relating self and affect. *Psychological Review*, 94, 319–40.

Higgins, E. T. (1996). Ideals, oughts, and regulatory focus: Affect and motivation from distinct pains and pleasures. In P. M. Gollwitzer and J. A. Bargh (Eds.), *The Psychology of Action: Linking Cognition and Motivation to Behavior* (pp. 91–114). New York: Guilford.

Hooker, K., Monahan, D., Shifren, K., and Hutchinson, C. (1992). Mental and physical health of spouse caregivers: The role of personality. *Psychology and Aging*, 7, 367–75.

Hsee, C. K., and Abelson, R. P. (1991). Velocity relation: Satisfaction as a function of the first derivative of outcome over time. *Journal of Personality and Social Psychology*, 60, 341–7.

Janoff-Bulman, R. (1992). *Shattered Assumptions*. New York: Free Press.

Johnson, J. E. (1996). Coping with radiation therapy: Optimism and the effect of preparatory interventions. *Research in Nursing and Health*, 19, 3–12.

King, K. B., Rowe, M. A., Kimble, L. P., and Zerwic, J. J. (1998). Optimism, coping, and long-term recovery from coronary artery bypass in women. *Research in Nursing and Health*, 21, 15–26.

Klinger, E. (1975). Consequences of commitment to and disengagement from incentives. *Psychological Review*, 82, 1–25.

Kukla, A. (1972). Foundations of an attributional theory of performance. *Psychological Review*, 79, 454–70.

Lau, R. R., and Hartman, K. A. (1983). Common sense representations of common illnesses. *Health Psychology*, 2, 167–85.

Lawrence, J. W., Carver, C. S., and Scheier, M. F. (2002). Velocity toward goal attainment in immediate experience as a determinant of affect. *Journal of Applied Social Psychology*, 32, 788–802.

Lazarus, R. S. (1966). *Psychological Stress and the Coping Process*. New York: McGraw-Hill.

Leedham, B., Meyerowitz, B. E., Muirhead, J., and Frist, W. H. (1995). Positive expectations predict health after heart transplantation. *Health Psychology*, 14, 74–9.

Leventhal, H., and Carr, S. (2001). Speculations on the relationship of behavioral theory to psychosocial research on cancer. In A. Baum and B. L. Andersen (Eds.), *Psychosocial Interventions for Cancer* (pp. 375–400). Washington, DC: American Psychological Association.

Leventhal, H., Leventhal, E. A., and Cameron, L. (2001). Representations, procedures and affect in illness self regulation: A perceptual-cognitive model. In A. Baum, T. Revenson, and J. Weinman (Eds.), *Handbook of Health Psychology* (pp. 19–48). Hillsdale, NJ: Erlbaum.

Leventhal, H., Meyer, D., and Nerenz, D. (1980). The common sense representation of illness danger. In S. Rachman (Ed.), *Medical Psychology* (Vol. 2, pp. 7–30). New York: Permagon Press.

Linville, P. (1985). Self-complexity and affective extremity: Don't put all of your eggs in one cognitive basket. *Social Cognition*, 3, 94–120.

Linville, P. (1987). Self-complexity as a cognitive buffer against stress-related illness and depression. *Journal of Personality and Social Psychology*, 52, 663–76.

Litt, M. D., Tennen, H., Affleck, G., and Klock, S. (1992). Coping and cognitive factors in adaptation to *in vitro* fertilization failure. *Journal of Behavioral Medicine*, 15, 171–87.

Little, B. R. (1989). Personal projects analysis: Trivial pursuits, magnificent obsessions, and the search for coherence. In D. M. Buss and N. Cantor (Eds.), *Personality Psychology: Recent Trends and Emerging Directions* (pp. 15–31). New York: Springer-Verlag.

MacNair, R. R., and Elliott, T. R. (1992). Self-perceived problem-solving ability, stress appraisal, and coping over time. *Journal of Research in Personality*, 26, 150–64.

Major, B., Richards, C., Cooper, M. L., Cozzarelli, C., and Zubek, J. (1998). Personal resilience, cognitive appraisals, and coping: An integrative model of adjustment to abortion. *Journal of Personality and Social Psychology*, 74, 735–52.

Markus, H., and Nurius, P. (1986). Possible selves. *American Psychologist*, 41, 954–69.

Meyer, D., Leventhal, H., and Gutmann, M. (1985). Common-sense models of illness: The example of hypertension. *Health Psychology*, 4, 115–35.

Miller, G. A., Galanter, E., and Pribram, K. H. (1960). *Plans and the Structure of Behavior*. New York: Holt, Rinehart, and Winston.

Miller, L. C., and Read, S. J. (1987). Why am I telling you this? Self-disclosure in a goal-based model of personality. In V. J. Derlega and J. Berg (Eds.), *Self-disclosure: Theory, Research, and Therapy* (pp. 35–58). New York: Plenum.

Moskowitz, J., Folkman, S., Collette, L., and Vittinghoff, E. (1996). Coping and mood during AIDS-related caregiving and bereavement. *Annals of Behavioral Medicine*, 18, 49–57.

Murphy, P. E., Ciarrocchi, J. W., Piedmont, R. L., Cheston, S., Peyrot, M., and Fitchett, G. (2000). The relation of religious belief and practices, depression, and hopelessness in persons with clinical depression. *Journal of Consulting and Clinical Psychology*, 68, 1102–6.

Oettingen, G. (1996). Positive fantasy and motivation. In P. M. Gollwitzer and J. A. Bargh (Eds.), *The Psychology of Action: Linking Cognition and Motivation to Behavior* (pp. 219–35). New York: Guilford Press.

Park, C. L., Moore, P. J., Turner, R. A., and Adler, N. E. (1997). The roles of constructive thinking and optimism in psychological and behavioral adjustment during pregnancy. *Journal of Personality and Social Psychology*, 73, 584–92.

Pervin, L. A. (1982). The stasis and flow of behavior: Toward a theory of goals. In M. M. Page and R. Dienstbier (Eds.), *Nebraska Symposium on Motivation* (Vol. 30, pp. 1–53). Lincoln: University of Nebraska Press.

Pervin, L. A. (Ed.) (1989). *Goal Concepts in Personality and Social Psychology*. Hillsdale, NJ: Erlbaum.

Peterson, C., and Seligman, M. E. P. (1984). Causal explanations as a risk factor for depression: Theory and evidence. *Psychological Review*, 91, 347–74.

Pettingale, K. W., Morris, T., and Greer, S. (1985). Mental attitudes to cancer: An additional prognostic factor. *Lancet*, 1, 750.

Pittman, T. S., and Pittman, N. L. (1980). Deprivation of control and the attribution process. *Journal of Personality and Social Psychology*, 39, 377–89.

Powers, W. T. (1973). *Behavior: The Control of Perception*. Chicago: Aldine.

Reed, G. M., Kemeny, M. E., Taylor, S. E., et al. (1994). "Realistic acceptance" as a predictor of decreased survival time in gay men with AIDS. *Health Psychology*, 13, 299–307.

Robbins, A. S., Spence, J. T., and Clark, H. (1991). Psychological determinants of health and performance: The tangled web of desirable and undesirable character-istics. *Journal of Personality and Social Psychology*, 61, 755–65.

Scheier, M. F., and Carver, C. S. (1985). Optimism, coping and health: Assessment and implications of generalized outcome expectancies. *Health Psychology*, 4, 219–47.

Scheier, M. F., and Carver, C. S. (1992). Effects of optimism on psychological and physical well-being: Theoretical overview and empirical update. *Cognitive Therapy and Research*, 16, 201–28.

Scheier, M. F., and Carver, C. S. (2001). Adapting to cancer: The importance of hope and purpose. In A. Baum and B. L. Andersen (Eds.), *Psychosocial Interventions for Cancer* (pp. 15–36). Washington, DC: American Psychological Association.

Scheier, M. F., Carver, C. S., and Bridges, M. W. (1994). Distinguishing optimism from neuroticism (and trait anxiety, self-mastery, and self-esteem): A reevaluatioon of the Life Orientation Test. *Journal of Personality and Social Psychology*, 67, 1063–78.

Scheier, M. F., Matthews, K. A., Owens, J. F. et al. (1989). Dispositional optimism and recovery from coronary artery bypass surgery: The beneficial effects on physical and psychological well-being. *Journal of Personality and Social Psychology*, 57, 1024–40.

Scheier, M. F., Matthews, K. A., Owens, J. F. et al. (1999). Optimism and rehospitaliza-tion following coronary artery bypass graft surgery. *Archives of Internal Medicine*, 159, 829–35.

Schulz, R., Bookwala, J., Knapp, J. E., Scheier, M. F., and Williamson, G. M. (1996). Pessimism, age, and cancer mortality. *Psychology and Aging*, 11, 304–9.

Seligman, M. E. P. (1991). *Learned Optimism*. New York: Knopf.

Shepperd, J. A., Maroto, J. J., and Pbert, L. A. (1996). Dispositional optimism as a predictor of health changes among cardiac patients. *Journal of Research in Personality*, 30, 517–34.

Shifren, K., and Hooker, K. (1995). Stability and change in optimism: A study among spouse caregivers. *Experimental Aging Research*, 21, 59–76.

Showers, C., and Ryff, C. (1996). Self-differentiation and well-being in a life transi-tion. *Personality and Social Psychology Bulletin*, 22, 448–60.

Smith, C. A., Wallston, K. A., and Dwyer, K. A. (1994). On babies and bathwater: Disease impact and negative affectivity in the self-reports of persons with rheum-atoid arthritis. *Health Psychology*, 14, 64–73.

Snyder, C. R. (1994). *The Psychology of Hope: You Can Get There from Here*. New York: Free Press.

Stanton, A. L., and Snider, P. R. (1993). Coping with breast cancer diagnosis: A prospective study. *Health Psychology*, 12, 16–23.

Steptoe, A., Wardle, J., Vinck, J., Tuomisto, M., Holte, A., and Wichstrøm, L. (1994). Personality and attitudinal correlates of healthy lifestyles in young adults. *Psychology and Health*, 9, 331–43.

Taylor, S. E., Kemeny, M. E., Aspinwall, L. G., Schneider, S. G., Rodriguez, R., and Herbert, M. (1992). Optimism, coping, psychological distress, and high-risk sexual behavior among men at risk for Acquired Immunodeficiency Syndrome (AIDS). *Journal of Personality and Social Psychology*, 63, 460–73.

Taylor, S. E., and Pham, L. B. (1996). Mental simulation, motivation, and action. In P. M. Gollwitzer and J. A. Bargh (Eds.), *The Psychology of Action: Linking Cognition and Motivation to Behavior* (pp. 219–35). New York: Guilford.

Taylor, S. E., Pham, L. B., Rivkin, I. D., and Armor, D. A. (1998). Harnessing the imagination: Mental simulation, self-regulation, and coping. *American Psychologist*, 53, 429–39.

Tedeschi, R. G., and Calhoun, L. G. (1995). *Trauma and Transformation: Growing in the Aftermath of Suffering*. Thousand Oaks, CA: Sage.

Thompson, S. C., and Spacapan, S. (1991). Perceptions of control in vulnerable populations. *Journal of Social Issues*, 47, 1–21.

Tompkins, C. A., Schulz, R., and Rau, M. T. (1988). Post-stroke depression in primary support persons: predicting those at risk. *Journal of Consulting and Clinical Psychology*, 56, 502–8.

Vallacher, R. R., and Wegner, D. M. (1985). *A Theory of Action Identification*. Hillsdale, NJ: Erlbaum.

Vallacher, R. R., and Wegner, D. M. (1987). What do people think they're doing? Action identification and human behavior. *Psychological Review*, 94, 3–15.

Wicklund, R., and Gollwitzer, P. (1982). *Symbolic self-completion*. Hillsdale, NJ: Lawrence Erlbaum Publishers.

Wills, T. A. (1981). Downward comparison principles in social psychology. *Psychological Bulletin*, 90, 245–71.

Wong, P. T. P., and Weiner, B. (1981). When people ask "why" questions, and the heuristics of attributional search. *Journal of Personality and Social Psychology*, 40, 650–63.

Wood, J. V. (1989). Theory and research concerning social comparisons of personal attributes. *Psychological Bulletin*, 106, 231–48.

Wood, J. V., Taylor, S. E., and Lichtman, R. R. (1985). Social comparison in adjustment to breast cancer. *Journal of Personality and Social Psychology*, 49, 1169–83.

Wortman, C. B., and Brehm, J. W. (1975). Responses to uncontrollable outcomes: An integration of reactance theory and the learned helplessness model. In L. Berkowitz (Ed.), *Advances in Experimental Social Psychology* (Vol. 8, pp. 277–336). New York: Academic Press.

Zeidner, M., and Hammer, A. L. (1992). Coping with missile attack: Resources, strategies, and outcomes. *Journal of Personality*, 60, 709–46.

PART IV

Adaptation to Stress and Chronic Illness

The Influence of Psychological Factors on Restorative Function in Health and Illness

Ashley W. Smith and Andrew Baum

University of Pittsburgh

Introduction

Stress and related syndromes such as burnout have been shown to cause emotional disturbances and have deleterious health effects. As a result, considerable attention has been focused on methods of intervention to reduce or prevent stress or its effects. Stress management represents a large clinical concentration and an active research area. Interestingly, one important way that people can relieve distress and ease its consequences is not a new intervention at all. Participation in restorative activities such as sleep, exercise, relaxation, vacation, social interaction, and spending time in natural environments that support restoration all appear to be good ways of reducing stress. Several psychological factors may be related to these effects of restoration on health and illness, including coping, self-efficacy, motivation, perceived control and personality factors, and a major pathway underlying these psychological factors is positive emotion. This chapter discusses the importance of engaging in restorative functions to promote improved mental and physical health. We review research suggesting that restorative behaviors lead to better physical and emotional functioning and discuss potential psychological mechanisms that may be involved in the relationship between restoration and health.

Restorative Function in the Context of "Positive Psychology"

"Treatment is not just about fixing what is broken, it is nurturing what is best" (Seligman and Csikszentmihalyi, 2000: 7).

Positive Psychology and Health

The last few years have been marked by renewed interest in positive psychology and of applications of positive psychological states and situations. Many researchers have examined the beneficial effects of positive behaviors, qualities, emotions and attributes on psychological and physical well-being (e.g. Fredrickson, 2001; Folkman, 2000; Gillham and Seligman, 1999; Salovey et al., 2000; Seligman, 2000; Seligman and Csikszentmihalyi, 2000; Sheldon and King, 2001; Taylor et al., 2000). An important aspect of this is the concept of restoration – that is, engaging in activities that allow one to "recharge his or her batteries" to replenish energies that support optimal behavior and thought.

The biological underpinnings of restoration can be illustrated by considering basic physiological processes involving refraction. Restoration refers to the fact that physiological systems (such as the nervous system and its constituent neurons) need time to restore their ability to react. A neuron that has fired cannot fire again until refraction is accomplished. After refraction, neurons can respond fully and rapidly. Similar effects are seen with skeletal muscle and its ability to respond and grow. During physical training, muscle hypertrophy occurs in which repeated injury to muscle fibers results in overcompensation of protein synthesis during rest. After resting, muscle fibers are able to respond with similar or increased strength. Similar processes appear to govern behavior and well-being. Restoration is also a useful method for buffering, reducing, and coping with the harmful effects of stress on the body.

Historically, psychologists have been narrowly focused on negative states leading to pathology and disorder, generally neglecting the influence of positive qualities on life satisfaction, quality of life, and health (Gillham and Seligman, 1999). While understanding that pathology and disease are important and essential topics for psychologists, they only explain part of human experience. To create more complete models and explanatory theories of behaviors and of physiological and psychological contributors to health and illness, our focus needs to be broad enough to include stress and its effects, as well as methods of restoration and optimal functioning (Gillham and Seligman, 1999; Seligman and Csikszentmihalyi, 2000).

Although an emphasis on physical and psychological damage rather than on fortitude and resiliency may help scientists and practitioners understand negative states, it does not always provide solutions (Gillham and Seligman, 1999). Under-researched areas such as creativity, hope, and persistence are as important as research on anxiety, depression and helplessness in understanding and explaining psychological health and well-being. The goals for developing a new, more positive psychology are to foster skill development, talent, and creativity, and to promote emotional states including happiness, contentment, optimism, and hope, that facilitate a more holistic health in all people (Seligman and Csikszentmihalyi, 2000).

Health Promotion and Positive Mood

Extreme stressors, trauma, bereavement or major illnesses can cause grievous harm and lead people to experience profound mental and physical dysfunction. However, even in cases of severe stress, victims show considerable variability in response and many recover from them readily. Research on post-traumatic stress disorder (PTSD) suggests that fewer than half of those exposed to traumatic stressors experience PTSD, and we have many examples of people returning from adversity (e.g. Folkman, 1997; Frankl, 1963; Janoff-Bulman and Berg, 1998; Janoff-Bulman and McPherson Frantz, 1997; Davis et al., 1998; Tedeschi et al., 1998). It is essential that scientists learn from these examples to better understand how to promote resiliency and assist in recovery from stressful or traumatic experiences. For researchers and practitioners, encouraging resiliency and psychological health can be encompassed in a more general emphasis on positive health.

An important development over the past 20 years has been a focus on health promotion (Breslow, 1999; National Center for Health Statistics, 1999; Ryff and Singer, 1998; USDHHS, 1991). The Surgeon General's report, *Healthy People 2000* (USDHHS, 1991), outlined comprehensive initiatives designed to increase the span of healthy life, decrease health disparities, and increase healthier behaviors for all Americans. Guidelines were established to provide prescriptions for health promotion targeted at areas such as physical activity, nutrition, mental healthcare, reduced tobacco use, disease prevention, and environmental health and safety. Breslow (1999) broadened this call by asking scientists to persuade the scientific community to focus on health maintenance and promotion. He encouraged them to promote specific behavior changes for American adults in order to achieve health balance. Recommended behavioral changes reflected public health messages; striving for moderate daily physical activity in at least 30 percent of Americans, a reduction in cigarette smoking to no more than 15 percent of adults, and a reduction of alcohol use in adolescents to less than 13 percent, and development of social strategies at various social levels (e.g., individual, community, state, policy; Breslow and Breslow, 1993).

One of the major forces identified by psychologists in establishing connections between mind and body and more holistic human health is emotion (Ryff and Singer, 1998). Extensive research on mood states and emotions have focused on negative emotions such as anger and fear, but recent interest in the effects of positive mood offers new perspectives (Ekman and Davidson, 1994; Folkman and Moskowitz, 2000; Fredrickson, 1998; Lewis and Haviland, 2000). Happiness has received increased attention as an outcome as well as an important emotion related to well-being (Panskepp, 1998; Salovey et al., 2000; Spiegel, 1998), and research suggests that positive emotions may be qualitatively different from negative emotions (Fredrickson, 1998; Folkman, 2000). Positive emotions may be related to physiological pathways that help to regulate responses to stress through release of endogenous opioids (Drolet et al., 2001;

McCubbin et al., 1992). State happiness associated with humor has also been shown to assist people in coping with stress (Martin, 2001; Moran, 1996).

There is more evidence that positive mood may be an integral part of the stress/illness relationship. Research has shown that positive mood may be one factor that helps to buffer stress (e.g. Fredrickson and Levenson, 1998; Smith et al., 2000). Research has also shown more direct links between positive emotion and the immune system (Booth and Pennebaker, 2000; Stone et al., 1987; 1994). Salovey and colleagues (2000) suggest that positive emotions generate psychological resources by promoting resilience, endurance and optimism. Positive mood may be a factor contributing to participation in or initiation of positive health behaviors. In this chapter we discuss the role of mood as an antecedent and consequence of various restorative health behaviors such as exercise.

Need for Restoration

Theorists have long debated whether the world we live in is more stressful than the world of our parents or grandparents. Regardless of how one resolves this debate, it is clear that we live in an increasingly complex, fast-paced world. Stress associated with increased modern technology has been related to both psychological symptoms and physiological arousal, and accidents or malfunctions of technological systems are also stressful (Arnetz and Wiholm, 1997; Baum and Fleming, 1993; Hudiburg and Necessary, 1996). A recent report by the American Public Health Association (2001) noted that people in the United States work longer hours and take fewer vacations, feel more stressed, have heavier workloads and experience less control over schedules than ever before. Increasing job dissatisfaction may be related to changes in job security and lack of skill development. Americans often face work environments in which the demands overwhelm resources, and leaving work does not always provide relief. Many people face stressors such as traffic congestion, car and home repairs, housework, childcare, balancing finances or other home-based stressors. Opportunities for restoration seem increasingly limited.

Work Stress
Occupational stress and burnout are characteristic of our modern industrialized society. Syndromes such as job strain are often produced by jobs that are high in demand, but low in control (Karasek and Thorerell, 1990), and were associated with several negative health outcomes. Job strain predicted physical and psychological health in a national, cross-sectional sample (Lerner et al., 1994) More recent data suggest that job strain is related to psychological symptoms such as stress, anxiety, irritability and fatigue (Cropley et al., 1999; Vedhara et al., 2000). There is also evidence that job strain is associated with increased risk of hypertension and cardiovascular disease (see Theorell and Karasek, 1996 for review; Pickering et al., 1996; Cropley et al., 1999; Weidner et al., 1997).

Burnout is an extreme form of job stress characterized by overwhelming exhaustion and incapacitation (Leiter and Maslach, 2001; Maslach et al., 2001).

In addition to work absenteeism and turnover, burnout has been associated with poor health and health indices (Guglielmi and Tatrow, 1998; Leiter and Maslach, 2001; Iskra-Golec et al., 1996). Although qualitative distinctions have been made, burnout is often related to chronic stress (Brill, 1984; Pines et al., 1981), suggesting incomplete adaptation to stressors that make it conceptually closer to chronic rather than acute stress.

Home Stress

While much stress research has focused on occupational stressors, stress is not confined solely to the workplace. Household duties such as domestic work have been shown to produce exhaustion, insomnia, and increases in blood pressure (Brisson et al., 1999; Tierney et al., 1990). There is also a growing literature detailing psychological and physiological effects of stress associated with caregiving (Folkman et al., 1994; Schulz et al., 1995; Vitaliano et al., 1997). Other stressors that often occur at home include the pressure of financial burdens (Krause and Baker, 1992; Vinokur et al., 1996; Walker, 1996) and childcare responsibilities (Deater-Deckard and Scarr, 1996).

For people who have multiple roles (e.g., employee, community member, and caregiver for children and elderly parents) stress can be compounded (McLaughlin et al., 1988; Stephens et al., 1994; Stephens and Townsend, 1997). Role strain can result from a variety of mixtures of roles, some of which may conflict or require overlapping resources. Women who try to balance home and work appear to be disproportionately affected by strains that occur at home and this can interact with work or other social stressors to produce a formidable burden. For example, women who have both job and home-based responsibilities reported having less recreational time and exhibited higher norepinephrine levels than did men in similar occupations (Lundberg and Frankenhauser, 1999). There is also evidence that women's health is affected by stress associated with multiple roles (Chesney and Ozer, 1995; Orth-Gomér et al., 1998).

Stress and Disease

Stress can affect disease at any point in its development, from etiology and progression to treatment and recovery or recurrence (Dougall and Baum, 2001). There is considerable evidence that stress affects heart disease (see Rozanski et al., 1999, for review). Stress has also been implicated in the etiology and progression of cancer (Baum and Anderson, 2001), infectious illness (Biondi and Zannino, 1997; Cohen and Williamson, 1991), diabetes (Ionescu-Tirgoviste et al., 1987) and autoimmune disorders (Affleck et al., 1997; Zautra et al., 1997; 1998). These effects are presumably products of biological changes that occur during or after stressful encounters and changes in health-impairing behaviors (e.g., smoking) and health protective behaviors (including restorative activities). Behaviors that provide quick relief, such as smoking, alcohol or drug use, may be increased and more restful or anabolic behaviors like sleep, relaxation, and exercise may not fit into a busy schedule. These relationships highlight the need to intervene to reduce stress and its consequences.

Stress and Restoration

Psychological theories of stress can accommodate constructs such as restorative activities as affecting people's perceptions and appraisal of stressors or as emotion-focused coping (Lazarus and Folkman, 1984; Long, 1993). Restorative activities may also distract people from pain or distress. Other researchers have made similar assertions, suggesting that restorative activities may provide an outlet for emotional or physical tension (Bharke and Morgan, 1978; Gal and Lazarus, 1975; Goodway, 1987). The important role of positive emotions as a means of buffering stress or disrupting its ill effects has received less attention. There is some evidence that, after exercising, individuals report improved mood and "feeling better" (Berger and Owen, 1983; Byrne and Byrne, 1993; Yeung, 1996). Positive mood and endogenous opioid release are associated with lower acute stress reactivity (Frederickson and Levenson, 1998; McCubbin et al., 1992; Smith et al., 2000).

In addition to affecting stress appraisal and response, restorative activities often cluster, leading to broad interactive and cumulative behavioral effects. Vacations are often opportunities to relax, sleep, eat better, exercise and interact with friends and family. Alternatively, people who participate in other restorative behaviors, such as exercise, may be more likely to adopt positive health behaviors such as good nutrition and social support development, and reduce negative health behaviors such as cigarette smoking, alcohol use, sedentary behavior (Dienstbier, 1984). Exercise may also have cognitive effects and influence stress appraisal as it enhances self-efficacy, overall self-esteem and perceptions of control (Dienstbier, 1984).

Biological mechanisms explaining the effects of restorative activities on stress often emphasize different pathways, but the results are similar. For example, relaxation and sleep provide time in which heart rate (HR) is slowed and blood pressure (BP) may be reduced. Exercise, on the other hand, may act like a stressor; in its acute phase, it increases heart rate and BP. However, there is evidence that exercise has longer-lasting relaxation effects (DeVries, 1981). Further, increased fitness levels are associated with lower overall sympathetic arousal in exercisers, particularly compared to non-exercisers during periods of stress (Crews and Landers, 1987; Boutcher et al., 1995; Sothmann et al., 1987).

The remainder of this chapter describes evidence that particular restorative activities and environments are beneficial and reduce the effects of daily or ongoing stress. As discussed previously, there are several behaviors that prevent or help relieve stress and are essential to restoring and therefore maintaining physical health and well-being. Activities such as social interaction, relaxation, sleeping, going on vacation, and spending time in natural environments have been shown to improve health.

Social Interaction as Restoration

There is considerable research on the effects of social support and social relationships on health. Reviews of these literatures have reported associations between the amount and quality of social relationships and psychological and physical morbidity (Berkman, 1995; Broadhead et al., 1983; Cohen, 1988; Cohen and Wills, 1985; House et al., 1988). Data suggest that social relationships are related to decreased risk of mortality (Berkman and Syme, 1979), affect psychological and physical functioning in cardiovascular risk and disease (Ford et al., 2000; Kaplan et al., 1988), cancer (Helgeson and Cohen, 1996), and HIV disease (Lutgendorf et al., 1998).

Stress and Social Support

The possibility that interpersonal relations affect physical health and stress buffering has been of interest for many years, but work in this area was not particularly coherent until about 30 years ago, when systematic analyses of social support began to appear (e.g., Cassel, 1976; Cobb, 1976). These analyses provided broad definitions of social support that focused on psychological benefits of comfortable social interactions, and animal research has provided some evidence of the notion that stress associated with disruption of relationships increases risk of disease (e.g., Kaplan and Manuck, 1999; Sachser et al., 1998). In humans, laboratory research suggests that the presence of a friend is associated with reduced cardiovascular reactivity to psychological stressors (Glynn, Christenfeld, and Gerin, 1999; Kamarck et al., 1991; Uchino and Garvey, 1997). Social support has also been associated with faster cardiovascular recovery from stressors (Roy et al., 1998).

Data also suggest that social support reduces or eliminates effects of stress in everyday settings. Social support buffered the relationship between perceived job stress and job strain among 636 men in various occupations, reducing physical complaints, depression and anxiety, and irritability (LaRocco et al., 1980). In a sample of psychiatric nurses, social support was significantly related to health as well as job satisfaction and protected nurses against occupational stress (Munro et al., 1998). A recent study of ambulatory blood pressure and heart rate over the course of a working day suggested that those who reported the most social support over the day showed no significant increase in physiological markers of stress (Steptoe, 2000). Among police officers, better quality of social support derived from interactions at work was associated with less negative mood at the end of the day (Buunk and Verhoeven, 1991).

Extensive evidence that social support provided by close friends and family members has important benefits for people experiencing stress does not suggest universal benefits of social support. Several studies of cancer patients and their families have shown that both the source of support (close family, friends, physicians) and the type of support (e.g., emotional versus informational support) may effect whether the support is perceived as positive (Dakof and Taylor, 1990; Manne et al., 1997; Wortman and Dunkel-Schetter, 1979). For example, advice from friends and family has been shown to be associated with distress in parents who have children with cancer (Smith et al., 2002). Although social support often buffers distress, it may contribute to maladaptive perceptions of dependency, debt, and personal inadequacy under some circumstances.

Interventions that enhance social interaction and support have marked psychological and physiological effects in individuals diagnosed with disease (Cruess et al., 2000; Spiegel et al., 1981; Fawzy et al., 1990). Despite discrepancies in the literature regarding survival associated with supportive group therapy (e.g., Goodwin et al., 2001; Spiegel et al., 1981), there is consistent evidence that group therapy has important psychological effects, including mood and quality of life benefits in late stage cancer patients (Classen et al., 2001; Goodwin et al., 2001; Spiegel et al., 1981). Earlier stage breast cancer patients may benefit more from education than from peer group discussions (Helgeson et al., 2001), but this may be due to a greater need for informational rather than emotional support during early stages of treatment. Several sources of benefit can be identified and go beyond the information and perceived control components of the interventions (see Helgeson and Cohen, 1996). For example, those who are lacking a good social network benefit more from peer discussion groups than those who have effective social networks (Helgeson et al., 1999). Research on support groups provides evidence that social support can improve physiological and psychological adjustment to illness.

Restorative Effects of Social Interactions

One explanation of the benefit of social support is that it increases gratifying social encounters, and there is evidence that increased social contact helps restore individuals. For example, when asked about the kinds of activities they find restorative, elderly respondents commonly report that social interactions such as socializing with friends, family or other residents are activities that they participate in to feel restored (Travis and McCauley, 1998). Research has also shown that interventions involving personal contact and interaction, even over the telephone, are more beneficial than similar interventions delivered by mail (Pelletier et al., 1999).

A review by Cohen and Wills (1985) suggests that the stress-buffering effects of social support are based on the perception that others will provide needed resources (not necessarily based on those needs being fulfilled). However, there is also research that suggests that social interactions may be more important than perceived support in buffering stress. More recent work by Cohen and colleagues (1997) suggested that social contacts (measured as the number of different types of social contacts the respondent interacted with in the previous two weeks) buffered upper respiratory illness. In a study of students preparing to take medical school entrance exams, the number of leisure forms of social interaction (with friends, neighbors and social groups) buffered exam stress, while perceived support did not (Bolger and Eckenrode, 1991). This study also showed that leisure forms of social contact buffered stress whereas obligatory contacts at work did not. Similar research has shown that social contact in the form of leisure companionship reduces stress-related physical health problems (Iso-Ahola and Park, 1996). Both amount of social interaction *and* the perception that that interaction is helpful or that social support is available are independently and synergistically beneficial for psychological and physical health.

Pathways Explaining the Benefits of Social Interactions

Models to explain the effects of social relationships on psychological and physical health suggest that social support may positively affect cognition (e.g., stressor appraisal), health behaviors (e.g., diet, exercise), emotion, neuroendocrine and immune responses, as well as coping (see Cohen et al., 2000; Ryff and Singer, 2001). It has been suggested that one way in which social support and supportive group interactions may exert their beneficial effects on physical health is through increased positive health behaviors and through better medical decision-making (Spiegel and Kimerling, 2001). Low social support has been related to negative health behaviors (Allgoewer et al., 2001). In a study of undergraduates preparing for exams, Steptoe and colleagues (1996) found that social support moderated the effects of stress on smoking and alcohol consumption, although there was no effect on physical activity. In a group of 854 blue-collar women workers, social network and support were associated with physical activity, better nutrition and health care screening (Kelsey et al., 2000).

Social interactions and support may be more useful for some personality types than for others. For example, extroverts are more likely to seek social interactions, while introverts may find these experiences uncomfortable (Bolger and Eckenrode, 1991). Further, there is evidence that highly cynical individuals do not benefit from social support during acute stress (Lepore, 1995). Those higher in neuroticism tend to perceive lower levels of support during stress than those who are less neurotic (Bolger and Eckenrode, 1991). Cognitive appraisals and perceptions are also related to the effects of social support on stress and health (Thoits, 1986; see Lakey and Cohen, 2000 for a recent discussion of the effects of social support on appraisal, social cognition and coping). Further, research has suggested that social interactions may be beneficial because they promote self-esteem and potentially self-efficacy (Lakey and Cohen, 2000).

Not surprisingly, emotional response to social interactions is related to the quality of the interaction (Berry and Hanson, 1996). Both positive and negative affect are associated with the number of interactions and the amount of time spent in social interactions (Berry and Hanson, 1996), although the quality of the interaction may be perceived as better when individuals experience positive emotion. Recent studies of emotion suggest that positive and negative affect are qualitatively different (Folkman and Moskowitz, 2000; Fredrickson, 1998). While intuitively we would expect that positive affect during an interaction is associated with better health outcomes, it may be that negative mood generated by catharsis or venting frustration may be adaptive in certain contexts. Future research needs to systematically explore the effects of positive versus negative interactions and examine the long-term effects of both positive and negative affect associated with those interactions.

Natural Environments as Restoration

Much of restoration research has its origin in the study of the psychologically positive values of the natural environment. To some extent this represents a search for explanations for the intuitive proposition that natural settings are restful and relaxing. Scientists have attempted to understand characteristics of environments that are stressful and have studied psychological and physiological responses to these environments and environmental features. Crowding, noise, commuting, pollution, natural disasters and industrial accidents have been studied (Baum and Fleming, 1993; Cohen et al., 1986; Evans and Cohen, 1987; Ironson et al., 1997; Schaeffer et al., 1988; Singer et al., 1974). Research has also examined whether more relaxing physical environments have opposite effects and may relieve stress.

A substantial body of literature suggests that natural environments (i.e. those containing mostly vegetation and water) are more psychologically and physiologically restorative than those that contain human-made structures such as sidewalks, buildings, and cars (see Parsons and Hartig, 2000). This literature has included recreation in natural settings, (e.g. hiking; Hartig et al., 1991; Hull and Stewart, 1995), simply experiencing wilderness or favorite natural settings (Lutz et al., 1999; Korpela and Hartig, 1996), views of natural settings from windows (Travis and McAuley, 1998; Ulrich, 1984; Verderber, 1986), and pictures or films about nature (Hartig et al., 1996; Parsons et al., 1998; Staats et al., 1997; Ulrich et al., 1991). It suggests that natural stimuli can have substantial benefit in these contexts.

Ulrich and colleagues (1991: 202) conceptualized restoration from the natural environment as including "positive changes in psychological states, in levels of activity in physiological systems, and often in behaviors or functioning, including cognitive functioning or performance." They suggest that a key element of restoration is an increase in positive emotions and decrease in negative emotions. Much of the "environment as restoration" literature has shown that natural environments improve psychological well-being or positive emotion (e.g. Hartig et al., 1991; 1996; Ulrich et al., 1991; Staats et al., 1997). These studies suggest that views or pictures that contain more vegetation and fewer urban structures are related to better mood.

Parallel to research on stress, scientists have measured the effects of restoration on several different outcomes, including physiological recovery. In one study, participants watched a stressful film and were then randomly assigned to watch a nature film, a film including traffic, or a film dominated by pedestrian activity (Ulrich et al., 1991). Heart period, pulse transit time, electrocardiogram activity, and skin conductance recovered faster and returned closer to baseline levels among participants watching the nature film. A similar study by Parsons and colleagues (1998) required college students to participate in two stressors before and after randomly assigning them to watch one of four films (views from car windows that had varying amounts of nature and urban content). Heart period and skin conductance recovered faster and more completely in those who watched films dominated by natural surroundings (forest or golf greens) than in those who watched films with more urban content. Watching the natural films also reduced the magnitude of HR, systolic blood pressure and skin conductance response to a subsequent stressor suggesting that the restorative effects of natural environments help to buffer future stress as well.

The quality of views or the extent to which natural views are available also affects stress and well-being. Moore (1981) found that prisoners whose cells faced the internal area of the prison were more likely to have health complaints (such as skin, respiratory, orthopedic, and gastrointestinal problems) than those who had windows that faced farmland outside of the prison. Research in hospital settings has shown that staff and patients prefer views that include natural settings and that windows which are obscured or too high are unsatisfactory and similar to having no window at all (Verderber, 1986). In a landmark study by Ulrich (1984), hospital room windows were shown to have even stronger palliative effects. Gall-bladder surgery patients who had windows that looked out on trees had shorter post-operative stays, received fewer negative comments in nurses' notes, reported less pain and took fewer doses of pain medication than did patients whose windows faced a brick wall. These results were supported by a more recent study of elderly people recovering from hip surgery (Travis and McAuley, 1998), confirming that patients were more likely to use windows with scenes of nature as a source of relaxation. Other research has shown that job stress (and its concomitant negative health effects such as headaches and illnesses) is lower in people who have access to the natural environment by way of windows or other areas in the workplace (R. Kaplan, 1983; S. Kaplan, 1988).

Vacations overlap with natural environments in several ways, most notably as an opportunity to get away from social and non-social sources of stress and because one way in which the natural environment may be accessed is on vacation. In its very definition, vacation is a respite from work with the express purpose of restoration. While focused on recuperation, vacation is a broad concept that can include a number of different restorative elements.

Vacations allow people to restore control over their social experience. By removing oneself from stressful contexts, vacations can offer time to recover, reflect and reorient. Studies suggest at least temporary benefits of such respites. A recent study of 53 aluminum hardware factory workers, ten days before, three days after and five weeks after two-week vacations, found that physical complaints were significantly lower after vacation and these benefits persisted five weeks later (Strauss-Blanche et al., 2000). An earlier study found that life and job satisfaction improved after vacation in a diverse sample of 128 employees. Satisfaction with, but not length of vacation was related to increased life satisfaction (Lounsbury and Hoopes, 1986). Similarly, clerical workers reported less burnout during and three days after a two-week vacation, but were closer to their pre-vacation levels three weeks after the vacation (Westman and Eden, 1997). Women reported more burnout before and three weeks after the vacation than men, but they also reported less burnout during their vacation then men. In the whole sample, those who reported the most satisfaction with their vacation received the most benefit.

Understanding the restorative nature of vacations is difficult because they can provide relief for many different kinds of stressors and they can include a number of different types of activities, all of which may have independent and synergistic effects on psychological well-being and health. Taking time away from work may be helpful simply as a break from daily job stressors, disrupting the cumulative effects of burdens at work. Vacations can also serve as a distraction from those daily stressors. People often choose to participate in enjoyable activities during vacation that can promote relaxation and enhance mood. Some of these activities may include more sleep, physical activity, more relaxing social interaction, and general relaxation.

Sleep, Restoration, and Health

A common element in restoration associated with these activities is sleep. One reason for this is that many people typically do not get enough sleep. A recent Gallup poll indicated that 36 percent of Americans report experiences of insomnia and 9 percent indicate that their insomnia is chronic (Ancoli-Israel and Roth, 1999). In the United States, the typical number of hours of sleep has decreased from 9 hours per night to 7.5 hours per night (Webb and Agnew, 1975) and a review of the sleep literature suggests that at least one-third of normal adults suffer from sleep loss (Bonnet and Arand, 1995). Higher workload and little flexibility in sleep time are associated with poor sleep in shift workers (Smith et al., 1999) and psychological and physical complaints are increased when workers change shifts earlier as opposed to later morning (Tucker et al., 1998). While many individuals may choose to limit sleep in order to maximize social and work activities (Broman et al., 1996), they may then face psychological or physical consequences.

A review of the effects of sleep on restoration is beyond the scope of this chapter. It needs to be mentioned because it is a pervasive and powerful source of restoration at several different levels, but it is neither a social phenomenon under most circumstances, nor are its benefits unique to social stressors. Regardless, it is a major factor in biological replenishment and psychological rejuvenation. There is evidence that sleep deprivation causes increased sympathetic responses associated with sleep loss, such as heart rate, blood pressure and norepinephrine in normotensive people (Lusardi et al., 1996; Tochikubo et al., 1996) and in hypertensive individuals (Lusardi et al., 1999). Sleep deprivation is also associated with heightened cortisol levels on the evening after sleep has been deprived (Leproult et al., 1997). It is possible that the HPA axis does not recover from stressors as readily when individuals are deprived of sleep.

In a study of people living near the Three Mile Island (TMI) nuclear facility, participants reported more sleep disturbances and more psychological and physical stress symptoms than control participants (Davidson et al., 1987). Stress was associated with poor sleep quality among all participants, but TMI-area residents reported problems with waking during the night, and reported less overall sleep than did control participants. Similar results were found for people who were present during Hurricane Andrew (Mellman et al., 1995). Those who experienced the storm reported more sleep disturbances than less-affected controls. In a sleep laboratory, hurricane victims experienced higher levels of arousal and more eye movements during REM was associated with trauma and distress. Epidemiological data suggest that shorter sleep duration (less than four hours/night) or longer sleep (greater than ten hours/night) is associated with a shorter life-span than a normal duration of eight hours of sleep/night (Kripke et al., 1979). Lack of sleep is related to health complaints in older adults (Habte-Gabr et al., 1991) and in adolescents (Mahon, 1995). Sleep disturbances are also related to fatigue, digestive, and cardiovascular disorders (Appels and Schouten, 1991; Carney et al., 1990; Koller, 1983; Knuttson, 1989; Smith et al., 1999).

Physical Activity as Restoration

Increasing people's physical activity has long been a centerpiece of health promotion campaigns, and evidence links physical activity to positive health outcomes and intermediate health-related outcomes including effects on the immune system (Gleeson, 2000; Pederson and Hoffman-Goetz, 2000), decreased cancer risk (Cottreau, Ness, and Kriska, 2000; Shepard and Shek, 1998), weight loss (Zelasko, 1995), diabetes (Wallberg-Henriksson, 1992), HIV disease (Mustafa et al., 1999), and lower all cause and cardiovascular morbidity and mortality (Blair et al., 1989; 1995; Lee et al., 1995).

Results from laboratory research provide support for exercise as an intervention for acute stress. Several studies have shown that acute bouts of exercise reduce psychological, hemodynamic, and neuroendocrine reactivity to acute stressors in athletes, and in healthy and hypertensive adults (Probst et al., 1997; Rejeski et al., 1991; 1992; Smith et al., 2000; West et al., 1998). Similar research has suggested that fitness is related to smaller responses during acute stress (see Crews and Landers, 1987 for a review; van Doornen and de Geus, 1989; Sothmann et al., 1987). Lower HR and BP reactivity to acute stress has also been produced after 10 to 12-week exercise programs (Anshel, 1996; Holmes and McGilley, 1987; Sherwood et al., 1989). Longer-term exercise programs also reduce anxiety and stress as well as enhance coping in individuals suffering from work stress (Gronningsaeter et al., 1992).

The stress-reducing and health-enhancing effects of exercise have led researchers to explore mechanisms explaining these effects. Exercise promotes enhanced mood, which may have lasting effects and assist individuals in feeling restored. Several reviews have suggested that acute exercise has positive mood effects (Byrne and Byrne, 1993; Ekkekakis and Petruzzello, 1999; Paluska and Schwenk, 2000; Petruzzello et al., 1991; Salmon, 2001; Yeung, 1996). Exercise decreases tension, depression, anger, confusion, and increases vigor up to four hours after exercise (Yeung, 1996), in various ages and in both men and women (Petruzello et al., 1991; Yeung, 1996). These mood effects of acute exercise may be an important element in stress buffering or restoration (Smith et al., 2000).

A key component of the restorative effects of exercise may be its association with social relationships. While exercise is not an inherently social activity, there is evidence that social contact helps to improve maintenance in physical activity programs, and that, at least for women, social interaction during exercise is an important factor governing outcomes (Gilette, 1988). Epidemiological data suggest that individuals with more friends and family and more contact with them report higher levels of physical activity (Spanier and Allison, 2001). Marital/cohabitation status was associated with lower levels of physical activity, but in a population-based sample, King and colleagues (1998) found that the transition from being single to being married was associated with increases in physical activity relative to remaining single. Intervention studies also suggest that spousal support increases physical activity (O'Reilly and Thomas, 1989; Wallace et al., 1995). Sources of support (e.g. friends versus family) may have differential effects on physical activity in African Americans versus Caucasian Americans (Treiber et al., 1992). However, several investigators have found that both friends and family are important in determining physical activity (Dishman and Sallis, 1994; King et al., 1990; Sallis et al., 1992).

Not surprisingly, social support that is specific to exercise has been more effective at predicting exercise adherence than more general social support (Eyler et al., 1999; Oka et al., 1995). Social support has also been shown to be an effective strategy to increase adherence to exercise programs in weight loss studies. The use of personal trainers to support individuals in exercise programs has been shown to assist with adherence (Jeffrey et al., 1998). One study experimentally manipulated social support to determine if it is an important factor in weight loss (Wing and Jeffrey, 1999). Participants recruited with friends reported exercising with friends more and had better weight loss maintenance than those recruited alone. Similar effects were found for those who participated with actual or assigned friends versus those who participated alone. These data are compelling because they suggest that social support is an important component of exercise adherence.

Some of the psychological mechanisms associated with exercise as a restorative activity have been discussed earlier in this chapter. Prominent psychological theories that explain the effects of exercise on stress include self-efficacy (Bandura, 1977). Exercising may lead to feelings of confidence in one's abilities and this may be transferable to other kinds of positive health behaviors (e.g., better diet, less smoking). General transfer of self-efficacy is an extension of original conceptions of efficacy and research has not confirmed it; most research on exercise self-efficacy is related to motivation specifically to exercise (e.g., Marcus and Owen, 1992).

Personality variables may also explain some of these effects. There is evidence that those who exercise may be more generally optimistic (e.g., Kavussanu and McAuley, 1995), but it is not clear whether this trait is linked to restorative effects of exercise. Other personality characteristics affecting exercise relate to control. Those people who initiate and adhere to exercise are higher in per-ceived control (Dienstbier, 1984), but it is not clear whether exercising itself enhances perceptions of control in other areas. Future research should be aimed at clarifying the roles of internal versus external control and exercise to deter-mine if perception of control enhances the restorative function of exercise.

Conclusions: Psychological Aspects of Restorative Function

Throughout this chapter we have argued that restorative activities have inde-pendent effects on psychological and physical health and well-being. One important feature of each of the activities discussed is their relationship to relaxation. Although there is an abundance of evidence suggesting that re-laxation training is helpful for stress-reduction it is often unlikely that people will choose to participate in structured relaxation sessions in order to reduce stress (Bellarosa and Chen, 1997). However, many of the activities that are restorative also promote relaxation. It is likely that these activities may inter-act and have synergistic effects on health as well. For example, when people are on vacation, they are likely to participate in a variety of activities includ-ing sleep, exercise, socializing, and having experiences in nature, that appear to be relaxing. The individual and combined effects of these activities need to be systematically studied in order to better determine optimal ways of recuperating from stress.

Another important factor related to the restorative function of these activ-ities may be individual choice and perceived control. For example, leisure physical activity is more effective at reducing stress than fitness level (Carmack et al., 1999), and social interactions are most beneficial when the desired type of support is provided (Bolger and Eckenrode, 1991). Restorative activities often provide people with more control over their time and the activities they participate in or attempt. Future research should investigate the effects of choice and perceptions of control on restoration to determine if these factors are more important than the activity itself.

Another cross-cutting theme in this chapter is emotion. Most restorative activ-ities are related to increased positive and/or decreased negative emotions. Recent psychophysiological models suggest that emotional states affect the integra-tion of cognition, behavior, and physiological arousal and affect health (Mayne, 2001). Emotion has also been shown to affect neuroendocrine responses (Cacioppo et al., 1993), the immune system (Booth and Pennebaker, 2000), and may have implications for development and behavioral genetic research (Rende, 2000). Beneficial effects of emotion may be related to the balance between positive and negative emotion, suggesting the importance of having the "right" amount of each in order to promote positive health (Mayne, 2000).

The stress-reducing effects of many of the activities discussed in this chapter have not historically been conceptualized in terms of restorative function. As a result, there is a wealth of research opportunity to determine the amount, type, and combination of effects each restorative activity has on job and home stress and strain. Future research should be designed to specifically test the effects of restorative activities on psychological and physical health outcomes in more naturalistic studies. This is an exciting time for research on positive and adaptive forms of psychological and physical functioning. Research focused on more positive human qualities is developing and there is much of importance to learn and apply. These themes will likely assist behavioral scientists in better understanding and promoting optimal human functioning by nurturing those qualities that are best in all of us.

Social processes, particularly those related to interpersonal relationships, offer another attractive explanation for the restorative effects of many activities. Respite from interpersonal stressors, social conflict, and overload is important, as are direct restorative benefits of social contact, integration, and social support that were discussed. Social interactions reinforce our sense of self-efficacy and beliefs that we are valued, cared for, and esteemed, providing relaxing moments and gratifying contacts. Because a good deal of one's quality of life reflects the balance of satisfying and frustrating interactions, the centrality of social contacts in restoration and overall happiness may be particularly important. More attention to these social psychological processes in the context of self-efficacy, perceived control, and other explanatory constructs should provide a more comprehensive view of restoration and how it works.

Acknowledgments

This chapter was supported in part by a grant from the National Heart Lung and Blood Institute (# HL65112).

Correspondence concerning this chapter should be sent to: Ashley Smith MS, Behavioral Medicine and Oncology, University of Pittsburgh, 3600 Forbes Avenue, 405 Iroquois, Pittsburgh, PA 15213, USA; e-mail: ashleys@imap.pitt.edu

References

Affleck, G., Urrows, S., Tennen, H., Higgins, P., Pav, D., and Aloisi, R. (1997). A dual pathway model of daily stressor effects on rheumatoid arthritis. *Annals of Behavioral Medicine*, 19, 161–70.

Allgoewer, A., Wardle, J., and Steptoe, A. (2001). Depressive symptoms, social support, and personal health behaviors in young men and women. *Health Psychology*, 20, 223–7.

Ancoli-Israel, S., and Roth, T. (1999). Characteristics of insomnia in the United States: Results of the 1991 National Sleep Foundation Survey. *Sleep*, 22, S347–53.

Anshel, M. H. (1996). Effect of chronic aerobic exercise and progressive relaxation on motor performance and affect following acute stress. *Behavioral Medicine*, 21, 186–96.

APHA (American Public Health Association). (2001). Public health impacts of job stress. *American Journal of Public Health*, 91, 502–3.

Appels, A., and Schouten, E. (1991). Waking up exhausted as risk indicator of myocardial infarction. *American Journal of Cardiology*. 68, 395–8.

Arnetz, B. B., and Wiholm, C. (1997). Technological stress: Psychophysiological symptoms in modern offices. *Journal of Psychosomatic Research*, 43, 35–42.

Bandura, A. (1977). Self-efficacy: Toward a unifying theory of behavioral change. *Psychological Review*, 84, 191–215.

Baum, A., and Andersen, B. L. (Eds.). (2001). *Psychosocial Interventions for Cancer*. Washington, DC: American Psychological Association.

Baum, A., and Fleming, I. (1993). Implications of psychological research on stress and technological accidents. *American Psychologist*, 48, 665–72.

Bellarosa, C., and Chen, P. Y. (1997). The effectiveness of occupational stress management interventions: A survey of subject matter expert opinions. *Journal of Occupational Health Psychology*, 2, 247–62.

Berger, B. G., and Owen, D. R. (1983). Mood alteration with swimming: Swimmers really do "feel better." *Psychosomatic Medicine*, 45, 425–33.

Berkman, L. F. (1995). The role of social relations in health promotion. *Psychosomatic Medicine*, 57, 245–54.

Berkman, L. F., and Syme, S. L. (1979). Social networks, host resistance, and mortality: A nine-year follow-up study of Alameda County residents. *American Journal of Epidemiology*, 109, 186–204.

Berry, D. S., and Hanson, J. S. H. (1996). Positive affect, negative affect, and social interaction. *Journal of Personality and Social Psychology*, 71, 796–809.

Bharke, M. S., and Morgan, W. P. (1978). Anxiety reduction following exercise and meditation. *Cognitive Therapy and Research*, 2, 323–33.

Biondi, M., and Zannino, L. (1997). Psychological stress, neuroimmunomodulation, and susceptibility to infectious diseases in animals and man: A review. *Psychotherapy and Psychosomatics*, 66, 3–26.

Blair, S. N., Kohl, H. W., Barlow, C. E., Paffenbarger, R. S. Jr., Gibbons, L. W., and Macera, C. A. (1995). Changes in physical fitness and all-cause mortality: A prospective study of healthy and unhealthy men. *Journal of the American Medical Association*, 273, 1093–8.

Blair, S. N., Kohl, H. W., Paffenbarger, R. S. Jr., Clark, D. G., Cooper, K. H., and Gibbons, L. W. (1989). Physical fitness and all-cause mortality: A prospective study of healthy men and women. *Journal of the American Medical Association*, 262, 2395–401.

Bolger, N., and Eckenrode, J. (1991). Social relationships, personality, and anxiety during a major stressful event. *Journal of Personality and Social Psychology*, 61, 440–9.

Bonnet, M. H., and Arand, D. L. (1995). We are chronically sleep deprived. *Sleep*, 18, 908–11.

Booth, R. J., and Pennebaker, J. W. (2000). Emotions and immunity. In M. Lewis and J. M. Haviland (Eds.), *Handbook of Emotions* (pp. 119–42). New York: Guilford Press.

Boutcher, S. H., Nugent, F. W., and Weltman, A. L. (1995). Heart rate response to psychological stressors of individuals possessing resting bradycardia. *Behavioral Medicine*, 21, 40–6.

Breslow, L. (1999). From disease prevention to health promotion. *Journal of the American Medical Association*, 281, 1030–3.

Breslow, L., and Breslow, N. (1993). Health practices and disability: Some evidence from Alameda County. *Preventive Medicine*, 22, 86–95.

Brill, P. L. (1984). The need for an operational definition of burnout. *Family and Community Health*, 6, 12–24.

Brisson, C., Laflamme, N., Moisan, J., Milot, A., Masse, B., and Vezina, M. (1999). Effect of family responsibilities and job strain on ambulatory blood pressure among white-collar women. *Psychosomatic Medicine*, 61, 205–13.

Broadhead, W. E., Kaplan, B. H., James, S. A. et al. (1983). The epidemiologic evidence for a relationship between social support and health. *American Journal of Epidemiology*, 117, 521–37.

Broman, J. E., Lundh, L. G., and Hetta, J. (1996). Insufficient sleep in the general population. *Neurophysiologie Clinique*, 26, 30–9.

Buunk, B. P., and Verhoeven, K. (1991). Companionship and support at work: A microanalysis of the stress-reducing features of social interaction. *Basic and Applied Social Psychology*, 12, 243–58.

Byrne, A., and Byrne, D. G. (1993). The effect of exercise on depression, anxiety and other mood states: A review. *Journal of Psychosomatic Research*, 37, 565–74.

Cacioppo, J. T., Klein, D. J., Berntson, G. G., and Hatfield, E. (1993). The psychophysiology of emotion. In M. Lewis and J. M. Haviland (Eds.), *Handbook of Emotions* (pp. 119–42). New York: Guilford Press.

Carmack, C. L., Boudreaux, E., Amaral-Melendez, M., Brantley, P. J., and de Moor, C. (1999). Aerobic fitness and leisure physical activity as moderators of the stress-illness relation. *Annals of Behavioral Medicine*, 21, 251–7.

Carney, R. M., Freedland, K. E., and Jaffe, A. S. (1990). Insomnia and depression prior to myocardial infarction. *Psychosomatic Medicine*, 52, 603–9.

Cassel, J. (1976). The contribution of the social environment to host resistance. *American Journal of Epidemiology*, 104, 107–23.

Chesney, M. A., and Ozer, E. M. (1995). Women and health: In search of a paradigm. *Women's Health: Research on Gender, Behavior, and Policy*, 1, 3–26.

Classen, C., Butler, L. D., Koopman, C. et al. (2001). Supportive-expressive group therapy and distress in patients with metastatic breast cancer: A randomized clinical intervention trial. *Archives of General Psychiatry*, 58, 494–501.

Cobb, S. (1976). Social support as a moderator of life stress. *Psychosomatic Medicine*, 38, 300–14.

Cohen, S. (1988). Psychosocial models of social support in the etiology of physical disease. *Health Psychology*, 7, 269–97.

Cohen, S., Evans, G. W., Stokols, D., and Krantz, D. S. (1986). *Behavior, Health and Environmental Stress*. New York: Plenum Press.

Cohen, S., Gottlieb, B. H., and Underwood, L. G. (2000). Social relationships and health. In S. Cohen, L. G. Underwood and B. H. Gottlieb (Eds.), *Social Support Measurement and Intervention* (pp. 3–28). New York: Oxford University Press.

Cohen, S., Doyle, W. J., Skoner, D. P., Rabin, B. S., and Gwaltney, J. M. Jr. (1997). Social ties and susceptibility to the common cold. *Journal of the American Medical Association*, 277, 1940–4.

Cohen, S., and Williamson, G. M. (1991). Stress and infectious disease in humans. *Psychological Bulletin*, 109, 5–24.

Cohen, S., and Wills, T. A. (1985). Stress, social support, and the buffering hypothesis. *Psychological Bulletin*, 98, 310–57.

Cottreau, C. M., Ness, R. B., and Kriska, A. M. (2000). Physical activity and reduced risk of ovarian cancer. *Obstetrics and Gynecology*, 96, 609–14.

Crews, D. J., and Landers, D. M. (1987). A meta-analytic review of aerobic fitness and reactivity to psychosocial stressors. *Medicine and Science in Sports and Exercise*, 19, S114–20.

Cropley, M., Steptoe, A., and Joekes, K. (1999). Job strain and psychiatric morbidity. *Psychological Medicine*, 29, 1411–16.

Cruess, S., Antoni, M., Cruess, D. et al. (2000). Reductions in herpes simplex virus type 2 antibody titers after cognitive behavioral stress management and relationships with neuroendocrine function, relaxation skills, and social support in HIV-positive men. *Psychosomatic Medicine*, 62, 828–37.

Dakof, G. A., and Taylor, S. E. (1990). Victims' perceptions of social support: What is helpful from whom? *Journal of Personality and Social Psychology*, 58, 80–9.

Davidson, L. M., Fleming, R., and Baum, A. (1987). Chronic stress, catecholamines, and sleep disturbance at Three Mile Island. *Journal of Human Stress*, 13, 75–83.

Davis, C. G., Nolen-Hoeksema, S., and Larson, J. (1998). Making sense of loss and benefiting from the experience: Two construals of meaning. *Journal of Personality and Social Psychology*, 75, 561–74.

Deater-Deckard, K., and Scarr, S. (1996). Parenting stress among dual-earner mothers and fathers: Are there gender differences? *Journal of Family Psychology*, 10, 45–59.

DeVries, H. A. (1981). Tranquilizer effect of exercise: A critical review. *The Physician and Physical Medicine*, 51, 47–55.

Dienstbier, R. (1984). The effects of exercise on personality. In M. H. Sachs and G. W. Buffone (Eds.), *Running as Therapy*. London: University of Nebraska Press.

Dishman, R. K., and Sallis, J. F. (1994). Determinants and interventions for physical activity and exercise. In C. Bouchard, R. J. Shephard, and T. Stephens (Eds.), *Physical Activity, Fitness, and Health: International Proceedings and Consensus Statement*. Champaign, IL: Human Kinetics Publishers.

Dougall, A. L., and Baum, A. (2001). Stress, health, and illness. In A. Baum, T. A. Revenson, and J. E. Singer (Eds.), *Handbook of Health Psychology* (pp. 321–37). Mahwah, NJ: Lawrence Erlbaum.

Drolet, G., Dumont, E. C., Gosselin, I., Kinkead, R., Laforest, S., and Trottier, J. (2001). Role of endogenous opioid system in the regulation of the stress response. *Progress in Neuro-Psychopharmacology and Biological Psychiatry*, 25, 729–41.

Ekkekakis, P., and Petruzzello, S. J. (1999). Acute aerobic exercise and affect: Current status, problems and prospects regarding dose-response. *Sports Medicine*, 28, 337–74.

Ekman, P., and Davidson, R. J. (Eds.). (1994). *The Nature of Emotion: Fundamental Questions*. New York: Oxford University Press.

Evans, G. W., and Cohen, S. (1987). Environmental stress. In D. Stokols and I. Altman (Eds.), *Handbook of Environmental Psychology* (pp. 571–610). New York: John Wiley.

Eyler, A. A., Brownson, R. C., Donatelle, R. J., King, A. C., Brown, D., and Sallis, J. F. (1999). Physical activity social support and middle- and older-aged minority women: results from a US survey. *Social Science and Medicine*. 49, 781–9.

Fawzy, F. I., Kemeny, M. E., Fawzy, N. W. et al. (1990). A structured psychiatric intervention for cancer patients, II: Changes over time in immunological measures. *Archives of General Psychiatry*, 47, 729–35.

Folkman, S. (1997). Positive psychological states and coping with severe stress. *Social Science and Medicine*, 45, 1207–21.

Folkman, S. (2000). *Positive Emotion in the Coping Process: When? Why? How?* Paper presented at the meeting of the American Psychological Association, Washington, DC.

Folkman, S., Chesney, M. A., Cooke, M., Boccellari, A., and Colette, L. (1994). Caregiver burden in HIV-positive and HIV-negative partners of men with AIDS. *Journal of Consulting and Clinical Psychology*, 62, 746–56.

Folkman, S., and Moskowitz, J. (2000). Positive affect and the other side of coping. *American Psychologist*, 55, 647–54.

Ford, E. S., Ahluwalia, I. B., and Galuska, D. A. (2000). Social relationships and cardiovascular disease risk factors: Findings from the third national health and nutrition examination survey. *Preventive Medicine*, 30, 83–92.

Frankl, V. E. (1963). *Man's Search for Meaning*. New York: Washington Square Press.

Fredrickson, B. L., and Levenson, R. W. (1998). Positive emotions speed recovery from the cardiovascular sequelae of negative emotions. *Cognition and Emotion*, 12, 191–220.

Fredrickson, B. L. (1998). What good are positive emotions? *Review of General Psychiatry*, 2, 300–19.

Fredrickson, B. L. (2001). The role of positive emotions in positive psychology: The broaden-and-build theory of positive emotions. *American Psychologist*, 56, 218–26.

Gal, R., and Lazarus, R. S. (1975). The role of activity in anticipating and confronting stressful situations. *Journal of Human Stress*, 4–20.

Gillett, P. A. (1988). Self-reported factors influencing exercise adherence in overweight women. *Nursing Research*, 37, 25–9.

Gillham, J. E., and Seligman, M. E. P. (1999). Footsteps on the road to a positive psychology. *Behaviour Research and Therapy*, 37, S163–73.

Gleeson, M. (2000). Overview: Exercise immunology. *Immunology and Cell Biology*, 78, 483–4.

Glynn, L. M., Christenfeld, N., and Gerin, W. (1999). Gender, social support, and cardiovascular responses to stress. *Psychosomatic Medicine*, 61, 234–42.

Goodway, R. (1987). Exercise, the stressor that reduces stress. *Occupational Health, May*, 164–7.

Goodwin, P. J., Leszcz, M., Ennis, M. et al. (2001). The effect of group psychosocial support on survival in metastatic breast cancer. *New England Journal of Medicine*, 345, 1719–26.

Gronningsaeter, H., Hytten, K., Skauli, G., Christensen, C. C., and Ursin, H. (1992). Improved health and coping by physical exercise or cognitive behavioral stress management training in a work environment. *Psychology and Health*, 7, 147–63.

Guglielmi, R. S., and Tatrow, K. (1998). Occupational stress, burnout, and health in teachers: A methodological and theoretical analysis. *Review of Educational Research*, 68, 61–99.

Habte-Gabr, E., Wallace, R. B., Colsher, P. L., Hulbert, J. R., White, L. R., and Smith, I. M. (1991). Sleep patterns in rural elders: Demographic, health, and psychobehavioral correlates. *Journal of Clinical Epidemiology*, 44, 5–13.

Hartig, T., Boeoek, A., Garvill, J., Olsson, T., and Gerling, T. (1996). Environmental influences on psychological restoration. *Scandinavian Journal of Psychology*, 37, 378–93.

Hartig, T., Mang, M., and Evans, G. W. (1991). Restorative effects of natural environment experiences. *Environment and Behavior*, 23, 3–26.

Helgeson, V. S., and Cohen, S. (1996). Social support and adjustment to cancer: Reconciling descriptive, correlational, and intervention research. *Health Psychology*, 15, 135–48.

Helgeson, V. S., Cohen, S., Schulz, R., and Yasko, J. (1999). Education and peer discussion group interventions and adjustment to breast cancer. *Archives of General Psychiatry*, 56, 340–7.

Helgeson, V. S., Cohen, S., Schulz, R., and Yasko, J. (2001). Long-term effects of educational and peer discussion group interventions on adjustment to breast cancer. *Health Psychology*, 20, 387–92.

Holmes, D. S., and McGilley, B. M. (1987). Influence of a brief aerobic training program on heart rate and subjective response to a psychologic stressor. *Psychosomatic Medicine*, 49, 366–74.

House, J. S., Landis, K. R., and Umberson, D. (1988). Social relationships and health. *Science*, 241, 540–5.

Hull, R. B., and Stewart, W. P. (1995). The landscape encountered and experienced while hiking. *Environment and Behavior*, 27, 404–26.

Hudiburg, R. A., and Necessary, J. R. (1996). Coping with computer-stress. *Journal of Educational Computing Research*, 15, 113–24.

Ionescu-Tirgonstei, C., Simion, P., Mariana, C., Dan, C. M., and Iulian, M. (1987). The signification of stress in aetiopathogenesis of Type-sub-2 diabetes mellitus. *Stress Medicine*, 3, 277–84.

Ironson, G., Wynings, C., Schneiderman, N. et al. (1997). Posttraumatic stress symptoms, intrusive thoughts, loss, and immune function after Hurricane Andrew. *Psychosomatic Medicine*, 59, 128–41.

Iskra-Golec, I., Folkard, S., Marek, T., and Noworol, C. (1996). Health, well-being and burnout of ICU nurses on 12- and 8-h shifts. *Work and Stress*, 10, 251–6.

Iso-Ahola, S. E., and Park, C. J. (1996). Leisure-related social support and self-determination as buffers of stress-illness relationship. *Journal of Leisure Research*, 28, 169–87.

Janoff-Bulman, R., and Berg, M. (1998). Disillusionment and the creation of value: From traumatic losses to existential gains. In J. H. Harvey (Ed.), *Perspectives on Loss: A Sourcebook* (pp. 35–47). Philadelphia: Brunner/Mazel.

Janoff-Bulman, R., and McPherson Frantz, C. (1997). The impact of trauma on meaning: From meaningless world to meaningful life. In M. J. Power and C. R. Brewin (Eds.), *The Transformation of Meaning in Psychological Therapies: Integrating Theory and Practice* (pp. 91–106). Chichester, England: John Wiley and Sons.

Jeffrey, R. W., Wing, R. R., Thorson, C., and Burton, L. R. (1998). Use of personal trainers and financial incentives to increase exercise in a behavioral weight-loss program. *Journal of Consulting and Clinical Psychology*, 66, 777–83.

Kamarck, T. W., Manuck, S. B., and Jennings, J. R. (1990). Social support reduces cardiovascular reactivity to psychological challenge: A laboratory model. *Psychosomatic Medicine*, 52, 42–58.

Kaplan, G. A., Salonen, J. T., Cohen, R. D., Brand, R. J., Syme, S. L., and Puska, P. (1988). Social connections and mortality from all causes and from cardiovascular disease: Prospective evidence from eastern Finland. *American Journal of Epidemiology*, 128, 370–80.

Kaplan, J. R., and Manuck, S. B. (1999). Status, stress, and atherosclerosis: The role of environment and individual behavior. *Annals of the New York Academy of Sciences*, 896, 145–61.

Kaplan, R. (1983). The role of nature in the urban context. In I. Altman and J. F. Wohlwill (Eds.), *Human Behavior and Environment: Advances in Theory and Research*, Vol 6, 127–61. New York: Plenum.

Kaplan, S. (1988). A model of person-environment compatibility. *Environment and Behavior*, 15, 311–32.

Karasek, R. A., and Theorell, T. (1990). *Healthy Work*. New York: Basic Books.

Kavussanu, M., and McAuley, E. (1995). Exercise and optimism: Are highly active individuals more optimistic? *Journal of Sport and Exercise Psychology*, 17, 246–58.

Kelsey, K. S., Campbell, M. K., Tessaro, I. et al. (2000). Social support and health behaviors among blue-collar women workers. *American Journal of Health Behavior*. 24, 434–43.

King, A. C., Kieran, M., Anh, D., and Wilcox, S. (1998). The effects of marital transitions on changes in physical activity: Results from a 10-year community study. *Annals of Behavioral Medicine*, 20, 64–9.

King, A. C., Taylor, C. B., Haskell, W. L., and DeBusk, R. F. (1990). Identifying strategies for increasing employee physical activity levels: Findings from the Stanford/Lockheed Exercise Survey. *Health Education Quarterly*. 17, 269–85.

Koller, M. (1983). Health risks related to shiftwork. An example of time-contingent effects of long-term stress. *International Archives of Occupational and Environmental Health*, 53, 59–75.

Korpela, K., and Hartig, T. (1996). Restorative qualities of favorite places. *Journal of Environmental Psychology*, 16, 221–33.

Knuttson, A. (1989). Shiftwork and coronary heart disease. *Journal of Social Medicine Supplement*, 44, 1–36.

Krause, N., and Baker, E. (1992). Financial strain, economic values, and somatic symptoms in later life. *Psychology and Aging*, 7, 4–14.

Kripke, D. F., Simons, R. N., Garfinkel, L., and Hammond, C. (1979). Short and long sleep and sleeping pills: Is increased mortality associated? *Archives of General Psychiatry*, 36, 103–16.

Lakey, B., and Cohen, S. (2000). Social support theory and measurement. In S. Cohen, L. G. Underwood, and B. H. Gottlieb (Eds.), *Social Support Measurement and Intervention*, New York: Oxford University Press.

LaRocco, J. M., House, J. S., and French, J. R. (1980). Social support, occupational stress, and health. *Journal of Health and Social Behavior*, 21, 202–18.

Lazarus R. S., and Folkman, S. (1984). *Stress, Appraisal, and Coping*. New York: Springer.

Lee, I. M., Hsieh, C. C., and Paffenbarger, R. S. Jr. (1995). Exercise intensity and longevity in men: The Harvard Alumni Health Study. *Journal of the American Medical Association*, 273, 1179–84.

Leiter, M. P., and Maslach, C. (2001). Burnout and health. In A. Baum, T. A. Revenson, and J. E. Singer (Eds.), *Handbook of Health Psychology* (pp. 415–26). Mahwah, NJ: Lawrence Erlbaum.

Lepore, S. J. (1995). Cynicism, social support and cardiovascular reactivity. *Health Psychology*, 14, 210–16.

Leproult, R., Copinschi, G., Buxton, O., and Van Cauter, E. (1997). Sleep loss results in an elevation of cortisol levels the next evening. *Sleep*, 20, 865–70.

Lerner, D. J., Levine, S., Malspeis, S., and D'Agostino, R. B. (1994). Job strain and health-related quality of life in a national sample. *American Journal of Public Health*, 84, 1580–5.

Lewis, M., and Haviland, J. M. (Eds.). (2000). *Handbook of Emotions*. New York: Guilford Press.

Long, B. C. (1993). A cognitive perspective on the stress-reducing effects of physical exercise. In P. Sereganian (Ed.), *Exercise Psychology: The Influence of Physical Exercise on Psychological Processes* (pp. 339–57). New York: John Wiley and Sons.

Lounsbury, J. W., and Hoopes, L. L. (1986). A vacation from work: Changes in work and nonwork outcomes. *Journal of Applied Psychology*, 71, 392–401.

Lundberg, U., and Frankenhauser, M. (1999). Stress and workload of men and women in high-ranking positions. *Journal of Occupational Health Psychology*, 4, 142–51.

Lusardi, P., Mugellini, A., Preti, P., Zoppi, A., Derosa, G., and Fogari, R. (1996). Effects of a restricted sleep regimen on ambulatory blood pressure monitoring in normotensive subjects. *American Journal of Hypertension*, 9, 503–5.

Lusardi, P., Zoppi, A., Preti, P., Pesce, R. M., Piazza, E., and Fogari, R. (1999). Effects of insufficient sleep on blood pressure in hypertensive patients: a 24-h study. *American Journal of Hypertension*, 12, 63–8.

Lutgendorf, S. K., Antoni, M. H., Ironson, G. et al. (1998). Changes in cognitive coping skills and social support during cognitive behavioral stress management intervention and distress outcomes in symptomatic human immunodeficiency virus (HIV)-seropositive gay men. *Psychosomatic Medicine*, 60, 204–14.

Lutz, A. R., Simpson-Housley, P., and deMan, A. F. (1999). Wilderness: Rural and urban attitudes and perceptions. *Environment and Behavior*, 31, 259–66.

Mahon, N. E. (1995). The contribution of sleep to perceived health status during adolescence. *Public Health Nursing*, 12, 127–33.

Manne, S. L., Taylor, K. L., Dougherty, J., and Kemeny, N. (1997). Supportive and negative responses in the partner relationship: Their association with psychological adjustment among individuals with cancer. *Journal of Behavioral Medicine*, 20, 101–25.

Marcus, B. H., and Owen, N. (1992). Motivational readiness, self-efficacy and decision-making for exercise. *Journal of Applied Social Psychology*, 22, 3–16.

Martin, R. A. (2001). Humor, laughter, and physical health: Methodological issues and research findings. *Psychological Bulletin*, 127, 504–19.

Maslach, C., Wilmar, W. B., and Leiter, M. P. (2001). Job burnout. *Annual Review of Psychology*, 52, 397–422.

Mayne, T. J. (2000). Negative affect and health: The importance of being earnest. *Cognition and Emotion*, 13, 601–35.

Mayne, T. J. (2001). Emotions and health. In T. J. Mayne and G. A. Bonanno (Eds.), *Emotions: Current Issues and Future Directions* (pp. 361–97). New York: The Guilford Press.

McCubbin, J. A., Cheung, R., Montgomery, T. B., Bulbulian, R., and Wilson, J. F. (1992). Aerobic fitness and opioidergic inhibition of cardiovascular stress reactivity. *Psychophysiology*, 29, 687–97.

McLaughlin, M., Cormier, L. S., and Cormier, W. H. (1988). Relation between coping strategies and distress, stress, and marital adjustment of multiple-role women. *Journal of Counseling Psychology*, 35, 187–93.

Mellman, T. A., David, D., Kulick-Bell, R., Hebding, J., and Nolan, B. (1995). Sleep disturbance and its relationship to psychiatric morbidity after Hurricane Andrew. *American Journal of Psychiatry*, 152, 1659–63.

Moore, E. (1981). A prison environment's effect on health care service demands. *Journal of Environmental Systems*, 11, 17–34.

Moran, C. C. (1996). Short-term mood change, perceived funniness, and the effect of humor stimuli. *Behavioral Medicine*, 22, 32–38.

Munro, L., Rodwell, J., and Harding, L. (1998). Assessing occupational stress in psychiatric nurses using the full job strain model: The value of social support to nurses. *International Journal of Nursing Studies*, 35, 339–45.

Mustafa, T., Sy, F. S., Macera, C. A. et al. (1999). Association between exercise and HIV disease progression in a cohort of homosexual men. *Annals of Epidemiology*, 9, 127–31.

National Center for Health Statistics (1999). *Healthy People 2000 Review, 1998–1999*. Hyattsville, MD: Public Health Service.

Oka, R. K., King, A. C., and Young, D. R. (1995). Sources of social support as predictors of exercise adherence in women and men ages 50 to 65 years. *Women's Health*, 1, 161–75.

O'Reilly, P., and Thomas, H. E. (1989). Role of support networks in maintenance of improved cardiovascular health status. *Social Science and Medicine*, 28, 249–60.

Orth-Gomér, K., Wenger, N., and Chesney, M. (Eds.). (1998). *Women, Stress and Heart Disease*. Mahwah, NJ: Erlbaum.

Paluska, S. A., and Schwenk, T. L. (2000). Physical activity and mental health: Current concepts. *Sports Medicine*, 29, 167–80.

Panskepp, J. (1998). The quest for long term health and happiness: To play or not to play, that is the question. *Psychological Inquiry*, 9, 56–66.

Parsons, R., and Hartig, T. (2000). Environmental Psychology. In J. T. Cacioppo, L. G. Tassinary, and G. G. Bernston (Eds.), *Handbook of Psychophysiology* (2nd edn., pp. 815–46). New York: Cambridge University Press.

Parsons, R., Tassinary, L. G., Ulrich, R. S., Hebl, M. R., and Grossman-Alexander, M. (1998). The view from the road: Implications for stress recovery and immunization. *Journal of Environmental Psychology*, 18, 113–40.

Pederson, B. K., and Hoffman-Goetz, L. (2000). Exercise and the immune system: regulation, integration, and adaptation. *Physiological Reviews*, 80, 1055–81.

Pelletier, K. R., Rodenburg, A., Vinther, A., Chikamoto, Y., King, A. C., and Farquhar, J. W. (1999). Managing job strain: A randomized, controlled trial of an intervention conducted by mail and telephone. *Journal of Occupational and Environmental Medicine*, 41, 216–23.

Petruzzello, S. J., Landers, D. M., Hatfield, B. D., Kubitz, K. A., and Salazar, W. (1991). A meta-analysis on the anxiety-reducing effects of acute and chronic exercise. *Sports Medicine*, 11, 143–82.

Pickering, T. G., Devereux, R. B., James, G. D. et al. (1996). Environmental influences on blood pressure and the role of job strain. *Journal of Hypertension*, 14, S179–85.

Pines, A. M., Aronson, E., and Kafry, D. (1981). *Burnout: From Tedium to Personal Growth*. New York: Free Press.

Probst, M., Bulbulian, R., and Knapp, C. (1997). Hemodynamic responses to the stroop and cold pressor tests after submaximal cycling exercise in normotensive males. *Physiology and Behavior*, 62, 1283–90.

Rejeski, W. J., Gregg, E., Thompson, A., and Berry, M. J. (1991). The effects of varying doses of acute aerobic exercise on psychophysiological stress responses in highly trained cyclists. *Sport and Exercise Psychology*, 13, 188–99.

Rejeski, W. J., Thompson, A., Brubaker, P. H., and Miller, H. S. (1992). Acute exercise: Buffering psychosocial stress responses in women. *Health Psychology*, 11, 355–62.

Rende, R. (2000). Emotion and behavior genetics. In M. Lewis and J. M. Haviland (Eds.), *Handbook of Emotions* (pp. 119–42). New York: Guilford Press.

Roy, M. P., Steptoe, A., and Kirschbaum, C. (1998). Life events and social support as moderators of individual differences in cardiovascular and cortisol reactivity. *Journal of Personality and Social Psychology*, 75, 1273–81.

Rozanski, A., Blumenthal, J. A., and Kaplan, J. (1999). Impact of psychological factors on the pathogenesis of cardiovascular disease and implications for therapy. *Circulation*, 99, 2192–217.

Ryff, C. D., and Singer, B. (1998). Human health: New directions for the next millennium. *Psychological Inquiry*, 9, 69–85.

Ryff, C. D., and Singer, B. H. (Eds.). (2001). *Emotion, Social Relationships, and Health*. New York: Oxford University Press.

Sachser, N., Duerschlag, M., and Hirzel, D. (1998). Social relationships and the management of stress. *Psychoneuroendocrinology*, 23, 891–904.

Sallis, J. F., Hovell, M. F., and Hofstetter, C. R. (1992). Predictors of adoption and maintenance of vigorous physical activity in men and women. *Preventive Medicine*. 21, 237–51.

Salmon, P. (2001). Effects of physical exercise on anxiety, depression, and sensitivity to stress: A unifying theory. *Clinical Psychology Review*, 21, 33–61.

Salovey, P., Rothman, A., Detweiler, J., and Steward, W. T. (2000). Emotional states and physical health. *American Psychologist*, 55, 110–21.

Schaeffer, M. H., Street, S. W., Singer, J. E., and Baum, A. (1988). Effects of control on the stress reactions of commuters. *Journal of Applied Social Psychology*, 18, 944–57.

Schulz, R., O'Brien, A. T., Bookwala, J., and Fleissner, K. (1995). Psychiatric and physical morbidity effects of dementia caregiving: Prevalence, correlates, and causes. *The Gerontologist*, 35, 771–91.

Seligman, M. E. P. (2000). Positive psychology. In J. E. Gillham (Ed.), *The Science of Optimism and Hope: Research Essays in Honor of Martin E. P. Seligman*. (pp. 415–29). Radnor, PA: Templeton Foundation Press.

Seligman, M. E. P., and Csikszentmihalyi, M. (2000). Positive psychology: An introduction. *American Psychologist*, 55, 5–14.

Sheldon, K. M., and King, L. (2001). Why positive psychology is necessary. *American Psychologist*, 56, 216–17.

Shepard, R. J., and Shek, P. N. (1998). Associations between physical activity and susceptibility to cancer: possible mechanisms. *Sports Medicine*, 26, 293–315.

Sherwood, A., Light, K. C., and Blumenthal, J. A. (1989). Effects of aerobic exercise training on hemodynamic responses during psychosocial stress in normotensive and borderline hypertensive Type A men: A preliminary report. *Psychosomatic Medicine*, 51, 123–36.

Singer, J. E., Lundberg, U., and Frankenhaeuser, M. (1974). Study on the train: A study of urban commuting. Reports from the Department of Psychology, University of Stockholm, No. 425.

Smith, A. W., Bellows, R. K., Wing, R. R., and Baum, A. (2002). Mood, quality of life, and social support in parents of cancer patients. Paper presented at the Society of Behavioral Medicine, Washington, DC.

Smith, C. S., Robie, C., Folkard, S. et al. (1999). A process model of shiftwork and health. *Journal of Occupational Health Psychology*, 4, 207–18.

Smith, A. W., Sward, K. L., and Baum, A. (2000). Acute aerobic exercise as a stress-buffer: Is positive mood a factor? Paper presented at the American Psychological Association Divisions of Health Psychology and Exercise and Sports Psychology (co-listed), Washington, DC.

Sothmann, M., Horn, T., Hart, B., and Gustafson, A. (1987). Comparison of discrete cardiovascular fitness groups on plasma catecholamine and selected behavioral responses to psychological stress. *Psychophysiology*, 24, 47–54.

Spanier, P. A., and Allison, K. R. (2001). General social support and physical activity: An analysis of the Ontario Health Survey. *Canadian Journal of Public Health*, 92, 210–13.

Spiegel, D. (1998). Getting there is half the fun: Relating happiness to health. *Psychological Inquiry*, 9, 66–8.

Spiegel, D., Bloom, J. R., and Yalom, I. (1981). Group support for patients with metastatic cancer: A randomized outcome study. *Archives of General Psychiatry*, 38, 527–33.

Spiegel, D., and Kimerling, R. (2001). Group psychotherapy for women with breast cancer: Relationships among social support, emotional expression, and survival. In C. D. Ryff and B. H. Singer (Eds.), *Emotion, Social Relationships, and Health*. New York: Oxford University Press.

Staats, H., Gatersblen, B., and Hartig, T. (1997). Change in mood as a function of environmental design: Arousal and pleasure on a simulated forest hike. *Journal of Environmental Psychology*, 17, 283–300.

Stephens, M. A., Franks, M. M., and Townsend, A. L. (1994). Stress and rewards in women's multiple roles: The case of women in the middle. *Psychology and Aging*, 9, 45–52.

Stephens, M. A. P., and Townsend, A. L. (1997). Stress of parent care: Positive and negative effects of women's other roles. *Psychology and Aging*, 12, 376–86.

Steptoe, A. (2000). Stress, social support and cardiovascular activity over the working day. *International Journal of Psychophysiology*, 37, 299–308.

Steptoe, A., Wardle, J., Pollard, T. M., Canaan, L., and Davies, G. J. (1996). Stress, social support and health-related behavior: A study of smoking, alcohol consumption and physical exercise. *Journal of Psychosomatic Research*, 41, 171–80.

Stone, A. A., Cox, D. S., Valdimarsdottir, H., Handorf, L., and Neale, J. M. (1987). Evidence that secretory IgA antibody is associated with daily mood. *Journal of Personality and Social Psychology*, 52, 988–93.

Stone, A. A., Neale, J. M., Cox, D. S., Napoli, A., Valdimarsdottir, H., and Kennedy-Moore, E. (1994). Daily events are associated with secretory immune response to an oral antigen in men. *Health Psychology*, 13, 440–6.

Strauss-Blanche, G., Ekmekcioglu, C., and Marktl, W. (2000). Does vacation enable recuperation? Changes in well-being associated with time away from work. *Occupational Medicine*, 50, 167–72.

Taylor, S. E., Kemeny, M. E., Reed, G. M., Bower, J. E., and Gruenwald, T. L. (2000). Psychological resources, positive illusions, and health. *American Psychologist*, 55, 5–14.

Tedeschi, R. G., Park, C. L., and Calhoun, L. G. (Eds.). (1998). *Posttraumatic growth: Positive changes in the aftermath of crisis*. Mahwah, NJ: Lawrence Erlbaum Associates.

Theorell, T., and Karasek, R. A. (1996). Current issues relating to psychosocial job strain and cardiovascular disease research. *Journal of Occupational Health Psychology*, 1, 9–26.

Thoits, P. A. (1986). Social support as coping assistance. *Journal of Consulting and Clinical Psychology*, 54, 416–23.

Tierney, D., Romito, P., and Messing, K. (1990). She ate not the bread of idleness: Exhaustion is related to domestic and salaried working conditions among 539 Quebec hospital workers. *Women's Health*, 16, 21–42.

Tochikubo, O., Ikeda, A., Miyajima, E., and Ishii, M. (1996). Effects of insufficient sleep on blood pressure monitored by a new multibiomedical recorder. *Hypertension*, 27, 1318–24.

Travis, S. S., and McAuley, W. J. (1998). Mentally restorative experiences supporting rehabilitation of high functioning elders recovering from hip surgery. *Journal of Advanced Nursing*, 27, 977–85.

Treiber, F. A., Baranowski, T., Braden, D. S., Strong, W. B., Levy, M., and Knox, W. (1991). Social support for exercise: Relationship to physical activity in young adults. *Preventive Medicine*, 20, 737–50.

Tucker, P., Smith, L., Macdonald, I., and Folkard, S. (1998). The impact of early and late shift changeovers on sleep, health, and well-being in 8- and 12-hour shift systems. *Journal of Occupational Health Psychology*, 3, 265–75.

Uchino, B. N., and Garvey, T. S. (1997). The availability of social support reduces cardiovascular reactivity to acute psychological stress. *Journal of Behavioral Medicine*, 20, 15–27.

Ulrich, R. S. (1984). View through a window may influence recovery from surgery. *Science*, 224, 420–1.

Ulrich, R. S., Simons, R. F., Losito, B. D., Fiorito, E., Miles, M. A., and Zelson, M. (1991). Stress recovery during exposure to natural and urban environments. *Journal of Environmental Psychology*, 11, 201–30.

USDHHS (1991). *Healthy People 2000: National Health Promotion and Disease Prevention Objectives*, Rockville, MD: US Department of Health and Human Services.

van Doornen, L. J., and de Geus, E. J. (1993). Stress, physical activity and coronary heart disease. *Work and Stress*, 7, 121–39.

Vedhara, K., Shanks, N., Anderson, S., and Lightman, S. (2000). The role of stressors and psychosocial variables in the stress process: A study of chronic caregiver stress. *Psychosomatic Medicine*, 62, 374–85.

Verderber, S. (1986). Dimensions of person-window transactions in the hospital environment. *Environment and Behavior*, 18, 450–66.

Vinokur, A. D., Price, R. H., and Caplan, R. D. (1996). Hard times and hurtful partners: How financial strain affects depression and relationship satisfaction of unemployed persons and their spouses. *Journal of Personality and Social Psychology*, 71, 166–79.

Vitaliano, P. P., Schulz, R., Kiecolt-Glaser, J., and Grant, I. (1997). Research on physiological and physical concomitants of caregiving: Where do we go from here? *Annals of Behavioral Medicine*, 19, 117–23.

Walker, C. M. (1996). Financial management, coping and debt in households under financial strain. *Journal of Economic Psychology*, 17, 789–807.

Wallace, J. P., Raglin, J. S., and Jastremski, C. A. (1995). Twelve month adherence of adults who joined a fitness program with a spouse versus without a spouse. *Journal of Sports Medicine and Physical Fitness*, 35, 206–13.

Wallberg-Henriksson, H. (1992). Exercise and diabetes mellitus. *Exercise and Sport Sciences Reviews*, 20, 339–68.

Webb, W. B., and Agnew, H. W. (1975). Are we chronically sleep deprived? *Bulletin of the Psychonomic Society*, 6, 47–48.

Weidner, G., Boughal, T., Connor, S. L., Pieper, C., and Mendell, N. (1997). Relationship of job strain to standard coronary risk factors and psychological characteristics in women and men of the Family Heart Study. *Health Psychology*, 16, 239–47.

West, S. G., Brownley, K. A., and Light, K. C. (1998). Postexercise vasodilation reduces diastolic blood pressure responses to stress. *Annals of Behavioral Medicine*, 20, 77–83.

Westman, M., and Eden, D. (1997). Effects of a respite from work on burnout: Vacation relief and fade-out. *Journal of Applied Psychology*, 82, 516–27.

Wing, R. R., and Jeffrey, R. W. (1999). Benefits of recruiting participants with friends and increasing social support for weight loss and maintenance. *Journal of Consulting and Clinical Psychology*, 67, 132–8.

Wortman, C. B., and Dunkel-Schetter, C. (1979). Interpersonal relationships and cancer: A theoretical analysis. *Journal of Social Issues*, 35, 120–55.

Yeung, R. R. (1996). The acute effects of exercise on mood state. *Journal of Psychosomatic Research*, 40, 123–41.

Zautra, A. J., Hoffman, J. M., Matt, K. S. et al. (1998). An examination of individual differences in the relationship between interpersonal stress and disease activity among women with rheumatoid arthritis. *Arthritis Care and Research*, 11, 271–9.

Zautra, A. J., Hoffman, J. M., Potter, P. T., Matt, K. S., Yocum, D., and Castro, W. L. (1997). Examination of changes in interpersonal stress as a factor in disease exacerbations among women with rheumatoid arthritis. *Annals of Behavioral Medicine*, 19, 279–86.

Zelasko, C. J. (1995). Exercise for weight loss: What are the facts? *Journal of the American Dietetic Association*, 95, 1414–17.

CHAPTER 17

Coping and Adjustment to Rheumatoid Arthritis

Craig A. Smith, Kenneth A. Wallston, and
Kathleen A. Dwyer

Vanderbilt University

Introduction

Coping – defined as a person's cognitive and behavioral efforts to manage the stress-producing aspects of one's circumstances, including those that are illness-related – should be a central construct in the study of how individuals adjust, or fail to adjust, to chronic illnesses. A key puzzle for health psychologists is to explain the large, easily observable individual differences in people's adjustment to chronic and acute medical conditions, as well as to other forms of adversity. Across a wide variety of conditions, including rheumatoid arthritis (e.g., Brown et al., 1989; C. A. Smith and Wallston, 1992; 1996), cancer (e.g., Carver et al., 1993; Helgeson and Cohen, 1996; Stanton and Snider, 1993), diabetes (e.g., Grey et al., 1991; Macrodimitris and Endler, 2001), sickle cell disease (e.g., Thompson et al., 1992), and HIV/AIDS (e.g., Kurdek and Siesky, 1990; Pakenham et al., 1994), and at any given level of pain and/ or physical symptomatology, some individuals appear to be minimally affected by their condition, and manage to maintain relatively active lives and good psychological adjustment. Others, however, demonstrate considerable functional impairment and relatively poor psychological adjustment. Such individuals may severely restrict their daily activities, become depressed and/or become profoundly dissatisfied with their lives.

A variety of constructs and variables have been proposed and shown to be relevant to understanding these individual differences. Included have been self-efficacy and control-related beliefs (e.g., Jensen and Karoly, 1991; Jensen et al., 1991a; C. A. Smith et al., 1991; Wallston and Wallston, 1978), optimism (e.g., Brenner et al., 1994; Taylor et al., 1992), self-esteem (e.g., Bernard et al., 1996; Malcarne et al., 1999), and social support (e.g., Affleck et al., 1988; Helgeson and Cohen, 1996). However, coping should be central among these constructs because coping represents the behavioral interface where these beliefs and resources are translated into thoughts and behaviors that impact directly on health, well-being, and adjustment.[1] Thus, it is through coping that beliefs that one is capable of effectively managing one's arthritis and the flares that go with it are translated into attempts to actively maintain one's lifestyle, despite those flares, just as it is through coping that one's feelings of helplessness about the condition are translated into more passive, detrimental behaviors, such as taking to bed and isolating oneself. In recognition of the central role of coping in adjustment to chronic illness, biopsychosocial models of adjustment, often based on the stress and coping framework advanced by Lazarus and Folkman (1984), typically depict the effects of psychosocial resources (e.g., one's control beliefs and social support) as being mediated by one's coping behaviors (see, e.g., C. A. Smith and Wallston, 1992).

In fact, coping has been a commonly studied construct in investigations of health and adjustment. For example, a recent (March 2002) search of the online PsychInfo database using the keywords "coping and health" yielded just under 9,000 citations of articles, books, and book chapters published since 1977.

However, all is not well with the study of coping. In fact, coping research has been characterized as being "in crisis" (cf. Somerfield and McCrae, 2000). At present, the dominant method for assessing coping involves administering standardized questionnaires, such as the Ways of Coping (WOC, Folkman and Lazarus, 1988), the COPE (Carver et al., 1989) or similarly designed, more health/condition-relevant inventories such as the Cognitive Strategies Questionnaire (CSQ, Rosensteil and Keefe, 1983) or the Vanderbilt Multidimensional Pain Coping Inventory (VMPCI, C. A. Smith et al., 1997). These scales yield numeric estimates of the degree to which individuals employ various coping strategies, which are then typically compared across groups of individuals, and/or correlated with measures of constructs theoretically related to coping, such as psychological adjustment, social support, and the like. This quantitative methodology has recently come under strong attack (e.g., Coyne, 1997; Coyne and Gottlieb, 1996; Coyne and Racioppo, 2000; Stone et al., 1991). In fact, one prominent coping researcher (Coyne, 1997; Coyne and Gottlieb, 1996; Coyne and Racioppo, 2000) has gone so far as to argue that almost nothing has been learned from the numerous studies involving coping checklists, and has called for a moratorium on such research.

Although we agree the use of coping checklists has had its problems, we find the verdict that little of value has been learned from such research to be far too dour, and the recommendation to abandon this type of research to be premature. Thus, in this chapter we draw on our own work on coping and adjustment to rheumatoid arthritis (C. A. Smith and Wallston, 1992; 1996; C. A. Smith et al., 1997) to consider a number of the potentially troublesome issues associated with the study of coping, and ways in which these issues might be addressed to strengthen the use of coping inventories. In addition, we illustrate some findings that have emerged from this research that we believe to be informative and useful.

Nonetheless, we also agree with recent commentators (e.g., Coyne and Racciopo, 2000; Somerfield, 1997) that the exclusive use of coping inventories is somewhat limited, and that the development of alternative, convergent methodologies is called for. Therefore we conclude this chapter by discussing some of our own recent efforts to supplement and integrate the more traditional, quantitative use of a coping inventory with alternative methodologies. First, we describe a project in which we sought to combine a quantitative coping assessment with a qualitative methodology (Dwyer et al., 1996); second, we describe a model that has been developed using a more purely qualitative approach (Dwyer, 2001a; 2001b); and third, we describe a coping based intervention that we and our colleagues developed and tested (Sinclair et al., 1998). Through these examples we illustrate the value of these alternative methodologies, how effective use of these methodologies can be informed by the use of quantitative coping inventories, and how those inventories themselves can be validated through the alternative methodologies.

Broad Dimensions versus Narrow Strategies

One issue confronting the coping researcher concerns the level of specificity at which to assess coping. In what might be termed the "first generation" of research using coping checklists, coping tended to be analyzed, and often assessed, in terms of broad coping dimensions corresponding to "problem-focused" versus "emotion-focused" coping (e.g., Folkman and Lazarus, 1980) or "active" versus "passive" coping (e.g., Brown and Nicassio, 1987).

The use of such broad dimensions, however, has had drawbacks. These broad dimensions necessarily encompass a range of potentially distinct coping strategies. For example, passive strategies might include such things as taking to bed, assuming the worst, restricting one's activities, and the like, whereas active strategies might include such things as attempting to maintain one's activities in the face of pain or stress, using distraction to ignore the stressor, actively seeking advice or help from others, and the like. By combining such strategies into a single score, broad coping scales may obscure and underestimate the relations between coping and adjustment. For instance, the use of broad summary scales does not allow one to determine which of several strategies is most responsible for any observed relations (see also, Jensen et al., 1991b; 1992). In addition, strategies subsumed by a broad scale could have opposing effects on adjustment that would tend to cancel out one or another coping strategy when combined into a single score. Finally, in developing broad summary scales, potentially important strategies might be overlooked, ignored, or dropped from consideration if they fail to contribute cleanly to a simple factor structure.

In response to these considerations, there has more recently been a move away from the use of broad summary scales to an examination of the specific coping strategies subsumed by those scales. In the general coping literature and for health coping, this move has been supported by the development of multidimensional coping instruments, such as the WOC (Folkman and Lazarus, 1988) and COPE (Carver et al., 1989) for general coping; and the Vanderbilt Multidimensional Pain Coping Inventory (VMPCI; C. A. Smith et al., 1997) and the Pain Response Inventory (PRI; Walker et al., 1997) for more health-specific coping. A clear finding to emerge from this shift is that different forms of emotion-focused coping (i.e., attempts to manage the distress resulting from stressful circumstances; cf. Lazarus and Folkman, 1984) differ in their relations to psychological adjustment. For instance, positive reappraisal (emphasizing the positive aspects of one's circumstances) generally has been found to be associated with relatively good psychological adjustment, whereas wishful thinking, distancing, and avoidance have been associated with relatively poor adjustment (e.g., Affleck and Tennen, 1991; Carver et al., 1993; Long and Sangster, 1993; C. A. Smith et al., 1997; Stanton and Snider, 1993; Walker et al., 1997). These findings should not be taken as necessarily indicating that these different forms of coping cause the observed differences in adjustment. Most of the relevant work has been cross-sectional; thus it is possible that differences in adjustment influence these forms of coping. In addition, in interpreting these findings the possibility that at least some of the coping items are at least partially confounded with measures of adjustment needs to be carefully considered (e.g., Stanton et al., 1994). Nonetheless, such findings clearly support the utility of adopting a multidimensional approach to the assessment of coping.

Of course, a potential drawback of adopting a multidimensional approach is that one's assessment instruments can quickly become unwieldy. Each of the individual subscales is typically assessed with three or four items, which from a psychometric standpoint is quite minimalist (DeVellis, 1991). Often, 10 to 15 distinct coping strategies might be assessed in a given inventory. For instance, the published version of the COPE (Carver et al., 1989) is comprised of 14 subscales; that of the VMPCI (C. A. Smith et al., 1997) is comprised of 11 subscales; and that of the PRI (Walker et al., 1997) is comprised of 14 subscales. Moreover, as we will argue below, a truly thorough assessment of coping would involve several more subscales than are typically assessed. Thus, existing coping inventories often include 60 or more items, and more comprehensive ones could easily expand to upwards of 100 items. Employing such inventories is very costly in terms of time and participant goodwill, and when such an inventory is included it may often come at the expense of other measures of alternative relevant constructs. Using such long measures may also often be impractical in chronically ill populations where the attention and effort a participant can devote to completing such measures may be quite limited.

One alternative to using such extensive inventories would be to revert to using a shorter measure assessing broader subscales, perhaps systematically including items representative of each of the multidimensional subscales. Such a solution would, of course, retain all the drawbacks of using the original broad subscales, as discussed above. An alternative solution would be to adopt the finer-grained multidimensional approach and retain the use of the individual subscales, but to be selective in the subscales that are assessed. Not all coping strategies are equally relevant to all situations; depending on the problem area and specific questions under study, the investigator could construct an abbreviated measure by strategically selecting the individual subscales likely to be most relevant and informative (see Coyne and Gottlieb, 1996, for a similar suggestion). Naturally, to make such selections effectively would require careful consideration of the nature of the problem being studied and of the observations that are likely to be made. However, as discussed subsequently, there are additional good reasons for doing a careful task analysis of the problem area one is studying before using a coping inventory in that area. Thus, the strategic selection of specific coping strategy measures for a given research problem may not be as onerous, or as potentially hit or miss, as it may first appear.

Assessing Strategies versus Functions

A second issue, closely related to the assessment of broad versus narrow dimensions, concerns whether one should directly assess the specific strategies used by an individual or the coping functions served by those strategies. Some of the labels given to the broader coping dimensions, such as "emotion-focused coping" and "problem-focused coping" (e.g., Folkman and Lazarus, 1980; Lazarus and Folkman, 1984) refer fairly directly to the coping functions served by the strategies subsumed by these broad dimensions. In particular, the labels "problem-focused" and "emotion-focused" refer to two distinct routes by which stress might be alleviated (Lazarus and Folkman, 1984). Thus "problem-focused" coping strategies reflect the person's efforts to alleviate stress by attempting to change directly the problematic circumstances or conditions. Examples of problem-focused coping might include efforts to raise additional money during a financial crisis, or engaging in therapeutic exercise to retard or reverse the progression of a chronic illness. "Emotion-focused" strategies, on the other hand, reflect efforts to alleviate the stress through internal, often cognitive, activities and adjustments that do not necessarily change the actual circumstances or conditions. Examples of emotion-focused coping might include reappraising the circumstances in a more positive light, attempting to shut out or ignore the circumstances, or changing one's priorities and goals such that the problematic circumstances become less important. In contrast, most of the subscales assessed in multidimensional coping inventories do not refer to such overarching coping functions, but rather refer to the specific behavioral and cognitive strategies in which persons might engage, such as seeking social support, avoidance, positive reappraisal, and the like.

Our position is that it is very important for the coping researcher to keep in mind the distinction between the specific strategies in which a person might engage and the overarching coping functions that might be served by those strategies. Moreover, although we believe that an appreciation of the distinctions among the overarching coping functions is invaluable for a theoretical understanding of the processes associated with coping and adjustment, we believe efforts at assessing coping should be directed at measuring the specific coping strategies in which a person engages rather than in attempting to directly assess the coping functions served by those strategies.

There are at least two reasons for taking this position. First, respondents are likely to be better able to report on which specific strategies they engaged in rather than on which functions those strategies served, as the specific strategies represent concrete behaviors and cognitions in a way that the more abstract functions served by those behaviors and cognitions do not. The use of coping inventories is no less prone to the limitations of self-report data than are other self-report measures, and in some ways are more susceptible to these limitations. One especially notable issue in assessing coping is whether respondents have access to all of their coping activities, and thus have the ability to report on them accurately. The effective use of some coping strategies, such as repression and denial, essentially precludes the person from being fully aware that he or she is employing the strategy. For instance, being aware that one is in denial can greatly reduce that strategy's effectiveness (e.g., Mehlman and Slane, 1994; Myers, 2000). Clearly, the careful and accurate assessment of such relatively inaccessible strategies would require the use of alternative, convergent methodologies beyond direct self-report. However, respondents do seem to have some awareness of their efforts at denial and related strategies (perhaps when their use is ineffective; as evidenced by consistent links between self-reported habitual use of denial/avoidance and poor adaptational outcomes, e.g., Carver et al., 1993; Lutgendorf et al., 1994). Other strategies (e.g., positive reappraisal, seeking social support, etc.) are more accessible to the respondent, and the assessment of them via self-report is less problematic. Thus, because many coping activities, especially the more internal, emotion-focused ones, do not have clear external manifestations, attempting to assess these strategies, even the relatively inaccessible ones, via self-report remain a worthwhile endeavor in our view. Nonetheless, given the difficulties and problems associated with this methodology, it seems prudent to keep the respondent's assessment task as easy as possible, and we believe that the more one focuses on the assessment of concrete behaviors and thoughts, the more likely it is that reliable and valid data will result.

Second, there is not necessarily a one-to-one mapping between coping strategies and the functions they serve. Sometimes a given strategy can serve both problem-focused and emotion-focused functions simultaneously. For instance, in seeking social support a person may often be looking for both problem-focused instrumental help with her problem and emotion-focused reassurance to help her reappraise the circumstances in a more benign manner. In addition, the function served by a particular strategy may often depend on the context in which it is used. For example, in many contexts the use of distraction can be conceptualized as an avoidant emotion-focused strategy that is often associated with relatively poor adaptational outcomes (e.g., Folkman et al., 1986); however, within the context of pain coping, the use of distraction is often a very effective problem-focused strategy, one that tends to be correlated with other problem-focused strategies and is associated with relatively good adaptational outcomes (see McCaul and Malott, 1984, for an analysis of when distraction will be more and less effective in coping with pain). In fact, within the pain domain, items assessing distraction were among the key defining items on the broad "active coping" subscale of the Vanderbilt Pain Management Inventory (Brown and Nicassio, 1987).

Moreover, even more extreme avoidant strategies, such as denial, can be beneficial under certain circumstances (e.g., Lazarus, 1983). For instance, in results that we report in more detail below, the avoidance/denial subscale of the VMPCI was found to be correlated positively with active coping, and to be associated with positive outcomes (C. A. Smith et al., 1997). Although relatively uncommon, such a result is not limited to pain coping. For example, denial has been found to be positively associated with positive adjustment in persons with end-stage renal failure (Fricchione et al., 1992) and cancer (Meyerowitz et al., 1986). In addition, in a meta-analysis examining the efficacy of coping strategies over time, Suls and Fletcher (1985) found that avoidant coping strategies might often be quite effective in the short term, but become less so for the longer term.

In a similar manner, in many contexts, catastrophizing (expecting the worst; complaining; Keefe et al., 1989; Rosensteil and Keefe, 1983) is considered to be a passive and largely maladaptive emotion-focused coping strategy. However, in several samples of children the catastrophizing subscale of the PRI (Walker et al., 1997) was found to load on the higher order "active" as well as "passive" scales described by the scale's developers. In interpreting this finding, the authors speculated that, in young children, the complaining and other activities associated with catastrophizing might well often serve as an effective problem-focused way of getting attention and assistance by persons who are otherwise relatively powerless to exert control over their health condition or circumstances (Walker et al., 1997).

The concerns regarding the methodological issues surrounding self-reports, combined with the observation that the precise functions served by individual coping strategies may often be context-dependent, lead us to recommend that investigators attempt to assess the actual coping strategies used in as direct and concrete a manner as possible, and then to use those data to infer the coping functions being served, rather than attempting to assess those functions directly.

Specificity Imbalance in Current Inventories vis-à-vis Emotion- versus Problem-focused Strategies

Careful consideration of the existing multidimensional coping measures in light of the above arguments reveals a glaring weakness and imbalance in these inventories. In particular, as originally noted by Lazarus and Folkman (1984) with regard to the inventories that existed at that time, it remains the case that currently available coping inventories do a much better job of assessing strategies associated with emotion-focused coping than they do assessing strategies associated with problem-focused coping. Emotion-focused strategies are largely intra-personal, representing a variety of ways that a person can adjust or adapt to stressful conditions without actually changing those conditions. As such, they in some sense transcend particular stress-producing conditions, and can be potentially utilized by the person (albeit not with equal effectiveness) across a broad range of conditions. Accordingly, it has proven to be a relatively straightforward matter to identify some of the major strategies a person might employ to adjust to stressful circumstances in an emotion-focused manner, and to develop scales to assess these strategies as part of a general-purpose coping inventory.

In contrast, problem-focused strategies, reflecting efforts to change the actual conditions to make them less stressful, are inherently context/task specific. The problem-focused strategies that might be effective and relevant in one set of conditions (e.g., managing one's blood sugar in diabetes) may be quite different from those that are effective and relevant in other contexts (e.g., in coping with arthritis-related pain and impairment or dealing with a financial shortfall due to unemployment). The upshot is that although existing coping inventories commonly include one or two problem-focused strategies that appear to have broad cross-situational applicability (notably seeking instrumental social support), the assessment of problem-focused coping strategies on these inventories is far less developed and differentiated than the assessment of emotion-focused strategies.

Instead, problem-focused strategies have largely been represented by a single subscale assessing something akin to "active problem-solving," which assesses the degree to which the respondent attempted to do anything (without specifying what was actually done) to try to change the stressful conditions. Such assessments, by failing to take into account the specific strategies that were used, or the specific context in which they were used, necessarily provide a very blurry picture of the links between problem-focused coping and adjustment. Such blurriness might underlie the fact that the observed relations between the use of problem-focused strategies and positive adaptational outcomes has been considerably weaker and less consistent than typically hypothesized (see C. A. Smith et al., 1997). In general, the ways in which one might succeed at a task are more constrained than the ways in which one might fail.

Accordingly, in order to examine the effectiveness of problem-focused coping, beyond knowing that a person did *something* to try to change the circumstances, it is important to know what specific strategies were attempted as well as whether those strategies were effectively executed. This last point is especially important to address because it has seldom been considered in the coping literature. Yet it is readily evident that even if a person knows what to do in a situation, and attempts to perform a highly effective coping strategy, those efforts will most likely come to naught if the strategy is performed incompetently (see also, Suls and David, 1996). For example, diligently taking one's prescribed medications can be quite harmful if one is confused about what and how much one should be taking at any given time.

Gaining the desired specificity in assessing problem-focused coping will come at a cost, however. First, because the relevant problem-focused strategies can be expected to differ as a function of the problem or condition to be contended with, and probably even the different stages of a chronic condition(Costa and McCrae, 1993; Coyne and Racioppo, 2000; de Ridder and Schreurs, 1996), considerable knowledge about the situation, and the coping strategies likely to be most relevant to contending with it, is highly desirable for developing specific problem-focused coping subscales for that problem or condition. This fact argues for a need to use convergent methodologies, beyond coping inventories, in the study of coping, because if coping inventories satisfactory for providing such information were available, they would not need to be developed. Below we will argue that the use of qualitative methodologies can be quite useful for the development of specific and relevant quantitative subscales for assessing problem-focused coping (see also Coyne and Gottlieb, 1996; Somerfield, 1997).

Second, the use of subscales that vary systematically across conditions and problems will necessarily preclude the use of omnibus, general-purpose coping inventories that allow straightforward comparisons of findings across a wide variety of contexts. As desirable as such general-purpose measures obviously are, we would caution against placing too high a premium on them. In our view the push to develop general purpose measures of problem-focused coping strategies has, ironically, impeded the study of problem-focused coping precisely because the relevance and efficacy of specific problem-focused strategies is highly context-dependent. For those problems and conditions deemed worthy of intensive study, we believe it is worthwhile to sacrifice some generalizability across contexts to gain a good understanding of the particular context (see also Coyne and Gottlieb, 1996). Especially if one studies coping with an eye toward developing interventions designed to assist those faring relatively poorly within a given context, then it is of vital importance to have a clear understanding of which particular coping strategies are most relevant, and which are most likely to prove efficacious within that context.

Assessment of Dispositional versus Situated Coping

There is some debate in the literature as to whether it is adequate to measure coping at a trait-dispositional level that summarizes the person's typical approach to coping with various forms of stress, as has often been done in the past (e.g., C. A. Smith and Wallston, 1992; C. A. Smith et al., 1997), or whether it is better assessed in a highly situation-specific manner in which the person's coping efforts within a specific encounter are assessed (e.g., Lazarus and Folkman, 1987). Our view on this issue is that neither approach to coping assessment is inherently superior to the other; both have their respective strengths and weaknesses; and which approach(es) one should adopt in a given study depends on one's research questions.

If one's interests are primarily in examining the process of coping – for instance, examining how one's coping activities unfold over the course of an encounter, or attempting to link coping activities to the short-term resolution of the encounter – then a highly situated, encounter-specific assessment of coping is called for. Dispositional measures that summarize coping activities across multiple encounters are clearly inappropriate for modeling the coping activities that are performed, and the factors that influence them, within a specific encounter (Lazarus and Folkman, 1987).

On the other hand, except for extreme situations, it is unlikely that a person's coping efforts in any single encounter are likely to strongly influence the person's long-term adjustment. Instead, it is more likely that the cumulative effects of how the person copes with repeated encounters are likely to influence such outcomes as overall life-satisfaction, depression, functional impairment, and the like. Therefore, if one's interests are in relating a person's coping activities to such outcomes, a more dispositional assessment of the person's coping style would usually be called for.

Such assessments could be obtained either by aggregating across multiple assessments of situated coping (e.g., Schwartz et al., 1999), or by using a measure such as the COPE (Carver et al., 1989) or VMPCI (C. A. Smith et al., 1997) that attempts to directly assess the person's usual style of coping. A question for future research is whether these two methods of estimating a person's coping style are comparably reliable and valid. The results of Schwartz et al. (1999) suggest that the aggregation of situated coping assessments may be superior, but this is a result that clearly needs replication. It is often much easier and cheaper to obtain a single assessment of coping style than it is to obtain the multiple situated assessments that would go into an aggregated measure. Therefore an important issue to assess is whether aggregating multiple situated measures provides an increase in validity substantial enough to justify the added effort and expense of obtaining multiple situated assessments.

In many instances, it can be valuable to assess coping at both the situated and dispositional levels within the same study (e.g., Carver and Scheier, 1994). Assessing coping at both levels allows one to address a number of theoretically relevant issues that cannot be addressed using either type of assessment by itself. For instance, one can explicitly model the degree to which dispositional coping styles can predict the use of individual coping strategies within specific encounters. Similarly, if such data are combined with additional data describing the specific encounter, one can explicitly model the situational factors that systematically influence coping such that it deviates from a person's dispositional coping style.

Some Representative Findings Using a Multidimensional Coping Inventory

As noted at the outset, in response to several of the concerns discussed above, we developed a multidimensional pain coping inventory, the VMPCI (C. A. Smith et al., 1997), to allow us to make a more fine-grained examination of coping and adjustment in persons with rheumatoid arthritis (RA) than we had been able to do with the Vanderbilt Pain Management Inventory (VPMI, Brown and Nicassio, 1987). This latter instrument only distinguished between active and passive pain coping strategies, while the newer one had 11 subscales. In this section we review some of the findings that have emerged from our use of this instrument that we believe highlight the utility of using a multi-dimensional coping inventory.

Dispositional Antecedents of Coping: Perceptions of Control and Social Support

As a set of behaviors or behavioral strategies, coping does not occur in a vacuum. In fact, like many constructs in social psychology, coping is best conceived of as having both antecedents – i.e., "causal" factors that precede it – as well as consequences – i.e., outcomes that are "caused" (or affected) by coping (such as changes in health status). The search for antecedents of coping has a rich history in social psychology (Folkman et al., 1986; Jerusalem and Schwarzer, 1989; Long et al., 1992; Mikulincer and Solomon, 1989; C. A. Smith and Wallston, 1992; Wanberg, 1997), but it is not the purpose of this chapter to review that literature. Instead, we will concentrate on some of the findings from our own research to illustrate a few of the factors that may predispose a person with RA to cope one way or the other with the pain that is characteristic of this condition.

In our depiction of a theoretical (path) model representing the general variables involved in adjustment to a chronic illness such as arthritis, we (i.e., C. A. Smith and Wallston, 1992) posited that there are three direct causal influences on coping: (1) primary appraisal (e.g., "is this painful condition or episode a threat to my well-being or a challenge that I need to overcome?"); (2) generalized beliefs and expectations regarding one's abilities and other internal resources (e.g., "do I have what it takes to cope with the pain?"); and (3) perceived availability of external resources, including social support (by which was meant "are there other people available whom I can call on for coping assistance?"). The model we put forth also contained paths from generalized expectancies and external resources to appraisal, thus setting up this latter construct as the main pathway to coping. "Although appraisal is posited to be the primary influence on coping, both beliefs and external influences can influence coping directly" (C. A. Smith and Wallston, 1992: 152). In the remainder of this section, we present some new longitudinal findings that speak to this latter assertion.

The data in our 1992 *Health Psychology* article came from the first of two longitudinal panel studies of persons with RA that we conducted. The analyses reported in that paper covered the first eight waves of data collection. We began wave 1 in 1983 and collected data for wave 8 in 1987, approximately four years later. Subsequent to that, we continued studying this same panel of individuals through wave 12, which ended in 1993–94. The main question being examined in this section is, "can we predict how subjects will cope with their arthritis pain in wave 12 from knowledge about their internal and external coping resources assessed at an earlier point in the study?"

For the purposes of these analyses, we first take an overly simplistic position and pretend that pain coping can be adequately captured by the two global dimensions identified by our colleagues Greg Brown and Perry Nicassio

when they developed the VPMI using data from waves 1 and 2 of our longitudinal study (see Brown and Nicassio, 1987). By the time wave 12 rolled
around, we had shortened the active and passive pain coping scales so as
not to overwhelm our subjects who, by that time, were also asked to fill out
the 60-item VMPCI. However, the reliability and concurrent validity of the
shortened versions of the active (5 items) and passive (6 items) pain coping
scales were still pretty impressive (see C. A. Smith et al., 1997).

In addition, we further test the links between potential antecedents and the
more specific subscales of the VMPCI to examine whether the results of these
analyses can refine any results observed based on the broader coping subscales. The version of the VMPCI that we used in these analyses, as well as
the analyses we report in subsequent sections of the chapter, consisted of
11 subscales, 5 of which (planful problem-solving, positive reappraisal, distraction, distancing/denial and stoicism) were found to be correlated with the
active subscale of the VPMI, 5 of which (confrontative coping, self-blame,
self-isolation, wishful thinking, and disengagement) were found to be correlated with the passive subscale, and one of which (use of religion) was only
weakly correlated with either scale. Recall that the relation between distanc-
ing/denial and active coping is somewhat unusual and might be specific to the
context of coping with pain (see discussion above).

The two main coping resource constructs our research team concentrated
on back in the early 1980s were locus of control beliefs and social support.
Locus of control (LOC) is a subset of a larger construct, perceived control (see
Wallston, 1989; 2001, for more about the relationship and distinction between these constructs). *Locus* refers to perceptions of the *place* where control
resides, and is usually dichotomized into "internal" versus "external." Generally, individuals with an internal locus of control orientation believe that
control over the important things that happen to them (i.e., their reinforcements) lie within them, either as a function of who they are or what they
do. Such individuals are thought to have control over their reinforcements.
Persons with an external locus of control orientation believe that control of
valued outcomes lies outside of themselves, residing either with other people
or being left totally up to fate, luck or chance. Externals are thought to be low
on perceived control.

In the early 1970s, Hannah Levenson, a clinical psychologist in Los Angeles,
recognized that, rather than being polar opposites, internality and externality
were essentially independent dimensions. She developed the I, P, and C scales
as a means of separately measuring internal (I) from external belief orientations,
and further distinguishing externality into two separate dimensions: powerful
others (P) and chance (C). A few years later, Ken and Barbara Wallston
modeled their Multidimensional Health Locus of Control (MHLC) Scales after
Levenson's work (see Wallston et al., 1978). The MHLC has three subscales –
IHLC (assessing persons' beliefs/expectancies that their health status is determined by their own behavior); PHLC (beliefs/expectancies that one's health
status is determined by the actions of "powerful other" persons, such as
family, friends, or health care professionals); and CHLC (beliefs/expectancies
that one's health status is determined by fate, luck or chance).

Given the obvious difference between these two multidimensional measures – that is, the I, P, and C scales assess generalized LOC beliefs while the MHLC is specific to the health domain – Levenson's scales are considered to be more "trait" or "personality" – like than the MHLC and, thus, less likely to change as a function of health-related experiences. Another difference is that the two external MHLC subscales were designed to be more empirically independent of one another than are Levenson's P and C scales. It is not unusual to find the P and C scales intercorrelating about 0.60, while it is rare to find that the PHLC and CHLC subscales share more than 10 percent common variance.

We gave Form B of the MHLC scales to our subjects in wave 1 of our longitudinal study, and the complete set of I, P, and C scales to the same subjects in wave 2, six months later. Based on those data, we shortened both sets of LOC measures and administered all six subscales to subjects at wave 3, one year after obtaining wave 1 data. When we look cross-sectionally at how well the six LOC scores at wave 3 predict *active* pain coping at the same point in time (i.e., also at wave 3) we find we can account for an adjusted 13.4 percent of the variance in active pain coping, with I and CHLC being the only unique predictors. Regressing active pain coping at wave 12 on the same set of wave 3 predictors results in a reliable adjusted R^2 of 6 percent, but with none of the six individual predictors making a significant independent contribution to the model. By controlling for wave 3 active pain coping, we looked at how well LOC assessed at wave 3 predicts *change* in active pain coping over the nine-year period. Unfortunately, LOC scores at wave 3 did not predict change in active pain coping.

The picture is somewhat different when it comes to predicting *passive* pain coping. Cross-sectionally, the six LOC scores predict an adjusted 18.5 percent of the variance in wave 3 passive pain coping, with IHLC, P, and CHLC all making significant unique contributions. Almost 16 percent of the variance in passive pain coping at wave 12 can be explained by the combination of the six LOC scores at wave 3, but, as above, none of the individual LOC scales contributed uniquely to this solution. Controlling for wave 3 passive coping, to predict change, cut the variance explained in half, and, again, no one single predictor variable stood out as making a unique contribution to this prediction equation. Examining the zero-order correlations, however, made it quite clear that chance LOC beliefs (either assessed by the C or CHLC subscales) were the ones most associated with passive pain coping and an increase in such behavior over time.

We next examined to what extent the locus of control scores assessed at wave 3 predicted the more specific subscales of the VMPCI assessed at wave 12. These analyses were done to see if the LOC scales might be more strongly related to certain of the VMPCI subscales than others, and thus whether we could refine the above results based on the more global pain coping scales. The most substantative finding from this set of analyses was for the subscale labeled "confrontative coping," a passive strategy that is often labeled "maladaptive." The six LOC subscales at wave 3 predicted 12.3 percent of the variance in this strategy at wave 12, with three of the predictors making a unique contribution to the prediction: PHLC and IHLC were both negatively associated with confrontative coping, whereas I was positively associated with this coping strategy. Thus, it appears that persons who simultaneously believe that their own actions determine the outcomes they receive in life but also do not believe that their health is controllable by either their own actions or those of powerful other persons are the ones who are most likely to lash out either physically or verbally when in pain.

The next strongest finding was for the subscale labeled "distancing/denial." We were able to predict an adjusted 6.8 percent of the variance in how much our subjects reported using this strategy in 1993 from the six LOC subscales completed back in 1984. The internal health locus of control subscale was the only one that made a unique contribution to this model, but it should be noted that both internal subscales (IHLC and I) were in the same positive direction, while CHLC correlated negatively with using distancing/denial as a pain coping strategy. This finding further highlights and extends our observations that "distancing/denial" in the face of pain operates like an active, adaptive coping strategy rather than a maladaptive one. It is more likely to be used by individuals who feel in control of their health and their lives, than by people who feel their health status is a matter of fate, luck, or chance.

From these analyses we can conclude that locus of control beliefs are related in an antecedent fashion to pain coping behaviors, although the specific results differ according to which type of coping is being assessed (e.g., active versus passive) and which locus of control dimension is uniquely responsible for the prediction. We also have shown that these predictions hold up over time. What is also true is that other ways of operationalizing internal coping resources (i.e., other than LOC beliefs) do an equally good, if not better job, of predicting pain coping. For instance, in their 1992 *Health Psychology* paper C. A. Smith and Wallston used a 4-item measure of perceived competence as another means of assessing generalized expectancies/internal coping resources. The wave 3 assessment of perceived competence predicts 13 percent of wave 12 passive pain coping and 4 percent of wave 12 active pain coping. In fact, even with the six LOC scales from wave 3 in the prediction equation, adding perceived competence (also from wave 3) to the model predicts an additional 5 percent of the variance of passive pain competence assessed at wave 12. Thus, locus of control along with other operationalizations of internal coping resources can, indeed, play an antecedent role in driving pain coping behavior, especially what Brown and Nicassio (1987) call passive pain coping behavior.

What role, if any, do external coping resources play in predicting active or passive pain coping scores? As mentioned above, we have mostly conceived of external coping resources as social support, both functional and structural (see Cohen et al., 2000, for more about this distinction). In our study we relied on three measures of social support that were recommended to us by Bob and Brenda DeVellis, colleagues from UNC-Chapel Hill who were also studying adjustment to rheumatoid arthritis (DeVellis et al., 1986). To get at functional support, we used a 4-item scale assessing the respondent's perceived quality of emotional support (e.g., "How often are you bothered by not having someone who shows you love and attention?") along with a 3-item scale assessing perceived availability of instrumental support (e.g., "If you couldn't use your car or your usual way of getting around for a week, could you find someone who would take you wherever you needed to go?"). To assess structural support we administered a 3-item measure of the extensivity of the subject's social network (e.g., "How many close friends would you say you have?"). In the analyses that follow, we treat these as three separate measures of social support.

Regressing active pain coping at wave 3 on the three measures of support that were assessed at wave 3 results in predicting an adjusted 4.2 percent of the variance, with quality of emotional support being the only unique significant social support predictor of active pain coping. This same set of predictors accounts for none of the variance in active pain coping nine years later, nor any of the variance in *change* in active pain coping from wave 3 to wave 12.

As with the LOC analyses, however, the picture is different when the criterion variable is passive pain coping. When all of the variables were assessed at wave 3, social support accounts for an adjusted 15.5 percent of the variance in passive pain coping, with both emotional support and network size making independent, but opposite, unique contributions. Other things (such as availability of instrumental support) being equal, people with an extensive social support network who perceived little emotional support from their friends or family were the most likely to report engaging in passive pain coping. This same pattern of findings held up, albeit somewhat less strongly, when predicting future passive pain coping. Nevertheless, individuals with a larger support network who felt unsupported emotionally back in the early 1980s continued to engage in greater amounts of passive pain coping nine years later. This structural measure of social support also contributed to the prediction of *change* in passive pain coping over the nine-year interval. Other things being equal, those with a larger social support network at wave 3 reliably increased the amount of passive pain coping that they engaged in over the subsequent nine years (a 4.5 percent change in variance accounted for). A particularly interesting aspect of these findings is that the different types of social support appear to work in opposite fashions to promote this type of coping behavior. Rather than network size, a structural component of support, facilitating adaptive (e.g., active) pain coping, it appears to lead to maladaptive (e.g., passive) pain coping, especially in the face of feeling emotionally unsupported by those in one's social network.

In a follow-up set of analyses, we regressed each of the more specific VMPCI subscales at wave 12 on the three social support scales, measured at wave 3, to examine whether the use of broad subscales might be obscuring relations between social support and specific coping strategies, as well as whether the observed links of social network size and emotional support with passive coping were general to all passive coping strategies, or more specific to a subset of them. In these analyses, only one set of relations between social support and an active coping subscale was observed. The tendency to seek social support was negatively correlated with the perceived adequacy of the person's emotional support and there was a marginal tendency for seeking support to be associated with having a larger support network available. Interestingly, the positive correlation between network size and passive coping was not evident when the individual passive coping strategies were examined. Instead, there was a *negative* association with confrontative coping such that persons with larger support networks were less likely to engage in this form of coping. The difference in the findings for generalized passive coping versus the more specific coping strategies highlights a need to further examine the influence of the size of one's social network on one's coping activities. The relationship between perceived emotional support and passive coping, however, was found to be more general, with inadequate social support being associated with disengagement, self-isolation, and wishful thinking. Thus, as was the case for the locus of control variables, examination of the relations between these antecedent variables and the individual coping strategies represented on the VMPCI yielded a different, and somewhat more refined view of these relations than could be obtained using the broader subscales of the VPMI.

Relations Between Coping and Adjustment

Beyond examining the antecedents of coping, it is also important to examine the relations between coping and adjustment. In fact, as we noted at the outset, scientific interest in coping has largely sprung from the theoretically based belief that coping represents the behavioral interface whereby antecedent factors such as control beliefs and social support can exert their influence on adaptational outcomes. Therefore, in this section we examine some of the links that have emerged in our work on RA between coping and psychological adjustment outcomes, such as depressive symptoms, functional impairment, and life satisfaction. If anything, the relations we have observed between coping and adjustment highlight the value, even more forcefully than the previous section, of employing a truly multidimensional assessment of coping over a two-dimensional one.

Prior to our development of the VMPCI (C. A. Smith et al., 1997), it was already evident that coping was systematically related to adjustment in RA. Passive coping, as assessed by instruments such as the VPMI (Brown and Nicassio, 1987), had been repeatedly found to be associated with relatively poor adjustment – e.g., increased depressive symptoms, increased functional impairment, reduced life-satisfaction, etc. (e.g., Brown et al., 1989; Jensen et al., 1991; C. A. Smith and Wallston, 1992; T. W. Smith et al., 1988). Interestingly, however, theoretically predicted links between more active coping and positive adjustment had not been consistently demonstrated.

As we noted at the outset of this chapter, the use of broad coping scales have several drawbacks that could partially obscure valid relations between coping and adjustment, and we wondered whether the previously observed weak and inconsistent relations between active coping and positive adjustment might reflect those drawbacks. Therefore, we developed the VMPCI in part to examine whether a truly multidimensional coping inventory could better account for variation in psychological adjustment than a two-dimensional inventory, such as the VPMI. In doing so, we were especially interested in whether the examination of more specific coping strategies might help clarify the potential relations between more positive forms of coping and adjustment.

The initial validation of the VMPCI was performed in two distinct samples. The first sample ($N = 171$) consisted of participants in wave 10 (Year 7) of the longitudinal sample described in the previous section, and the second sample ($N = 207$) consisted of a cohort of more newly diagnosed persons with RA who were in the first wave of a second longitudinal study. The measures used for this second cohort were identical to those used at wave 10 in the first sample. The use of the two samples allowed us to examine the degree to which observed relations between coping and adjustment would generalize across two rather different samples of persons with RA.

In our initial set of analyses we examined the degree to which the specific subscales of the VMPCI could account for variation in adaptational outcomes, specifically depressive symptoms, life satisfaction, positive affect, and negative affect, beyond what could be accounted for by the broad subscales of the VPMI. In these analyses, which used multiple regression to perform set-wise analyses of partial variance, we first controlled for variations in the outcomes attributable to pain, and then we entered sequentially the two subscales of the VPMI and the eleven subscales of the VMPCI, and vice-versa. In evaluating the increment in explained variance attributable to adding the subscales associated with either measure we always adjusted the observed change in R^2 to account for the number of predictor variables associated with that measure (Cohen and Cohen, 1983).

The results of these analyses provided strong support for utilizing the more differentiated subscales of the VMPCI. In no case did adding the two subscales of the VPMI to those of the VMPCI increase the variance accounted for in the outcome variables. Adding the subscales of the VMPCI to those of the VPMI, however, substantially increased (by approximately 10–20 percent) the variance accounted for in each of the outcomes we examined (i.e., depressive symptoms, positive affect, and negative affect) except life-satisfaction, which demonstrated smaller increases that were inconsistent across the samples (C. A. Smith et al., 1997). These results clearly indicated that the more specific subscales of the VMPCI could account for all the variance in these outcomes that could be accounted for by the more general VPMI, and could also account for considerable additional variance in them that could not be captured by the VPMI.

To follow up on these results, we also conducted a number of correlation/regression analyses that examined in a variety of ways the relations between the individual subscales of the VMPCI and these adaptational outcomes. In the most conservative of these analyses we regressed each of the outcome variables simultaneously on any of the subscales of the VMPCI that were significantly correlated with that outcome in our two samples, and identified those coping strategies that made a significant, unique contribution of the outcome in both samples. These analyses were cross-sectional; thus causal conclusions should not be drawn from them. Nonetheless, they illustrate the utility of the additional information to be gained from the more specific subscales of the VMPCI.

In both samples, disengagement was found to be uniquely associated with each of the four outcome variables. It was positively associated with negative affect and depressive symptoms, and negatively associated with life satisfaction and positive affect. As the disengagement subscale was found to be especially highly correlated with the passive subscale of the VPMI ($r = 0.75$ and 0.80 in the two samples, respectively), this finding essentially replicates prior findings using the VPMI (e.g., Brown et al., 1989) that have generally linked passive coping with negative adaptational outcomes. However, for each of these outcome variables, a second coping variable also demonstrated a unique relation to the outcome, although which coping variable this was varied for the different outcomes. Both negative affect and depressive symptoms were uniquely predicted by a second form of passive coping. For negative affect, this predictor was confrontative coping, whereas for depression it was self-isolation. Neither of these additional relations could have been demonstrated with the VPMI because it only uses a single index of passive coping. Both life satisfaction and positive affect were further predicted by positive reappraisal. These latter findings replicate previous findings by Zautra et al. (1995) in which active coping was found to be associated with positive outcomes. However, they further extend and refine such findings by indicating that it is a particular form of active coping, positive reappraisal, that is especially closely related to the positive outcomes, a refinement that is not possible when one employs a single omnibus active coping scale.

Need for More Sophisticated Analytic Strategies

We believe that the representative results described above indicate the value of using multidimensional coping inventories in the study of adaptation to chronically stressful health conditions, such as RA. However, we also find such results, which are fairly representative of those obtained in the study of coping, as being mildly dissatisfying because they do not fully utilize the information that can be obtained through such inventories. Specifically, in typical analyses, each coping strategy and its relationship to antecedents and/or adaptational outcomes is often considered individually in univariate ANOVAs or simple correlations. When a more multivariate approach has been taken it has typically consisted of factor or canonical correlation analyses designed to reduce the dimensionality of the data, or, as in our own work reported above, multiple regression analyses designed to examine, for example, which individual coping strategies contribute uniquely to the prediction of the outcome(s) under study.

Such analyses can be highly informative, and thus are well worth doing and reporting. However, they do not take full advantage of the multivariate information available. For instance, these approaches do not address issues such as whether individuals tend to engage in preferred *patterns* of coping. Thus, they do not address whether individuals who tend to engage in, say, positive reappraisal, also engage in certain other coping strategies. This issue is an important one to evaluate as it has long been observed that in response to highly stressful circumstances, individuals typically engage in a combination of multiple problem- and emotion-focused strategies (e.g., Folkman and Lazarus, 1980). The more traditional approaches also do not address whether the influences of the individual coping strategies used in such combinations are simply additive, in that each strategy influences adaptation independently, or whether the use of certain coping strategies interact such that the impact of a given coping strategy on adaptation varies as a function of what other strategies are used with it. That is, traditional analytical approaches do not address the issue of whether certain patterns of coping are especially deleterious or beneficial, beyond the individual influences of the strategies contributing to those patterns.

We do not claim to have figured out how to take full advantage of the rich information provided by multidimensional coping inventories. Nonetheless we have made some preliminary efforts (e.g., C. A. Smith and Wallston, 1996) to move beyond the more traditional analytic approaches, and we briefly review the results of those efforts here.

As a first step, we sought to examine whether distinct groups of individuals could be characterized as using different combinations, or *profiles*, of coping strategies in response to their arthritis-related pain, and whether such coping profiles were differentially related to adaptational outcomes. To accomplish this, we employed a hierarchical cluster analysis (Ward's method; Aldenderfer and Blashfield, 1984) on the coping data, using all 11 subscales of the VMPCI, from the first cohort described above ($N = 165$ of the 171, who had complete data for the analysis).

An examination of the coping profile for the entire sample indicated that participants used relatively high levels (around 2 to 2.5 on a 0–4 point scale) of planful problem solving, positive reappraisal, distraction, distancing/denial, stocism, use of religion, and wishful thinking, and substantially lower levels (approximately 1 on the same scale) of confrontative coping, self-blame, self-isolation, and disengagement. Thus, overall, with the exception of wishful thinking, which was also used quite heavily, our respondents reported a general proclivity to utilize strategies associated with active coping, and to avoid those associated with passive coping.

The results of the cluster analysis, however, indicated that this overall profile masked the fact that our participants could each be classified as utilizing one of four distinct patterns of coping. The standardized (within each coping scale) profiles corresponding to these four patterns are illustrated in Figure 17.1. Although, such labels should be used with caution, we found that each of the four clusters could be given a descriptive label quite easily.

The first cluster ($n = 47$) can be characterized as "active copers" because they tend to report the use of the more active pain coping strategies, while avoiding the use of more passive ones. In direct contrast, the second cluster ($n = 63$) can be referred to as "passive copers" because they demonstrate the opposite pattern in their use of coping. The third cluster ($n = 18$) might be referred to as "minimal copers" because they report using relatively low levels (at or below the mean) of all 11 coping strategies. The final cluster ($n = 37$) can be classified as "self-blamers" due to their especially strong reported use

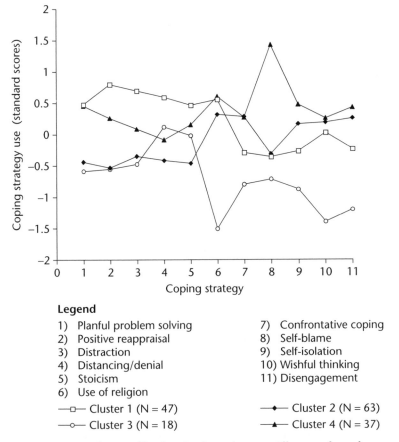

Figure 17.1   Mean coping profiles for the four clusters. All scores have been standardized.
From C. A. Smith and K. A. Wallston (1996). An analysis of coping profiles and adjustment in persons with rheumatoid arthritis. *Anxiety Stress and Coping*, 9, 107–22; http://www.tandf.co.uk. Reprinted with permission.

of this strategy. It should be noted, however, that this last group reports relatively high use of virtually all of the coping strategies.[2]

To examine whether these coping profiles were differentially associated with adaptational outcomes, we compared the four clusters in terms of pain and functional impairment, as well as the four indicators of psychological adjustment (life-satisfaction, depressive symptomatology, positive and negative affect) discussed above. The minimal copers demonstrated especially low levels of pain and impairment, and relatively high levels of psychological adjustment, whereas the self-blamers demonstrated the opposite pattern. The active and passive copers both had moderate, highly similar levels of pain and impairment, but differed substantially in terms of psychological adjustment; whereas the active copers demonstrated quite high levels of adjustment, the passive copers demonstrated quite low levels (C. A. Smith and Wallston, 1996).

Obviously, given the cross-sectional nature of these data, one must be very cautious in making causal inferences, and it is very unlikely that the coping activities represent unidirectional causal influences on adjustment. For instance, it is quite plausible that for the minimal copers, both the high levels of adjustment and the generally low levels of coping at least partially reflect the fact that these individuals are experiencing relatively little pain and impairment, and thus have relatively few stressors surrounding their condition with which to contend. Conversely, the high levels of all types of coping and relatively poor adjustment demonstrated by the self-blamers are likely to be, at least in part, a function of the especially high levels of pain and functional impairment experienced by these individuals. Nonetheless, in this context, and given their very similar levels of pain and impairment, the differences in psychological adjustment between the active and passive copers is very suggestive, and at the very least provides convergent validation of the previously observed linkages between passive coping and relatively poor adjustment, as well as the heretofore less well documented linkages between active coping and relatively good adjustment. Moreover, the existence of the distinctive profiles drives home the point that the individual coping strategies are not used in isolation, but are used in concert with other strategies, perhaps as an integrated coping effort.

Beyond documenting the existence of distinctive coping profiles, we were also interested in whether the particular *patterns* of coping used by an individual were associated with adjustment. That is, we were interested in whether particular combinations of coping were related to adaptational outcomes in synergistic ways that could not be accounted for by the independent, additive effects of the individual coping strategies contributing to the pattern. Statistically, this issue can be addressed by asking if the coping strategies interacted in predicting adjustment. To keep our initial approach to this issue computationally manageable, we limited ourselves to examining only the 55 potential two-way interactions among the 11 coping strategies for each outcome, and did not attempt to examine the many more potential multi-way interactions among the coping strategies.

Using the 0.05 level of significance, approximately twice as many of the tested interactions were found to be statistically reliable than would be expected by chance. However, relatively few interactions were observed in predicting either life-satisfaction or negative affect, whereas the majority of the observed interactions involved either depressive symptoms or positive affect. For instance, depressive symptoms were synergistically predicted by combinations of wishful thinking and confrontative coping, self-isolation and self-blame, self-isolation and wishful thinking, self-isolation and disengagement, disengagement and planful problem-solving, use of religion and distraction, self-isolation and stoicism, and confrontative coping and stoicism. Positive affect was synergistically predicted by combinations of self-blame and self-isolation, self-blame and distraction, confrontative coping and planful problem-solving, self-isolation and planful problem-solving, disengagement and planful problem-solving, use of religion and positive reappraisal, use of religion and stoicism, and positive appraisal and stoicism (C. A. Smith and Wallston, 1996).

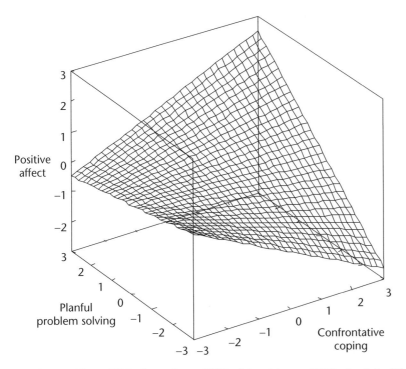

Positive = −.02 + −.01*Confrontative + .35*Planful problem + .17*Confrontative*Planful problem
affect   coping   solving   coping   solving

Figure 17.2   Regression surface depicting the interaction of planful problem solving and confrontative coping in predicting positive affect. All scores have been standardized.
From C. A. Smith and K. A. Wallston (1996). An analysis of coping profiles and adjustment in persons with rheumatoid arthritis. *Anxiety Stress and Coping*, 9, 107–22; http://www.tandf.co.uk. Reprinted with permission.

Such findings indicate that for these two outcomes in particular, the particular *combinations* of coping strategies that one employs are relevant to adaptational outcomes.

To provide a concrete example of how these combinations of coping strategies are related to coping outcomes, Figure 17.2 depicts the interaction of confrontative coping and planful problem-solving in predicting positive affect. In this instance, whether the use of confrontative coping was associated with increased or decreased positive affect depended on the degree to which the person also employed planful problem solving. As can be seen in the figure, looking at the front face of the cube, at very low levels of planful problem solving, increased levels of confrontative coping were associated with lower levels of positive affect. However, as indicated on the back face of the cube, at higher levels of planful problem-solving, increased confrontative coping was associated with increased positive affect.

We believe that these examples, both the cluster analysis and the interaction analysis, highlight the value of adopting a true multivariate approach to the study of coping and its relations to adjustment. Our results illustrate that individuals tend to use particular patterns of coping strategies in contending with their arthritis-related pain and impairment, and that the particular patterns of coping they employ are related to adaptational outcomes in ways that are not captured through traditional univariate analyses. However, we also view these initial analytical attempts as very preliminary. We believe that we have only begun to scratch the surface of what truly multidimensional approaches have to offer to the study of coping. Not only is there a need to develop more sophisticated methods for examining the relations between more complex patterns of coping and adjustment, but it is also important to dig beneath the surface of these relations and to ask about why particular combinations might have such synergistic effects. For instance, using the example presented above, how does the use of planful problem-solving moderate the influence of confrontative coping on positive affect? One speculative possibility is that in the relative absence of planful problem-solving, confrontative coping comes across as hostile complaining that serves little effect except, perhaps, to alienate those around the person using it. In contrast, in concert with planful problem-solving, such confrontation might serve as an activistic attempt to improve one's circumstances and might engender admiration in others. In any event, it is clear that it is important to document and seek to understand such synergistic effects among multiple coping strategies.

The Value of Multiple or Alternative Methodologies

Although we clearly disagree with those who would argue that the use of coping inventories in the study of adaptation to stress is misguided, it should also be clear from our discussion of the issues that we do not see the use of coping inventories as a panacea. Instead, we would agree with the critics of coping inventories that there are a number of important issues that such inventories are not well designed to address, and there are other issues for which information provided by complimentary methods can enrich the understanding gained through the use of coping inventories. As examples of this, we would first argue that combining the use of coping inventories with more qualitative methods can enrich our understanding of the context in which coping occurs (Greene et al., 1989; Morgan, 1998; Morse, 1991; Tashakkori and Teddlie, 1998). Not only might such qualitative methods be useful for identifying the specific coping strategies most relevant for a particular condition or context, but these techniques can also provide considerable information regarding the process of adaptation to stress and the manner in which one's coping activities contribute to this process. Second, used by themselves, especially in cross-sectional studies, but also in more longitudinal ones, coping inventories provide relatively weak evidence regarding the causal influence of coping on adaptation. In our theorizing we often assume that coping influences adaptation, and the data observed are often consistent with this assumption, but the empirical evidence directly supportive of this causal influence is often quite weak. Direct manipulation of coping through behavioral interventions in conjunction with the assessment of coping using inventories offers the promise of strengthening such evidence.

Below we describe three examples of our recent efforts to utilize mixed and alternative methodologies to begin to address some of these issues. In our first example, we describe our efforts to draw on data obtained using the VMPCI to guide a qualitative investigation of the process of adapting to RA (Dwyer et al., 1996); in our second example we describe a model of adjustment to RA that has emerged from a more purely qualitative examination of coping with RA (Dwyer, 2002a; 2002b), and in our third example we describe an intervention study in which coping was systematically assessed, if not directly manipulated (Sinclair et al., 1998).

Example 1: Combining Quantitative and Qualitative Methodologies

Led by Kathleen Dwyer, we sought to use qualitative methodology to try to further understand the differences between individuals displaying different coping profiles, such as those described in the previous section. To begin, we focused on the persons displaying the "active" and "passive" coping profiles described above. To do this, we drew upon the participants from our second longitudinal sample, whose data had not contributed to the original cluster analyses. Using data from the first wave collected from this sample ($N = 207$), we used the mean coping profiles derived from the first sample to classify the members of this second sample into the four profiles identified in the previous study. From this procedure, we identified 57 "active copers" and 71 "passive copers" who had also completed an initial telephone interview. Given that these participants were selected based on their coping profiles, it is not surprising that the coping profiles for these two groups were virtually identical to those observed in the original study. However, in a substantive replication of the original study, as in the original sample, these two groups were found to not differ in levels of pain and impairment, but to differ substantially in psychological adjustment, with the active copers demonstrating considerably better adjustment than the passive copers (Dwyer et al., 1996).

Each of the participants in this second sample had participated in a telephone interview within approximately three months of their having completed the first wave of data collection. As a part of this interview, the participants had been asked three open-ended questions: "What is it like for you to have arthritis?" "How is life different for you now than before you developed the arthritis?" and "What are the things about having arthritis that concern you the most – that you find yourself thinking about most often?" The responses given by the active and passive copers were transcribed verbatim and analyzed to identify major themes using the NUDIST software for analyzing qualitative data (QSR, 1997). The results of these analyses revealed that the members of the two groups were handling their arthritis very differently. The active copers appeared to approach their condition with a "can do" attitude. As one participant stated: "I struggle a little bit, but I have made my mind up that I am going to conquer this if I possibly can." The stories of the active copers are full of action-oriented statements that reflect their knowledge about their condition. They readily identified a variety of coping strategies that they used to manage their arthritis. The most commonly cited strategies included: active decision making (69 percent), regulating activities based on symptoms (56 percent), staying active (41 percent), and "don't dwell on it" (33 percent). They tended to engage supportive others in their social environment, generally felt that they had options in managing their condition, and voiced that they could influence the impact of the disease on them through the choices they made. The passive copers, in contrast, talked very little about coping strategies or efforts to contend with their disease; the few strategies that were discussed by passive copers were in reaction to symptoms rather than self-initiated. The passive copers tended to be very inwardly focused and relatively unlikely to call upon supportive others around them.

Further analysis of the interview data from this latter group suggested that there were actually two distinct subgroups within the passive copers. The majority of the passive copers used language that was quite similar to the active copers; however, they seemed to have difficulties accurately appraising their situation. As one individual commented, "it's like I have the mystery disease to me . . ." The inability to recognize and understand their situation appeared linked to the difficulties they described in managing their situation. This group took on a reactive approach to coping with their illness rather than the proactive stance described by the active copers. The second and much smaller subgroup of subjects were characterized by the words of one participant, "to me it was . . . your life taken away . . ." This small subgroup of subjects viewed themselves as unable to do anything to alter their situation. Their interviews focused on the numerous losses they had experienced and lacked any discussion of strategies to manage their condition. Thus, the portraits of these two groups of individuals that emerge from their own words not only validates the view of these groups as "active" and "passive" copers, respectively, but it also fills out and enriches the view of these two subgroups that had been obtained through more quantitative means.

Example 2: Using a Qualitative Approach to Understanding Coping

In two related studies, using qualitative research methods, a theoretical model describing how individuals live with their arthritis was developed and refined. The goal of these studies was to develop an even richer, more contextualized view of what it is like to live with and cope with RA than was obtained in the work we've described above. In the first study (Dwyer, 2001a), 44 younger women were interviewed on two occasions. The initial theoretical model was developed from these interviews. In the second study (Dwyer, 2001b), inter-view data from 36 younger and older men, and 52 older women were analyzed to refine the model.

The participants in both studies took part in a semi-structured telephone interview designed to explore the process of adjusting to and managing their RA. The audiotaped interviews were transcribed verbatim. The interviews were analyzed using procedures described by Strauss and Corbin (1990). After initially completing line-by-line coding, the codes were sorted and clus-tered based on similarities. Conceptual labels and definitions were developed for each of the clusters of initial codes. In the final step of the analysis, relational statements linking the major concepts were developed from the data. To enhance the trustworthiness of the study, multiple strategies were used including analyst triangulation, peer debriefing, and frequent coding checks (Miles and Huberman, 1994).

The major premise of the "Living with Rheumatoid Arthritis Model" (LWRAM) is that living with RA involves two related processes, a cognitive process referred to as "transforming self" and a behavioral process labeled "managing" (see Figure 17.3). The model suggests that individuals who are able to undergo a transformation of self subsequently engage in managing behaviors that result in the person's learning to live with their disease. In contrast, individuals who are unable to change their perceptions of self engage in managing behaviors that result in a continual struggle to live with the disease. These processes are cyclical and may be altered by changes that result from the waxing and waning of symptoms associated with the disease and its treatment.

When confronted with RA, adults engage in a series of three inter-related cognitive activities: learning about self; altering self-expectations; and developing self-confidence. First, individuals learn how their disease and its treatment affect them and how it might continue to affect them. This learning frequently occurs by trial-and-error. Individuals may attempt to engage in activities as though their lives were not altered by their illness and they may find them-selves unable to do so. The model also posits that learning includes develop-ing an awareness of one's body cues so that the individual can adjust activities as needed. Understanding the connection between the levels of stress experi-enced by the individual and how one feels physically is another important dimension of learning. Finally, the last aspect of learning involves learning specific interventions that can be used to treat disease- and treatment-related symptoms.

According to the LWRAM, the process of learning about oneself is an ante-cedent to the other two cognitive processes – an individual's ability to alter his/her self-expectations and to develop confidence in the self's ability to cope with the disease and life in general. Men and women are able to articulate self-expectations in terms of the roles they function in and how they perceive they should enact these roles. As a consequence of learning how their disease has affected them, individuals are able to engage in the second cognitive process, altering one's self-expectations such that there is a fit between one's capabilities and one's expectations. The ability to fulfill the role expectations

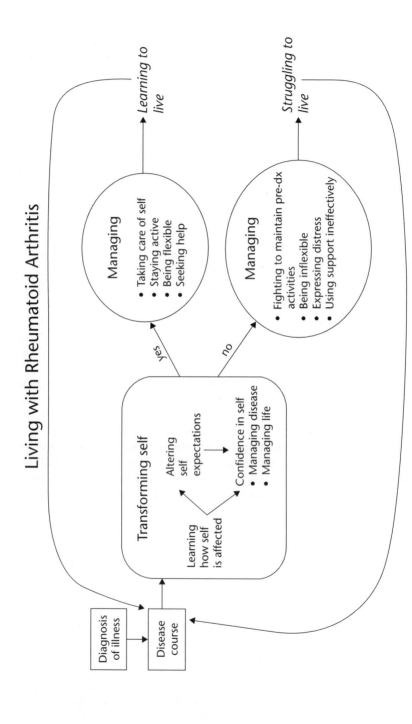

Figure 17.3 Graphical representation of the Living with Rheumatoid Arthritis Model (LWRAM).

one has, recognizing how the disease has affected the individual, and having a repertoire of strategies to use to manage the symptoms experienced, all contribute to the individual's ability to enact the third cognitive process, developing confidence in one's ability to cope with the illness and more generally, one's life.

Individuals who have successfully transformed the perception of self are those who discuss the various types of learning that have occurred, are able to articulate the various ways in which self-expectations had been altered, and characterize themselves as feeling confident, in control of their situation, and hopeful. In contrast, individuals who have not experienced a transformation of self have difficulty talking about how their disease has affected them and in identifying techniques that could be used to cope with the symptoms they experience. In addition, they describe significant emotional distress related to falling short of their self-expectations. Both scenarios have implications for the behavioral strategies employed to manage the disease.

Managing, the second process in the LWRAM, emphasizes the activities that are engaged in to try to deal with the day-to-day pattern of symptoms experienced following the completion of treatment for the chronic illness. Two distinctive clusters of managing activities, based on whether or not individuals have transformed their perceptions of themselves, are suggested. According to this model, each cluster is comprised of four interrelated processes that are described in detail below.

In those individuals whose selves have transformed, the LWRAM suggests there are four strategies involved in managing. These include taking care of self, staying active, being flexible and seeking help. Taking care of self involves engaging in behaviors that maximize one's ability to function and minimize the effects of symptoms. Individuals employing this strategy describe themselves as using a variety of specific strategies such as employing assistive devices to complete an activity, pacing one's activity level, following the treatment regimen, and making longer-term lifestyle changes to maximize their level of functioning. Staying active is a major theme in the descriptions of day-to-day living offered by these individuals. Their stories involve not only the physical actions of keeping busy, but also the act of staying connected with others. Dealing with the day-to-day symptoms requires frequent modifications to one's activities. Being flexible is the third managing strategy employed by those who have transformed. These individuals offer examples of how they are able to 'go with the flow' and adjust their activities based on how they are feeling. Seeking help and support from others (informational and instrumental support) is the fourth key aspect of managing according to the model. Based on the model, individual stories include examples of seeking help to complete various tasks as well as seeking comfort from someone who is "there and cares." These individuals characterize themselves as having learned to live with RA. They express confidence in their ability to cope and characterize themselves as in control.

In contrast, there are four different strategies involved in managing for those who are unable to transform the self. According to the LWRAM, the four strategies that are employed by these individuals include fighting to maintain the pre-diagnosis/pre-treatment level of activity, being inflexible, expressing distress and using support ineffectively. Common to all of these strategies is the individual's inability to realistically fit their activities with their capabilities. In fighting to maintain the pre-diagnosis/pre-treatment level of activity, the individual is unable to relinquish activities willingly. These individuals describe how they spend significant energy to maintain the status quo. Their stories also include examples of how they have maintained a rigid sense of what they should be able to do, in spite of their symptoms. Consistent with the model, these individuals characterize their experiences with strong emotional descriptors that capture the distress they experience. Finally, these individuals offer examples of ineffective use of support resources, including not seeking out support and declining offers of assistance from others including instrumental and emotional support. For this group of individuals, their stories depict an ongoing struggle to live with their disease. With the continued mismatch between their capabilities and their expectations of themselves, the LWRAM suggests that these individuals lack confidence in their own ability, report high levels of distress and see themselves as lacking control.

We believe that qualitatively derived models such as this one provide a richer, more contextualized understanding of coping than can be readily obtained through the exclusive use of quantitatively oriented coping inventories. Not only can one identify the major coping activities in which different individuals are engaged, but also one can obtain a wealth of information regarding the context in which that coping occurs, including a rich description of the specific issues or problems the individual is attempting to address through her coping efforts. This information, in turn, can be very valuable in designing the more strategically focused quantitative assessments of coping that we have advocated above.

Example 3: An Intervention Study

Surprisingly, despite the centrality of the construct of coping to the explanation of why people with RA either do or do not make a good adaptation to living with this chronic illness, there have been very few intervention studies specifically designed to help people cope more effectively with this condition (de Ridder and Schreurs, 2001). One exception to this was a study by Kraaimaat et al. (1995; cited by de Ridder and Schreurs) in which 77 Dutch patients with RA participated in ten weekly 120-minute group sessions consisting of either cognitive behavioral therapy (emphasizing active coping) or occupational therapy. Coping behavior changed very little during the course of that study, although those patients in the cognitive behavioral condition indicated a moderate increase in pain coping by distracting themselves with pleasant activities. This modest change in coping behavior, however, had no systematic effect on patients' outcomes.

While that study was being conducted in the Netherlands, Ken Wallston and Kathleen Dwyer, joined by their nursing colleague, Vaughn Sinclair, were carrying out their own cognitive behavioral intervention for Middle Tennessee women with RA under the auspices of a clinical sciences grant from the National Arthritis Foundation. Termed Mastery Effectiveness Training (MET), the purpose of the intervention was explicitly to strengthen subjects' personal coping resources (e.g., beliefs about control over their condition; self-efficacy beliefs; feelings of helplessness) and to alter the ways in which they coped with their arthritis pain. Most of the didactic content of the MET intervention was delivered via 90-minute videotapes that the participants watched at home prior to attending three 150-minute small group sessions held two weeks apart. The central theme presented throughout MET was that individuals always have some degree of control over their response to an upsetting event or problem, and these responses are modifiable (see Sinclair et al., 1998, for details of the intervention).

Ninety-one women participated in the MET program. The intervention was evaluated using a quasi-experimental design in which the women served as their own (wait-list) controls. A shortened, 37-item version of the VMPCI (C. A. Smith et al., 1997) was administered before and after the intervention to detect changes in 12 pain coping strategies. There was no significant change from immediately pre-MET to immediately post-MET in six of the pain coping strategies (blaming self, catastrophizing, denial, distraction, passivity, or venting emotions). There were, however, significant increases over the treatment period in problem solving and turning to religion, and significant decreases in acceptance and self-isolation. Plus there were trends ($p < 0.10$, 2-tailed) toward increases in reappraisal and use of social support. Interestingly, these significant changes in pain coping behavior were, by and large, uncorrelated with changes in psychological well-being of these participants over the course of the MET intervention. However, despite the fact that, in general, MET participants decreased their use of acceptance as a pain coping strategy, an increase in the use of acceptance was correlated with an increase in pain.

The results of this study indicate that it is possible through a systematic intervention to experimentally change the strategies an individual uses to cope with pain, and thus supports the potential for using such intervention studies to more experimentally examine the influence of coping on adjustment and well-being. Nonetheless, two characteristics of the present study that weaken its power to serve as such an experimental test itself should be noted. First, as evident in the above description, the MET intervention was primarily designed to alter coping-antecedent control-related beliefs, rather than to alter particular coping strategies, per se. Thus, the changes in coping that were observed lend support to the causal influence of such antecedent beliefs on coping, but they are not necessarily indicative of how much various coping strategies might change in the face of interventions that more directly emphasize changes in coping. Interventions more directly focused on coping might well produce considerably stronger changes in coping, which, in turn, could more strongly affect adaptational outcomes. Second, as the time-course by which one's coping activities might influence adaptational outcomes is not known, it is highly desirable to build into such studies more frequent assessments of coping and longer-term follow-ups in which the degree to which changes in coping and the longer-term impact of such coping changes on adjustment can be assessed. Nonetheless, as the results of the MET intervention study indicate, pain coping has the potential to be manipulated through well-designed interventions, and the use of such interventions hold the potential to more directly test the causal influence of coping on adjustment than is possible through other methods, even well-designed daily measurement studies such as those advocated by a number of our colleagues (see the following chapter by Tennen et al. in this volume).

Conclusions

We believe that the use of coping inventories in the study of adaptation to stress, and to adjustment to chronic health conditions in particular, continues to have considerable utility. In this chapter, in response to calls for the cessation of using such inventories (e.g., Coyne, 1997; Coyne and Racioppo, 2000), we have reviewed a number of theoretical and methodological issues relevant to using such inventories, and we have described some representative findings that have emerged from our own study of adjustment to RA that has used two such inventories. We believe that considerations of the issues we have discussed, and the findings we have reviewed, support the argument that, when used with care, coping inventories have much to contribute to our understanding of coping and adjustment, but that they are not a panacea.

For instance, one conclusion we would endorse is that it is seldom appropriate to employ a generic, all-purpose coping inventory for the study of one's particular problem (see also, Coyne and Gottlieb, 1996). Instead, the investigator should take steps to ensure that the coping strategies most relevant to the issue(s) under study, and especially the most relevant problem-focused strategies, are adequately assessed. Given realistic constraints on the research process (e.g., time constraints, participants' attentional capacities, etc.), this often will entail the researcher knowledgably and strategically selecting only a subset of the many coping strategies that could potentially be assessed. Although such strategic use of coping inventories necessarily reduces the degree to which results from different studies on somewhat different problems can be directly compared, we believe that this cost is offset by the wealth of data regarding coping and adaptation for particular conditions and circumstances that can be obtained.

One existing "problem" with the use of the more detailed, truly multidimensional coping inventories is that at present, typically used, analytic strategies (ANOVA, multiple regression, etc.) are not up to the task of fully taking advantage of the rich, multivariate data that such inventories can yield. We have attempted to illustrate the promise of using truly multivariate analytic strategies (e.g., cluster analysis) with our preliminary efforts in this direction. Nonetheless, our efforts are clearly very preliminary, and devising richer and more informative analytic strategies remains a challenge for the future.

Finally, we have attempted to emphasize that, although the use of coping inventories is important, informative, and valuable, they should not be used to the exclusion of other methodologies. We believe that intelligently combining the use of coping inventories with alternative methodologies can be far more informative than the use of either methodology by itself. For instance, the combined use of experimental coping interventions with the systematic assessment of coping and adjustment can help sort out issues of causal influence that can only weakly be addressed through the use of coping inventories alone. In a complementary manner, the combination of qualitative techniques with the more quantitative use of coping inventories can help flesh out the meaning of the statistically reliable relations between coping and adjustment revealed by the inventories. In addition, such qualitative data can be quite generative, suggesting additional potential coping strategies to assess that the investigator might otherwise miss, and yielding valuable information regarding the processes underlying coping and adaptation that can serve as hypotheses for subsequent investigations. Far from being a bane to the study of coping and adaptation, as some (e.g., Coyne, 1997) have suggested, we believe that the use of coping inventories maintains and deserves a prominent place in such research. Used appropriately, and in combination with complementary methodologies, such inventories have already contributed much, and will continue to contribute substantially, to our understanding of well-being in the face of chronic illness.

Authors' Note

Correspondence concerning this chapter should be sent to Craig A. Smith, Department of Psychology and Human Development, Vanderbilt University, Box 512 Peabody, Nashville, TN 37203, USA; e-mail: craig.a.smith@vanderbilt.edu

Notes

1. In emphasizing the importance of coping as the main cognitive and behavioral path of influence on well-being and adjustment we do not mean to deny the existence of other, more physiologically based pathways that also are potentially important. For instance, there is evidence to suggest that an optimistic outlook might enhance immune functioning in a fairly direct manner, whereas depression appears to impair it (e.g., Cohen and Rodriguez, 1995; Herbert and Cohen, 1993; Segerstrom et al., 1998). These pathways are important, and clearly worth pursuing. However, cognitive and behavioral responses to one's condition, such as engaging in effective health behaviors or ignoring one's doctor's advice, are also important influences on health and functioning and they are the ones we focus on here.

2. We were not the first to use cluster analysis to classify RA patients on the basis of their coping behaviors. Our colleague in London, Stan Newman, classified 158 RA patients into four groups on the basis of their responses to a specific 36-item "Coping with Arthritis Questionnaire" (Newman et al., 1990). Interestingly, their largest group, like ours, was labeled "passive copers" but their passive copers were described as not strongly embracing or rejecting any of the coping strategies.

References

Affleck, G., Pfeiffer, C., Tennen, H., and Fifield, J. C. (1988). Social support and psychological adjustment to rheumatoid arthritis: Quantitative and qualitative findings. *Arthritis Care and Research*, 1, 71–7.

Affleck, G., and Tennen, H. (1991). Appraisal and coping predictors of mother and child outcomes after newborn intensive care. *Journal of Social and Clinical Psychology*, 10, 424–47.

Aldenderfer, M. S., and Blashfield, R. K. (1984). *Cluster Analysis*. Sage University Paper Series on Quantitative Applications in the Social Sciences. (Series No. 07-044). Beverly Hills: Sage.

Bernard, L. C., Hutchison, S., Lavin, A., and Pennington, P. (1996). Ego-strength, hardiness, self-esteem, self-efficacy, optimism, and maladjustment: Health-related personality constructs and the "Big Five" model of personality. *Assessment*, 3, 115–31.

Brenner, G. F., Melamed, B. G., and Panush, R. S. (1994). Optimism and coping as determinants of psychosocial adjustment to rheumatoid arthritis. *Journal of Clinical Psychology in Medical Settings*, 1, 115–34.

Brown, G. K., and Nicassio, P. M. (1987). Development of a questionnaire for the assessment of active and passive coping strategies in chronic pain patients. *Pain*, 31, 53–63.

Brown, G. K., Nicassio, P. M., and Wallston, K. A. (1989). Pain coping strategies and depression in rheumatoid arthritis. *Journal of Consulting and Clinical Psychology*, 57, 652–7.

Carver, C. S., Pozo, C., Harris, S. D. et al. (1993). How coping mediates the effect of optimism on distress: A study of women with early stage breast cancer. *Journal of Personality and Social Psychology*, 65, 375–90.

Carver, C. S., and Scheier, M. F. (1994). Situational coping and coping dispositions in a stressful transaction. *Journal of Personality and Social Psychology*, 66, 184–95.

Carver, C. S., Scheier, M. F., and Weintraub, J. K. (1989). Assessing coping strategies: A theoretically-based approach. *Journal of Personality and Social Psychology*, 56, 267–83.

Cohen, J., and Cohen, P. (1983). *Applied Multiple Regression/Correlation Analysis for the Behavioral Sciences* (2nd edn.). Hillsdale, NJ: Erlbaum.

Cohen, S., and Rodriguez, M. S. (1995). Pathways linking affective disturbances and physical disorders. *Health Psychology*, 14, 374–80.

Cohen, S., Underwood, L. G., and Gottlieb, B. H. (2000). *Social Support Measurement and Intervention: A Guide for Health and Social Scientists*. New York: Oxford University Press.

Costa, P. T. Jr., and McCrae, R. R. (1993). Psychological stress and coping in old age. In L. Goldberger and S. Breznitz (Eds.), *Handbook of Stress: Theoretical and Clinical Aspects* (pp. 403–12). New York: Free Press.

Coyne, J. C. (1997). Improving coping research: Raze the slum before any more building! *Journal of Health Psychology*, 2, 153–72.

Coyne, J. C., and Gottlieb, B. H. (1996). The mismeasure of coping by checklist. *Journal of Personality*, 64, 959–91.

Coyne, J. C., and Racioppo, M. W. (2000). Never the twain shall meet? Closing the gap between coping research and clinical intervention research. *American Psychologist*, 55, 655–64.

de Ridder, D., and Schreurs, K. (1996). Coping, social support and chronic disease: A research agenda. *Psychology, Health, and Medicine*, 1, 71–82.

de Ridder, D., and Schreurs, K. (2001). Developing interventions for chronically ill patients: Is coping a helpful concept? *Clinical Psychology Review*, 21, 205–40.

DeVellis, R. F. (1991). *Scale Development: Theory and Applications*. Newbury Park, CA: Sage.

DeVellis, R. F., DeVellis, B. M., Sauter, S. V., Harring, K., and Cohen, J. L. (1986). Predictors of pain and function in arthritis. *Health, Education, and Research*, 1, 61–7.

Dwyer, K. A. (2001a). "Just learn to live with it:" The stories of younger women with RA. Manuscript in preparation. Vanderbilt University, Nashville, TN.

Dwyer, K. A. (2001b). Learning to live with rheumatoid arthritis: Age and gender differences. Manuscript in preparation. Vanderbilt University, Nashville, TN.

Dwyer, K. A., Bess, C., and Smith, C. (1996). Active versus passive coping: An in-depth exploration of the coping profiles. *Arthritis Care and Research*, 9, S9.

Folkman, S., and Lazarus, R. S. (1980). An analysis of coping in a middle-aged community sample. *Journal of Health and Social Behavior*, 21, 219–39.

Folkman, S., and Lazarus, R. S. (1988). *Manual for the Ways of Coping Questionnaire*. Palo Alto, CA: Consulting Psychologists Press.

Folkman, S., Lazarus, R. S., Dunkel-Schetter, C., DeLongis, A., and Gruen, R. J. (1986). Dynamics of a stressful encounter: Cognitive appraisal, coping, and encounter houtcomes. *Journal of Personality and Social Psychology*, 50, 992–1003.

Fricchione, G. L., Howanitz, E., Jandorf, L., Kroessler, D., Zervas, I., and Woznicki, R. M. (1992). Psychological adjustment to end-stage renal disease and the implications of denial. *Psychosomatics*, 33, 85–91.

Greene, J. C., Caracelli, V. J., and Graham, W. F. (1989). Toward a conceptual framework for mixed-method evaluation designs. *Educational Evaluation and Policy Analysis*, 11, 255–74.

Grey, M., Cameron, M. E., and Thurber, F. W. (1991). Coping and adaptation in children with diabetes. *Nursing Research*, 40, 144–9.

Helgeson, V. S., and Cohen, S. (1996). Social support and adjustment to cancer: Reconciling descriptive, correlational, and intervention research. *Health Psychology*, 15, 135–48.

Herbert, T. B., and Cohen, S. (1993). Depression and immunity: A meta-analytic review. *Psychological Bulletin*, 113, 472–86.

Jensen, M. P., and Karoly, P. (1991). Control beliefs, coping efforts, and adjustment to chronic pain. *Journal of Consulting and Clinical Psychology*, 59, 431–8.

Jensen, M. P., Turner, J. A., and Romano, J. M. (1991). Self-efficacy and outcome expectancies: Relationship to chronic pain coping strategies and adjustment. *Pain*, 44, 263–9.

Jensen, M. P., Turner, J. A., and Romano, J. M. (1992). Chronic pain coping measures: Individual vs. composite scores. *Pain*, 51, 273–80.

Jensen, M. P., Turner, J. A., Romano, J. M., and Karoly, P. (1991). Coping with chronic pain: A critical review of the literature. *Pain*, 47, 249–83.

Jerusalem, M., and Schwarzer, R. (1989). Anxiety and self-concept as antecedents of stress and coping: A longitudinal study with German and Turkish adolescents. *Personality and Individual Differences*, 10, 785–92.

Keefe, F. J., Brown, G. K., Wallston, K. A., and Caldwell, D. S. (1989). Coping with rheumatoid arthritis pain: Catastrophizing as a maladaptive strategy. *Pain*, 37, 51–6.

Kraaimaat, F. W., Brons, M. R., Geenen, R., and Biljsma, J. W. (1995). The effect of behavior therapy in patients with rheumatoid arthritis. *Behavior Research and Therapy*, 33, 487–95.

Kurdek, L. A., and Siesky, G. (1990). The nature and correlates of psychological adjustment in gay men with AIDS-related conditions. *Journal of Applied Social Psychology*, 20, 846–60.

Lazarus, R. S. (1983). The costs and benefits of denial. In S. Breznitz (Ed.), *The Denial of Stress* (pp. 1–30). New York: International Universities Press.

Lazarus, R. S., and Folkman, S. (1984). *Stress, Appraisal, and Coping*. New York: Springer.

Lazarus, R. S., and Folkman, S. (1987). Transactional theory and research on emotions and coping. *European Journal of Personality*, 1, 141–69.

Long, B. C., Kahn, S. E., and Schutz, R. W. (1992). Causal model of stress and coping: Women in management. *Journal of Counseling Psychology*, 39, 227–39.

Long, B. C., and Sangster, J. I. (1993). Dispositional optimism/pessimism and coping strategies: Predictors of psychosocial adjustment of rheumatoid and osteoarthritis patients. *Journal of Applied Social Psychology*, 23, 1069–91.

Lutgendorf, S., Anotoni, M. H., Schneiderman, N., and Fletcher, M. A. (1994). Psychosocial counseling to improve quality of life in HIV infection. *Patient Education and Counseling*, 94, 217–35.

Macrodimitris, S. D., and Endler, N. S. (2001). Coping, control, and adjustment in type 2 diabetes. *Health Psychology*, 20, 208–16.

Malcarne, V. L., Hansdottir, I., Greenbergs, H. L., Clements, P. J., Weisman, M. H. (1999). Appearance self-esteem in systemic sclerosis. *Cognitive Therapy and Research*, 23, 197–208.

McCaul, K. D., and Malott, J. M. (1984). Distraction and coping with pain. *Psychological Bulletin*, 95, 516–33.

Mehlman, E., and Slane, S. (1994). Validity of self-report measures of defense mechanisms. *Assessment*, 1, 189–97.

Meyerowitz, B. E., Burish, T. G., and Wallston, K. A. (1986). Health psychology: A tradition of integration of clinical and social psychology. *Journal of Social and Clinical Psychology*, 4, 375–92.

Mikulincer, M., and Solomon, Z. (1989). Causal attributions, coping strategies, and combat-related post-traumatic stress disorder. *European Journal of Personality*, 3, 269–84.

Miles, M. B., and Huberman, A. M. (1994). *Qualitative Data Analysis: An Expanded Source Book* (2nd edn). Newbury Park: Sage.

Morgan, D. L. (1998). Practical strategies for combining qualitative and quantitative methods: Applications to health research. *Qualitative Health Research*, 8, 362–76.

Morse, J. M. (1991). Approaches to qualitative-quantitative methodological triangulation. *Nursing Research*, 40, 120–3.

Myers, L. B. (2000). Identifying repressors: A methodological issue for health psychology. *Psychology and Health*, 15, 205–14.

Newman, S., Fitzpatrick, R., Lamb, R., and Shipley, M. (1990). Patterns of coping in rheumatoid arthritis. *Psychology and Health*, 4, 187–200.

Pakenham, K. I., Dadds, Mark, R., and Terry, D. J. (1994). Relationship between adjustment to HIV and both social support and coping. *Journal of Consulting and Clinical Psychology*, 62, 1194–203.

QSR (Qualitative Solutions and Research Pty Ltd) (1997). *QSR NUD*IST User's Guide, Version 4.0*. Thousand Oaks, CA: Scolari-Sage Publications Software.

Rosenstiel, A. K., and Keefe, F. J. (1983). The use of coping strategies in chronic low back pain patients: Relationship to patient characteristics and current adjustment. *Pain*, 17, 33–40.

Schwartz, J. E., Neale, J., Marco, C., Shiffman, S. S., and Stone, A. (1999). Does trait coping exist? A momentary assessment approach to the evaluation of traits. *Journal of Personality and Social Psychology*, 77, 360–9.

Segerstrom, S. C., Taylor, S. E., Kemeny, M. E., and Fahey, J. L. (1998). Optimism is associated with mood and immune change in response to stress. *Journal of Personality and Social Psychology*, 74, 1646–55.

Sinclair, V. G., Wallston, K. A., Dwyer, K. A., Blackburn, D. S., and Fuchs, H. (1998). Effects of a cognitive-behavioral intervention for women with rheumatoid arthritis. *Research in Nursing and Health*, 21, 315–26.

Smith, C. A., Dobbins, C. J., and Wallston, K. A. (1991). The mediational role of perceived competence in psychological adjustment to rheumatoid arthritis. *Journal of Applied Social Psychology*, 21, 1218–47.

Smith, C. A., and Wallston, K. A. (1992). Adaptation in patients with chronic rheumatoid arthritis: Application of a general model. *Health Psychology*, 11, 151–62.

Smith, C. A., and Wallston, K. A. (1996). An analysis of coping profiles and adjustment in persons with rheumatoid arthritis. *Anxiety, Stress, and Coping*, 9, 107–22.

Smith, C. A., Wallston, K. A., Dwyer, K. A., and Dowdy, S. W. (1997). Beyond good and bad coping: A multidimensional examination of coping with pain in persons with rheumatoid arthritis. *Annals of Behavioral Medicine*, 19, 11–21.

Smith, T. W., Peck, J. R., Milano, R. A., and Ward, J. R. (1988). Cognitive distortion in rheumatoid arthritis: Relation to depression and disability. *Journal of Consulting and Clinical Psychology*, 56, 412–16.

Somerfield, M. R. (1997). The utility of systems models of stress and coping for applied research: The case of cancer adaptation. *Journal of Health Psychology*, 3, 133–51.

Somerfield, M. R., and McCrae, R. R. (2000). Stress and coping research: Methodological challenges, theoretical advances, and clinical applications. *American Psychologist*, 55, 620–5.

Stanton, A. L., Danoff-Burg, S., Cameron, C. L., and Ellis, A. P. (1994). Coping through emotional approach: Problems of conceptualization and confounding. *Journal of Personality and Social Psychology*, 66, 350–62.

Stanton, A. L., and Snider, P. R. (1993). Coping with a breast cancer diagnosis: A prospective study. *Health Psychology*, 12, 16–23.

Stone, A. A., Greenberg, M. A., Kennedy-Moore, E., and Newman, M. G. (1991). Self-report, situation-specific coping questionnaires: What are they measuring? *Journal of Personality and Social Psychology*, 61, 648–58.

Strauss, A., and Corbin, J. (1990). *Basics of Qualitative Research: Grounded Theory Procedures and Techniques*. Thousand Oaks, CA: Sage.

Suls, J., and David, J. P. (1996). Coping and personality: Third time's the charm? *Journal of Personality*, 64, 993–1005.

Suls, J., and Fletcher, B. (1985). The relative efficacy of avoidant and nonavoidant coping strategies: A meta-analysis. *Health Psychology*, 4, 249–88.

Tashakkori, A., and Teddlie, C. (1998). Mixed methodology: Combining qualitative and quantitative approaches. Thousand Oaks, CA: Sage Publications.

Taylor, S. E., Kemeny, M. E., Aspinwall, L. G., Schneider, S. G., Rodriguez, R., and Herbert, M. (1992). Optimism, coping, psychological distress, and high-risk sexual behavior among men at risk for Acquired Immunodeficiency Syndrome (AIDS). *Journal of Personality and Social Psychology*, 63, 460–73.

Thompson, R. J., Gil, K. M., Abrams, M. R., Philips, G. (1992). Stress, coping, and psychological adjustment of adults with sickle cell disease. *Journal of Consulting and Clinical Psychology*, 60, 433–40.

Walker, L. S., Smith, C. A., Garber, J., and Van Slyke, D. A. (1997). Development and validation of the Pain Response Inventory for Children. *Psychological Assessment*, 9, 392–405.

Wallston, K. A. (1989). Assessment of control in health care settings. In A. Steptoe and A. Appels (Eds.), *Stress, Personal Control and Health* (pp. 215–28). Chicester, England: Wiley.

Wallston, K. A. (2001). Conceptualization and operationalization of perceived control. In A. Baum, T. A. Revenson, and J. E. Singer (Eds.), *The Handbook of Health Psychology* (pp. 49–58). Mahwah, NJ: Erlbaum.

Wallston, B. S., and Wallston, K. A. (1978). Locus of control and health: A review of the literature. *Health Education Monographs*, 6, 107–17.

Wallston, K. A., and Wallston, B. S., and DeVellis, R. (1978). Development of the Multidimensional Health Locus of Control (MHLC) scales. *Health Education Monographs*, 6, 160–70.

Wanberg, C. R. (1997). Antecedents and outcomes of coping behaviors among unemployed and reemployed individuals. *Journal of Applied Psychology*, 82, 731–44.

Zautra, A. J., Burleson, M. H., Smith, C. A. et al. (1995). Arthritis and perceptions of quality of life: An examination of positive and negative affect in rheumatoid arthritis patients. *Health Psychology*, 14, 399–408.

CHAPTER 18

Daily Processes in Health and Illness

Howard Tennen, Glenn Affleck

University of Connecticut Health Center

and

Stephen Armeli

Pace University

Introduction

During the past twenty years there has been a surge of interest in the daily processes that maintain health, anticipate and prolong illness episodes, and reflect adaptation to illness. This area of inquiry has become increasingly daunting in its scope, methods, and analytic strategies. Scores of investigations in the medical literature have employed daily or multiple within-day reports to evaluate symptoms, side effects, life quality, health care seeking, treatment adherence, and treatment outcomes. An equally extensive psychological literature has turned to daily recording methods to address questions of interest to health psychologists.

In addition to these studies in the medical and psychological literatures, there is a growing body of investigation linking psychosocial processes to everyday health, illness, and health behavior. This area of research is the focus of our chapter. We hope to capture the breadth and depth of the daily process literature and the unique insights this work has generated into how we understand the temporal unfolding of illness symptoms and silent illness risk processes, adjustment to chronic illness, and health risk behaviors as they occur on a daily basis.

We begin with a description of the daily process paradigm and a synopsis of evidence documenting the advantages of measuring health related phenomena close to the time they occur. We then review four substantive areas in which daily process studies have made substantial contributions: (1) daily stress and risk for cardiovascular disease; (2) the measurement and temporal dynamics of coping; (3) everyday adjustment to chronic pain, with special attention to the pursuit of personal goals; and (4) daily processes in substance use including a demonstration of the flexibility of daily process designs to answer phenomenologically and conceptually meaningful questions. Throughout, we provide detailed examples from our own work to portray the research questions, methods, and statistical approaches unique to daily process studies.

The Daily Process Paradigm

The daily process paradigm provides investigators with new methodological and statistical tools for exploring the social foundations of health and illness. This approach pursues sources of individual differences in within-person relations between variables that are thought to change in meaningful ways from day-to-day or within a day. Readers interested in a more detailed evaluation of the methodological and statistical options now available for such studies can consult several reviews and commentaries appearing in the literature in personality psychology (e.g., Nezlek, 2001; West and Hepworth, 1991); health psychology and behavioral medicine (e.g., Brown and Moskowitz, 1998; Schwartz and Stone, 1998), clinical psychology (e.g., Affleck et al., 1999b), and social psychology (e.g., Kenny et al., 1997).

Many investigators working at the interface of social and health psychology have turned to a daily process paradigm to examine the relation between daily experiences and physical symptoms, including episodes of minor illness (e.g., Stone et al., 1987) and migraine headaches (e.g., Kohler and Haimerl, 1990), and the ebb and flow of symptoms of chronic illnesses such as diabetes (Aikens and Wallander, 1994); rheumatoid arthritis (Affleck et al., 1994); fibromyalgia (Hazlett, 1992); dermatitis (King and Wilson, 1991); irritable bowel syndrome (Suls et al., 1994); and lupus (Adams et al., 1994). Members of our research group have examined the correspondence between disease changes and mood in rheumatoid arthritis patients (Affleck et al., 1992) and in asthma patients (Affleck et al., 2000), and pain coping strategies in rheumatoid arthritis patients (Keefe et al., 1997).

Within- versus Across-person Relations: The Difference that Makes a Difference

The unique contributions to the study of health and illness that can be made by daily process studies went too long under-appreciated because of psychology's dominant tradition of nomothetic inquiry, or, the search for lawful relations among variables across populations of persons. The nomothetic approach can be contrasted with the idiographic approach, which seeks relations among variables *within* a single individual over time and has occasionally been employed in some extraordinarily well-documented and revealing case studies (e.g., Potter and Zautra, 1997).

To appreciate what a daily process paradigm can contribute to our understanding of health and illness is to understand first the difference between an across-persons association and a within-person association. We and several other investigators have commented extensively on this fundamental distinction (e.g., Larsen and Kasimatis, 1991; Shiffman and Stone, 1998; Tennen and Affleck, 1996; West and Hepworth, 1991). Nevertheless, we continue to witness enough confusion about it among our colleagues (not to mention the occasional manuscript or grant application reviewer) to warrant another reminder.

We, like many, have been tempted to draw within-person inferences from across-person associations. For example, in early cross-sectional studies of stressful life events, correlations between the number of events and health problems were taken to mean that when a person experiences a stressful event, he or she would be more likely to become ill. No such inference can be made without observing people when they are under stress and when they are not. An across-person correlation, moreover, can depart markedly from a within-person correlation (Snijders and Bosker, 1999). We cannot emphasize this enough. Tennen and Affleck (1996) and Kenny et al. (1998) have illustrated (and we will again later in this chapter in relation to substance use) that across-persons and within-person correlations can differ not only in magnitude, but also in direction, and that a statistically significant positive across-person association can emerge when not a single individual in the group shows a positive within-person association!

Consider, for example, the findings from our study of rheumatoid arthritis patients who kept daily diaries of their desirable and undesirable events for 75 consecutive days. After aggregating the scores to generate mean levels of both types of events, we found a moderately high across-person correlation of 0.50 between them; participants who reported more desirable events also reported more undesirable events. But as we might suspect for many across-person correlations appearing in the stress and health literature, this association could be confounded by characteristics of the participants. Conceivably, a reporting bias could confound the association, inasmuch as some people simply differ in their thresholds for what they call *any* event, desirable or undesirable. But one need not turn to nuances in response tendencies to explain this finding. Three background factors – gender, work outside the home, and children living at home – accounted fully for the desirable event–undesirable event correlation. When we controlled for these factors, the correlation approached zero! The moderately positive association is apparently due to the fact that women who work outside the home and have young children experience more events, whether desirable or undesirable.

The question addressed by the across-person correlation is whether people who experience more undesirable daily events also experience more desirable daily events. Quite a different question is "how are desirable and undesirable events patterned in an *individual's* life?" Is a day with more undesirable events also a day with more desirable events? The across-person analysis cannot answer this question. It requires calculation of a within-person measure of association. As a moment of self-reflection would suggest, desirable and undesirable events connected within individuals in an *inverse* way. Not a single participant exhibited the statistically significant positive association between desirable and undesirable events that was found when the data were analyzed across persons. In fact, the mean within-person correlation was −0.25, with a preponderance of significant *negative* correlations. Even many of those who reported a large number of both desirable and undesirable events showed an inverse relation when these events were examined on a within-person basis.

This comparison of across-person and within-person correlations highlights three points: (1) within-person analysis eliminates potential sources of across-person confounding; (2) both the magnitude and direction of associations can change when research questions are framed in within-person terms; and (3) although it is common to draw within-person inferences from across-person associations, they address different questions. Some of the most interesting and clinically relevant questions demand within-person analytic strategies.

Other benefits of time-intensive idiographic studies have been advanced by us elsewhere (Affleck et al., 1999b; Tennen et al., 1991) and by others (e.g., Larsen and Kasimatis, 1991; Brown and Moskowitz, 1998). They allow investigators to capture proximal events, behaviors, and adaptational outcomes closer to their actual occurrence and to track changes in rapidly fluctuating processes such as physical symptoms and mood closer to their moments of change. These studies also minimize recall error, including systematic error in which individuals who differ on measured or unmeasured variables provide differentially accurate data or use different cognitive heuristics to assist their recall (Neisser, 1991). Because these studies track adaptational processes as they unfold, they offer unique opportunities to test the elegant process-oriented models of stress, coping, and health now in the literature and to narrow the gap between theory and research (Tennen et al., 2000). Additional benefits of daily process studies include the ability to mitigate some forms of confounding by using informants as their own controls and to establish temporal precedence as a foundation for causal inference (Tennen and Affleck, 1996).

The Idiographic–nomothetic Hybrid Design

Several authors (Epstein, 1983; Larsen and Kasimatis, 1991; Tennen and Affleck, 1996) have advocated combining the best of the idiographic and nomothetic traditions in a mixed design that is a hallmark of the daily process paradigm. This encourages investigators to ask: "Are there relations between social/psychological and health variables within individuals over time that generalize across individuals or that relate to differences between individuals?" Answering this question requires that we first examine relations among the daily variables over time for each individual we study. We can then return to the population of individuals in two ways: by determining if the within-person relations generalize across persons, and by discerning how they relate to differences between individuals.

Fortunately, recent developments in multilevel data analysis now allow investigators to simultaneously examine sources of variation in data sets containing both within- and across- person observations (e.g., Schwartz and Stone, 1998). The typical daily process study will generate a multilevel data matrix containing data from at least two sampling units hierarchically arranged such that one is "nested" in the other. With sufficient amounts of these data in hand, investigators can draw reliable statistical inferences about relations at each level of the analysis as well as across the levels. In the vernacular of multilevel modeling, the repeated observations (the daily reports) are called "level 1 (or lower level) variables". These level 1 observations are organized within level 2 units, that is, persons, whose characteristics are called "level 2 (or upper level) variables."

A general class of multilevel modeling methods – known variously as random-effects models (Laird and Ware, 1983), hierarchical linear models (Bryk and Raudenbush, 1992), multilevel models (Goldstein, 1987), random coefficient models (de Leeuw and Kreft, 1986), and random regression models (Bock, 1989) – allow one to estimate the level 1 effects of one daily observation on another and the level 2 effects of individual differences that may "modify" the strength and direction of the relation. An important advantage of these statistical methods is their ability to take into account the likely lack of independence between the daily observations and the person providing them. They can also accommodate "unbalanced" designs in which participants provide varying numbers of observations and missing observations.

Now that we described the daily process paradigm, we turn our attention to four areas in which daily process studies have made substantial contributions. The first area is daily stress and risk for cardiovascular disease.

Daily Stress and Risk for Cardiovascular Disease: Myocardial Ischemia, Stress-reactive Blood Pressure Changes, and the Effects of Job Strain on Ambulatory Blood Pressure

The lay public has for many years viewed sudden and chronic stress a risk factor for cardiovascular events, particularly myocardial infarction (MI). Yet, until recently, the medical community has been reluctant to acknowledge that acute stress might trigger a cardiac event, even among vulnerable individuals, or that chronic stress might set into motion pathophysiologic processes that anticipate later coronary disease. As Krantz et al. (1996) note, anecdotal reports and epidemiological research, although provocative, are compromised by the potential role of retrospection error. Efforts to reconstruct events and experiences prior to sudden death or the occurrence of a MI, for example, are fraught with potential recall bias. Accurate recollection is a particularly thorny problem for studies of stress and cardiac events, where widely held causal theories increase the likelihood that a cardiac event will prime individuals to "recall" stressful antecedents (Ross, 1989). Even studies that compare patients' experiences just prior to an MI with their usual daily experiences are vulnerable to retrospection bias, because a participant searching for a satisfying cause of his or her MI is more likely to interpret pre-MI experiences as stressful (Krantz et al., 1996). These limitations have created fertile ground for studies of how everyday stress and stress-related emotions anticipate cardiac events. We now summarize this literature in three areas: Daily stress as a precipitant of myocardial ischemia; stress-reactive blood pressure changes; and the effects of job strain on ambulatory blood pressure.

Myocardial Ischemia

Coronary artery disease (CAD) is the leading cause of death among men and women in the United States (American Heart Association, 1998). Whereas individuals with a history of MI or angina are often under a physician's care, many people with CAD are asymptomatic because MI and angina appear rather late in the course of coronary atherosclerosis. Until recently, our understanding of the role of behavioral and social factors contributing to CAD was limited by reliance on clinical manifestations (angina, MI, sudden cardiac death) and after-the-fact speculation regarding precursors and risk factors. Over the past decade, Krantz and colleagues have examined ways in which myocardial ischemia may be a significant link between the development of CAD and its precipitous life threatening clinical manifestations. Myocardial ischemia is a temporarily insufficient coronary blood supply. Although brief ischemic episodes do not permanently damage the heart, they represent a significant risk for MI and sudden cardiac death, and individuals with stable angina who experience ischemia in response to mental stress have a greatly increased risk of cardiac death, MI, and angioplasty (Krantz et al., 2000). The transient and repeated quality of myocardial ischemia, combined with new technologies allowing ambulatory electrocardiogram monitoring, make it an ideal target for daily process studies.

Krantz and colleagues (described in Krantz et al., 1993) tracked the daily lives of CAD patients whose 24–48 hour ambulatory electrocardiogram revealed transient ischemia. While wearing a Holter monitor, these patients completed a diary that assessed their activities and moods multiple times over the course of a day. Krantz et al. found that, for the most part, ischemia occurred during light exercise, such as slow walking, and during an array of mental activities. Ischemic time tended to be greatest when patients were more angry. These findings, combined with evidence that silent ischemia occurs more frequently during stressful encounters (Freeman et al., 1987), led Krantz et al. to conclude that mental stress and anger may be important triggers of silent ischemia. Their structured diary method also allowed these investigators to determine that symptomatic ischemic episodes (i.e., episodes with angina pain) occurred during higher levels of physical activity and when the individual was standing, whereas silent episodes occurred at lower activity levels and when the individual was sitting or reclining. Krantz et al. also found that, beyond physical activity, time of day made an independent contribution to the prediction of ischemia, with the greatest amount of ischemic time occurring in the morning. Although these diary studies cannot be interpreted unambiguously because participants initiated diary entries (and thus the number of entries varied across participants), these daily studies of myocardial ischemia in daily life demonstrate that ischemic events are typically silent and that they appear to be linked to mental stress and affective disruption.

Helmers et al. (1995) extended these findings by examining whether the combined personality traits of defensiveness and hostility predicted ischemic episodes in daily life. Individuals with functionally severe coronary artery disease were identified as defensive and hostile, low hostile, high hostile, and defensive based on their scores on the Cook-Medley Hostility Inventory and the Marlowe-Crowne Social Desirability Scale. As anticipated, patients who were defensive and hostile exhibited the most frequent ischemic episodes during ambulatory electrocardiographic monitoring. They also showed the most severe mental stress-induced ischemia in the laboratory. This line of inquiry is important for several reasons. First, it extends the study of myocardial ischemia to include personality predictors. Second, it demonstrates how individual differences and other across-person factors can be used in daily process studies to predict physical processes such as ischemia. Third, it hints at the potential of daily process methods to examine how person and social factors may predict not only univariate processes such as ischemic events, but also bivariate processes such as the temporal contingency between stressful experiences and ischemia in daily life. New technologies that allow investigators to measure physiological, emotional, behavioral, and interpersonal processes as they unfold day-to-day promise to substantially increase our knowledge of the mechanisms underlying risk for clinically meaningful, and potentially life threatening, cardiovascular events.

A final example of how daily diary methods and ambulatory electrocardiograhic monitoring can yield unique findings regarding the immediate triggers of cardiac events is seen in Gabbay et al.'s (1995) study of daily physical activities, anger, and smoking among patients with coronary artery disease. Gabbay et al. found that although these patients spent most of their time in low-intensity physical and mental activities, ischemia was most likely during intense physical and mental episodes. Intense anger was, as anticipated, a reliable trigger of ischemic episodes. Smokers in this patient sample were five times more likely to experience ischemia when they were smoking. By using daily process methods to document the temporal patterning of activities, emotions, and smoking, this study demonstrates that, among coronary artery patients, anger and smoking are as potent as strenuous activity in triggering day-to-day ischemic episodes.

Cardiovascular Reactivity Assessed through Ambulatory Blood Pressure Monitoring

An excellent example of how the study of cardiovascular risk factors in daily life can be extended to include bivariate processes appears in Kamarck and colleagues' (1998a) studies of psychosocial influences on ambulatory cardio-vascular activity. As Kamarck et al. note, the ambulatory assessment of blood pressure (BP) allows clinicians to evaluate BP levels and variability *in situ* and over time, and it allows investigators to examine how psychological and social factors influence the ebb and flow of an individual's blood pressure beyond the confines of the laboratory. The fact that ambulatory BP predicts cardio-vascular events and mortality among individuals with hypertension, and that its prognostic value is above and beyond that of clinic BP readings (Kamarck et al., 1998a), adds to the potential significance of this line of biobehavioral inquiry.

The unique prognostic value of ambulatory BP led to the hypothesis that individuals who manifest excessive cardiovascular reactivity and who face recurring daily stressors are at increased risk to develop hypertension and coronary heart disease. The "reactivity hypothesis" (Matthews et al., 1986) can be viewed as a diathesis-stress model, in which vulnerable (cardiovascularly reactive) individuals who experience recurrent stressors have transient blood pressure elevations in response to the stressors. These repeated changes eventually produce structural changes and an increase in vascular resistance, which produces higher blood pressure levels even in the absence of stressful encounters. Kamarck et al. (1998a) reasoned that since the very nature of cardiovascular reactivity involves only brief fluctuations in BP in response to everyday stressors, adequate tests of this phenomenon require investigators to monitor stressors and cardiovascular activity in real time. Whereas laboratory investigations demonstrate that cardiovascular reactivity is a fairly reliable phenomenon, only *in situ* repeated measurement via daily process studies allows ecologically valid tests of the reactivity hypothesis. This method also allows investigators to assess differential exposure to stressful encounters, and to evaluate the possibility that some individuals select environments that are more likely to trigger acute pressor responses.

Kamarck et al. (1998a) developed the Diary of Ambulatory Behavioral States (DABS) to measure in real time three aspects of everyday life that are relevant to cardiovascular reactivity and disease risk: task demands and control, social interaction characteristics, and affective states. Task demands and control were included based on Karasek and colleagues' (1988) demonstration that workers who appraise their work as involving high task demands and low control over job-related decisions are at increased risk for hypertension or CAD. Social interaction characteristics (measured with items selected from existing social interaction diaries, e.g., Reis and Wheeler, 1991) were included in the DABS based on evidence that social threats affect acute cardiovascular activation, that interpersonal harassment during exposure to laboratory stressors increases cardiovascular reactivity, and, based on epidemiological evidence, that social support increases the risk of post-MI survival (see Kamarck et al., 1998a for details). Emotional activation was included in the DABS based on evidence that negative affect and arousal may be associated with variation in cardiovascular activity in everyday life. Also included in the DABS are items that assess activity, posture, recent alcohol and caffeine use and food intake, whether the individual was speaking at the time of the assessment, and an estimate of ambient temperature. Each of these variables have been independently linked to daily changes in cardiovascular activity. The DABS is completed by participants in the form of an electronic diary via a palmtop computer. The clock on the palmtop was synchronized with an ambulatory blood pressure monitor that measured blood pressure every 45 minutes for 4 days (in one study) or every hour for six days (in a second study). DABS data was time stamped to assure that it was entered at the time ambulatory BP was being measured.

The repeated within-person data produced by the synchronized DABS and ambulatory BP monitor were well suited for random effects regression analysis, and preliminary analyses revealed that changes in negative affect and arousal were independently linked to within-day fluctuations in blood pressure, even after controlling for posture, activity, and other momentary influences on BP. Karmack et al. demonstrated that the effect of negative affect and arousal was substantial: systolic BP increases of 6.4 mm Hg, and diastolic BP increases of 7.4 mm Hg across the range of negative affect and arousal measured by the DABS (see also Kamarck et al., 1998b).

Echoing the findings of most daily process studies in the area of psychosocial factors influencing health and illness, Kamarck et al. (1998a) found a wide range of cardiovascular reactivity in response to everyday emotional activation. They note that the most reactive individuals, those in the top 10 percent, had average changes of 20 mm Hg in diastolic blood pressure across the range of negative affect and arousal. We are encouraged by the mounting evidence that daily process methods can identify what may be stable individual differences in within-person dynamic patterns and contingencies, in this case the within-person relationship between emotional activation and changes in BP. These dynamic individual differences can be used as predictors of long-term, clinically meaningful health outcomes such as hypertension and coronary artery disease. Even if Kamarck et al. had found no reliable within-person relationship between emotional activation and BP across their entire sample, there may still have been a subgroup displaying clinically significant cardiovascular reactivity. By examining their findings participant by participant, investigators of daily processes in health and illness can discover at risk subgroups, or identify moderators of individual differences in within-person dynamic relationships.

Jamner et al. (1998) note that, across studies, the relationship between mood and cardiovascular activity has been modest, with some studies showing no reliable association. This difference across studies may be attributed, in part, to a failure to distinguish within-person from across-person relationships. Although the cardiovascular reactivity hypothesis by its very nature captures a within-person phenomenon, some studies have examined the across-person relationship between mood and BP. As we explained earlier, there is no reason to anticipate a correspondence between within-person and across-person relationships. In fact, Kamarck et al. (1998a), whose carefully designed electronic diary study demonstrated substantial within-person associations between emotional activation and BP, found no consistent evidence for the across-person associations between emotion and BP based on the same data.

Jamner et al. (1998) argued that the relationship between ambulatory mood and BP in daily diary studies may be masked by how investigators typically measure affective states. They note that daily affect measures are often created on an ad hoc basis, and that when participants are free to check as many momentary mood items as apply to them, the majority actually endorse none of the items. Jamner et al. note that advances in the technology of in vivo monitoring, including paging systems and palmtops, have not been matched by advances in the content of daily process indicators, including the measurement of mood. They compared a Likert scale mood assessment with one that used mood adjectives, in which participants selected one mood from each of seven mood groups that best described their current state. Jamner et al. also explored the use of mood adjective scales that were derived for each participant based on his or her own lexicon. They found that mood adjective scales yielded a greater correspondence between mood and BP (and heart rate) than Likert scales. Individually derived adjective scales showed a marginal advantage over group derived scales. We anticipate that these promising findings, and those reported by Kamarck et al. (1998a) will encourage further methodological investigations of daily processes in the area of cardiovascular reactivity, and more generally in the study of daily processes in health and illness.

One mechanism through which stress, particularly interpersonal stress, might lead to transient changes in BP is through the experience of anger. Converging evidence supports the hypothesis that frequent and intense episodes of suppressed anger can, over time, contribute to the development of cardiovascular disease and its manifestations, including elevated BP, lipid concentration, and coronary stenosis (e.g., Engebrestson and Stoney, 1995). Although intuitively appealing, this line of inquiry has produced inconsistent findings, with support for the suppressed anger hypothesis emerging only when BP is assessed with a single (less reliable) BP measurement (see Suls et al., 1995 for a meta-analysis summarizing research studies). Porter et al. (1999) reasoned that these inconsistent findings may reflect, in part, the assumption that anger expression is a stable personality disposition. This guiding principle has led investigators to assess anger expression via personality scales. Porter et al. supplemented a trait measure of anger expression with seven days of state measures, in which participants described each anger-provoking situation as it occurred, rated the intensity of their anger, the target of their anger, and, if the target was another person, their relationship with the target. Ambulatory BP was measured during one weekday. Although trait and state anger expression were moderately correlated, neither predicted ambulatory BP. Unfortunately, Porter et al. could not verify when state anger ratings were made, and as they note, ratings made several days after the anger-arousing situation might be influenced by memory decay and systematic bias. Despite these null findings, we highlight this study because it demonstrates the potential application of daily process conceptualizations and methods to emotional dynamics thought to anticipate cardiovascular disease. These dynamics, which unfold over brief periods in everyday life, demand the application of real time assessments and within-person analytic strategies.

One might reasonably ask if laboratory studies might be a better way to evaluate inherently dynamic processes such as cardiovascular reactivity or anger expression. In the lab, stressors or anger-provoking circumstances can be well controlled and comparable for all participants. Moreover, daily process studies are messy affairs. Their ecological validity notwithstanding, the timing of assessments, their potential intrusiveness, and the relative infrequency of theoretically critical circumstances in everyday life compromise the daily process approach. Although it is tempting to retreat to the lab as a way to secure control over key variables, recent evidence suggests that rather than being a well-controlled surrogate for the real world in the prediction of cardiac events, the lab may provide findings that supplement those obtained from daily process studies. Kop et al. (2000) demonstrated the unique contributions of laboratory and in vivo studies in their investigation of factors related to left ventricular mass (LVM), a risk factor for cardiac morbidity. Kop et al. found that both ambulatory BP and laboratory assessments of mental stress-induced systolic BP responses predicted LMV, and that each made an independent contribution to the prediction of this clinically meaningful condition. We encourage investigators to turn to both laboratory and daily process designs to better understand those health-related phenomena that fluctuate in everyday life, such as BP, and those phenomena that are in essence a relationship between two processes, such as cardiovascular reactivity.

Possible Futures of the Cardiovascular Reactivity Hypothesis: A Daily Process View

Despite the intuitive appeal of the BP reactivity hypothesis, and its track record as a catalyst for research, support for the hypothesis has been inconsistent. Pickering, Gerin and colleagues have argued that the hypothesis is insufficiently developed to explain vulnerability to hypertension and cardiovascular disease (Gerin et al., 2000; Pickering, 1993; Pickering and Gerin, 1990), and they have turned to daily process designs to support their claim (Friedman et al., 2001; Gerin et al., 1993; 1998).

Until relatively recently, evidence of blood pressure reactivity was derived solely from the lab. Pickering, Gerin and associates have argued that whereas laboratory findings are assumed to generalize to real life circumstances, the concordance between laboratory and daily life indicators of reactivity is rather modest. Although more recent versions of the reactivity hypothesis have been refined to include situational, moderational, person X situation models, Gerin et al. (2000: 373) argued cogently that:

> "[i]f reactivity is to be implicated as a cause of hypertension, it must occur with some frequency in the person's natural environment. If, however, the laboratory-based reactivity does not predict reactivity in the real world . . . there is little reason to assume that the people identified as high reactors in the laboratory will be the ones who suffer more damaging reactive episodes in the real world."

Gerin et al. have suggested that although BP reactivity, that is, the BP response that occurs while the stressor is present, may play some role in the development of hypertension and cardiovascular disease, more important factors may include recovery of pre-stress resting levels, BP variability, and hemodynamic changes. Although the measurement of recovery and underlying hemodynamic changes present genuine challenges, these are inherently within-person, over-time phenomena that demand daily process formulations and methods, and we anticipate that real world daily studies will be playing an increasingly important role in our understanding of the social and psychological foundations of cardiovascular health and illness. Evidence of the potential of daily process studies to uncover these social and psychological factors can be found in studies of job strain and blood pressure, to which we now turn.

Job Strain, Household Characteristics, and Ambulatory Blood Pressure

Karasek et al.'s (1988) heralded "job strain" model of the link between work-related stress and health has generated a spate of studies examining the association between job strain and cardiovascular illness or risk for CVD. Daily studies employing ambulatory BP monitoring have added significantly to our appreciation of how job strain influences CVD and CVD risk factors. As we mentioned previously, according to the job strain model, individuals at greatest risk for stress-related illness are those whose jobs involve high work-load demands while providing low job-decision latitude, that is, low levels of control of work-related decisions. One proposed mediational pathway through which job strain promotes cardiovascular disease is through its influence on blood pressure. Pickering and colleagues (see Landsbergis et al., 1994; Schnall et al., 1998) reviewed evidence for the link between job strain and ambulatory BP, and they extended this area of inquiry by examining the relationship prospectively, and by using four different operationalizations of job strain. The most widely used procedure involves defining as under high strain those individuals who fall above the sample (or national) median on demands and below the median on latitude/control. Landsbergis et al. (1994) refer to this as the quadrant definition of job strain. Another approach involves creating a continuous job strain metric that is the quotient created by dividing demands by latitude. A third operationalization is the multiplicative interaction term controlling for the main effects of demands and latitude. Finally, job strain can be examined in terms of nonlinear effects of demand and latitude. Landsbergis et al. (1994) found that each of these four formulations of job strain were associated with elevated ambulatory systolic BP. This association was independent of SES, and interestingly, the link between job strain and BP was greater among lower SES groups.

In a three-year follow-up of the workers in this study, Schnall et al. (1998) replicated the Time 1 cross-sectional associations at Time 2. Most important, however, was the finding that workers in high strain jobs during both waves of the study showed higher work, home, and sleep ambulatory BP than workers who were categorized as experiencing high work strain during neither wave. Remarkably, the effect sizes were twice the difference between blacks and whites, and larger than the effect of aging 25 years or gaining 50 pounds. Moreover, individuals experiencing high job strain at Time 1, but not three years later, showed a decrease in ambulatory BP at work and home after controlling for other common risk factors. Comparing these effect sizes to those of commonly investigated risk factors revealed that the effect on ambulatory BP of no longer experiencing job strain at Time 2 was comparable (though in the opposite direction) to aging 15 years or gaining more than 40 pounds, and larger than the treatment effect in weight reduction trials. These rather remarkable findings underscore the unique contributions of daily process studies to our understanding of cardiovascular disease risk, but also how daily study designs can be incorporated into longitudinal studies. We see great promise in the use of multi-wave daily designs to study changes in health-related phenomena.

Although individuals with high job strain are particularly vulnerable to ambulatory BP elevations and cardiovascular disease, differences between work and home BP are common, particularly among men. Daily process studies have enhanced our understanding of this difference between work and home BP, and have offered clues to its underlying mechanisms. Pickering and colleagues have conjectured that this change in BP is a reflection of less stress in the home environment than at work. James et al. (1993) reasoned that if differences in stress lead to differences in work and home BP, the higher levels of stress at work should produce increased catecholamine output, which in turn should increase blood pressure. Although these linkages among stress, catecholamine output, and blood pressure have been produced reliably in the laboratory, their association in everyday life requires daily and within-day monitoring.

James et al. (1993) evaluated whether the work–home BP differences found in men also emerged among working women, and whether these changes were linked to changes in epinepherine and norepinephine activity. Eighty working women provided work (11 a.m.–3 p.m.), home (6 p.m.–10 p.m.), and sleep (upon awakening; approximately 6 a.m.) urine samples and their ambulatory BP was monitored. Based on their ratings of perceived stress during the work and home periods, each woman was characterized as "work-stressed" if she characterized the work period as more stressful than the home period, or "home-stressed" if the home period was rated as equally stressful or more stressful than the work period. Throughout the work, home, and sleeping periods, ambulatory BP was recorded. Work-stressed women, who were more often white and without children, showed a greater change in BP over the day than their home-stressed counterparts. And, as predicted, the BP change among work-stressed women was associated with a comparable change in catecholamines. These findings not only extend to women our understanding of how perceived work environments influence variations in BP, but they also demonstrate how intensive daily designs can offer clues to mediational processes, and how such study designs can bridge laboratory findings and intervention efforts.

Finally, Marco et al. (2000) combined momentary diary reports via palm-top computer and ambulatory BP monitoring to examine how gender and having children influence BP. The electronic diary provided momentary assessments of participants' location, posture, mood, stressful events, and perceived stress during one weekend day and two weekdays. Marco et al. (2000) found that men's ambulatory BP was higher at work than at home. Women without children also showed higher ambulatory BP (ABP) at work than at home, whereas ABP was similar across settings for women with children at home. These findings replicate those in previous daily BP monitoring studies. New findings included no difference in ABP across settings for men without children, and similar work and non-workday ABP for women without children. Interestingly, men with children at home had the highest APB. Marco et al. speculated that, for men, having children at home may confer a risk for developing hypertension, whereas women without children may have higher ABP across the week than women with children, thus increasing their risk for developing hypertension later in life. These provocative findings could only have been obtained through real-time (BP, mood, location, posture) or close to real-time (stress and perceived stress) assessments of health-related parameters.

The Measurement and Temporal Dynamics of Coping

The concept of coping plays a central role in almost every model of adaptation to illness. Yet serious concerns have been raised about how coping is measured in most studies of adjustment to threatening encounters or illness episodes. Two major concerns have emerged. First, it is not clear whether individuals can retrospectively report their coping efforts accurately. If coping reports are not a reliable reflection of people's thoughts and behaviors during a stressful encounter or illness episode, statistical connections between coping and health cannot be valid. Second, coping research has essentially ignored the coping's temporal dynamics. Daily coping studies have begun to address both of these concerns.

Studies Comparing Retrospective and "Real-time" Coping Reports

In all but a few of the hundreds of empirical studies of coping, participants are asked to recall how they coped with a particular event or how they typically cope with stressful encounters. Five studies have compared recalled coping, the approach to coping measurement that permeates the literature, to coping reports made closer to their real-time occurrence. Ptacek et al. (1994) had a group of college students use a coping inventory to record every day for a week the ways in which they were coping with an anticipated course examination. Five days following the exam, participants again completed the coping inventory, but this time they were asked to describe how they had coped with the examination during the time they had completed daily coping reports. Ptacek et al. concluded that there was only modest concordance across daily and retrospective methods, even for an event that occurred less than a week before retrospective ratings were made. In a follow-up study, Smith et al. (1999) obtained daily coping reports as students prepared for a demanding exam, and compared these daily reports to those obtained with a 7-day retrospective measure of coping that covered the same time frame as the daily reports. Again, the daily and retrospective coping reports shared only 25 percent of their variance, and among students who reported the highest levels of exam stress, daily coping predicted less than 10 percent of the variation in recalled coping. Smith et al. also found that recalled coping consistently overestimated daily coping attempts. These studies suggest that investigators interested in how people cope with illness, or how coping with stressful events influences health, should not rely solely on recalled coping reports.

Stone, Shiffman and colleagues, leaders in the study of individuals in their daily lives, also found that recollected coping does not correspond well with coping reported close to its real-time occurrence. Remarkably, Stone et al. (1998) found limited correspondence between these coping assessment methods even when recall was limited to 48 hours. Individuals experiencing high levels of work or marital stress used palmtop computers to report their coping on multiple occasions over two days. Stone et al. found only modest agreement between these real-time and short-term retrospective coping reports. After only two days, 30 percent of the participants did not report strategies they had reported on the palmtop, and almost the same proportion of participants endorsed a strategy they had not recorded during the two study days.

Using the same study sample and data reported by Stone et al. (1998), Schwartz et al. (1999) took this line of inquiry further by examining whether real time coping reports support the concept of trait coping, which permeates the literature on coping with illness. They found that self-reported measures of trait coping accounted for a very small portion of the variation in momentary coping. In fact, only 2 of 17 trait coping indicators accounted for more than 3 percent of real time coping variance. Moreover, they found only modest support for the concept of trait coping: Only 15–30 percent of the variability in momentary coping with a current stressor was attributable to individual differences in coping. This is a provocative finding, because many theories of health-related behavior, including theories of risky alcohol use that we will review subsequently, are based on trait conceptions of coping.

In a more nuanced test of the concept of trait coping, Porter et al. (2000) used their rich data set to evaluate whether the gender differences regularly reported in the coping literature emerged when coping was assessed close to its real-time occurrence. They found that traditional trait measures of coping replicated previous findings, with women reporting greater use of support seeking and catharsis than men. Momentary assessments, however, revealed no gender differences in coping. However, in another study in which the coping reports of osteoarthritis and rheumatoid arthritis patients were collected each day, Affleck et al. (1999a) found that women used more emotion-focused strategies each day than men, even after controlling for their greater pain.

The Temporal Dynamics of Coping

Folkman and Lazarus's (1980) distinction between coping efforts aimed at the perceived source of stress, that is, "problem-focused coping," and efforts to regulate one's emotions as a way of adapting to a stressful encounter, that is, "emotion-focused coping," has with occasional modifications guided coping theory and research for more than 20 years. Yet the temporal unfolding of these two forms of coping could not be examined through traditional retrospective coping reports. Rothbaum et al.'s (1982) "fallback hypothesis" posits that whereas problem-focused coping strategies will be employed regularly in the absence of emotion-focused strategies, emotion-focused strategies are less likely to be employed unless problem-focused strategies have also been attempted.

Tennen et al. (2000) used daily coping reports to test the fallback hypothesis in the context of coping with chronic pain from rheumatoid arthritis. These arthritis sufferers reported their pain coping strategies and pain intensity every day for 75 days. Consistent with the fallback hypothesis, Tennen et al. found that whereas problem-focused strategies were employed regularly without emotion-focused strategies over thousands of person-days, emotion-focused strategies were employed quite infrequently without problem-focused strategies. The likelihood of emotion-focused coping was 4.4 times greater on a problem-focused coping day than on a day without problem-focused coping. Tennen et al. were also able to predict emotion-focused coping days from the presence or absence of the *previous* day's problem-focused coping. Not only was today's emotion-focused coping predicted by yesterday's problem-focused coping, but this cross-day association was itself a function of the change in pain from yesterday to today. An increase in today's pain over yesterday's pain increased the likelihood that problem-focused coping yesterday would be followed by emotion-focused coping today. In other words, when efforts to directly influence pain are not successful (as evidenced by an increase in next-day pain), the next day people may try harder to adjust to that which cannot be readily changed. These theory-driven processes could not have been ascertained through traditional coping reports or in-depth interviews.

Together, these daily process studies of coping demonstrate that: (a) coping as traditionally measured by retrospective report bears only modest resemblance to coping efforts described in real time, even when the recall period is as little as 48 hours; (b) whereas the literature on coping with illness and health threats continues to rely on trait conceptions of coping, studies examining the momentary assessment of coping find no support for trait coping; (c) gender differences in coping, a centerpiece of the coping literature, deserve more careful attention using daily process designs; and (d) problem- and emotion-focused coping unfold temporally in ways that are consistent with current theory. Thus, although daily process studies of coping provide daunting challenges to cherished (recall-based) methods and conceptualizations (such as trait coping and socialization-based gender differences in coping), this area of daily inquiry has demonstrated for the first time hypothesized temporal patterns in how individuals cope with pain associated with a chronic illness. We believe that the study of daily coping will continue to influence how we understand coping, how it is measured, and how clinicians attempt to modify their patients' coping efforts.

The Pursuit of Personal Goals in Daily Life with Chronic Pain

Theory and much research in personality, social, and health psychology underscore the critical place of personal goals in the dynamics of everyday life. Personal goals are "motivational units" that are less global than broad cognitive representations or personality characteristics, but more integrative than isolated behaviors or attitudes (Karoly, 1991). The pursuit of personal goals figures prominently in psychological adaptation to life with chronic pain. Karoly and Jensen (1987) argued that chronic pain patients can develop "self-defeating schemas" of pain in relation to the accomplishment of cherished goals. The perception of pain-related barriers to goal progress can thus be as critical a factor in adapting to life with chronic pain as is the pain itself.

We have studied the dynamics and individual differences underlying the daily pursuit of personal goals in women with fibromyalgia syndrome. Henriksson et al. (1992) found that most individuals with fibromyalgia experience pain and fatigue each day and claim that both states affect their ability to accomplish daily goals. A qualitative study (Henriksson, 1995) revealed several common stressors of living with fibromyalgia, including the burden it imposes on achieving personal goals and the hardship of abandoning their most cherished life plans. Efforts to cope with these burdens included changing daily routines, reorganizing daily priorities, and pursuing new goals and interests. We now describe two of our recent studies of how individuals pursue personal goals in daily life while facing chronic pain. The design, methods, and findings of these studies capture the unique strengths and potential of daily process research for understanding illness behavior.

For our first study (Affleck et al., 1998), we hypothesized that daily changes in sleep, pain, and fatigue would be linked with variations in daily goal pursuit, and, in turn, that daily goal pursuit would influence emotional well-being. We believe that this study, which broke new ground in assessing goal attainment with a prospective daily methodology, offers fresh possibilities for research on personal goals and health (Karoly, 1991) and yet another focus for health psychology's attention to the significant experiences of everyday life.

This study targeted the pursuit of "medium range" health and social goals in daily life with chronic pain. These goals concern the improvement or maintenance of health and fitness (e.g., eating a low fat diet, following a regular exercise routine) and the enhancement of social relationships (e.g., spending more time with one's children, being more patient with co-workers). The movement toward and away from these goals is generally easier to monitor than is the fulfillment of more global and distant aspirations (e.g., becoming a better person), and is more likely to influence psychological well-being than is carrying out the more mundane tasks of everyday life (e.g., to get to the supermarket after work) (Karoly, 1999). Health and social goals may also be construed differently. For example, individuals have been shown to attach greater value to their social goals than to their health goals, but to reward themselves more often when they make progress in their health goals than when they move toward their social goals (Karoly and Ruehlman, 1995).

For this study, 50 women meeting American College of Rheumatology criteria for primary fibromyalgia syndrome supplied data from both end-of-day summaries (using paper-and-pencil diaries) and within-day electronic interviews (using hand-held computers) for 30 consecutive days. As an initial foray, we thought it reasonable to measure goal-related processes once a day. On the other hand, pain, fatigue, and mood are likely to change over the course of a day and may be contaminated by systematic retrospection errors in subjective averaging across a day (Hedges et al., 1985). Accordingly, pain, fatigue, and both positive and negative mood were assessed as "momentary" processes at randomly selected moments during the morning, afternoon, and evening.

Before beginning the study, participants were asked to describe one health and fitness goal, and one social goal. Each night before retiring to bed, they rated how much effort they made toward the goal that day, how much their fibromyalgia pain and/or fatigue interfered with their progress toward the goal, and how much progress they made toward achieving the goal. During the month of data collection, participants also carried a palm-top computer programmed as an electronic interviewer (ELI), which requested information about their previous night's sleep quality once a day after awakening and their pain, mood, and fatigue three times a day.

Our first research question concerned the within-person association between daily changes in pain intensity, fatigue, and sleep quality with patients' efforts to accomplish their personal goals, their perception that goal attainment was hindered by pain and fatigue, and their evaluation of progress made toward their goals each day. These within-person relations were modeled by multi-level random effects regressions (Bryk and Raudenbush, 1992).

As we anticipated, days following a poorer night's sleep were associated with a decline in the next day's effort to accomplish health/fitness goals. Although goal effort was not diminished on days with increasing pain and fatigue, the perception that goal progress was hindered by pain and fatigue was greater on days with mounting pain and fatigue as well as on days following a less restorative night's sleep. And, for social/interpersonal goals, an increase in pain during the day was associated with the perception of less daily goal progress at day's end. Thus, while daily progress toward health/fitness goals may have been regulated by the quality of the previous night's sleep, progress toward social/interpersonal goals may have been affected by changes in the course of pain across the day.

Our second research question concerned the role that goal-related activities might play in daily mood changes. On days during which participants believed that their daily progress toward health and fitness goals was impeded by pain and fatigue, they showed a decline in positive mood from morning to evening regardless of that day's pain and fatigue. And on days when participants saw greater progress in their social and interpersonal goals, they showed improvements in positive mood across the day, also independent of that day's pain and fatigue. Interestingly, equivalent findings were not obtained when changes in daily negative mood were examined, suggesting that daily goal pursuits might play a more prominent part in the waxing and waning of positive affect as opposed to negative affect.

Our first study ignored sources of individual differences in goal effort, barriers, and progress and in the extent to which these goal processes track the vicissitudes of pain and fatigue. Larger numbers of subjects would enable a combination of idiographic and nomothetic approaches. Accordingly, our second study (Affleck et al., 2001b) included 39 additional women, and sampled individual difference constructs from value-expectancy models of motivation to explain how and when women with fibromyalgia remain engaged in the pursuit of their goals, particularly when they face elevated levels of daily pain and fatigue.

Although there is little disagreement among goal theorists that the meaningfulness of a goal should predict the initiation and persistence of goal-directed effort (e.g., Carver and Scheier, 1998; Karoly, 1999), there has been debate over the determinants of goal outcome expectancies (cf., Carver, et al., 2000; Snyder, et al., 1991; Tennen and Affleck, 2000). Therefore, in addition to evaluating the importance of goal valuation in the pursuit of daily goals in the face of pain and fatigue, we examined two constructs which have been theorized to influence goal outcome expectancies: self-efficacy appraisals and dispositional optimism.

Self-efficacy Appraisals

In Karoly's taxonomy of goal construal, self-efficacy is a critical appraisal directing the choice to actively pursue a goal (Karoly and Ruehlman, 1995). Self-efficacy is the appraisal that one has the capacity to do what it requires to accomplish a specific goal. Believing that one possesses the knowledge, skills, or abilities required to achieve that goal is thought to instill confidence in goal attainment and spur goal-directed efforts (Bandura, 1997). A sense of self-efficacy in overcoming the challenges of living with chronic pain has repeatedly been shown to predict psychological and physical well-being (e.g., Keefe et al., 1996). Lefebvre et al. (1999) found that self-efficacy appraisals regarding one's ability to manage pain, fatigue, and functional limitations associated with rheumatoid arthritis were associated with less daily pain, more positive daily mood, and greater confidence in the effectiveness of one's daily coping strategies.

Dispositional Optimism and Pessimism

Carver and Scheier (Carver et al., 2000; Carver and Scheier, 1998) contend that self-efficacy judgments and related personal control appraisals are not the only perceptions that increase people's confidence that they can meet their goals. They draw attention to the expectation itself that the goal will be achieved, an appraisal that can depend on circumstances that have little to do with a sense of personal control or self-efficacy. The critical element in Carver and Scheier's model of goal attainment is thus "*whether* the desired outcome seems likely to occur, not *how* it is to occur" (Carver et al., 2000: 141). People's estimates of the probability that a goal will be achieved can turn on their personal history of having met similar goals. They can also turn on their personality: namely, their disposition to hold generalized positive outcome expectancies (optimism) or negative outcome expectancies (pessimism) about the future (Carver and Scheier, 1998).

Scheier and Carver (1992) have summarized effects of optimism on physical well-being, which span the appearance of physical symptoms in healthy individuals to milestones of recovery from life-saving surgery. A daily process study of individuals with rheumatoid arthritis or fibromyalgia has also documented some of the benefits of optimism for adapting to daily life with chronic pain (Affleck et al., 2001a; Tennen et al., 1992). Optimists did not report less daily pain, but they did cite significantly higher levels of positive daily mood, more frequent positive daily events, and fewer pain-related activity limitation days, and greater confidence in the effectiveness of their daily pain coping strategies. Most pertinent to the present study is evidence that optimism may motivate the changes in behavior which help people achieve their health-related goals. This includes evidence that optimism predicts health-promoting behaviors (Robbins et al., 1991) and heart patients' adherence to cardiac rehabilitation regimens (Shepperd et al., 1996).

One week before beginning the daily diary portion of the study (which we described earlier), participants completed several questionnaires assessing their goal valuation (Karoly and Ruehlman, 1995), goal-specific self-efficacy appraisals (Karoly and Ruehlman, 1995), and dispositional optimism/pessimism (Scheier and Carver, 1985). We found that goal valuation, but not self-efficacy judgments or dispositional optimism/pessimism, was a unique predictor of how much effort participants expended on the average day to attain both health and social goals. The same was true for the average day's estimate of health and social goal progress. This salutary effect of goal valuation on goal effort and goal progress was displayed evenhandedly across days; it did not differ on days that were more or less painful or fatiguing.

In contrast, the ability of dispositional optimism to predict goal effort and goal progress became apparent only on days that presented greater obstacles to goal progress. The less optimistic person reported less effort and progress in reaching health goals than did the more optimistic person on days when she was more tired. In other words, in the face of greater fatigue, the more optimistic individual was less likely to retreat from her health goals.

Many studies reviewed by Carver and Scheier (1998) support the view that optimists can more readily rise above adversity. Our findings, derived from a mixed idiographic–nomothetic design, extend this evidence of the optimist's superior ability to surmount obstacles to goal accomplishment. This study's ability to document the role of optimism in the dynamic within-person relations of goal obstacles with goal effort and goal progress makes these findings unique in the literature on optimism and pessimism.

Another finding offers a clue why optimists, at least those who live with chronic pain, persist in goal-directed activity. The optimists among the women in our study – despite reporting levels of daily pain and fatigue no different from those of their less optimistic counterparts – were less apt to identify their pain and fatigue as obstacles in the path to their health goals. This finding, if elaborated further, may prove to be cogent evidence of the capacity of dispositional optimism to interrupt the formation of a self-handicapping chronic pain schema in which pain not only makes goal attainment difficult but becomes a schematic cue for retreating from one's goals (Karoly and Jensen, 1987).

In arriving at these findings, we followed the increasingly common practice of treating optimism and pessimism as independent constructs (e.g., Chang et al., 1994). Pessimism did figure independently in one of our findings: pessimistic women, compared to those who were less pessimistic, were more apt to cite barriers to health and social goals on days that were less painful than usual. Hence, whereas optimism predicted the *positive* outcome of sustaining progress toward goals even on days with more fatigue, pessimism predicted the *negative* outcome of perceiving pain as a goal barrier even on days with less pain.

Although goal valuation, optimism, and pessimism each contributed independently to the dynamics of daily goal pursuit, goal self-efficacy did not. This cannot be attributed to substantial shared variances in the measures; the two goal self-efficacy scores were only modestly correlated with goal valuation and with optimism or pessimism. And even when we examined it alone as a predictor in all multilevel analyses, self-efficacy predicted only the perception of lesser barriers to health goals on the average day. Thus, although self-efficacy has repeatedly been demonstrated to predict psychological and physical well-being among individuals with chronic pain (e.g., Keefe, et al., 1996; Lefebvre et al., 1999), it failed to account for individual differences in the short-term goal pursuits of women with fibromyalgia. Our study's 30-day time frame for monitoring goal processes and outcomes may be an important limiting factor here; over a longer time span, self-efficacy appraisals might be a more robust predictor of goal attainment. This limitation notwithstanding, our findings are in line with Carver and Scheier's proposal that outcome expectancies – the perception that desired outcomes will be achieved – are better predictors of the movement toward goals in the face of barriers than are self-efficacy expectancies – the perception that one can do what it takes to reach desired outcomes (Carver et al., 2000). And most relevant to the goals of this chapter, these findings demonstrate the important ways in which daily process designs and methods can contribute to theory testing, and how these designs and methods offer insights into the dynamics of everyday life in health and illness.

Daily Processes in Substance Use

The association between daily experience and addictive behaviors lies squarely at the intersection of social psychology, health psychology, and public health, and is ideally suited for daily process investigation. Much theory and research, for example, has focused on the role of daily stress and negative affect as precursors to drinking and smoking (Conger, 1956; Greeley and Oei, 1999) and as psychological triggers for lapses from abstinence (Shiffman et al., 1999). Voluminous literature is also devoted to the role of alcohol and smoking in altering affective states: that is, reducing negative affective states and enhancing positive affective states (Greeley and Oei, 1999; Shiffman, 2000). To date, however, the preponderance of empirical work on these topics has used research designs that are inadequate for assessing such dynamically unfolding processes (see Affleck et al., 1999b; Shiffman et al., 1999; Tennen at al., 2000).

In the following sections, we review theoretical questions relevant to the social and psychological foundations of substance use and, where appropriate, we compare previously held notions (mostly derived from cross-sectional designs) to recent findings from studies using daily process designs. We also present findings from our ongoing studies of alcohol use. Although some research (e.g., Klatsky, 1994) suggests that moderate drinking might help prevent coronary heart disease, recent studies (e.g., Britton and McPherson, 2001) indicate that such benefits are largely limited to older adults (> 55 years of age) and that any benefits are outweighed by costs associated with increasing risk for other ailments (e.g., liver cirrhosis; hemorrhagic stroke) and alcohol dependence, and negative alcohol-related outcomes (e.g., traffic crashes, interpersonal aggression) (Gordis, 1999).

Daily Substance Use and the "Level of Analysis Problem"

Even if we neglect the overwhelming evidence in the literature, and assume that individuals can recall average levels of alcohol use and smoking, and that they can estimate their characteristic mood states, depressive and anxious symptoms and life stress, issues related to the "level of analysis" in substance use research represents a significant area of confusion. Specifically, many of the theoretical models of alcohol consumption and cigarette smoking are "multilevel" in nature, spanning both within-person and across-person levels of analysis.

For example, Cooper and colleagues' (1992) stressor-vulnerability model asserts that men, individuals with stronger positive alcohol-outcome expectancies, and those with limited coping skills, will drink relatively more during high stress periods compared to low stress periods. The preponderance of field research (e.g., Cooper et al., 1992) to date, however, has relied on retrospective, cross-sectional designs, with the central goal being the uncovering of differential associations between recent life stress and average drinking levels across high- and low-risk (i.e., based on expectancies and coping dimensions) individuals.[1] Although results from such studies are informative, a stronger positive association between overall life stress and average alcohol consumption found among high-risk individuals, compared to low-risk individuals, cannot be interpreted as evidence for their greater propensity towards stress-induced drinking. As we cautioned earlier in this chapter, it is inappropriate to make inferences about contingencies at one level of analysis (e.g., the within-person contingency that people drink when stressed) from results obtained at another level of analysis (e.g., across-person). Such associations might have little in common.

To illustrate the level of analysis problem, we examined data from 34 drinkers (16 women) whose alcohol consumption put them at risk for alcohol-related problems; these individuals are a subset of those examined in Armeli et al. (2000a). Because we were interested in the associations among smoking and alcohol consumption, we only examined individuals who reported smoking at least once during the course of the study. For 60 days, participants recorded their smoking, alcohol consumption, and desire to drink (example item *"I felt like I could really use a drink"*) in structured nightly diaries, which they returned in postage-paid return envelopes the next day.

As shown in Table 18.1, the within- and across-person associations share little in common. At the within-person level of analysis, individuals show positive associations among all three variables. That is, on days when participants reported greater alcohol consumption, they also tended to smoke more and report a greater desire to drink. Conversely, at the across-person level of analysis, no association was found between average smoking levels and average consumption levels. Of even greater interest, we found a negative across-person association between average smoking levels and average levels of desire to drink. Thus, making inferences about within-person associations from across-person results, one might surmise that individuals have a lower desire to drink when they smoke, contrary to findings at the appropriate within-person level of analysis.

Recognizing the problems associated with drawing inferences about daily substance use processes from aggregate level data, researchers have begun to take advantage of the power and flexibility offered by daily process research designs and multilevel analytical techniques. We now turn our attention

Table 18.1 Within-person versus across-person associations among smoking, drinking, and desire to drink

	1	2	3
1. Smoking	–	0.45*	0.34*
2. Alcohol consumption	0.05	–	0.59*
3. Desire to drink	−0.46*	0.52*	–

Note: Above diagonal are within-person associations, below diagonal are aggregate across-person associations. Within-person values represent the square root of percentage reduction of within-person residual variances obtained in multilevel model. Multilevel models containing daily alcohol consumption as the dependent variable controlled for day of the week by including six orthogonal dummy codes. * $p < 0.01$.

to recent studies re-examining existing theoretical models of drinking and smoking using such approaches. Although several early field studies employed within-person or daily research designs to address the aforementioned level of analysis problems (e.g., Stone et al., 1985), we focus only on more recent work using multilevel analytic frameworks (i.e., simultaneous examinations of within- and across-person factors).

Daily Diary Studies of Substance Use

Armeli et al. (2000b) used a daily diary design to re-examine Cooper et al.'s (1992) stressor-vulnerability model (SVM). As stated earlier, according to SVM certain individuals are prone to stress-induced drinking. In Cooper et al.'s (1992) original study, results showed significant interactive effects of stress, gender, alcohol expectancies, and avoidant coping style in predicting average consumption levels. However, the cross-sectional nature of Cooper et al.'s data limited inferences about at-risk individuals' drinking behavior during high stress versus low stress periods, an inherently within-person question which is the crux of tension reduction hypothesis (Conger, 1956).

Armeli et al. (2000b) had 88 heavy drinkers[2] record for 60 days in struc-tured nightly diaries the stressfulness of the day's most negative event, their desire to drink, and their alcohol consumption. Prior to this phase of the study, participants completed measures of alcohol expectancies and avoidant coping style. As predicted by SVM, the within-person associations between event stress and desire to drink and consumption varied as a function of across-person risk factors. Specifically, men who expected drinking to result in general positive feelings or feelings of careless unconcern (i.e., a sense of irresponsibility and lack of concern for doing things well) drank more and had a greater desire to drink on high stress days compared to low stress days.

Although findings for gender and expectancies reinforce predictions made by SVM, little support was found for predicted moderating effects of avoidant coping style. In fact, several findings indicated that avoidant coping style actually buffered the exacerbating effect of careless unconcern on the stress-drinking relation. That is, individuals with an avoidant coping style, which heretofore has been deemed an important risk factor for problem drinking, might not demonstrate a stronger tendency to drink when stressed.[3] Although this finding was not predicted and is in need of replication, it highlights the necessity of examining theory-driven predictions at the appropriate level of analysis.

Carney et al. (2000) used a daily diary design to re-examine Cooper et al.'s (1995) motivational model of alcohol use positing both tension-reduction and positive experience enhancement pathways to consumption. Using a sub-sample from Armeli et al. (2000b), Carney et al. (2000) examined how daily alcohol consumption and desire to drink covaried with positive and negative daily events in the domains of work, health, and non-work (encompassing daily experiences with spouse, family, friends, as well as social and recre-ational events). Carney et al. found that individuals drank more on days on which they reported more positive and negative non-work events, and they drank less on days when they reported more positive and negative health events and positive work events. Similar results for the effects of positive and negative daily events and mood states on daily consumption were found in Armeli et al.'s (2000b) diary study of drinkers meeting criteria for alcohol dependence. Findings from these studies provide initial support – at the daily level of analysis – for Cooper et al.'s (1995) motivational model of drinking and further illustrate the complexity of this process, heretofore undetected in studies using more traditional cross-sectional research designs.

Within-day "Real-time" Studies of Daily Substance Use and Abuse

In contrast to the interval contingent nature of these once-a-day diary studies, several recent studies have used event and signal contingent recording strategies to examine daily substance abuse (see Wheeler and Reis, 1991 for detailed distinctions among these methods). As Shiffman (2000) suggests, such methods have several advantages over daily diaries, including real-time assessment and more rigorous compliance verification.

Collins et al. (1998) examined the association between positive and negative mood states and excessive drinking among heavy drinkers enrolled in an eight-week behavioral drinking moderation program. At the beginning of drinking episodes, which were individually defined based on time between drinks and changes of location, participants rated their positive and negative affect, the type of activity in which they were involved (e.g., work, leisure, etc.), and their social context (i.e., presence of family, friends, etc.). They also rated their affect at the end of the drinking episodes. Most of the drinking episodes took place in leisure contexts and in the presence of others, and more excessive drinking occurred when participants were in a more positive mood at the beginning of a drinking episode. Interestingly, excessive drinking was also associated with lower levels of post-episode positive affect.

Swendsen et al. (2000) had 100 heavy drinkers (55 women; mean age 33.9 years) record their mood states and alcohol consumption for 30 days on palmtop computers. Mood states were assessed three times a day (participants were randomly prompted during morning, afternoon, and early evening intervals) and alcohol consumption was recorded as it occurred. Swendsen et al. (2000) found that for men, nervous mood in the early evening predicted greater alcohol consumption later in the evening (controlling for prior consumption), and the more alcohol participants consumed the less nervous they were at the end of the drinking episode. This "tension-reduction" effect, which demands the temporal sequencing of variables, could only be examined faithfully using a within-day event and signal contingent daily process design.

Mohr et al. (2001) provide another illustration of the flexibility of daily process technology in the study of daily substance use. Mohr et al. assessed how daily positive and negative interpersonal experiences were associated with drinking in different locations and social situations. Specifically, during in vivo recording of alcohol consumption, participants also recorded their location (e.g., home versus away) and social context (e.g., alone versus interacting with others). Positive and negative interpersonal experiences were measured in nightly booklets. Mohr et al. found that on days with more negative interpersonal experiences, participants engaged in more solitary drinking (i.e., drinking at home and alone), whereas on days with more positive interpersonal experiences they drank more in social contexts.

A final study of interest dealing with daily substance use is Shiffman et al.'s (1999) examination of the relation between alcohol consumption and cigarette smoking. The goal of this study was to re-examine several theoretical models pertaining to the link between alcohol consumption and cigarette smoking. For example, the conditioned learning model states that alcohol consumption and smoking become associated through repeated pairing in social situations (e.g., smoking and drinking while socializing with others or in bars).

In this study 57 cigarette smokers carried palmtop computers and recorded their cigarette smoking and alcohol consumption for a week. Participants initiated electronic interviews when they were about to smoke a cigarette; five smoking situations per day were prompted with additional questions including alcohol consumption, mood states, and activities. These smokers were also beeped randomly during the day to obtain non-smoking baseline data. Thus, this study combined signal contingent and event contingent recording methods. Results showed that smoking was 2.1 times more likely when subjects had been drinking than when they had not been drinking. This association held even after controlling for possible situational confounds such as day of week, being with others, and in places where smoking was permitted.

The Flexibility of Daily Process Designs

The aforementioned studies illustrate the advantages of daily process methodologies in the study of daily substance use. In addition to facilitating the examination of moment to moment and day to day covariation between substance use and its hypothesized correlates, such designs offer a great deal of flexibility in modeling the temporal sequence among constructs such as daily events, mood states, and substance use. This is especially relevant in the study of alcohol consumption, which is restricted by a host of legal and social factors to certain times and situations. In Carney et al.'s (2000) study of heavy drinkers, for example, approximately 40 percent of the total drinks were consumed on Fridays and Saturdays. Thus, the form of the association between daily negative events, mood states, and alcohol consumption might not conform to the same-day design employed in many of the aforementioned studies.

In some instances, the temporal lag between stress, negative affect, and alcohol consumption might cycle on a weekly basis (i.e., weekend consumption might be a function of average weekday stress). This might be especially so in the case of work stress. Neither Carney et al. (2000) nor Armeli et al. (2000a) found that daily drinking was associated with daily work stress. One possibility is that work stress is associated with increased responsibility and time constraints (e.g., working overtime, project deadlines) that might make alcohol use on a given day less likely. Another possible model is that individuals relieve their work stress via alcohol consumption on the weekends. Thus, having data at the moment or daily level does not necessitate examination of within-day associations, but allows researchers to explore other possible lag sequences.

To illustrate the flexibility of daily process data, we re-examined work stress and alcohol consumption data from Carney et al. (2000) at the weekly level of analysis. Specifically, we aggregated data from weekdays (Monday to Thursday) and weekends (Friday to Saturday). This allowed us to examine whether weekday positive and negative work events predicted weekend alcohol use controlling for weekday alcohol use. We also examined weekday levels of perceived stress as measured by Cohen et al.'s (1983) four-item version of the Perceived Stress Scale.

All 83 participants had at least seven full weeks of data. We surmised that weekday stress might have the strongest effect on alcohol use at the earliest part of the weekend, thus we examined Friday's alcohol consumption as a separate outcome.[4] We also examined Saturday and Sunday consumption and total weekend consumption (Friday, Saturday, and Sunday). Because the number of within-person observations was small (i.e., 7–8 level 1 observations), we examined each predictor separately (i.e., each predictor paired with weekday alcohol use separately).

As shown in Table 18.2, weekday work stress did not predict changes in consumption from weekdays to weekend. In contrast, positive work experiences, such as completing a task, solving a work-related problem, or being helped by a fellow employee, predicted changes in drinking from weekdays to Saturday and Sunday alcohol consumption. Additionally, weekday perceived stress was related to change in consumption from weekdays to Friday, but not Saturday and Sunday consumption.

Although these findings are exploratory, they illustrate the flexibility of daily data in examining associations among constructs that might coincide with the ebb and flow of individuals' weekly responsibilities and social opportunities. Interestingly, the *daily* associations among negative work events, perceived stress and drinking using the Monday to Thursday data indicated

Table 18.2 Weekday events predicting weekend consumption

Predictor	Friday	Alcohol use Saturday–Sunday	Total weekend
Weekday positive work events	0.01	0.11*	0.08*
Weekday negative work events	−0.03	−0.05	−0.04
Weekday perceived stress	0.34**	−0.03	−0.09

Note: Coefficients represent unstandardized pooled within-person partial regression coefficients. All models controlled for weekday alcohol use (Monday–Thursday) and Saturday–Sunday outcome also controlled for Friday alcohol consumption. Based on Carney et al.'s (2000) findings, all models controlled for positive and negative health events occurring on the outcome days. * $p < 0.10$, ** $p < 0.05$.

that overall perceived stress was higher on days with more negative work events. These findings, along with the weekly results, suggest the possibility of a complex indirect effect in which work stress might influence overall levels of stress during the week, which in turn influences alcohol use at the first opportunity when responsibilities are diminished (i.e., Friday evening).

Table 18.2 also reveals that positive weekday work events anticipated greater Saturday and Sunday consumption. Yet, several studies (Armeli et al., 2000a; Carney et al., 2000) found that individuals drank less on days characterized by more positive work experiences compared to days with less positive work experiences. The combined findings provide another demonstration of the importance of level of analysis. Specifically, examining the association between positive work experience and alcohol consumption at daily versus weekly levels of analyses provides drastically different results. Taken together, these findings suggest that individuals might restrain their alcohol consumption during the work week, even drinking less on days characterized by high accomplishments, but then celebrate such exploits on the weekend by consuming alcohol in response to positive work week experiences.

Conclusions

We have highlighted the strengths, unique virtues and benefits of employing daily process designs to study how psychosocial factors influence health, illness and health risk behaviors, and how in turn these factors are influenced by physical health. Yet, as we have noted previously (Tennen et al., 1991; 2000), studying daily processes in health and illness is difficult for investigators and participants. For investigators, data collection and management represent a substantial undertaking, and for participants, repeated recording of symptoms, thoughts, emotional states, and behaviors can be onerous. We also have lingering concerns that our study participants, who meet every challenge we place in their path, are perhaps more agreeable, motivated, and perhaps better adjusted (see Waite et al., 1998). Although investigators should remain alert to the possibility that intensive self-monitoring might influence the health or illness phenomena being monitored, studies designed specifically to examine reactive effects of diary assessment seem to be finding no evidence that intensive self-assessment affects health-related processes (Cruise et al., 1996; von Baeyer, 1994). We remain confident that daily process research holds enormous promise in our efforts to uncover the psychological and social factors that maintain health and healthful behaviors and those that initiate, maintain, and respond to illness episodes.

Acknowledgments

The order of authorship is arbitrary. Grants R29-AA09917, T32-AA07290, and P50-AA03510 from the National Institute of Alcohol Abuse and Alcoholism supported preparation of this chapter.

Correspondence concerning this chapter should be addressed to Howard Tennen, Department of Community Medicine and Health Care, University of Connecticut Health Center, Farmington, CT 06030-6325, USA; e-mail: tennen@nso1.uchc.edu

Notes

1. We do not mean to imply that there are no studies of substance use employing within-person, longitudinal designs. However, much of this work has focused on changes in substance use over long periods of time. Such studies do not truly address the moment to moment or day to day questions posed by theories outlining tension-reduction and experience enhancement processes.
2. Subjects did not meet DSM III-R criteria for abuse or dependence, but 50 percent did meet the following generally accepted criteria for risky drinking levels: more than 3 or 4 standard drinks in any day for women and men, respectively; and more than 12 or 16 standard drinks in any week for women and men, respectively.
3. Such a finding does not necessarily contradict results suggesting avoidant coping to be a general risk factor for increased alcohol consumption. It could be that high avoidant-copers drink more on average, but do not drink more on high stress versus low stress days. Avoiding everyday stressful situations, in ways other than consuming alcohol, might lead to increased depressive or anxious symptoms, which in turn might influence overall drinking levels over time.
4. All participants worked traditional hour jobs (i.e., Monday to Friday, 9 to 5). Only 13 percent of the negative work events and 9 percent of the positive work events occurred on Saturday and Sundays.

References

Adams, S., Dammers, P., Saia, T., Brantley, P., and Gaydos, G. (1994). Stress, depression, and anxiety predict average symptom severity and daily symptom fluctuation in Systemic Lupus Erythematosus. *Journal of Behavioral Medicine*, 17, 459–77.

Affleck, G., Apter, A., Tennen, H. et al. (2000). Mood states associated with transitory changes in asthma symptoms and peak expiratory flow. *Psychosomatic Medicine*, 62, 61–8.

Affleck, G., Tennen, H., and Apter, A. (2001a). Optimism, pessimism, and daily life with chronic illness. In E. Chang (Ed.), *Optimism and Pessimism: Implications for Theory, Research, and Practice* (pp. 147–68). Washington, DC: American Psychological Association Books.

Affleck, G., Tennen, H., Keefe, F. et al. (1999a). Everyday life with osteoarthritis or rheumatoid arthritis: Independent effects of disease and gender on pain, mood, and coping. *Pain*, 83, 601–9.

Affleck, G., Tennen, H., Urrows, S., and Higgins, P. (1992). Neuroticism and the pain-mood relation in rheumatoid arthritis: Insights from a daily prospective study. *Journal of Consulting and Clinical Psychology*, 60, 119–26.

Affleck, G., Tennen, H., Urrows, S., and Higgins, P. (1994). Person and contextual features of stress reactivity: Individual differences in relations of undesirable daily events with mood disturbance and chronic pain intensity. *Journal of Personality and Social Psychology*, 66, 329–40.

Affleck, G., Tennen, H., Urrows, S. et al. (1998). Fibromyalgia and the pursuit of personal goals: A daily process analysis. *Health Psychology*, 17, 40–7.

Affleck, G., Tennen, H., Zautra, A., Urrows, S., Abeles, M., and Karoly, P. (2001b). Women's pursuit of personal goals in daily life with fibromyalgia: A value-expectancy analysis. *Journal of Consulting and Clinical Psychology*, 69, 587–96.

Affleck, G., Zautra, A., Tennen, H., and Armeli, S. (1999b). Multilevel daily process designs for consulting and clinical psychology: A preface for the perplexed. *Journal of Consulting and Clinical Psychology*, 67, 746–54.

Aikens, J., and Wallander, J. (1994). A nomothetic-idiographic study of daily psychological stress and blood glucose in women with type-I diabetes-mellitus. *Journal of Behavioral Medicine*, 17, 535–48.

American Heart Association (1998). *Heart and Stroke Statistical Update*. Dallas, TX: American Heart Association.

Armeli, S., Carney, M. A., Tennen, H., Affleck, G., and O'Neil, T. (2000a). Stress and alcohol use: A daily process examination of the stressor-vulnerability model. *Journal of Personality and Social Psychology*, 78, 979–94.

Armeli, S., Tennen, H., Affleck, G., and Kranzler, H. (2000b). Does affect mediate the association between daily events and alcohol use? *Journal of Studies on Alcohol*, 61, 862–71.

Bandura, A. (1997). *Self-efficacy: The Exercise of Control*. New York: Freeman.

Bock, R. (1989). *Multilevel Analysis of Educational Data*. New York: Academic Press.

Britton, A., and McPherson, K. (2001). Mortality in England and Wales attributable to current alcohol consumption, *Journal of Epidemiology and Community Health*, 55, 383–8.

Brown, K., and Moskowitz, D. (1998). It's a function of time: A review of the process approach to behavioral medicine research. *Psychosomatic Medicine*, 20, 109–17.

Bryk, A. S., and Raudenbush, S. W. (1992). *Hierarchical Linear Models*. Newbury Park, CA: Sage.

Carney, M. A., Armeli, S., Tennen, H., Affleck, G., and O'Neil, T. (2000). Positive and negative daily events, perceived stress, and alcohol use: A diary study. *Journal of Consulting and Clinical Psychology*, 68, 788–98.

Carver, C., Harris, S., Lehman, J. et al. (2000). How important is the perception of personal control? Studies of early stage breast cancer patients. *Personality and Social Psychology Bulletin*, 26, 139–49.

Carver, C., and Scheier, M. (1998). *On the Self-regulation of Behavior*. Cambridge: Cambridge University Press.

Chang, E., D'Zurilla, T., and Maydeu-Olivares, A. (1994). Assessing the dimensionality of optimism and pessimism using a multimeasure approach. *Cognitive Therapy and Research*, 18, 143–60.

Cohen, S., Kamarck, T., and Mermelstein, R. (1983). A global measure of perceived stress. *Journal of Health and Social Behavior*, 24, 385–96.

Collins, R. L., Morsheimer, E. T., Shiffman, S., Paty, J. A., Gnys, M., and Papandonatos, G. (1998). Ecological momentary assessment in a behavioral drinking moderation training program. *Experimental and Clinical Psychopharmacology*, 6, 306–15.

Conger, J. J. (1956). Reinforcement theory and the dynamics of alcoholism. *Quarterly Journal of Studies on Alcohol*, 17, 296–305.

Cooper, M. L., Frone, M. R., Russell, M., and Mudar, P. (1995). Drinking to regulate positive and negative emotions: A motivational model of alcohol use. *Journal of Personality and Social Psychology*, 69, 990–1005.

Cooper, M. L., Russell, M., Skinner, J. B., Frone, M. R., and Mudar, P. (1992). Stress and alcohol use: Moderating effects of gender, coping and alcohol expectancies. *Journal of Abnormal Psychology*, 101, 139–52.

Cruise, C. E., Broderick, J., Porter, L., Kaell, A., and Stone, A. A. (1996). Reactive effects of diary assessment in chronic pain patients. *Pain*, 67, 253–8.

de Leeuw, J., and Kreft, I. (1986). Random coefficient models for multilevel analysis. *Journal of Educational Statistics*, 11, 57–85.

Engebrestson, T. O., and Stoney, C. M. (1995). Anger expression and lipid concentrations. *International Journal of Behavioral Medicine*, 2, 281–98.

Epstein, S. (1983). A research paradigm for the sutdy of personality and emotions. In M. Page (Ed.), *Personality – Current Theory and Research: 1982 Nebraska Symposium on Motivation* (pp. 91–154). Lincoln, NE: University of Nebraska Press.

Folkman, S., and Lazarus, R. S. (1980). An analysis of coping in a middle-aged community sample. *Journal of Health and Social Behavior*, 21, 219–39.

Freeman, L. J., Nixon, P. G., Sallabank, P. et al. (1987). Psychological stress and silent myocardial ischemia. *American Heart Journal*, 114, 447–82.

Friedman, R., Schwartz, J. E., Schnall, P. L. et al. (2001). Psychological variables in hypertension: Relationship to casual or ambulatory blood pressure in men. *Psychosomatic Medicine*, 63, 19–31.

Gabbay, F. H., Krantz, D. S., Kop, W. et al. (1996). Triggers of myocardial ischemia during daily life in patients with coronary artery disease: Physical and mental activities, anger, and smoking. *Journal of the American College of Cardiology*, 27, 585–92.

Gerin, W., Christenfeld, N., Pieper, C. et al. (1998). The generalizability of cardiovascular responses across settings. *Journal of Psychosomatic Research*, 44, 209–18.

Gerin, W., Pickering, T. G., Glynn, L. et al. (2000). An historical context for behavioral models of hypertension. *Journal of Psychosomatic Research*, 48, 369–77.

Gerin, W., Pieper, C., and Pickering, T. G. (1993). Measurement reliability of cardiovascular reactivity changes scores: A comparison of intermittent and continuous forms of assessment. *Journal of Psychosomatic Research*, 37, 493–501.

Goldstein, H. (1987). *Multilevel Models in Educational and Social Research*. New York: Oxford University Press.

Gordis, E. (1999). Alcohol and coronary heart disease. *Alcohol Alert, National Institute on Alcohol and Alcoholism*, No. 45.

Greeley, J., and Oei, T. (1999). Alcohol and tension reduction. In K. E. Leonard and H. T. Blane (Eds.), *Psychological Theories of Drinking and Alcoholism* (pp. 14–53). New York: Guilford Press.

Hazlett, R. (1992). Fibromyalgia: A time-series analysis of the stressor-physical symptom association. *Journal of Behavioral Medicine*, 15, 541–58.

Hedges, S., Jandorf, L., and Stone, A. A. (1985). Meaning of daily mood assessments. *Journal of Personality and Social Psychology*, 48, 428–34.

Helmers, K. F., Krantz, D. S., Merz, C. N. et al. (1995). Defensive hostility: Relationship to multiple markers of cardiac ischemia in patients with coronary disease. *Health Psychology*, 14, 202–9.

Henricksson, C. (1995). Living with continuous muscular pain: Patient perspectives. *Scandinavian Journal of Caring Sciences*, 9, 67–76.

Henricksson, C., Gundmark, I., Bengtsson, A., and Ek, A. (1992). Living with fibromyalgia: Consequences for daily life. *Clinical Journal of Pain*, 8, 138–44.

James, G. D., Schlussel, Y. R., and Pickering, T. G. (1993). The association between daily blood pressure and catecholamine variability in normotensive working women. *Psychosomatic Medicine*, 55, 55–60.

Jamner, L., Shapiro, D., and Alberts, J. (1998). Mood, blood pressure, and heart rate: Strategies for developing a more effective ambulatory mood diary. In D. S. Krantz and A. Baum (Eds.), *Technology and Methods in Behavioral Medicine* (pp. 195–220). Mahwah, NJ: Erlbaum.

Kamarck, T. W., Shiffman, S. M., Smithline, L. et al. (1998a). The diary of ambulatory behavioral states: A new approach to the assessment of psychosocial influences on ambulatory cardiovascular activity. In D. S. Krantz and A. Baum (Eds.), *Technology and Methods in Behavioral Medicine* (pp. 163–93). Mahwah, NJ: Erlbaum.

Kamarck, T. W., Shiffman, S. M., Smithline, L., Goodie, J. L., and Jong, J. (1998b). The effects of strain, social conflict, and emotional activation on ambulatory cardiovascular activity: Daily life consequences of "recurring stress" in a multiethnic sample. *Health Psychology*, 17, 1–13.

Karasek, R. A., Theorell, T., Schwartz, J. E., Schnall, P. L., Pieper, C. F., and Michela, J. L. (1988). Job characteristics in relation to the prevalence of myocardial infarction in the US Health Examination Survey (HES) and Health and Nutrition Examination Survey (HANES). *American Journal of Public Health*, 78, 910–19.

Karoly, P. (1991). Goal systems and health outcomes across the life span: A proposal. In H. E. Schroeder (Ed.), *New Directions in Health Psychology Assessment* (pp. 65–93). New York: Hemisphere.

Karoly, P. (1999). A goal systems-self-regulatory perspective on personality, psychopathology, and change. *Review of General Psychology*, 3, 264–91.

Karoly, P., and Jensen, M. (1987). *Multimethod Assessment of Chronic Pain*. New York: Pergamon.

Karoly, P., and Ruehlman, L. (1995). Goal cognition and its clinical implications: Development and preliminary validation of four motivational assessment instruments. *Assessment*, 2, 113–29.

Keefe, F., Affleck, G., Lefebvre, J., Starr, K., Caldwell, D., and Tennen, H. (1997). Pain coping strategies and coping efficacy in rheumatoid arthritis: A daily process analysis. *Pain*, 69, 35–42.

Keefe, F., Caldwell, D., Baucom, D. et al. (1996). Spouse-assisted coping skills training in the management of osteoarthritic knee pain. *Arthritis Care and Research*, 9, 279–91.

Kenny, D., Kashy, D., and Bolger, N. (1997). Data analysis in social psychology. In D. Gilbert, S. Fiske, and G. Linzey (Eds.), *Handbook of Social Psychology* (4th edn., pp. 233–65). New York: McGraw-Hill.

King, R., and Wilson, G. (1991). Use of a diary technique to investigate psychosomatic relations in atopic dermatitis. *Journal of Psychosomatic Research*, 35, 697–706.

Klatsky, A. L. (1994). Epidemiology of coronary heart disease: Influence of alcohol. *Alcohol: Clinical and Experimental Research*, 18, 88–96.

Kohler, T., and Haimerl, C. (1990). Daily stress as a trigger of migraine attacks: Results of thirteen single-subject studies. *Journal of Consulting and Clinical Psychology*, 58, 870–2.

Kop, W. J., Gottdiener, J. S., Patterson, S. M., and Krantz, D. S. (2000). Relationship between left ventricular mass and hemodynamic responses to physical and mental stress. *Journal of Psychosomatic Research*, 48, 79–88.

Krantz, D. S., Gabbay, F. H., Hedges, S. M., Leach, S. G., Gottdiener, J. S., and Rozanski, A. (1993). Mental and physical triggers of silent myocardial ischemia: Ambulatory studies using self-monitoring diary methodology. *Annals of Behavioral Medicine*, 15, 33–40.

Krantz, D. S., Kop, W. J., Santiago, H. T., and Gottdiener, J. S. (1996). Mental stress as a trigger of myocardial ischemia and infarction. *Cardiology Clinics*, 14, 271–87.

Krantz, D. S., Sheps, D. S., Carney, R. M., and Natelson, B. H. (2000). Effects of mental stress in patients with coronary artery disease. *Journal of the American Medical Association*, 283, 1800–2.

Laird, N., and Ware, J. (1982). Random-effects models for longitudinal data. *Biometrics*, 38, 963–74.

Landsbergis, P. A., Schnall, P. L., Warren, K., Pickering, T. G., and Schwartz, J. E. (1994). Association between ambulatory blood pressure and alternative formulations of job strain. *Scandinavian Journal of Work, Environment and Health*, 20, 349–63.

Larsen, R., and Kasimatis, M. (1991). Day-to day physical symptoms: Individual differences in the occurrence, duration, and emotional concomitants of minor daily illnesses. *Journal of Personality*, 59, 387–424.

Lefebvre, J., Keefe, F., Affleck, G. et al. (1999). The relationship of arthritis self-efficacy to daily pain, daily mood, and daily pain coping in Rheumatoid Arthritis patients. *Pain*, 80, 425–35.

Marco, C., Schwartz, J., Neale, J., Shiffman, S., Catley, D., and Stone, A. A. (2000). Impact of gender and having children in the household on ambulatory blood pressure in work and nonwork settings: A partial replication and new findings. *Annals of Behavioral Medicine*, 22, 110–15.

Matthews, K. A., Weiss, S. M., Detre, T. et al. (Eds.) (1986). *Handbook of Stress, Reactivity, and Cardiovascular Disease*. New York: Wiley.

Mohr, C. D., Armeli, S., Tennen, H., Carney, M. A., Affleck, G., and Hromi, A. (2001). Daily interpersonal experiences, context, and alcohol consumption: Crying in your beer and toasting good times. *Journal of Personality and Social Psychology*, 80, 489–500.

Neisser, U. (1991). A case of misplaced nostalgia. *American Psychologist*, 46, 34–6.

Nezlek, J. B. (2001). Multilevel random coefficient analyses of event- and interval-contingent data in social and personality psychology research. *Personality and Social Psychology Bulletin*, 27, 771–85.

Pickering, T. G. (1993). Applications of ambulatory blood pressure monitoring in behavioral medicine. *Annals of Behavioral Medicine*, 15, 26–32.

Pickering, T. G., and Gerin, W. (1990). Cardiovascular reactivity in the laboratory and the role of behavioral factors in hypertension: A critical review. *Annals of Behavioral Medicine*, 12, 3–16.

Porter, L. S., Marco, C. A., Schwartz, J. E., Neale, J. M., Shiffman, S., and Stone, A. A. (2000). Gender differences in coping: A comparison of trait and momentary assessments. *Journal of Social and Clinical Psychology*, 19, 480–98.

Porter, L. S., Stone, A. A., and Schwartz, J. E. (1999). Anger expression and ambulatory blood pressure: A comparison of state and trait measures. *Psychosomatic Medicine*, 61, 454–63.

Potter, P., and Zautra, A. (1997). Stressful life events' effects on rheumatoid arthritis disease activity. *Journal of Consulting and Clinical Psychology*, 65, 319–23.

Ptacek, J. T., Smith, R. E., Espe, K., and Raffety, B. (1994). Limited correspondence between daily coping reports and retrospective coping recall. *Psychological Assessment*, 6, 41–9.

Reis, H. T., and Wheeler, L. (1991). Studying social interaction with the Rochester Interaction Record. *Advances in Experimental Social Psychology*, 24, 269–317.

Robbins, A., Spence, J., and Clark, H. (1991). Psychological determinants of health and performance: The tangled web of desirable and undesirable characteristics. *Journal of Personality and Social Psychology*, 61, 755–65.

Ross, M. (1989). Relation of implicit theories to the construction of personal histories. *Psychological Review*, 96, 341–57.

Rothbaum, F., Weisz, J., and Snyder, S. (1982). Changing the world and changing the self: A two process model of perceived control. *Journal of Personality and Social Psychology*, 42, 5–37.

Ruehlman, L. S., and Karoly, P. (1991). With a little flak from my friends: Development and preliminary validation of the Test of Negative Social Exchange (TENSE). *Psychological Assessment*, 3, 97–104.

Scheier, M., and Carver, C. (1985). Optimism, coping, and health: assessment and implications of generalized outcome expectancies. *Health Psychology*, 4, 219–47.

Scheier, M., and Carver, C. (1992). Effects of optimism on psychological and physical well-being: Theoretical overview and empirical update. *Cognitive Therapy and Research*, 16, 201–28.

Schnall, P. L., Schwartz, J. E., Landsbergis, P. A., Warren, K., and Pickering, T. G. (1998). A longitudinal study of job strain and ambulatory blood pressure: Results from a three-year follow-up. *Psychosomatic Medicine*, 60, 697–706.

Schwartz, J. E., Neale, J. M., Marco, C. A., Shiffman, S., and Stone, A. A. (1999). Does trait coping exist? A momentary assessment approach to the evaluation of traits. *Journal of Personality and Social Psychology*, 77, 360–9.

Schwartz, J., and Stone, A. (1998). Strategies for analyzing ecological momentary assessment data. *Health Psychology*, 17, 6–16.

Shepperd, J., Maroto, J., and Pbert, L. (1996). Dispositional optimism as a predictor of health changes among cardiac patients. *Journal of Research in Personality*, 30, 517–34.

Shiffman, S. (2000). Real-time self-report of momentary states in the natural environment: computerized ecological momentary assessment. In A. A. Stone, J. S. Turkkan, C. A. Bachrach, J. B. Jobe, H. S. Kurtzman, and V. S. Cain (Eds.), *The Science of Self-report: Implicaitons for Research and Practice* (pp. 277–96). Mahwah, NJ: Lawrence Erlbaum Associates.

Shiffman, S., Fischer, L., Paty, J., Gnys, M., Hickcox, B. A., and Kassel, M. S. (1999). Drinking and smoking: A field study of their association. *Annals of Behavioral Medicine*, 16, 203–9.

Shiffman, S., and Stone, A. (1998). Introduction to the special section: Ecological momentary assessment in health psychology. *Health Psychology*, 17, 3–5.

Smith, R. E., Leffingwell, T. R., and Ptacek, J. T. (1999). Can people remember how they coped? Factors associated with discordance between same-day and retrospective reports. *Journal of Personality and Social Psychology*, 76, 1050–61.

Snijders, T., and Bosker, R. (1999). *Multilevel Analysis: An Introduction to Basic and Advanced Multilevel Modeling*. Thousand Oaks: Sage Publications.

Snyder, C., Harris, C., Anderson, J. et al. (1991). The will and the ways: Development and validation of an individual difference measure of hope. *Journal of Personality and Social Psychology*, 60, 570–85.

Stone, A. A., Lennox, S., and Neale, J. M. (1985). Daily coping and alcohol use in a sample of community adults. In S. Shiffman and T. A. Wills (Eds.), *Coping and Substance Use* (pp. 199–220). New York: Academic Press.

Stone, A., Reed, B., and Neale, J. (1987). Changes in daily event frequency precede episodes of physical symptoms. *Journal of Human Stress*, 13, 70–4.

Stone, A. A., Schwartz, J. E., Neale, J. M. et al. (1998). A comparison of coping assessed by ecological momentary assessment and retrospective recall. *Journal of Personality and Social Psychology*, 74, 1670–80.

Suls, J., Wan, C., and Blanchard, E. (1994). A multilevel data-analytic approach for evaluation of relationships between daily life stressors and symptomatology: Patients with irritable bowel syndrome. *Health Psychology*, 13, 103–13.

Suls, J., Wan, C. K., and Costa, P. T. (1995). Relationship of trait anger to resting blood pressure: A meta-analysis. *Health Psychology*, 14, 444–56.

Swendsen, J., Tennen, H., Carney, M. A., Affleck, G., Willard, A., and Hromi, A. (2000). Mood and alcohol consumption: An experience sampling test of the self-medication hypothesis. *Journal of Abnormal Psychology*, 109, 198–204.

Tennen, H., and Affleck, G. (1996). Daily processes in coping with chronic pain: Methods and analytic strategies. In M. Zeidner and N. Endler (Eds.), *Handbook of Coping* (pp. 151–80). New York: Wiley.

Tennen, H., and Affleck, G. (2000). The perception of personal control: Sufficiently important to warrant careful scrutiny. *Personality and Social Psychology Bulletin*, 26, 152–6.

Tennen, H., Affleck, G., Armeli, S., and Carney, M. (2000). A daily process approach to coping: Linking theory, research, and practice. *American Psychologist*, 55, 626–36.

Tennen, H., Affleck, G., Urrows, S., Higgins, P., and Mendola, R. (1992). Perceiving control, construing benefits, and daily processes in rheumatoid arthritis. *Canadian Journal of Behavioral Science*, 24, 186–203.

Tennen, H., Suls, J., and Affleck, G. (1991). Personality and daily experience: The promise and the challenge. *Journal of Personality*, 59, 313–38.

von Baeyer, C. (1994). Reactive effects of measurement of pain. *The Clinical Journal of Pain*, 10, 18–21.

Waite, B. M., Claffey, R., and Hillbrand, M. (1998). Differences between volunteers and nonvolunteers in a high demand self-recording study. *Psychological Reports*, 83, 199–210.

West, S. G., and Hepworth, J. T. (1991). Statistical issues in the study of temporal data: Daily experiences. *Journal of Personality*, 59, 609–62.

Wheeler, L. and Reis, H. T. (1991). Self-recording of everyday life events: Origins, types, and uses. *Journal of Personality*, 59, 339–54.

CHAPTER 19

Scenes from a Marriage: Examining Support, Coping, and Gender within the Context of Chronic Illness

Tracey A. Revenson

The Graduate Center of the City University of New York

Introduction

The past quarter century of stress and coping research has produced a wealth of studies examining how individuals cope with stressful events, the predictors and correlates of coping behavior, and the relation of coping to physical and mental health outcomes. Terminology such as "emotion-focused coping" and "threat appraisals" has become part of any serious coping researchers' lexicon. As a graduate student, I entered "coping" into one of the Library of Congress' new computer search systems. Nearly a hundred titles appeared on the terminal, including "Coping with your leaky roof." Twenty years later, a search on *PsychLit* produced an output of over a thousand studies. However, most focused almost exclusively on the coping efforts of *individuals*. Relatively few investigated how family members cope with the stressors they face *as a couple* or *as a family*, or how the coping efforts of family members mutually influence each other, for better or for worse. As many chronic stressors and life strains involve the whole family – if not the neighborhood, community and school – it is time to extend the study of stress, coping, and adaptation beyond the individual level of analysis.

When one family member is experiencing ongoing complex stressors or life strains, other members of the family are affected as well – by the stressor itself, by its psychological impact on the affected individual, and by its cumulative effect on family functioning. An essential step towards clarifying the relationship between coping and health involves examining coping as it naturally occurs within the context of significant, intimate relationships. This often results in complex analyses involving direct, indirect, and reciprocal effects – analyses that are necessary for understanding adaptational processes and not simply outcomes.

The chronic illness of one member of a married couple provides a good opportunity for exploring the intersection of naturalistic dyadic coping processes and gender.[1] Chronic illness can be conceptualized as a chronic stressor (Lepore, 1997) or chronic strain (Pearlin, 1989). It is not a transient event but a life circumstance involving a series of interrelated life strains – some of which can be addressed by individual or family coping efforts and others that are outside of the realm of personal control.

In this chapter I present a framework for studying married couples' coping, summarize some of my colleagues' work that has spurred my own, and present some of my own work. I weave two questions throughout the chapter that are central to understanding marital coping processes: first, how does context – specifically, the interpersonal, medical, and temporal contexts – affect couples' patterns of coping with chronic illness? Second, how does gender fit into the equation? Is the experience of living with a chronically ill spouse the same for men and women?

Coping with Chronic Illness

Mirroring the zeitgeist of the time, my own study of coping started out at the individual level of analysis. After thrashing around my first year of graduate school, I was lucky enough to become involved in a longitudinal study of coping and adaptation to chronic illness in middle and late life. The research project was designed by my mentor, Barbara J. Felton, who understood that physical illness was a, if not *the*, major life strain confronting older people. Theories in social gerontology suggested that illness, disability, and health declines affect older people's psychological well-being and those cognitive and behavioral coping efforts should mediate this connection (see, for example, Felton and Revenson, 1989). Moreover, as different illness conditions pose different degrees of life threat, controllability, uncertainty, and intrusiveness into daily life, we included context in the study by comparing four different chronic conditions: hypertension, diabetes, systemic blood cancers, and rheumatoid arthritis.

Until the late 1970s, coping was viewed largely as a dispositional construct (e.g., Haan, 1977). Richard Lazarus challenged that with his stress and coping paradigm (Lazarus, 1981; Lazarus and Launier, 1978; Lazarus and Folkman, 1984), which brought together two ideas: first, that individuals' experience of stress is dependent on their cognitive and affective appraisals of the event, and second, that coping was shaped by both personal resources (or dispositions) and situational determinants. The Berkeley Stress and Coping Project had developed the Ways of Coping scale (Lazarus and Cohen, 1977) to test this paradigm, and we added this new measure to our battery of more dispositional coping measures. In several papers we presented empirical evidence that coping efforts did affect individual adjustment, that coping affected mental health outcomes more strongly than the reverse causal possibility, and that personal and situational factors such as age, level of disability, the nature of the illness, and social support also affected coping processes (e.g., Felton and Revenson, 1984; 1987; Felton et al., 1984; Revenson et al., 1983).

In our attempts to be sensitive to respondents' health status, the study interviews took place in kitchens, living rooms, and diners across the five boroughs of New York City. Often, the patient's husband or wife would ask, "What about me? Don't you want to know how *I* feel about the illness? Aren't you going to talk to me, too?" Being a dutiful graduate student and novice researcher, I adhered to the study's protocol, banning the partner to the den for fear of contaminating the patient's responses. However, I often stayed an extra hour once the formal interview was completed, to talk with the spouse, pretend to record the information, and even ask a few of the study's questions. And as any good researcher knows, the most interesting material occurs after the interview is formally over. It was these conversations over coffee and cookies (and in one case, figs picked from a backyard tree in Brooklyn) that fueled my interest in how illness affects the patient, the spouse, *and* the marital relationship. At the same time, an article by Wortman and Dunkel-Schetter (1979) piqued my interest further by laying forth their theory of the possible "negative" effects of social support – that, unintentionally, family members may not be able to provide needed support because the relative's cancer creates a sense of personal threat or discomfort.

It seemed that the spouses[2] of people with chronic illness were caught between a rock and a hard place. Marriage is a primary relationship because it is (hopefully) long term, affords a central role identity, and provides a fundamental resource of social support. Husbands and wives of chronically ill persons experience unique stressors. Some emanate directly from caregiving, where spouses are inextricably involved in decision-making about treatment and day-to-day care. Other stresses emerge from the need to restructure family roles and responsibilities as the disease progresses or presents new challenges. Still other stresses are filtered through the lens of the patient's experience, as in the case of a spouse feeling helpless at seeing her or his partner in pain (Revenson and Majerovitz, 1990). There are also societal or normative expectations that the healthy spouse care for his or her ill partner. In fact, the provision of support may be conceptualized as a stressor for the spouse in its own right, particularly when, as in the case of chronic illness, it is a lifelong task.

One central aspect of couples' coping involves the transaction of social support (Burman and Margolin, 1992; Cutrona, 1996). Thoits (1986) refers to support as coping assistance and Bodenmann (1997) as supportive dyadic coping. Spouses provide love and affection, especially the assurance that the patient is loved despite any adverse changes that illness has wrought on the physical body, personality, or quality of the marriage. They provide tangible assistance with day-to-day responsibilities and special needs created by treatment, validate their partners' emotions or coping choices, and help their partners reappraise the meaning of the illness. Spouses share the existential and practical concerns about how the illness may affect the marriage and family in the future. They provide continuity and security in a life disrupted by the physical indications and emotional meanings of illness.

Thus, spouses occupy a dual role in the coping process: as primary provider of support to the ill partner, helping her or him to cope, and as a family member who needs support in coping with the illness-related stressors she or he is experiencing. Role conflict is likely to occur, and the amount of support the spouse is able to provide may be limited by the stressors she or he is facing.

Examining Marital Coping within an Ecological Framework

Since that early research, I have advocated that coping with chronic illness can be studied best within an ecological or contextual perspective. A plea for including context has a long history in psychology from Lewin (1943/1997) and Murray (1938) to Mischel (1968) and Bronfenbrenner (1977; 1986). Within the stress context, it continues with vigor in the work of Bradbury (Bradbury and Fincham, 1991; Pasch et al., 1997), Coyne (Coyne and Fiske, 1992; Lyons et al., 1998); DeLongis (O'Brien and DeLongis, 1997), Hobfoll (1989); Lepore, (1997); Repetti (Repetti et al., 2002; Repetti and Wood, 1997), and T. W. Smith (Brown and Smith, 1992; Smith, 1995).

My perspective (Revenson, 1990; see also Anderson and McNeilly, 1991; Ickovics et al., 2001) views psychosocial adaptation as a function of the ecological niche that the person, or in this case the couple, occupies. The ecological niche involves several interdependent and overlapping systems, which I have labeled the sociocultural, interpersonal, situational, and temporal contexts (see Figure 19.1). This ecological or contextual approach serves as a framework that exposes the interconnections among factors that influence couples' coping.

The *sociocultural context* includes molar variables such as age, gender, socioeconomic status, and educational level. These demographic markers may be proxy variables denoting health-promoting or health-damaging psychological processes (Matthews, 1989) or may serve as moderators of the relationship between stress and coping; they also may reflect the coping resources available to the couple. Culture also may define the acceptability of particular coping responses: for example, the acceptability of emotional expression as an adaptive mechanism varies widely.

The *interpersonal context* represents both the marital relationship itself as well as interpersonal relationships that connect with either partner or the couple as a unit. Although most researchers focus on one aspect of the interpersonal context – naturally occurring support systems (i.e., family and friends) – interpersonal aspects of the health care environment, such as the patient-physician relationship, also may affect coping and adaptation. Because my focus is on the couple as a unit, the interpersonal context includes aspects of the relationship that existed before the diagnosis as well as those that have emerged as a consequence of the illness.

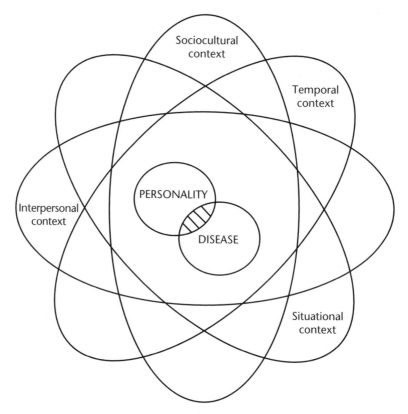

Figure 19.1 An ecological framework for studying personality-disease relationships. Reprinted from T. A. Revenson (1990). *All other things are not equal: An ecological perspective on the relation between personality and disease*. In H. S. Friedman (Ed.), *Personality and Disease* (pp. 65–94). Copyright © 1990 John Wiley & Sons. Reprinted by permission of John Wiley & Sons, Inc.

The *situational context* encompasses those aspects of the proximal environment that create or alleviate stress. It includes both the specific stressors that a particular illness presents (such as pain, disability, or life-threat) as well as other major and minor stressors that couples confront as they live with the illness. For example, unemployment may affect the ability to pay for medical treatment; at the same time, disability may affect employment status.

The *temporal context* can be conceptualized in a number of ways and, in my opinion, is the most understudied in research. It encompasses both the timing of illness within the individual's life and the progression (or "life") of the illness. Life transitions or unexpected events that occur "off-time" in the "normative" life cycle are likely to be perceived as more stressful than those that are experienced "on-time" (Neugarten, 1979), particularly if they occur prematurely, leaving the individual no time for anticipatory coping or planning. With off-time events, relatively few age peers are simultaneously experiencing the same life situation.

Similarly, disease staging and progression of illness provide clues as to what coping tasks are most salient. A newly diagnosed breast cancer patient may be dealing with the meaning of the illness, recovery from surgery, and weekly radiation therapy; two years later she may have no physical symptoms but be dealing with the uncertainty and threat of recurrence. A slower disease progression (for example, a slower-growing tumor) may allow a gradual and smoother adaptation, as people cope with their illness in smaller bites and as anticipatory coping efforts are made for future problems. A disease course marked with frequent transitions from health to illness – sometimes without warning – may prove a harder road to follow. This suggests that individual coping efforts must accommodate to rapidly changing illness demands.

Three aspects of this contextual perspective are worth noting with regard to couples' coping. First, a couple constitutes a social system in itself, but also exists within a number of interdependent social systems. In thinking about a contextual model of marital coping with illness, the interpersonal context might be thought of as forming the larger structure under which all other contextual systems fall.

Second, an ecological approach addresses the reciprocal relationships between individuals and the social systems with which they interact. The fundamental characteristic of a marital relationship is *behavioral interdependence* – that is, each person's overt behavior affects the overt behavior and subjective perceptions of the other. However, any relationship that endures long enough to allow both partners to form attitudes and beliefs about each other and about the relationship (as most marriages do) also can be viewed as exhibiting *psychological interdependence* (Huston and Robins, 1982). Psychological interdependence indicates that attitudes, beliefs, and behavior are the result, at least in part, of the interactions between the spouses.

The coping process involves transactions between two individuals (husband and wife) or between a couple and a social system (for example, the extended family or the health care system). The psychosocial effects of illness extend in a ripple effect: each family member's reaction to illness and coping responses reverberate throughout the whole family and back again. Thus, in examining coping at the marital level, researchers must look not only at the reaction of one spouse to the other's coping behavior, but at how each spouse directly or covertly influences the other spouse's cognitions, emotions, and actions. For example, it is not enough to know that the one partner was trying to be supportive; it is also critical to know whether that support was perceived as helpful by the recipient (Lanza et al., 1995).

Third, variables beyond the level of the individual are critical to understanding an ecological perspective. Individual coping choices do more than affect both partners individually – they affect the marital relationship. Admittedly, it is conceptually and methodologically difficult to untangle the effects of the illness on each spouse from the effects of illness on the marriage. Methodologically, this can be done in a number of ways: collecting parallel data from both spouses and examining fit or congruence, or asking each spouse about marital-level variables.

Translating from the individual to the marital level, each coping task that patients confront has a counterpart in marital functioning. The medical uncertainty about prognosis and disease progression is mirrored in uncertainty about the future functioning of the marriage and the family. What will happen to daily life if the ill spouse becomes severely disabled? Which family activities may be sacrificed in order to accommodate a demanding treatment regimen or its effects? Even small chores or events, such as doing laundry or going to a cocktail party, may become transformed into chronic strains that overshadow other aspects of family life. As Pearlin has written, "disruptive events acquire much of their stressful character not by their own *direct* impact but by disrupting and dislocating the more structured elements of peoples' lives" (Pearlin and Turner, 1987: 148; see also Pearlin, 1991; Pearlin et al., 1981).

Spouses may be forced to take on new or additional responsibilities when the patient becomes physically disabled. Further, these changes in role responsibilities may lie outside traditional gender roles. For example, when married women are afflicted with disabling illnesses such as rheumatoid arthritis or multiple sclerosis, husbands need to take on a greater share of household chores and childcare. Similarly, some wives of men whose employment is terminated by disability find that they need to work outside the home.

Although I have focused so far on the negative consequences of chronic illness on marriage, there are positive aspects as well, and as researchers, it is important to study them. While some patients and spouses report that the illness has a negative effect on family life, others report that it brought them closer together (Schmaling and Sher, 2000). Illness narratives and personal stories are replete with examples of personal growth, of how people changed their lives with the onset of illness. Some studies have documented that strong marriages become stronger and weak marriages deteriorate, but others have found that close families can become severely strained and less enmeshed families are able to adapt with less effort (Patterson and Garwick, 1994).

This leads to the conclusion that illness should be conceptualized at the familial-, or in this case marital-, level of analysis, and the research questions must begin to focus on the contextual influences that enhance or inhibit a couples' coping efforts. The question becomes not *whether* coping works, but *when, for whom, and under what circumstances* certain coping efforts promote adaptation. Rosnow and Rosenthal (1989: 1280) have noted that "there is a growing awareness in psychology that just about everything under the sun is context dependent in one way or another", but I believe that this statement diminishes the importance of context: to understand adaptation to adversity, we must treat coping as a process that *unfolds in particular relationships and within specific sociocultural, interpersonal, situational, and temporal contexts.*

Couples' Coping with Rheumatic Disease

With that as prologue, I now address some of these marital-level coping issues with data from a study of couples' coping with rheumatic disease. Rheumatic diseases, such as rheumatoid arthritis, are chronic auto-immune disorders which pose no immediate life threat but create a complex set of illness-related stressors, including severe and often unpredictable pain, joint swelling and stiffness, physical disability, and uncertainty about disease progression (Newman et al., 1996). The symptoms and progression of rheumatic diseases are manageable, but not curable by current medical treatment. Persons with rheumatic disease must adjust their lifestyle to accommodate frequent medical care, ongoing pain and stiffness in joints, unpredictable symptom flares, and increasing physical disability. The rheumatic diseases occur 3–4 times as often among women as men, creating an interesting context in which to study the role of gender in coping (Revenson and Danoff-Burg, 2000).

The findings of the multiple disease coping study described previously and of a longitudinal study of women with rheumatoid arthritis which I conducted with Kathleen Schiaffino (Revenson et al., 1991; Schiaffino and Revenson, 1992; 1995a; 1995b; Schiaffino et al., 1991) provided information about the range of coping strategies used and their effects on psychological adjustment. At the same time, I felt that I didn't have a grasp on the specific issues faced by the spouses of these individuals.

As a first step, Deborah Majerovitz and I interviewed the husbands of the 63 married patients in the Revenson and Schiaffino study, asking them to reflect on how the illness had affected not only their well-being, but also their marriage (Revenson and Majerovitz, 1990).

The five most frequently reported stressors involved the husbands' emotional reactions to the way that illness had affected their wives, themselves, and the marital relationship: Seeing their wife in pain and feeling helpless to do anything about it; frustration with their wife's physical limitations and the impact the disability had on daily life; reductions in shared pleasurable activities, including socializing, recreational activities, and sex; watching their wife become more depressed; and worries regarding their wife's future health and how the marriage would be affected.

We also found that social support from the spouse affected the ill wife's adjustment. Husbands provided more support to wives who were in greater pain or were more depressed (Revenson and Majerovitz, 1991). Thus, husbands weren't driven away by the emotional needs of their wives, but appeared to be responsive to them. However, the effectiveness of spousal support was moderated by how the wife appraised her illness: for wives who viewed their illness as uncontrollable and severe, spousal support was linked to increased depression; in contrast, for wives who felt they could handle their illness, spousal support was linked to lower depression (Schiaffino et al., 1995). One thing was clear: living with a spouse with rheumatic disease creates a life situation of ongoing concerns that affect social and sexual interactions between husband and wife (Majerovitz and Revenson, 1994; Revenson and Gibofsky, 1995).

Our next step could have been to examine how one partner's coping affected the other's well-being. But a more intriguing and pressing theoretical question seemed to be that of dyadic coping – looking at the couple's coping patterns *as a unit*.

Conceptual Models of Marital-level Coping

In the past decade, a number of studies have examined couples' coping with illness at the dyadic level of analysis. This research has studied heart disease (Coyne and Smith, 1991; Coyne et al., 2001; Lyons et al., 1998; Michaela, 1987; Rankin-Esquer et al. (2000); Rohrbaugh et al., 2002; Suls et al., 1997), end-stage renal disease (Gray et al., 1985), infertility (Berghuis and Stanton, 2002; Levin et al., 1997; Pasch and Christensen, 2000); rheumatoid arthritis (Bermas et al., 2000; Danoff-Burg and Revenson, 2000; Manne and Zautra, 1989; 1990; Revenson, 1994; 1995; Tucker et al., 1999) and cancer (Baider et al., 1998; Hagedoorn et al., 2000; Halford et al., 2000; Manne et al., 1999; Northouse et al., 1995; Pistrang and Barker, 1995), as well as other health conditions (Schmaling and Sher, 2000). These studies can be characterized by three different approaches to couples' coping: relationship-focused coping; mutual influence; and coping congruence ("fit"). All three approaches can be applied to couples confronting a health-related stressor, all integrate elements of family systems theory, and all require the researcher to obtain data from both husbands and wives. No one approach is more "correct" than others, and some studies use more than one approach.

Relationship-focused Coping

An exciting approach to couples' coping focuses on maintaining the quality of the marital relationship as a focus of coping (Coyne and Fiske, 1992; DeLongis and O'Brien, 1990; Lyons et al., 1998; O'Brien and DeLongis, 1996; 1997). This approach extends the individualistic stress and coping paradigm to dyadic-level coping and also considers coping within the interpersonal context of the health care system.

Within the stress and coping paradigm (Lazarus, 1981; 1999; Lazarus and Folkman, 1984; Lazarus and Launier, 1978), coping strategies have been described as serving problem and emotion-focused functions. In the former, coping efforts are aimed at managing or eliminating the source of stress; in the latter, coping is directed toward managing the emotional distress that arises from stress appraisals. Supportive relationships are conceptualized primarily as available resources that can aid the individual's coping in a number of ways – by providing information about coping options, feedback validating or criticizing the individual's coping choices, instrumental assistance in carrying out the coping actions, or emotional sustenance to help sustain coping efforts. As such, social support has been conceptualized as coping assistance (Thoits, 1986).

This reformulation of the stress and coping paradigm adds a third and possibly superordinate coping function: *relationship-focused coping*. Relationship-focused coping involves attending to the other partner's emotional needs while maintaining the integrity of the marital relationship, and managing one's own stress without creating upset or problems for others. It involves a balance between self and other, with the goal of maintaining the integrity of the marital relationship above either partner's needs. Relationship-focused coping modes include negotiating or compromising with others, considering the other person's situation, and being empathic (DeLongis and O'Brien, 1990).

A couple of studies have examined relationship-focused among couples in which the husband had experienced a myocardial infarction (Coyne and Smith, 1991; Suls et al., 1997). Both focused on a particular relationship-focused coping strategy, *protective buffering*, that involves "hiding concerns, denying worries, and yielding to the partner to avoid disagreements" (Coyne and Smith, 1991: 405). Although protective buffering is ostensibly used to avoid disagreements and "protect" the relationship, it appears to exact psychological costs for the person using it, in terms of increased psychological distress. Thus, wives' coping efforts to shield husbands from stress in the post-MI period may have contributed to their own distress (Coyne and Smith, 1991), as did husbands' efforts to protect their wives (Suls et al., 1997). Perhaps this happens because the partner using protective buffering feels constrained to express negative emotions or worries to the other person (cf., Lepore's idea of social constraints, 1997). However, protective buffering does not appear to harm the spouse, that is, the person being "protected" (Suls et al., 1997). Thus, relationship-focused coping may require a tradeoff between protecting one's own well-being and one's partner's.

Mutual Influence Models

Mutual influence models do not specify a particular function of coping, but focus on the effects of one partner's coping on the other partner's coping and adjustment (e.g., Manne and Zautra, 1990). A recent study by Berghuis and Stanton (2002) of adjustment to infertility provides a nice illustration, in that it attempts to untangle three possible mechanisms through which each partner's coping influences her or his adjustment as well as the other partner's adjustment. The first mechanism is essentially an additive, or separate influence model: each person's adjustment is independently affected by her or his coping and her or his spouse's coping. The two other mechanisms are interaction models in which the relation between one partner's coping and her or his adjustment is tempered by what the other person is (or is not) doing. One version of this model posits that if partners use similar coping strategies then adjustment would be greater. The other version suggests that one partner's use of an effective strategy might predominate, either nudging the other partner's coping in the same direction or "canceling out" the effects of the partner's less effective strategies.

These models were tested in a prospective study of couples seeking treatment for infertility (Berghuis and Stanton, 2002). Husbands and wives completed measures of coping, depression, and marital satisfaction prior to participating in a medical procedure (artificial insemination by the husband) and after receiving a negative pregnancy test result. All three models were supported to some extent with regard to coping through emotional approach, a coping mode that involves both emotional processing and emotional expression. The relationship between women's use of emotional approach coping and depression was a function of their husbands' use of that same strategy. If women coped primarily through emotional approach, their husbands' use of that strategy was less influential on (the woman's) level of depression. In contrast, if women used very little emotional approach coping, their husbands' coping through emotional approach coping was more strongly related to the woman's depression level.

Conversely, if husbands engaged in emotional approach coping – while the wives did *not* – the women had relatively low depression scores. But if husbands also did not use this strategy – that is both members of the couple coped very little through emotional approach, women were more depressed after the failed insemination attempt. This pattern of findings suggests a *compensatory coping* model, in which one person in the family has to use an effective coping strategy (effective, that is, relative to the target stressor).

Coping Congruence

Conceptualizing couples' coping in terms of congruence is drawn from person-environment fit theory (French et al., 1974) and family systems theories (e.g., Patterson and Garwick, 1984). Within family system theories, stressors such as illness are seen as exerting a disorganizing influence on the family, which then requires a reorganization effort. Couples' coping involves these reorganization efforts, to maximize congruence or "fit" between the partners' coping styles, in order to cope most effectively as a couple. Strategies that work in direct opposition or cancel each other out are incongruent and would lead to worse psychosocial outcomes.

Congruence, however, can involve either similarity or complementarity of coping styles. If spouses use similar coping strategies it might be easier to contend with stress: coping efforts are coordinated and mutually reinforcing – that is, one partner's efforts will not impede the other's. At the same time, complementary coping styles can be congruent when they work in concert to reach a desired goal, either enhancing the other person's strategy or filling a coping "gap." In fact, complementary strategies may be more effective than when husband and wife use identical strategies because the couple, as a unit, would have a broader coping repertoire. Dissimilar strategies would be seen as non-congruent if one partner's coping efforts undermined the other partner's or effectively "cancelled them out."

On with the Dance: Couples' Coping with Rheumatic Disease

To illustrate coping congruence theory, as well as to address questions of gender, context, and the confluence of coping and social support provision, I will use data from my own study of 113 heterosexual married couples with rheumatic disease. This study was designed with the goals of describing the dyadic coping strategies of couples faced with a chronic physical illness and those aspects of the medical, interpersonal, and temporal contexts that are associated with those coping efforts. We looked at how partners support each other in their coping efforts, and how dyadic or marital coping was associated with psychological adjustment. Three central questions undergirded the study: (1) Was the congruence (or similarity) of partners' coping efforts more important than which strategies were used?; (2) How did the couples' current life context influence current coping efforts?; and (3) How did gender play out in couples' coping processes, particularly in the provision of emotional and tangible support?

The primary measure of coping was the Revised Ways of Coping (WOC-II) Scale (Folkman et al., 1986), a 66-item self-report measure that contains a broad range of cognitive and behavioral strategies that husbands and wives completed independently. Rather than assessing coping with response to a self-named stressor or assessing global, dispositional coping styles, we made the scale situation-specific by eliciting coping responses in response to "your illness" (for the patient) or "your partner's illness" (for the spouse). Although most studies have adopted the factor structures found with samples of healthy, young adult married couples and older couples (Folkman et al., 1986), we found these structures did not fit our data, and conducted our own factor analysis, producing a seven-factor solution that included a broad range of strategies. A brief description of the strategies follows.[3]

Positive Problem-solving is an instrumental coping strategy with an optimistic tone. It includes items involving forward-looking problem-focused cognitions and behaviors, such as planning for action, and reappraising the illness as a time of personal growth. *Escape into Fantasy*, a cognitive avoidance strategy, describes a more passive coping style of wishing that things had happened differently and imagining a better life situation. *Distancing* describes efforts to minimize or avoid the threat and detach oneself from the emotional distress caused by the illness. *Rational Thinking* reflects a calm, collected approach to managing the stressful situation. *Seeking Support* involves actions to mobilize social resources for reassurance and confirmation. *Passive Acceptance* includes a number of non-actions that may not make things better, but prevent the situation from becoming worse. This strategy reflects the coping mode of "inhibition of action" that Lazarus (1981) described in his original paradigm, but which has seldom been included in coping measures. *Finding Blame* describes expressions of anger toward a person or circumstances responsible for the stresses of illness.

Theme and Variations: Descriptions of Couples' Coping

Cluster analysis was used to describe dyadic processes of coping and test the notion of congruence by analyzing the similarity and differences in spouses' coping efforts. The couple was the unit of analysis, with the wife and husband's scores on each of the seven coping strategies linked under a single identification

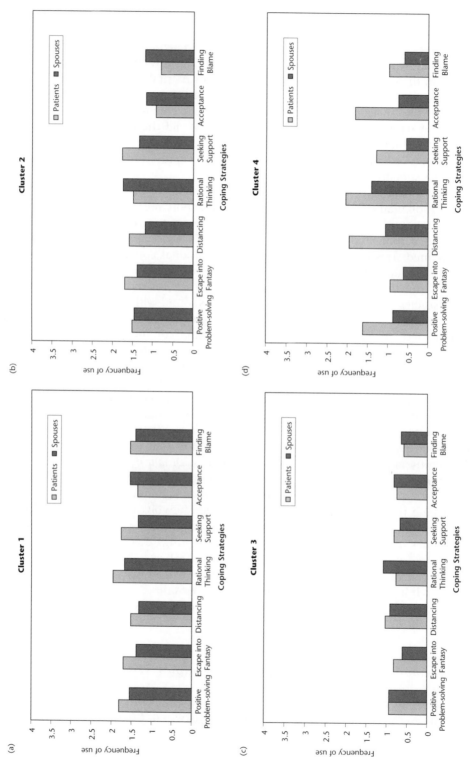

Figure 19.2 Couples cluster profiles.

number. Thus the cluster analysis grouped *couples* – not individuals – with respect to their patterns of coping. The cluster profiles in Figure 19.2a–d provide information about couples' coping. From these profiles we can glean information about the types of coping strategies used by couples in a particular cluster, the degree to which each strategy was used (mean score), whether any strategy or strategies are predominant, and whether husbands' and wives' coping styles are similar or dissimilar. Most importantly, cluster analysis – though primarily a descriptive strategy – is able to portray complex patterns among a set of coping strategies rather than examining them independently (see also Danoff-Burg et al., 2000).

A fairly high level of congruence in their coping characterizes couples in Cluster 1 (Figure 19.2a), although patients used slightly more of each strategy than their healthy spouses. These couples are using a number of coping strategies to a fairly high degree, particularly Positive Problem-solving and Rational Thinking. Thus, the couples in this cluster could be characterized as effortful partnerships, that is, both partners are coping actively with the illness and using some of the same strategies.

Couples who were grouped in Cluster 2 (Figure 19.2b) show a moderate degree of congruence in their coping, particularly with respect to the strategies of Positive Problem-solving and Rational Thinking. Patients and healthy spouses differed, however, in the intensity with which they used other strategies. Patients used the strategies of Escape into Fantasy and Finding Blame to a greater degree than did their spouses, and Distancing to a lesser degree.

In Cluster 3 (Figure 19.2c), there was again a high degree of congruence but, in this case, the congruence was in the degree of coping (of any kind) and not in the type of strategies used. Both partners did fairly little coping of any kind, and no single strategy or strategies predominated.

Cluster 4 (Figure 19.2d) included those couples whose coping efforts were most dissimilar. Patients used a combination of Distancing, Rational Thinking, and Passive Acceptance, and tended not to use the strategies of Escape into Fantasy or Finding Blame. In contrast, their healthy spouses exerted fewer coping efforts across the board, although they used Rational Thinking to a moderate degree. In this cluster, spouses differ in both intensity and content of their coping.

Thus, the cluster analysis suggests that there are patterns of coping depicted by the use of multiple coping strategies, or even coping modes, and that by combining husbands' and wives' scores one can get a picture of the similarity or dissimilarity of their coping efforts.

Contextual Correlates of Coping

These cluster profiles provide a description of couples' coping patterns, but leave unanswered many questions of determinants and outcomes: what contextual factors are linked to particular coping profiles? To examine context I drew on my theoretical model (see Figure 19.1) of the sociocultural, interpersonal, situational, and temporal contexts. The situational context was conceptualized in two domains – the medical context (e.g., illness severity and functional disability) and the stress context (e.g., other stressful events and chronic strains, caregiver burden, depression). The temporal context was operationalized not only as the length of illness and disease stage, but also as whether the illness had been diagnosed before or after the couple was married.

Coping cluster differences were found in some contexts but not others. There were no differences between the four coping clusters in any of the social support measures, including the amounts of positive and problematic (negative) social support received from or provided to the partner (or, in parallel measures, the close social network). Nor were there differences among coping clusters on more evaluative dimensions such as satisfaction with support received.

The medical context – pain, disease severity, disease activity, or disability – was not related to a couples' membership in any particular coping cluster. There was, however, a consistent and meaningful pattern of cluster differences in the stress content, that is, the couples' *subjective* experience of the illness. Couples in Cluster 1 – the one in which couples were doing a good deal of coping and using a lot of active, problem-focused strategies – stood apart from the other three clusters in a number of meaningful ways. Patients in this cluster had greater levels of depressive symptoms than patients in any of the other three clusters, with half having scores indicative of clinical depression. Spouses in this cluster perceived a much greater degree of stress in their lives – specifically interpersonal stress with family and friends and ways in which the partner's illness intruded into their daily lives. Cluster 1 spouses also reported a higher degree of caregiver burden than spouses in two of the other three clusters. Within the sociocultural context, Cluster 1 couples were slightly younger, married for a shorter length of time, and the least affluent.

What did this signify about the influence of context on couples coping? I have described social support processes among couples facing chronic illness as a tango, a stylized "dance" in which partners must coordinate the offering and receipt of help in a fluid way that recognized the emotional context surrounding the transaction (Revenson, 1993; 1995; Revenson et al., 1991). But, as my colleague Suzanne Ouellette pointed out to me, not all couples tango so elegantly. The cluster analyses and the way that context influences coping patterns suggest that there are a number of ways of "dancing" to the beat of chronic stress.

Patients in Cluster 1 were more distressed than patients in any other cluster and their spouses felt a greater degree of stress was placed on them by virtue of living with an ill partner. If we were to adopt a traditional stress and coping model, we might conclude that the problem-focused efforts of these couples may have not been able to manage the ongoing burdens of pain and increasing disability, and that the efforts by these couples to improve their situation may have left them feeling worse. Perceiving the ineffectiveness of their coping efforts, they may have tried many different types of coping strategies, also without success (Aldwin and Revenson, 1987). Either the indiscriminate use of every strategy within their repertoire led to poorer adaptive outcomes, or emotional distress led these couples to try every coping strategy they could think of in an attempt to manage that distress.

An alternative interpretation would be that the wide range of coping strategies reflects flexibility in coping. These couples' coping efforts may not have minimized distress, but gave them hope because they were actively doing *something*. More importantly, they were doing *it as a team* – they tangoed, even if it wasn't an elegantly executed tango. And, although the base rate of seeking counseling was low within the full sample (approximately 23 percent of patients and 19 percent of spouses), the majority of these individuals tended to be in Cluster 1. It is possible that Cluster 1 couples may have been at the stage of confronting the meaning of the illness, which may have (temporarily) heightened their emotional distress, but we know little about their long-term outcomes.

One other finding suggests yet another interpretation of the data. Patients and spouses in Cluster 1 had higher scores on a measure of personal growth developed to assess the positive outcomes of illness (Felton and Revenson, 1984). Thus, despite their distress, these actively coping couples were able to reappraise their illness in a more positive light and could see benefits from their struggle. Dyadic, contextual coping analyses may reveal a resilience that may not be apparent from approaches that examine the effect of individual-level coping strategies on individual-level outcome measures.

Cluster 4 showed the most dissimilarity between wives and husbands. Patients were actively coping with their illness, but their partners were reporting few coping efforts overall. These couples were the oldest in the sample and had been coping with the illness for the longest time. And, in most cases, the illness had been diagnosed after they had been married for some time. This suggests that, over time, the couples had developed styles of coping that were independent yet complementary. And, in all likelihood, their coping has become more effortless, part of the way they habitually interact. This finding was not altogether surprising: in close relationships, we see a certain degree of synchrony or orchestration that takes place as each person seeks to cope with a common stressor or when one spouse attempts to support the other's coping (Eckenrode, 1991).

The less vigorous coping efforts of the three less-distressed clusters may simply reflect a coping response that is appropriate to the (lower) level of illness-related stress. This is consistent with Lazarus' stress and coping paradigm, emphasizing the importance of psychological appraisal processes and the situation-specificity of coping (Lazarus, 1999; Lazarus and Folkman, 1984). With long-term, non-life-threatening illness and effective treatment, perceptions of illness stress may lessen or stabilize over time, or couples may learn to accommodate to the vicissitudes of the illness. A calmer, more graceful waltz, rather than a rigid, stylized tango may better describe the coping efforts of most couples in this study.[4]

From the data presented, dissimilar coping styles within a couple do not signal a greater level of psychological or marital problems. It is likely that the partners' different modes of coping did not cancel each other out, but more likely complemented each other, producing a wider repertoire of coping options.

The answer to the question of whether the fit between husbands' and wives' coping is a greater predictor of adjustment than simply knowing which strategies were used remains unanswered; couples in one cluster characterized by high similarity (1) were highly distressed, while in another cluster (3) they were not.

What these data do indicate is the importance of understanding couples' life context and *their perceptions of it*, as they cope with a serious illness. Coping seems less dependent on the objective circumstances of the illness, and more on the couple's integration of those circumstances into their life. For example, although features of the medical context did not differentiate couples' coping patterns, the experience of pain or disability spilled over to distress experienced by the healthy spouse.

Even this contextual analysis, however, cannot answer questions about couples' coping and long-term adaptation to illness. With cross-sectional data, we can see the resulting patterns of congruence or incongruence of couples' coping, but not the evolution of those patterns over time. Did one spouse's choice of coping strategy change how the other spouse coped? Do partners knowingly coordinate coping efforts – whether capitalizing on similarity or complementarity – to achieve desired outcomes? Does partners' coping become more congruent over time, as ineffective strategies or strategies that impeded the other partners' coping efforts are discarded and successful ones are adopted or recycled? These are the questions of the next generation of coping research.

The Missing Variable of Gender

The study I described examined married couples' coping within a number of contexts, including the interpersonal and sociocultural contexts. However, the rheumatic diseases affect women to a much greater extent than men. Three-quarters of the patients were women – were the results reflecting, and thus only generalizable to, female patient–male spouse dyads? Had I been conceptualizing coping from an androcentric perspective, focusing on what actions individuals and couples purposefully did and didn't do? Had I ignored the fact that particular types of coping are used more frequently by women and may be more effective for women (Stanton et al., 2000)? Were there other variables – variables more gender-relevant than self-report checklists of a small set of cognitions and behaviors – that can provide a different approach to couples' coping processes (Revenson, 2001)?

In part because of funding priorities and practical constraints, most health psychology studies focus on a specific disease. Because many diseases vary in their prevalence among men and women, most studies of coping with illness include respondents of only one sex. Thus, if we detect differences in patients' or spouses' adjustment, we cannot disentangle the influences of the illness context and of gender, or conclude whether the experience of coping with the "same" illness differs for men and women.

Wives face a greater burden than husbands, whether they are the partner with the illness or the spouse-caregiver (Schmaling and Sher, 2000). In an early study, Hafstrom and Schram (1984) compared couples in which the husband or wife had a chronic condition to couples in which neither spouse was ill. Wives who were chronically ill did more housework, compared to wives in non-ill families (although they spent fewer hours in the paid labor force). There were no differences in marital satisfaction, although women with chronic illness were less satisfied with their role performance as wives and mothers. Wives whose husbands had a chronic illness were less satisfied with their marriages than wives in non-ill families. Wives whose husbands were ill were less satisfied in many areas – with their husband's understanding of their feelings, the amount of attention received from their husbands, with their husband's help around the house and his role performance as a husband and father, and with the amount of time the couple spent together and the way they spent it. They were also less satisfied with their role performance as a mother, but surprisingly, not with their performance as a wife. Clearly the women with ill husbands felt a responsibility to keep the family and home intact, but at great personal cost.

In contrast, the situation where the wife has a chronic illness appears to take less of a toll on the husband and the marriage. In Hafstrom and Schram's (1984) study, a wife's illness has a weaker impact on the marital relationship than a husband's illness – on the time husbands spent listening to their spouses' problems and feelings, giving attention, or carrying out his roles as husband and father. Studies of couples coping with a myocardial infarction present a similar picture. (The majority of these studies are of male patients and female spouses.) After a heart attack, men tend to reduce their work activities and responsibilities and are nurtured by their wives. In contrast, after returning home from the hospital, women resume household responsibilities more quickly, including taking care of other family members, and report receiving a greater amount of help from adult daughters and neighbors than from their healthy husbands. Michela (1987) found such substantial differences in husbands' and wives' experience that he wrote, "*His* experience is filtered through concerns about surviving and recovering from the MI with a minimum of danger or discomfort, while *her* experience is filtered through the meaning of the marital relationship to her – what the marriage has provided and, hence, what is threatened by the husband's potential death or what is lost by his disability" (p. 272). Is this a result of gender-role socialization? Or is it because of differences between being a patient and being the caregiver?

The cluster analyses didn't give strong hints about the influence of gender. I had wondered if some of the differences I found between patients and spouses' coping were a reflection of gender. Although the sample included too few male patient–female spouse couples to analyze separately, we were able to redo the cluster analysis with only the female patient–male spouse couples. The findings were essentially identical to those reported for the full sample. We also looked at the proportion of couples in each cluster in which the wife versus the husband was ill. The proportion of women patients in each cluster was different: Cluster 1 – the most congruent cluster – included six times more couples in which the wife was ill; this ratio was 2 : 1 in Cluster 2,

3 : 1 in Cluster 3 and 4 : 1 in Cluster 4. Thus, it seems that the pattern of couples' coping we found may be shaded by gender.

We also examined the interaction of gender and patient–spouse role. Role (patient or spouse) was seen as a within-couple source of variance and patient gender as the between-couple factor. There were no significant effects on any of the seven coping strategies. However, there were significant findings for a number of measures of psychosocial adjustment. In terms of gender differences, women had significantly higher scores than men on depressive symptoms, psychological distress, and sexual dissatisfaction; there were no differences in marital satisfaction. This suggests that gender has an influence on adjustment, regardless of whether one is the person with rheumatic disease or their spouse.

However, there were a number of interesting interactions between gender and patient status. Comparing the four groups (female patients, male patients, female spouses, and male spouses), female patients had the highest levels of depression and male patients the lowest. In fact, female patients were the only group to approach the scale score that indicated clinical depression. Mirroring this effect, female patients had the lowest well-being scores and male patients the highest. Although there was not a significant interaction effect for marital satisfaction, there was a main effect for patient status: Patients (male and female) reported *greater* marital satisfaction than their healthy spouses did.

The finding that female patients had lower psychological well-being than their male counterparts mirrors the literature on gender differences in depression in the general population (Gore and Colten, 1991). Although depression is often related to pain, disability, and disease severity, there were no differences between female and male patients on any of these medical variables. I then turned to more interpersonal explanations.

An Alternate Conceptualization of Social Support: The Division of Household Labor

Thoits (1986) has conceptualized social support as coping assistance, instrumental and emotional support assisting with problem-focused and emotion-focused coping, respectively. In addition to questions assessing receipt and provision of tangible support in more traditional ways, Ana Abraído-Lanza and I decided to think of the division of household labor as a way to capture couples' support transactions (Revenson and Lanza, 1994).

The division of household labor reflects a broader and more gendered approach to coping, as adjustment to illness reflects the need to redistribute family roles and responsibilities (Patterson and Garwick, 1994). Many sociological studies (e.g., Hochschild, 1989) have documented a gender gap in men and women's sharing of household responsibilities. Even with the growing proportion of women in the paid labor force, women spend an average of 15 more hours a week on household responsibilities than do men. This gender inequity has been found to have important mental health implications for women (e.g., Crosby and Jaskar, 1993).

We felt that we would find a gender inequity among couples coping with illness, and that this inequity would be related to psychological well-being, support satisfaction, and marital satisfaction. In marriages where women were ill, there would be a narrowing of the gender gap in the division of household labor; that is, men would pick up more of the ongoing household responsibilities. In contrast, in marriages where the husband was ill, women would take on even more responsibilities.

We asked the wives and husbands (separately) about the division of household labor on 14 different household tasks. For each task, respondents were asked to divide 100 percent into the proportion of that task done by themselves, their spouse, and others (either family members or paid help). Using those proportions, we compared how the distribution of household labor differs across couples in which the wives were ill and couples in which the husbands were ill, comparing them to a sample of couples matched for age and socio-economic status with no chronic illness.

Overall, the data mirrored the gender gap in the division of household labor found in other sociological studies: for most tasks, wives did over half of the work. This finding did not differ whether we use the wife or husband's report. In fact, in most cases, wives and husbands agreed about how household work was shared, so we combined their data to produce a couple's score.

Our first hypothesis addressed whether division of household labor shifts when wives are ill; specifically, that it moves toward greater gender equity. It did: women with rheumatic disease relinquished or were relieved of some of their household responsibilities, particularly when disability was more severe. However, this occurred only in specific areas. In fact, women with rheumatic disease did no less of the daily cooking or dishes as compared to healthy wives (either in couples where the husband is ill or in healthy couples), and about two-thirds of the social planning. Husband and wives in all three types of couples shared responsibility equally for domestic finances.

The second part of the hypothesis predicted not only a shift in the pattern of women's work among couples in which the wife has a chronic illness, but a move toward greater gender equity. This part of the hypothesis was only partially supported and, again, differed by type of task. For some tasks, such as running errands and grocery shopping, husbands picked up the slack, increasing their proportion of work done. For others, such as laundry and heavy cleaning, the decrease in work by ill wives was filled by a combination of the husband doing more and use of outside (paid or unpaid) help. With regard to childcare and routine cleaning, couples tended to rely on outside help (either paid or family help) to compensate for the ill wives' decrease. For traditionally male tasks (taking out garbage, household repairs, outside chores, car maintenance), we found little difference in the distribution of labor among couples where the wife was ill and healthy comparison couples: men continued to do these tasks.

What happens to the division of labor when the *husbands* have rheumatic disease? Based on earlier literature, we had predicted that wives would assume many of the traditionally male responsibilities. We were wrong. Ill men did reduce their contribution, doing less than healthy husbands or husbands of ill wives. Wives picked up the garbage, and did a bit more of the household repairs, but outside chores and car maintenance were given over almost wholly to outside help. Thus, women do not take on all of their husband's responsibilities.

These analyses underline the fact that married couples' experience of coping with illness cannot be extricated from gender. Most of the couples appeared to be resourceful in taking some of the burden off the ill partner and in getting household responsibilities done. This may have been possible because this sample had the financial resources to do so; the picture may be different in families with fewer economic resources. Although there was clearly a responsiveness of couples to adjust how household responsibilities are shared when one partner has a chronic illness, women – even those who are ill – were still responsible for many of the around-the-clock maintenance tasks such as cooking, cleaning and child care. Rose et al. (1996) reached a similar conclusion in their study of spouses of survivors of acute myocardial infarction; husbands of ill women increased their responsibilities, while ill women decreased theirs. However, wives recovering from MI carried a heavier burden of household responsibilities than their male counterparts.

The manner in which household tasks are shared even in ill couples suggests that a gender-based typology persists despite illness, and that certain tasks remain forever the province of husband or wife. Women do more of the tasks that need either daily or immediate attention and fix women's lives into a more rigid routine, such as feeding the family and attending to children's needs. Whether this is really what women want is an open question. Clearly, being saddled with household chores can become problematic and even detrimental to health when one has a rheumatic disease, as pain, joint swelling, and symptom flares are not predictable, controllable, or time-limited. Others have suggested, however, that women (and men) may view maintaining this traditional role and keeping charge of the household may be one way that wives support the person who is able to be in the work force. Similarly, Abraído-Lanza (1997) has shown that keeping a culturally and personally valued social role improves well-being.

Emotional Support: Giving, Receiving, and Judging

The gender differences in adjustment to illness we found also may be shaped by the degree to which female and male patients feel supported by their partners. In the early study of women with rheumatoid arthritis and their spouses I described previously in this chapter, a number of wives of ill men confided that they had lessened their own requests for emotional support, for fear of increasing their ill husbands' distress (Revenson and Majerovitz, 1990; 1991; Schiaffino et al., 1995). Since then, we have learned that emotional-approach coping, involving both the processing and expression of emotions, may be more advantageous for women than men (Stanton et al., 2000), and that being unable to express one's feelings – what Lepore (1997) terms *social constraints* – may result in dissatisfaction with support and decreased well-being. Thus we looked at whether there were gender differences in the perceptions of support transactions, and whether a less than desired level of emotional support may be related to adjustment difficulties.

We asked husbands and wives about the degree to which they received positive and problematic support from their partners, the degree to which they gave positive and problematic support to their partners, and the degree to which they were satisfied with the instrumental and emotional support received from their partners. (Problematic support was conceptualized and measured as the transactions of "support that are seen [by the recipient] as non-supportive, even though the provider's actions may have been well-intended . . . for example, when it is neither desired nor needed, or when the type of support offered does not match the recipient's needs", Revenson et al., 1991: 807–8). Again we examined the separate and combined effects of gender and role (patient versus spouse).

There were no gender differences among patients in the degree to which positive *or* problematic support was received. However, there were significant differences between male and female *spouses*. Husbands of ill women reported receiving more positive support than wives of ill men. Mirroring this finding, wives of ill men reported receiving more problematic support than did husbands of ill wives. There were no differences among men and women in the amount of positive or problematic support that they reported *giving* to their partner.

Ill wives and their husbands were equally satisfied with the instrumental and emotional support they received from each other. However, there was a large discrepancy between ill husbands and their wives: ill husbands were extremely satisfied with the support received but, more importantly, their wives were extremely dissatisfied. In fact, wives of ill men were the least satisfied of all respondents, and they reported receiving less emotional support, more problematic spousal support, and were dissatisfied with the emotional and tangible support they were receiving from their partners.

Can this be linked to the discrepancies in household responsibilities? Perhaps it was the feeling of never-ending responsibilities that led women caring for ill husbands to feel dissatisfied with the instrumental and emotional support they were receiving from their spouses. Women who had a rheumatic disease enjoyed greater sharing of household labor with their husbands, but the couples also relied more on outside help. In contrast, in couples where men were ill, wives were more likely to add some around-the-clock maintenance tasks to their prior household tasks, perhaps leading to feelings of burden and a lack of appreciation.

Woven together, these analyses suggest that a traditional gender-typed division of labor exists even when chronic illness affects a marriage, and may reveal only the visible surface of deeper emotional issues: what should a husband and a wife contribute to a family when one person is ill or disabled? How appreciated does each feel? And how does each develop a gender strategy for coping with these issues at home? These are the underlying issues that deserve further research attention in order to increase our knowledge about the specific ways in which gender is part of couples' adaptation to illness.

Concluding Remarks

Couples' experience of coping with illness can be extricated neither from gender nor from the interpersonal, sociocultural, or temporal contexts in which that experience is embedded. Whether they are the patient or the caregiver, women assume a disproportionate share of the responsibilities for maintaining the family's organization and providing nurturance to family members. Gilligan (1982) has noted that women tend to be socialized into caretaking roles in close relationships and are more responsive to the well-being of others; Wethington et al. (1987) have shown that women react not only to their own stressors, but view others' stressors as their own.

Differing gender roles and their influence on family coping processes have implications for both family functioning and health behaviors. Whereas family coping responsibilities may be natural extensions of women's roles, they create added stress for wife-caregivers. When their husbands are ill, wives do not reap the same benefits of increased caregiving and support from their husbands. They may be compelled to cope in different ways to complement the husband's style. On a more optimistic note, however, gender roles have changed in a major way over the past quarter century. Cohort studies point to less differentiation in gender roles today, which might suggest more flexibility for families coping with stress in the future. Current studies of chronic illness, including my own, often involve individuals in middle and old age, whose early gender-role socialization is likely to be different than their respective cohorts of tomorrow.

This points to a glaring inadequacy in our current conceptions of coping: if we continue to focus only on the patient's coping efforts and their relation to adjustment, and on the instrumental or problem-solving aspects of coping, we will miss the critical influence of gender. If we focus on patients' individual efforts without considering their meaning as part of a couples' coping efforts, we will miss the critical influences of significant others. Coping with illness does not simply mean *having illness* – it involves caring for family members with illness. With the exception of the Alzheimer disease literature, which has focused a great deal on the concept of caregiver burden, coping research has avoided issues of gender and family, choosing instead to focus on motivations, emotions, and self-regulation processes.

The study of coping on a dyadic level represents a next step in understanding process as well as outcome, particularly when individuals are coping with a chronic stressor that affects both spouses. We cannot continue to separate the study of coping processes from that of social support. Whether we choose to conceptualize social support as a form of coping assistance (Thoits, 1986) or as a mode of coping (Bodenmann, 1997; DeLongis and O'Brien, 1997), much of what is considered coping involves the appraisals, actions, emotions, and feedback of others (Lazarus, 1999).

It is important to begin to assemble a literature that examines the multiple influences of family members on adaptation while considering the influence of gender and gender roles, even if that research gets methodologically messy.

The mandate of this research would be to learn the specific ways in which gender is part of couples' adaptation to illness in order for health psychology to most effectively maximize family adaptation and provide guidance to medical practitioners.

Acknowledgments

I should have subtitled this chapter "Work, Interrupted." It is one of the more personal pieces I have written, revealing the interrupted, non-linear process of coming up with and discarding research ideas. The editors of this volume, Ken Wallston and Jerry Suls, gave authors a wide berth to present past and current research. I took this opportunity to gain closure on a study that I have been involved with for a decade.

The research described in this chapter was funded by grants from the National Institute of Health (AM36679), the Cornell University Medical College Arthritis and Musculoskeletal Disease Center (AR38520), the City University of New York PSC-CUNY Research Award Program, and the New York Chapter of the Arthritis Foundation. More valuable than the funding, however, was the energy, enthusiasm, and intellectual input of former students who collaborated on the studies described here, particularly S. Deborah Majerovitz and Ana F. Abraído-Lanza. The words on these pages may be mine, but the couples study was a joint production. In more measured ways, Ann Cameron, Lisa Kurata, Chandra Mason, Judith Schor, Vita Rabinowitz, Jennifer Ayala, Caren Jordan, and Sharon Danoff-Burg all made important contributions. Allan Gibofsky, MD and Stephen Paget, MD, provided patients *and* patience over a decade of research. My colleagues Robert DeVellis, Craig Smith, and Joan Tucker, graciously offered ideas about the cluster analysis, and Stanton Newman provided helpful feedback on the manuscript. I will always thank my lucky stars for the early and continued mentoring of Barbara J. Felton, who taught me not only about doing research, but also about the lives of women researchers.

Correspondence concerning this chapter should be sent to: Tracey A. Revenson, PhD, Doctoral Program in Psychology, City University of New York Graduate Center, 365 Fifth Avenue, New York, NY 10016-4309, USA; e-mail: Trevenson@gc.cuny.edu

Notes

1. This chapter focuses on heterosexual couples, and thus the conclusions may not apply to same-sex couples. Similarly, many of the issues may apply to adult child caregivers.
2. Throughout this chapter, the term "patient" will be used for the spouse with the rheumatic disease and the term "spouse" will be used to connote the healthy spouse.
3. A complete description of the factor analysis procedures and results can be obtained from the author. Interestingly, the structure was very similar to those found in other studies of chronic illness (Dunkel-Schetter et al., 1992; Felton et al., 1984).

4. A caveat is in order here: although family members' responses to illness are important determinants of adaptation, it is important to emphasize that the family's coping repertoire may be constrained by the medical context. Pain and imminent death may be stronger determinants of family coping than either individual attributes or family interactional styles. For example, even the most adaptive families may not be able to cope in the short run with the demands of certain illnesses, such as end-stage Alzheimer's disease.

References

Abraído-Lanza, A. F. (1997). Latinas with arthritis: Effects of illness, role identity, and competence on psychological well-being. *American Journal of Community Psychology, 25,* 601–27.

Aldwin, C. M., and Revenson, T. A. (1987). Does coping help? A re-examination of the stress-buffering role of coping. *Journal of Personality and Social Psychology, 53,* 337–48.

Anderson, N. B., and McNeilly, M. (1991). Age, gender, and ethnicity as variables in psychophysiological assessment: Sociodemographics in context. *Psychological Assessment, 3,* 376–84.

Baider, L., Koch, U., Eascson, R., and Kaplan De-Nour, A. (1998). Prospective study of cancer patients and their spouses: The weakness of marital strength. *Psycho-Oncology, 7,* 49–56.

Berghuis, J. P., and Stanton, A. L. (2002). Adjustment to a dyadic stressor: A longitudinal study of coping and depressive symptoms in infertile couples over an insemination attempt. *Journal of Consulting and Clinical Psychology, 70,* 433–8.

Bermas, B. L., Tucker, J. S., Winkelman, D. K., and Katz, J. N. (2000). Marital satisfaction in couples with rheumatoid arthritis. *Arthritis Care and Research, 13,* 149–55.

Bodenmann, G. (1995). A systemic-transactional view of stress and coping in couples. *Swiss Journal of Psychology, 54,* 34–49.

Bodenmann, G. (1997). Dyadic coping: A systemic-transactional view of stress and coping among couples: Theory and empirical findings. *Revue Européenne de Psychologie Appliqueé, 47,* 137–40.

Bradbury, T., and Fincham, F. D. (1991). A contextual model for advancing the study of marital interaction. In G. J. O. Fletcher and F. D. Fincham (Eds.), *Cognition in Close Relationships* (pp. 127–47). Hillsdale, NJ: Erlbaum.

Bronfenbrenner, U. (1977). Toward an experimental ecology of human development. *American Psychologist, 32,* 513–31.

Bronfenbrenner, U. (1986). Ecology of the family as a context for human development: Research perspectives. *Developmental Psychology, 22,* 723–42.

Brown, P. C., and Smith, T. W. (1992). Social influence, marriage, and the heart: Cardiovascular consequences of interpersonal control in husbands and wives. *Health Psychology, 11,* 88–96.

Burman, B., and Margolin, G. (1992). Analysis of the association between marital relationships and health problems: An interactional perspective. *Psychological Bulletin, 112,* 39–63.

Coyne, J. C., and Fiske, V. (1992). Couples coping with chronic and catastrophic illness. In M. A. P. Stephens, S. E. Hobfoll, and J. Crowther (Eds.), *Family Health Psychology* (pp. 129–49). Washington DC: Hemisphere.

Coyne, J. C., Rohrbaugh, M. J., Shoham, V., Sonnega, J., Nicklas, J. M., and Cranford, J. A. (2001). Prognostic importance of marital quality for survival of congestive heart failure. *American Journal of Cardiology, 88,* 526–9.

Coyne, J. C., and Smith, D. A. (1991). Couples coping with a myocardial infarction: A contextual perspective on wives' distress. *Journal of Personality and Social Psychology*, 61, 404–12.

Crosby, F., and Jaskar, K. (1993). Women and men at home and at work: Realities and illusions. In S. Oskamp and M. Costanzo (Eds.), *Gender Issues in Social Psychology* (pp. 143–71). Newbury Park, CA: Sage.

Cutrona, C. E. (1996). *Social Support in Couples*. Thousand Oaks, CA: Sage.

Danoff-Burg, S., and Revenson, T. A. (2000). Rheumatic illness and relationships: Coping as a joint venture. In K. B. Schmaling and T. G. Sher (Eds.), *The Psychology of Couples and Illness* (pp. 105–34). Washington DC: American Psychological Association.

Danoff-Burg, S., Revenson, T. A., and Ayala, J. (2000). Researcher knows best? Toward a closer match between the concept and measurement of coping. *Journal of Health Psychology*, 5, 183–94.

DeLongis, A., and O'Brien, T. B. (1990). An interpersonal framework for stress and coping: An application to the families of Alzheimer's patients. In M. A. P. Stephens, J. H. Crowther, S. E. Hobfoll, and D. L. Tennenbaum (Eds.), *Stress and Coping in Later-life Families* (pp. 221–39). Washington, DC: Hemisphere.

Dunkel-Schetter, C., Feinstein, L. G., Taylor, S. E., and Falke, R. L. (1992). Patterns of coping with cancer. *Health Psychology*, 11, 79–87.

Eckenrode, J. (Ed.) (1991). *The Social Context of Coping*. New York: Plenum Press.

Felton, B. J., and Revenson, T. A. (1984). Coping with chronic illness: A study of illness controllability and the influence of coping strategies on psychological adjustment. *Journal of Consulting and Clinical Psychology*, 52, 343–53.

Felton, B. J., and Revenson, T. A. (1987). Age differences in coping with chronic illness. *Psychology and Aging*, 2, 164–70.

Felton, B. J., and Revenson, T. A. (1989). The psychology of health: Issues in the field with special focus on the older person. In I. Parham, L. W. Poon and I. G. Siegler, (Eds.), *Curriculum Content for Education in the Social-behavioral Sciences* (pp. 4.1–4.54). New York: Springer.

Felton, B. J., Revenson, T. A., and Hinrichsen, G. A. (1984). Stress and coping the explanation of psychological adjustment among chronically ill adults. *Social Science and Medicine*, 18, 889–98.

Folkman, S., Lazarus, R. S., Dunkel-Schetter, C., DeLongis, A., and Gruen, R. J. (1986). Dynamics of a stressful encounter: Cognitive appraisal, coping, and encounter outcomes. *Journal of Personality and Social Psychology*, 50, 992–1003.

French, J. R. P., Jr., Rodgers, W., and Cobb, S. (1974). Adjustment as person-environment fit. In G. V. Coelho, D. A. Hamburg, and J. E. Adams (Eds.), *Coping and Adjustment* (pp. 316–33). New York: Basic Books.

Gilligan, C. (1982). *In a Different Voice: Psychological Theory and Women's Development*. Cambridge, MA: Harvard University Press.

Gore, S., and Colten, M. E. (1991). Gender, stress, and distress. In J. Eckenrode (Ed.), *The Social Context of Coping* (pp. 139–63). New York: Plenum Press.

Gray, H., Brogan, D., and Kutner, N. G. (1985). Status of life areas: Congruence/noncongruence in ESRD patient and spouse perceptions. *Social Science and Medicine*, 20, 341–6.

Haan, N. (1977). *Coping and Defending*. New York: Academic Press.

Hafstrom, J. L., and Schram, V. R. (1984). Chronic illness in couples: Selected characteristics, including wife's satisfactions with and perception of marital relationships. *Family Relations*, 33, 195–203.

Hagedoorn, M., Kuijer, R. G., Buunk, B. P., DeJong, G. M., Wobbes, T., and Sanderman, R. (2000). Marital satisfaction in patients with cancer: Does support from intimate partners benefit those who need it most? *Health Psychology*, 19, 274–82.

Halford, W. K., Scott, J. L., and Smythe, J. (2000). Helping each other through the night: Couples and coping with cancer. In K. B. Schmaling and T. G. Sher (Eds.), *The Psychology of Couples and Illness* (pp. 135–70). Washington DC: American Psychological Association.

Hobfoll, S. E. (1989). Conservation of resources: A new attempt at conceptualizing stress. *American Psychologist*, 44, 513–24.

Hochschild, A. (1989). *The Second Shift*. New York: Viking Penguin.

Huston, T. L., and Robins, E. (1982). Conceptual and methodological issues in studying close relationships. *Journal of Marriage and the Family*, 44, 901–25.

Ickovics, J. R., Thayaparan, B., and Ethier, K. A. (2001). Women and AIDS: A contextual analysis. In A. Baum, T. A. Revenson, and J. E. Singer (Eds.), *Handbook of Health Psychology* (pp. 817–39). Mahwah, NJ: Erlbaum.

Lanza, A. F., Cameron, A. E., and Revenson, T. A. (1995). Helpful and unhelpful support among individuals with rheumatic diseases. *Psychology and Health*, 10, 449–62.

Lazarus, R. S. (1981). The stress and coping paradigm. In C. Edisdorfer, D. Cohen, A. Kleinman, and P. Maxim (Eds.), *Models for Clinical Psychopathology* (pp. 177–214). New York: Spectrum Medical and Scientific Books.

Lazarus, R. S. (1999). *Stress and Emotion*. New York: Springer.

Lazarus, R. S., and Cohen, J. B. (1977). Coping questionaire. Unpublished questionnaire, Berkeley Stress and Coping Project, University of California, Berkeley (unnumbered).

Lazarus, R. S., and Folkman, S. (1984). *Stress, Appraisal and Coping*. New York: Springer.

Lazarus, R. S., and Launier, R. (1978). Stress-related transactions between person and environment. In L. A. Pervin and M. Lewis (Eds.), *Perspectives in Interactional Psychology* (pp. 287–327). New York: Plenum.

Lepore, S. J. (1997). The social context of coping with chronic stress. In B. Gottlieb (Ed), *Coping with Chronic Stress* (pp. 133–60). New York: Plenum Press.

Levin, J. B., Sher, T. G., and Theodos, V. (1997). The effect of intracouple coping concordance on psychological and marital distress in infertility patients. *Journal of Clinical Psychology in Medical Settings*, 4, 361–72.

Lewin, K. (1943/1997). *Resolving Social Conflicts and Field Theory in Social Science*. Washington, DC: American Psychological Association.

Lyons, R. F., Mickelson, K. D., Sullivan, M. J., and Coyne, J. C. (1998). Coping as a communal process. *Journal of Personal and Social Relationships*, 15, 579–605.

Majerovitz, S. D., and Revenson, T. A. (1994). Sexuality and rheumatic disease: The significance of gender. *Arthritis Care and Research*, 7, 29–34.

Manne, S. L., Alfieri, T., Taylor, K. L., and Dougherty, J. (1999). Spousal negative responses to cancer patients: The role of social restriction, spouse mood and relationship satisfaction. *Journal of Consulting and Clinical Psychology*, 67(3), 352–61.

Manne, S. L., and Zautra, A. J. (1989). Spouse criticism and support: Their association with coping and psychological adjustment among women with rheumatoid arthritis. *Journal of Personality and Social Psychology*, 56, 608–17.

Manne, S. L., and Zautra, J. (1990). Couples coping with chronic illness: Women with rheumatoid arthritis and their husbands. *Journal of Behavioral Medicine*, 13, 327–42.

Matthews, K. A. (1989). Are sociodemographic variables markers for psychological determinants of health? *Health Psychology*, 8, 641–8.

Michela, J. L. (1987). Interpersonal and individual impacts of a husband's heart attack. In A. Baum, and J. E. Singer, (Eds.), *Handbook of Psychology and Health* (Vol. 5, pp. 255–301). Hillsdale, NJ: Erlbaum.

Mischel, W. (1968). *Personality and Assessment*. New York: Wiley.

Murray, H. (1938). *Explorations in Personality*. New York: Oxford University Press.

Neugarten, B. (1979). Time, age and the life cycle. *American Journal of Psychiatry*, 136, 887–94.

Newman, S., Fitzpatrick, R., Revenson, T. A., Skevington, S., and Williams, G. (1996). *Understanding Rheumatoid Arthritis*. London: Routledge, Kegan, Paul.

Northouse, L. L., Templin, T., Mood, D., and Oberst, M. (1995). Couples' adjustment to breast cancer and benign breast disease. *Psycho-oncology*, 7, 37–48.

O'Brien, T. B., and DeLongis, A. (1996). The interactional context of problem-, emotion-, and relationship-focused coping: The role of the big five personality factors. *Journal of Personality*, 64, 775–813.

O'Brien, T. B., and DeLongis, A. (1997). Coping with chronic stress: An interpersonal perspective. In B. Gottlieb (Ed.), *Coping with Chronic Stress* (pp. 161–90). New York: Plenum Press.

Pasch, L. A., Bradbury, T. N., and Sullivan, K. T. (1997). Social support in marriage: An analysis of intraindividual and interpersonal components. In G. R. Pierce, B. Lakey, I. G. Sarason, and B. R. Sarason (Eds.), *Sourcebook of Social Support and Personality* (pp. 229–56). New York: Plenum.

Pasch, L. A., and Christensen, A. (2000). Couples facing fertility problems. In K. B. Schmaling and T. G. Sher (Eds.), *The Psychology of Couples and Illness* (pp. 241–68). Washington DC: American Psychological Association.

Patterson, J. M., and Garwick, A. W. (1994). The impact of chronic illness on families: A family systems perspective. *Annals of Behavioral Medicine*, 16, 131–42.

Pearlin, L. I. (1989). The sociological study of stress. *Journal of Health and Social Behavior*, 30, 241–56.

Pearlin, L. I. (1991). The study of coping: An overview of problems and directions. In J. Eckenrode (Ed.), *The Social Context of Coping* (pp. 261–76). New York: Plenum Press.

Pearlin, L. I., Liberberman, M. L., Menaghan, E., and Mullan, J. T. (1981). The stress process. *Journal of Health and Social Behavior*, 22, 337–56.

Pearlin, L. I., and Turner, H. A. (1987). The family as a context of the stress process. In S. V. Kasl and C. L. Cooper (Eds.), *Stress and Health: Issues in Research Methodology* (pp. 143–65). New York: John Wiley and Sons.

Pistrang, N., and Barker, C. (1995). The partner relationship in psychological response to breast cancer. *Social Science and Medicine*, 40, 789–97.

Rankin-Esquer, L. A., Deeter, A., and Taylor, C. B. (2000). Coronary heart disease and couples. In K. B. Schmaling and T. G. Sher (Eds.), *The Psychology of Couples and Illness* (pp. 43–70). Washington DC: American Psychological Association.

Repetti, R. L., Taylor, S. E., and Seeman, T. E. (2002). Risky families: Family social environments and the mental and physical health of offspring. *Psychological Bulletin*, 128, 330–66.

Repetti, R. L., and Wood, J. (1997). Families accommodating to chronic stress: An interpersonal perspective. In B. Gottlieb (Ed.), *Coping with Chronic Stress* (pp. 191–220). New York: Plenum Press.

Revenson, T. A. (1990). All other things are *not* equal: An ecological perspective on the relation between personality and disease. In H. S. Friedman (Ed.), *Personality and Disease* (pp. 65–94). New York: John Wiley.

Revenson, T. A. (1993). The role of social support with rheumatic disease. In S. Newman and M. Shipley (Eds.), *Psychological Aspects of Rheumatic Disease*. (*Balliere's Clinical Rheumatology* Vol. 7, No. 2, pp. 377–96). London: Bailliere Tindal.

Revenson, T. A. (1994). Social support and marital coping with chronic illness. *Annals of Behavioral Medicine*, 16, 122–30.

Revenson, T. A. (1995). On with the dance: Couples' coping with illness. Invited Address to the Division of Aging and Human Development, Annual Meeting of the American Psychological Association, New York, August.

Revenson, T. A. (2001). Chronic illness adjustment. In J. Worrell (Ed.), *Encyclopedia of Women and Gender* (Vol. 1, pp. 245–56). San Diego, CA: Academic Press.

Revenson, T. A., and Danoff-Burg, S. (2000). Arthritis. In A. Kazdin (Editor-in-Chief.), *Encyclopedia of Psychology* (Vol. 1, pp. 240–2). Washington DC: American Psychological Association.

Revenson, T. A., and Gibofsky, A. (1995). Marriage, social support and adjustment to rheumatic diseases. *Bulletin of the Rheumatic Diseases*, 44, 5–8.

Revenson, T. A., and Lanza, A. F. (1994). Married with illness: Influence of gender on support and coping. In T. A. Revenson and N. P. Bolger (Co-Chairs), *Stress, Coping and Support Processes in the Context of Marriage.* Paper presented at the Annual Meeting of the American Psychological Association, Los Angeles, CA, August.

Revenson, T. A., and Majerovitz, S. D. (1990). Spouses' support provision to chronically ill patients. *Journal of Social and Personal Relationships*, 7, 575–86.

Revenson, T. A., and Majerovitz, D. M. (1991). The effects of chronic illness on the spouse: Social resources as stress buffers. *Arthritis Care and Research*, 4, 63–72.

Revenson, T. A., Schiaffino, K. M., Majerovitz, S. D., and Gibofsky, A. (1991). Social support as a double-edged sword: The relation of positive and problematic support to depression among rheumatoid arthritis patients. *Social Science and Medicine*, 33, 807–13.

Revenson, T. A., Wollman, C. A., and Felton, B. J. (1983). Social supports as stress buffers for adult cancer patients. *Psychosomatic Medicine*, 45, 321–30.

Rohrbaugh, M. J., Cranford, J. A., Shoham, V., Nicklas, J. M., Sonnega, J., and Coyne, J. C. (2002). Couples coping with congestive heart failure: Role and gender differences in psychological distress. *Journal of Family Psychology*, 16, 3–13.

Rose, G., Suls, J., Green, P. J, Lounsbury, P., and Gordon, E. (1996). Comparison of adjustment, activity, and tangible social support in men and women patients and their spouses during the six months post-myocardial infarction. *Annals of Behavioral Medicine*, 18, 264–72.

Rosnow, R. L., and Rosenthal, R. (1989). Statistical procedures and the justification of knowledge in psychological science. *American Psychologist*, 44, 1276–84.

Schiaffino, K. M., and Revenson, T. A. (1992). The role of perceived self-efficacy, perceived control, and causal attributions in adaptation to rheumatoid arthritis: Distinguishing mediator vs. moderator effects. *Personality and Social Psychology Bulletin*, 18, 709–18.

Schiaffino, K. M., and Revenson, T. A. (1995a). Relative contributions of spousal support and illness appraisals to depressed mood in arthritis patients. *Arthritis Care and Research*, 8, 80–7.

Schiaffino, K. M., and Revenson, T. A. (1995b). Why me? The persistence of negative illness cognitions over time. *Journal of Applied Social Psychology*, 25, 601–18.

Schiaffino, K. M., Revenson, T. A., and Gibofsky, A. (1991). Assessing the role of self-efficacy beliefs in adaptation to rheumatoid arthritis. *Arthritis Care and Research*, 4, 150–7.

Schmaling, K. B., and Sher, T. G. (2000). *The Psychology of Couples and Illness.* Washington DC: American Psychological Association.

Smith, T. W. (1995). Assessment and modification of coronary-prone behavior: A transactional view of the person in social context. In A. J. Goreczny (Ed.), *Handbook of Health and Rehabilitation Psychology* (pp. 197–217). New York: Plenum.

Stanton, A. L., Kirk, S. B., Cameron, C. L., and Danoff-Burg, S. (2000). Coping through emotional approach: Scale construction and validation. *Journal of Personality and Social Psychology*, 78, 1150–69.

Suls, J., Green, P., Rose, G., Lounsbury, P., and Gordon, E. (1997). Hiding worries from one's spouse: Associations between coping via protective buffering and distress in male post-myocardial infarction patients and their wives. *Journal of Behavioral Medicine*, 20, 333–49.

Thoits, P. A. (1986). Social support as coping assistance. *Journal of Consulting and Clinical Psychology*, 54, 416–23.

Tucker, J. S., Winkelman, D. K., Katz, J. N., and Bermas, B. L. (1999). Ambivalence over emotional expression and psychological well-being among rheumatoid arthritis patients and their spouses. *Journal of Applied Social Psychology*, 29, 271–90.

Wethington, E., McLeod, J. D., and Kessler, R. (1987). The importance of life events for explaining sex differences in mental health. In R. C. Barnett, L. Biener, and G. K. Baruch (Eds.), *Gender and Stress* (pp. 144–55). New York: Free Press.

Wortman, C. B., and Dunkel-Schetter, C. (1979). Interpersonal relationships and cancer: A theoretical analysis. *Journal of Social Issues*, 35, 120–55.

Index